WITHDRAWN

THE DRAMATIC WORKS IN
THE BEAUMONT AND
FLETCHER CANON

Already published

VOLUME I

The Knight of the Burning Pestle
The Masque of the Inner Temple and Gray's Inn
The Woman Hater   The Coxcomb
Philaster   The Captain

VOLUME II

The Maid's Tragedy   A King and No King
Cupid's Revenge   The Scornful Lady
Love's Pilgrimage

THE
DRAMATIC WORKS IN
THE BEAUMONT AND
FLETCHER CANON

GENERAL EDITOR
FREDSON BOWERS
Linden Kent Professor of English Literature, University of Virginia

VOLUME III

LOVE'S CURE   THE NOBLE GENTLEMAN   BEGGARS' BUSH
THE TRAGEDY OF THIERRY AND THEODORET
THE FAITHFUL SHEPHERDESS

CAMBRIDGE UNIVERSITY PRESS
CAMBRIDGE
LONDON · NEW YORK · MELBOURNE

Published by the Syndics of the Cambridge University Press
The Pitt Building, Trumpington Street, Cambridge CB2 1RP
Bentley House, 200 Euston Road, London NW1 2DB
32 East 57th Street, New York, NY 10022, USA
296 Beaconsfield Parade, Middle Park, Melbourne 3206, Australia

First published 1976

Printed in Great Britain
at the
University Printing House, Cambridge
(Euan Phillips, University Printer)

Library of Congress cataloguing in publication data (Revised)

Beaumont, Francis, 1584–1616.
The dramatic works in the Beaumont and Fletcher canon.

I. Fletcher John, 1579–1625, joint author.
II. Bowers, Fredson Thayer, ed.
III. Title.

PR2420 1966   822'.3'09   66–74421
ISBN 0 521 20730 4 (vol. 3)

CONTENTS

Foreword   *page* vii

LOVE'S CURE   1

Edited by GEORGE WALTON WILLIAMS, *Professor of English, Duke University*

THE NOBLE GENTLEMAN   113

Edited by L. A. BEAURLINE, *Professor of English, University of Virginia*

BEGGARS' BUSH   225

Edited by FREDSON BOWERS, *Linden Kent Professor of English Literature, University of Virginia*

THE TRAGEDY OF THIERRY AND THEODORET   363

Edited by ROBERT K. TURNER, JNR, *Professor of English, Milwaukee University*

THE FAITHFUL SHEPHERDESS   483

Edited by CYRUS HOY, *Professor of English, University of Rochester*

v

FOREWORD

These volumes contain the text and apparatus for the plays conventionally assigned to the Beaumont and Fletcher canon, although in fact Fletcher collaborated with dramatists other than Beaumont in numerous plays of the canon and some of the preserved texts also represent revision at a later date by various hands. The plays have been grouped chiefly by authors; this arrangement makes for an order that conveniently approximates the probable date of composition for most of the works.

The texts of the several plays have been edited by a group of scholars according to editorial procedures set by the general editor, who closely supervised in matters of substance as well as of detail the initially contrived form of the texts. Thereafter the individual editors have been left free to develop their concepts of the plays according to their own views. We hope that the intimate connection of one individual, in this manner, with all the different editorial processes will lend to the results some uniformity not ordinarily found when diverse editors approach texts of such complexity. At the same time, the peculiar abilities of the several editors have had sufficient free play to ensure individuality of point of view in its proper role; and thus, we hope, the deadness of compromise that may fasten on collaborative effort has been avoided, even at the risk of occasional internal disagreement.

The principles on which each text has been edited have been set forth in detail in 'The Text of this Edition' prefixed to volume I, pp. ix–xxv, followed by an account on pp. xxvii–xxxv of the Folio of 1647. Necessary acknowledgements will be found in the present volume in each Textual Introduction.

F.B.

Charlottesville, Virginia
1975

LOVE'S CURE

edited by

GEORGE WALTON WILLIAMS

TEXTUAL INTRODUCTION

Love's Cure, or The Martial Maid (Greg, *Bibliography*, no. 661) was one in the list of plays by Beaumont and Fletcher entered to Humphrey Moseley in the Stationers' Register between 4 and 15 September 1646. The play was printed in the 1647 Folio, this text being the only one of authority.[1]

The Prologue 'At the reviving of this Play' and the Epilogue give indication of being later additions. The Prologue (set in large type so as to fill page 5S6) speaks of the passage of some time between the writing of the play and its revival:[2]

> The minds art has this preheminence,
> She still retaineth her first excellence.

The Epilogue (page 5S5ᵛ) concludes the play in a tone of general neutrality. It speaks of 'Our Author', and it sounds as if it might serve as epilogue to any comedy. Indeed, it does serve also as epilogue to Lodowick Carlell's *Deserving Favorite*, published in 1629, though perhaps written any time between 1622 and 1629.[3] If the Epilogue was originally written for *Love's Cure*, its reference to the singular 'author' is puzzling, as it might be assumed that the value of double authorship was greater than that of single authorship.[4] If, on the other hand, the Epilogue betokens a revival and the 'author' is in fact merely the reviser, another puzzle develops. In short, it seems wisest not to attempt to draw information from these two pieces, but to interpret them in the light of information drawn from less nebulous sources. Professor Bentley's hypothesis is prob-

[1] R. C. Bald, *Bibliographical Studies in the Beaumont and Fletcher Folio of 1647* (Oxford, 1938).

[2] R. Warwick Bond ('On Six Plays in Beaumont and Fletcher, 1679', *R.E.S.*, xi (July, 1935), 267) suggests that the Prologue belongs to *The Queen of Corinth*, the play designed to follow *Love's Cure* in Moseley's original scheme, but the bibliographical evidence of the assignment of plays to Griffin vitiates this suggestion.

[3] Charles H. Gray, *Lodowick Carliell* [*sic*] (Chicago, 1905).

[4] Mr Hoy has pointed to other examples of this situation ('The Shares of Fletcher and his Collaborators in the Beaumont and Fletcher Canon (vi)', *SB*, xiv (1961), 48).

ably correct (for reasons that will appear below): 'The prologue
and epilogue, therefore, indicate that *Love's Cure* was originally a
collaboration by Beaumont and Fletcher, and was later revised by a
single dramatist, presumably Philip Massinger.'[1]

Mr Hoy's linguistic demonstration of the various shares of
authorship sheds a clear light into one of the more confused and
uncertain areas of the canon. He regards the play as originally a
collaborative effort of Beaumont and Fletcher, Acts I, IV, and V
being a revision by Massinger 'so extensive as to amount to re-
writing'.[2]

I.i	Rewritten by Massinger
I.ii	Fletcher revised by Massinger
I.iii	Rewritten by Massinger
II.i	Beaumont and Fletcher ('essentially the work of Beaumont')
II.ii.1–120	Fletcher ('essentially, the unaided work of Fletcher')
121–68	Fletcher revised by Massinger
168–259	Beaumont and Fletcher ('essentially, unaided Beaumont')
III.i	Beaumont ('wholly [Beaumont's]')
III.ii	Fletcher revised by Massinger
III.iii.1–17	Fletcher
18–77	Beaumont
78–123	Fletcher revised by Massinger
III.iv	Fletcher revised by Massinger
III.v	Fletcher
IV.i	Rewritten by Massinger
IV.ii	Rewritten by Massinger
IV.iii.1–19	Rewritten by Massinger
20–71	Fletcher revised by Massinger ('basically the work of Fletcher')
71–132	Rewritten by Massinger
IV.iv	Rewritten by Massinger
V.i	Rewritten by Massinger
V.ii	Rewritten by Massinger
V.iii.1–194	Beaumont and Fletcher revised by Massinger
195–256	Beaumont and Fletcher
257–62	Massinger

[1] G. E. Bentley, *The Jacobean and Caroline Stage*, III (Cambridge, 1954), 365. The
thesis that the double title indicates two stages of the development of the text does not
seem persuasive (cf. Baldwin Maxwell, *Studies in Beaumont, Fletcher, and Massinger*
(Chapel Hill, N.C., 1939), pp. 1–3).

[2] Hoy, 'Fletcher and his Collaborators', p. 49. The assignments are taken from
pp. 48–56, *passim*.

These observations on authorship yield deductions on the date and the construction of the play. If the play contains the collaborative work of Beaumont and Fletcher, it must have been written prior to 1613, when Beaumont retired; and Mr Hoy has argued strongly that it probably is 'one of the earliest' of their collaborations, earlier even than *The Woman Hater*, written in the first half of 1606. Oliphant had already reached the same conclusion, arguing that Maurice (I.ii.33) would not have been titled 'Graf' after 1609 and that the character of Lazarillo in *Love's Cure* is a preliminary sketch of the character of the same name in *The Woman Hater*, a 'more complete and finished creation'.[1]

The main situation of the play, involving the transvestite siblings, however, derives from the Spanish comedy *La fuerza de la costumbre* by Guillén de Castro y Bellris, published in 1625 in Valencia.[2] As this publication could not have reached England in time for Beaumont or Fletcher to have used it, the conclusion must be that the remarkable parallels between the Spanish comedy and *Love's Cure* are due to the reviser, Philip Massinger.[3]

An analysis of the play based on the authorship tests discloses that the sections for which Beaumont is primarily responsible are

[1] E. H. C. Oliphant, *Plays of Beaumont and Fletcher* (New Haven, 1927), p. 418, and 'Three Beaumont and Fletcher Plays', *R.E.S.*, XII (April, 1936), 200; see below, p. 6, n. 2. The popularity of the name 'Lazarillo' on the English stage traces its appearance from *Blurt, Master Constable* (1602), where Lazarillo is a braggart soldier who has a hungry servant. The name then appears in *Love's Cure* and *The Woman Hater*, and in *Match Me in London* and *All's Lost by Lust*. See Thomas L. Berger, 'A Critical Old-spelling Edition of Thomas Dekker's *Blurt, Master Constable* (1602)' (unpublished doctoral dissertation, Duke University, Durham, N.C., 1969). See also John Shirley, 'The Parasite, the Glutton, and the Hungry Knave in English Drama to 1625' (unpublished doctoral dissertation, University of Iowa, Iowa City, 1937). Bond notices several verbal parallels between *Blurt* and *Love's Cure* (pp. 268–9).

[2] The comedy was probably written 1610–15(?), but it seems unnecessary to invent the thesis that a manuscript version had preceded the printed edition to England. See Courtney Bruerton, 'The Chronology of the "Comedias" of Guillén de Castro', *Hispanic Review*, XII (April, 1944), 89–151. See also Martin E. Erickson, 'A Review of Scholarship Dealing with the Problem of a Spanish Source for *Love's Cure*', in Waldo F. McNeir (ed.), *Studies in Comparative Literature*, Louisiana State University Studies, Humanities Series, no. 11 (Baton Rouge, 1962), pp. 102–19.

[3] His biographers have concluded that Massinger was probably able to read Spanish (T. A. Dunn, *Philip Massinger* (London, 1957), p. 12; Donald S. Lawless, *Philip Massinger and His Associates* (Muncie, Ind., 1967), p. 7).

those of Malroda and the Alguazier (III.i, iii) with the necessary associations of Vitelli and Piorato; Mr Hoy has described Beaumont's contribution in Malroda's 'finely extravagant speech' and in Vitelli's reply (III.iii.32–77) as 'the finest things in the play'. Beaumont also treats the romantic interest in material now assigned to Clara and Vitelli (II.ii.168–259). Fletcher's sections treat primarily of the four low-comedy figures – Pachieco, Mendoza, Metaldi, and Lazarillo (III.v; IV.iii.20–71) – though he seems to have joined with Beaumont in treating Vitelli and Malroda (III. iii.78–123), and Beaumont seems to have joined with him in depicting the four comics (II.i). Acts II and III contain, as Mr Hoy has said, 'much composite writing'. Fletcher is perhaps also responsible for the situations of Lucio and Bobadilla in I.ii and in II.ii (with Clara); his preferred 'ye' is found in the latter scene.

It is evident then that the two groups of characters consisting on the one hand of Malroda, Vitelli, Piorato, and the Alguazier and on the other of Mendoza, Metaldi, Pachieco, and Lazarillo constitute the vestigial remains of a Beaumont and Fletcher collaboration, dating from the early years of the century, probably between 1602 (the publication of *Blurt, Master Constable*) and 1606 (the date of *The Woman Hater*). It is possible also that these characters formed plots and/or subplots of a play the main plot of which turned on reversals of the sexes and transvestitism involving Clara, Lucio, and Bobadillo. Amazonian maidens were known from classical times, but Bond has noticed the presence of martial maids on both warring sides during the siege of Ostend.[1] It may be suggested further that twenty years later, Massinger undertook to refurbish this old and apparently not popular[2] comedy by revising it in light of his knowledge of *La fuerʒa de la costumbre*, another play referring to the Spanish wars in Flanders, and of Leonard Digges' translation

---

[1] Bond, 'Six Plays', p. 266. Bentley dates the 'historic setting of the play' during the years following the Spanish siege of Ostend (which took place 1601–4), to which conspicuous reference is made in the opening scene (p. 364). If Beaumont and Fletcher are responsible for this historic setting, they were writing of a contemporary moment.

[2] If *Love's Cure* had not been popular when presented in its *ur*-version, Beaumont and Fletcher might have felt no qualms in extracting from it what of merit could be rescued – the character of Lazarillo – and in re-using it almost immediately, consigning the rest of their work to the files.

of the Spanish romance *Gerardo*, published in 1622.[1] To the latter
source Massinger had already turned in preparing with Fletcher *The
Spanish Curate*, and he used it again for the situation involving
Vitelli and Malroda (IV.ii). From it he may have taken the names
Sayavedra and Mendoza (though neither is uncommon); in historical materials on the Siege of Ostend he could have found the names
of Spinola, Alvarez, Vitelli, Pacheco, and Lamoral. No names
derive from *La fuerza de la costumbre*, but twice in the opening
scenes of *Love's Cure* does Bobadilla mention the force of custom
(I.ii.47; II.ii.95; in the latter instance the Fletcherian 'ye' is immediately adjacent). The most reasonable conclusion is that already
advanced by Mr Hoy: the Folio text presents a composite play the
sub-plots of which, joint efforts of Beaumont and Fletcher in *ca.*
1605, have been revised, rewritten, reordered, and fitted into a main
plot by Philip Massinger after 1625. Original material in this re-
working has been assigned to new characters, all names have been
made uniform, and the whole has been given a final integrity surprising in light of its fragmented composition. 'The play has been
re-worked, in some degree, from beginning to end, but it has been
re-worked much more extensively in some places than in others.
Massinger's revision of the first and the last two acts has been so
extensive as to amount to re-writing...His handling of Acts II and
III was much less thoroughgoing; there he had been content to
stitch some of his favorite turns of phrase on to a textual fabric
clearly not of his own devising.'[2]

There is little evidence on which to found a description of the
manuscript that served as printer's copy for the Folio, but what
there is would suggest that the copy was itself, or was based on, a
prompt book. Many critics have noted the marginal stage direction
'2 *Torches* | *ready*' (beside III.iv.76), anticipating by 60 lines their
use; this clearly derives from actual prompt condition. Mr Hoy
adds that 'The long final scene has apparently been marked for two
theatrical cuts...which were never actually made in the prompt
book, but the cues for which survive in the folio text in the otherwise inexplicable repetition of two speeches. Genevora's line:

[1] Bond, 'Six Plays', pp. 266–7.
[2] Hoy, 'Fletcher and his Collaborators', p. 49.

'*Lamorall*: you have often sworne | You'ld be commanded by me"
[V.iii. after line 137*a*] is repeated...later [V.iii.150–1], where
following Lamorall's answer, her reply "Your hearing for six
words" [after 'in me.', line 153] anticipates...[line 174] at which
it is repeated, this time in a speech of Eugenia's.'[1] Another indication
of prompt origin is the appearance of entry directions a few lines
in advance of the moment of actual entry (as marked by the speech
of the entering character). This phenomenon is so frequent as to
constitute almost a policy on the matter. Yet another example of
this sort of anticipation occurs at I.iii.40 where the 'Musick' presumably accompanying Eugenia's entrance at line 40 is cited in a
direction at line 38.[2] The copy can hardly have served as a
thoroughly acceptable prompt book, however, for it lacks many
exit directions and a few entry directions; regularity in these matters
one would have assumed a prerequisite for intelligent prompting.

It should be mentioned in passing that there is evidence that the
play was written to be performed with an interval between Acts IV
and V (and thus presumably between the other acts as well), for the
text requires a character's exit at the end of one scene and his im-
mediate re-entry at the beginning of the succeeding scene. Such
going and coming are meaningless unless an interval (of music?)
intervenes. (This particular interval, according to Lamorall (V.i.1),
represents the passing of six hours.)

The text as preserved in the 1647 Folio frequently prints a dash
(——) to indicate, presumably, the deletion of an oath or assevera-
tion. Such spaces, variously filled by editors ('Heav'n', 'pox'),
have been reprinted as dashes in the present edition. No reconstruction suggests itself immediately for the two dashes at IV.ii.37.

Love's Cure, or The Martial Maid was printed in the 1647 Folio
in Section 5, the section assigned to Edward Griffin.[3] The play was

---

[1] Hoy, 'Fletcher and his Collaborators', pp. 55–6. See Textual Notes.

[2] Dyce was the first editor to notice this anticipation. For another of his comments
on the music of the play, see the Textual Note to III.ii.118.

[3] The comments that follow on the printing and press-work of *Love's Cure* are
much indebted to Professor Standish Henning, whose unpublished analysis of
Section 5, kindly made available to me, has confirmed some of my own findings and
illuminated others. I have also benefited from the insights of Mr (now Dr) Thomas L.
Berger in compositor analysis.

originally intended by Moseley to conclude the section, for it bears on the last page the catchword 'Queene of *Corinth*.', the title of the first play in section 6 following. In fact, it is followed by *The Honest Man's Fortune*, a play evidently added to Griffin's share after the original assignments had been made and perhaps after *Love's Cure* had been completely printed off.

The play occupies signatures 5Q3 through 5S6 (5S6^v is blank); quires 5Q and 5R are in fours, the normal pattern of the folio, but quire 5S is in sixes, another indication that it was designed to conclude the section.

The running-title analysis suggests three-skeleton work for the three quires, with three verso titles and three recto titles appearing in a reasonable sequence.

Verso:	I	Q3^v, R4^v, S5^v	*Loves Cure, or*[1]
	III	Q4^v, R1^v, S2^v, S4^v	*Loves Cure, or*[2]
	V	R2^v, R3^v, S1^v, S3^v	*Loves Cure, or*
Recto:	II	Q4, R4, S3, S5	*the Martiall Mayde.*
	IV	R1, S1, S2	*The Martiall Maid.*
	VI	R2, R3, S4	*The Martiall Maid.*

The inner and outer formes of the outer sheet of 5S are each printed in a skeleton from which one running title has been removed (i.e., from 5S6 and 6^v). As both these skeletons appear complete in the middle or inner sheets of the quire, it must follow that the middle and inner sheets were imposed before the outer sheet.[3] (To suppose that two skeletons were dismantled for the outer sheet and then reassembled for the middle and inner sheets, both of them correctly, would be to strain conjecture.) In consequence it should follow that printing began, as is now thought customary, from the innermost sheet (probably the innermost forme) of quires 5S and proceeded to the outermost. The same method obtained probably for 5Q and 5R.

---

[1] Title I is changed on S5^v to read '*Loves Cure, &c.*'

[2] Title III is pied between quires Q and R, '*Loves*' only remaining constant.

[3] Though the running title was removed to print page 5S6, the page number was not; in consequence, '143' appears on page 5S4 and again, erroneously, on page 5S6. The error demonstrates that 5S4 was printed before 5S6. Another error in pagination, '128' for '127' on 5Q4 (University of Texas, copy 2), is an error of verso for recto, occasioned perhaps by changing from one play to another.

Compositorial analysis suggests that three compositors set the type for *Love's Cure*; their stints are as follows:

Comp. *A*:   Q4^v, R1, 1^v, 2,   4^v, S1, 1^v
     B: R2^v, 3, 3^v, 4,
     C: Q3, 3^v, 4,
     A: S5, 5^v, 6
     B: S3^v, 4, 4^v,
     C: S2, 2^v, 3,

The indifference to distinctions of forme or quire argues for assignments based primarily on time and availability; it suggests successive (not simultaneous) work and points to seriatim setting as the method of composition used.[1]

The linguistic preferences that distinguish the compositors from one another are these:

A	*B*	*C*
I'le (Ile)	Ile	I'le (Ile)
i'le	ile	i'le
'tis, 'twas, 'twill, *etc.*	tis, twas, twill	'tis, 'twas, 'twill
beleeve	believe	believe
Country	Countrey	Country
Mistresse	Mistris	Mistris
doe (do)	do (doe)	do
goe	go (goe)	go
will	will (wil)	wil (will)

Attempts to relate these distinctions to the authorial divisions have not been fruitful; apparently the manuscript underlying the printed edition is in the hand of a single writer which yet preserves the varying linguistic formations of the several authors.

[1] The seeming random succession of stints of varying length in the *Love's Cure* quires is thoroughly consistent with the 'pattern' in the rest of Griffin's section, as Mr Henning's analysis makes clear. Though this pattern does not preclude the possibility of setting by formes in the play, it renders it unlikely; normally, that method of setting should reveal itself (one would suppose) in a pattern of shared work based on formes. The actual pattern here seems to be based on time, without regard to formes or quires.

Mr Henning notes (privately) that, as a general rule, types do not recur within the same quire; from this negative evidence he concludes tentatively that many pages were left standing (waiting to be printed or distributed) as the composition proceeded. Such a thesis is congruent with the proposition of seriatim setting and with the observation already advanced that printing proceeded from innermost forme (i.e., the first available) to outermost.

Though it is likely that *Love's Cure* was performed in its original condition – perhaps by the Children of Paul's – there is no record of a performance by the Children and no record of its ever having been licensed for the stage. It must be supposed, however, that it did enjoy a performance in its revised form, for a Prologue was written for the occasion (1626?). In a warrant issued by the Lord Chamberlain on 7 August 1641, prohibiting the publication of sixty plays the property of the King's Men,[1] *Love's Cure* was included as in their repertory. It was not performed between 1660 and 1710, and 'the 1778 editors stated that it had not been acted "for many years past." On May 22, 1793, the Drury Lane Company, performing in the Haymarket Theater, gave *The Female Duellist*, "never acted before."'[2] This 'poor farce' seems to have been inspired by *Love's Cure*.

The present text is based on a collation of sixteen copies of the 1647 Folio. In addition, four copies now at the Library of the University of Illinois and five copies (as well as the one fully collated) in the Library of the University of Texas have been sporadically examined for variants.

The Historical Collation includes the two seventeenth-century folio editions, the eighteenth-century collected editions, and the sole separate quarto edition (reprinting F2) of the play: 'Love's Cure: or, the Martial Maid. A Comedy. Written by Mr. Francis Beaumont, and Mr. John Fletcher. London, Printed for J. T. And Sold by J. Brown at the Black Swan without Temple-Bar. 1718.'

The only modern edition of the play of which I am aware is that of Professor Guy A. Battle, submitted as a master's thesis at Duke University in 1947, but the edition has not been published. Though I have not included this edition in the Historical Collation, I have profited much by its suggestions. I am indebted also to Mr L. A. Beaurline who has called to my attention the various manuscripts and musical settings of the song at III.ii.119–26; of the five settings, only one (Rosenbach) is without the music of John Wilson.

---

[1] Bald, *Bibliographical Studies*, pp. 5–8.

[2] Guy A. Battle (ed.), 'Loves Cure, or the Martiall Maid...A Critical Text with Comment' (unpublished master's thesis, Duke University, Durham, N.C., 1947), pp. 178, 177–80.

THE PERSONS REPRESENTED IN THE PLAY.

ASSISTANT, or Governor
VITELLI, *a young Gentleman, enemy to* Alvarez,
LAMORAL, *a fighting Gallant, friend to* Vitelli.
ANASTRO, *an honest Gentleman, friend to* Vitelli,
DON ALVAREZ, *a noble Gentleman Father to* Lucio, *and* Clara.
SIAVEDRA, *a friend to* Alvarez.
LUCIO, *Son to* Alvarez, *a brave young Gentleman in womans habit.*
ALGUAZIER, *a sharking pandarly Constable.*
[PIORATO, *a swordsman*]
PACHIECO, *a Cobler* ⎫
MENDOZA, *a Botcher,* ⎬ *of worship.*   10
METALDIE, *a Smith,* ⎭
LAZARILLO, Pachieco *his hungry servant*
BOBBADILLA, *a witty knave, servant to* Eugenia, *and Steward to*
Alvarez.
HERALD,
OFFICER.
[SERVANTS, PAGES, WATCH, GUARD, ATTENDANTS.]
   WOMEN.
EUGENIA, *a virtuous Lady, wife to* Don Alvarez.   20
CLARA, *Daughter to* Eugenia, *a martial Maid, valiant and chaste,*
enamoured of Vitelli.
GENEVORA, *Sister to* Vitelli, *in love with* Lucio.
MALRODA, *a wanton Mistirise of* Vitelli.

The Scene Sevil.

The Persons. . .Sevil.] F2; *om.* F1   5, 7 *Gentleman*] Gent. F2
   8 ALGUAZIER] ALGUAZEIR F2   14 *Steward*] Steward vant F2

Love's Cure
or,
The Martial Maid.

Enter Vitelli, Lamorall, Anastro.

Vitelli.   *Alvarez* pardon'd?

Anastro.   And return'd.

Lamorall.   I saw him land
At St. *Lucars,* and such a generall welcome
Fame, as harbinger to his brave actions,
Had with the easie people, prepard for him,
As if by his command alone, and fortune,
Holland with those low Provinces, that hold out
Against the Arch-Duke, were again compel'd
With their obedience to give up their lives
To be at his devotion.

Vitelli.   You amaze me,
For though I have heard, that when he fled from *Civill*   10
To save his life (then forfeited to Law
For murthering *Don Pedro* my deer Uncle)
His extreame wants inforc'd him to take pay
In th' Army sat down then before *Ostend,*
'Twas never yet reported, by whose favour
He durst presum to entertain a thought
Of comming home with pardon.

Anastro.   'Tis our nature
Or not to hear, or not to give beliefe
To what we wish far from our enemies.

Lamorall. Sir 'tis most certaine the Infantas letters   20
Assisted by the Arch-Dukes, to King *Philip*
Have not alone secur'd him from the rigor
Of our Castillian Justice, but return'd him
A free man, and in grace.

Vitelli.   By what curs'd meanes

10 *Civill*] i.e., Seville   14 *Ostend*] F2; Ostena F1

13

Could such a fugitive arise unto
The knowledge of their highnesses? much more
(Though known) to stand but in the least degree
Of favour with them?

Lamorall.   To give satisfaction
To your demand, though to praise him I hate,
Can yeild me small contentment, I will tell you,   30
And truly, since should I detract his worth,
'Twould argue want of merit in my self.
Briefly, to passe his tedious pilgrimage
For sixteene years, a banish'd guilty-man,
And to forget the stormes, th'affrights, the horrors
His constancy, not fortune overcame,
I bring him, with his little son, grown man
(Though 'twas said here he took a daughter with him)
To *Ostends* bloody seige that stage of war
Wherein the flower of many Nations acted,   40
And the whole Christian world spectators were;
There by his son, or were he by adoption
Or nature his, a brave Scene was presented,
Which I make choyce to speak of, since from that
The good successe of *Alvarez*, had beginning.

Vitelli.   So I love vertue in an enemy
That I desire in the relation of
This young mans glorious deed, you'ld keep your self
A friend to truth, and it.

Lamorall.   Such was my purpose;
The Town being oft assaulted, but in vaine,   50
To dare the prow'd defendants to a sally,
Weary of ease, *Don Inigo Peralta*
Son to the Generall of our Castile forces
All arm'd, advanc'd within shot of their wals,
From whence the muskateers plaid thick upon him,
Yet he (brave youth) as carelesse of the danger,
As carefull of his honor, drew his sword,
And waving it about his head, as if
He dar'd one spirited like himself, to triall

14

Of single valor, he made his retreat   60
With such a slow, and yet majestique pace,
As if he still cald low'd, dare none come on?
When sodainly from a posterne of the town
Two gallant horse-men issued, and o're-took him,
The army looking on, yet not a man
That durst relieve the rash adventurer,
Which *Lucio*, son to *Alvarez* then seeing,
As in the vant-guard he sat bravely mounted,
Or were it pity of the youths misfortune,
Care to preserve the honour of his Country,   70
Or bold desire to get himselfe a name,
He made his brave horse, like a whirle wind bear him,
Among the Combatants: and in a moment
Discharg'd his Petronell, with such sure aime
That of the adverse party from his horse,
One tumbled dead, then wheeling round, and drawing
A faulchion, swift as lightning he came on
Upon the other, and with one strong blow
In view of the amazed Town, and Campe
He strake him dead, and brought *Peralta* off   80
With double honour to himselfe.
Vitelli.   'Twas brave:
But the successe of this?
Lamorall.   The Campe receiv'd him
With acclamations of joy and welcome,
And for addition to the faire reward
Being a massy chain of gold given to him
By yong *Peralta's* Father, he was brought
To the Infantas presence, kiss'd her hand,
And from that Lady, (greater in her goodnesse
Then her high birth) had this encouragement:
Go on youngman; yet not to feed thy valour   90
With hope of recompence to come, from me,
For present satisfaction of what's past,
Aske any thing that's fit for me to give,
And thee to take, and be assur'd of it.

15

Anastro.   Excellent princesse.

Vitelli.   And stil'd worthily
The heart bloud, nay the soule of Souldiers.
But what was his request?

Lamorall.   That, the repeale
Of *Alvarez* makes plaine: he humbly begd
His Fathers pardon, and so movingly
Told the sad story of your uncles death   100
That the Infanta wept, and instantly
Granting his suit, working the Arch-duke to it,
Their Letters were directed to the King,
With whom they so prevaild, that *Alvarez*
Was freely pardon'd.

Vitelli.   'Tis not in the King
To make that good.

Anastro.   Not in the King? what subject
Dares contradict his power?

Vitelli.   In this I dare,
And wil: and not call his prerogative
In question, nor presume to limit it.
I know he is the Master of his Lawes,   110
And may forgive the forfeits made to them,
But not the injury done to my honour;
And since (forgeting my brave Uncles merits
And many services, under Duke *D'Alva*)
He suffers him to fall, wresting from Justice
The powerfull sword, that would revenge his death,
I'le fill with this *Astrea's* empty hand,
And in my just wreake, make this arme the Kings.
My deadly hate to *Alvarez*, and his house,
Which as I grew in years, hath still encreas'd,   120
As if it cal'd on time to make me man,
Slept while it had no object for her fury
But a weak woman, and her talk'd of Daughter:
But now, since there are quarries, worth her flight
Both in the father, and his hopefull son,

124 flight] Sympson; sight F 1–2

16

I'le boldly cast her off, and gorge her full
With both their hearts: to further which, your friendship
And oathes will your assistance: let your deedes
Make answer to me; uselesse are all words
Till you have writ performance with your Swords.   130

Exeunt.

Enter Bobadilla, *and* Lucio [*in woman's attire*].   [I.] ii

Lucio.   Go fetch my work: this ruffe was not well starch'd,
So tell the maid, 't has too much blew in it,
And look you that the Partrich and the Pullen
Have cleane meat, and fresh water, or my Mother
Is like to hear on't.
Bobadilla.   O good St. *Jaques* helpe me: was there ever such an
Hermaphrodite heard of? would any wench living, that should
hear and see what I do, be wrought to believe, that the best of a
man lies under this Petticoate, and that a Cod-peece were far
fitter here, then a pind-Placket?   10
Lucio.   You had best talk filthily: do, I have a tongue
To tell my Mother, as well as ears to heare
Your ribaldry.
Bobadilla.   Nay you have ten womens tongues that way I am
sure: why my yong Master or Mistris, Madam, Don, or what
you wil, what the devill have you to do with Pullen, or Partrich?
or to sit pricking on a clowt all day? you have a better needle,
I know, and might make better work, if you had grace to use it.
Lucio.   Why, how dare you speak this before me, sirha?
Bobadilla.   Nay rather, why dare not you do what I speak?— 20
though my Lady your mother, for fear of *Vitelli* and his faction,
hath brought you up like her daughter, and h'as kept you this
twentie year, which is ever since you were born, a close prisoner
within dores, yet since you are a man, and are as wel provided as
other men are, methinks you should have the same motions of the
flesh, as other Cavaliers of us are inclin'd unto.
Lucio.   Indeed you have cause to love those wanton motions,

6 St.] F2; Sir F1
14 Nay] F2; May F1

17

They having holp you to an excellent whipping,
For doing something, I but put you in mind of it,
With the Indian mayd, the governour sent my mother   30
From *Mexico*.

Bobadilla. Why, I but taught her a Spanish trick in charity,
and holp the King to a subject that may live to take *Grave Maurice*
prisoner, and that was more good to the State, then a thousand
such as you are ever like to do: and I wil tell you, (in a fatherly
care of the Infant I speak it) if he live (as blesse the babe, in
passion I remember him) to your years, shall he spend his time in
pinning, painting, purling, and perfuming as you do? no, he shall
to the wars, use his Spanish Pike, though with the danger of the
lash, as his father has done, and when he is provoked, as I am now, 40
draw his Toledo desperatly, as——

Lucio. You will not Kill me? oh.

Bobadilla [*aside*]. I knew this would silence him: how he hides
his eyes? if he were a wench now, as he seems, what an advantage
had I, drawing two Toledos, when one can do this? but oh me,
my Lady: I must put up:——young Master I did but jest:——
O custom, what ha'st thou made of him?

Enter Eugenia, [*with* Stephano] *and* [*other*] *Servants.*

Eugenia. For bringing this, be still my friend; no more
A servant to me.

Bobadilla.   What's the matter?

Eugenia.   Here,
Even here where I am happy to receive   50
Assurance of my *Alvarez* returne,
I wil kneell down: and may those holy thoughts
That now possesse me wholy, make this place
A Temple to me, where I may give thanks
For this unhop'd for blessing Heavens Kind hand
Hath pour'd upon me.

Lucio.   Let my duty Madam
Presume, if you have cause of joy, to entreat
I may share in it.

28 holp] Sympson; hope F1–2 *33 *Grave*] F2; grave F1 [i.e., *Graf* (or Count)]

18

Bobadilla [*aside*].   'Tis well, he has forgot how I frighted him yet.
Eugenia.   Thou shalt: but first kneel with me *Lucio*,   60
No more *Posthumina* now, thou hast a Father,
A Father living to take off that name,
Which my too credulous fears, that he was dead,
Bestow'd upon thee; thou shalt see him *Lucio*,
And make him young again, by seeing thee,
Who only hadst a being in my Womb
When he went from me, *Lucio*: O my joyes,
So far transport me, that I must forget
The ornaments of Matrons, modesty
And grave behaviour; but let all forgive me   70
If in th'expression of my soules best comfort
Though old, I do a while forget mine age,
And play the wanton in the enterteinment
Of those delights I have so long despair'd of.
Lucio.   Shall I then see my Father?
Eugenia.   This houre *Lucio*;
Which reckon the begining of thy life,
I mean that life, in which thou shalt appeare
To be such as I brought thee forth: a man,
This womanish disguise, in which I have
So long conceal'd thee, thou shalt now cast off,   80
And change those qualities thou didst learn from me,
For masculine virtues, for which seek no tutor,
But let thy fathers actions be thy precepts;
And for thee *Zancho*, now expect reward
For thy true service.
Bobadilla.   Shall I?——you hear fellow *Stephano*, learne to know
me more respectively; how do'st thou think I shall become the
Stewards chaire ha? will not these slender hanches show well with
a gold chaine, and a night-Cap after supper when I take the
accompts?   90
Eugenia.   Haste, and take down those blacks, with which my
          chamber
Hath like the widow, her sad Mistris, mourn'd,

89 gold chaine, and a] Colman; chaine, and a gold F1–2

And hang up for it, the rich Persian arras,
Us'd on my wedding night: for this to me
Shall be a second marriage: send for Musique,
And will the cooks to use their best of cunning
To please the palat.

Bobadilla. Will your Ladiship have a Potato-pie, tis a good
stirring dish for an old Lady, after a long Lent.

Eugenia. Be gon I say: why sir, you can go faster?   100

Bobadilla. I could Madam: but I am now to practise the Stewards
pace, that's the reward I look for: every man must fashion his
gate, according to his calling:——you fellow *Stephano*, may walk
faster, to overtake preferment: so, usher me. [*Exit with Servant.*]

Lucio. Pray Madam, let the wascoat I last wrought
Be made up for my Father: I wil have
A cap and boote-hose sutable to it.

Eugenia.   Of that
Wee'l think hereafter *Lucio*: our thoughts now
Must have no object, but thy Fathers welcome,
To which thy helpe——

Lucio.   With humble gladnesse Madam.   110
                                        Exeunt.

Enter Alvarez, Clara [*in man's attire*].   [I.] iii

Alvarez. Where lost we *Syavedra*?

Clara.   He was met
Entring the City by some Gentlemen
Kinsmen, as he said of his own, with whom
For complement sake (for so I think he term'd it)
He was compel'd to stay: though I much wonder
A man that knowes to do, and has done well
In the head of his troop, when the bold foe charg'd home,
Can learn so sodainly to abuse his time
In apish entertainment: for my part
(By all the glorious rewards of war)   10
I had rather meet ten enemies in the field
All sworn to fetch my head, then be brought on

98 Potato-pie] i.e., an aphrodisiac   103 gate] i.e., gait

To change an houres discourse with one of these
Smooth City fools, or tissue Cavaliers,
The only Gallants, as they wisely think,
To get a Jewell, or a wanton Kisse
From a Court-lip, though painted.
Alvarez.   My lovd *Clara*
(For *Lucio* is a name thou must forget
With *Lucios* bold behaviour) though thy breeding
I'the camp may plead something in the excuse   20
Of thy rough manners, custome having chang'd,
Though not thy Sex, the softnesse of thy nature,
And fortune (then a cruell stepdame to thee)
Impos'd upon thy tender sweetnesse, burthens
Of hunger, cold, wounds, want, such as would crack
The sinewes of a man, not borne a Souldier:
Yet, now she smiles and like a naturall mother
Looks gently on thee, *Clara*, entertaine
Her proffer'd bounties with a willing bosome;
Thou shalt no more have need to use thy sword;   30
Thy beauty (which even *Belgia* hath not alter'd)
Shall be a stronger guard, to keep my *Clara*,
Then that has bin, (though never us'd but nobly)
And know thus much——
Clara.   Sir, I know only that
It stands not with my duty to gaine-say you,
In any thing: I must, and will put on
What fashion you think best: though I could wish
I were what I appeare.
Alvarez.   Endeavour rather
To be what you are, *Clara*, entring here
As you were borne, a woman.

15 The] F2; Then F1   15 Gallants] F2; Gallans F1
17 lovd] Sympson; Love F1–2   26 borne] i.e., born

Enter Eugenia, Lucio, *Servants.*

Eugenia.   Let choice Musick   *Musick.* 40
  In the best voyce that ere touch'd humane eare,
  For joy hath tide my tongue up, speak your welcome.
Alvarez. My soule, (for thou giv'st new life to my spirit)
  Myriads of joyes, though short in number of
  Thy vertues, fall on thee; Oh my *Eugenia*,
  Th'assurance, that I do embrace thee, makes
  My twenty years of sorrow but a dreame,
  And by the Nectar, which I take from these,
  I feele my age restor'd, and like old *Æson*,
  Grow young againe.
Eugenia.   My Lord long wish'd for, welcome,   50
  Tis a sweet briefnesse, yet in that short word
  All pleasures which I may call mine, begin,
  And may they long increase, before they finde
  A second period: let mine eyes now surfet
  On this so wish'd for object, and my lips
  Yet modestly pay back the parting kisse
  You trusted with them, when you fled from *Civill*
  With little *Clara* my sweet daughter: lives she?
  Yet I coul'd chide my selfe, having you here
  For being so coveteous of all joyes at once,   60
  T'enquire for her, you being alone, to me
  My *Clara*, *Lucio*, my Lord, my selfe,
  Nay more then all the world.
Alvarez.   As you, to me are.
Eugenia. Sit down, and let me feed upon the story
  Of your past dangers, now you are here in safety
  It will give rellish, and fresh appetite
  To my delights, if such delights can cloy me.
  Yet do not *Alvarez*, let me first yeild you
  Accompt of my life in your absence, and
  Make you acquainted how I have preserv'd   70
  The Jewell left lock'd up in my womb,

22

When you, in being forc'd to leave your country,
Suffer'd a civill death.
Alvarez.　　　　　Doe my *Eugenia,*
'Tis that I most desire to heare.
Eugenia.　　　　　Then know——

　　Within Clashing swords. Sayavedra [*calls*] *within.*

Alvarez.　What voyce is that?
Sayavedra [*within*].　　　　If you are noble Enemies,
Oppresse me not with odds, but kill me fairely.
Vitelli (*within*).　Stand off, I am too many of my selfe.

　　　　　　Enter Bobadilla.

Bobadilla.　Murther, murther murther, your friend my Lord,
Don *Syavedra* is set upon in the Streets, by your enemies *Vitelli,*
and his Faction: I am almost kill'd with looking on them.　　80
Alvarez.　Ile free him, or fall with him: draw thy sword
And follow me.　　　　　　　　　　[*Exit.*]
Clara.　　　　Fortune I give thee thankes
For this occasion once more to use it.　　　　　*Exit.*
Bobadilla.　Nay, hold not me Madam; if I doe any hurt, hang me.
Lucio.　Oh I am dead with feare! let's flye into
Your Closet, Mother.
Eugenia.　　　　　No houre of my life
Secure of danger? heav'n be mercifull,
Or now at once dispatch me.

　　　Enter Vitelli, *pursued by* Alvarez, *and* Sayavedra,
　　　　　　Clara *beating of* Anastro.

Clara [*to Alvarez*].　　　　Follow him:
Leave me to keepe these off.
Alvarez.　　　　　Assault my friend
So neere my house?
Vitelli.　　　　Nor in it will spare thee,　　90

74 heare] F2; he are F1　　　75 *Sayavedra.*] F2; *om.* F1
77 *Vitelli.*] F2; *om.* F1
*88 *beating of*] i.e., beating off　　90 my] F2; by F1

23

Though 'twere a Temple: and Ile mak it one,
I being the Priest, and thou the sacrifice,
Ile offer to my uncle.
Alvarez.   Haste thou to him,
And say I sent thee.   [Alvarez *and* Sayavedra *attack* Vitelli.]
Clara [*apart*].   'Twas put bravely by,
And that: and yet comes on, and boldly rare:
In the warres, where emulation and example
Joyn to encrease the courage, and make lesse
The danger; valour, and true resolution
Never appear'd so lovely: brave againe:
Sure he is more then man, and if he fall,   100
The best of vertue, fortitude would dye with him:
And can I suffer it? forgive me duty,
So I love valour, as I will protect it
Against my Father, and redeeme it, though
'Tis forfeited by one I hate.   [*She joins* Vitelli.]
Vitelli [*to Clara*].   Come on,
All is not lost yet: You shall buy me deerer
Before you have me: keep off.
Clara.   Feare me not,
Thy worth has tooke me Prisoner, and my sword
For this time knowes thee onely for a friend,
And to all else I turne the point of it.   110
Sayavedra.   Defend your Fathers Enemy?
Alvarez.   Art thou mad?
Clara.   Are you men rather? shall that valour, which
Begot you lawfull honour in the warres,
Prove now the parent of an infamous Bastard
So foule, yet so long liv'd, as murther will
Be to your shames? have each of you, alone
With your own dangers onely, purchas'd glory
From multitudes of Enemies, not allowing
Those neerest to you, to have part in it,
And doe you now joyn, and lend mutuall helpe   120
Against a single opposite? hath the mercy
Of the great King, but newly wash'd away

24

The blood, that with the forfeit of your life
Cleav'd to your name, and family like an ulcer,
In this againe to set a deeper dye
Upon your infamy? you'll say he is your foe,
And by his rashnesse call'd on his own ruine;
Remember yet, he was first wrong'd, and honour
Spur'd him to what he did: and next the place
Where now he is, your house, which by the lawes   130
Of hospitable duty should protect him;
Have you been twenty yeeres a stranger to it,
To make your entrance now in blood? or thinke you
Your country-man, a true born Spaniard, will be
An offring fit, to please the genius of it?
No, in this i'le presume to teach my Father,
And this first Act of disobedience shall
Confirme I am most dutifull.
Alvarez [*aside*].   I am pleas'd
With what I dare not give allowance to.——
Unnaturall wretch, what wilt thou doe?
Clara.   Set free   140
A noble Enemy: come not on, by —
You passe to him, through me:——[*To* Vitelli] the way is open:
Farwell: when next I meet you, doe not look for
A friend, but a vow'd foe; I see you worthy,
And therefore now preserve you, for the honour
Of my sword onely.
Vitelli [*aside*].   Were this man a friend,
How would he win me, that being my vow'd foe
Deserves so well?——I thanke you for my life;
But how I shall deserve it, give me leave
Hereafter to consider.   *Exit.*
Alvarez [*to Eugenia*].   Quit thy feare,   150
All danger is blown over: I have Letters
To the Governour, in the Kings name, to secure us,
From such attempts hereafter: yet we need not
That have such strong guards of our own, dread others;
And to encrease thy comfort, know, this young man

Whom with such fervent earnestnesse you eye,
Is not what he appeares, but such a one
As thou with joy wilt blesse, thy daughter *Clara*.
Eugenia.   A thousand blessings in that word.
Alvarez.   The reason
Why I have bred her up thus, at more leisure   160
I will import unto you: wonder not
At what you have seen her doe, it being the least
Of many great and valiant undertakings
She hath made good with honour.
Eugenia.   Ile returne
The joy I have in her, with one as great
To you my *Alvarez*: you, in a man
Have given to me a daughter: in a woman,
I give to you a Sonne: this was the pledge
You left here with me, whom I have brought up
Different from what he was, as you did *Clara*,   170
And with the like successe; as she appeares
Alter'd by custome, more then woman, he
Transform'd by his soft life, is lesse then man.
Alvarez.   Fortune, in this gives ample satisfaction
For all our sorrowes past.
Lucio.   My deerest Sister.
Clara.   Kinde brother.
Alvarez.   Now our mutuall care must be
Imploy'd to help wrong'd nature, to recover
Her right in either of them, lost by custome:
To you I give my *Clara*, and receive
My *Lucio* to my charge: and we'll contend   180
With loving industry, who soonest can
Turne this man woman, or this woman man.
                             Exeunt.

Enter Pachieco, *and* Lazarillo.

Pachieco.   Boy: my Cloake, and Rapier; it fits not a Gentleman
of my ranck, to walke the streets in *Querpo.*
Lazarillo.   Nay, you are a very ranck Gentleman. *Signior,* I am
very hungry, they tell me in *Civill* here, I looke like an Eele, with
a mans head: and your neighbour the Smith here hard by, would
have borrowed me th'other day, to have fish'd with me, because
he had lost his angle-rod.
Pachieco.   Oh happy thou *Lazarillo* (being the cause of other mens
wits) as in thine own: live leane, and witty still: oppresse not thy
stomach too much: grosse feeders, great sleepers: great sleepers, 10
fat bodies; fat bodies, lean braines: No *Lazarillo,* I will make thee
immortall, change thy humanitie into deitie, for I will teach thee
to live upon nothing.
Lazarillo.   Faith *Signior,* I am immortall then already, or very
neere it, for I doe live upon little or nothing: belike that's the
reason the Poets are said to be immortall, for some of them live
upon their wits, which is indeed as good as little or nothing:
But good Master, let me be mortall still, and let's goe to supper.
Pachieco.   Be abstinent; shew not the corruption of thy generation:
he that feeds, shall die, therefore he that feeds not, shall live.   20
Lazarillo.   I; but how long shall be live? ther's the question.
Pachieco.   As long as he can without feeding: did'st thou read of
the miraculous maid in *Flanders?*
Lazarillo [*aside*].   No, nor of any maid else; for the miracle of
virginitie now a daies ceases, ere the virgin can read virginitie.
Pachieco.   She that liv'd three yeere without any other sustenance
then the smell of a Rose.
Lazarillo.   I heard of her *Signior;* but they say her guts shrunk
all into Lute-strings, and her neather-parts cling'd together like a
Serpents Taile, so that though she continued a woman still above 30
the girdle, beneath that she was monster.
Pachieco.   So are most women, beleeve it.

*2 *Querpo*] i.e., undress (Sp. *cuerpo*)
12 deitie] F 2; dietie F 1
*31 that] yet F 1–2

Laɀarillo. Nay all women *Signior*, that can live onely upon the smell of a Rose.

Pachieco. No part of the History is fabulous.

Laɀarillo. I thinke rather no part of the Fable is Historicall: but for all this, sir, my rebellious stomach will not let me be immortall: I will be as immortall, as mortall hunger will suffer: put me to a certaine stint sir, allow me but a red herring a day.

Pachieco. O' de dios: would'st thou be gluttonous in thy deli- 40 cacies?

Laɀarillo. He that eats nothing but a red herring a day, shall ne'ere be broyl'd for the devils rasher: a Pilcher, *Signior*, a Surdiny, an Olive, that I may be a philosopher first, and immortall after.

Pachieco. Patience *Laɀarillo*; let contemplation be thy food a while: I say unto thee, one Peaze was a Souldiers provant a whole day, at the destruction of *Jerusalem*.

Laɀarillo. I; and it were any where, but at the destruction of a place, i'le be hang'd.

Enter Metaldi, *and* Mendoza.

Metaldi. *Signior Pachieco Alasto*, my most ingenious Cobler of 50 *Civill*, the *bonos noxios* to your *Signiorie*.

Pachieco. *Signior Metaldi de Forgio*, my most famous Smith, and man of mettle, I returne your curtesie ten fold, and do humble my Bonnet beneath the Shooe-soale of your congie: the like to you *Signior Mendoɀa Pediculo de Vermini*, my most exquisite Hose-heeler.

Laɀarillo [*aside*]. Her's a greeting betwixt a Cobler, a Smith, and a Botcher: they all belong to the foot, which makes them stand so much upon their Gentrie.

Mendoɀa. Signior Laɀarillo. 60

Laɀarillo. Ah *Signior* see: nay, we are all *Signiors* here in *Spaine*, from the Jakes-farmer to the Grandee, or *Adelantado*: —— this botcher looks as if he were dowgh-bak'd; a little butter now, and I could eate him like an oaten-Cake: his fathers diet was new Cheese and Onions when he got him: what a scallion-fac'd rascall 'tis?

Metaldi. But why *Signior Pachieco*, do you stand so much on the

43 ne'ere] F2; neere F1   61 see] i.e., *si*

28

prioritie, and antiquitie of your qualitie (as you call it) in comparison of ours?

Mendoza. I; your reason for that.

Pachieco. Why thou Iron-pated Smith: and thou wollen-witted 70
Hose heeler: heare what I will speak indifferently (and according
to Ancient writers) of our three professions: and let the upright
Lazarillo be both judge, and moderator.

Lazarillo. Still am I the most immortally hungrie, that may be.

Pachieco [to Metaldi]. Suppose thou wilt derive thy pedigree, like
some of the old Heroes, (as *Hercules*, *Æneas*, *Achilles*) lineally
from the Gods, making *Saturne* thy great Grand-father, and
Vulcan thy Father: *Vulcan* was a God——

Lazarillo [aside]. He'll make *Vulcan* your God-father by and by.

Pachieco. Yet I say *Saturne* was a crabbed block-head, and 80
Vulcan a limping horn-head, for *Venus* his wife was a strumpet,
and *Mars* begat all her Children; therefore however, thy originall
must of necessitie spring from Bastardie: further, what can be a
more deject spirit in man, then to lay his hands under every ones
horses feet, to doe him service, as thou do'st? [*To Mendoza*] For
thee, I will be briefe: thou do'st botch, and not mend, thou art a
hider of enormities, *viz.* scabs, chilblaines, and kibed heeles:
much proane thou art to Sects, and Heresies, disturbing state, and
government; for how canst thou be a sound member in the
Common-wealth, that art so subject to stitches in the anckles?—— 90
Blush, and be silent then, Oh ye Machanick, compare no more with
the politique Cobler: For Coblers (in old time) have prophesied,
what may they doe now then, that have every day waxed better,
and better? have we not the length of every mans foot? are we not
daily menders? yea, and what menders? not horse-menders——

Lazarillo [aside]. Nor manners-menders.

Pachieco. But soule-menders: Oh divine Coblers; doe we not
like the wise man spin our own threds, (or our wives for us?)
doe we not by our sowing the hide, reape the beefe? are not we of
the gentle craft, whil'st both you are but crafts-men? You will say 100
you feare neither Iron nor steele, and what you get is wrought out
of the fire, I must answer you againe, though, all this is but forgery.

97 soule-menders] F1(c); soule-members F1(u)

You may likewise say, a mans a man, that has but a hose on his head: I must likewise answer, that man is a botcher, that has a heel'd-hose on his head: to conclude there can be no comparison with the Cobler, who is all in all in the Common-wealth, has his politique eye and ends on every mans steps that walkes, and whose course shall be lasting to the worlds end.

Metaldi. I give place: the wit of man is wonderfull: thou hast hit the naile on the head, and I will give thee six pots for't though I 110 ne'ere clinch shooe againe.

Enter Vitelli *and* Alguazier.

Pachieco [*apart*]. Who's this? Oh our *Alguazier*: as arrant a knave as e're wore one head under two offices: he is one side *Alguazier*——

Metaldi [*apart*]. The other side Serjeant.

Mendoza [*apart*]. That's both sides carrion I am sure.

Pachieco [*apart*]. This is he apprehends whores in the way of justice, and lodges 'em in his own house, in the way of profit: he with him, is the *Grand-Don Vitelli*, 'twixt whom and *Fernando Alvarez* the mortall hatred is: he is indeed my *Dons* Bawd, and 120 do's at this present lodge a famous Curtizan of his, lately come from *Madrill*.

Vitelli. Let her want nothing Signior, she can aske:
What losse, or injury you may sustaine
I will repaire, and recompence your love:
Onely that fellowes coming I mislike,
And did fore-warn her of him: beare her this
With my best love, at night i'le visit her.

Alguazier. I rest your Lordships Servant.

Vitelli.   Good ev'n, Signior:——
[*Apart*] Oh *Alvarez*, thou hast brought a Sonne with thee   130
Both brightens, and obscures our Nation,
Whose pure strong beames on us, shoot like the Suns
On baser fires: I would to heaven my blood

111 ne'ere] F2; neere F1   *111 clinch] F2; clinth F1
113 one head] F2; ont head F1   122 *Madrill*] i.e., Madrid
129 *Signior*] Dyce; Signiors F1–2   131 brightens] F2; brightnes F1

30

Had never stain'd thy bold unfortunate hand,
That with mine honour I might emulate
Not persecute such vertue: I will see him
Though with the hazard of my life: no rest
In my contentious spirits can I finde
Till I have gratefide him in like kinde.   *Exit.*

Alguazier. I know you not: what are ye? hence ye base Besegnios. 140

Pachieco. Marry, *Catzo: Signior Alguazier,* do'ye not know us?
why, we are your honest neighbours, the Cobler, Smith, and
Botcher, that have so often sate snoaring cheeke by joll with your
Signiorie in rug at midnight.

Lazarillo. Nay, good *Signior,* be not angry: you must understand,
a Cat and such an Officer see best in the dark.

Metaldi. By this hand, I could finde in my heart to shooe his
head.

Pachieco. Why then we know you *Signior;* thou mongrill begot at
midnight, at the Goale gate, by a Beadle, on a Catch-poles wife, 150
are not you he that was whipt out of *Toledo* for perjury?

Mendoza. Next, condemn'd to the Gallies for pilfery, to the buls
pizell?

Metaldi. And after call'd to the Inquisition, for Apostacie?

Pachieco. Are not you he that rather then you durst goe an
industrious voyage being press'd to the Islands, skulk'd till the
fleet was gone, and then earn'd your royall a day by squiring
puncks, and pruncklings up and down the City?

Lazarillo. Are not you a Portuguize borne, descended o'the
Moores, and came hither into *Civill* with your Master, an errant 160
Taylor, in your red Bonnet, and your Blew Jacket lowsie: though
now your block head be cover'd with the Spanish Block, and
your lashed Shoulders with a Velvet Pee?

Pachieco. Are not you he, that have been of thirty callings, yet
ne're a one lawfull? that being a Chandler first, profess'd sincerity,
and would sell no man Mustard to his beefe on the Sabbath, and
yet sold Hypocrisie all your life time?

Metaldi. Are not you he, that were since a Surgeon to the

141 Marry] Sympson; *Mary* F 1–2
149 we] Sympson; *om.* F 1–2   163 Pee] i.e., pea (a short coat)

Stewes, and undertooke to cure what the Church it selfe could not,
strumpets? that rise to your Office by being a great *Dons* Baw'd? 170
Laȝarillo. That commit men nightly, offencelesse, for the gaine
of a groat a Prisoner, which your Beadle seemes to put up, when
you share three pence?
Mendoȝa. Are not you he, that is a kisser of men, in drunkennesse,
and a berrayer in sobriety?
Alguaȝier [aside]. *Diabolo:* they'll raile me into the Gallyes again.
Pachieco. Yes *Signior,* thou art even he we speake of all this while:
thou maist by thy place now, lay us by the heeles: 'tis true: but
take heed, be wiser, pluck not ruine on thine own head: for never
was there such an Anatomy, as we shall make thee then: be wise 180
therefore, Oh thou Childe of the night! be friends and shake
hands, thou art a proper man, if they beard were redder: remember
thy worshipfull function, a Constable, though thou turn'st day
into night, and night into day, what of that? watch lesse, and pray
more: gird thy beares skin (*viȝ.* thy Rug-gowne) to thy loynes,
take thy staffe in thy hand, and goe forth at midnight: Let not thy
mittens abate the talons of thy authority, but gripe theft and
whoredom, wheresoever thou meet'st 'em: bear 'em away like a
tempest, and lodge 'em safely in thine own house.
Laȝarillo. Would you have whores and theeves lodg'd in such a 190
house?
Pachieco. They ever doe so: I have found a theefe, or a whore
there, when the whole Suburbs could not furnish me.
Laȝarillo. But why doe they lodge there?
Pachieco. That they may be safe, and forth-coming: for in the
morning usually the theefe is sent to the Goale, and the whore
prostrates her selfe to the Justice.
Mendoȝa. Admirable *Pachieco.*
Metaldo. Thou Cobler of Christendom.
Alguaȝier [aside]. There is no railing with these rogues: I will 200
close with 'em, till I can cry quittance.——Why *Signiors,* and
my honest neighbours, will you impute that as a neglect of my
friends, which is an imperfection in me? I have been Sand-blinde
from my infancie: to make you amends, you shall sup with me.

170 rise] i.e., rose (dialect 'riz')

Lazarillo.   Shall we sup with 'ye sir?——O' my conscience, they
have wrong'd the Gentleman extreamly.

Alguazier.   And after supper, I have a project to employ you in
shall make you drink, and eat merrily this moneth: I am a little
knavish: why and doe not I know all you to be knaves?

Pachieco.   I grant you, we are all knaves, and will be your knaves: 210
But, oh, while you live, take heed of being a proud knave.

Alguazier.   On then passe: I will beare out my staffe, and my
staffe shall beare out me.

Lazarillo.   Oh *Lazarillo,* thou art going to supper.

                                                         Exeunt.

        Enter Lucio [*in man's attire*], *and* Bobadilla.   [II.] ii

Lucio.   Pray be not angry.

Bobadilla.   I am angry, and I will be angry: *diablo*'what should you
doe in the Kitchin, cannot the Cooks lick their fingers without
your overseeing? nor the maids make pottage, except your dogs-
head be in the pot? *Don Lucio, Don Quot-queane, Don Spinster,*
weare a Petti-coate still, and put on your smock a' monday: I will
have a babie o' clouts made for it, like a great girl: nay, if you will
needs be starching of Ruffs, and sowing of black-work, I will
of a milde, and loving Tutor, become a Tyrant. Your Father has
committed you to my charge, and I will make a man, or a mouse on   10
you.

Lucio.   What would you have me doe? this scurvy sword
So gals my thigh: I would 'twer burnt: pish, looke
This cloak will ne'r keep on: these boots too hidebound,
Make me walk stiffe, as if my leggs were frozen,
And my Spurs gingle, like a Morris-dancer:
Lord, how my head akes, with this roguish hat;
This masculine attire, is most uneasie,
I am bound up in it: I had rather walke
In folio, againe, loose, like a woman.   20

Bobadilla.   In Foolio, had you not?
Thou mock to heav'n, and nature, and thy Parents,
Thou tender Legge of Lamb; Oh, how he walkes

  2 *Bobadilla.*] F2; *om.* F1   7 babie] F2; badie F1

                            33

As if he had be-piss'd himselfe, and fleares!
Is this a gate for the young Cavalier,
Don Lucio, Sonne and heire to Alvarez?
Has it a corne? or do's it walke on conscience,
It treads so gingerly? Come on your wayes,
Suppose me now your Fathers foe, Vitelli,
And spying you i'th' street, thus I advance,   30
I twist my Beard, and then I draw my sword.
Lucio.   Alas.
Bobadilla.   And thus accost thee: ——traiterous brat,
How dur'st thou thus confront me? impious twig
Of that old stock, dew'd with my kinsmans gore,
Draw, for i'le quarter thee in peeces foure.
Lucio.   Nay, Prethee Bobadilla, leave thy fooling,
Put up thy sword, I will not meddle with'ye;
I, justle me, I care not: I'le not draw,
Pray be a quiet man.
Bobadilla.   Do'ye heare: answer me, as you would doe Don Vitelli, 40
or i'le be so bold as to lay the pomell of my sword over the hilts of
your head:
My name's Vitelli, and i'le have the wall.
Lucio.   Why then i'le have the kennell: what a coyle you keepe?
Signior, what happen'd 'twixt my Sire and your
Kinsman, was long before I saw the world,
No fault of mine, nor will I justifie
My Fathers crimes: forget sir, and forgive,
'Tis Christianity: I pray put up your sword,
Ile give you any satisfaction   50
That may become a Gentleman; however
I hope you are bred to more humanity
Then to revenge my Fathers wrong on me
That crave your love, and peace:——law you now Zancho
Would not this quiet him, were he ten Vitellies?
Bobadilla.   Oh craven-chicken of a Cock o'th' game: well, what
remedy? did thy father see this, O' my conscience, he would cut of
thy Masculine gender, crop thine eares, beat out thine eyes, and
set thee in one of the Peare-trees for a scar-crow: As I am Vitelli,

I am satisfied, but as I am *Bobadilla Spindola Zancho*, Steward of 60
the house, and thy fathers servant, I could finde in my heart to
lop of the hinder part of thy face, or to beat all thy teeth into thy
mouth: Oh thou whay-blooded milk-sop, Ile waite upon thee no
longer, thou shalt ev'n waite upon me: come your wayes sir, I
shall take a little paines with ye else.

Enter Clara [*in woman's attire*].

Clara. Where art thou Brother *Lucio?* ran tan tan ta ran tan ran
tan tan, ta ran tan tan-tan. Oh, I shall no more see those golden
dayes, these clothes will never fadge with me: a — o' this filthie
vardingale, this hip-hape: [*to Bobadilla*] brother why are womens
hanches onely limited, confin'd, hoop'd in, as it were with these 70
same scurvy vardingales?
Bobadilla. Because womens hanches onely are most subject to
display and fly out.
Clara [*to Lucio*]. *Bobadilla*, rogue, ten Duckets, I hit the prepuse
of thy Cod-peice.
Lucio. Hold, if you love my life, Sister: I am not *Zancho Bobadilla*,
I am your brother *Lucio*: what a fright you have put me in?
Clara. Brother? and wherefore thus?
Lucio. Why, Master Steward here, *Signior Zancho*, made me
change: he do's nothing but misuse me, and call me Cowheard, 80
and sweares I shall waite upon him.
Bobadilla. Well: I doe no more then I have authority for:——
[*aside*] would I were away though: for she's as much too mannish,
as he too womanish: I dare not meddle with her, yet I must set a
good face on't (if I had it).——I have like charge of you Maddam,
I am as well to mollifie you, as to qualifie him: what have you to
doe with Armors, and Pistols, and Javelins, and swords, and such
tooles? remember Mistresse: nature hath given you a sheath onely,
to signifie women are to put up mens weapons, not to draw them:
looke you now, is this fit trot for a Gentlewoman? You shall see 90
the Court Ladies move like Goddesses, as if they trod ayre; they
will swim you their measures, like whiting-mops as if their feet
were finnes, and the hinges of their knees oyld: doe they love to

*69–77 see Textual Note

ride great horses, as you doe? no, they love to ride great asses
sooner: faith, I know not what to say to'ye both: Custome hath
turn'd nature topsie-turvy in you.

Clara. Nay but Master Steward——

Bobadilla. You cannot trot so fast, but he ambles as slowly.

Clara. *Signior Spindle*, will you heare me?

Bobadilla. He that shall come to bestride your virginitie, had 100
better be afoot o're the Dragon.

Clara. Very well.

Bobadilla. Did ever Spanish Lady pace so?

Clara. Hold these a little.

Lucio. Ile not touch 'em, I.

Clara. First doe I breake your Office o're your pate,
You Dog-skin-fac'd rogue, pilcher, you poore *John*,
Which I will beat to Stock-fish. [*Beats him.*]

Lucio. Sister.

Bobadilla. Maddam.

Clara. You Cittern-head, who have you talk'd to, hah?
You nasty, stincking, and ill-countenanc'd Cur.

Bobadilla. By this hand, Ile bang your brother for this, when 110
I get him alone.

Clara. How? kick him *Lucio*:——he shall kick you *Bob*,
Spight o' the nose, that's flat:—— kick him, I say,
Or I will cut thy head off.

Bobadilla [*aside to Lucio*]. Softly y'had best. [*Lucio kicks him.*]

Clara. Now, thou leane, dride, and ominous visag'd knave,
Thou false and peremptory Steward, pray,
For I will hang thee up in thine own Chaine.

Lucio. Good Sister, doe not choake him.

Bobadilla. Murder, murder. *Exit.* 120

Clara. Well: I shall meet with'ye:——*Lucio*, who bought this?
'Tis a reasonable good one; but there hangs one
Spaines Champion ne're us'd truer: with this Staffe
Old *Alvarez* has led up men so close,
They could almost spit in the Canons mouth,
Whil'st I with that, and this well mounted, scurr'd

126 scurr'd] i.e., skirred

A Horse-troope through, and through, like swift desire,
And seen poor rogues retire, all gore, and gash'd
Like bleeding Shads.
Lucio.   'Blesse us, Sister *Clara*,
How desperately you talke: what do'ye call   130
This Gun, a dag?
Clara.   Ile give't thee: a French petronell:
You never saw my Barbary, the *Infanta*
Bestow'd upon me, as yet *Lucio?*
Walke down, and see it.
Lucio.   What into the Stable?
Not I, the Jades wil kick: the poore Groom there
Was almost spoyled the other day.
Clara.   Fie on thee,
Thou wilt scarce be a man before thy mother.
Lucio.   When wil you be a woman?
Clara.   Would I were none.
But natures privy Seale assures me one.   [*They talk apart.*]

Enter Alvarez *and* Bobadilla.

Alvarez.   Thou angerst me: can strong habituall custome   140
Work with such Magick on the mind, and manners
In spight of sex and nature? finde out sirha,
Some skilfull fighter.
Bobadilla.   Yes sir.
Alvarez.   I wil rectifie,
And redeem eithers proper inclination,
Or bray 'em in a morter, and new mold 'em.
Bobadilla.   Believe your eyes sir; I tell you, we wash an Ethiop.
                                                          Exit.
Clara.   I strike it for ten Duckets.
Alvarez.   How now *Clara*,
Your breeches on still? and your petticote
Not yet off *Lucio?* art thou not guelt?
Or did the cold Muscovite beget thee,   150
That lay here Lieger in the last great frost?

148–149 breeches on...petticote | Not yet off] i.e., figuratively

Art not thou *Clara*, turn'd a man indeed
Beneath the girdle? and a woman thou?
Ile have you search'd by —, I strongly doubt;
We must have these things mended: come go in.   *Exit.*

Enter Vitelli, *and* Bobadilla.

Bobadilla. With *Lucio* say you? there is for you.   [*Pointing.*]
Vitelli. And there is for thee.   [*Giving money.*]
Bobadilla. I thank you: you have now bought a little advice of
me; if you chance to have conference with that lady there, be very
civill, or looke to your head: she has ten nailes, and you have but 160
two eyes: If any foolish hot motions should chance to rise in the
horizon under your equinoctiall there, qualifie it as well as you
can, for I feare the elevation of your pole will not agree with the
Horoscope of her constitution: she is Bell the Dragon I assure you.
                                                                Exit.

Vitelli. Are you the *Lucio*, sir, that sav'd *Vitelli?*
Lucio. Not I indeed sir, I did never brable;
There walks that *Lucio*, metamorphosed.
Vitelli. Do ye mock me?   *Exit* [Lucio].
Clara.   No, he do's not: I am that
Suposed *Lucio* that was, but *Clara*
That is, and daughter unto *Alvarez.*   170
Vitelli. Amazement daunts me; would my life were riddles,
So you were still my faire Expositor:
Protected by a Lady from my death.
Oh I shall weare an everlasting blush
Upon my cheek from this discovery:
Oh you the fairest Souldier, I ere saw;
Each of whose eyes, like a bright beamy shield
Conquers, without blowes, the contentious.
Clara. Sir, guard yourself, you are in your enemies house,
And may be injur'd.
Vitelli.   Tis impossible: 180
Foe, nor oppressing odds dares prove *Vitelli*,
If *Clara* side him, and wil call him friend;
I would the difference of our bloods were such

As might with any shift be wip'd away:
Or would to Heaven your selfe were all your name;
That having lost blood by you, I might hope
To raise blood from you. But my black-wing'd fate
Hovers aversely over that fond hope:
And he, whose tongue thus gratifies the daughter,
And sister of his enemy, weares a Sword   190
To rip the father and the brother up.
Thus you, that sav'd this wretched life of mine,
Have savd it to the ruine of your friends.
That my affections should promiscuously
Dart love and hate at once, both worthily!
Pray let me kisse your hand.
Clara.   You are treacherous,
And come to do me mischiefe.
Vitelli.   Speake on still:
Your words are falser (faire) then my intents,
And each sweet accent far more treacherous; for
Though you speak ill of me, you speak so well,   200
I doe desire to heare you.
Clara.   Pray be gone:
Or kill me, if you please.
Vitelli.   Oh, neither can:
For to be gone, were to destroy my life;
And to kill you, were to destroy my soule:——
I am in love, yet must not be in love:
Ile get away apace:——yet valiant Lady,
Such gratitude to honour I do owe,
And such obedience to your memory,
That if you will bestow something, that I
May weare about me, it shall bind all wrath,   210
My most inveterate wrath, from all attempts,
Till you and I meet next.
Clara.   A favour sir?
Why I wil give ye good councell.

*202 can] *stet* F1   206 apace] F2; a pace F1

Vitelli.   That already
You have bestowd: a Ribbon, or a Glove.
Clara.   Nay those are tokens for a waiting-maid
To trim the Butler with.
Vitelli.   Your feather.
Clara.   Fie;
The wenches give them to their Serving-men.
Vitelli.   That little ring.
Clara.   Twill hold you but by th' finger;
And I would have you faster.
Vitelli.   Any thing
That I may weare, and but remember you.   220
Clara.   This smile: my good opinion, or my self.
But that it seems you like not.
Vitelli.   Yes, so well,
When any smiles, I will remember yours;
Your good opinion shall in weight poize me
Against a thousand ill: Lastly, your selfe,
My curious eye now figures in my heart,
Where I wil weare you, till the Table breake.
So, whitest Angels guard you.
Clara.   Stay sir, I
Have fitly thought to give, what you as fitly
May not disdaine to weare.
Vitelli.   What's that?
Clara.   This Sword.——   230
[*Aside.*] I never heard a man speak till this houre.
His words are golden chaines, and now I feare
The Lyonesse hath met a tamer here:
Fie, how this tongue chimes:——what was I saying?
Oh: this favour I bequeath you, which I tie
In a love-knot, fast, nere to hurt my friends;
Yet be it fortunate 'gainst all your foes
(For I have neither friend, not foe, but yours)
As ere it was to me: I have kept it long,
And value it, next my Virginity: 240

234 this] Dyce; his F1-2

40

But good, return it, for I now remember
I vow'd, who purchas'd it, should have me too.
Vitelli. Would that were possible: but alas it is not;
Yet this assure your selfe, most honour'd *Clara*,
Ile not infringe an Article of breath
My vow hath offerd to ye: nor from this part
Whilst it hath edge, or point, or I a heart.   *Exit.*
Clara. Oh leave me living:——what new exercise
Is crept into my breast, that blauncheth clean
My former nature? I begin to finde   250
I am a woman, and must learn to fight
A softer sweeter battaile, then with Swords.
I am sick me thinks, but the disease I feele
Pleaseth, and punisheth: I warrant love
Is very like this, that folks talke of so;
I skill not what it is, yet sure even here,
Even in my heart, I sensibly perceive
It glows, and riseth like a glimmering flame,
But know not yet the essence on't nor name.

                                                              Exit.

                    Enter Malroda, *and* Alguazier.   III. i

Malroda.   He must not, nor he shall not? who shall let him?
You? politique *Diego*, with your face of wisdome;
Don-blirt, the — on your aphorismes,
Your grave, and sage Ale physiognomy:
Do not I know thee for the *Alguazier*
Whose dunghill all the Parish Scavengers
Could never rid? thou Comedy to men,
Whose serious folly is a but for all
To shoot their wits at; whilst thou hast not wit,
Nor heart, to answer, or be angry.
Alguazier.   Lady.   10
Malroda.   Peace, peace, you rotten rogue, supported by
A staffe of rottener office: dare you check

                    1 let] i.e., hinder
                    8 but] i.e., butt

4   41   B D W

Anys accesses, that I wil allow?
Piorato is my friend, and visits me
In lawfull sort to espouse me as his wife;
And who wil crosse, or shall, our enter-viewes?
You know me sirha, for no Chambermaid,
That cast her belly, and her wastcote lately;
Thou thinkst thy Constableship is much: not so,
I am ten offices to thee: I, thy house,   20
Thy house, and Office is maintain'd by me.
Algua̧zier. My house of office is maintain'd ith' garden:
Go too, I know you, and I have conniv'd;
Y'are a delinquent, but I have conniv'd;
A poyson, though not in the third degree:
I can say, blacks your eye, though it be grey;
I have connivd at this your friend, and you:
But what is got by this connivency?
I like his feather well: a proper man,
Of good discourse, fine conversation,   30
Valiant, and a great carrier of the businesse,
Sweet breasted, as the Nightingale, or Thrush:
Yet I must tell you, you forget your selfe;
My Lord *Vitellies* love, and maintenance
Deserves no other Jack ith' box, but he:
What though he gather'd first the golden fruit,
And blew your pigges-coat up into a blister,
When you did wait at Court upon his mother;
Has he not wel provided for the barne?
Beside, what profit reap I by the other?   40
If you wil have me serve your pleasure, Lady,
Your pleasure must accommodate my service;
As good be vertuous and poore, as not
Thrive by my knavery: all the world would be
Good, prosper'd goodnesse like to villany.
I am the Kings vice-gerent by my place;

13 Anys] i.e., Anyone's
23, 24 conniv'd] Dyce; contriv'd F1-2
*29 feather] i.e., manner, character   39 barne] i.e., bairn

42

His right Lieutenant in mine owne precinct.

Malroda.   Thou art a right rascall in all mens precincts;
Yet now my paire of twins, of fools, and knave,
Looke we are friends; there's Gold for thee, admit   50
Whom I wil have, and keep it from my *Don*;
And I will make thee richer then thou art wise:
Thou shalt be my Bawd, and my Officer:
Thy children shall eate still, my good night Owle,
And thy old wife sell Andyrons to the Court,
Be countenanced by the *Dons*, and weare a hood,
Nay keepe my garden-house; Ile call her mother,
Thee father, my good poysonous red-har'd Dill,
And Gold shall daily be thy Sacrifice,
Wrought from a fertill Island of mine owne,   60
Which I wil offer, like an Indian Queen.

Alguazier.   And I wil be thy divel, thou my flesh,
With which Ile catch the world.

Malroda.   Fill some Tobacco,
And bring it in: if *Piorato* come
Before my *Don*, admit him; if my *Don*
Before my Love, conduct him, my deere devill.

Alguazier.   I wil my dear flesh: first come, first serv'd. Wel said.

                                              Exit [Malroda].

O equall Heaven, how wisely thou disposest
Thy severall gifts? one's born a great rich foole,
For the subordinate knave to worke upon: 70
Anothers poore, with wits addition,
Which wel or ill us'd, builds a living up;
And that too from the Sire oft discends:
Onely faire vertue, by traduction
Never succeeds, and seldome meets successe;
What have I then to do with't? My free will
Left me by Heaven, makes me or good, or ill:
Now since vice gets more in this vicious world
Then piety, and my stars confluence

47 owne] F2; owe F1
*58 Dill] *see Textual Note*

Enforce my disposition to affect   80
Gaine, and the name of rich, let who wil practice
War, and grow that way great: religious,
And that way good: my chiefe felicity
Is wealth the nurse of sensuality:
And he that mainly labours to be rich,
Must scratch great scabs, and claw a Strumpets itch.

                                                    Exit.

         Enter Piorato, *and* Bobadilla, *with Letters.*   [III.]

Piorato.   To say sir, I wil wait upon your Lord,
    Were not to understand my selfe.
Bobadilla.   To say sir
    You wil doe any thing but wait upon him,
    Were not to understand my Lord.
Piorato.   Ile meet him
    Some halfe houre hence, and doubt not but to render
    His sonne a man againe: the cure is easie,
    I have done divers.
Bobadilla.   Women do ye mean, sir?
Piorato.   Cures I do mean sir: be there but one sparke
    Of fire remaining in him unextinct,
    With my discourse Ile blow it to a flame;   10
    And with my practice, into action:
    I have had one so full of childish feare,
    And womanish-hearted sent to my advice,
    He durst not draw a Knife to cut his meat.
Bobadilla.   And how sir, did you help him?
Piorato.   Sir, I kept him
    Seaven daies in a darke room by Candle-light,
    A plenteous Table spread with all good meats,
    Before his eyes, a case of keen broad Knives,
    Upon the board, and he so watchd, he might not
    Touch the least modicum, unlesse he cut it: 20
    And thus I brought him first to draw a knife.
Bobadilla.   Good.

                          44

Piorato.　　　　Then for ten daies did I diet him
Onely with burnt Porke sir, and gammons of Bacon;
A pill of Caveary now and then,
Which breeds choler adust you know.
Bobadilla.　　　　　　　　　Tis true.
Piorato. And to purge phlegmatick humor, and cold crudities,
In all that time, he dranke me Aqua fortis,
And nothing else but——
Bobadilla.　　　　　　　Aqua vite *Signior*,
For Aqua fortis poysons.
Piorato.　　　　　Aqua fortis
I say again: what's one mans poyson *Signior*,　　　30
Is anothers meat or drinke.
Bobadilla.　　　　　　Your patience sir;
By your good patience, h'ad a huge cold stomacke.
Piorato. I fir'd it: and gave him then three sweats
In the Artillery-yard three drilling daies:
And now he'l shoot a Gun, and draw a Sword,
And fight with any man in Christendome.
Bobadilla. A receipt for a coward: Ile be bold sir
To write your good prescription.
Piorato.　　　　　　　Sir, hereafter
You shall, and underneath it put *probatum*:
Is your chaine right?
Bobadilla.　　　　　Tis both right and just sir;　　　40
For though I am a Steward, I did get it
With no mans wrong.
Piorato.　　　　　You are witty.
Bobadilla.　　　　　　So, so.
Could you not cure one sir, of being too rash
And over-daring? there now's my disease:
Fool-hardy as they say, for that in sooth
I am.
Piorato. Most easily.
Bobadilla.　　　　How?
Piorato.　　　　　　To make you drunke sir,
With smal Beere once a day; and beat you twice,

Till you be bruis'd all over: if that help not,
Knock out your braines.

Bobadilla.   This is strong Physick *Signior*,
And never wil agree with my weak body: 50
I finde the medcine worse then the malady,
And therefore wil remain fool-hardy stil:
You'l come sir?

Piorato.   As I am a Gentleman.

Bobadilla.   A man oth' Sword should never break his word.

Piorato.   Ile overtake you: I have onely sir
A complementall visitation
To offer to a Mistris lodgd hereby.

Bobadilla.   A Gentlewoman?

Piorato.   Yes sir.

Bobadilla.   Faire, and comely?

Piorato.   Oh sir, the Paragon, the Non-parill
Of *Civill*, the most wealthy Mine of *Spaine*,   60
For beauty, and perfection.

Bobadilla.   Say you so?
Might not a man entreat a curtesie,
To walke along with you *Signior*, to peruse
This dainty Mine, though not to dig in't *Signior*?
Hauh — I hope you'l not deny me, being a stranger;
Though I am Steward, I am flesh and blood,
And fraile as other men.

Piorato.   Sir, blow your nose:
I dare not for the world: no, she is kept
By a great *Don*, *Vitelli*.

Bobadilla.   How?

Piorato.   Tis true.

Bobadilla.   See, things wil veere about: this *Don Vitelli*   70
Am I to seeke now, to deliver Letters
From my young Mistris *Clara*: and I tell you,
Under the Rose, because you are a stranger,
And my speciall friend, I doubt there is

57 hereby] Langbaine; here by F 1–2

46

A little foolish love betwixt the parties,
Unknown unto my Lord.
Piorato [*aside*].   Happy discovery:
My fruit begins to ripen.———Hark you sir,
I would not wish you now, to give those Letters:
But home, and ope this to *Madona Clara*,
Which when I come Ile justifie, and relate   80
More amply, and particularly.
Bobadilla.   I approve
Your counsell, and wil practice it: *baʒi los manos*:———
Here's two chewres chewrd: when wisdome is imployd
Tis ever thus:———your more acquaintance, *Signior*:
I say not better, least you think, I thought not
Yours good enough.
Piorato.   Your servant excellent Steward.
                                        Exit [Bobadilla].
Would all the *Dons* in *Spain* had no more brains;
Here comes the *Alguaʒier.*

                    Enter Alguazier.

                    Dieu vous guard Mounsier.
Is my cuz stirring yet?
Alguaʒier.   Your cuz (good cosen)?
A whore is like a foole, akin to all   90
The gallants in the Town: Your cuz, good *Signior*,
Is gone abroad sir, with her other cosen,
My Lord *Vitelli*: since when there hath been
Some dozen cosens here to enquire for her.
Piorato.   She's greatly alli'd sir.
Alguaʒier.   Marry is she sir,
Come of a lusty kindred: the truth is,
I must connive no more: no more admittance
Must I consent to: my good Lord has threatned me,
And you must pardon.
Piorato.   Out upon thee man,
Turne honest in thine age? one foot ith' grave?   100

83 chewres] i.e., chores

47

Thou shalt not wrong thy selfe so, for a million:
Looke, thou three-headed *Cerberus* (for wit
I mean) here is one sop, and two, and three,
For every chop a bit.   [*Giving money.*]

Alguazier.   I marry sir:
Wel, the poore heart loves you but too wel.
We have been talking on you 'faith this houre:
Where, what I said, goe too: she loves your valour;
Oh and your Musicke most abominably:
She is within sir, and alone: what meane you?

Piorato.   That is your Sergeants side, I take it sir;   110
Now I endure your Constables much better;
There is lesse danger in't: for one you know
Is a tame harmlesse monster in the light,
The Sergeant salvage both by day, and night.

Alguazier.   Ile call her to you for that.

Piorato.   No, I wil charme her.

Enter Malroda.

Alguazier.   She's come.

Piorato.   My Spirit.

Malroda.   Oh my Sweet,
Leape hearts to lips, and in our kisses meet.

Piorato.   *Turn, turn thy beauteous face away,*   Song.
                    How pale and sickly looks the day,
                            In emulation of thy brighter beams!   120
            Oh envious light, fly, fly, be gone,
            Come night, and peece two breasts as one;
                    When what love does, we will repeat in dreams.
            Yet (thy eyes open) who can day hence fright,
            Let but their lids fall, and it will be night.

Alguazier.   Wel, I wil leave you to your fortitude;
And you to temperance: ah, ye pretty paire,
Twere sin to sunder you. Lovers being alone

*118 Song.] *see Textual Note*

48

Make one of two, and day and night all one.
But fall not out, I charge you, keep the peace;   130
You know my place else.   *Exit.*
Malroda.   No, you wil not marry:
You are a Courtier, and can sing (my Love)
And want no Mistrisses: but yet I care not,
Ile love you still; and when I am dead for you,
Then you'l believe my truth.
Piorato.   You kill me (faire)
It is my lesson that you speake: have I
In any circumstance deserv'd this doubt?
I am not like your false and perjur'd *Don*
That here maintains you, and has vowd his faith,
And yet attempts in way of marriage   140
A Lady not far off.
Malroda.   How's that?
Piorato.   Tis so:
And therefore Mistris, now the time is come
You may demand his promise; and I sweare
To marry you with speed.
Malroda.   And with that Gold
Which *Don Vitelli* gives, you'l walke some voyage
And leave me to my trade; and laugh, and brag,
How you ore-reach'd a whore, and guld a Lord.
Piorato.   You anger me extreamly: fare you wel.
What should I say to be believd? expose me
To any hazzard; or like jealous *Juno*   150
(Th' incensed step-mother of *Hercules*)
Designe me labours most impossible,
Ile doe 'em, or die in 'em; so at last
You wil believe me.
Malroda.   Come, we are friends: I doe.
I am thine, walk in: my Lord has sent me outsides,
But thou shalt have 'em, the colours are too sad.
Piorato.   'Faith Mistris, I want clothes indeed.
Malroda.   I have
Some Gold too, for my servant.

49

Piorato.   And I have
A better mettle for my Mistris.

> *Exeunt.*

Enter Vitelli *and* Alguazier, *at severall doors.*   [III.] ii

Alguazier [*aside*].   Undone — wit now or never help me: my
  Master
He wil cut my throat, I am a dead Constable;
And he'l not be hangd neither, there's the griefe:——
The party sir is here.
Vitelli.   What?
Alguazier.   He was here;
I cry your Lordship mercy: but I rattled him;
I told him here was no companions
For such deboshd, and poor-condition'd fellows;
I bid him venture not so desperately
The cropping of his eares, slitting his nose,
Or being gelt.
Vitelli.   Twas wel done.
Alguazier.   Please your honour,   10
I told him there were Stewes, and then at last
Swore three or foure great oathes she was remov'd,
Which I did thinke I might in conscience,
Being for your Lordship.
Vitelli.   What became of him?
Alguazier.   Faith sir, he went away with a flea in's eare,
Like a poore cur, clapping his trindle taile
Betwixt his legs.—*A chi ha, a chi ha, a chi ha*—now luck.

> [*Stands apart.*]

Enter Malroda *and* Piorato.

Malroda.   Tis he, do as I told thee: 'Blesse thee *Signior.*——

> [*Piorato stands apart.*]

[*To Vitelli*] Oh, my deare Lord.
Vitelli.   *Malroda*, what alone?
Malroda.   She never is alone, that is accompanied   20

With noble thoughts, my Lord; and mine are such,
Being onely of your Lordship.

Vitelli.   Pretty Lasse.

Malroda.   Oh my good Lord, my picture's done: but 'faith
It is not like; nay this way sir, the light
Strikes best upon it here.

Piorato [apart].   Excellent wench.   *Exit.*

Alguazier [apart].   I am glad the danger's over.   *Exit.*

Vitelli.   Tis wondrous like,
But that Art cannot counterfeit what Nature
Could make but once.

Malroda [aside].   All's cleare: another tune
You must heare from me now.——*Vitelli,* thou'rt
A most perfidious and a perjur'd man,   30
As ever did usurpe Nobility.

Vitelli.   What meanst thou *Malroda?*

Malroda.   Leave your betraying smiles,
And change the tunes of your inticing tongue
To penitentiall prayers; for I am great
In labour even with anger, big with child
Of womans rage, bigger then when my wombe
Was pregnant by thee: goe seducer, fly
Out of the world, let me the last wretch be
Dishonoured by thee: touch me not, I loath
My very heart, because thou layst there long;   40
A woman's wel helpt up, that's confident
In ere a glittering outside on you all:
Would I had honestly been matchd to some
Poore Countrey-swaine, ere known the vanity
Of Court: peace then had been my portion,
Nor had been cozend by an houres pompe
To be a whore unto my dying day.

Vitelli [aside].   Oh the uncomfortable waies such women have,
Their different speech and meaning, no assurance
In what they say or do: Dissemblers   50
Even in their prayers, as if the weeping Greeke

33 tongue] Sympson; tongues F1–2

51

That flatter'd *Troy* afire had been their *Adam*;
Lyers, as if their mother had been made
Onely of all the falshood of the man,
Dispos'd into that rib: Do I know this,
And more: nay, all that can concern this Sex,
With the true end of my creation?
Can I with rationall discourse sometimes
Advance my spirit into Heaven, before
'T has shook hands with my body, and yet blindly   60
Suffer my filthy flesh to master it,
With sight of such faire fraile beguiling objects?
When I am absent, easily I resolve
Nere more to entertaine those strong desires
That triumph ore me, even to actuall sin;
Yet when I meet again those sorserers eyes,
Their beames my hardest resolutions thaw,
As if that cakes of Ice and July met,
And her sighes powerfull as the violent North,
Like a light feather twirle me round about   70
And leave me in mine own low state again.——
What aylst thou? prethee weep not: Oh, those tears
If they were true, and rightly spent, would raise
A flowry spring ith' midst of January:
Celestiall Ministers with Christall cups
Would stoop to save 'em for immortall drink:
But from this passion; why all this?
Malroda.   Do'ye ask?
You are marrying: having made me unfit
For any man, you leave me fit for all:
Porters must be my burthens now, to live;   80
And fitting me your selfe for Carts and Beadles,
You leave me to 'em: And who of all the world
But the virago, your great Arch-foes daughter?
But on: I care not, this poore rush: 'twill breed
An excellent comedy: ha, ha: 't makes me laugh:
I cannot choose: the best is, some report
It is a match for feare, not love o' your side.

Vitelli [*aside*].   Why how the devill knows she, that I saw
This Lady? are all whores, peec'd with some witch?
I will be merry.———'Faith 'tis true, sweet heart,   90
I am to marry!
Malroda.   . Are you? you base Lord.
By — i'le Pistoll thee.
Vitelli.   A roaring whore?
Take heed, there's a correction house hard by:
You ha' learn'd this o' your swordman, that I warn'd you of,
Your fencers, and your drunkards: but whereas
You upbraid me with oathes, why I must tell you
I ne're promis'd you marriage, nor have vow'd,
But said I lov'd you, long as you remain'd
The woman I expected, or you swore,
And how you have fail'd of that (sweet heart) you know.   100
You faine would shew your power, but fare you well,
Ile keepe no more faith with an infidell.
Malroda.   Nor I my bosome for a Turk: do'ye heare?
Goe, and the devill take me, if ever
I see you more: I was too true.
Vitelli.   Come, pish:
That devill take the falsest of us two.
Malroda.   Amen.
Vitelli.   You are an ill Clerk; and curse your selfe:
Madnesse transports you: I confesse, I drew you
Unto my will: but you must know that must not
Make me doat on the habit of my sin.   110
I will, to settle you to your content,
Be master of my word: and yet he li'd
That told you I was marrying, but in thought:
But will you slave me to your tyranny
So cruelly I shall not dare to looke
Or speake to other women? make me not
Your smocks Monopolie: come, let's be friends:
Looke, her's a Jewell for thee: I will come
At night, and——
Malroda.   What 'yfaith: you shall not sir.

Vitelli.   'Faith, and troth, and verily, but I will.   120
Malroda.   Halfe drunck, to make a noise, and raile?
Vitelli.   No, no,
Sober, and dieted for the nonce: I am thine,
I have won the day.
Malroda.   The night (though) shall be mine.
                              Exeunt [*severally*].

        Enter Clara *and* Bobadilla *with Letters.*
                                                    [III.] iv
Clara.   What said he sirha?
Bobadilla.   Little, or nothing: faith I saw him not,
  Nor will not: he doth love a strumpet, Mistresse,
  Nay, keeps her spitefully, under the Constables nose,
  It shall be justifi'd by the Gentleman
  Your brothers Master, that is now within
  A' practising: there are your Letters: come
  You shall not cast your selfe away, while I live,
  Nor will I venture my right worshipfull place
  In such a businesse — here's your Mother: downe: 10
  And he that loves you: another'gates fellow,
  I wis. If you had any grace——
Clara.   Well rogue. [*She sits down and sews.*]
Bobadilla.   Ile in, to see *Don Lucio* mannage: he'll make
  A pretty peece of flesh; I promise you,
  He do's already handle his weapon finely.   *Exit.*

        Enter Eugenia *and* Sayavedra.

Eugenia.   She knows your love sir, and the full allowance
  Her Father and my selfe approve it with,
  And I must tell you, I much hope it hath
  Wrought some impression, by her alteration;
  She sighes, and saies forsooth, and cries heigh ho,   20
  She'll take ill words oth' Steward, and the Servants,
  Yet answer affably, and modestly:

        12 I wis] Dyce; I wish F1-2
                    54

Things sir, not usuall with her: there she is,
Change some few words.
Sayavedra.   Maddam, I am bound to'ye:——

                              [*Eugenia stands apart.*]

How now, faire Mistresse, working?
Clara.   Yes forsooth,
Learning to live another day.
Sayavedra.   That needs not.
Clara.   No forsooth: by my truly but it do's,
We know not what we may come too.
Eugenia [apart].   'Tis strange.
Sayavedra.   Come, I ha beg'd leave for you to play.
Clara.   Forsooth
'Tis ill for a faire Lady to be idle.   30
Sayavedra.   She had better be well-busied, I know that.
Turtle: me thinkes you mourne, shall I sit by you?
Clara.   If you be weary sir, you had best be gone;
I work not a true stitch, now you'r my mate.
Sayavedra.   If I be so, I must doe more then side you.
Clara.   Ev'n what you will, but tread me.
Sayavedra.   Shall we bill?
Clara.   Oh no, forsooth.
Sayavedra.   Being so faire, my *Clara*,
Why do'ye delight in black-worke?
Clara.   Oh white sir,
The fairest Ladies like the blackest men:
I ever lov'd the colour: all black things   40
Are least subject to change.
Sayavedra.   Why, I doe love
A black thing too: and the most beauteous faces
Have oftnest of them: as the blackest eyes,
Jet-arched browes, such haire: i'le kisse your hand.
Clara.   'Twill hinder me my work sir: and my Mother
Will chide me, if I doe not doe my taske.
Sayavedra.   Your Mother, nor your Father shall chide: you

45 me my work] F2; me work my F1

55

Might have a prettier taske, would you be rul'd,
And looke with open eyes.
Clara.   I stare upon you:
And broadly see you: a wondrous proper man,   50
Yet 'twere a greater taske for me to love you
Then I shall ever work sir, in seven yeer.
[*Aside.*] — o' this stitching, I had rather feele
Two, then sow one: this rogue h'as giv'n me a stitch
Cleane crosse my heart.—— Good faith sir: I shall prick you.
Sayavedra.   In goodder faith, I would prick you againe.
Clara.   Now you grow troublesome.——Pish; the man is foolish.
Sayavedra.   Pray weare these trifles.
Clara.   Neither you, nor trifles,
You are a trifle, weare your selfe, sir, out,
And here no more trifle the time away.   60
Sayavedra.   Come; you're deceived in me, I will not wake,
Nor fast, nor dye for you.
Clara.   Goose, be not you deceiv'd,
I can not like, nor love, nor live with you,
Nor fast, nor watch, nor pray for you.
Eugenia [*apart*].   Her old fit.
Sayavedra [*aside*].   Sure, this is not the way.——Nay, I will breake
Your melancholie.
Clara.   I shall breake your pate then,
Away, you sanguine scabbard.
Eugenia.   Out upon thee
Thou'lt breake my heart, I am sure.
Sayavedra.   She's not yet tame.

Enter Alvarez, Piorato [*fencing with*] Lucio: *and* Bobadilla.

Alvarez.   On sir; put home: or I shall goad you here
With this old Fox of mine, that will bite better.   70
Oh, the brave age is gone; in my young daies
A Chevalier would stock a needles point
Three times together: strait ith' hams?
Or shall I giv'ye new Garters?
Bobadilla.   Faith old Master.

There's little hope: the linnen sure was danck
He was begot in, he's so faint, and cold:
Ev'n send him to *Toledo*, there to study,
For he will never fadge with these *Toledos*.——
Beare ye up your point there; pick his teeth: Oh'base.
Piorato.   Fie: you are the most untoward Scholler: beare   80
Your body gracefully: what a posture's there?
You lie too open breasted.
Lucio.   Oh!
Piorato.   You'ld never
Make a good States-man.
Lucio.   Pray, no more.
I hope to breath in peace, and therefore need not
The practise of these dangerous qualities,
I doe not meane to live by't; for I trust
You'l leave me better able.
Alvarez.   Not a Button:
Eugenia, Let's goe get us a new heire.
Eugenia.   I by my troth: your daughter's as untoward.
Alvarez.   I will breake thee bone by bone, and bake thee,   90
Ere i'le ha' such a woodden Sonne, to inherit:
[*To Piorato*] Take him a good knock; see how that will work.
Piorato.   Now, for your life *Signior*:
Lucio.   Oh: alas, I am kill'd
My eye is out: looke Father: *Zancho*:——
Ile play the foole no more thus, that I will not.
Clara.   'Heart: nere a rogue in *Spaine* shall wrong my brother
Whil'st I can hold a sword.   [*She turns on* Piorato.]
Piorato.   Hold, Maddam, Maddam.
Alvarez.   *Clara.*
Eugenia.   Daughter.
Bobadilla.   Mistresse.
Piorato.   Bradamante.
Hold, hold I pray.   [*They part.*]
Alvarez.   The devil's in her, o'the other side: sure.   100

76 cold:] F2; cold: 2 *Torches* | *ready.* F1

[*To Piorato*] There's Gold for you:——they have chang'd what
    ye calt's:
Will no cure help? well, I have one experiment,
And if that faile, Ile hang him, then here's an end on't.——
Come you along with me: and you sir.
Bobadilla.   Now are you going to drowning.

                Exeunt Alvarez, Eugenia, Lucio, Bobadilla.
Sayavedra.   Ile ev'n along with ye: she's too great a Lady
For me, and would prove more then my match.   *Exit.*
Clara.   You'r he spoke of *Vitelli* to the Steward?
Piorato.   Yes: and I thank you, you have beat me for't.
Clara.   But are you sure you doe not wrong him?
Piorato.   Sure?   110
So sure, that if you please venture your selfe
Ile show you him, and his Cockatrice together,
And you shall heare 'em talke.
Clara.   Will you? by — sir
You shall endeere me ever: and I ask
You mercy.
Piorato.   You were somewhat boystrous.
Clara.   There's Gold to make you amends: and for this paines,
Ile gratifie you further: i'le but masque me
And walke along with ye: faith let's make a night on't.

                             Exeunt.

Enter Alguazier, Pachieco, Mendoza, Metaldi, Lazarillo.   [III.]

Alguazier.   Come on my brave water-Spaniels: you that hunt
Ducks in the night: and hide more knavery under your gownes
then your betters: observe my precepts, and edifie by my doctrine:
at yond corner will I set you; if drunkards molest the street, and fall
to brabling, knock you down the malefactors, and take you up
their cloaks and hats, and bring them to me: they are lawfull
prisoners, and must be ransom'd ere they receive liberty: what
else you are to execute upon occasion, you sufficiently know: and
therefore I abbreviat my Lecture.
Metaldi.   We are wise enough, and warme enough.   10

Mendoza. Vice this night shall be apprehended.

Pachieco. The terror of rug-gownes shall be known: and our bils discharge us of after recknings.

Lazarillo. I will doe any thing, so I may eat.

Pachieco. *Lazarillo,* We will spend no more; now we are growne worse, we will live better: let us follow our calling faithfully.

Alguazier. Away, then the Common-wealth is our Mistresse: and who would serve a common Mistresse, but to gaine by her?

                                                        Exeunt.

Enter Vitelli, Lamorall, Genevora, Anastro,   IV. i
          and two Pages with lights.

Lamorall. I pray you see the Masque, my Lord.

Anastro. 'Tis early night yet.

Genevora. O if it be so late, take me along:
 I would not give advantage to ill tongues
 To tax my being here, without your presence
 To be my warrant.

Vitelli.   You might spare this, Sister,
 Knowing with whom I leave you; one that is
 By your allowance, and his choice, your Servant,
 And may my councell and perswasion work it,
 Your husband speedily. [*To Lamorall*] For your entertainment 10
 My thankes; I will not rob you of the meanes
 To doe your Mistresse some acceptable service
 In waiting on her to my house.

Genevora.   My Lord——

Vitelli. As you respect me, without further trouble
 Retire, and taste those pleasures prepar'd for you,
 And leave me to my own wayes.

Lamorall.   When you please sir.

                                        Exeunt [*severally*].

                        59   5-2

Enter Malroda, *and* Alguazier   [IV.]

Malroda.   You'l leave my Chamber?

Alguaƶier.   Let us but bill once,
My Dove, my Sparrow, and I, with my office
Will be thy slaves for ever.

Malroda.   Are you so hot?

Alguaƶier.   But taste the difference of a man in place,
You'l finde that when authoritie pricks him forward,
Your *Don*, nor yet your *Diego* comes not neere him
To doe a Lady right: no men pay deerer
For their stolne sweetes, then we: three minutes trading
Affords to any sinner a protection
For three yeeres after: thinke on that: I burne;   10
But one drop of your bounty.

Malroda.   Hence you rogue,
Am I fit for you? is't not grace sufficient
To have your staffe, a bolt to bar the doore
Where a *Don* enters, but that you'l presume
To be his taster?

Alguaƶier.   Is no more respect
Due to this rod of justice?

Malroda.   Doe you dispute?
Good Doctoɪ of the Dungeon, not a word more,
— if you doe, my Lord *Vitelli* knowes it.

Alguaƶier.   Why I am bigge enough to answer him,
Or any man.

Malroda.   'Tis well.

Vitelli (*within*).   *Malroda.*

Alguaƶier.   How?   20

Malroda.   You know the voice, and now crowch like a Cur
Tane worrying sheepe: I now could have you guelded
For a Bawd rampant: but on this submission
For once I spare you.

Alguazier.   I will be reveng'd.——

Enter Vitelli.

My honourable Lord.

Vitelli.   There's for thy care.   [*Giving money.*]

Alguazier [*aside*].   I am mad, starck mad: proud Pagan scorn her
     host?
I would I were but valiant enough to kick her,
Il'd wish no manhood else.

Malroda.   What's that?

Alguazier.   I am gone.   *Exit.*

[Malroda *and* Vitelli *talk apart.*]

Enter Piorato *and* Clara, *above.*

Piorato.   You see, I have kept my word.

Clara.   But in this object
Hardly deserv'd my thanks.

Piorato.   Is there ought else   30
You will command me?

Clara.   Onely your sword
Which I must have: nay, willingly; I yet know
To force it, and to use it.

Piorato.   'Tis yours Lady.

Clara.   I ask no other guard.

Piorato.   If so, I leave you:
[*Aside.*] And now, if that the Constable keepe his word,
A poorer man may chance to gull a Lord.   *Exit* [*above*].

Malroda.   By this good — you shall not.

Vitelli.   By this —
I must, and will, *Malroda*; What, doe you make
A stranger of me?

Malroda.   Ile be so to you,
And you shall find it.

Vitelli.   These are your old arts   40
T'endeere the game you know I come to hunt for,
Which I have borne too coldly.

24.1 *Enter* Vitelli.] F2; *om.* F1

61

Malroda.   Doe so still,
For if I heat you, hang me.
Vitelli.   If you doe not
I know who'll starve for't: why, thou shame of women,
Whose folly, or whose impudence is greater
Is doubtfull to determine; this to me
That know thee for a whore.
Malroda.   And made me one,
Remember that.
Vitelli.   Why, should I but grow wise
And tye that bounty up, which nor discretion
Nor honour can give way too; thou wouldst be   50
A Bawd e're twenty, and within a moneth
A barefoot, lowzie, and diseased whore,
And shift thy lodgings oftner then a rogue
That's whipt from post to post.
Malroda.   Pish: all our Colledge
Know you can raile well in this kinde.
Clara [apart].   For me
He never spake so well.
Vitelli.   I have maintain'd thee
The envy of great fortunes, made thee shine
As if thy name were glorious: stuck thee full
Of jewels, as the firmament of Starrs,
And in it made thee so remarkable   60
That it grew questionable, whether vertue poore,
Or vice so set forth as it is in thee,
Were even by modesties selfe to be prefer'd;
And am I thus repaid?
Malroda.   You are still my debtor;
Can this (though true) be weigh'd with my lost honour,
Much lesse my faith? I have liv'd private to you,
And but for you, had ne're known what lust was,
Nor what the sorrow for't.
Vitelli.   'Tis false.
Malroda.   'Tis true,

64 *Malroda.*] F2; *om.* F1

But how return'd by you, thy whole life being
But one continued act of lust, and Shipwrack   70
Of womens chastities.
Vitelli.   But that I know
That she that dares be damn'd dares any thing,
I should admire thy tempting me: but presume not
On the power you thinke you hold o're my affections,
It will deceive you: yeeld, and presently
Or by the inflamed blood, which thou must quench
Ile make a forcible entrie.
Malroda.   Touch me not:
You know I have a throat, — if you doe
I will cry out a rape, or sheath this here,
Ere i'le be kept, and us'd for Julip-water   80
T'allay the heate which lushious meats and wine
And not desire hath rais'd.
Vitelli [*aside*].   A desperate devill,
My blood commands my reason: I must take
Some milder way.
Malroda [*aside*].   I hope (deere *Don*) I fit you.
The night is mine, although the day was yours:
You are not fasting now.——This speeding trick
Which I would as a principle leave to all,
That make their maintenance out of their own *Indies*
As I doe now, my good old mother taught me;
Daughter, quoth she, contest not with your lover   90
His stomach being empty; let wine heat him,
And then you may command him: 'tis a sure one:
His lookes shew he is coming.
Vitelli.   Come this needs not,
Especially to me: you know how deere
I ever have esteemed you.
Clara [*apart*].   Lost again.
Vitelli.   That any sigh of yours, hath power to change
My strongest resolution, and one teare
Sufficient to command a pardon from me,

96 sigh] Colman; sight F 1–2

63

For any wrong from you, which all mankinde
Should kneel in vaine for.

Malroda.   Pray you pardon those   100
That need your favour, or desire it.

Vitelli.   Prethee,
Be better temper'd: Ile pay as a forfeit
For my rash anger, this purse fil'd with Gold.
Thou shalt have servants, gownes, attires, what not?
Only continue mine.

Malroda [*aside*].   'Twas this I fish'd for.

Vitelli. Look on me, and receive it.

Malroda.   Well, you know
My gentle nature, and take pride t'abuse it:
You see a trifle pleases me, we are friends;
This kisse, and this confirmes it.

Clara [*apart*].   With my ruine.

Malroda. I'le have this dyamond, and this pearle.

Vitelli.   They are yours. 110

Malroda. But wil you not, when you have what you came for,
Take them from me to morrow? tis a fashion
Your Lords of late have us'd.

Vitelli.   But Ile not follow.

Clara [*apart*]. That any man at such a rate as this
Should pay for his repentance.

Vitelli.   Shall we to bed now?

Malroda. Instantly, Sweet: yet now I think on't better
Ther's something first that in a word or two
I must acquaint you with.   [*They talk apart.*]

Clara.   Can I cry ayme,
To this against my selfe? Ile break this match,
Or make it stronger with my bloud.   *Descends.*

        Enter Alguazier, Piorato, Pachieco, Metaldi,
            Mendoza, Lazarillo, *and others*.

Alguazier.   I am yours, 120

118 cry ayme] i.e., cry encouragement

64

A *Don*'s not priviledgd here more then yourself,
Win her, and weare her.
Piorato.   Have you a Priest ready?
Alguazier.   I have him for thee, Lad.——[*Aside*] And when I have
Married this scornefull whore to this poor gallant,
She wil make suit to me; there is a trick
To bring a high-priz'd wench upon her knees.——
For you my fine neat Harpyes stretch your tallons
And prove your selves true night-Birds.
Pachieco.   Take my word
For me and all the rest.
Lazarillo.   If there be meat
Or any banquet stirring, you shall see   130
How ile bestow my selfe.
Alguazier.   When they are drawn,
Rush in upon 'em: al's faire prize you light on:
I must away: your officer may give way
To the Knavery of his watch, but must not see it.
You all know where to finde me.
Metaldi.   There look for us.
                                        Exit [Alguazier].

Vitelli.   Who's that?
Malroda.   My *Piorato*, welcome, welcome:
Faith had you not come when you did, my Lord
Had done I know not what to me.
Vitelli [*aside*].   I am gul'd,
First cheated of my Jewels, and then laugh'd at.——
Sirha, what make you here?
Piorato.   A businesse brings me,   140
More lawfull then your own.
Vitelli.   How's that, you slave?
Malroda.   He's such, that would continue her a whore
Whom he would make a wife of.
Vitelli.   Ile trea'd upon
The face you doat on, strumpet.
Pachieco.   Keep the peace, there.

Vitelli.   A plot upon my life too?
Metaldi.   Down with him.

Enter Clara [*with a sword*].

Clara.   Show your old valour, and learn from a woman,
    One Eagle has a world of odds against
    A flight of Dawes, as these are.
Piorato.   Get you off,
    Ile follow instantly.
Pachieco.   Run for more help there.
                            Exeunt all but Vitelli *and* Clara.
Vitelli [*aside*].   Losse of my gold, and jewels, and the wench too   150
    Afflicts me not so much, as th'having *Clara*
    The witnesse of my weaknesse.
Clara [*aside*].   He turns from me,
    And yet I may urge merit, since his life
    Is made my second gift.
Vitelli [*aside*].   May I ne'r prosper
    If I know how to thank her.
Clara.   Sir, your pardon
    For pressing thus beyond a Virgins bounds
    Upon your privacies: and let my being
    Like to a man, as you are, be th'excuse
    Of my solliciting that from you, which shall not
    Be granted on my part, although desir'd   160
    By any other: sir, you understand me,
    And 'twould shew nobly in you, to prevent
    From me a farther boldnesse, which I must
    Proceed in, if you prove not mercifull,
    Though with my losse of blushes, and good name.
Vitelli.   Madam, I know your wil, and would be thankfull
    If it were possible I could affect
    The Daughter of an enemy.
Clara.   That faire false one
    Whom with fond dotage you have long pursu'd
    Had such a father: she to whom you pay   170
    Deerer for your dishonour, then all titles

66

Ambitious men hunt for are worth.
Vitelli.   'Tis truth.
Clara.   Yet, with her, as a friend you still exchange
  Health for diseases, and to your disgrace
  Nourish the rivals to your present pleasures,
  At your own charge, us'd as a property
  To give a safe protection to her lust,
  Yet share in nothing but the shame of it.
Vitelli.   Grant all this so, to take you for a wife
  Were greater hazard, for should I offend you   180
  (As tis not easy still to please a woman)
  You are of so great a spirit, that I must learn
  To weare your petticoat, for you wil have
  My breeches from me.
Clara.   Rather from this houre
  I here abjure all actions of a man,
  And wil esteem it happinesse from you
  To suffer like a woman: love, true love
  Hath made a search within me, and expel'd
  All but my naturall softnesse, and made perfect
  That which my parents care could not begin.   190
  I wil show strength in nothing, but my duty,
  And glad desire to please you, and in that
  Grow every day more able.
Vitelli [*aside*].   Could this be,
  What a brave race might I beget? I finde
  A kind of yeelding; and no reason why
  I should hold longer out: she's yong, and faire,
  And chast for sure, but with her leave the Devil
  Durst not attempt her.——Madam, though you have
  A Souldiers arme, your lips appear as if
  They were a Ladies.
Clara.   They dare sir from you   200
  Endure the tryall.   [*He kisses her.*]
Vitelli.   Ha: once more I pray you.   [*He kisses her.*]
  [*Aside.*] The best I ever tasted; and tis said
  I have prov'd many, 'tis not safe I feare

67

To aske the rest now: wel, I will leave whoring,
And luck heaven send me with her.——Worthiest Lady,
Ile wait upon you home, and by the way
(If ere I marry, as ile not forswear it)
Tell you, you are my wife.
Clara.   Which if you do,
From me all man-kinde women, learne to woe.

Exeunt.

Enter Alguazier, Pachieco, Metaldi,   [IV.]
Mendoza, Lazarillo.

Alguazier.   A cloak? good purchase, and rich hangers? well,
Wee'l share ten Pistolets a man.
Lazarillo.   Yet still
I am monstrous hungry: could you not diduct
So much out of the grosse some, as would purchase
Eight loynes of Veale, and some two dozen of Capons?
Pachieco.   O strange proportion for five.
Lazarillo.   For five? I have
A legion in my stomach that have kept
Perpetuall fast these ten years: for the Capons,
They are to me but as so many black Birds:
May I but eate once, and be satisfied,   10
Let the fates call me, when my ship is fraught,
And I shall hang in peace.
Alguazier.   Steale well to night,
And thou shalt feed to morrow; so, now you are
Your selves againe, ile raise another watch
To free you from suspition: set on any
You meet with boldly: ile not be far off,
T'assist you, and protect you.   *Exit.*
Metaldi.   O brave officer.
Pachieco.   Would every ward had one but so well given,
And we would watch, for rug, in gownes of velvet.

Enter Alvarez, Lucio, Bobadilla.

205 heaven] Dyce; herein F 1–2

68

Mendoza.   Stand close: a prize.

Metaldi.   Satten, and gold Lace, Lads.   20

                              [*They stand apart.*]

Alvarez.   Why do'st thou hang upon me?

Lucio.   'Tis so darke

I dare not see my way: for heaven sake father

Let us go home.

Bobadilla.   No, ev'n here wee'l leave you:

Let's run away from him, my Lord.

Lucio.   Oh 'las.

Alvarez.   Thou hast made me mad: and I wil beat thee dead

Then bray the in a morter, and new mold thee

But I wil alter thee.

Bobadilla.   'Twill never be:

He has bin three dayes practising to drink,

Yet still he sips, like to a waiting woman,

And looks as he were murdring of a fart   30

Among wild Irish swaggerers.

Lucio.   I have still

Your good word, *Zancho.* ——Father.

Alvarez.   Milk-sop, coward;

No house of mine receives thee: I disclam thee:

Thy mother on her knees shall not entreat me

Hereafter to acknowledge thee.

Lucio.   Pray you speak for me.

Bobadilla.   I would; but now I cannot with mine honour.

Alvarez.   Ther's only one course left, that may redeem thee,

Which is, to strike the next man that you meet,

And if we chance to light upon a woman,

Take her away, and use her like a man,   40

Or I wil cut thy hamstrings.

Pachieco [*apart*].   This makes for us.

Alvarez.   What do'st thou do now?

Lucio.   Sir, I am saying my prayers;

For being to undertake what you would have me,

I know I cannot live.

26 new] F2; now F1

69

Enter Lamorall, Genevora, Anastro, *and*
Pages with lights.

Lamorall.   Madam, I fear
You'l wish you had usd your coach: your brothers house
Is yet far off.
Genevora.   The better sir: this walk
Will help digestion after your great supper,
Of which I have fed largely.
Alvarez [*to Lucio*].   To your task,
Or els you know what followes:
Lucio.   I am dying:
Now Lord have mercy on me:——by your favour,   50
Sir I must strike you.
Lamorall.   For what cause?
Lucio.   I know not:
And I must likewise talke with that young Lady,
An houre in private.
Lamorall.   What you must, is doubtfull,
But I am certain sir, I must beat you.   [*Beats him.*]
Lucio.   Help, help.
Alvarez.   Not strik againe?
Lamorall.   How, *Alvarez*?
Anastro.   This for my Lord *Vitelli's* love.   [*Strikes* Alvarez.]
Pachieco.   Break out,
And like true theeves, make pray on either side,
But seem to help the stronger.
Bobadilla.   Oh my Lord,
They have beat him on his knees.
Lucio.   Though I want courage:
I yet have a sons duty in me, and   60
Compassion of a fathers danger; that,
That wholy now possesses me.   [*Attacks* Anastro.]
Alvarez.   Lucio.
This is beyond my hope.

58 stronger] Colman; stranger F 1–2

70

Metaldi.   So *Lazarillo,*
Take up all boy: well done.
Pachieco.   And now steale off
Closely, and cunningly.
Anastro.   How? have I found you?——
Why Gentlemen, are you madde, to make your selves
A prey to Rogues?
Lazarillo.   Would we were off.
Bobadilla.   Theeves, theeves.
Lamorall.   Defer our own contention: and down with them.
Lucio.   Ile make you sure.
Bobadilla.   Now he playes the Devil.
Genevora.   This place is not for me.   *Exit* [*with Pages*].
Lucio.   Ile follow her   70
Half of my pennance is past ore.   *Exit.*

Enter Alguazier [*and Watches at one door; at the other door*],
     Assistente *and other Watches* [*and stand apart*].

Alguazier.   What noyse?
What tumult's there? keep the Kings peace I charge you.
Pachieco.   I am glad he's come yet.
Alvarez.   O, you keep good Guard
Upon the City, when men of our ranck
Are set upon in the streetes.
Lamorall.   The *Assistente*
Shall heare of't be assur'd.
Anastro.   And if he be
That carefull Governour he is reported,
You will smart for it.
Alguazier.   Patience, good *Signiours:*
Let me survey the Rascals: O, I know them,
And thank you for them: they are pillfring rogues   80
Of *Andaluzia,* that have perus'd
All Prisons in *Castile:* I dare not trust

67 *Lazarillo.*] Dyce; *Lam.* F 1–2
75 *Assistente*] Langbaine (Assistant); assistance F 1; assistants F 2

71

The dungeon with them: no, ile have them home
To my own house.

Pachieco. We had rather go to prison.

Alguazier. Had you so, dog-bolts? yes, I know you had:
You there would use your cunning fingers on
The simple locks; you would: but ile prevent you.

Lamorall. My Mistris lost? good night. *Exit* [*with* Anastro].

Bobadilla. Your Son's gon to,
What should become of him?

Alvarez. Come of him, what will:
Now he dares fight, I care not: i'le to bed: 90
Look to your prisoners *Alguazier.* *Exit with* Bobadilla.

Alguazier. Al's cleer'd:
Droop not for one disaster: let us hug,
And triumph in our knaveries.

Assistente [*apart*]. This confirmes
What was reported of him.

Metaldi. 'Twas done bravely.

Alguazier. I must a little glory in the meanes
We officers have, to play the Knaves, and safely:
How we breake through the toyles, pitch'd by the Law,
Yet hang up them that are far lesse delinquents:
A simple shopkeeper's carted for a baud
For lodging (though unwittingly) a smock-Gamster: 100
Where, with rewards, and credit I have kept
Malroda in my house as in a cloyster,
Without taint, or suspition.

Pachieco. But suppose
The Governour should know't?

Alguazier. He? good Gentleman,
Let him perplex himself with prying into
The measures in the market, and th'abuses
The day stands guilty of: the pillage of the night
Is only mine, mine own fee simple;
Which you shall hold from me, tennants at will,
And pay no rent for't.

Pachieco. Admirable Landlord. 110

Alguazier.   Now wee'l go search the taverns, commit such
  As we finde drinking: and be drunk our selves
  With what we take from them: these silly wretches
  Whom I for forme sake only have brought hither
  Shall watch without, and guard us.
Assistente.   And we wil
  See you safe lodg'd, most worthy *Alguazier*,
  With all of you his comrads.
Metaldi.   Tis the Governour.
Alguazier.   We are betray'd?
Assistente.   My guard there: bind them fast:
  How men in high place, and authority
  Are in their lives and estimation wrong'd   120
  By their subordinate Ministers? yet such
  They cannot but imploy: wrong'd justice finding
  Scarce one true servant in ten officers.
  T'expostulate with you, were but to delay
  Your crimes due punishment, which shall fall upon you
  So speedily, and severely, that it shall
  Fright others by th'example: and confirme
  However corrupt officers may disgrace
  Themselves, 'tis not in them to wrong their place.——
  Bring them away.
Alguazier.   Wee'l suffer nobly yet,   130
  And like to Spanish Gallants.
Pachieco.   And wee'l hang so.
Lazarillo.   I have no stomach to it: but i'le endeavour.

                                          Exeunt.

                Enter Lucio, *and* Genevora.   [IV.] iv

Genevora.   Nay you are rude; pray you forbeare; you offer now
  More then the breeding of a Gentleman
  Can give you warrant for.
Lucio.   Tis but to kisse you,

                1 you offer] F2; your offer F1

And think not ile receive that for a favour
Which was enjoyn'd me for a pennance, Lady.
Genevora.   You have met a gentle confessor, and for once
(So then you wil rest satisfied) I vouchsafe it.
Lucio.   Rest satisfide with a kisse? why, can a man
Desire more from a woman? is there any
Pleasure beyond it? may I never live   10
If I know what it is.
Genevora [*aside*].   Sweet Innocence.   [*They kisse.*]
Lucio.   What strange new motions do I feele? my veines
Burn with an unknown fire: in every part
I suffer alteration: I am poysond,
Yet languish with desire againe to taste it,
So sweetly it works on me.
Genevora [*aside*].   I ne'r saw
A lovely man, till now.
Lucio.   How can this be?
She is a woman, as my mother is,
And her I have kiss'd often, and brought off
My lips unscortch'd; yours are more lovelie, Lady,   20
And so should be lesse hurtfull: pray you vouchsafe
Your hand to quench the heat tane from your Lip,
Perhaps that may restore me.
Genevora.   Willinglie.
Lucio.   The flame increases: if to touch you, burne thus,
What would more strict embraces do? I know not,
And yet methinks to die so, were to ascend
To Heaven, through Paradise.
Genevora [*aside*].   I am wounded too,
Though modesty forbids that I should speake
What ignorance makes him bold in.——Why do you fix
Your eyes so stranglie on me?
Lucio.   Pray you stand still,   30
There is nothing els, that is worth the looking on:
I could adore you, Ladie.
Genevora.   Can you love mee?

*30 stranglie] stronglie F 1–2

Lucio. To waite on you, in your chamber, and but touch
What you, by wearing it, have made divine,
Were such a happinesse. I am resolv'd,
Ile sell my libertie to you for this glove,
And write my selfe your slave.

Enter Lamorall.

Genevora.   On easier termes,
Receive it as a friend.
Lamorall.   How! giving favour!
I'le have it with his heart.   [*Takes the glove.*]
Genevora.   What will you doe?
Lucio. As you are mercifull, take my life rather.   40
Genevora. Will you depart with't so?
Lucio.   Do's that grieve you?
Genevora. I know not: but even now you appeard valiant.
Lucio. Twas to preserve my father: in his cause
I could be so again.
Genevora.   Not in your own?
Kneel to thy rivall and thine enemy?
Away unworthy creature, I begin
To hate my selfe, for giving entrance to
A good opinion of thee: For thy torment,
If my poore beauty be of any power,
Mayst thou doat on it desperately: but never   50
Presume to hope for grace, till thou recover
And weare the favour that was ravish'd from thee.
Lamorall. He weares my head to then.   [*Exit.*]
Genevora.   Poore foole, farewell.
Exit.

Lucio. My womanish soul, which hitherto hath governd
This coward flesh, I feele departing from me;
And in me by her beauty is inspir'd
A new, and masculine one: instructing me
What's fit to doe or suffer; powerfull love
That hast with loud, and yet a pleasing thunder

41 *Lucio.*] Sympson; *Lam.* F 1–2   42 appeard] Langbaine; appeare F 1–2

Rous'd sleeping manhood in me, thy new creature,   60
Perfect thy worke so that I may make known
Nature (though long kept back) wil have her owne.

Exit.

Enter Lamorall [*with* Genevora's *glove in his hat*] *and* Lucio.   V. i

Lamorall.   Can it be possible, that in six short houres
The subject still the same, so many habits
Should be remov'd? or this new *Lucio*, he
That yesternight was baffeld and disgrac'd,
And thankt the man that did it, that then kneeld
And blubberd like a woman, should now dare
On terms of honour seeke reparation
For what he then appear'd not capable of?
Lucio.   Such miracles, men that dare doe injuries
Live to their shames to see, for punishment   10
And scourge to their proud follies.
Lamorall.   Prethee leave me:
Had I my Page, or foot-man here to flesh thee,
I durst the better heare thee.
Lucio.   This scorn needs not:
And offer such no more.
Lamorall.   Why say I should,
You'l not be angry?
Lucio.   Indeed I think I shal,
Would you vouchsafe to shew your selfe a Captaine,
And lead a little further, to some place
That's lesse frequented.
Lamorall.   He looks pale.
Lucio.   If not,
Make use of this.
Lamorall.   There's anger in his eyes too:
His gesture, voyce, behaviour, all new fashion'd;   20
Wel, if it does endure in act the triall
Of what in show it promises to make good,

7 On terms] F2; One terme F1   10 for] Sympson; and for F1–2

Ulysses Cyclops, *Io's* transformation,
Eurydice fetcht from Hell, with all the rest
Of *Ovids* Fables, ile put in my Creed;
And for proofe all incredible things may be,
Write down that *Lucio*, the coward *Lucio*,
The womanish *Lucio* fought.

Lucio.   And *Lamorall*,
The stil imployd great duellist *Lamorall*
Took his life from him.

Lamorall.   Twill not come to that sure: 30
Methinks the onely drawing of my Sword
Should fright that confidence.

Lucio.   It confirmes it rather.
To make which good, know you stand now oppos'd
By one that is your Rivall, one that wishes
Your name and title greater, to raise his;
The wrong you did, lesse pardonable then it is,
But your strength to defend it, more then ever
It was when justice friended it; the Lady
For whom we now contend, *Genevora*
Of more desert, (if such incomparable beauty   40
Could suffer an addition); your love
To *Don Vitelli* multipli'd; and your hate
Against my father and his house increas'd;
And lastly, that the Glove which you there wear,
To my dishonour, (which I must force from you)
Were deerer to you then your life.

Lamorall.   You'l finde
It is, and so ile guard it:

Lucio.   All these meet then
With the black infamy, to be foyld by one
That's not allowd a man: to help your valour,
That falling by your hand, I may, or die,   50
Or win in this one single opposition
My Mistris, and such honour as I may
Inrich my fathers Armes with.

25 my] Sympson; your F1–2   26–27 be, Write] F2; be Writ F1

Lamorall.   Tis said Nobly;
My life with them are at the stake.
Lucio.   At all then.
                         Fight. [Lucio *takes his sword.*]
Lamorall.   She's yours: this, and my life to, follow your fortune,
                         [*Giving his hat with the glove.*]
And give not onely back that part the looser
Scorns to accept of——
Lucio.   What's that?
Lamorall.   My poor life,
Which do not leave me as a further torment,
Having dispoild me of my Sword, mine honour,
Hope of my Ladies grace, fame, and all else   60
That made it worth the keeping.
Lucio.   I take back
No more from you, then what you forc'd from me;
And with a worser title: yet think not
That Ile dispute this, as made insolent
By my successe, but as one equall with you,
If so you wil accept me; that new courage,
Or call it fortune if you please, that is
Confer'd upon me by the onely sight
Of fair *Genevora*, was not bestow'd on me
To bloody purposes: nor did her command   70
Deprive me of the happinesse to see her
But till I did redeem her favour from you;
Which onely I rejoyce in, and share with you
In all you suffer else.
Lamorall.   This curtesie
Wounds deeper then your Sword can, or mine owne;
Pray you make use of either, and dispatch me.
Lucio.   The barbarous Turke is satisfied with spoile;
And shall I, being possest of what I came for,
Prove the more Infidell?
Lamorall.   You were better be so,

55 life to,] F2 (too); life, to F1

78

Then publish my disgrace, as tis the custome,   80
And which I must expect.
Lucio.   Judge better on me:
I have no tongue to trumpet mine owne praise
To your dishonour: tis a bastard courage
That seekes a name out that way, no true born one;
Pray you be comforted, for by all goodnesse
But to her vertuous selfe, the best part of it,
I never wil discover on what termes
I came by these: which yet I take not from you,
But leave you in exchange of them, mine own,
                    [Lucio *gives his own hat and sword.*]
With the desire of being a friend; which if   90
You wil not grant me but on further triall
Of manhood in me, seeke me when you please,
(And though I might refuse it with mine honour)
Win them again, and weare them: so good morrow.   *Exit.*
Lamorall.   I nere knew what true valour was till now;
And have gain'd more by this disgrace, then all
The honours I have won: they made me proud,
Presumptuous of my fortune; a meere beast,
Fashion'd by them, onely to dare and doe:
Yeelding no reasons for my wilfull actions   100
But what I stuck on my Swords point, presuming
It was the best Revenew. How unequall
Wrongs wel maintain'd makes us to others, which
Ending with shame teach us to know our selves.
I wil think more on't.

                    Enter Vitelli.

Vitelli.   *Lamorall.*
Lamorall.   My Lord?
Vitelli.   I came to seeke you.
Lamorall.   And unwillingly
You nere found me till now: your pleasure sir?
Vitelli.   That which wil please thee friend: thy vowd love to me
Shall now be put in action: means is offer'd

                    79

To use thy good Sword for me; that which still   110
Thou wearst, as if it were a part of thee.
Where is it?
Lamorall.   Tis changd for one more fortunate:
Pray you enquire not how.
Vitelli.   Why, I nere thought
That there was majick int, but ascribd
The fortune of it to the arme.
Lamorall.   Which is
Grown weaker too. I am not (in a word)
Worthy your friendship: I am one new vanquish'd,
Yet shame to tell by whom.
Vitelli.   But Ile tell thee
'Gainst whom thou art to fight, and there redeeme
Thy honour lost, if there be any such: 120
The King, by my long suit, at length is pleas'd
That *Alvarez* and my self, with eithers Second,
Shall end the difference between our houses,
Which he accepts of. I make choice of thee;
And where you speak of a disgrace, the means
To blot it out, by such a publique triall
Of thy approved valour, wil revive
Thy ancient courage. If you imbrace it, doe;
If not, Ile seeke some other.
Lamorall.   As I am
You may command me.
Vitelli.   Spoke like that true friend   130
That loves not onely for his private end.

                                        Exeunt.

            Enter Genevora *with a Letter and* Bobadilla.   [V.] i

Genevora.   This from *Madona Clara?*
Bobadilla.   Yes, and't please you.
Genevora.   *Alvarez* daughter?
Bobadilla.   The same, Lady.

        114 majick] Sympson; musick F 1–2   114 ascribd] Dyce; ascribe F 1–2

Genevora.   She,
That sav'd my brothers life?
Bobadilla.   You are still in the right,
She wil'd me wait your walking forth: and knowing
How necessary a discreet wise man
Was in a businesse of such weight, she pleas'd
To think on me: it may be in my face
Your Ladiship not acquainted with my wisdome
Finds no such matter: what I am, I am;
Thought's free: and think you what you please.
Genevora.   Tis strange,   10
Bobadilla.   That I should be wise, Madam?
Genevora.   No, thou art so;
There's for thy paines: [*giving money*] and prethee tell thy Lady
I wil not faile to meet her: Ile receive
Thy thanks and duty in thy present absence:
Farewell, farewel, I say, now thou art wise.   *Exit* Bobadilla.
She writes here, she hath something to impart
That may concerne my brothers life; I know not,
But generall fame does give her out so worthy,
That I dare not suspect her: yet wish *Lucio*
Were Master of her mind: but fie upon't;   20
Why do I think on him?

                    Enter Lucio.

                    See, I am punish'd for it,
In his unlookd for presence: Now I must
Endure another tedious piece of Courtship,
Would make one forsweare curtesie.
Lucio.   Gracious Madam, [*Kneels.*]
The sorrow paid for your just anger towards me
Arising from my weaknesse, I presume
To presse into your presence, and dispaire not
An easie pardon.
Genevora [*aside*].   He speaks sence: oh strange.
Lucio. And yet believe, that no desire of mine,
Though all are too strong in me, had the power   30

                         81

For their delight, to force me to infringe
What you commanded, it being in your part
To lessen your great rigour when you please,
And mine to suffer with an humble patience
What you'l impose upon it.
Genevora [*aside*].   Courtly too.
Lucio.   Yet hath the poore, and contemn'd *Lucio*, Madam,
(Made able onely by his hope to serve you)
Recover'd what with violence, not justice,
Was taken from him: and here at your feet
                    [*Laying down* Lamorall's *hat and sword.*]
With these, he could have laid the conquer'd head   40
Of *Lamorall* (tis all I say of him)
For rudely touching that, which as a relique
I ever would have worship'd, since twas yours.
Genevora [*aside*].   Valiant, and every thing a Lady could
Wish in her servant.
Lucio.   All that's good in me,
That heavenly love, the opposite to base lust,
Which would have all men worthy, hath created;
Which being by your beames of beauty form'd,
Cherish as your own creature.
Genevora [*aside*].   I am gone
Too far now to dissemble.——Rise, or sure   [*He rises.*] 50
I must kneele with you too: let this one kisse
Speake the rest for me: tis too much I doe,
And yet, if chastity would, I could wish more.
Lucio.   In overjoying me, you are grown sad;
What is it Madam? by —
There's nothing that's within my nerves (and yet
Favour'd by you, I should as much as man)
But when you please, now or on all occasions
You can think of hereafter, but you may
Dispose of at your pleasure.
Genevora.   If you breake   60
That oath again, you lose me. Yet so wel
I love you, I shall never put you to't;

And yet forget it not: rest satisfied
With that you have receiv'd now; there are eyes
May be upon us: till the difference
Between our friends are ended, I would not
Be seen so private with you.
Lucio.   I obey you.
Genevora.   But let me heare oft from you, and remember
I am *Vitellies* sister.
Lucio.   What's that Madam?
Genevora.   Nay nothing, fare you well: [*Exit* Lucio.]
                                    who feeles loves fire,   70
Would ever aske to have means to desire.

                                                  Exit.

          Enter Assistente, Sayavedra, Anastro, Herald,   [V.] iii
                          Attendants.

Assistente.   Are they come in?
Herald.   Yes.
Assistente.   Read the Proclamation,
That all the people here assembled may
Have satisfaction, what the Kings deere love,
In care of the Republique, hath ordained;
Attend with silence: read aloud.

Herald reads.   *Forasmuch as our high and mighty Master,* Philip,
the potent and most Catholique King of Spaine, *hath not onely in his*
own Royall person, been long, and often sollicited, and grieved, with
the deadly and uncurable hatred, sprung up betwixt the two ancient
and most honourably discended Houses of these his two deerely and 10
equally beloved subjects, Don Ferdinando de Alvarez, *and* Don
Pedro de Vitelli: (*all which in vaine his Majesty hath often*
endeavoured to reconcile and qualifie:) *But that also through the*
debates, quarrels, and outrages daily arising, falling, and flowing
from these great heads, his publique civill Government is seditiously
and barbarously molested and wounded, and many of his chiefe
Gentry (no lesse tender to his Royall Majesty then the very branches
of his own sacred blood) spoyld, lost, and submerged, in the impious

inundation and torrent of their still-growing malice: It hath therefore
pleased His sacred Majesty, out of His infinite affection to preserve 20
his Common-wealth, and generall peace, from farther violation,
(as a sweet and heartily loving father of his people) and on the earnest
petitions of these Arch-enemies, to Order, and Ordaine, That they
be ready, each with his welchosen and beloved friend, arm'd at all
points like Gentlemen, in the Castle of St. Iago, *on this present*
Munday morning betwixt eight and nine of the clocke; where (before
the combatants be allowed to commence this granted Duell) This to be
read aloud for the publique satisfaction of his Majesties welbeloved
Subjects.

'Save the King. 30

Drums within.

Sayavedra. Hark how their Drums speak their insatiate thirst
Of blood, and stop their eares 'gainst pious peace,
Who gently whispering, implores their friendship?
Assistente. Kings, nor authority can master fate;
Admit 'em then, and blood extinguish hate.

Enter severally, Alvarez *and* Lucio,
Vitelli *and* Lamorall.

Sayavedra. Stay, yet be pleasd to think, and let not daring
Whei ein men nowadaies exceed even beasts,
And think themselves not men else, so transport you
Beyond the bounds of Christianity:
Lord *Alvarez, Vitelli,* Gentlemen, 40
No Town in *Spaine,* from our Metropolis
Unto the rudest hovell, but is great
With your assured valours daily proofes:
Oh wil you then, for a superfluous fame,
A sound of honour, which in these times, all
Like heretiques professe (with obstinacy
But most erroneously) venture your soules,
Tis a hard tasque, thorough a Sea of blood
To saile, and land at Heaven?
Vitelli. I hope not
If justice be my Pilot: but my Lord, 50

84

You know, if argument, or time, or love,
Could reconcile, long since we had shook hands;
I dare protest, your breath cooles not a veine
In any one of us, but blowes the fire
Which nought but blood reciprocall can quench.
Alvarez. 　Vitelli, thou sayst bravely, and sayst right,
And I wil kill thee for't, I love thee so.
Vitelli. 　Ha, ha, old man: upon thy death Ile build
A story (with this arme) for thy old wife
To tell thy daughter *Clara* seven yeeres hence　　　　60
As she sits weeping by a winter fire,
How such a time *Vitelli* slew her husband
With the same Sword his daughter favour'd him,
And lives, and weares it yet: Come *Lamorall*,
Redeeme thy selfe.
Lamorall. 　　　　　*Lucio, Genevora*
Shall on this Sword receive thy bleeding heart,
For my presented hat, laid at her feet.
Lucio. 　Thou talkst wel *Lamorall*, but tis thy head
That I wil carry to her to thy hat:
Fie father, I do coole too much.
Alvarez. 　　　　　　　Oh boy:　　　　70
Thy fathers true sonne:
Beat Drums, — and so good morrow to your Lordship.
Sayavedra. 　Brave resolutions.
Anastro. 　　　　　Brave, and Spanish right.

　　　Enter above Eugenia, Clara, Genevora.

Genevora. 　*Lucio.*
Clara. 　　　　　*Vitelli.*
Eugenia. 　　　　*Alvarez.*
Alvarez. 　　　　　How the devill
Got these Cats into th' gutter? my pusse too?
Eugenia. 　Heare us.
Genevora. 　　　　We must be heard.
Clara. 　　　　　　　We will be heard.
　Vitelli; looke, see *Clara* on her knees

85

Imploring thy compassion.——Heaven, how sternly
They dart their emulous eyes, as if each scorn'd
To be behind the other in a look!——   80
Mother, death needs no Sword here: oh my sister
(Fate faine would have it so) perswade, entreat,
A Ladies teares are silent Orators
(Or should be so at least) to move beyond
The honiest-tongu'd Rethoritian.——
[*To Vitelli*] Why will you fight? why do's an uncles death
Twentie yeare old, exceed your love to me
But twentie daies? whose forc'd cause, and faire manner
You could not understand, onely have heard.
Custome, that wrought so cunningly on nature   90
In me, that I forgot my sex, and knew not
Whether my body femall were, or male,
You did unweave, and had the power to charme
A new creation in me, made me feare
To think on those deeds I did perpetrate,
How little power though you allow to me
That cannot with my sighes, my teares, my prayers
Move you from your own losse, if you should gaine.
Vitelli.   I must forget you *Clara*, 'till I have
Redeem'd my uncles blood, that brands my face   100
Like a pestiferous Carbuncle: I am blinde
To what you doe: deafe to your cries: and Marble
To all impulsive exorations.
When on this point, I have pearch'd thy fathers soule,
Ile tender thee this bloody reeking hand
Drawne forth the bowels of that murtherer:
If thou canst love me then, i'le marry thee,
And for thy father lost, get thee a Sonne;
On no condition else.
Assistente.   Most barbarous.
Sayavedra.   Savage.
Anastro.   Irreligious.
Genevora.   Oh *Lucio*!   110

85 honiest] Colman; honest F1-2
86

Be thou more mercifull: thou bear'st fewer yeers,
Art lately wean'd from soft effeminacy,
A maidens manners, and a maidens heart
Are neighbours still to thee: be then more milde,
Proceed not to this combat; bee'st thou desperate
Of thine owne life? yet (deerest) pitty mine:
Thy valour's not thine owne, I gave it thee,
These eyes begot it, this tongue bred it up,
This breast would lodge it: doe not use my gifts
To mine own ruine: I have made thee rich,　　　　120
Be not so thanklesse, to undoe me for't.

Lucio.　Mistresse, you know I doe not weare a vaine
I would not rip for you, to doe you service:
Life's but a word, a shadow, a melting dreame,
Compar'd to essentiall, and eternall honour.
Why, would you have me value it beyond
Your brother? if I first cast down my sword
May all my body here, be made one wound,
And yet my soule not finde heaven thorough it.

Alvare{z} [*to Eugenia*].　You would be catter-walling too, but peace, 130
Goe, get you home, and provide dinner for
Your Sonne, and me: we'l be exceeding merry:
Oh *Lucio*, I will have thee cock of all
The proud *Vitellies* that doe live in *Spaine*:
Fie, we shall take cold: hunch: — I am hoarse
Already.

Lamorall [*to Vitelli*].　How your Sister whets my spleene!
I could eate *Lucio* now.

Genevora.　　　　　　　*Vitelli*, Brother,
Ev'n for your Fathers soule, your uncles blood,
As you doe love my life: but last, and most
As you respect your own Honour, and Fame,　　　　140
Throw downe your sword; he is most valiant
That herein yeelds first.

---

122 vaine] i.e., veine　　　*135 hunch] *stet* F1
*137 now.] F2; now: | *Gen. Lamorall*: you have often sworne | You'ld be com-
manded by me. F1

Vitelli.   Peace, you foole.

Clara.   Why *Lucio*,
Doe thou begin; 'tis no disparagement:
He's elder, and thy better, and thy valour
Is in his infancy.

Genevora.   Or pay it me,
To whom thou ow'st it: Oh, that constant time
Would but goe back a week, then *Lucio*
Thou would'st not dare to fight.

Eugenia.   *Lucio*, thy Mother,
Thy Mother beggs it: throw thy sword down first.

Alvarez.   Ile throw his head downe after then.

Genevora.   *Lamorall.*   150
You have often sworne you'ld be commanded by me.

Lamorall.   Never to this: your spight, and scorn *Genevora*,
H'as lost all power in me.

Assistente, Sayavedra, Anastro.   Strange obstinacy!

Alvarez, Vitelli, Lucio, Lamorall.   We'l stay no longer.

Clara.   Then by thy oath *Vitelli*,
Thy dreadfull oath, thou wouldst returne that sword
When I should aske it, give it to me, now,
This instant I require it.

Genevora.   By thy vow,
As dreadfull, *Lucio*, to obey my will
In any one thing I would watch to challenge,
I charge thee not to strike a stroake: now he   160
Of our two brothers that loves perjurie
Best, and dares first be damn'd, infringe his vow.

Sayavedra.   Excellent Ladies.

Vitelli.   Pish, you tyrannize.

Lucio.   We did equivocate.

Alvarez.   On.

Clara.   Then *Lucio*,
So well I love my husband, for he is so,
(Wanting but ceremony) that I pray

151 sworne] Dyce; swore F1–2 [*but see preceding note*]
*153 me.] me. | Gen. Your hearing for six words. F1–2

88

His vengefull sword may fall upon thy head
Succesfully for false-hood to his Sister.
Genevora.　I likewise pray (*Vitelli*) *Lucio's* sword
(Who equally is my husband, as thou hers)　　　　　　170
May finde thy false heart, that durst gage thy faith,
And durst not keepe it.
Assistente.　　　　　Are you men, or stone.
Alvarez.　Men, and we'l prove it with our swords.
Eugenia.　Your hearing for six words, and we have done.——
Zancho come forth.——We'l fight our challenge too:

　　　　Enter Bobadilla *with two swords and a Pistoll.*

Now speake your resolutions.
Genevora.　　　　　These they are,
The first blow given betwixt you, sheathes these swords
In one anothers bosomes.
Eugenia.　　　　　And rogue, looke
You at that instant doe discharge that Pistoll
Into my breast: if you start back, or quake,　　　　　180
Ile stick you like a Pigge.
Alvarez.　　　　　——hold: you are mad.
Genevora.　This we said: and by our hope of blisse
This we will doe: speake your intents.
Clara, Genevora.　　　　　Strike.
Eugenia.　　　　　Shoot.
Alvarez, Vitelli, Lucio, Lamorall.　Hold, hold: all friends.
Assistente.　Come downe.　[*Exeunt those above.*]
Alvarez.　　　　　These devillish women
Can make men friends and enemies when they list.
Sayavedra.　A gallant undertaking and a happie;
Why this is noble in you: and will be
A wellcomer present to our Master *Philip*
Then the returne from his *Indies.*

　　　Enter [*below*] Clara, Genevora, Eugenia, *and* Bobadilla.

Clara.　Father your blessing.

Alvarez.   Take her: if ye bring not   190
Betwixt you, boyes that will finde out new worlds,
And win 'em too I'm a false Prophet.
Vitelli.   Brother.
There is a Sister: long divided streames
Mix now at length, by fate.   [*They talk apart with* Assistente.]
Bobadilla.   I am not regarded: I was the carefull Steward that
provided these Instruments of peace, I put the longest weapon in
your Sisters hand, (my Lord) because she was the shortest Lady:
For likely the shortest Ladies, love the longest — men: And for
mine own part, I could have discharged it: my Pistoll is no ordin-
ary Pistoll, it has two ramming Bullets; but thought I, why should 200
I shoot my two bullets into my old Lady? if they had gon, I
would not have staid long after: I would ev'n have died too,
bravely y'faith, like a Roman-Steward: hung my selfe in mine
owne Chaine, and there had been a story of *Bobadilla Spindola
Zancho,* for after ages to lament: hum: I perceive I am not onely
not regarded, but also not rewarded.
Alvarez.   Prethee peace: 'shalt have a new chaine, next Saint
Jaques day, or this new gilt.
Bobadilla.   I am satisfied: let vertue have her due: And yet I am
melancholy upon this atonement: pray heaven the State rue it 210
not: I would my Lord *Vitellies* Steward, and I could meet: they
should find it should cost 'em a little more to make us friends:
well, I will forsweare wine, and women for a yeere: and then I
will be drunk to morrow, and runne a whoring like a dogge with a
broken bottle at's taile; then will I repent next day, and forsweare
'em againe more vehemently: be for-sworne next day againe,
and repent my repentance: for thus a melancholy Gentleman doth,
and ought to live.
Assistente.   Nay, you shall dine with me: and afterward
Ile with 'ye to the King: But first, I will   220
Dispatch the Castles businesse, that this day
May be compleat. Bring forth the malefactors.

190 ye] F2; he F1

90

Enter, Alguazier, Pachieco, Metaldi, Mendoza, Lazarillo, Piorato,
Malroda, *and Guard.*

You *Alguazier*, the Ringleader of these
Poore fellowes, are degraded from your office,
You must restore all stolne goods you receiv'd,
And watch a twelve moneth without any pay:
This, if you faile of, (all your goods confiscate)
You are to be whipt, and sent into the Gallies.

Alguazier. I like all, but restoring: that Catholique doctrine
I doe dislike: Learn all ye officers   230
By this to live uprightly (if you can).   *Exit.*

Assistente. You Cobler, to translate your manners new,
Are doom'd to th' Cloyster of the Mendicants,
With this your brother botcher, there for nothing
To cobble, and heel hose for the poor Friers,
Till they allow your pennance for sufficient,
And your amendment; then you shall be freed,
And may set up againe.

Pachieco.   *Mendoza*, come.
Our soules have trod awry in all mens sight,
We'l underlay 'em, till they goe upright.   240

                    Exeunt Pachieco *and* Mendoza.

Assistente. Smith, in those shackles you for your hard heart
Must lye by th' heeles a yeer.

Metaldi.   I have shod your horse, my Lord.

                              Exit [Metaldi].

Assistente. Away: for you, my hungry white-loaf'd face,
You must to th' Gallies, where you shall be sure
To have no more bits, then you shall have blowes.

Lazarillo. Well, though herrings want, I shall have rowes.

Assistente. Signior, you have prevented us, and punish'd
Your selfe severelier then we would have done.
You have married a whore: may she prove honest.

Piorato. 'Tis better my Lord, then to marry an honest woman   250
That may prove a whore.

Vitelli.   'Tis a hansome wench: and thou canst keepe her tame
Ile send you what I promis'd.
Piorato.   Joy to your Lordships.
Alvarez.   Here may all Ladies learne, to make of foes
The perfect'st friends: and not the perfect'st foes
Of deerest friends, as some doe now a dayes.
Vitelli.   Behold the power of love: lo, nature lost
By custome irrecoverably, past the hope
Of friends restoring, love hath here retriv'd
To her own habit, made her blush to see   260
Her so long monstrous metamorphoses.
May strange affaires never have worse successe.

Exeunt.

EPILOGUE

Our Author feares there are some Rebell hearts,
Whose dulnesse doth oppose loves peircing darts;
Such will be apt to say there wanted wit,
The language low, very few scænes are writ
With spirit and life; such odde things as these
He cares not for, nor ever meanes to please;
For if your selves, a Mistresse, or loves friends,
Are lik't with this smooth Play he hath his ends.

FINIS

257 lo] Dyce; to F1-2

92

A PROLOGUE

At the reviving of this Play.

Statues and Pictures challenge price and fame;
If they can justly boast, and prove they came
From *Phidias* or *Apelles*. None deny,
Poets and Painters hold a sympathy;
Yet their workes may decay and lose their grace,
Receiving blemish in their limbs or face.
When the minds art has this preheminence,
She still retaineth her first excellence.
Then why should not this deere peece be esteem'd
Child to the richest fancies that ere teem'd?   10
When not their meanest off-spring, that came forth,
But bore the image of their fathers worth,
Beaumonts, and *Fletchers*, whose desert outwayes
The best applause, and their least sprig of Bayes
Is worthy *Phœbus*; and who comes to gather
Their fruits of wit, he shall not rob the treasure.
Nor can you ever surfeit of the plenty,
Nor can you call them rare, though they be dainty.
The more you take, the more you do them right,
And wee will thanke you for your own delight.   20

93

TEXTUAL NOTES

I.ii

33 *Grave*] 'In the manuscript of *Sir John Van Olden Barnavelt* the name is written "Grave Maurice," line 109. And so it probably was in this manuscript [for *Love's Cure*]' (Battle, 'Loves Cure', p. 100).

I.iii

88 *beating of* Anastro] I.e., beating off; Anastro is probably not visible on stage – or if so, for a brief skirmish only.

II.i

2 in *Querpo*] Mr Beaurline has noted this form in *Love's Pilgrimage* and in Jonson's *The New Inn* (II. 572–3).

31 that] As an improvement over the Folio 'yet' which he retained, Dyce conjectured 'it', 'the MS. having had "yt"'. Dyce's reconstruction of the manuscript I accept, but I read 'that'. The same emendation was proposed by Sympson in notes 1 and 7 (pp. 395, 400) for two other presumed erroneous 'yet' forms, but these proposals have not been adopted generally. The passage recalls *King Lear*, IV.vi.128–9: 'But to the girdle do the gods inherit, Beneath is all the fiend's.'

111 clinch] The F2 correction has been generally adopted; it depends on the common *t:c* misreading.

II.ii

69–77 This is a difficult passage to visualize. In both of her speeches, Clara addresses one man and the other answers. Evidently, she has mistaken Bobadilla for Lucio (lines 74–7), whence I conclude that she has also already mistaken Lucio for Bobadilla (lines 69–73). She does not, of course, recognize her brother in man's attire, but it is not clear why she does not recognize that he is not Bobadilla (or Bobadilla he). Mr Battle suggests (p. 59) that Bobadilla at line 64 dresses Lucio in some article of clothing that marks him a servant, but the suggestion does not carry conviction.

202 can] The F2 reading 'neither can I', followed by all editions, not only suggests the erroneous 'I can't do it either' but also is hypermetrical.

III.i

29 feather]   Editors reject the F1 reading following Sympson and Seward (p. 424), but Mr Battle cites as parallel the modern expression: 'He was in fine feather' (p. 117).

58 Dill]   A dill is a wench, but such a gloss seems inapposite in this context. Dyce suggested 'drill, a Baboon, or over-grown Ape'. Sympson printed 'Deel', and Weber modernized to 'devil'. This is perhaps the likeliest interpretation.

III.ii

118 *Song*.]   Dyce conjectures that the song should follow immediately Piorato's 'I wil charme her' (line 115), thus becoming the charm itself. As a charm, the song succeeds in drawing first the lady – 'She's come' – and then a kiss (its own proper punctuation). The Alguazier's words interrupt this pretty picture. This staging of the song provides a more effective dramatic context than that of the Folio, but there is insufficient justification to adopt Dyce's conjecture in this edition. The song with its music is preserved in several manuscripts (see Historical Collation).

IV.iv

30 stranglie]   This common *o*:*a* misreading is anticipated in reverse at IV.iii.58 where Colman and Dyce read 'stronger' for folio 'stranger'.

V.iii

135 hunch]   Probably the same expletive that appears as 'Hauh' at III.ii.65; it is evidently the equivalent of modern 'hunh'.

137 After 'now:' F1 inserts the speech of Genevora which it prints again at lines 150–1. The presumed erroneous anticipation suggests, as Weber observed, that 'the intermediate speeches were omitted in the representation'. See also next note.

153 After 'me:' F1 (followed by all editions) inserts a speech which it prints again at line 174. Like the anticipation discussed in the preceding note, this repetition also seems to suggest an omission in the representation. The present crux involves, however, a change in speaker. Presumably, the assignment to Eugenia at line 174 is correct, as she is the ranking matron

of the trio, and the speech of highest melodramatic content is fittingly
given to her. The assignment of the speech to Genevora at line 153 may be
due to the assumption that Lamorall's preceding speech, addressed to her,
requires an answer from her. The omission of this insertion restores the
meter to the surrounding lines.

PRESS-VARIANTS IN F1 (1647)

[Copies Collated: Bodl (Bodleian Library B.1.8.Art.), Camb¹ (Cambridge University Library Aston a. Sel.19), Camb² (Cambridge University Library SSS.10.8); CSmH (Henry E. Huntington Library 112111), DFo¹ (Folger Shakespeare Library copy¹), DFo² (Folger Shakespeare Library copy²), NCD (Duke University), NCU (University of North Carolina), NN¹ (New York Public Library, Berg Collection/Beaumont Copy¹), NN² (New York Public Library, Berg Collection/Beaumont Copy²), NN³ (New York Public Library, Berg Collection/Beaumont Copy³), NN⁴ (New York Public Library, *KC/1647/Beaumont (Astor Copy)), NN⁵ (New York Public Library, Arents Collection 232, Acc. 3583), TxU (University of Texas Ah/B 384/C647/copy²), ViU¹ (University of Virginia 217972), ViU² (University of Virginia 570973).]

Quire Q (*outer sheet, inner forme*)

Corrected: the rest
Uncorrected: TxU

Sig. 5Q4
heading 127] 128
I.ii.91 which] whtch
96 cooks] cooks,
I.iii.68 *Alvarez*] *Alvarezi*
68.1 c.w. Accompt] Accomp

Quire R (*inner sheet, inner forme*)

Corrected: the rest
Uncorrected: CSmH

Sig. 5R2ᵛ
II.ii.180 Tis] Ti3

Quire R (*outer sheet, outer forme*)

Corrected: Bodl, Camb², CSmH, DFo¹, NCD, NCU, NN¹,²,⁴, TxU
Uncorrected: Camb¹, DFo², NN³,⁵, ViU¹,²
Sig. 5R1
II.i.97 foule-menders] foule-members

97

QUIRE S (*middle sheet, outer forme*)

Corrected: Bodl, Camb², DFo¹, NN⁴,⁵, ViU¹
Uncorrected: Camb¹, CSmH, DFo², NCD, NCU, NN¹⁻³, TxU, ViU²
Sig. 5S2
IV.ii.124 gallant,] gallant.

QUIRE S (*outer sheet, inner forme*)

Corrected: the rest
Uncorrected: ViU²

Sig. 5S1ᵛ
IV.ii.56 *Vit.*] *Vit.*

EMENDATIONS OF ACCIDENTALS

I.i

I.i Actus Primus—— *Scæna Prima.*
  F1
  1 *Vitelli.*] *centered in* F1
  5 fortune,] ~ ˌ F1–2
  12 *Don*] Don F2
  30 I] F2; 1 F1 (*often so*)
  74 Discharg'd] F2; Dischar'd F1
  77 faulchion,] F2; ~ ˌ F1
  77 lightningˌ] F2; ~ , F1

  87 presence,] F2; ~ ˌ F1
  89 encouragement:] F2; ~ ˌ F1
  97 That,] ~ ˌ F1–2
  98 *Alvareʒˌ*] F2; ~ , F1
  114 *D'Alva*] F2; D'*Alva* F1
  118 Kings.] ~ , F1–2
  119 *Alvareʒ*] F2; *Alvarʒ* F1
  127 which,] F2; ~ ˌ F1

I.ii

I.ii *Scæna Secunda.* F1
  2 't has] F2; 'thas F1
  10 pind-Placket] pind-|Placket F1;
    Pinn'd ˌ Placket F2
  43–47 F1–2 *line:* I knew...eyes?
    | If he...advantage | Had...
    this? | But...Master | I...
    him?
  43 hides] F2; hids F1

  44 eyes] F2 (eies); eys F1
  46 up:——] ~ : ˌ F1–2
  46 jest:——] ~ : ˌ F1–2
  54 A] F2; a F1
  69 modestyˌ] ~ , F1–2
  76 life,] ~ ˌ F1–2
  86 I?——] I? ˌ F1–2
  103 calling:——] ~ : ˌ F1–2
  110 helpe] F2; helfe F1

I.iii

I.iii] *Scæna Tertia.* F1
  14 tissue] F2; tisseu F1
  25 hunger] F2; hunder F1
  27 Yet,] ~ ˌ F1–2
  27 smilesˌ] ~ , F1–2
  34 much——] ~ . F1–2
  40 Eugenia] F2; *Eugnia* F1
  40 *Musick.*] *after line* 38 *in* F1–2
  50 Lord ˌ...for,] ~ ,...~ ˌ F1–2
  61 T'enquire] F2; 'Tenquire F1
  74 heare.] ~ , F1–2
  74 know——] ~ ˌ F1; ~ . F2

  74.1 *Within*...*swords.*] *after* death.
    (*line* 73) *in* F1–2
  74.1 *Within*] F2; *within* F1
  76 fairely.] ~ , F1–2
  77 *Vitelli* (*within*).] *Vitelli within.*
    F1 (*as* s.d. *after line* 75); Vitelli
    within.... Vit. F2 (*as* s.d. *after*
    line 75; *prefix line* 77)
  79–80 *Vitelli*...*them.*] *one line of*
    verse in F1–2
  88 him:] ~ ˌ F1–2
  95 rare:] ~ ˌ F1–2

100 fall,] ~ ; F1–2
129 did:] ~ , F1–2
139 to.——] ~ ; ‸ F1–2
142 me:——] ~ : ‸ F1–2

148 well?——] ~ ? ‸ F1–2
182 man woman,] F2; ~ ~ ‸ F1
182 woman ‸ man] F2; ~ , ~ F1

II.i

II.i] *Actus secundus. Scæna prima.* F1
3 Gentleman.] Gent. F1–2
25 virginitie.] ~ ? F1–2
40–41 *O' de dios*...delicacies?] *one line of verse in* F1; *prose in* F2
46–47 provant...*Jerusalem.*] F1 *lines:* provant...day, | at... *Jerusalem.*; F2 *lines:*... Provant a | whole day, | At... *Jerusalem.*
49 place,] F2; ~ ‸ F1
49.1 *after line* 47 *in* F1–2
50–51 *Signior...Signiorie.*] F1–2 *line:* Signior... ingenious | Cobler...*Signiorie.*
52 *Forgio*] F2; *forgio* F1
55 *Vermini*] vermim F1; *Vermim* F2
55–56 Hose-|heeler] Hose-heeler F1–2
62 *Adelantado:*——] ~ : ‸ F1–2
63 were] F2; w're F1
63 dowgh-bak'd;] ~ ‸ F1; ~ , F2
64 oaten-Cake] F2; oaten-|Cake F1
65 scallion-fac'd rascall] F2; scallion fac'd-rascall F1
70 wollen-witted] wollen-|witted F1–2
76 *Æneas*] F2; *Æeas* F1
78 God——] ~ . F1–2

81 *Vulcan*] F2; *Vulgan* F1
86 briefe:] ~ ‸ F1; ~ , F2
87 *viz.*] F2 (*viz,*); viz. F1
90–91 anckles?——Blush] ~ ? ‸ blush F1–2
95 horse-menders——] ~ . F1–2
102 though,] F2; ~ ‸ F1
102 forgery.] ~ , F1; ~ : F2
109 *Metaldi.*] F2; *Net.* F1
112–114 Who's...*Alguazier*] F1 *lines:* Who's...knave as | E're ...side | *Alguazier; prose in* F2
114 *Alguazier*——] ~ . F1–2
129 *Signior:*——] Signiors: ‸ F1–2
140 I know...Besegnios.] *one line of verse in* F1–2
141 Marry,] *Mary* ‸ F1–2
141 *Catzo:*] ~ ‸ F1–2
144 *Signiorie*] signiorie F1; *Signiorie* F2
151 out‸] F2; ~ , F1
151 perjury?] ~ . F1–2
153 pizell?] ~ . F1–2
154 Apostacie?] ~ . F1–2
170 strumpets?] ~ ‸ F1–2
170 *Dons*] Dons F1–2
183 Constable,] ~ ‸ F1; ~ ; F2
185 loynes] loyes F1; *om.* F2
201 quittance.——Why] ~ : ‸ why F1–2
205 sir?——] ~ ? ‸ F1–2

II.ii

II.ii] *Scæna Secunda.* F 1
2 angry:] ~ ∧ F 1–2
2 *diablo*'what] *diablo*': what F 1;
  ~ ∧ : ~ F 2
4–5 dogs-|head] dogs-head F 1–2
9 Tyrant.] ~ , F 1–2
32 thee:——] ~ : ∧ F 1–2
43 *prose in* F 1–2
54 peace:——] ~ : ∧ F 1–2
55 *Vitellies?*] ~ . F 1–2
68 o'] O' F 1–2
75 Cod-peice] F 2 (Codpiece);
  Cod-peicu F 1
82 for:——] ~ : ∧ F 1–2
85 it).——] ~) ∧∧ F 1–2
97 Steward——] ~ . F 1–2
99 me?] ~ , F 1–2
106 ∧ rogue] F 2; -rogue F 1
112 *Lucio*:——] ~ , ∧ F 1–2
113 flat:——] ~ : ∧ F 1–2
121 with'ye:——] ~ : ∧ F 1–2
131 Gun,] ~ ∧ F 1–2

139.1 *Enter*...*Bobadilla.*] *after*
  woman? (*line* 138) *in* F 1–2
158–164 F 1–2 *line*: I thank...advice
  | Of...that | Lady...has | Ten
  ...foolish | Hot...horizon |
  Under...as | You...will | Not
  ...constitution: | She...you.
168 *Exit.*] *after line* 167 *in* F 1–2
169 *Lucio* ∧ that was,] F 2; *Lucio*,
  that was ∧ F 1
169 *Clara*∧] ~ , F 1–2
195 worthily!] ~ ? F 1–2
204 soule:——] ~ : ∧ F 1–2
206 apace:——] ~ : ∧ F 1–2
214 bestowd:] ~ ; F 2; ~ . F 1
216–217 Fie;...Serving-men.] *one*
  line in F 1–2
222 well,] ~ : F 1–2
230 Sword.——] ~ . ∧ F 1–2
233 here:] F 2; ~ ; F 1
234 chimes:——] ~ : ∧ F 1–2
239 kept] F 2; kepit F 1
248 living:——] ~ : ∧ F 1–2

III.i

III.i] *Actus tertius, Scæna prima.* F 1
1 must not,] ~ ? F 1–2
1 shall not?] ~ , F 1–2
5 *Alguazier*] F 2; *Alquazier* F 1
16 shall,] ~ ∧ F 1–2
24 conniv'd;] ~ ∧ F 1–2

27 this∧] ~ . F 1; ~ , F 2
33 tell you,...selfe;] ~ ;...~ ,
  F 1–2
54 still,] F 2; ~ ∧ F 1
67.1 *Exit.*] *after line* 66 *in* F 1–2

III.ii

III.ii] *Scæna secunda.* F 1
13 womanish-hearted] F 2; ~ ∧ ~
  F 1
26 crudities,] ~ ; F 1–2
64 *Signior*] F 2; Sgnior F 1
77 ripen.—— Hark] ~ : ∧ hark
  F 1–2

82 *bazi los*] *bazilos* F 1–2
82 *manos*:——] ~ : ∧ F 1–2
84 thus:——] ~ : ∧ F 1–2
86.1 *Exit.*] *after* enough. (*line* 86)
  in F 1–2
87 brains;] ~ , F 1–2
88 *Alguazier.*] ~ : F 1–2

88 *Enter* Alguazier.] *after* enough.   89 cosen)?] cosen?) F1–2
  (*line* 86) *in* F1–2   118 *Song.*] Song. F1–2
88 *Dieu*] *dieu* F1–2   124 *Yet*] c.w. *Yee* F1

III.iii

III.iii] *Scena tertia.* F1   81 Carts_∧] ~ , F1–2
  3 griefe:——] ~ : _∧ F1–2   81 Beadles,] F2; ~ _∧ F1
  18 *Signior.*——] ~ . _∧ F1–2   84 poore] F2; poorc F1
  29 now.——] ~ : _∧ F1–2   85 't] F2; 't' F1
  32 *Malroda*] *Mal.* F1; *Mal* _∧ F2   90 merry.——'Faith] ~ , _∧ 'faith
  71 again.——] ~ . _∧ F1–2   F1–2
  73 rightly] F2; righly F1   91 marry!] ~ ? F1–2
  80 live;] ~ _∧ F1; ~ , F2

III.iv

III.iv] *Scæna quarta.* F1   65 way.——Nay] ~ : _∧ nay F1;
  11–12 And he...I wis.] *one line of*   ~ , _∧ nay F2
  verse in F1–2   68.1 *in right margin beside lines*
  12 wis.] ~ _∧ F1; ~ , F2   67–68 *in* F1; *after* sure. (*line* 68)
  12 grace——] ~ . F1–2   *in* F2
  15.1 *in right margin beside lines* 9–12   68.1 Piorato_∧] ~ , F1–2
  in F1; *after* grace. (*line* 12) *in*   74 giv'ye] gi'v'ye F1; give ye F2
  F2   78 *Toledos.*——] ~ ; _∧ F1–2
  24 to'ye:——] ~ ; _∧ F1–2   83 Pray,] ~ _∧ F1–2
  33 gone;] ~ _∧ F1–2   88 *Eugenia*] *indented as if a prefix*
  34 I...stitch,] (I...stitch) F1–2   F1; *om.* F2
  42 and the] F2; andthe F1   100 sure.] ~ , F1–2
  52 yeer.] ~ , F1–2   103 on't.——] ~ . _∧ F1–2
  55 heart.——Good] ~ : _∧ good   105.1 *Exeunt*] F2; *Exit* F1
  F1–2   105.1 *in right margin beside lines*
  57 troublesome.——Pish] ~ : _∧   104–6 F1–2
  pish F1–2   118.1 *Exeunt.*] *Exit.* F1–2
  57 is_∧] F2; ~ , F1

III.v

III.v] *Scæna quinta.* F1   17–18 Away,...her?] F1–2 *line:*
  12–13 The terror...recknings.]   Away,...who | Would...her?
  F1–2 *line:* The...bils | Dis-
  charge...recknings.

IV.i

IV.i] *Actus quartus. Scæna prima.* F1   13 Lord———] ~ , F1–2
10 speedily.] ~ : ᴧ F1–2

IV.ii

IV.ii] *Scæna secunda.* F1
10 that:] ~ , F1–2
18 if] If F1–2
20 well.] well. *Vitelli within.* F1–2
20 (*within*)] om. F1–2
23 rampant] F2; rampani F1
24 will] F2; Will F1
24 reveng'd.———] ~ ᴧᴧ F1; ~ ᴧ
——— F2
26 host?] F2; ~ ᴧ F1
28.2 *after line 27 in* F1–2
32 nay, willingly;] ~ ᴧ ~ ᴧ F1–2
38 What,] ~ ᴧ F1–2
48 Why,] ~ ᴧ F1–2
63 prefer'd;] ~ , F1–2
85 yours:] ~ ᴧ F1–2
86 now.———This] ~ : ᴧ this F1–2

89 now,] ~ ; F1–2
89 me;] ~ , F1–2
101 Prethee,] F2; ~ . F1
120 *and others*] &c F1–2
123 Lad.———And] ~ ; ᴧ and F1–2
124 gallant,] F2; ~ . F1
126 knees.———] ~ : ᴧ F1–2
135.1 *Exit.*] *after* finde me. (*line* 135)
in F1–2
139 at.———] ~ : ᴧ F1–2
145.1 *after* strumpet. (*line* 144) *in*
F1–2
164 mercifull] F2; mercifuil F1
198 her.———] ~ : ᴧ F1–2
201 you.] ~ : F1–2
205 her.———Worthiest] ~ : ᴧ
worthiest F1–2

IV.iii

IV.iii] *Scæna Tertia.* F1
0.2 Lazarillo] F2; Lararillo F1
13 so,] ~ ᴧ F1–2
19 watch,] F2; ~ ᴧ F1
19.1 *after line* 17 *in* F1–2
32 Zancho.———Father] ~ , ᴧ
father F1–2
33 disclam thee:] ~ , F1–2
34 motherᴧ] F2; ~ ; F1
50 me:———] ~ : ᴧ F1–2

56 *Vitelli's*] F2; *Vitell's* F1
65 you?———] ~ ? ᴧ F1–2
71 *Enter*] F2; *Entes* F1
71 *Watches*] F2; *Watchcs* F1
85 so,] ~ ᴧ F1–2
108 fee simple] F2; feesimple F1
115 wilᴧ] F2; ~ . F1
124 T'expostulate] 'T'expostulate
F2; 'T'xpostulate F1
129 place.———] ~ . ᴧ F1–2

IV.iv

IV.iv] *Scæna Quarta.* F1
8 why,] ~ ᴧ F1–2
29 in.———Why] ~ : ᴧ why F1–2
35 resolv'd] F2; resov'd F1

44–45 Not...enemy?] *one line in*
F1–2
62.1 *Exit*] *Exeunt* F1–2

V.i

V.i] *Actus Quintus. Scæna prima.* F 1
26 proofe‸] ~ , F 1–2
26 be,] F 2: ~ ‸ F 1
38 it; the] ~ . The F 1–2
41 addition);] ~) ‸ F 1–2
42 multipli'd;] ~ , F 1–2

43 Against] F 2; Aagainst F 1
104 selves.] ~ , F 1–2
106 unwillingly‸] ~ ; F 1–2
115–116 Which...word)] *one line
in* F 1–2

V.ii

V.ii *Scæna secunda.* F 1
21 s.d. *after line* 19 *in* F 1–2
34 with] F 2; wirh F 1
50 dissemble.——Rise] ~ : ‸ rise
F 1–2

64 now;] ~ : F 1–2
65 us:] ~ , F 1–2
66 ended,] ~ : F 1–2
71.1 *Exit.*] *Exeunt.* F 1–2

V.iii

V.iii] *Scena tertia.* F 1
6 Herald reads.] *as* s.d. *in* F 1–2
6–30 *in slightly larger type in* F 1
7 Spaine] F 2; *Spaine* F 1
21 Common-wealth] *defective
hyphen prints as a dot in some
copies*
24 welchosen] wel-|chosen F 1;
well-chosen F 2
25 *St.*] St. F 1–2
25 Iago] Jago F 1–2
30.1 *after* King. (*line* 30) *in* F 1–2
46 obstinacy‸] ~) F 1–2
47 erroneously)] ~ , F 1; ~ ‸ F 2
61 winter] wintet F 1; winters F 2
73.1 *after line* 72 *in* F 1–2
76 will be heard.] ~ ‸ F 1–2
78 compassion.——] ~ : ‸ F 1–2
80 look!——] ~ ! ‸ F 1–2
85 honiest-tongu'd Rethoritian.
——] honest tongu'd-Rethori-
tian: ‸ F 1–2
98 should] F 2; shoule F 1

116 mine:] ~ ‸ F 1–2
122 vaine‸] ~ . F 1–2
127 brother?] ~ : F 1–2
174 done.——] ~ , ‸ F 1–2
175 forth.——We'l] ~ ‸ ——we'l
F 1–2
188 wellcomer] F 2; well comer F 1
189.1 Genevora, Eugenia,] F 2; ~ ‸
~ ‸ F 1
204 *Bobadilla Spindola*] ~ , ~ , F 1–
2
209 yet I] F 2; yet i F 1
229 restoring:] ~ ‸ F 1–2
234 brother‸] ~ , F 1–2
235 botcher, there‸] F 2; ~ ‸ ~ ,
F 1
240.1 *Exeunt.*] *Exe.* F 2; *Enit.* F 1
241 Smith] *Smith* F 1–2
252 tame‸] F 2; ~ : F 1
257 love:] ~ , F 1–2
257 lo,] ~ ‸ F 1–2
261 metamorphoses.] ~ , F 1–2

Epilogue

1–8 *in italic in* F 1–2

1 Author] F 2; *Auhor* F 1

7 selves, a Mistresse,] ~ ∧ ~ ∧ F 1–2

Prologue

12 worth,] ~ . F 1–2

HISTORICAL COLLATION

[This collation against the present text includes the two seventeenth-century folio texts (F 1, 1647, F 2 1679), the single quarto (Q 1718), and the editions of Langbaine (L, 1711), Theobald–Seward–Sympson (S, 1750), Colman (C, 1778), Weber (W, 1812), Dyce (D, 1843). For the song at III.ii.118–125 these texts are also included: John Wilson, *Cheerful Ayres* (1660) (CA), Bodleian Library MS Mus b. 1 28v (MSB), Edinburgh University MS Dc 1, 69 p. 78 (MSE), Rosenbach MS 243/4 p. 55 (MSR). Omission of a siglum indicates that the text concerned agrees with the reading of the lemma.]

I.i

10 *Civill*] *Sevil* F 2+
14 In th'] I' th' F 2+(− W, − D)
14 *Ostend*] Ostena F 1
44 make] made W
48 you'ld] you'll L, Q, S, C
80 strake] struck F 2+(− D)
110 the] *om.* F 2, L, Q
124 flight] sight F 1, F 2, L, Q

127 which,...friendship_∧] which _∧
...friendship, F 1, F 2; which,
...friendship, L, S, C, W (±);
which,...friendship; Q
128 oathes _∧...assistance:] oathes _∧
...assistance, F 1, F 2; oathes;
...assistance, L, Q, C, W (±)

I.ii

6 St.] Sir F 1
14 Nay] May F 1
22 h'as] has F 2+; hath Q
22–23 this...year] these...years F 2+(− D)

28 holp] hope F 1–2, L
61 *Posthumina*] *Posthumia* F 2+
89 gold chaine, and a] chaine, and a gold F 1–2, L, Q, S

I.iii

4 complement] compliment F 2 +
15 The] Then F 1
15 Gallants] Gallans F 1
17 lovd] Love F 1–2, L, Q
44 joyes] joy C, W
57 *Civill*] *Sevil* F 2+
61 T'enquire] To enquire W, D

71 in] within S, C, W
74 heare] he are F 1
74.1 *Within Clashing swords.*] after death. (*line* 73) F 1–2, L, Q; after that? (*line* 75) S, C, W
74.1 Sayavedra *within.*] *om.* S +
75 voyce] noise F 2+

106

75 *Sayavedra.*] *om.* F 1
75 Enemies,] Enemies, *Vitelli with-in.* F 1-2, L
77 *Vitelli.*] *om.* F 1

79 enemies] Enemy S
90 my] by F 1
95 and yet] yet he S, C, W
113 you] ye L, Q, S, C, W

II.i

1 my] and F 2, L, Q
4 *Civill*] *Sevil* F 2+
10 great sleepers: great sleepers,] great sleepers: F 2, L, Q
12 deitie] dietie F 1
26 yeere] years F 2+(−D)
31 beneath that] yet beneath S
31 that] yet F 1 +
43 ne'ere] neere F 1
48 and] an C, W, D
51 *Civill*] *Sevil* F 2 +
57 Her's] Here's F 2+
82 begat] begot F 2, L, Q, S
83 be] shew C
91 Machanick] Mechanicks F 2+
97 soule-menders] F 1(c)+; soule-members F 1(u)
98 spin] spin out F 2, L, Q, S
102 is] *om.* S
111 ne'ere] neere F 1
111 clinch] clinth F 1; clench W

113 one head] ont head F 1
121 do's] does F 2+
129 *Signior*] *Signiors* F 1+(−D)
131 brightens] brightnes F 1
140 you not] ye not C, W
141 Marry] *Mary* F 1-2
141 do'ye] d'ye F 2, L, Q, S; d'you C; do you W, D
144 *Signiorie*] Signior L, Q
149 we] *om.* F 1-2, L, Q
152 pilfery,] pilfery, there S
160 *Civill*] *Sevil* F 2+
170 strumpets?] strumpets ᴧ F 1-2, L, Q
170 rise] riss D
175 berrayer] betrayer L
181 Oh] *om.* F 2, L, Q, S
185-186 gird...midnight:] *om.* F 2, L, Q, S
185 beares skin] bear-skin C, W
202 you] ye C, W

II.ii

2 *Bobadilla.*] *om.* F 1
7 babie] badie F 1
36 leave] leaving L, Q, S, C, W
37 ye] you W, D
40 Do'ye] D'ye F 2, L, Q, S, C; Do ye W; Do you D
54 law] La D
59 of] off Q, W
65 ye] you C, W, D
67 tan, ta] tan ta, ta F 2, L, Q, S, C
68 a —] a pox C, W, D
80 Cowheard] Coward L, Q, S+
85 you] *om.* F 2, L, Q

95 to'ye] t'ye F 2, L, S, C; 't ye Q; to ye W, D
113 the] thy Q, S+
114 cut] kick W
121 with 'ye] with ye F 2, L, Q, W; w'ye S, C; with you D
126 scurr'd] scour'd F 2, L, Q; skirr'd S, C, W
130 do'ye] d'ye F 2, L, Q, S, C; do ye W; do you D
150 did] did not S
151 Lieger] leger C
154 by —] by Heaven C, W, D

156 is] he's S, C; he is W
164 Bell] Bell and L, Q, S, C, W
202 can] can I F 2+
206 apace] a pace F 1–2, L
210 all] my S, C
217 their] the S, C, W

219 have] have have F 2
234 this] his F 1+(−D)
234 saying] a saying S
239 I have] I've F 2+(−W, −D)
245 an Article] a particle F 2, L, Q, S

III.i

3 the —] the pox C+
3 on] upon S+
8 but] Butt F 2+
13 Anys] Any F 2, L
23, 24 conniv'd] contriv'd F 1+
    (−D)

26 blacks] black's F 2+
29 feather] feature S+
40 by] be L
47 owne] owe F 1
52 thou art] thou'rt F 2+(−D)
58 Dill] Deel S, C; devil W

III.ii

7 ye] you C, W, D
16 by] by a F 2, L, Q
32 h'ad] h'had F 2, C; he 'ad L, Q,
    S; he had W
40 Tis] It is S+
42 You are] You're very S
57 hereby] here by F 1, F 2
60 Civill] Sevil F 2+
66 I am] I am a L, Q; I'm a S, C
74 speciall] especial W, D
82 bazi los] Beso las W, D
90 akin] a Kin F 2; a-kin L
104 chop] chap C
105 too] too too S

115 Ile] I will C
115 I wil] I'll C, W
118 Turn, turn] Turne, turne, turne
    CA, MSB, MSE; Turn MSR
121 fly, fly] fly hence MSR
122 peece...as] joyne...in CA,
    MSB, MSE, MSR
122 breasts] breaths MSR
123 When] And MSR
123 does] dooth MSR
124 Yet] keepe MSR
124 thy] thine W; CA, MSE, MSR
125 their] thy MSR
129 night] might F 2

III.iii

7 deboshd] debauch'd F 2, L, Q,
    S, C
33 tongue] tongues F 1–2, L, Q
42 on] of S, C, W
77 Do'ye] Do ye F 2, L, Q; D'ye
    S; D'you C; Do you W, D

92 By —] By Heav'n C, W, D
98 I lov'd] I'd love S, C; I love W
103 do'ye] d'ye F 2, L, Q, S, C; Do
    ye W; Do you D
118 her's] here's Q, S+
120 'Faith] I'faith S, C, W; Faith D

III.iv

11 he] ye L
12 I wis] I wish F1+(−D)
15 do's] does F2+
24 to'ye] t'ye F2, L, Q, S; t'you C;
    to you W, D
27 do's] does F2+
28 know] knew F2
38 do'ye] d'ye F2, L, Q, S; d'you
    C; do you W, D
45 me my work] me work my F1
53 — o'] Plague o' C, W; Pox o'
    D
54 h'as] has L+
55-56 Good...againe.] om. F2, L,
    Q

72 needles] needless F2, L, Q;
    Needle's S+
74 ye] you C, W, D
76 cold:] cold: 2 Torches ready.
    F1
79 ye] y' S, C; you D
88 Eugenia,] om. F2, L, Q, S
94 —] Pox D; om. F2+
113 by —] By Heaven C, W, D
115 You mercy] Your mercy L, Q,
    S
116 you] y' S, C; ye W
117 further] farther F2, L, Q, S
118 with ye] w'ye S, C; with you D

III.v

12 bils] Bliss L, Q; bilss F2

IV.i

14 further] farther F2, L, Q, S

IV.ii

6 nor yet] not yet L; nor S
9 sinner] finner F2
16 this] his F2, L, Q
18 — if] Pox if C, W, D
24.1 Enter Vitelli.] om. F1
27 I would I] Would I S
28 Il'd] I'll F2, L, Q; I'd S, C, D;
    I would W
37 good —] good kiss C, W; good
    light D
37 this —] this kiss C, W; this
    light D

55 For] 'Fore S, C
64 Malroda.] om. F1
78 — if] By Heaven, if C, W;
    pox, if D
96 sigh] sight F1-2, L, Q, S
118 ayme] ay me F2; ah me L, Q
126 high-priz'd] high-pric'd C+
140 make] makes F2, L, Q, S, C
142 her] his F1
143 upon] on S
163 farther] further C, W
205 heaven] herein F1+(−D)

IV.iii

4 some] sum F2+
26 the] thee F2+
26 new] now F1
42 do] *om.* S
42 Sir, I am saying] I'm saying, Sir,
  S; Sir, I'm saying C
54 sir,] sir, that S
57 pray] prey F2+
58 stronger] stranger F1–2, L, Q,
  S

67 *Lazarillo.*] *Lam.* F1+(−D)
75 *Assistente*] Assistant L, Q, S, C,
  W; assistants F2; assistance F1
76 of't] on't F2+(−W, −D); of
  it W
88 to] *om.* L, Q
108 fee simple] feesimple F1
120 estimation] estimations F2+
125 upon] on S

IV.iv

1 you offer] your offer F1
21 you] *om.* S
30 stranglie] stronglie F1+
30 you] *om.* S

41 *Lucio.*] *Lam.* F1–2, L, Q
41 Do's] Does S+
42 appeard] appeare F1–2

V.i

7 On terms] One terme F1
7 seeke] to seek S, C
10 for] and for F1–2, L, Q,
17 further] farther F2, L, Q, S
24 fetcht] fetch F2
25 my] your F1–2, L, Q
27 Write] Writ F1
47 meet] must meet F2, L, Q, S
55 life ∧ to,] life, to ∧ F1–2, L;
  life ∧ to ∧ Q
56 looser] loser L+

58 further] farther F2, L, Q, S
70 purposes] purpose S
81 on] of S, C, W
91 further] farther F2, L, Q, S
103 makes] make C, W, D
107 till] tell F2
109 is] are W
111 thee] that L, Q
114 majick] musick F1–2, L, Q
114 ascribd] ascribe F1+(−D)
115 the] thy S

V.ii

1 and't] an't F2+
2 same,] same ∧ L, Q, S
29 desire] desires C+
38 what] that L, Q

46 heavenly] havenly F2
55 by —] by Heav'n C, W; by
  my soul, I swear, D
61 lose] loose F2

V.iii

9 *uncurable*] *honorable* F2, L, Q
10 *honourably*] *uncurable* F2, L, Q
11 Ferdinando] Fernando D
21 *farther*] *further* C
22 *a*] *om.* L, Q
24 *be*] *by* F2
31 how] *om.* F2, L, Q
48 Tis] It is W
48 thorough] through F2+(−S, −D)
61 winter fire] winters fire F2; Winter's fire L, Q, S; winter-fire C
85 honiest] honest F1–2, L, Q, S
86 do's] does C+
104 on] in F2, L, Q
111 more] *om.* F2, L, Q
129 thorough] through W
135 — I am] By Heav'n, I'm C; By Heaven, I am W; pox, I am D

137 now.] now: | *Gen. Lamorall*: you have often sworne | You'ld be commanded by me. F1
151 sworne] swore F1+(−D)
153 in] on S, C
153 me.] me. *Genevora.* Your hearing for six words F1+
172 stone] stones S
181 — hold] By Heaven! Hold W
182 we] we have S, C, W, D
190 ye] he F1
198 ——] *om.* C, W
210 melancholy] me-| Q
219 shall] stall F2
225 restore] return F2, L, Q, S
233 Cloyster] Cloisters F2+
236 your] you F2, L, Q
246 though] though I S+
252 and] an C+
254 Here] Hear F2
257 lo, nature] Nature, tho' C; So Nature W; to nature F1–2, L, Q, S

Prologue

14 Bayes] Boyes F2

THE NOBLE GENTLEMAN

edited by

L. A. BEAURLINE

TEXTUAL INTRODUCTION

Almost nothing is certain about the textual history of *The Noble Gentleman* except that Sir Henry Herbert licensed it 3 February 1625/6, 'by John Fletcher...acted at the Blackfriars', according to Malone's extracts from the Office Book of the Master of the Revels (J. Q. Adams (ed.), p. 31). This was five months after Fletcher died, and in the absence of a specification that it was 'new', 'old', 'renewed', 'corrected', or 'with scenes added', the entry appears to be a regular one for a new play, like dozens of others. The prologue to the first printing of the 1647 Folio presents it as a revival of the sort of play in fashion 'some twenty yeare agoe', worthy of the noble memory of its authors. Since the same prologue, in a slightly different text, was used for Q2 1649 of *Thierry and Theodoret*, G. E. Bentley thought its applications to *The Noble Gentleman* were 'doubtful', but the prologue and epilogue to *Thierry* were inserted in the second issue of Q2, and an inserted epilogue was also borrowed, this from Shirley's *The Changes* (1632). Similarly the epilogue to *The Noble Gentleman* reappears, again on an inserted fold, in Q2 1649 of *The Woman Hater* (see Greg's *Bibliography*). Therefore, it seems likely that the other plays were the borrowers and ours the lender; hence I presume the prologue was written for *The Noble Gentleman*. Nevertheless, we certainly cannot conjecture with any confidence that the original drama was written in 1606 and then twenty years later Herbert licensed a revision. Composition in 1624–5 and a revival in the 1630s are just as probable, when Beaumont and Fletcher flourished on the stage.

Various allusions in the text suggest a date much later than 1606. The exasperated Cozen, objecting to a woman's education at court, says

> Sir, I had rather send her to *Virginia*
> To help to propagate the English nation (I.i.90–1)

referring to a proposal of the Virginia Company to recruit females and transport them to the colony, first thought of in 1619 and not generally known until about 1621–2. The story of Shattillion and

his Love parallels the fortunes of Lady Arabella Stuart, her right to
the throne by a female line from Henry VII, her imprisonment by
the king, her attempted escape disguised as a boy, and her marriage to
William Seymour, also of royal lineage, that audiences could not fail
to recognize. Longavile says of Shattillion, whose Love stands 'very
near the crown':

> He is strong opinion'd that the wench he loved
> Remaines close prisoner by the Kings command,
> Fearing her title.   (I.ii.96–8)

And Shattillion makes the allusion as explicit as possible:

> if his Majesty had suffered me
> To marry her, though she be after him,
> The right heire generall to the Crowne of *France*,
> I would not have convayed her into *Spaine*,
> As it was thought, nor would I ere have joyn'd,
> With the reformed Churches to make them
> Stand for my cause.   (IV.iii.20–6)

It seems unlikely that this would have been tolerated on the stage
between 1610 and Arabella's death in the Tower in 1615. We know
that *Epicoene* and probably *The Knight of the Burning Pestle* were
suppressed, apparently for allusion to her and the Prince of
Moldavia in 1609; moreover, the whole sub-plot of *The Noble
Gentleman* is involved in this case.[1] The main plot, a fantastic
practical joke about a gentleman's rapid acquisition of noble titles –
knight, baron, earl, and duke – would have had the most point for
an English audience after 1623, when George Villiers climaxed his
sudden rise from gentleman, to knight, baron, earl, marquis, and
duke. There had not been an English duke since the execution of the
Duke of Norfolk in 1572.[2] Finally, a mention of the Lord of Lorn

---

[1] See Baldwin Maxwell's analysis of most of these allusions, *Studies in Beaumont,
Fletcher, and Massinger* (Chapel Hill, 1939), pp. 147–65. Marion A. Taylor, 'Lady
Arabella Stuart and Beaumont and Fletcher', *Papers in Language and Literature*, VIII
(1972), 252–60, presents the evidence from *The Knight of the Burning Pestle*.

[2] Oddly, no one has remarked on this particularly obvious contemporary theme,
of undeserved and preposterous honors granted by the king, nor can the instance
of Robert Carr be offered with much force, since he never rose beyond an earl.
I grant that he was 'disgraced' in a way vaguely suggestive of the undoing of
our noble gentleman, in a kind of trial and through the machinations of a much

seems to refer to the ill-fated Duke of Argyll and Lord of Lorn, who was declared a traitor in 1619.[1] Until further evidence comes to light, the *terminus a quo* must be 1623, not just for revisions but for the entire play, which is, after all, a cleverly constructed farce that is remarkably integrated, in spite of some roughness in the text. This conclusion differs from Maxwell's because he assumed that only limited parts of the text were affected by the allusions he considered. But the analogy with poor Arabella's life pervades the sub-plot and the sub-plot is necessary to the main plot at two critical places. Act V would be a shambles without the sub-plot. The *raison d'être* of the main story is the Gentleman's belief that he has been elevated to a dukedom. It cannot be mere coincidence that the highly specific allusions point to the same years or a little later.

Conjecture about the identity of the authors has been contaminated by misuse of the 'some twenty yeare agoe' passage in the prologue and by feeble guesses that the style of the play is not mature Fletcher; it must be 'early' Fletcher or 'early' Beaumont – presumably while he was in the country writing verse letters to Ben Jonson – or both. Therefore we need not inspect Oliphant's house of cards very closely.[2] Cyrus Hoy's analysis of linguistic forms in the text requires serious consideration, however, because he has attended to some real and pertinent facts.[3] He concludes that the licence in 1626 was for a revised play, since the extant text was 'certainly' not Fletcher's unaided work, because the verbal forms do not accord with his habits sufficiently to allow us to take Herbert's words 'by John Fletcher' exclusively. But Hoy does not mention that the play could as easily have been a collaboration from the start, it could have been completed by another hand after Fletcher's death, or the text we have could be a later revision, since the epilogue says that the players have done their best for the audience's pleasure 'to fit | With new paines, this old monument of wit'. I am not prepared to say who may have been the other author,

worse woman than our Lady, but in any case a reference to Carr's fall would put the play after 1615.   [1] See the textual note on V.i.86.
  [2] *The Plays of Beaumont and Fletcher* (New Haven, 1927), pp. 183–200; and see another plea for Beaumont's authorship in Robert F. Willson, Jr's 'Francis Beaumont and the "Noble Gentleman"', *English Studies*, XLIX (1968), 525–9.
  [3] *Studies in Bibliography*, XI (1958), 85–99.

but I think that Hoy, although usually sure-footed, has slipped in his interpretation of the statistics. He suggests that the figures look like those for *The Woman Hater*, a joint work of the two dramatists about 1607, for which we have characteristic clumps of Fletcherian 'ye's' in five scenes and none or one in the remaining twelve scenes: in order 0, 0, 0, 0, 0, 13, 0, 1, 0, 0, 13, 18, 1, 9, 0, 0, 23; totalling 78. *The Noble Gentleman* has a smaller number of 'ye's', however, and they are sprinkled more evenly through successive scenes: 7, 5, 2, 1, 4, 2, 1, 3, 0, 2, 0, 0, 1, 1, 1, 8; totalling 38. If we presume, as Hoy does, that Beaumont wrote the first draft and Fletcher revised later, the incidence of 'ye's' probably should be greater; and Hoy admits that even Beaumont used an occasional 'ye'. Nor can we affirm that other linguistic habits in the text are distinctively Beaumont's, for he was eclectic in his preferences, flexible, and various, making it, in Hoy's words, 'quite impossible to establish for Beaumont a neat pattern of linguistic preferences'. 'Hath', 'doth', ''em' and other elisions are little help in distinguishing the two dramatists (pp. 86–7), as they were in distinguishing Fletcher from Massinger. The whole demonstration must rest on the incidence of 'ye', a low incidence, which may be tolerable for collaborations with Beaumont only if they are supported by early publication dates or known early productions. Since the 'ye/you' evidence is slight, and all we have to go by is the license in 1626 for *The Noble Gentleman*, we 'can only assume that Sir Henry Herbert knew what he was talking about when he licensed the play as Fletcher's' and that it was new, possibly finished by someone else. I concur with this, Bentley's opinion, and the conclusion is strengthened by full consideration of the post-1619 allusions mentioned above.

Printer's copy must not have been theatrical, for the stage directions say nothing of props and actors; exits are often left out. R. C. Bald thought *The Noble Gentleman* had the look of a private transcript, because a prompt copy would have had to be tidier with speech prefixes. There seem to be some gaps too. Act I scene iv ends with Jaques' convincing Cozen to speak with the Gentleman about wasting his estate while keeping up with the court. But the very next scene shows the Gentleman ready to return to the

country. Something must also be omitted at the beginning of
IV.ii, as Oliphant noticed. R. W. Bond remarked that a number of
asides or addresses to the audience contain rhyme tags where the
sentiments are inconsistent with the Lady's character, especially her
sympathy with Shattillion (See II.i.203–16; III.ii.98–106; III.ii.113–
51; III.iv.14–20; V.i.446–50); he also cited Cozen's speech at
V.i.128–37. But rhyme tags crop up in other sententious passages,
and the Lady could be expected to admire a love-smitten and high-
born Shattillion who grovels before his mistress.

William Wilson printed the play for section two of the First
Folio. The same two compositors who set other plays in the section
did their typical work here, Compositor *A* responsible for the
largest portion: D2–D3 (I.i.1–I.iii.33), D4 (II.i.10–126), E1–E3
(II.ii.28–III.iv.58), F1 (IV.iv.19–142), perhaps F1ᵛ column *b*
(IV.v.43–V.i.21), F2ᵛ–F3ᵛ (V.i.134–end). Compositor *B*, as usual
the more careless worker, set the other parts.[1] Compositor *B*'s
pages average at least twice as many substantive errors – some
pages with as many as seven mistakes, and numerous examples of
omission, turned letters, foul case, and inadequate punctuation. It
is also worth noting that we can lay the ghost of Massinger's supposed use of odd periods in this play, periods in the midst of stage
directions, first noticed by W. J. Lawrence; alas, they occur only
in Compositor *B*'s pages. Presswork seems to have been fairly
regular, and only a few stop-press corrections have been detected:
a wrong running title and a handful of small errors.

The most obvious difference between this edition and its pre-
decessors is in its treatment of names in entrances and speech
prefixes. The history of editions since 1647 has been characterized
by a gradual shift from generic to proper names. F1 used (with
slightly varying abbreviations in prefixes) *Gentleman* (later *Duke*),

---

[1] My assignments are the same as Robert K. Turner's except that he gives F1ᵛ
doubtfully to compositor *B*, and I hesitantly divide F1ᵛ, because column *b* has four
test forms for *A* and two for *B*; column *a* has five of *B*'s forms, one of *A*'s. Turner
gives F2 doubtfully to *B*, but I put more weight on the habitual forms for *B* (23
instances of *Dutch.* and one *Coz.* prefix) than on typographic evidence; whereas I
think E4 is the doubtful page because it has only one of *B*'s test forms, but Turner is
fairly confident that it is *B*'s page on account of typographic evidence. Needless to
say, I am deeply indebted to Turner's analysis in his 'The Printers and the Beaumont
and Fletcher Folio of 1647, Section 2', *Studies in Bibliography*, xx (1967), 35–59.

Cozen, Servant, Wife, Lady (later *Duchess*), *Love, Doctor, Groom, Page, Man,* etc...., but F1 used proper names for five other characters: *Longavile, Bewfort, Maria, Shattillion,* and *Jaques.* F2 first introduced other proper names among 'The Persons represented in the Play': 'Monsieur Marine', 'Clerimont', 'Marine's *Wife*', 'Clerimont's *Wife*', and 'Shattillion's *Mistriss*'. The Servant to Marine's Wife is called 'A Gentleman'. Colman first substituted these names for the generic ones in stage directions and prefixes, except that he left the Gentleman's Wife 'Lady'. Weber changed Cozen's servant to 'Anthony' and he supplied scene locations. Dyce finished the process, changing 'Lady' to 'Madame Marine'. These novelistic identifications obscure the elemental force of the original drama, for it seems appropriate for the main figures of the play to remain almost anonymous. A theatre audience listening to the dialogue could hardly be expected to pick up the names from their occasional mention, and prominent characters like *Servant, Love,* and Cozen's *Wife,* are never named other than generically. The effect on stage would be of a morality play transformed into a farce. Therefore, I have tried to keep the original forms of F1 as much as possible, consistent with the editorial procedures of this edition and with clarity. Prefixes are normalized to their most frequent forms for each, and to avoid giving a character two forms of prefixes I reluctantly eliminated *Duke* and *Duchess* in favor of *Gentleman* and *Lady. Servant* is made into *Her Servant* to avoid confusion with the household help.

Since the copy was apparently rough and Compositor *B* acted according to his wont, the number of emendations is larger than usual, but the editor has tried to avoid the excesses of those who came before, appealing to contemporary usage to justify some idioms in the original text. One conjectural emendation ('Duchy top-man' for 'Duchy lope-man', III.iv.8) is a notable correction of an error in F1 that taxed the ingenuity of lexicographers since Nares' *Glossary.* The University of Virginia copy 2 of F1 served as copy text, and it has been compared with twenty others. I am grateful to Robert K. Turner for his generous help in finding press variants and for his careful analysis of the printing of the first folio. A noble gentleman indeed.

[The Persons represented in the Play

The NOBLE GENTLEMAN, but none of the wisest, Monsieur Marine.

HER SERVANT, Madam Marine's gallant.

LONGAVILE ⎱ two Courtiers that plot to abuse the Gentleman.
BEWFORD   ⎰

SHATTILLION, a Lord, Mad for Love.

COZEN to the Gentleman, Cleremont, a Gull.

JAQUES, an old servant to the Gentleman's family.

Gentlemen disguised as Citizens.

Doctor, Page, Groom, Man.

LADY, Madam Marine, a witty wanton.

Shattillion's LOVE, a virtuous Virgin.

WIFE, Cozen's wife, a simple country Gentlewoman.

MARIA, the Lady's Servant.

The Scene: France]

The Persons. . .France] *based on* F2; *om.* F1

The Prologue

Wit is become an anticke: and puts on
As many shapes of variation,
To court the times applause, as the times dare
Change severall fashions; nothing is thought rare
Which is not new and follow'd, yet we know
That what was worne some twenty yeare agoe,
Comes into grace againe, and we pursue
That custome, by presenting to your view
A play in fashion then, not doubting now
But 'twill appeare the same, if you allow   10
Worth to their noble memory, whose name,
Beyond all power of death live in their fame.

6 yeare] *stet* F1; years F2, Q1649 *Thierry*
11 memory...name] *stet* F1-2; memories...names *Thierry*
*12 live] *stet* F1-2, *Thierry*; lives Colman

122

THE NOBLE GENTLEMAN

Enter Gentleman *and* Jaques.

Gentleman.   What happiness waits on the life at Court,
What dear content, greatness, delight and ease?
What ever-springing hopes, what tides of honour,
That raise their fortunes to the height of wishes?
What can be more in man, what more in nature,
Then to be great and fear'd? A Courtier,
A noble Courtier? 'Tis a name that drawes
Wonder, and dutie, from all eyes and knees.
Jaques.   And so your Worships land within the walls,
Where you shall have it all inclos'd and sure.   10
Gentleman.   Peace knave; dull creature, bred of sweate and smoke,
These mysteries are far above thy faith:
But thou shalt see——
Jaques.   And then I shall believe
Your faire revenues, turn'd into fair suites,
I shall believe your Tenants bruis'd and rent
Under the weight of Coaches, all your state
Drawn through the streets in triumph, suits for places
Plied with a mine of gold, and being got
Fed with a great streame, I shall believe all this.
Gentleman.   You shall believe, and know me glorious.   20
                                        [*Exit* Jaques.]

Enter Cozen.

Cozin good day and health.
Cozen.   The same to you Sir,
And more, without my wishes, could you know
What calm content dwels in a private house:
Yet looke into your selfe, retire: this place
Of promises, and protestations, fits
Minds only bent to ruine; you should know this,

You have their language perfect, you have tutors
I doe not doubt sufficient: but beware.
Gentleman.   You are merry Couzin.
Cozen.   Yet your patience,
You shall learn that too, but not like it selfe   30
Where it is held a vertue; tell me Sir,
Have you cast up your state, rated your land,
And finde it able to endure the change
Of time and fashion? is it always harvest?
Always vintage? have you ships at Sea
To bring you gold, and stone from rich *Peru*
Monthly returning treasure? doth the King
Open his large Exchequer to your hands
And bid you be a great man? can your wife
Coyne off her beauty? or the weeke allow   40
Suites to each day? and know no ebb in honour?
If these be possible, and can hold out,
Then be a Courtier still, and still be wasting.
Gentleman.   Cozen, pray give me leave.
Cozen.   I have done.
Gentleman.   I could requite your gall, and in a straine
As bitter, and as full of Rubarb, preacht
Against your Countrey life, but 'tis below me
And only subject to my pitty; know
The eminent court, to them that can be wise,
And fasten on her blessings, is a sunne   50
That drawes men up from course and earthly being,
(I meane these men of merit that have power
And reason to make good her benefits)
Learns them a manly boldnesse, gives their tongues
Sweetnesse of language, makes them apt to please;
Files of all rudenesse, and uncivill haviour,
Shews them as neat in carriage as in cloaths;
Cozen have you ever seen the Court?
Cozen.   No Sir,
Nor am I yet in travaile with that longing.

*46 preacht] *stet* F 1; preach F 2

124

Gentleman.   O the state, and greatnesse of that place   60
Where men are found
Only to give the first creation glory!
Those are the models of the ancient world
Left like the Roman statues to stir up
Our following hopes; the place it selfe puts on
The brow of Majestie, and flings her lustre
Like the aire newly lightned; forme, and order,
Are only there themselves, unforc't, and sound,
As they were first created to this place.
Cozen.   You nobly came, but wil goe from thence base.   70
Gentleman.   'Twas very pretty, and a good conceite;
You have a wit good Cozen, I do joy in't,
Keep it for Court: but to my selfe againe,
When I have view'd these pieces, turn'd these eyes,
And with some taste of superstition,
Lookt on the wealth of Nature, the faire dames,
Beauties, that lights the Court, and makes it shew
Like a faire heaven, in a frosty night,
And mongst these mine, not poorest, 'tis for tongues
Of blessed Poets, such as *Orpheus* was,   80
To give their worth and praises. O deare Cozen:
You have a wife, and faire, bring her hither,
Let her not live to be the Mistris of
A Farmers heir and be confined ever
To a serge, farre courser then my horse-cloath.
Let her have Velvets, Tiffinies, Jewels, Pearls,
A Coach, an Usher, and her two Lacquies,
And I will send my Wife to give her rules,
And reade the rudiments of Court to her.
Cozen.   Sir, I had rather send her to *Virginia*   90
To help to propagate the English nation.

Enter Page.

Gentleman.   Sirra, how slept your Mistris, and what visitants
Are to pay service?

125

Page.   Sir, as I came out,
Two Counts were newly entered.
Gentleman.   This is greatnesse,
But few such servants waite a Countrey beauty.
Cozen.   They are the more to thank their modesty.
God keep my wife, and all my Issue female
From such uprisings.

                Enter a Doctor.

Gentleman.   What? my learned Doctor?
You will be welcome, give her health and youth
And I will give you gold.   *Exit* Doctor. 100
Cozen, how savours this? is it not sweet?
And very great, tasts it not of Noblenesse?
Cozen.   Faith Sir my pallat is too dull and lazie,
I cannot taste it, 'tis not for my relish,
But be so still, since your own misery
Must first reclaime ye, to which I leave you Sir.
If you will yet be happy, leave the humour
And base subjection to your Wife, be wise,
And let her know with speed you are her husband,
I shall be glad to heare it.
            My horse is sent for.   *Exit.* 110
Gentleman.   Even such another countrey thing as this
Was I, such a piece of durt, so heavy,
So provident to heap up ignorance,
And be an asse: such musty cloaths wore I,
So old and threed-bare: I do yet remember
Divers young Gallants lighting at my gate,
To see my honoured wife, have offered pence,
And bid me walk their horses, such a slave
Was I in shew then: but my eyes are open'd.

         Enter [Lady] *Gentlemans Wife.*

Many sweet morrows to my worthy Wife.   120

         *107 humour] *stet* F 1–2

126

Lady. 'Tis well, and aptly given, as much for you.
But to my present businesse, which is money——
Gentleman.   Lady I have none left.
Lady.   I hope you dare not say so, nor imagin
So base and lowe a thought: I have none left.
Are these words fitting for a man of worth,
And one of your full credite? Do you know
The place you live in? me, and what I labour
For, you and your advancement?
Gentleman.   Yes my dearest.
Lady.   And do you pop me off with this slight answer,   130
In troth I have none left? in troth you must have;
Nay stare not, 'tis most true; send speedily
To all that love you, let your people flye
Like thunder through the Citie, and not return
Under five thousand crownes. Try all, take all,
Let not a wealthy merchant be untempted
Or any that hath the name of money,
Take up at any use, give band, or land,
Or mighty statutes able by their strength
To tye up *Sampson* were he now alive.   140
There must be money gotten; for be perswaded,
If we fall now, or be but seen to shrinke,
Under our faire beginnings, 'tis our ruine,
And then good-night to all, (but our disgrace)
Farewell the hope of comming happinesse,
And all the aimes we levied at so long.
Are ye not mov'd at this? no sense of want,
Towards your selfe yet breeding? Be old,
And common, jaded to the eyes
Of groomes, and pages, chamber-maides, and garders,   150
And when you have done, put your poor house in order
And hang your selfe, for such must be the end
Of him that willingly forsakes his hopes
And hath a joy to tumble to his ruine.

*146 levied] *stet* F1; levell'd Sympson

127

All that I say is certaine; if ye faile
Do not impute me with it, I am cleare.
Gentleman.   Now heaven forbid I should do wrong to you
My dearest Wife, and Madam; yet give leave
To your poore creature to unfold himselfe.
You know my debts are many more then meanes,   160
My bands not taken in, my friends at home
Drawn dry with these expences, my poore Tenants
More full of want then we; then what new course
Can I beget to raise those crowns by? speake,
And I shall execute.
Lady.   Pray tell me true,
Have you not land in the Countrey?
Gentleman.   Pardon me,
I had forgot it.
Lady.   Sir, you must remember it,
There is no remedy, this land must be
In *Paris* ere to morrow night.
Gentleman.   It shall,
Let me consider, some three hundred acres   170
Will serve the turne.
Lady.   'Twill furnish at all points.
Now you speak like your selfe, and know like him,
That meanes to be man, suspect no lesse
For the return will give ye five for one;
You shall be great to morrow, I have said it.
Farewell, and see this businesse be a-foote
With expedition.
Gentleman.   Health, all joy, and honour
Waite on my lovely wife.   *Exit* Lady.
                    What? *Jaques, Jaques.*

                    Enter Jaques.

Jaques.   Sir did you call?
Gentleman.   I did so, hie the *Jaques,*
Downe to the Bancke, and there to some good Merchant   180

173 man] *stet* F1; a man F2

128

(Conceive me well good *Jaques*, and be private)
Offer three hundred acres of my land:
Say it is choise, and fertile, aske upon it
Five thousand Crowns; this is the businesse
I must employ thee in, be wise and speedy.
Jaques.   Sir do not do this.
Gentleman.   Knave I must have money.
Jaques.   If you have money thus, your knave must tell ye
You will not have a foote of land left, be more warie
And more friend to your selfe, this honest land
Your Worship has discarded, has been true,   190
And done you loyall service.
Gentleman.   Gentle *Jaques*,
You have a merry wit, employ it well
About the businesse you have now in hand.
When ye come backe, enquire me in the presence,
If not, in the Tennis-Court, or at my house.   *Exit.*
Jaques.   If this vaine hold, I know where to enquire ye.
Five thousand crowns, this with good husbandry
May hold a month out, then five thousand more,
And more land a bleeding for't, as many more
And more land laid aside. God and St. *Dennis*   200
Keep honest minded young men Bachellers.
'Tis strange My Master should be yet so young
A puppy, that he cannot see his fall
And got so neare the sun. I'le to his Cozen
And once more tell him on't, if he faile,
Then to my mortgage, next unto my sale.

                                                    Exit.

           Enter Longavile, Bewford, *and* Her Servant.   [I. ii]

Her Servant.   Gentlemen, hold on discourse a while,
I shall return with knowledge how and where
We shall have best accesse unto my Mistris
To Tender your devotions.

204 And] i.e. as though he   o.1 Her Servant] *the Servant* F 1-2
3 We] *stet* F 1-2; Ye Sympson

Longavile.   Be it so:——   *Exit.*
Now to our first discourse.
Bewford.   I prethee peace;
Thou canst not be so bad, or make me know
Such things are living, doe not give thy selfe
So common and so idle, so open vile,
So great a wronger of thy worth, so low,
I cannot, nor I must not credite thee.   10
Longavile.   Now by this light I am a Whore-master,
An open and an excellent Whore-master,
And take a speciall glory that I am so:
I thank my stars I am a Whore-master,
And such a one as dare be known and seen,
And pointed at to be a noble wencher.
Bewford.   Do not let all eares heare this, harke ye Sir,
I am my selfe a Whore-master, I am;
Believe it Sir (in private be it spoken)
I love a Whore directly; most men are Wenchers,   20
And have profest the science, few men
That looks upon ye now, but Whore-masters,
Or have a full desire to be so.
Longavile.   This is noble.
Bewford.   It is without all question, being private,
And held as needfull as intelligence,
But being once discover'd, blown abroad,
And known to common senses, 'tis no more
Then geometrical rules in Carpenters
That only know some measure of an art,   30
But are not grounded: be no more deceived,
I have a conscience to reclaim you, Sir.
Mistake me not: I do not bid you leave
Your whore or lesse to love her; God forbid it
I should be such a villain to my friend,
Or so unnaturall: 'twas never harbor'd here;
Learn to be secret first, then strike your Deere.
Longavile.   Your faire instructions *Monsieur* I shall learn.

*34 God] om. F1-2; Heaven Colman

130

Bewford.   And you shall have them: I desire your eare.

Longavile.   They are your servants.

Bewford.   You must not love.

Longavile.   How Sir?   40

Bewford.   I meane a Lady, theres danger:
  Shee hath an Usher and a Waiting-Gentlewoman,
  A page, a Coach-man, these are feed, and fee'd
  And yet for all that will be prating.

Longavile.   So.

Bewford.   You understand me Sir, they will discover't,
  And there is a losse of credite: table talke
  Will be the end of this, or worse, then that;
  Will this be worthy of a Gentleman?

Longavile.   Proceed good Sir.

Bewford.   Next leave your City Dame;
  The best of that tribe are most meerly coy,   50
  Or most extreamely foolish, both which vices
  Are no great stirrers up, unlesse in husbands
  That owe this Cattle, fearing her thats coy
  To be but seeming, her that's foole too forward.

Longavile [aside].   This is the rarest fellow, and the soundest,
  I meane in knowledge, that ere wore a Codpiece;
  H'as found out that will passe all *Italy,*
  All *France* and *England* (to their shames I speake
  And to the griefes of all their Gentlemen)
  The noble theory of luxury.

Bewford.   Your patience,   60
  And I will lay before your eyes a course
  That I my selfe found out, 'tis excellent,
  Easy, and full of freedome.

Longavile.   O good Sir,
  You rack me till I know it.

Bewford.   This it is:
  When your desire is up, your blood well heated
  And apt for sweet encounter, chuse the night
  And with the night your wench, the streets have store,

---

*39 eare] Sympson; care F 1–2   53 owe] i.e. own

There seize upon her, get her to your chamber,
Give her a cardecew, 'tis royall payment;
When ye are dull, dismisse her, no man knows   70
Nor she her selfe, who hath encountered her.
Longavile.   O but their faces.
Bewford.   Nere talke of faces:
The night allows her equall with a Dutches,
Imagination doth all: think her faire,
And great, clapt in velvet, she is so.
Sir, I have tryed those, and do find it certaine,
It never failes me, 'tis but twelve nights since
My last experience.
Longavile [*aside*].   O my meiching varlet,
I'le fit ye as I live.——
'Tis excellent, I'le be your Scholler Sir.   80

Enter Lady *and* Her Servant.

Lady.   You are fairly welcome both: troth Gentlemen
You have been strangers, I could chide you for't,
And taske ye with unkindness, what's the news?
The towne was never empty of some novelty;
Servant, what's your intelligence?
Her Servant.   Faith nothing.
I have not heard of any worth relating.
Bewford.   Nor I sweet Lady.
Longavile.   Then give me attention:
Monsieur Shattillion's mad.
Lady.   Mad?
Longavile.   Mad as May-butter,
And which is more, mad for a wench.
Lady.   'Tis strange, and full of pitty.
Longavile.   All that comes neare him   90
He thinks are come of purpose to betray him,
Being full of strange conceite, the wench he loved
Stood very near the Crowne.

<hr>

69 payment;] F2; ~ ∧ F1
*75 clapt] *stet* F1–2; yclad Sympson (*conj.*)

Lady.   Alas good *Monsieur*;
A' was a proper man, and faire demean'd,
A person worthy of a better temper.
Longavile.   He is strong opinion'd that the wench he loved
Remaines close prisoner by the Kings command,
Fearing her title: when the poore grieved Gentlewoman
Follows him much lamenting, and much loving
In hope to make him well, he knows her not,   100
Nor any else that comes to visite him.
Lady.   Let's walk in Gentlemen, and there discourse
His further miseries; you shall stay dinner,
In truth you must obey.
Omnes.   We are your servants.

                                        Exeunt.

                    Enter Couzen.   [I. iii]

Cozen.   Ther's no good to be done, no cure to be wrought
Upon my desperate kinsman: I'le to horse
And leave him to the fooles whip, misery.
I shall recover twenty miles this night,
My horse stands ready, I'le away with speed.

                    Enter Shattillion.

Shattillion.   Sir, may I crave your name?
Cozen.   Yes Sir you may:
My name is *Cleremon.*
Shattillion.   'Tis wel, your faction?
What party knit you with?
Cozen.   I know no parties,
Nor no factions Sir.
Shattillion.   Then weare this crosse of white:
And where you see the like they are my friends,   10
Observe them well, the time is dangerous.
Cozen.   Sir keep your crosse, I'le wear none. [*Aside*] Sure this fellow
Is much beside himselfe, grown mad.
Shattillion.   A word Sir;
You can pick nothing out of this; this crosse

                        .133

Is nothing but a crosse, a very crosse,
Plaine without spell or witch-craft, search it,
You may suspect, and well, there's poyson in't,
Powder, or wild-fire, but 'tis nothing so.
Cozen.   I do beleeve you Sir, 'tis a plain crosse.
Shattillion.   Then do your worst, I care not, tell the King,   20
Let him know all this, as I am sure he shall;
When you have spit your venome, then will I
Stand up a faithfull, and a loyall subject,
And so God save His Grace, this is no Treason.
Cozen [*aside*].   He is March mad.——Farewell *Monsieur.*
Shattillion.   Farewell;
I shall be here attending.——   *Exit* Couzen.
                    'Tis my life
They aime at, there's no way to save it, well
Let 'em spread all their nets: they shall not draw me
Into any open Treason, I can see,
And can beware, I have my wits about me,   30
I thanke heaven for't.

                    Enter [Shattillion's] Love.

Love [*aside*].   There he goes,
That was the fairest hope the *French* Court bred,
The worthiest and the sweetest temper'd spirit,
The truest, and the valiantest, the best of judgment,
Till most unhappy I sever'd those vertues
And turn'd his wit wild with a coy deniall,
Which heaven forgive me, and be pleas'd, O heaven
To give againe his senses, that my love
May strike off all my follies.
Shattillion.   Lady.
Love.   I Sir.
Shattillion.   Your will with me sweete Lady.
Love.   Sir I come——   40
Shattillion.   From the dread sovraigne King, I know it Lady;

                    39 Sir] F2; Sis F1

                    134

He is a gracious Prince, long may he live.
Pertaine you to his chamber?

Love.　　　　　　　　No indeed Sir,
That place is not for women. Do you know me?

Shattillion.　Yes, I do know you.

Love.　Whats my name? pray you speake.

Shattillion.　Thats all one, I do know you and your businesse,
You are discovered Lady, I am warie,
It stands upon my life; pray excuse me,
The best man of this kingdome sent you hither,　　　　50
To dive into me; have I toucht you? ha?

Love.　You are deceiv'd Sir, I come from your love,
That sends you faire commends, and many kisses.

Shattillion.　Alas poore soule how does she? is she living?
Keepes she her bed still?

Love.　　　　　　　　Still Sir. She is living,
And well, and shall do so.

Shattillion.　　　　　Are ye in counsell?

Love.　No Sir, nor any of my sex.

Shattillion.　　　　　　Why so,
If you had been in counsell, you would know,
Her time to be but slender; she must die.

Love.　I do believe it Sir.

Shattillion.　　　　　And suddainely,　　　　60
She stands too neare a fortune.

Love.　　　　　　　Sir?

Shattillion.　　　　　　　'Tis so,
There is no jesting with a Princes title.
Would we had both been borne of common parents
And liv'd a private and retired life,
In homely cottage, we had then enjoyed,
Our loves, and our embraces, these are things,
That cannot tend to treason——

Love [*aside*].　　　　　I am wretched.

Shattillion.　O I pray as often for the King as any,
And with as true a hart, for's continuance,
And do moreover pray his heires may live,　　　　70

135

And their faire issues, then as I am bound
For all the states and commons; if these prayers
Be any wayes ambitious, I submit,
And lay my head downe, let 'em take it off;
You may informe against me, but withall
Remember my obedience to the crowne,
And service to the state.
Love.   Good Sir, I love yee.
Shattillion.   Then love the gratious King, and say with me
Heaven save his grace.
Love.   Heaven save his grace.
Shattillion [*aside*].   This is strange——
A woman should be sent to undermine me,   80
And buz love into me to try my spirit;
Offer me kisses and enticing follies,
To make me open and betray my selfe;
It was a subtle and a dangerous plot,
And very soundly followed.——Farewell Lady,
Let me have equall hearing, and relate
I am an honest man. Heaven save the King.   *Exit.*
Love.   I'le never leave him, till by art or prayer
I have restorde his senses. If I make
Him perfect man againe, he's mine, till when   90
I here abjure all loves of other men.

                                            Exit.

                Enter Cozen, *and* Jaques.   [I. iv

Jaques.   Nay, good Sir be perswaded, go but back,
And tell him hee's undone; say nothing else,
And you shall see how things will worke upon't.
Cozen.   Not so good *Jaques*, I am held an asse,
A countrey foole, good to converse with durte
And eate course bread, weare the worst wooll,
Know nothing but the high way to *Paris*,

And wouldst thou have me bring these staynes,
And imperfections to the rising veiw
Of the right worshipfull thy worthy Master?   10
They must be bright and shine, their cloathes
Soft velvet and the Tyrian purple, sweet
Like the Arabian gums, hung like the Sun,
Their golden beames on all sides; such as these
May come and know, thy Master, I am base
And dare not speake unto him, hee's above me.
Jaques.   If ever you did love him, or his state,
His name, his issue, or your selfe, go backe:
'Twill be an honest and a noble part
Worthy a kinsman, save three hundred acres   20
From present execution; they have had sentence,
And cannot be repriev'd, be mercifull.
Cozen.   Have I not urg'd already all the reasons
I had to draw him from his will? his ruine?
But all in vaine, no counsell will prevaile,
Has fixt himselfe, ther's no removing, *Jaques,*
'Twil prove but breath and labour spent in vaine,
I'le to my horse, farewell.
Jaques.   For Gods sake Sir,
As ever you have hope of joy turne backe;
I'le be your slave for ever, do but go,   30
And I will lay such faire directions to you
That if hee be not doting on his fall,
He shall recover sight, and see his danger,
And ye shall tell him of his wives abuses,
I feare, to foule against him; how she plots,
With our young Mounsiers, to milke dry her husband,
And lay it on their backs, the next her pride,
Then what his debts are, and how infinite
The curses of his tenants; this will worke.

12 Tyrian purple,] F2; trojan purple_Λ F1
*12 sweet] *om.* F1–2; smell Seward (*conj.*)
*13 hung] *stet* F1–2; Seward *suggested* flung *or* fling

I'le pawne my life and head, he cryes, away,   40
I'le to my house in the Countrey.
Cozen.   Come I'le go,
And once more try him; if he yeild not, so,
The next that tryes him shall be want and woe.

                                                    Exeunt.

                    Enter Gentleman *Solus.*   II.[i]

Gentleman.   *Jaques.*
Jaques (within).   Sir.
Gentleman.   Rise *Jaques,* 'tis growne day.——
The country life is best, where quietly
Free from the clamour of the troubled Court,
We may enjoy our own greene shadowed walkes,
And keepe a moderate diet without art.
Why did I leave my house and bring my wife,
To know the manner of this subtile place?
I would when first the lust to fame and honour,
Possest me, I had met with any evill
But that, had I been tyed to stay at home   10
And earn the bread for the whole family
With my own hand happy had I been.

                    Enter Jaques.

Jaques.   Sir this is from your wonted course at home,
When did ye there keep such inordinate hours?
Goe to bed late? start thrice? and call on me?
Would you were from this place; our Countrey sleepes,
Although they were but of that moderate length
That might maintain us in our daily worke,
Yet were they sound and sweet.
Gentleman.   I *Jaques,* there
We dreamt not of our wives, wee lay together,   20
And needed not; now at length my Cozins words,
So truly ment, mixt with thy timely prayers

                    8 and] F2; an F1

                        138

So often urged, to keepe me at my home,
Condemne me quite.
Jaques.   'Twas not your fathers course:
He liv'd and dy'd in *Orleance*, where he had
His Vines as fruitfull as experience
(Which is the art of husbandry) could make;
He had his presses for 'em, and his wines
Were held the best, and out-sold other mens,
His corne and cattell serv'd the neighbour Townes   30
With plentifull provision, yet his thrift
Could misse one beast amongst the heard, he rul'd
More where he liv'd, then ever you will here.
Gentleman. 'Tis true, why should my wife then 'gainst my good,
Perswade me to continue in this course?
Jaques.   Why did you bring her hither? At the first,
Before you warm'd her blood with new delights,
Our countrey sports could have contented her;
When you first married her, a puppet-play
Pleas'd her as well as now the tilting doth.   40
She thought her selfe brave in a bugle chaine,
Where Orient pearle will scarce content her now.
Gentleman. Sure *Jaques*, she sees something for my good
More then I doe, she oft will talk to me
Of offices, and that she shortly hopes
By her acquaintance with the friends she hath
To get a place shall many times outway
Our great expences, and if this be so——
Jaques.   Think better of her words, she doth deceive you,
And only for her vaine and sensuall ends   50
Perswade ye thus. Let me be set to dwell
For ever naked in the barest soile
So you will dwell from hence.
Gentleman.   I see my folly,
Packe up my stuffe, I will away this morne.
Haste—haste.
Jaques.   I, Now I see your Fathers honours

36 hither? At] Langbaine; ~ ‸ at F1–2

139   10-2

Trebling upon you, and the many prayers
The countrey spent for him, which almost now
Begun to turne to curses, turning backe,
And falling like a timely shower upon ye.
Gentleman. Goe, call up my wife.
Jaques. But shall she not prevaile, 60
And sway you, as she oft hath done before?
Gentleman. I will not heare her, but raile on her
Till I be ten miles off.
Jaques. If you be forty,
'Twill not be worse Sir.
Gentleman. Call her up.
Jaques. I will Sir. *Exit.*
Gentleman. Why what an Asse was I that such a thing
As a wife is could rule me? Know not I
That woman was created for the man,
That her desires, nay all her thoughts should be
As his are? is my sense restor'd at length?
Now she shall know, that which she should desire, 70
She hath a husband that can govern her,
If her desires leades me against my will.

Enter Lady.

Are you come?
Lady. What sad unwonted course
Makes you raise me so soone, that went to bed
So late last-night?
Gentleman. O you shall goe to bed
Sooner hereafter, and be rais'd againe
At thriftie hours; in Summer-time wee'l walke
An houre after our supper, and to bed,
In winter you shall have a set at Cards,
And set your maids to worke.
Lady. What do you meane? 80
Gentleman. I wil no more of your new tricks; your honours,
Your offices, and all your large preferments,
Which still you beate into my eares, hang ore me.

140

I'le leave behind for others, the great sway
Which I shall beare at Court: my living here
With countenance of your honoured friends
I'le be content to loose: for you speake this
Only that you may still continue here
In wanton ease, and draw me to consume
In cloaths and other things idle for shew   90
That which my Father got with honest thrift.
Lady.   Why, who hath been with you Sir, that you talke
Thus out of Frame?
Gentleman.   You make a foole of me:
You provide one to bid me forth to supper
And make me promise; then must some one or other
Invite you forth; if you have borne your selfe
Loosely to any Gentleman in my sight
At home, you ask me how I like the carriage,
Whether it were not rarely for my good,
And open'd not a way to my preferment?   100
Come I perceive all: talke not, we'le away.
Lady.   Why Sir, you'le stay till the next triumph Day
Be past?
Gentleman.   I, you have kept me here triumphing
This seven yeares, and I have ridden through the streetes,
And bought embroyderd hose and foote-cloths too;
To shew a subjects zeale, I rode before
In this most gorgeous habit, and saluted
All the acquaintance I could espie
From any window, these were wayes ye told me
To raise me; I see all: make you ready straight,   110
And in that gowne which you came first to Town in,
Your safe-guard, cloake, and your hood sutable:
Thus on a duble gelding shall you amble,
And my man *Jaques* shall be set before you.
Lady.   But will you goe?
Gentleman.   I will.
Lady.   And shall I too?

*90 idle for] *stet* F 1–2; for idle Sympson

141

Gentleman.   And you shall too.
Lady.   But shall I by this light?
Gentleman.   Why by this light you shall.
Lady.   Then by this light
You have no care of your estate, and mine.
Have we been seven years venturing in a ship,
And now upon return with a faire winde   120
And a calme sea, full fraught with our own wishes
Laden with wealth and honour to the brim,
And shall we flye away and not receive it?
Have we been tilling, sowing, labouring
With paine and charge a long and tedious winter,
And when we see the corne above the ground,
Youthfull as is the morne and the full eare
That promises to stuffe our spatious garners,
Shall we then let it rot, and never reap it?
Gentleman.   Wife talke no more, your Retoricke comes too late,   130
I am inflixable; and how dere you
Adventure to direct my course of life?
Was not the husband made to rule the wife?
Lady.   'Tis true, but where the man doth misse his way,
It is the womans part to set him right;
So Fathers have a power to guide their Sonnes
In all their courses, yet you oft have seene
Poore litle children that have both their eyes
Lead their blind Fathers.
Gentleman [*aside*].   She has a plaguy witt.——
I say you'r but a little piece of man.   140
Lady.   But such a peice, as being tane away
Man cannot last: the fairest and tallest ship,
That ever saild, is by a little peice
Of the same wood, steerd right, and turnd about.
Gentleman [*aside*].   'Tis true she sayes, her answers stand with
         reason.
Lady.   But Sir, your Cozin put this in your head

127 the full] F2; full F1   130 *Gentleman.*] F2; I *Gent.* F1
*131 I am] F2; am F1   133 made] F2; mad F1

142

Who is an enemie to your preferment,
Because I should not take place of his wife;
Come by this kisse thou shalt not go sweete heart.
Gentleman.   Come, by this kisse I will goe Sweet-heart,   150
On with your riding stuffe; I know your tricks,
And if preferment fall ere you be ready,
'Tis welcome, else adue the Citie life.
Lady.   Well Sir I will obey.
Gentleman.   About it then.
Lady.   To please your humour I would dresse my selfe,
In the most loathsome habit you could name
Or travell any whether ore the world
If you command me; it shall neere be said
The fraylty of a woman whose weake minde,
Is often set on loose delights and shewes,   160
Hath drawne her husband to consume his state,
In the vaine hope of that which never fell.
Gentleman.   About it then, [*aside*] women are pleasant creatures,
When once a man begins to know himselfe.
Lady.   But harke you Sir because I wilbe sure,
You shall have no excuse, no word to say
In your defence hereafter, when you see
What honours were preparde for you and me
Which you thus willingly have throwne away:
I tell you I did looke for present honour,   170
This morning for you, which I know had come,
But if they do not come ere I am ready
(Which I will be the sooner least they should)
When I am once set in a countrey life,
Not all the power of earth shall alter me,
Not all your prayers or threats shall make me speak
The Least words to my honourable freinds
To do you any grace.
Gentleman.   I will not wish it.
Lady.   And never more hope to be honourable.
Gentleman.   My hopes are lower.
Lady.   As I live you shall not,   180

You shall be so farr from the name of noble
That you shall never see a Lord againe;
You shall not see a maske, or Barriers,
Or tilting or a solemn christning,
Or a great marriage, or new fire-works,
Or any bravery; but you shall live
At home bespotted with your owne loved durt
In scurvy cloathes as you were wont to doe,
And to content you I will live so too.

Gentleman.   'Tis all I wish, make hast the day drawes on,   190
It shall be my care to see your stuffe pact up.   *Exit* Gentleman.

Lady.   It shal be my care to gul you: you shal stay,
And more then so, intreat me humbly too.
You shall have honours presently.——*Maria.*

                    Enter Maria.

Maria.   Madam.
Lady.   Bring hither, pen, inke, and paper.
Maria.   'Tis here.
Lady.   Your Master Will not stay,
Unlesse preferment come within an houre.   [*Writes.*]
Maria.   Let him commande one of the Citie gates
In time of mutiny, or you may provide him
To be one of the counsell for invading
Some savage countrey to plant christian faith.   200
Lady.   No, no, I have it for him, call my page.   *Exit* Maria.
Now my deare husband there it is will fit you,
And when the world shall see what I have done,
Let it not move the spleene of any wife,
To make an asse of her beloved husband
Without good ground, but if they will be drawne
To any reason by you, do not gull them;
But if they grow conceited of themselves,
And be fine Gentlemen, have no mercie,
Publish them to the world, 'twill do them good   210
When they shall see their follies understood.

                    [*Enter* Page.]

                    144

Go beare these letters to my servant,
And bid him make hast.   [*Exit* Page.]
                    I will dresse my selfe
In all the journey cloathes I used before,
Not to ride but to make the laughter more.

                                                    Exit.

            Enter Gentleman *and* Jaques.   [II. ii]

Gentleman.   Is all pact up?
Jaques.   All, all Sir, there is no tumbler,
   Runs throw his hoop with more dexteritie
   Then I aboute this businesse: tis a day
   That I have long longd to see——
Gentleman.   Come wheres my spurs?
Jaques.   Here Sir——and now 'tis come.
Gentleman.   I *Jaques* now
   I thanke my fates, I can command my wife.
Jaques.   I am glad to see it Sir.
Gentleman.   I do not love
   Always to be made a puppie, *Jaques.*
Jaques.   But yet me thinkes your worship does not looke
   Right like a countrey Gentleman.
Gentleman.   I will,   10
   Give me my tother hat.
Jaques.   Here.
Gentleman.   So, my Jerkin.
Jaques.   Yes Sir.
Gentleman.   On with it *Jaques*; thou and I
   Will live so finely in the countrey, *Jaques*,
   And have such pleasant walks into the woods
   A mornings, and then bring home riding rods,
   And walking staves——
Jaques.   And I will beare them Sir,
   And skurdge-sticks for the children.
Gentleman.   So thou shalt,

            15 home] F2; whom F1

                        145

And thou shalt do all, over see my worke folkes
And at the weekes end pay them all their wages.
Jaques.   I will Sir, so your worship give me mony.   20
Gentleman.   Thou shalt receive all too: give me my drawers.
Jaques.   They are ready Sir.
Gentleman.   And I will make thy Mistriss,
My wife, looke to her landrie and her dayry,
That we may have our linnen cleane on Sundayes.
Jaques.   And holy dayes.
Gentleman.   I, and ere we walke about the grounds
Provide our breake-fast, or she shall smoke, I'le have
Her a good huswife. She shall not make a voyage
To her sisters, but she shall live at home,
And feed her pullen fat, and see her maides   30
In bed before her, and locke all the doores.
Jaques.   Why that will be a life for Kings and Queenes.
Gentleman.   Give me my Scarfe with the great button quickly.
Jaques.   'Tis done Sir.
Gentleman.   Now my Mittens.
Jaques.   Here they are Sir.
Gentleman.   'Tis well! now my great dagger.
Jaques.   There.
Gentleman.   Why so;
Thus it should be, now my riding rod.
Jaques.   There's nothing wanting Sir.
Gentleman.   Another, man,
To sticke under my girdle.
Jaques.   There it is.
Gentleman.   All is well.
Jaques.   Why now me thinks your Worship looks
Like to your selfe, a man of meanes and credit,   40
So did your grave and famous Ancestors,
Ride up and down to faires, and cheapen cattell.
Gentleman.   Goe, hasten your Mistrisse, Sirra.
Jaques.   It shall be done.
                                        Exit Jaques.

          Enter [Her] Servant *and* Page.

Her Servant.   Who's that? who's that boy?

Page.   I thinke it be my Master.

Her Servant.   Who, he that walkes in gray whisking his riding rod?

Page.   Yes Sir, 'tis he.

Her Servant.   'Tis he indeed; he is prepar'd
  For his new journey; when I wink upon you
  Runne out and tell the Gentlemen 'tis time.——
  Monsieur good day.   50

Gentleman.   *Monsieur*
  Your Mistrisse is within, but yet not ready.

Her Servant.   My businesse is with you Sir; 'tis reported,
  I know not whether by some enemie
  Maliciously that envies your great hopes,
  And would be ready to sow discontents
  Betwixt his Majesty and you, or truly,
  (Which on my faith I would be sorry for)
  That you intend to leave the Court in hast.

Gentleman.   Faith Sir within this halfe houre.——*Jaques?*

Jaques (within).   Sir?   60

Gentleman.   Is my wife ready?

Jaques [within].   Presently.

Her Servant.   But Sir,
  I needs must tell you as I am your friend,
  You should have tane your journey privater
  For 'tis already blaz'd about the Court.

Gentleman.   Why Sir, I hope it is no Treason, is it?

Her Servant.   'Tis true Sir, but 'tis grown the common talk,
  There's no discourse else held, and in the presence
  All the Nobility and Gentry
  Have nothing in their mouths but only this,
  Monsieur Marine that noble Gentleman,   70
  Is now departing hence; every mans face
  Looks ghastly on his fellows, such a sadnesse
  (Before this day) I nere beheld in Court,
  Mens hearts begin to faile them when they heare it,

49 Gentlemen] Dyce; Gentleman F1-2
*67 discourse] Sympson (*sugg.*); discovery F1-2

147

In expectation of the great event
That needs must follow it; pray heaven it be good!
Gentleman.   Why I had rather all their hearts should faile
Then I stay here untill my purse faile me.
Her Servant.   But yet you are a Subject, and beware,
I charge you by the love I beare to you,   80
How you doe venture rashly on a course
To make your soveraign jealous of your deeds,
For Princes jealousies where they love most,
Are easily found, but they be hardly lost.
Gentleman.   Come these are tricks, I smell 'em, I will goe.
Her Servant.   Have I not still profest my selfe your friend?
Gentleman.   Yes, but you never shewd it to me yet.
Her Servant.   But now I will, because I see you wise,
And give ye thus much light into a businesse
That came to me but now; be resolute,   90
Stand stifly to it that you will depart,
And presently.
Gentleman.   Why so I meane to doe.
Her Servant.   And by this light you may be what you will;
Will you be secret Sir?
Gentleman.   Why? what's the matter?
Her Servant.   The King does feare you.
Gentleman.   How?
Her Servant.   And is now in
                                                Counsell.
Gentleman.   About me?
Her Servant.   About you, and you be wise,
You'l finde hee's in Counsell about you.
His Councellours have told him all the truth.
Gentleman.   What truth?
Her Servant.   Why that which now he knows too well.
Gentleman.   What is't?
Her Servant.   That you have followed him seven years   100
With a great traine: and though he have not grac't you,
Yet you have div'd into the hearts of thousands,
With liberality and noble carriage;

148

And if you should depart home unprefer'd,
All discontented, and seditious spirits
Would flocke to you and thrust you into action:
With whose help, and your Tenants, who doth not know
(If you were so dispos'd:) how great a part
Of this yet fertile peaceful realm of *France*
You might make desolate? But when the King   110
Heard this——
Gentleman.   What said he?
Her Servant.   Nothing, but shook,
As never Christian Prince did shake before.
                              [*Winks to* Page, *who exits.*]
And to be short you may be what you will,
But be not ambitious Sir, sit downe
With moderate honours, least you make your selfe
More feard.
Gentleman.   I know Sir what I have to doe
In mine own businesse.

                    Enter Longavile.

Longavile.   Where's *Monsieur Mount Marine.*
Her Servant.   Why there he stands, will you ought with him?
Longavile.   Yes.——
Good day *Monsieur Marine.*
Gentleman.   Good day to you.
Longavile.   His Majesty doth commend himselfe,   120
Most kindly to you Sir, and hath by me,
Sent you this favour: kneele downe, rise a Knight.
Gentleman.   I thank his Majesty.
Longavile.   And he doth further
Request you, not to leave the Court so soone,
For though your former merits have been slighted,
After this time there shall no Office fall
Worthy your spirit, as he doth confesse
There's none so great, but you shall surely have it.
Her Servant.   Do you heare? if you yield yet you are an asse.
Gentleman.   I'le shew my service to his Majesty   130

                    149

In greater things then these, but for this small one
I must intreat his Highnesse to excuse me.
Longavile. I'le beare your Knightly words unto the King,
And bring his Princely answer backe againe.   *Exit* Longavile.
Her Servant. Well said, be resolute a while, I know
There is a tide of honours comming on,
I warrant you.

                    Enter Bewford.

Bewford.   Where is this new made Knight?
Gentleman. Here Sir.
Bewford.   Let me enfold you in my arms,
Then call you Lord, the King will have it so,
Who doth entreat your Lordship to remember   140
His message sent to you by *Longavile.*
Her Servant. If ye be durty, and dare not mount aloft;
You may yield now, I know what I would do.
Gentleman. Peace, I will fit him.——Tell his Majesty
I am a Subject, and I do confesse
I serve a gracious Prince, that thus hath heapt
Honours on me without desert, but yet
As for the message, businesse urgeth me,
I must be gone, and he must pardon me,
Were he ten thousand Kings and Emperours.   150
Bewford. I'le tell him so.
Her Servant.   Why, this was like your selfe.
Bewford [*aside*]. As he hath wrought him, 'tis the finest fellow
That ere was Christmas Lord, he carries it
So truly to the life, as though he were
One of the plot to gull himselfe.   *Exit* Bewford.
Her Servant.   Why so,
You sent the wisest and the shrewdest answer
Unto the King, I swear, my honoured friend
That ever any Subject sent his Liege.

*142 durty] *stet* F1–2; durt-ty'd Sympson (*sugg.*)
156 answer] F2; *om.* F1

Gentleman.   Nay now I know I have him on the hip,
I'le follow it.

Enter Longavile.

Longavile.   My honourable Lord,   160
  Give me your noble hand right courteous Peer,
  And from henceforth be a courtly Earl;
  The King so wills, and Subjects must obey:
  Only he doth desire you to consider
  Of his request.
Her Servant.   Why faith you'r well my Lord,
  Yield to him.
Gentleman.   Yield? why 'twas my plot——
Her Servant [*aside*].   Nay 'twas your wives plot.
Gentleman.   To get prefer-
                                            ment by it,
  And thinks he now to pop me ith mouth
  But with an Earldome? Ile be one step higher.
Her Servant [*aside*].   'Tis the finest Lord! I am afraid anon   170
  He will stand upon't to share the Kingdome with him.

Enter Bewford.

Bewford.   Wher's this Courtly Earle?
  His Majesty commends his love unto you;
  And will you but now grant to his request,
  He bids you be a Duke, and chuse of whence.
Her Servant.   Why if you yield not now, you are undone;
  What can you wish to have more, but the Kingdome?
Gentleman.   So please his Majesty, I would be Duke of *Burgundy*
  Because I like the place.
Bewford.   I Know the King is pleas'd.
Gentleman.   Then will I stay and kisse his Highnesse hand.   180
Bewford.   His Majesty wil be a glad man when he hears it.
Longavile [*to Serv.*].   But how shall we keep this from the worlds
      eare
  That some one tell him not, he is no Duke?
Her Servant.   Wee'l think of that anon.——Why Gentlemen,

151

Is this a gracious habit for a Duke?
Each gentle body set a finger to
To pluck the clouds of this his riding weeds
From off the orient sunne of his best cloths;
I'le pluck one boot and spur off.
Longavile.   I another.
Bewford.   Ile pluck his Jerkin off.
Her Servant.   Sit down my Lord.   190
Both his spurs off at once good *Longavile.*
And *Bewford* take that scarfe off, and that hat
Doth not become his largely sprouting fore-head.
Now set your gracious foot to this of mine,
One pluck will do it, so, off with the other.
Longavile.   Loe thus your servant *Longavile* doth pluck
The trophy of your former gentry off.——
Off with his Jerkin *Bewford.*
Her Servant. [*aside*].   Didst thou never see
A nimble footed Taylor stand so in his stockings,
Whilst some friend helpt to pluck his Jerkin off,   200
To dance a Jigg?

Enter Jaques.

Longavile.   Here's his man *Jaques* come,
Booted and ready still.
Jaques.   My Mistris stayes;
Why how now Sir? what do your Worship mean,
To plucke your grave and thrifty habit off?
Gentleman.   My slippers, *Jaques.*
Longavile.   O thou mighty Duke pardon this man,
That thus hath trespassed in ignorance.
Gentleman.   I pardon him.
Longavile.   His Graces slippers, *Jaques.*
Jaques.   Why what's the matter?
Longavile.   Foot, man, hee's a Duke:
The King hath rais'd him above all his land.   210

*199 Taylor] *stet* F1-2   200 helpt] help F1; help'd F2
*209 Foot, man] Weber (*sugg.*); Foot-man F1-2

Jaques.   I'le to his Couzen presently, and tell him so;
O what a dung-hill countrey rogue was I!   *Exit* Jaques.

Enter Lady.

Her Servant.   See, see, my Mistrisse.
Longavile.   Let's observe their greeting.
Lady.   Unto your will as every good wife ought,
I have turnd all my thoughts, and now am ready.
Gentleman.   O Wife I am not worthy to kisse the least
Of all thy toes, much lesse thy thumb,
Which yet I would be bold with; all thy counsell
Hath been to me Angelicall, but mine
To thee hath been most durty like my mind: 220
Deare Duchesse I must stay.
Lady.   What, are you mad
To make me dresse, and undresse, turne and winde me,
Because you find me plyant? said I not
The whole world should not alter me, if once
I were resolv'd? and now you call me Duchesse:
Why what's the matter?
Gentleman [*kneels*].   Loe a Knight doth kneel.——
Lady.   A Knight?
Gentleman.   A Lord——
Lady.   A foole.
Gentleman.   I say doth kneele
An Earle, a Duke.
Longavile.   In drawers.
Bewford.   Without shoes.
Lady.   Sure you are lunatick.
Her Servant.   No honoured Duchesse,
If you dare but believe your servants truth,   230
I know he is a Duke.
Longavile.   God save his Grace.
Lady.   I aske your Graces pardon.
Gentleman [*rises*].   Then I rise,
And here in token that all strife shall end
'Twixt thee and me, I let my drawers fall

And to thy hands I do deliver them:
Which signifies, that in all acts and speeches,
From this time forth my wife shall wear the breeches.
Her Servant.   An honourable composition.

Exeunt omnes.

Enter Couzen *and* Jaques.   III.[i]

Cozen.   Shall I beleeve thee *Jaques.*
Jaques.   Sir you may.
Cozen.   Didst thou not dreame?
Jaques.   I did not.
Cozen.   Nor imagine?
Jaques.   Neither of both: I saw him great and mighty,
I saw the *Monsieurs* bow, and heard them cry
Good health and fortune to my Lord the Duke.
Cozen. A Duke art sure? a Duke?
Jaques.   I am sure a Duke,
And so sure as I know my selfe for *Jaques.*
Cozen.   Yet the sun may dazell! *Jaques*, was it not
Some leane Commander of an angry Block-house
To keep the Fleamish Eele-boats from invasion,   10
Or some bold Baron able to dispend
His fifty pounds a yeare, and meet the foe
Upon the Kings command in gilded canvas,
And do his deeds of worth? or was it not
Some place of gaine, as Clerk to the great Band
Of maribones, that people call the Switzers?
Men made of beufe, and sarcenet?
Jaques.   Is a Duke,
His chamber hung with Nobles like a presence!
Cozen.   I am something wavering in my faith;
Would you would settle me, and sweare 'tis so,   20
Is he a Duke indeed?

10 Fleamish] ſleamish F1; Fleemish F2
*17 beufe] *stet* F1–2; beef Langbaine; buff Sympson
*17 Is a Duke,] ∼ ∧ F1–2

154

Jaques.   I sweare he is.
Cozen.   I am satisfied, he is my Kinsman, *Jaques,*
    And I his poor unworthy Couzen.
Jaques.   True Sir.
Cozen.   I might have been a Duke too, I had meanes,
    A wife as faire as his, and as wise as his,
    And could have brookt the Court as well as his,
    And laid about her for her husbands honour:
    O *Jaques,* had I ever dreamt of this,
    I had prevented him.
Jaques.   Faith Sir it came
    Above our expectation; we were wise   30
    Only in seeking to undoe this honour,
    Which shewed our dung-hill breeding and our durt.
Cozen.   But tell me *Jaques,*
    Why could we not perceive? what dull Divell
    Wrought us to crosse this noble course, perswading
    'Twould be his overthrow? 'For me, a Courtier
    Is he that knows all, *Jaques,* and does all,
    'Tis as his noble Grace hath often said,
    And very wisely, *Jaques,* we are fooles,
    And understand just nothing.
Jaques.   I, as we were,   40
    I confesse it. But rising with our great Master,
    We shall be call'd to knowledge with our places;
    'Tis nothing to be wise, not thus much there; [*Snaps his fingers.*]
    Ther's not the least of the billet dealers,
    Nor any of the Pastry, or the Kitchin,
    But have it in measure delicate.
Cozen.   Me thinks this greatness of the Dukes my Couzens
    (I aske you mercy, *Jaques,* that near name
    Is too familiar for me) should give promise
    Of some great benefits to his attendants.   50
Jaques.   I have a suite my selfe, and it is sure,
    Or I mistake my ends much.

                36 'For me,] 'for me, F2; for me ∧ F1

                              155   11-2

Cozen.   What is't *Jaques*,
May I not crave the place?
Jaques.   Yes Sir you shall,
'Tis to be but his Graces Secretary,
Which is my little all, and my ambition,
Till my known worth shall take me by the hand
And set me higher; how the fates may do
In this poor threed of life is yet uncertaine;
I was not born I take it for a trencher,
Nor to espouse my Mistris Dairy-maid.   60
Cozen.   I am resolv'd my wife shall up to Court;
I'le furnish her, that is a speeding course,
And cannot chuse but breed a mighty fortune;
What a fine youth was I, to let him start,
And get the rise before me? I'le dispatch
And put my selfe in moneys.
Jaques.   Masse 'tis true,
And now you talke of money, Sir my businesse
For taking up those Crowns must be dispatcht.
This litle plot in the Countrey lies most fit
To do his Grace such serviceable uses,   70
I must about it.
Cozen.   Yet before you goe
Give me your hand, and bear my humble service
To the great Duke your Master, and his Duchesse,
And live your selfe in favour: say my wife
Shall there attend them shortly, so farewell.
Jaques.   I'le see you mounted Sir.
Cozen.   It may not be,
Your place is far above it, spare your selfe,
And know I am your servant, fare ye well.
Jaques.   Sir I shall rest to be commanded by you.   *Exit* Cousen.
This place of Secretary will not content me,   80
I must be more and greater: let me see,
To be a Baron is no such great matter
As people take it: for say I were a Count,

*68 taking up] Sympson; taking F 1-2

156

I am still an under person to this Duke,
Which me thinks sounds but harshly: but a Duke?
O I am strangely taken, 'tis a Duke
Or nothing, I'le advise upont, and see
What may be done by wit and industry.

Exit.

Enter Lady, Longavile, Bewford, [Her] Servant.　　[III. ii]

Lady.　It must be carried closely with a care
That no man speak unto him, or come near him
Without our private knowledge, or be made
Afore-hand to our practice. My good husband
I shall entreat you now to stay a while,
And prove a noble coxcomb. Gentlemen,
Your counsell and advice about this carriage.
Her Servant.　Alas good man, I do begin to mourn
His dire massacre: what a persecution
Is pouring down upon him? sure he is sinfull.　　10
Longavile.　Let him be kept in's chamber under shew
Of state and dignity, and no man sufferd
To see his noble face, or have accesse,
But we that are Conspirators.
Bewford.　　　　　　　　Or else
Down with him into the countrey amongst his Tenants,
There he may live far longer in his greatnesse,
And play the foole in pomp amongst his fellows.
Lady.　No, he shall play the foole in the City, and stay;
I will not loose the greatnesse of this jest
That shal be given to my wit for the whole revenues.
Her Servant.　Then thus wee'l have a guard about his person,
That no man come too neare him, and our selves　　20
Always in company; have him into the City
To see his face swell; whilst in divers corners,
Some of our own appointing shall be ready
To cry heaven blesse your Grace, long live your Grace.

0.1 Servant] Servants F 1–2

157

Lady. Servant, your counsells excellent good,
And shall be followed, 'twill be rarely strange
To see him stated thus, as though he went
A shroving through the City, or intended   30
To set up some new stake: I shall not hold
From open laughter when I heare him crye
Come hither my sweet Dutchesse: let me kisse
Thy gracious lips: for this will be his phrases!
I feare me nothing but his legs will breake
Under his mighty weight of such a greatnesse.
Bewford. Now me thinks dearest Lady you are too cruell;
His very heart will freeze in knowing this.
Lady. No, no, the man was never of such deepnesse
To make conceite his Master: Sir I'le assure ye   40
He will out-live twenty such pageants.
Were he but my Cozen or my Brother,
And such a desperate killer of his fortune,
In this beliefe he should dye, though it cost me
A thousand crowns a day to hold it up;
Or were I not known his wife, and so to have
An equall feeling of this ill he suffers,
He should be thus till all the boyes i'th Towne
Made sute to weare his badges in their hats,
And walke before his Grace with sticks and nose-gayes;   50
We married women hold——
Her Servant.   'Tis well, no more.
The Duke is entring, set your faces right,
And bow like Countrey prologues: here he comes.
Groom [*within*].   Make roome afore, the Duke is entring.

Enter [Gentleman *as*] *Duke* [*and* Groom].

Longavile.   The choisest fortunes waite upon our Duke——
Her Servant.   And give him all content and happinesse.
Bewford.   Let his great name live to the end of time.
Gentleman.   We thank you, and are pleas'd to give you notice

*31 stake] *stet* F 1; wake F 2   *54 *Groom.* Make] Dyce; Make F 1–2
57 his] F 1 *cor*; this F 1 *uncor*

We shall at fitter times wait on your Loves,
Till when, be neare Us.
Longavile.   'Tis a valiant purge,   60
And works extreamly; 'tas delivered him
Of all Right worshipfull and gentle humours,
And left his belly full of noblenesse.
Gentleman. It pleased the King my Master
For sundry vertues not unknown to him,
And the all-seeing state, to lend his hand
And raise me to this Emminence; how this
May seeme to other men, or stir the mindes
Of such as are my fellow Peers, I know not;
I would desire their loves in just designes.   70
Lady. Now by my faith he does well, very well:
Beshrew my heart I have not seen a better
Of a raw fellow, that before this day
Never rehearst his state: 'tis marvellous well.
Her Servant. Is he not Duke indeed? see how he lookes
As if his spirit were a last, or two
Above his veines, and stretcht his noble hide.
Longavile. Hee's high brac't like a drum, pray God he breake not.
Bewford. Why let him break, ther's but a Calves-skin lost.
Longavile. May it please your Grace to see the City,   80
'Twill be to the minds and much contentment
Of the doubtfull people.
Gentleman. I am determin'd so, till my returne
I leave my honoured Dutchesse to her chamber.——
Be carefull of your health, I pray you be so.
Her Servant. Your grace shall suffer us your humble servants
To give attendance fit so great a person
Upon your body.
Gentleman.   I am pleased so.
Longavile. Away good *Bewford*, raise a guard sufficient
To keep him from the reach of tongues, be quicke;   90
And do you heare, remember how the streets

77 stretcht] F1 *cor*; stretch F1 *uncor*

Must be dispos'd with for cryes, and salutations.—— [*Exit*
Your grace determines not to see the King—— Bewford.]
Gentleman. Not yet, I shall be ready ten dayes hence
To kisse his highnesse hand, and give him thanks,
As it is fit I should for his great bounty.
Set forward Gentlemen.
Groom. Room for the Duke there. *Exeunt Duke*
and traine.

Lady. 'Tis fit he should have room to shew his mightinesse,
He swels so with his poyson.——'Tis better to
Reclaim ye thus, then make a sheeps-head of you, 100
It had been but your due; but I have mercy Sir,
And mean to reclaim you by a directer course.
That woman is not worthy of a soule
That has the soveraign power to rule her husband,
And gives her title up, so long provided
As there be faire play, and his state not wrongd.

Enter Shattillion.

Shattillion. I would be glad to know whence this new Duke
springs,
The people buz abroad, or by what title
He received his dignity; 'tis very strange
There should be such close jugling in the State, 110
But I am tyed to silence, yet a day
May come, and soone to perfect all these doubts.
Lady [*aside*]. It is the mad *Shattillion*; by my soule
I suffer much for this poor Gentleman;
I'le speake to him, may be he yet knows me.——
Monsieur Shattillion.
Shattillion. Can you give me reason
From whence this great Duke sprang that walkes abroad?
Lady. Even from the King himselfe.
Shattillion. As you are a woman,
I think you may be coverd: Yet your prayer
Would do no harm good woman.

*92 with for cryes] *stet* F 1–2; for cryes Sympson

Lady.   God preserve him.

Enter Shattillions Love.

Shattillion.   I say Amen, and so say all good subjects.
Love.   Lady as ever you have lov'd, or shall,
As you have hope of heaven lend your hand,
And wit to draw this poore distracted man
Under your roofe from the broad eyes of people,
And wonder of the streets.
Lady.   With all my heart;
My feeling of his griefe and losse is much.
Love.   Sir now you are come so neare the prison, wil ye
Goe in, and visit your fair Love? poore soule
She would be glad to see you.
Shattillion.   This same Duke   130
Is but apocryphall, there's no creation
That can stand where titles are not right.
Love.   'Tis true Sir.
Shattillion.   This is another draught upon my life;
Let me examine well the words I spake.
The words I spake were, that this novell Duke
Is not o'th true making, 'tis to me most certaine——
Lady.   You are as right Sir as you went by line.
Shattillion.   And to the griefe of many thousands more——
Lady.   If there be any such, God comfort them.   140
Shattillion.   Whose mouths may open when the time shall please;
I'me betraid, commend me to the King,
And tell him I am sound, and crave but justice;
You shall not need to have your guard upon me,
Which I am sure are plac'd for my attachment;
Lead on; I'm obedient to my bonds.
Love.   Good Sir be not displeased with us;
We are but servants to his highnesse will,
To make that good.
Shattillion.   I doe forgive you even with my heart;   150
Shall I entreat a favour?
Lady.   Any thing.

Shattillion.   To see my love before that fatall stroake,
And publish to the world my christian death,
And true obedience to the Crown of *France*.
Love.   I hope it shall not need Sir, for there is mercy
As well as justice in his Royall heart.

Exeunt.

Enter three Gentlemen [dressed as Citizens].   [III.

1. Gentleman.   Every man take his corner, here am I,
You there, and you in that place, so be perfect;
Have a great care your cryes be loud, and faces
Full of dejected feare and humblenesse.
He comes.

Enter Jaques.

Jaques.   Fye how these streets are charg'd and swell'd
With these same rascally people? give more room,
Or I shall have occasion to distribute
A martial almes amongst you; as I am a Gentleman
I have not seen such rude disorder,
They follow him like a prize, there's no true gaper   10
Like to your Citizen, he will be sure
The beares shall not passe by his door in peace,
But he and all his family will follow.
Roome there afore!   *Sound* [*trumpets*].

Enter [*the* Gentleman *as*] *Duke and his company.*

Give roome, and keep your places
And you may see enough; keep your places.
Longavile.   These people are too far unmanner'd, thus
To stop your Graces way with multitudes.
Gentleman.   Rebuke them not good *Monsieur*, 'tis their loves
Which I will answer, if it please my stars
To spare me life and health.   20

14 *Sound.*] Dyce (Sympson *conj.*); Sound? F1–2 *print as part of the dialogue
following* afore!   14 Give] *Jaques.* Give F1–2

2. Gentleman.   Blesse your Grace.

Gentleman.   And you with all my heart.

1. Gentleman.   Now heaven preserve your happy days.

Gentleman.   I thank you too.

3. Gentleman.   Now heaven save your Grace.

Gentleman.   I thanke you all.

Bewford.   On there before.

Gentleman.   Stand Gentlemen, stay yet a while,
For I am minded to impart my love
To these good people, and my friends   30
Whose love and prayers for my greatnesse,
Are equall in abundance.——Note me well,
And with my words, my heart! for as the tree——

Longavile.   Your Grace had best beware, 'twil be inform'd
Your greatnesse with the people.

Gentleman.   I had more
My honest and ingenious people——but
The weight of businesse hath prevented me.
I am call'd from you: but this tree I spake of
Shall bring forth fruit I hope to your content,
And so I share my bowels amongst you all.   40

People.   A noble Duke, a very noble Duke.

Enter fourth Gentleman [*as a Citizen*].

Her Servant.   Afore there Gentlemen.

4. Gentleman.   You'r faithfully met good *Monsieur Mount Marine.*

Her Servant.   Be advis'd, the time is alter'd.

4. Gentleman.   Is he not the same man he was afore?

Gentleman.   Still the same man to you Sir.

Longavile.   You have received mighty grace, be thankfull.

4. Gentleman.   Let me not dye in ignorance.

Longavile.   You shall not.
Then know the King out of his love hath pleased
To stile him Duke of *Burgundy.*

4. Gentleman [*kneeling*].   O great Duke,   50

41.1 *fourth*] a F1–2

163

Thus low, I plead for pardon, and desire
To be enrol'd amongst your poorest slaves.
Gentleman [*raising him*].   Sir you have mercy, and withall my hand.
From henceforth let me call you one of mine.
Her Servant.   Make room afore there, and dismisse the people.
Gentleman.   Every man to his house in peace and quiet.
People.   Now heaven preserve the Duke, heaven blesse the Duke.

Exeunt Omnes.

Enter Lady [*with a letter*].   [III.

Lady.   This letter came this morn from my Cozen.——
To the great Lady, high and mighty Duchesse
Of *Burgundy*, be these delivered.——
O, for a stronger lace to keep my breath
That I may laugh the nine dayes till the wonder
Fall to an ebb: the high and mighty Duchesse!
The high and mighty! God, what a stile is this?
Methinks it goes like a Duchy top-man,
A ladder of a hundred rounds will faile
To reach the top on't. Well my Gentle Cozen   10
I know by these contents your itch of honour;
You must to the Court, you say, and very shortly:
You shall be welcome; and if your wife have wit
I'le put her in a thriving course, if not
Her own sin on her owne head, not a blot
Shall staine my reputation, only this:
I must for healths sake sometimes make an asse
Of the tame moyle my husband; 'twill do him good,
And give him fresher brains, me fresher blood.
Now for the noble Duke, I heare him comming.   20

Enter [Gentleman *as*] Duke, *his traine.*

Your Grace is well return'd.
Gentleman.   As well as may be:
Never in younger health, never more able:

7 mighty! God,] Weber; mighty ∧ God? F1–2
*8 top-man] lope-man F1–2   18 moyle] i.e. mule

I meane to be your bed-fellow this night,
Let me have good encounter.

Bewford.   Blesse me heaven,
What a hot meat this greatnesse is?

Longavile.   It may be so, for I'le be sworn he hath
Not got a snap this two months on my knowledge,
Or her woman is damd for swearing it.

Gentleman.   I thank you Gentlemen for your attendance
And also your great paines; pray know my lodgings   30
Better and oftner, do so Gentlemen.
Now by my honour, as I am a Prince,
I speake sincerely, know my lodgings better,
And be not strangers; I shall see your service
And your deservings, when you least expect.

Omnes.   We humbly thank your Grace for this great favor.

Gentleman.   Jaques?

Jaques.   Your Grace.

Gentleman.   Be ready for the Countrey,
And let my Tenants know the Kings great love:
Say I would see them, but the waight at Court
Lyes heavy on my shoulders: let them know   40
I do expect their duties in attendance
Against the next feast, wait for my comming.
Go take up post horse, and be full of speed.   *Exit* Jaques.

Lady.   I would desire your Grace——

Gentleman.   You shall desire,
And have your full desire, sweet Duchesse speak.

Lady.   To have some conference with a Gentleman
That seems not altogether void of reason.
He talks of titles, and things neare the Crown,
And knowing none so fit as your good Grace,
To give the difference in such points of State——   50

Gentleman.   What is he? If he be noble, or have any part
That's worthy our converse, We do accept him.

Lady.   I can assure your Grace his straine is noble,
But he's very subtle.

42–43 comming. | Go] Sympson (*conj.*); ~ ₐ | To F1–2

Gentleman.   Let him be so.
Let him have all the braines, I shall demonstrate
How this most Christian Crown of *France* can beare
No other show of title then the Kings.
I will goe in and meditate for halfe an houre,
And then be ready for him presently,
I will convert him quickly or confound him.   [*Exit.*] 60
Her Servant.   Is mad *Shattillion* here?
Lady.   Is here, and's Lady.
I prethee servant fetch him hither.
Her Servant.   Why,
What do you meane to put him to?
Lady.   To chat
With the mad lad my husband; 'twill be brave
To heare them speake, babl, stare, and prate. [*Exit* Her Servant.]
Bewford.   But what shall be the end of all this, Lady?

          Enter Shattillion, *and* [Her] Servant

Lady.   Leave that to me, now for the grand dispute,
For see here comes *Shattillion*: as I live
Me thinks all *France* should beare part of his griefes.
Longavile.   I'le fetch my Lord the Duke.   [*Exit* Longavile.] 70
Shattillion.   Where am I now, or whether will you lead me?
To my death? I crave my priviledge,
I must not dye but by just course of law.
Her Servant.   His Majesty hath sent by me your pardon,
He meant not you should dye; but would intreate you
To lay the full state of your Title open,
Unto a grave and noble Gentleman.

          Enter [Gentleman *as*] *Duke, and* Longavile.

The Duke of *Burgundy* who here doth come,
Who either by his wisedome will confute you,
Or else informe and satisfie the King.   80
Bewford.   May't please your grace, this is the Gentleman.

          66 Is here] *stet* F 1–2; He's here Langbaine
          66.1 Her Servant] Servant F 1; Lady F 2

                              166

Gentleman.   Is this he that chops Logicke with my liege?
Shattillion.   D'ee mocke me? you are great, the time will come
When you shall be as much contemned as I.
Where are the ancient complements of *France*,
That upstarts brave the Princes of the bloud?
Gentleman.   Your title Sir, in short.
Shattillion.   He must Sir, be
A better states man then your selfe, that can
Trip me in any thing, I will not speake
Before these witnesses.
Gentleman.   Depart the roome,   90
For none shall stay, no not my dearest Dutches.
Lady [aside].   Wee'le stand behind the Arras and heare all. *Exeunt.*
Gentleman.   In that chaire take your place, I in this;
Discourse your title now.
Shattillion.   Sir you shall know,
My loves true title, mine by marriage.
Setting aside the first race of French Kings
Which will not here concerne us, as *Pharamond*,
With *Clodion, Merov,* and *Chilperik*,
And to come downe unto the second race,
Which we will likewise slip——
Gentleman.   But take me with you.   100
Shattillion.   I pray you give me leave: ——of *Martell Charles*,
The Father of King *Pippin*, who was Sire
To *Charles*, the great and famous *Charlemaine*;
And to come to the third race of *French* Kings,
Which will not be greatly pertinent in this cause,
Betwixt the King and me, of which you know
Hugh Capet was the first,
Next his Sonne *Robert, Henry* then, and *Phillip*
With *Lewis*, and his Sonne a *Lewis* too,
And of that name the seventh, but all this   110
Springs from a female as it shall appeare.
Gentleman.   Now give me leave; I grant you this your title

*98 *Clodion, Merov*] *Clodian, Meron* F 1; *Clodian, Meroveus* F 2
102 was ∧ Sire∧] ~ , Sir, F 1; ~ , Sire ∧ F 2   110 seventh] F 2; seventy F 1

167

At the first sight carryes some shew of truth;
But if ye weigh it well ye shall finde light.
Is not his Majestie possest in peace,
And justice executed in his name,
And can you thinke the most Christian King
Would do this if he saw not reason for it?

Shattillion.   But had not the tenth *Lewis* a sole daughter?

Gentleman.   I cannot tell.

Shattillion.   But answer me directly.   120

Gentleman.   It is a most seditious question.

Shattillion.   Is this your justice?

Gentleman.   I stand for my King.

Shattillion.   Was ever heire apparant thus abus'd?
I'le have your head for this.

Gentleman.   Why, do your worst.

Shattillion.   Will no one stir to apprehend this traytor?
A guard about my person! will none come?
Must my owne royall hands performe the deede?
Then thus I do arrest you.   [*Seizes him.*]

Gentleman.   Treason, help.

Enter Lady, Longavile, Bewford *and* [Her] Servant.

Lady.   Help, help, my Lord and husband.

Gentleman.   Help thy Duke.

Longavile.   Forbeare his graces person.

Shattillion.   Forbeare you   130
To touch him that your heire apparent weds,
But by this hand I will have all your heads.   *Exit.*

Her Servant.   How doth your grace?

Gentleman.   Why? well.

Her Servant.   How do
You finde his title?

Gentleman.   'Tis a dangerous one,
As can come by a female.

Her Servant.   I, 'tis true,
But the law *Salicke*, cuts him off from all.

126 person] will₋] ~ ₋ ~ ? F1; ~ , ~ ₋ F2   129 thy] *stet* F1; the F2

Longavile. I do beseech your grace how stands his title?

Gentleman. Pew, nothing, the law *Shallicke* cuts him off from all.

Lady. My gracious husband you must now prepare,
  In all your graces pomp to entertaine   140
  Your cozen, who is now a convertite,
  And followes here, this night he will be here.

Gentleman. Be ready all in hast; I do intend,
  To shew before my cozens wondring face
  The greatnesse of my pomp, and of my place.

                                        Exeunt omnes.

                Enter Cozen, *his* Wife [*and his Manservant*].   IV. [i]

Cozen. Sirra is all things carried to the Taylor,
  The measure and the fashion of the gowne
  With the best trim?

Man.   Yes Sir and 'twill be ready
  Within this two dayes.

Cozen.   For my selfe I care not,
  I have a suite or two of ancient velvet,
  Which with some small correcting and addition
  May steale into the presence.

Wife. Would my Gowne were ready!
  Husband, I'le lay my life, to make you something
  Ere to morrow night.

Cozen.   It must not bee   10
  Before we see the *Duke*, and have advice,
  How to behave our selves: lets in the while,
  And keep our selves from knowledge till time shall call us.

                                             Exeunt.

                Enter Longavile *and* Bewford.   [IV. ii]

Longavile. I much admire the fierce masculine spirit,
  Of this dread Amazon.

Bewford.   This following night
  I'le have a wench in solace.

                0.1 Cozen,] ~ . F1; Cozen *and* F2

Longavile.   Sir, I heare you,
And will be with you if I live, no more.

Enter Maria.

Maria.   My Lady would intreate your presence Gentlmen.
Bewford.   We will obey your Lady, she is worthy.   [*Exit.*]
Longavile.   You light alove, a word, or two.
Maria.   Your will Sir.
Longavile.   Harke in your eare, wilt thou be maried?
Speake, wilt thou marry?
Maria.   Maried? to whom Sir?
Longavile.   To a proper fellow, landed, and able bodied?   10
Maria.   Why do you flout me Sir?
Longavile.   I sweare I do not;
I love thee for thy Ladies sake, be free.
Maria.   If I could meet such matches as you speake of,
I were a very child to loose my time, Sir.
Longavile.   What saiest thou to *Monsieur Bewford*?
Maria.   Sir
I say hee's a proper Gentleman, and far
Above my meanes to looke at.
Longavile.   Dost thou like him?
Maria.   Yes Sir, and ever did.
Longavile.   He is thine owne.
Maria.   You are too greate in promises.
Longavile.   Be rul'd
And follow my advice, he shall be thine.   20
Maria.   Would you would make it good Sir.
Longavile.   Do but thus,
Get thee a cushion underneath thy cloathes,
And leave the rest to me.
Maria.   I'le be your scholler,
I cannot loose much by the venture sure.
Longavile.   Thou wilt loose a prettie maiden head, my rogue,
Or I am much o'th bow hand. You'le remember

5 Gentlmen] F2; Gentlman | F1
*7 light alove] light o' love Sympson; light alone F1-2

If all this take effect, who did it for you,
And what I may deserve for such a kindnesse?
Maria.　Yours Sir.

Exeunt.

Enter Jaques *and* Shattillion *severally.*　　　　[IV. iii]

Jaques.　Save ye Sir.
Shattillion.　Save the King.
Jaques.　I pray you Sir, which is the nearest way——
Shattillion.　Save the King, this is the nearest way.
Jaques.　Which is the nearest way to the post house?
Shattillion.　God save the King and his post house.
Jaques.　I pray Sir direct me to the house.
Shattillion.　Heaven save the King, you cannot catch me Sir.
Jaques.　I do not understand you Sir.
Shattillion.　You do not, I say you cannot catch me Sir.　　10
Jaques.　Not catch you Sir?
Shattillion.　　　　　　No Sir, nor can the King,
With all his stratagems, and his forced tricks,
Although he put his nobles in disguise,
Never so oft to sift into my words,
By course of law, lay hold upon my life.
Jaques [*aside*].　It is businesse that my Lord the *Duke*
Is by the King imployed in, and he thinks
I am acquainted with it.
Shattillion.　　　　　　I shall not need
To ripp the cause up, from the first to you,
But if his Majesty had suffered me　　　　　20
To marry her, though she be after him,
The right heire generall to the Crowne of *France*,
I would not have convayed her into *Spaine*,
As it was thought, nor would I ere have joyn'd,
With the reformed Churches to make them
Stand for my cause.
Jaques.　　　　　　I do not thinke you would.

6 house] F2; horse F1

Shattillion.   I thanke you Sir, and since I see you are
A favorer of vertues, kept in bondage,
Tell directly to my soveraigne King,
For so I will acknowledge him for ever,   30
How you have found my staid affections
Setled for peace, and for the present state.
Jaques.   Why Sir?
Shattillion.   And good Sir tell him further this,
That notwithstanding all suggestions
Brought to him against me and all his suspitions,
(Which are innumerall) to my treasons,
If he will warrant me but publique tryall,
I'le freely yeild my selfe into his hands;
Can he have more then this?
Jaques.   No by my troth.
Shattillion.   I would his Majesty would heare but reason,   40
As well as you.
Jaques.   But Sir you do mistake me,
For I never saw the King
In all my life but once, therefore good Sir,
May it please you to shew me which is the post house.
Shattillion.   I cry you mercie Sir, then you'r my freind.
Jaques.   Yes Sir.
Shattillion.   And such men are very rare with me,
The post house is hard by, farewell.
Jaques.   I thanke you Sir, I must ride hard to night,
And it is darke already.
Shattillion [*aside*].   I am cruell
To send this man directly to his death   50
That is my freind, and I might easily save him.
He shall not dye.——Come backe my freind, come backe.
Jaques.   What is your will?
Shattillion.   Do you not know?
Jaques.   Not I.
Shattillion.   And do you gather nothing by my face?
Jaques.   No Sir.
Shattillion.   Vertue is ever innocent.

172

Lay not the fault on me, I greive for you,
And wish that all my teares might win your safety.
Jaques. Why Sir?
Shattillion.   Alas good freind you are undone,
The more ill fortune mine, to be the meanes
Of your sad overthrow: you know not me?   60
Jaques. No truely Sir.
Shattillion.   Would you had never seene me,
I am a man pursu'd by the whole state
And sure some one hath seene me talke with you.
Jaques. Yes divers Sir.
Shattillion.   Why then your head is gon.
Jaques. I'le out of towne.
Shattillion.   Would it were soone enough;
Stay if you love your life, or else you are taken.
Jaques. What shall I do?
Shattillion [*aside*].   I'le venture deeply for him,
Rather then to cast away an innocent.——
Take courage friend, I will preserve thy life,
With hazard of mine owne.
Jaques.   I thanke you Sir.   70
Shattillion. This night thou shalt be lodg'd within my doores,
Which shall be all lockt fast, and in the morne
I'le so provide, you shall have free accesse,
To the Sea side and so be shipt away,
Ere any know it.
Jaques.   Good Sir suddainly
I am afraide to dye.
Shattillion.   Then follow me.   *Exeunt.*

Enter Shattillions Love.

Love. This way he went, and there's the house; I hope
His better Angell hath directed him
To leave the wandring streetes, poore Gentleman.
Would I were able with as free a hart,   80
To set his soule right, as I am to grieve

77 house; I hope∧] Langbaine; ~ ∧ ~ , F1; ~ , ~ , F2

The ruine of his fame, which God forgive me.——
Sir if you be within, I pray Sir speake to me.

[*Enter* Shattillion *and* Jaques *above.*]

Shattillion.   I am within and will be, what are you?
Love.   A friend.
Shattillion.   No Sir you must pardon me,
I am acquainted with none such.——[*To* Jaques] Be speedy,
Friend there is no other remedy.
Love.   A word Sir, I say I am your friend.
Shattillion.   You cannot scape by any other meanes,
Be not feareful.   [*Exit* Jaques.]
              God save the King.   90
What's your businesse Sir?
Love.   To speake with you.
Shattillion.   Speake out then.
Love.   Shall I not come up?
Shattillion.   Thou shalt not.——Flye if thou beest thine own
   friend,
There lyes the sute and all the furniture
Belonging to the head, on with it friend.
Love.   Sir do you heare?
Shattillion.   I do, God blesse the King.——
It was a habit I had laid aside,
For my owne person if the state had forced me.
Love.   Good Sir unlocke your dore.
Shattillion.   Be full of speede,
I see some twenty Musketeeres in ambush.——   100
What ere thou art, know I am here and will be;
Seest thou this bloody sword that cryes revenge?——
Shake not my friend, through millions of these foes
I'le be thy guard and set thee safe aboard.
Love.   Dare you not trust me Sir?
Shattillion.   My good sword before me,
And my alleagance to the King, I tell thee
Captaine (for so I guesse thee by thy armes

*105 sword] F2; *om.* F1

174

And the loose flancks of halberdeeres about thee),
Thou art too weake and foolish to attempt me.——
If you be ready follow me, and harke you   110
Upon your life speake to no living wight,
Except my selfe.
Love.   *Monsieur Shattillion?*
Shattillion.   Thou shalt not call agen; thus with my sword,
And the strong faith I beare unto the King,
Whom God preserve, I will descend my chamber,
And cut thy throate, I sweare I'le cut thy throate.——
Steale after me and live.   [*Exit above.*]
Love.   I will not stay
The furie of a man so farr distracted.   *Exit* Love.

                    Enter Shattillion.

Shattillion.   Where's the Officer that dares not enter,
To intrap the life of my distressed friend?   120
I, have you hid your selfe? you must be found;
What do you feare? is not authority
On your side? Nay, I know the Kings command
Will be your warrant, why then feare you? speake.
What strange designes are these? *Shattillion,*
Be resolute and beare thy selfe upright,
Though the whole world despise thee: soft, me thinks
I heard a rushing which was like the shake
Of a discovered Officer, I'le search
The whole streete over, but I'le finde thee out.   *Exit.* 130

                    Enter Jaques *in womens aparrell.*

Jaques.   How my joyntes do shake, where had I been
But for this worthy Gentleman, that hath
Some touch of my infortunes: would I were
Safe under hatches once for *Callicut*;
Farewell the pomp of Court, I never more
Can hope to be a Duke or any thing,

                119 *Shattillion.*] Sympson; *om.* F 1–2

                            175

I never more shall see the glorious face
Of my faire spreading Lord that loved me well.

Enter Shattillion.

Shattillion.   Flye you so fast? I had a sight of you,
But would not follow you; I was too wise;   140
You shall not lead me with a cunning tricke,
Where you may catch me; poore *Shattillion*;
Hath the Kings anger left thee never a friend?
No, all mens loves move by the breath of Kings.
Jaques.   It is the Gentleman that sav'd my life.——
Sir?
Shattillion.   Blesse *Shattillion*, another plot.
Jaques.   No Sir, 'tis I.
Shattillion.   Why, who are you?
Jaques.   Your friend whom you preserved.
Shattillion.   Whom I preserved?
My friend? I have no woman friend but one,
Who is to close in prison to be here;   150
Come neere let me looke on you.
Jaques.   'Tis I.
Shattillion.   You should not be a woman by your stature.
Jaques.   I am none Sir.
Shattillion.   I know it, then keepe off.——
Strange men and times! how I am still preserv'd!
Here they have sent a yeoman of the guard
Disguis'd in womans cloathes to worke on me,
To make love to me, and to trap my words,
And so insnare my life.——I know you Sir,
Stand back upon your perill.——Can this bee
In christian common weales? from this time forth   160
I'le cut off all the meanes to worke on me.
I'le nere stirr from my house, and keep my doores
Lockt day and night, and cheapen meat and drink
At the next shops by signes, out of my window,
And having bought it draw it up in my garters.

137 the…face ₐ] F2; thy…face; F1

Jaques.   Sir, will you help me?
Shattillion.   Do not follow me.——
I'le take a course to live despight of men.   *Exit* Shattillion.
Jaques.   He dares not venture for me; wretched *Jaques*,
Thou art undone for ever and for ever,
Never to rise againe: what shall I do?   170

                    Enter Bewford.

Where shall I hide me? heres one to take me,
I must stand close, and not speake for my life.
Bewford.   This is the time of night, and this the haunte,
In which I use to catch my wastcoatieres;
It is not very darke, no I shall spie 'em;
I have walkt out in such a pitchy night
I could not see my fingers this farr off,
And yet have brought home venson by the smell;
I hope they have not left their old walke, ah?
Have I spied you sitting? by this light   180
To me theres no such fine sight in the world,
As a white-apron twixt twelve and one;
See how it glisters? do you thinke to scape?
So now I have you fast; come and do not strive,
It takes away the edge of appetite;
Come I'le be liberall every way,
Take heed you make no noyse for waking of the watch.

                                        Exeunt.

                    Enter Cozen *and his* Wife.   [IV. iv]

Cozen.   Now the blessing of some happy guide,
To bring us to the Duke and we are ready.

                    Enter Longavile *and* [Her] Servant.

Come forward, see the doore is opend,
And two of his Gentlemen, I'le speake to them,

        176 night ₐ] ~ . F 1-2   178 home] F 2; whom F 1
        180 sitting? by this light ₐ] ~ ₐ ~ ? F 1-2

                                177

And marke how I behave my selfe.——God save yee;
For lesse I cannot wish to men of sort,
And of your seeming: are you of the Dukes?
Longavile.   We are Sir, and your servants, your salutes,
We give you backe againe with many thanks.
Cozen.   When did you heare such words before wife? peace,   10
Do you not dare to answer yet; is't fit
So meane a Gentleman as my selfe should crave,
The presence of the great Duke your Master?
Her Servant.   Sir you may.
Longavile.   Shall we desire your name and businesse Sir,
And wee will presently informe him of you.
Cozen.   My name is *Cleremont.*
Her Servant.   You are his graces kinsman,
Or I am much mistaken.
Cozen.   You are right,
Some of his noble blood runs through these veines,
Though far unworthy of his graces knowledge.   20
Longavile.   Sir we must all be yours; his graces kinsman,
And we so much forgetfull? 'twas a rudenesse,
And must attend your pardon; thus I crave it,
First to this beauteous Lady, whom I take   [*kisses.*]
To be your wife Sir, next your mercie.
Cozen.   You have it Sir.——I do not like this kissing,
It lyes so open to a world of wishes.
Her Servant.   This is the merry fellow, this is he
That must be noble too.
Longavile.   And so he shall.
If all the art I have can make him noble,
I'le dub him with a Knight-hood, if his wife
Will be but forward, and joyne issue;   30
I like her above excellent.
Her Servant.   Wilt please you
To walke a turne or two, whilst to the Duke
We make your comming known?

11 is't] F2; s't F1

178

Cozen.   I shal attend, Sir.
                    Exit [Her] *Servant and* Longavile.
Wife [*aside.*]   These Gentlemen are very proper men,
    And kisse the best that ere I tasted.——
    For goodnesse-sake husband let us never more
    Come neare the Countrey, what so ere betide us;
    I am in malice with the memory   40
    Of that same stinking dung-hill.
Cozen.   Why now you are
    My chicken and my dear, love where I love,
    Hate where I hate: now you shall have twenty gownes,
    And twenty chaines; see, the doore is opening.
Groom [*within*].   Roome afore there, the Duke is entring.

Enter Gentleman [*mounting a state*], Lady, Longavile, [Her] Servant,
    Maria.

Cozen.   'Tis the Duke, even he himselfe; be merry,
    This is the golden age the Poet speaks on.
Wife.   I pray it be not brazen'd, by their faces,
    And yet me thinks they are the neatest pieces
    For shape and cutting that ere I beheld.   50
Cozen.   Most gracious Duke, my poor Spouse and my selfe
    Do kisse your mighty foote, and next to that
    The great hand of your Duchesse, ever wishing
    Your honours ever-springing, and your yeares.
Gentleman.   Cozen?
Cozen.   Your Graces vassall, far unworthy
    The nearnesse of your blood.
Gentleman.   Correct me not,
    I know the word I speake, and know the person.
    Though I be something higher then the place
    Where common men have motion, and discending
    Down with my eye, their formes are lessened to me,   60
    Yet from this pitch can I behold my owne,
    From millions of those men that have no marke,
    And in my fearfull stoop, can make them stand,

179

When others feele my souse and perish. Cozen
Be comforted, you are very welcome, so
Is your faire wife: the charge of whom I give
To my own dearest and best beloved.
Tell me, have you resolv'd your selfe for Court,
And utterly renounc'd the slavish Countrey,
With all the cares thereof?

Cozen.   I have sir.   70

Gentleman.   Have you dismist your eating houshold, sold
  Your hangings of *Nebuchadnezar*, for such they were,
  As I remember, with the furnitures
  Belonging to your beds and chambers?

Cozen.   I Sir.

Gentleman.   Have you most carefully tane off the lead,
  From your roofe weake with age, and so prevented
  The ruine of your house, and clapt him in
  A summer suite of thatch to keepe him coole?

Cozen.   All this I have perform'd.

Gentleman.   Then lend me all your hands [*comes down*], I will
        embrace my Cozen   80
  Who is an understanding Gentleman,
  And with a zeale mighty as is my name,
  Once more I bid you welcome to the Court.——
  My state againe.   [*Resumes his seat.*]

Lady.   As I was telling you your husband
Must be no more Commander, looke to that.
Be severall at meate, and lodging, let him have
Boord-wages and dyet 'mongst his men i'th towne;
For pleasure if he be given too't let him have it,
Else as your own fancie shall direct you.   90
Cozen, you see this mighty man here: he was an asse
When he came first to towne: indeed he was
Just such another coxcomb as your husband,
God blesse the mark and every good mans childe!
This must not stir you Cozen.

Wife.   Heaven forbid!

*64 souse] Sympson; soule F1; feet F2   *69 renounc'd] F2; renounce F1

Longavile.   Sweet *Maria*, provide the cushion ready for it.
Maria.   It shall be done.   [*Exit*.]
Gentleman.   Receive all your advices from our selfe,
  Be once a day with us, and so farewell
  For this time, my faire Cozen. Gentlemen   100
  Conduct him to his lodging.
Lady.   Farewell, and think upon my words.
Wife.   I shall observe them.
Cozen.   Health, and the Kings continuall love attend you.
                                    Exit Gentleman *and* Lady.
Her Servant.   O for a private place to ease my lungs!
  Heaven give me patience, such a paire of Jades
  Were never better ridden to this houre;
  Pray heaven they hold out to the journeys end.
Longavile.   Twitch him aside good *Monsieur*, whilst I breake
  Upon the body of his strength, his wife;   110
  I have a constant promise: she is my own.
Her Servant.   Ply her to wind-ward.——*Monsieur*, you have
      taken
  The most compendious way to raise your selfe,
  That could have been delivered by a councell.
Cozen.   I have some certaine aimes Sir: but my wife——
Her Servant.   Your wife? you must not let that trouble you.
Cozen.   It will Sir, to see her in a strangers armes.
Her Servant.   What mean you?
  Let her alone, be wise, stir not a foot,
  For if you do, all your hopes are buryed: 120
  I sweare you are a lost man if you stir.
Cozen.   I thanke you Sir, I will be more advis'd.
Her Servant.   But what great Office do you levell at?
Cozen.   Sir, they are kissing.
Her Servant.   Let them kisse,
  And much may't do their good hearts; they must kisse
  And kisse, and double kisse, and kisse againe,
  Or you may kisse the post for any rising:
  Had your noble Kinsman ever mounted

*125 may't] may F 1–2

To these high Spheres of honour, now he moves in,
But for the kisses of his wife?
Cozen.   I Know not.   130
Her Servant.   Then I doe; credite me, he had been lost,
A fellow of no mark, and no repute,
Had not his wife kist soone, and very sweetly:
She was an excellent woman, and dispatcht him
To his full being, in a moment Sir—— *Exit* Longavile *and* Wife.
Cozen.   But yet me thinks he should not take her Sir
Into a private roome.
Her Servant.   Now stand and flourish,
You are a made man for ever. I doe
Envy you: if you stand your fortunes up,
You are the happiest man, but your great Cozen,   140
This day in Court: well I will marry surely,
And not let every man out-run me thus.
'Tis time to be mine owne friend; I'll not live
In towne here, and direct the readiest way,
To other men, and be a slave my selfe.
Cozen.   Nay good Sir be not mov'd; I am your servant,
And will not be ungratefull for this knowledge.
Her Servant.   Will you be walking home?
Cozen.   I would desire
To have my wife a long.
Her Servant.   You are too raw;
Be gon and take no notice where you left her,   150
Let her returne at leisure, if she stay
A moneth 'twill be the better; understand me,
This Gentleman can doe't.
Cozen.   I will Sir, ——and wife
Remember me a Duke, a Duke wife.   *Exit* Cozen.
Her Servant.   Aboard her *Longaveile*, shee's thine owne,——
To me the fooling of this foole is venerie.
                                        Exit Servant.

135 full ᴀ being,] F2; ~ , ~ ᴀ F1   *135 *Exit* Longavile *and* Wife.] stet F1–2
143 I'll not] Sympson; I F1–2

Enter Bewford *and* Jaques.

Bewford.   Come, preethe come, have I not crownes? behold
And follow me, here; not a word, go in;
Grope by the walls, and you shall finde a bed,
Lye downe there, see, see.   [*Exit* Jaques.]
                    A turne or two to give
My blood some heate; and I am presently
For action, darkenesse by thy leave I come.   *Exit* Bewford.

Enter Maria.

Maria.   I am perfect in my lesson; be my speed,
Thou God of marriage, this is the doore, I'le knock.
Bewford (*within*).   Whose there? I cannot come yet.
Maria.   *Monsieur*
                                Bewford?
Bewford [*within*].   Stay 'till I light a candle, who are ye?   10
Maria.   Sir? a poore Gentlewoman.

Enter Bewford.

Bewford.   O come in,
I'le finde a time for you too, be not loude.
Maria.   Sir you have found that time already, shame
On my soule therefore.
Bewford.   Why? what's the matter?
Maria.   Do you not see Sir, is your light so dim?
Bewford.   Do you not waite on the Lady *Mount Marine?*
Maria.   I do Sir, but my love on you.
Bewford.   Poore soule!
How cam'st thou by this big belly?
Maria.   By your selfe.
Bewford.   By heaven I ne're toucht your body.
Maria.   Yes,
Unsweare that oath agen, I'le tell you all;   20
These two yeares I have lov'd you, but the meanes
How to enjoy you, I did never know
Till twelfe night last, when hearing of your game

183

To take up wenches private in the night,
I apprehended straight this course to make
My selfe as one of them, and waite your coming;
I did so, and enjoyed you, and now this child
That now is quicke within me: hide my shame,
And marry me: or else I must be forc't——
Longavile (*within*).   *Monsieur Bewford, Monsieur Bewford.*
Bewford.   Whose
                                              that calls? 30

Longavile (*within*).   Are you a bed?
Bewford.   No Sir.——The hangings.
                    [Maria *hides behind the arras.*]

Enter Longavile.

Longavile.   Nay *Monsieur*, I'le forbid that, we'le have fair play.
Lend me your candle, are you taken *Bewford*?
A lecher of your practice, and close carriage
To be discovered thus? I am a sham'd
So great a Master in his art should faile,
And stagger in his grounds.
Bewford.   Your wide,
This woman and my selfe are man and wife,
And have been so this halfe yeare.
Where are you now? have I been discovered?   40
You cannot breake so easily on me Sir,
I am to wary to be opend by you.
Longavile.   But these are but illusions to give couler
To your most misticke leacherie, but Sir
The belly hath betray'd you, it all must out.
Bewford.   Good *Longavile* believe me on my faith,
I am her husband.
Longavile.   On my faith I cannot
Unlesse I saw your hands fast and your heartes.
Bewford.   Why *Longavile* when did I give that to your eares
That was not truth? by all the world she's mine,   50

28 me: hide ‿] F1 *cor*; ~ ‿ ~ : F1 *uncor*; ~ , ~ ‿ F2
*45 you, it all] Dyce; you ‿ all, it F1–2; you, all Sympson

184

She is my wife and to confirme you better
I give my selfe againe.——Here take my hand
And I yours, we are once more married.——
Will this content you?
Longavile.   Yes, I am believing, and God give you joy.
Bewford.   My loving wife I will not wrong thee,
Since I am thine and only loved of thee,
From this houre I vow my selfe a new man,
Be not jealous: for though I had a purpose,
To have spent an hower or two in solace otherwise,   60
And was provided for it, yet thy love
Shall put a better temper to my blood.
Come out thou woman of unholsome life,
Be sorry for thy sinnes, and learne to mend,

[*Enter* Jaques.]

Nay never hide your face, you shall be seene.
Longavile.   *Jaques*, why *Jaques*, art thou that *Jaques*,
The very staffe, and right hand of our Duke?
Speake, thou bearded *Venus*.
Jaques.   I am he,
By miracle preserv'd to be that *Jaques*.
Within this two houres Gentlemen, poor *Jaques*   70
Was but as coarse in grave: a man of wisedome,
That of my conscience if he had his right
Should have a pretty state, but that's all one,
That noble Gentleman did save this life,
I keepe it for him, 'tis his owne.
Longavile.   Oh *Bachus*!
Is all the world drunke? come wee'le to the Duke
And give thankes for this delivery.

[*Exeunt.*]

61 thy] Dyce; my F1-2

Enter [Gentleman *as*] *Duke, and* Jaques.   V. [i

Gentleman.   Not gon unto my Tenants to relate
  My grace and honour, and the mightynesse
  Of my new name which would have struck a terrour
  Through their course doublets, to their very hearts?
Jaques.   Alas great Lord and Master, I could scarce
  With safety of my life returne againe
  Unto your graces house, and but for one
  That had some mercie, I had sure been hang'd.
Gentleman.   My house?
Jaques.   Yes Sir, this house, your house 'ith towne.
Gentleman.   *Jaques* we are displeas'd, hath it no name?   10
Jaques.   What name?
Gentleman.   Dull rogue; what hath the King bestowed
  So many honours, open'd all his springes,
  And showerd his graces downe upon my head,
  And has my house no name? no title yet?
  Burgundy house you Asse.
Jaques.   Your graces mercy.——
  And when I was come off, and had recover'd
  Burgundy house, I durst not yet be seene,
  But lay all night for feare of pursuivants
  In *Burgundy* privie house.
Gentleman.   O Sir, 'tis well;
  Can you remember now? but *Jaques* know   20
  Since thy intended journey is so croste,
  I will go downe my selfe this morning.
Jaques.   Sir?
Gentleman.   Have I not said this morning?
Jaques.   But consider,
  That nothing is prepared yet for your journey;
  Your graces teames not here to draw your cloathes;
  And not a carrier yet in town to send by.
Gentleman.   I say once more go about it.
  You'r a wise man, you'de have me linger time,
  Till I have worne these cloathes out: will ye go?   *Exit* Jaques.

186

Enter Lady.

Make ye ready wife.

Lady.   I am so, mighty Duke.

Gentleman.   Nay for the Countrey.

Lady.   How? for the Countrey?

Gentleman.   Yes I am resolv'd
To see my Tenants in this bravery,
Make them a sumptuous feast, with a slight shew
Of *Dives and Laʒarus*, and a squib or two,
And so returne.

Lady.   Why Sir? you are not mad?

Gentleman.   How many Dukes have ye known mad? I pray speake.

Lady.   You are the first Sir, and I hope the last,
But you are stark horne mad.

Gentleman.   Forbeare good wife.

Lady.   As I have faith you'r mad: your hornes   40
Have been to heavy for you, and have broke
Your skull in pieces, if you be in earnest.

Gentleman.   Well you shall know my skull and wits are whole
Ere I have done, and yet I am in earnest.

Lady.   Why, do you think I'le go?

Gentleman.   I know you shall.

Lady.   I shall? by what authority shall I?

Gentleman.   I am your husband.

Lady.   True I confesse it,
And by that name the world hath given you
A power to sway me; but Sir you shall know
There is a greater bond that tyes me here,   50
Alleagance to the King; has he not heapt
Those honours on you to no other end,
But to stay you here, and shall I have a hand
In the offending such a gracious Prince?
Besides, our owne undoings lyes uppon't.
Were there no other cause, I do not see,
Why you should go, if I should say you should not.

Gentleman.   Do you thinke so?

Lady.   Yes faith.

Gentleman.   Now good wife make
Me understand that point.
Lady.   Why that you shall,
Did I not bring you hither?
Gentleman.   Yes.
Lady.   And were   60
Not all those honours wrought out of the fire
By me?
Gentleman.   By you?
Lady.   By me; how strang you make it!
When you came first did you not walke the Town,
In a long cloake halfe compasse? an old hat,
Linde with vellure, and on it for a band,
A skeine of crimson cruell?
Gentleman.   I confesse it.
Lady.   And tooke base courses?
Gentleman.   Base?
Lady.   Base by this light,
Extreame base, and scurvie, monstrous base.
Gentleman.   What were these courses, wife?
Lady.   Why you shall know;
Did you not thus attired trot up and down,   70
Plotting for vild and lowsie offices,
And agreed with the Sergiant of the beares,
To buy his place? deny this if you can.
Gentleman.   Why it is true.
Lady.   And was not that monstrous base?
Gentleman.   Be advis'd wife, a beares a princly beast.
Lady.   A beare?
Gentleman.   Yes wife, and one side venson.
Lady.   You'r more then one side foole, I'm sure of that.
Gentleman.   But since you have vext me wife, know you shall go,
Nor you shall never have penny from me.
Lady.   Nay I have done, and though I know 'twill be   80
Your overthrow, I'le not forsake you now.
Gentleman.   Be ready then.
Lady.   I will.   *Exit* Gentleman.

Enter Bewford, Longavile, [Her] Servant, Maria.

Longavile.   What are you married *Bewford?*
Bewford.   I as fast
  As words, and hearts, and hands and Priest can make us.
Lady.   O Gentlemen, we are undone.
Longavile.   For what?
Lady.   This Gentleman, the Lord of Lorne, my husband,
  Will be gon downe to shew his play fellowes,
  Where he is gay.
Bewford.   What, downe into the Countrey?
Lady.   Yes faith, was ever foole but he so crosse?
  I would as faine be gracious to him,   90
  As he could wish me, but he will not let me;
  Speake faithfully, will he deserve my mercy?
Longavile.   According to his merits he should weare,
  A guarded coate, and a great wooden dagger.
Lady [*to the audience*].   If there be any woman that doth knowe,
  The duties 'twixt a husband and his wife,
  Will speake but one word for him he shall scape;
  Is not that reasonable? but ther's none.——
  Be ready therefore, to pursue the plot
  We had against a pinch, for he must stay.   100
Longavile.   Waite you here for him whilst I go
  And make the King acquainted with your sport,
  For feare he be incens'd for our attempting
  Places of so great honour.
Lady.   Go, be speedy.   *Exit* Longavile.

Enter [Gentleman *as*] *Duke*, Cozen, [his] Wife, Jaques, Man.

Gentleman.   Come let me see how all things are disposed of.
Jaques.   One Cart will serve for all your furniture,
  With roome enough behinde to ease the footman;
  A capcase for your linnen, and your plate,
  With a strange locke that opens with Amen;
  For my young Lord because of easie portage,   110

*86 Lorne] Colman; lorne F1; Lorgue F2

189

A quiver of your graces linde with Cunney,
Made to be hang'd about the Nurses neck,
Thus with a scarfe or towell.
Gentleman.   Very good.
Jaques.   Nay, 'tis well, but had you staid another weeke,
I would have had you furnisht in such pomp,
As never Duke of *Burgundy* was furnisht;
You should have had a sumpter though't had cost me
The laying on my selfe: where now you are faine,
To hire a rippers mare, and buy new dossers,
But I have got them painted with your armes,   120
With a faire darnex Carpet of my owne
Laid crosse for the more state.
Gentleman.   *Jaques* I thanke you:
Your Carpet shall be brusht and sent you home.——
What, are you ready wife?
Lady.   An houre agoe.
Gentleman.   I cannot chuse but kisse thy royall lips,
Deare Dutches mine, thou art so good a woman.
Bewford [*aside*].   Yould say so if you knew all, goodman Duckling.
Cozen [*aside*].   This was the happiest fortune could befall me;
Now in his absence will I follow close
Mine owne preferment, and I hope ere long,   130
To make my meane and humble name so strong,
As my great Couzens, when the world shall know,
I beare too hot a spirit to live low.
The next Spring wil I down my wife and houshold;
I'le have my Ushers, and my foure Lacquies,
Six spare caroches too: but mum, no more,
What I intend to do, I'le keep in store.
Gentleman.   Mountye, mountye——*Jaques*, be our querry.
Groom.   To horse there Gentlemen, and fall in couples.
Gentleman.   Come honoured Duchesse.   140

Enter Longavile.

119 rippers] i.e. reapers   136 caroches] F2; croches F1
138 Mountye...querry] i.e. *Montez...equerry*

190

Longavile.   Stand thou proud man.

Gentleman.   Thieves, *Jaques*, raise the
people.

Longavile.   No, raise no people, 'tis the Kings command,
  Which bids thee once more stand thou haughty man,
  Thou art a monster, for thou art ungratefull,
  And like a fellow of a rebell nature,
  Hast flung from his embraces: and for
  His honours given thee, hast not returnd
  So much as thanks, and to oppose his will,
  Resolv'd to leave the Court, and set the Realm
  A fire, in discontent, and open action: 150
  Therefore he bids thee stand thou proud man,
  Whilst with the whisking of my sword about
  I take thy honours off: this first sad whiske
  Takes off thy Duke-dome, thou art but an Earl.

Gentleman.   You are mistaken, *Longavile.*

Longavile.   O would I were, this second whiske divides
  Thy Earldome from thee, thou art yet a Baron.

Gentleman.   No more whisks if you love me *Longavile.*

Longavile. Two whisks are past, and two are yet behind,
  Yet all must come, but not to linger time,   160
  With these two whisks I end, now *Mount Marine*,
  For thou art now no more, so says the King,
  And I have done his Highnesse will with griefe.

Gentleman.   Disgraced from my honours?

Longavile.   'Tis too certaine.

Gentleman.   I am no Traitor sure that I know of;
  Speak *Jaques*? hast thou ever heard me utter word
  Tending to treason, or to bring in the enemy?

Jaques.   Alas sir I know nothing,
  Why should your Worship bring me in to hang me?
  God's my judge Gentlemen I never medled   170
  But with the brushing of his cloaths, or fetching
  In water in a morning for his hands.

Cozen.   Are these the honours of this place? *Antony*

191

Help me to take her gowne off quickly
Or I'le so swinge ye for't——
Wife.   Why husband? Sir?
Co{en.   I'le not loose a penny by this towne.
Longavile.   Why what do you meane sir, have her to her lodging,
And there undresse her, I will waite upon her.
Co{en.   Indeed you shall not, your moneth is out I take it.
Get you out before me wife: 180
Couzen farewell, I told you long agoe,
That pride begins with pleasure, ends with woe.
                                        Exit with's Wife.
Bewford.   Goe thy way sentences, 'twill be thy fortune
To live and dye a Cuckold and Church-warden.
Lady.   O my poor husband! what a heavy fortune
Is fallen upon him?
Bewford.   Me thinks 'tis strange,
That heaven fore-warning great men of their falls,
With such plaine tokens, they should not avoid them?
For the last night betwixt eleven and twelve,
Two great and hideous blazing stars were seen   190
To fight a long houre by the clocke, the one
Drest like a Duke, the other like a King,
Till at the last the crowned star ore-came.
Her Servant.   Why do ye stand so dead, *Monsieur Marine?*
Gentleman.   So *Caesar* fell when in the Capitoll
They gave his body two and thirty wounds.
[*To the audience*] Be warned all ye Peers, and by my fall,
Hereafter learn to let your wives rule all.
Her Servant.   *Monsieur Marine,* pray let me speak with you;
Sir I must wave you to conceale this party,   200
It stands upon my utter overthrow;
Seem not discontented, nor do not stir
A foote, for if you do, you and your hope——
I sweare you are a lost man if you stir.
And have an eye to *Bewford,* he'l tempt you.
Bewford.   Come, come, for shame goe downe;

200 wave] i.e. signal

Were I *Marine*, by heaven I would goe down:
And being there, I would rattle him such an answer
Should make him smoake.
Gentleman.   Good *Monsieur Bewford* peace,
Leave these rebellious words, or by the honours   210
Which I once enjoyed, and yet may sweare by,
I'le tell the King of your proceedings; I
Am satisfied.
Lady.   You talkt of going down
When 'twas not fit, but now let's see your spirit,
A thousand and a thousand will expect it.
Gentleman.   Why wife, are you mad?
Lady.   No nor drunk, but I'de have
You know your own strength.
Gentleman.   You talk like a most foolish
Woman wife; I tell you I will stay,
Yet I have a cratchet troubles me.
Longavile.   More cratchets yet?
Gentleman.   Follow me *Jaques*, I   220
Must have thy counsell.——I will returne againe,
Stay you there Wife.   [*Exit with* Jaques.]
Longavile.   I fear this losse of honour
Will give him some few stooles.
Lady.   No, no, he is resolv'd,
He will not stir a foote I'le lay my life.
Bewford.   I, but hee's discontented, how shall we
Resolve that and make him stay with comfort?
Lady.   Faith *Bewford* we must even let nature work,
For hee's the sweetest temper'd man for that
As one can wish, for let men but goe about to foole him,
And hee'l have his finger as deep in't as the best;   230
But see where he comes frowning, blesse us all!

           Enter [Gentleman *as*] *Duke.*

Gentleman.   Off with your hats, for here doth come
The high and mighty Duke of *Burgundy.*
What ever you may think, I have thought

And thought, and thought upon't, and I finde it plaine,
The King cannot take backe what he has given,
Unlesse I forfeit it by course of Law.
Not all the water in the river *Sene*,
Can wash the blood out of these Princely veines.
Lady.   Godamercy husband, thou art the best   240
To worke out a thing at a pinch, in *France*.
Gentleman.   I will ascend my state againe.———Duchesse
Take your place,———and let our Champion enter.
Longavile.   Has he his Champion? that's excellent.
Gentleman.   And let loud musick sound before his entrance.
                                        Sound Trumpet.

Enter Jaques *in armour, one carrying a Scuchion before him, and a*
                        two-handed sword.

Lady.   How well our Champion doth demean himselfe,
As if he had been made for such an action?
Me thinks his sturdy trunchion he doth wield,
Like *Mars* approaching to a bloody field.
Gentleman.   I think ther's no man so desperate   250
To dare encounter with our Champion,
But trust me, *Jaques*, thou hast pleas'd us well.———
Once more our warlike musick, then proceed.
                                    [*A Trumpet sounds.*]
                    Enter Shattillion.

Shattillion [*aside*].   What wondrous age is this? what close
        proceedings?
I heare the clang of Trumpets in this house,
To what intent do not our States-men search?
O no, they look not into simple truth;
For I am true, and they regard not me.
A man in armour too: God save the King.
The world will end, theres nought but treachery.   260
Jaques.   I *Jaques*, servant to the high and mighty *Godfrey* Duke of

245.1 *Sound Trumpet.*] Sympson (*conj.*); Sound Trumpet Ff *print as continuation*
of Gentleman's speech.

Burgundy, do come hither to prove by natural strength and
activity of my body, without the help of sorcery, inchantment,
or negromancy, that the said *Godfrey* late of *Mount Marine*, and
now of *Burgundy*, hath perfect right therto, notwithstanding the
Kings command to the contrary, and no other person whatsoever:
and in token that I wilbe ready to make good the same, I throw
down my gage, which is my honour. Pronounced the 37. of
February stilo novo. *God save the Duke.*

Shattillion [aside].   Of all the plots the King hath laid for me   270
This was the shrewdest, 'tis my life they seeke,
And they shall have it: if I should refuse
To accept the challenge in the Kings behalfe,
They have some cause to take away my life,
And if I do accept it, who can tell,
But I may fall by doubtfull chance of war?
'Twas shrewd, but I must take the least of evills.——
I take thy gauntlet up thou treacherous man,
That stands in armed coate against the King,
Whom God preserve, and with my single sword   280
Will justifie what ever he commands.——
I'le watch him for catching of my words.

Gentleman.   *Jaques* goe on, defend our Princely title.

Shattillion.   Why shrinkst thou backe? thou hast an evill cause;
Come forward man, I have a rocke about me,
I fight for my true Liege.

Gentleman.   Goe forward *Jaques*.

Jaques.   I do beseech your Grace to pardon me,
I will not fight with him, with any else
I'le shew my resolution speedily.

Shattillion.   Come do thy worst, for the King shall see   290
All is not true that is reported of me.

Jaques.   I may not fight with him by law of armes.

Gentleman.   What? shall my title fall? wilt thou not fight?

Jaques.   Never with him that once hath sav'd my life.

Shattillion.   Dar'st thou not fight? behold then I doe goe
Strong with the zeale I beare my Soveraign,

268–69 37. of *February*] stet F1–2

195

And seize upon that haughty man himselfe.
Descend the steps (that thou hast thus usurpt
Against the King and State) downe to the ground,
And if thou doe utter but a syllable   300
To crosse the Kings intent, thou art but dead;
There, lye upon the earth and pine and dye.——
[*Aside*] Did ever any man wade through such stormes,
To save his life, as poore *Shattillion?*
Longavile.   I feare this challenge hath spoil'd all.
Lady.   Ne're feare it, hee'l work it out againe.——Servant,

Enter Shattillions Love.

See where *Shattillions* Love, poor Lady, comes.
Gentleman.   Jaques.
Jaques.   Lye still sir if you love your life,
I'le whistle when he's gone.
Love.   O Gentlemen, I charge you by the love   310
Which you beare to women, take some pitty
On this distressed man, help to restore
That pretious jewell to him he hath lost.
Bewford.   Lady what ever power doth lye in us
By art or prayer, or danger, we are yours.
Love.   A strange conceite hath wrought this malady,
Conceites againe must bring him to himselfe,
My strict denyall to his will wrought this!
And if you could but draw his wilder thoughts
To know me, he would sure recover sense.   320
Longavile.   That charge I'le undertake.
Gentleman.   Looke *Jaques*, look,
For Gods sake let me rise; this greatnesse is
A Jade, I cannot sit it.
Jaques.   His sword is up,
And yet he watcheth you.
Gentleman.   I'le down again:
Pray for thy Master, *Jaques.*

*306 againe.——Servant,] Sympson; ~ ∧∧ servant. F1; ~ , ∧ servant. F2
*319 wilder] *stet* F1–2

Shattillion.   Now the King
  May see all the suggestions are not true,
  He hath receiv'd against my loyalty;
  When all men else refuse, I fight his battails,
  And thrust my body into dangers mouth;
  I am become his Champion, and this sword   330
  Has taught his enemies to know themselves;
  O that he would no more be jealous of me!
Longavile. *Monsieur Shattillion*, the King assures you,
  That for this valiant loyall act of yours,
  He hath forgot all jealousies and feares,
  And never more will tempt you into danger.
Shattillion. But how shall I believe this? what new token
  Of reconcilement will he shew me?
  Let him release my poor love from her torment,
  From her hard fare and strict imprisonment.   340
Longavile. He hath done this to win your after-love,
  And see your Lady sent you from the King
  By these two Gentlemen: be thankfull for her.
Shattillion. She lives, she lives, I know her by the power
  Shoots from her eyes.   [*Kneels.*]
Love.   Rise deare *Shattillion.*
Shattillion. I Know my duty, next unto my King,
  I am to kneele to you.
Love.   I'le have you rise.——
  Fetch me a chair.——Sit down *Shattillion.*
Shattillion [*sitting*]. I am commanded, and faith tell me Mistris,
  What usage have you had? pray be plaine?   350
Love. O my most lov'd *Shattillion*, paine enough,
  But now I am free, thanks to my God and King.
Longavile. His eyes grow very heavy, not a word,
  That his weak senses may come sweetly home.
Shattillion. The King is honourable.   [*Sleeps.*]
Gentleman. When do you whistle *Jaques?*
Jaques.   By and by.
Longavile. Come hither *Monsieur*, canst thou laugh a little?

*333 assures] F2; assigns F1

197

Her Servant.   Yes Sir.

Longavile.   So thou shalt then.—*Bewford* how dost thou?

Bewford.   Why well.

Longavile.   I'me glad on't, and how does thy wife?

Bewford.   Why you may see her Sir, she stands behind you.   360

Longavile.   By the mass she's there indeed, but wher's her belly?

Bewford.   Belly?

Longavile.   Her great belly man: what hast thou sent thee?

Her Servant.   A boy I'le lay my life, it tumbled so.

Bewford.   Catcht by this light.

Longavile.   I'le be a gossip *Bewford.*

Her Servant.   And I.

Longavile.   I have an odd Apostle spoone.

Bewford.   S'foote catcht.

Lady.   Why what's the matter Gentlemen?

Longavile.   He's married to your woman.

Lady.   And I not know it?

Her Servant.   'Twas a veniall sin.

Bewford.   Gall, gall, gall.   [*Maria kneels.*]

Lady.   Forgive her *Monsieur Bewford*, 'twas her love.   370

Bewford.   You may rise if you please, I must endure it.

Longavile.   See how my great Lord lyes upon the ground
And dare not stir yet?   *Jaques whistles.*

Gentleman.   *Jaques, Jaques,* is the Kings Champion gone yet?

Jaques.   No, but hee's asleep.

Gentleman.   Is he asleep, art sure?

Jaques.   I am sure he is, I heare him snore.

Gentleman.   Then by your favours Gentlemen I rise,
And know I am a Duke still.

Jaques.   And I am his Champion.

Lady.   Hold thee there, and all *France* cannot mend thee.

Gentleman.   I am a Prince as great within my thoughts   380
As when the whole state did adorn my person;
What tryall can be made to try a Prince?

373 Jaques *whistles.*] Langbaine; *Jaques,* whistles? Ff *print as continuation of
Longavile's speech*

I will oppose this noble corps of mine
To any danger that may end the doubt.
Lady.   Great Duke and husband there is but one way
To satisfie the world of our true right,
And it is dangerous.
Gentleman.   What may it be?
Were it to bring the great Turke bound in chaines
Through *France* in triumph: or to couple up
The Sophie, and great *Prester John* together,   390
I would attempt it Duchesse; tell the course.
Lady.   There is a strong opinion through the world,
And no doubt grounded on experience,
That Lyons will not touch a lawfull Prince,
If you be confident then of your right,
Amongst the Lions beare your naked body,
And if you come off cleare and never winch,
The world will say you are a perfect Prince.
Gentleman.   I thank you Duchesse for your kinde advice,
But know we do not affect those ravenous beasts.   400
Longavile.   A Lyon is a beast to try a King;
But for the triall of such a state like this
Pliny reports a mastive dog will serve.
Gentleman.   We will not deale with dogs at all: but men.
Her Servant.   You shall not need to deale with them at all,
Hark you Sir, the King doth know you are
A Duke.
Gentleman.   No, does he?
Her Servant.   Yes, and is content
You shall be, but with this caution, that
None know it but your selfe: for if ye do,
He'l take it away by act of Parliament.   410
Gentleman.   Here's my hand, and whilst I live or breath,
No living wight shall know I am a Duke.
Her Servant.   Marke me directly Sir, your wife may know it.
Gentleman.   May not *Jaques?*
Her Servant.   Yes, he may.

*400 know] Dyce; now F1-2

199

Gentleman.   May not my countrey Couzen?

Her Servant.   By no meanes sir,
If you love your life and state.

Gentleman.   Well then,
Know all I am no Duke.

Her Servant.   No I'le sweare it.

Longavile.   See he wakes.

Shattillion.   Where am I, or where have I been all this while?   420
Sleep hath not sate so sound upon mine eyes
But I remember well that face;
O thou too cruell, leave at length to scorne
Him that but looking on thy beauty dyes,
Either receive me, or put out my eyes.

Love [*kneeling*].   Dearest *Shattillion* see upon my knees,
I offer up my love, forget my wrongs.

Shattillion.   Art thou mine own?

Love.   By heaven I am.

Shattillion.   Then all the world is mine.

Love.   I have stranger things to tel thee, my dearest love.   430

Shattillion.   Tell nothing
But that thou art mine own: I do not care
To know where I have been, or how I have liv'd,
Or any thing, but that thou art my own.

Bewford.   Well wife, though 'twere a trick that made us wed,
Wee'l make our selves merry soone in bed.

Gentleman.   Know all I am no Duke.

Lady.   What say'e?

Gentleman.   *Jaques?*

Jaques.   Sir.   440

Gentleman.   I am a Duke.

Both.   Are yee?

Gentleman.   Yes faith, yes faith.
But it must only run amongst our selves,
And *Jaques* thou shalt be my Secretary still.

Lady.   Kinde Gentlemen, leade in *Shattillion,*
For he must needs be weak and sickly yet.——

438 say'e] F2; saye F1

Now all my labours have a perfect end
As I could wish: let all young sprightly wives
That have dull foolish Coxcombs to their husbands,
Learn by me their duties, what to doe,
Which is to make 'em fooles, and please 'em too.   450

[*Exeunt.*]

The Epilogue

The Monuments of vertue and desert,
Appeare more goodly when the glosse of art
Is eaten off by time, then when at first
They were set up, not censur'd at the worst.
We have done our best for your contents to fit
With new paines this old monument of wit.

TEXTUAL NOTES

Prologue

12 live] F1 ' their noble memory, whose name... live in their fame' need not be changed to create more explicit concord, as in Q1649 *Thierry and Theodoret* and Colman, since 'their memory' and 'whose name' had sufficient plural meaning for an early-seventeenth-century ear.

I.i

46 preacht] 'I could requite...and...preacht' needs no emendation if we assume an ellipsis 'could requite and have preacht'. The shift to past tense after 'should' and 'could' was common: 'We should...found it so' (*Coriolanus*, IV.vi.34–5, 1623 ed.).

107 humour] The meaning is clearly 'Leave the humour of a courtier and the base subjection to your wife'; hence I do not follow Sympson's suggestions 'this humour' or 'the humouring'. Another possibility is 'leave the humorous and base subjection', and the authors clipped '-ous' as Shakespeare did in expressions like 'venome mud' (*Rape of Lucrece*, line 850, 1594 ed.) and 'venome tooth' (*Richard III*, I.ii.291, 1597 ed.).

146 levied] 'Levy' was used for 'level', as 'winking with one eye, as though hee were levying at a Woodcocke'. Nicholas Breton, *The Court and Country* (1618), Sig. B1ᵛ.

I.ii

34 God forbid] F1–2 leave out 'God', though they do not indicate a break, and some editors supply 'Heaven', too mild an oath to be excised by a censor. Since Jaques uses 'God' elsewhere (I.i.200), it seems appropriate here.

39 eare] The usual expression is 'give me your ear', when someone wants attention. Editors changed 'eare' to 'ears' because the reply below is 'They are your servants.' But there are many examples in these plays of a plural 'they' referring to a singular noun.

75 clapt in velvet] Sympson's 'ycald' misses the mocking tone of the speech.

I.iii

78–79 say with me | Heaven save his grace.] Eye-skip is the simplest explanation for F1's omission.

I.iv

12 sweet like the Arabian gums] The rhetorical figure requires an adjective
or participle (omitted from F1) to parallel 'hung like the sun'; hence I find
Seward's suggested 'Smell like the Arabian gums' awkward. For use of
'sweet' see Herrick's 'Sweet as is that gum', *Hesperides* (ed. Martin), p. 57,
line 145.

13 hung like the Sun] Seward thought 'flung' or 'fling' would do better
here, and Dyce emended 'hung' to 'fling', probably to agree with 'shine' in
line 11, and he inserted 'smell' in line 13:

> They must be bright and shine,——
> Their clothes soft velvet and Tyrian purple,
> Smell like the Arabian gums; fling like the Sun,
> Their golden beams on all sides.

But F1 'hung like the Sun' is clearer and it accords with the passive
attributes in the description. A well furnished chamber is hung with rich
cloth, and the sun may be seen as if decorated with its beams. Longavile
later speaks of the 'orient sun' of the Gentleman's clothes (II.ii.188). The
sun's golden beams can do more than scatter, fling, cast, or glide in Elizabethan poetry. I think the sense is that would-be great men are pretentious
in their clothes, clothes gilded on all sides; thus their bodies are hung like
the sun with golden beams on all sides, recalling the symbol of the king.

II.i

90 things idle for shew] Sympson transposed the words to make the
ordinary phrase 'things for idle show', but there were idle things or things
idle enough in courtly life.

131 I am] The capital 'I' moved from line 131 up to line 130 in all copies
of F1 I have seen.

II.ii

67 discourse] F1's 'discovery...held' does not reappear in seventeenth-
century English, as far as I can tell, whereas 'discourse', first proposed by
Sympson, fits the context of 'common talk'. Compare 'Imagind worth
Holds in his bloud such swolne and hott discourse', *Troilus and Cressida*,
II.iii.183 (1609 ed.).

142 durty] Sympson suggested 'durt-ty'd', which explains the meaning, but
'durty' is used in the same way several times in this play. A dirty mind is
an attribute that most characters in this play wish to avoid – a mind tied to
the soil and to country ways. (See line 220 below.)

199 nimble footed Taylor]   Is the text corrupt or was there some now forgotten dancing tailor alluded to?

209 Floot, man]   Jaques is not called a 'foot-man' (F1's reading) elsewhere
in the play. He is the principal servant in the household and he aspires to be
the Duke's secretary. The exclamation (first proposed by Weber) is more
appropriate. 'Foote, man, let hym be ten thousand preists', Chapman's (?)
Charlemagne, *ca.* 1598–9, ed. Frank Schoell (1920), III.138.

III.i

17 beufe]   I presume that F1 'beufe' is a spelling variant of 'beef'. The
OED records 'boef', 'bœfe', and 'buefs' for the seventeenth century.
Dyce and Sympson preferred 'buff' – a serjeant's leather jerkin, but that
seems inappropriate for the fancy dress of a Switzler.

17 Is a Duke,]   The meaning must be 'He's a Duke'; 'Is' was a colloquial
substitution for 'He's' (see Abbot's *Shakespearean Grammar*, sec.
400).

68 taking up]   F1–2 'taking those Crowns' does not seem to be the
idiom, for I find no examples of 'take' in the sense 'to borrow money'.
OED v. 30 comes closest, meaning to originate, to take examples from, as
to borrow ideas. Sympson's emendation, which also repairs the meter,
seems best.

III.ii

31 set up some new stake]   F2 'wake' must be rejected and F1 'stake'
allowed to stand. At the Lord Mayor's or a magnifico's coming into office a
'new painted' stake or post was adorned before his door (See *The Fair
Maid of the Inn*, ed. Dyce, III.i, p. 45). Sympson also notes that there was a
great procession, with much pomp, at the setting up of a may pole, probably
what the Lady means to suggest here (See Brand's *Popular Antiquities*, 1905
ed., p. 403).

54 *Groom*...Make room...entring.]   F1–2 give this line to the Lady's
Servant, but, as Dyce noted, the Groom makes similar 'fore cries' at line 97
below and at IV.iv.45.

92 with for cryes]   A forecrier, like the Groom at line 54, cleared the way
for an important person. Hence I reject Sympson's dropping the preposi-
tion 'with' in an effort to simplify the passage. *The Middle English Dic-
tionary* gives several examples of this use, and the *OED* cites one from 1440.

III.iv

8 a Duchy top-man]   F1–2 'lope-man' has been interpreted by Nares as a
skipper and by Dyce as a leaping man or rope dancer (citing Middleton and

Rowley's *Spanish Gipsey*, IV.i, 'He that lopes on the ropes'), but the *OED* is content to identify him as a runner (citing only the passage from this play). The original reading was surely 'top-man', a sailing vessel with a topsail on its mast. Since the Lady goes on to say that 'A ladder of a hundred rounds will faile | To reach the top on't', the emendation clarifies her metaphor in a way that a rope dancer could not.

98 *Clodion, Merov*] F1 *Clodian, Meron* indicates that the manuscript contained an approximation of the native spellings of France's medieval kings, and Compositor *B* or a scribe misread 'Clodian' for 'Clodion' and 'Meron' for 'Merov' (or 'Merovee'). F2 turned 'Meron' into the Latin form 'Meroveus'.

IV.ii

7 light alove] F1–2 'light alone', a typical error for Compositor *B* like 'horse' for 'house' IV.iii.6, makes little sense and is not supported by other occurrences in seventeenth-century English. Sympson's emendation 'light o' love' is the right meaning, but the phrase in Henry Porter's *Two Angry Women* (1599), sig. C3ᵛ, 'light aloue' is probably the form of the original reading.

IV.iii

105 My good sword before me] F1 omits 'sword', supplied in F2 correctly, because Shattillion threatens with his sword at line 113 below.

IV.iv

64 feele my souse and perish] Since the Gentleman's speech is laced with expressions from falconry – 'pitch', 'marke', 'stoop', and 'stand' – Sympson must be right to change the meaningless F1 'feel my soule' and F2's unexpressive 'feel my feet'. The 'souse' is the stroke of the hawk descending violently upon its prey (Dyce). This happy emendation also explains F1's easy misreading.

69 renounc'd] I follow F2 because of its concord with the rest of Gentleman's questions here, but I do it reluctantly. F1 'renounce' recalls the baptismal ceremony better: 'Dost thou... renounce the devil and all his works, the vain pomp and glory of the world, and with all covetous desires of the same?'

125 And much may't do their good hearts] F1–2 'may' needs only the change to 'may't' to suggest the saying 'Much good may't do them.' All editors have followed Sympson's more drastic transposition 'And much good may't do their hearts.' Compare 'Much good dich thy good heart' (*Timon of Athens*, I.ii.73, 1623 ed.), and 'Much good doe it your good heart' (*Merry Wives of Windsor*, I.i.83, 1623 ed.). I have not found the

exact wording of our text elsewhere, but a transposed epithet was a recognized figure.

135 *Exit* Longavile *and* Wife.] I presume F1–2 are correct here and that Cozen and Her Servant shout to them through the door at lines 154–5.

IV.v

45 you, it all must out] F1–2 'you all, it must out' seems wrong because Longavile addresses only Bewford. Dyce's reordering is the smoothest.

V.i

86 Lord of Lorne] There is 'a pretty ballad of the Lord of Lorn and the false Steward' in the Roxburgh ballads (Dyce), but the reference is to the many misfortunes of the seventh Earl of Argyll and Lord of Lorn, who turned Catholic and served King Philip III of Spain (Weber). He was formally declared a traitor February 1618/19 and lost his property. Hence F2 'Lorgue' and F1 'lorn' need slight alteration.

268–269 37. of *February*] So in F1–2 and no doubt part of the mock heroic style.

306 againe.——Servant] F1–2 'againe servant' implies that Longavile is Her Servant; therefore I follow Sympson's punctuation.

319 wilder thoughts] F1–2 and all later editions let this reading stand, but the psychology of that day depended much upon dulcet methods of turning demented minds by appealing to 'milder' not 'wilder' thoughts. In lines 333ff. Longavile soothes Shattillion by appealing to his thankfulness to his Love and his trust of the king's grace. Of course it is possible that Love means to turn his unsteady thoughts toward her in order to calm them.

333 assures] F1 'assigns' is not supported by any appropriate meaning in the *OED*, so I follow F2.

400 know] F1–2 'now', followed by all editors until Dyce, deserves Mason's sharp question 'Was there any other time at which Marine *did* affect those ravenous beasts?' *Comments on the Plays of Beaumont and Fletcher* (1797). The Gentleman uses pompous expressions of this kind habitually: 'Jaques know...I will go downe' (V.i.20–3), 'know you shall go' (line 78), and 'know I am Duke still' (line 378).

PRESS-VARIANTS IN F1

[Copies collated: Bodl (Bodleian Library B.i.8.Art), Camb¹ (University Library Cambridge, Aston a.Sel.19), Camb² (SSS.10.8), CLU (University of California at Los Angeles), CLU-C (William Andrews Clark Library), CSmH (Huntington Library), Hoy (personal copy of Cyrus Hoy, University of Rochester), ICN (Newberry Library), IU¹ (University of Illinois 822/B38/1647), IU² (q822/B38/1647 cop. 2), MB (Boston Public Library), MnU (University of Minnesota), NcD (Duke University), NIC (Cornell University), NjP (Princeton University), ViU¹ (University of Virginia 570973), ViU² (217972), WaU (University of Washington), WMU¹ (University of Wisconsin–Milwaukee copy 1), WMU² (copy 2), WMU³ (copy 3), WU (University of Wisconsin–Madison)]

SHEET 2D i (*inner forme*)

First-stage corrected: Camb¹⁻², CLU, CLU-C, CSmH, Hoy, IU¹, MB, NjP, ViU¹, WaU, WMU¹⁻³, WU
Uncorrected: ICN

Sig. 2D4
II.i.112 safe-guard,] safe-guard ∧
         Second-stage corrected: Bodl, IU², MnU, NcD, NIC, ViU²
RT   *The Noble Gentleman*] *The Custome of the Countrey*

SHEET 2E ii (*inner forme*)

Corrected: Camb¹⁻², CLU, CLU-C, CSmH, Hoy, ICN, IU¹⁻², MB, MnU, NcD, NIC, ViU¹⁻², WaU, WMU¹⁻³, WU
Uncorrected: Bodl, NjP

Sig. 2E2ᵛ
III.ii.57 his] this
    77 stretcht] stretch

SHEET 2F i (*inner forme*)

Corrected: Camb², CLU, CLUC, Hoy, ICN, IU¹⁻², MB, MnU, NcD, NIC, ViU¹⁻², WaU, WMU²⁻³, WU
Uncorrected: Bodl, Camb¹, CSmH, NjP, WMU¹

Sig. 2F1^v
    IV.v.28 me: hide] me hide:
        29 forc't] for'ct
        30 Bewford, Monsieur] Bewford, Monsienr
        43 couler] couller

SHEET 2F ii (*outer forme*)

Corrected: Bodl, Camb², CLU, CSmH, Hoy, ICN, IU$^{1-2}$, MB,
MnU, NcD, NIC, ViU$^{1-2}$, WMU$^{1-3}$, WU
Uncorrected: Camb¹, CLU-C, NjP, WaU

Sig. 2F3^v
    One rule beneath cw] *Two rules beneath cw*

EMENDATIONS OF ACCIDENTALS

Prologue

3 dare∧] ~ , F1–2
4 fashions;] ~ , F1–2

5 know∧] F2; ~ , F1

I.i

I.i] *Actus Primus, Scæna Prima.* F1
7 Courtier?] ~ , F1–2
13 believe∧] ~ ; F1–2
21 Coʒen.] *His prefixes throughout the play vary among Couʒen, Coʒen, Cous, Co, Coʒ, and Cos.*
26 ruine;] ~ , F1–2
48 pitty;] ~ , F1–2
52–53 (I...benefits)] ∧ ~ ...~ , F1–2
65 hopes;] ~ , F1–2
67 lightned;] F2; ~ , F1
78 night,] ~ : F1–2
81 praises.] ~ ; F1–2
83–85 Let...cloath.] Ff *line* Let ...heir | And...serge, | Farre ...cloath.
90 Sir,] F2; ~ ∧ F1
91.1 Page] Servant F1–2
93 *Page.*] *Ser.* F1–2
93 Sir,] ~ ∧ F1 (F2 *omits* Sir)
96 modesty.] ~ , F1–2
103 lazie,] ~ ∧ F1–2
105 still,] ~ . F1–2
105–106 But...Sir.] Ff *line* But... still, | Since...ye, | To...Sir.
106 Sir.] ~ , F1–2

111 Gentleman. Even] *cw* F1, F2; Even F1
119.1 Gentlemans] Gent. F1–2
121 Lady.] *Wife. her prefixes in this scene*
121 you.] ~ , F1–2
124–125 I...left.] Ff *line* I...lowe | A...left.
125 lowe∧] ~ , F1–2
129 you∧] ~ ? F1–2
132 true;] ~ , F1–2
134–136 Like...untempted] Ff *line* Like...Citie, | And... crownes. | Try...untempted
140 alive.] ~ , F1–2
148 Be] be F1–2
149 common,] ~ ; F1–2
155 certaine;] ~ , F1–2
163 we;] ~ , F1–2
166–167 Pardon...it.] *One line in* Ff
169–170 It...acres] *One line in* Ff
171 points.] ~ , F1–2
174 one;] ~ , F1–2
178 *Exit* Lady.] *Exit* Wife. *printed as line* 177
179 Jaques,] ~ . F1–2
184 Crowns;] ~ , F1–2

I.ii

0.1 Longavile] Longovile F1–2
1 *Her Servant.*] *His prefixes throughout the play are Serv. or Ser. His entrances are all Servant.*

2 how∧] F2; ~ , F1
4 so:——] ~ : ∧ F1–2
4 *Exit.*] *One half line earlier in* Ff
18 am;] ~ ∧ F1–2

209

19 in] F2; In F1
20 directly;] ~ , F1–2
33–34 Mistake...it] Ff *line* Mistake
...whore | Or...it
36 here;] ~ , F1–2
41 danger:] ~ ₐ F1; ~ . F2
55 soundest,] F2; ~ ₐ F1
56 Codpiece;] ~ , F1–2
58–59 (to...Gentlemen)] ,~ ...
~ ₐ F1; ; ~ ...~ , F2
64 is:] ~ , F1–2
67 wench,] F2; ~ ₐ F1
74 all:] ~ ₐ F1–2

75 so.] ~ ₐ F1; ~, F2
76 certaine,] ~ ₐ F1–2
78–79 O...live.——] *One line in*
Ff
79 live.——] ~ . F1–2
81 *Lady.*] *Her first prefix in this*
scene is Wife., *thereafter* Lady.
(*as is her entrance at line* 80.1)
87 attention:] ~ , F1–2
92 conceit,] ~ : F1–2
97 command,] ~ : F1
98 title:] ~ , F1–2
103 miseries;] ~ , F1–2

I.iii

12 none. Sure] ~ , sure F1–2
14 this;] ~ , F1–2
25 mad.——Farewell] ~ , farewell
F1–2
26 attending.——] ~ , ₐ F1–2
26 *Exit* Couzen.] Ff *print as line* 25
35 Iₐ] ~ : F1–2
38 senses,] ~ : F1–2
40 come——] ~ . F1–2
41 Lady;] ~ , F1–2
42 live.] ~ , F1–2

44 women. Do] ~ , do F1; ~ , Do
F2
51 me;] ~ , F1–2
55 Sir.] ~ , F1–2
62 title.] ~ , F1–2
70 live,] ~ ; F1–2
72 commons;] ~ , F1–2
74 downe,] F2; ~ ₐ F1
85 followed.——Farewell] ~ , ₐ
farewell F1–2
89 senses.] ~ , F1–2

I.iv

0.1 *Enter*ₐ] F2; ~ . F1
2 undone;...else,] ~ , ~ ; F1–2
4 asse,] F2; ~ ₐ F1
14–16 Their...me.] Ff *line* Their
...sides; | Such...know, | Thy
...him, | Hee's...me.
23 reasonsₐ] ~ , F1–2

26 removing,] F2; ~ ₐ F1
39 tenants;] ~ , F1–2
39 worke.] ~ ₐ F1–2
40 cryes,] ~ ₐ F1–2
41–42 Come...so,] Ff *line* Come
...him; | If...so,
42 him;] ~ , F1–2

II.i

II.i] *Actus secundus.* F1
0.1 *Enter*ₐ] F2; ~ . F1
1 Rise *Jaques,*] ~ ₐ F1–2
1 day.——] ~ , ₐ F1–2
9 evillₐ] ~ . F1–2

19–20 I...together,] *One line in* Ff
20 together,] ~ ; F1–2
32–33 Could...here.] Ff *line*
Could...heard, | He...here.
37 delights,] ~ ! F1–2

38 her;] F2; ~ , F1
39 her,] ~ ; F1; ~ ∧ F2
59 And...ye.] Ff *line* And...
shower | Upon...ye.
66–67 As...man,] Ff *line* As...
me? | Know...man,
72 will.] ~ ; F1–2
72.1 *Enter* Lady.] *Enter* Wife.
printed as 71.1 F1–2
73 *Lady*.] *Wife. her prefixes in this
scene* F1–2
75 night?] ~ . F1–2
75–77 O...walke] Ff *line* O...
hereafter, | And...hours; | In
...walke
77 hours;] ~ , F1; ~ : F2
81 tricks;] ~ , F1–2
89 ease,] ~ : F1–2
92–93 Why...Frame?] Ff *line*
Why...Sir, | That...Frame.
93 Frame?] ~ F1–2
96 forth;] ~ , F1–2
102–103 Why...past?] Ff *line* Why
...triumph | Day...past?
105 too;] ~ , F1–2

126 ground] F2; gronnd F1
134 true,] ~ ∧ F1; ~ : F2
139 witt.——] ~ , ∧ F1–2
143–144 That...about.] Ff *line* That
...same | Wood...about.
158 me;] ~ , F1–2
167 hereafter,] ~ ; F1–2
169 away:] ~ , F1–2
171 come,] ~ ∧ F1; ~ : F2
191 *Exit* Gentleman.] Ff *print as line*
192.1
192 stay,] ~ . F1–2
193 so,] F2; ~ ∧ F1
193 too.] ~ ∧ F1; ~ , F2
194 presently.——] ~ ; ∧ F1–2
199 him∧] ~ , F1–2
200 invading∧] ~ , F1–2
202 page.] ~ ∧ F1; ~ ; F2
202 *Exit*∧] ~ . F1
202 *Exit* Maria.] Ff *print as line* 203
203 you,] ~ . F1–2
212 understood.] ~ , F1–2
214 hast.] ~ , F1–2
214 selfe∧] ~ , F1–2
215 before,] F2; ~ ∧ F1

II.ii

0.1 *Enter* ∧ Gentleman∧] ~ . ~ .
F1; ~ ∧ ~ , F2
4 see——] ~ . F1–2
5 Sir——] ~ , F1–2
7–8 I...*Jaques*.] Ff *line* I...
alwayes | To...*Jaques*.
8 Alwayes∧] ~ , F1–2
9 looke∧] ~ , F1–2
10–11 I...hat.] *One line in* Ff
12 *Jaques*;] ~ , F1–2
26 I,] ~ ∧ F1–2
27–29 Provide...home,] Ff *line*
Provide...-fast, | Or...hus-
wife. | She...sisters, | But...
home,
28 huswife.] ~ ∧ F1; ~ ; F2
35 well !] ~ ? F1; ~ : F2

35–36 Why...rod.] *One line in* Ff
37–38 Another...girdle.] *One line
in* Ff
49 time.——] ~ ∧—— F1–2
51–52 *Monsieur*...ready.] *One line
in* Ff
58 (Which...for)] ∧ ~ , F1–2
60 houre.——] ~ . ∧ F1–2
71 hence;] ~ , F1; ~ : F2
76 it;] ~ , F1–2
79 beware,] F2; ~ ∧ F1
80 you,] F2; ~ ∧ F1
82 deeds,] F2; ~ ∧ F1
90 now;] ~ , F1–2
96 me?] F2; ~ ; F1
97 you.] ~ ? F1; ~ : F2
99 Why∧] ~ ? F1; ~ , F2

102 hearts] F2; hea ts F1
104 unprefer'd,] F2; ~ ‸ F1
108–109 (If...France] Ff line (If...
    dispos'd:) | How...France
109 France] F2; Fran. | F1
110 But] but F1–2
113 will,] ~ ? F1–2
118 Yes.——] ~ : ‸ F1–2
118–119 Yes...Marine.] One line in
    Ff
123–124 And...soone,] Ff line And
    ...you, | Not...soone,
126 fall‸] ~ ; F1–2
129 heare?] F2; ~ , F1
136 on,] ~ . F1–2
144 him.——Tell] ~ ; ‸ tell F1–2
155–156 Why...answer] One line in
    Ff
165–166 Why...him.] One line in
    Ff
166 plot——] ~ . F1–2
169 Earldome?] F2; ~ , F1

170 Lord!] ~ , F1–2
176 undone;] ~ , F1–2
184 anon.——] ~ . ‸ F1–2
184–185 Wee'l...Duke?] Ff line
    Wee'l...anon.—— | Why...
    Duke?
190 Lord.] ~ ; F1–2
191 Longavile.] F2; ~ ‸ F1
197 off.——] ~ , ‸ F1; ~ . ‸ F2
201 come,] F2; ~ ‸ F1
206. O...man,] Ff line O...Duke |
    Pardon...man,
212.1 Lady] Wife F1–2
219–220 Hath...mind:] Ff line
    Hath...thee | Hath...mind:
221 What,] ~ ‸ F1–2
221–222 What...me,] Ff line What
    ...me | Dresse...me,
226 kneel.——] ~ . ‸ F1–2
227 Lord——] ~ . F1–2
227–228 I...Duke.] One line in Ff
229 Duchesse,] F2; ~ ‸ F1

III.i

III. i] Actus Tertius. F1
8 dazell!] ~ ? F1; ~ ; F2
17–18 Is...presence!] One line in
    Ff
18 presence!] ~ ? F1–2
22 Kinsman,] ~ . F1–2
25 wise as his,] ~ ; F2
28 Jaques,] F2; ~ ‸ F1
30 expectation;] ~ , F1–2

40–41 I...Master,] Ff line I...
    it. | But...Master,
42 places;] ~ , F1–2
43 there;] ~ , F1–2
68 dispatcht.] ~ ¿ F1; ~ : F2
79 you.] ~ ; F1–2
79 Exit Cousen.] Ff on line 78
81 greater:] F2; ~ , F1

III.ii

0.1 Lady] Wife so her entrances and
    prefixes in the whole of this act
    F1–2
0.1 Longavile] Longoveil F1–2
4 practice.] ~ : F1–2
4 Afore...husband] Ff line Afore
    ...practice. | My...husband

6 And...Gentleman,] Ff line And
    ...coxcomb. | Gentleman,
6 coxcomb.] F2; ~ : F1
14–15 Or...Tenants,] One line in Ff
18 stay;] ~ ‸ F1–2
31 To...hold] Ff line To...
    stake: | I...hold

34 phrases!] ~ ? F1–2
50 nose-gayes;] ~, F1–2
55 Duke——] ~, F1–2
58 *Gentleman*] *Duke or Du. his prefixes from here to the end of the play* F1–2
60–61 'Tis...him] Ff *line* 'Tis... extreamly; | 'Tas...him
67 Emminence;] ~, F1–2
69 not;] ~, F1–2
75 indeed?] ~, F1–2
81 'Twill] F2; Twill F1
84 chamber.——] ~ .ᴧ F1–2
92 salutations.——] ~ . F1–2
96 bounty.] F2; ~ ᴧ F1
97 Gentlemen] F2; Goentlemen F1
99–102 He...course.] Ff *line* He ...poyson.——| 'Tis...make | A...due; | But...you | By ...course.
99 poyson.——] ~, ᴧ F1–2
109 dignity;] ~, F1–2
113 *Shattillion*;] ~ ᴧ F1–2
115 me.——] me. ᴧ F1–2
116–120 Can...woman.] Ff *line* Can...whence | This... abroad? | Even...himselfe. | As...coverd: | Yet...woman.
119 coverd:] ~ ? F1–2
129 Love?] ~ : F1–2
130–131 This...creation] Ff *line* This...but | Apocryphall... creation
137 o'th] ot'h F1; o'th' F2
137 certaine——] ~ . F1–2
139 more——] ~ . F1–2

III.iii

2 perfect;] ~, F1–2
3 loud,] ~ ; F1–2
14 afore!] ~ ? F1–2
18 *Monsieur*,] F2;¹~ ᴧ F1
32 abundance.——Note] ~, ᴧ note F1–2
33 words,] ~ ; F1–2
33 heart!] ~ ? F1–2
36 people——but] ~ .——But F1–2
41 *People*.] *Omnes*. F1–2
43 *4. Gentleman*.] *Gen. as are all his prefixes to the end of the scene* Ff
53 hand.] ~, F1–2

III.iv

0.1 Lady] Wife *all her entrances and prefixes in this scene* F1–2
1 Cozen.——] ~ ᴧᴧ F1–2
3–4 Of...breath] Ff *line* Of... O, | For...breath
3 delivered.——] ~ .ᴧ F1–2
6 Duchesse!] ~ ? F1–2
9 a hundred] 100 F1–2
10 on't. Well] ~, well F1; ~ : well F2
16 this:] ~ ᴧ F1–2
17–19 I...blood.] F2; F1 *lines* I ...sometimes | Make...husband; | 'Twill...brains, | Me ...blood.
24 heaven,] ~ ᴧ F1–2
26–28 It...it.] Ff *line* It...so, | For...snap | This...woman | Is...it.
30 paines;] ~, F1–2
34 strangers;] ~, F1–2
44–45 You...speak.] Ff *line* You ...your | Full...speak.
47 reason.] F2; ~ ¿ F1

61 Lady.] ~ , F 1–2
62–65 Why...prate.] Ff *line* Why
   ...to? | To...husband; |
   'Twill...babl, | Stare, and
   prate.
66.1 *Enter*ᴧ] F 2; ~ . F 1
68–69 For...griefes.] Ff *line* For
   ...thinks | All...griefes.
77.1 Longavile] Longovile F 1–2
84 I.] ~ , F 1–2
87–88 He...can] Ff *line* He...
   Sir, | Be...can
90–91 Depart...Dutches.] Ff *line*
   Depart...stay, | No...
   Dutches.

93 this;] ~ , F 1–2
95 marriage.] ~ , F 1–2
101 leave:——] ~ , ᴧ F 1–2
103 *Charles*,] ~ ᴧ F 1–2
103 *Charlemaine*;] ~ . F 1–2
112 leave;] ~ , F 1–2
130–131 Forbeare...weds,] Ff *line*
   Forbeare...that | Your...
   weds,
131 thatᴧ] F 2; ~ , F 1
133–134 How do...title?] *One line*
   in Ff
135 I,] F 2; ~ ᴧ F 1
143 hast;] ~ , F 1–2

IV.i

IV.i] *Actus quartus.* F 1
3–4 Yes...dayes.] *One line in* Ff
5 velvet,] ~ ; F 1–2

8–10 Would...night.] Ff *line*
   Would...life, | To...night.
8 ready !] ~ ᴧ F 1–2

IV.ii

2–3 This...solace.] *One line in* Ff
8–9 Hearke...marry?] *One line in*
   Ff
10 bodied?] ~ , F 1–2
11–12 I sweare...free.] *One line in*
   Ff

11 not;] F 2; ~ , F 1
15 *Bewford?*] F 2; ~ . F 1
15–16 Sir...far] *One line in* Ff
19–20 Be...thine.] *One line in* Ff
26 hand. You'le] ~ , you'le F 1–2
28 kindnesse?] ~ . F 1–2

IV.iii

3 way——] ~ ? F 1; ~ . F 2
13 disguise,] ~ ; F 1–2
18–19 I...you,] Ff *line* I...up, |
   From...you,
22 *France*,] ~ . F 1–2
25 themᴧ] ~ , F 1–2
26–28 I...bondage,] Ff *line* I...
   Sir, | And...favorer | Of...
   bondage,
28 bondage,] ~ ; F 1–2
36 (Which...innumerall)] ᴧ ~ ...
   ~ ᴧ F 1–2
49–50 I...death] *One line in* Ff

51 him.] ~ , F 1–2
52 dye.——Come] ~ , come F 1–2
55 innocent.] ~ , F 1–2
56 Lay] F 2; La F 1
59 fortune ᴧ mine,] ~ , ~ ᴧ F 1–2
60 me?] ~ . F 1–2
65 enough;] ~ , F 1–2
68 innocent.——] ~ , ᴧ F 1–2
75–76 Good...dye.] *One line in* Ff
78 himᴧ] ~ , F 1–2
81 grieveᴧ] ~ , F 1–2
82 me.——] ~ ; ᴧ F 1–2

86 such.——Be] ~ : ₄ be F 1–2
88 Sir,] F 2; ~ ₄ F 1
90 feareful.] ~ , F 1–2
90 King.] ~ , F 1–2
92 then.] ~ ? F 1–2
93 not.——Flye] ~ ; ₄ fly eF 1;
  ~ : ₄ flye F 2
93 thine] F 2; thin | F 1
96 King.——] ~ , ₄ F 1–2
99–100 Be...ambush.——] *One*
  line in Ff
100 ambush.——] ~ , ₄ F 1; ~ ₄ ₄
  F 2
101 be;] ~ , F 1–2
102 revenge?——] ~ ? ₄ F 1–2
106 King,] ~ ₄ F 1–2
107–108 armes ₄...thee),] ~)...
  ~ ₄ , F 1–2
109 me.——] ~ . ₄ F 1–2
114 King,] ~ ; F 1–2
116 throate.——] ~ , ₄ F 1–2
117 stay ₄] ~ . F 1–2
121 found;] ~ , F 1–2
122–123 What...command] Ff *line*
  What...side? | Nay...com-
  mand

123 side?] ~ ₄ F 1–2
124 speake.] ~ ₄ F 1–2
127 thinks ₄] ~ . F 1–2
130.1 *Jaques* ₄] F 2; ~ . F 1
132–133 But...were] Ff *line* But
  ...that | Hath...were
134 *Callicut*;] ~ , F 1–2
140 wise;] ~ , F 1–2
145 Gentleman] F 2; Gent. F 1
145–146 It...Sir?] *One line in* Ff
145 life.——] ~ , ₄ F 1–2
146 Sir?] ~ . F 1–2
153 off.——] ~ , ₄ F 1–2
154 preserv'd!] ~ ? F 1–2
157 me,] ~ ; F 1–2
158 life.——] ~ , ₄ F 1–2
159 perill.——Can] ~ , ₄ can F 1–2
162 house,] ~ : F 1–2
166 me.——] ~ , ₄ F 1–2
168 me;] ~ , F 1–2
168 *Jaques*,] ~ ₄ F 1; ~ ! F 2
174 wastcoatieres;] ~ , F 2; wasc-
  coatieres, F 1
175 'em;] ~ , F 1–2
178 smell;] ~ , F 1–2
187.1 *Exeunt.*] Ff *place on line* 186

IV.iv

3 forward,] ~ ₄ F 1–2
4 Gentlemen,] Gent. F 1–2
5 selfe.——] ~ , ₄ F 1–2
6–7 For...Dukes?] Ff *line* For
  ...seeming: | Are...Dukes?
7 seeming:] F 2; ~ ₄ F 1
23 pardon;] ~ , F 1–2
23 it,] ~ : F 1–2
26 Sir.——] ~ , ₄ F 1–2
31 Knight-hood,] ~ ; F 1–2
32 issue;] ~ , F 1–2
35.1 *Exit*...Longavile.] Ff *place*
  one half line earlier
37 tasted.——] ~ . ₄ F 1–2
41–44 Why...opening.] Ff *line*

Why...dear, | Love...now |
You...chaines; | See...open-
ing.
43 hate:] F 2; ~ , F 1
44 chaines;] ~ , F 1–2
45.1 Gentleman, Lady] Duke, Wife
  Ff
46 himselfe;] ~ , F 1–2
56–57 Correct...person.] Ff *line*
  Correct...speake, | And...
  person.
63 stand,] ~ . F 1–2
64 perish.] ~ , F 1; ~ : F 2
71–72 Have...were,] Ff *line* Have
  ...household, | Sold...were,

215

77–78 The...coole?] Ff *line* The
...him | In...coole?
83 Court.——] ~ ; ∧ F1–2
85 *Lady.*] *Duch. her prefixes in this*
scene Ff
86 that.] ~ , F1–2
88 i'th] it'h F1; i'th' F2
88 towne;] ~ ∧ F1–2
95 forbid!] ~ ? F1–2
100 Cozen.] ~ ; F1–2
104.1 Gentleman *and* Lady.] *Duke*
and Duchesse. F1–2 *place on line*
103
107 houre;] ~ , F1–2
110 wife;] ~ , F1–2
112 wind-ward.——] ~ ∧∧ F1–2
118–119 What...foot,] *One line in*
Ff

119 foot,] ~ ∧ F1–2
133 sweetly:] F2; ~ ∧ F1
138–139 You...up,] Ff *line* You...
ever. | I...up,
139 you:] ~ ∧ F1–2
140 man,...Cozen,] ~ : ~ ∧ F1–2
143 friend;] ~ , F1–2
146 mov'd;] ~ , F1–2
148 I...a long.] *One line in* Ff
149 raw;] ~ , F1–2
152 better;] ~ , F1–2
152 me,] ~ ∧ F1–2
153 Sir,——] ~ , ∧ F1–2
153–154 I...wife.] *One line in* Ff
155 *Longaveile,*] F2; ~ ∧ F1–2
155 owne,——] ~ , ∧ F1–2
156 foole∧] F2; ~ , F1

IV.v

2 in;] ~ ∧ F1–2
4 see. A] ~ , a F1–2
7 lesson;] ~ , F1–2
11–12 O...loude.] *One line in* Ff
17–18 Poore...belly?] *One line in*
Ff
19–20 Yes...all;] *One line in* Ff
31 Sir.——The] ~ , the F1–2
32 play.] ~ ∧| F1; ~ , F2
39 yeare.] ~ , F1–2
47–48 On...heartes.] Ff *line* On
...saw | Your...heartes.

52 againe.——Here] ~ , ∧ here
F1–2
53 married.——] ~ , ∧ F1–2
57 thee,] ~ ∧ F1–2
58 I∧] F2; ~ , F1
62 blood.] ~ , F1–2
68–69 I...Jaques.] *One line in* Ff
69 *Jaques.*] ~ , F1–2
73 one,] ~ ∧ F1–2
75–76 Oh...Duke] *One line in* Ff

V.i

V.i] *Actus quintus.* F1
2 honour,] ~ ; F1–2
15 mercy.——] ~ , ∧ F1–2
19 well;] ~ , F1–2
24 journey;] ~, F1–2
27 it.] ~ , F1–2
29 *Exit*∧] F2; ~ . F1

29.1 *Enter* Lady.] *Enter* Wife.
printed as 30.1 F1–2
31 *Lady.*] *Dutches. Dutch. Duch.*
her prefixes in this scene (except
for 438 and 444) Ff
31 Duke] F2; *Duke* F1
32–33 Yes...bravery,] *One line in* Ff

33 bravery,] F2; ~ ∧ F1
34 shew∧] ~ , F1–2
35 *Dives and Lazarus*] *Dives,* and *Lazarus* F1; *Dives* and *Lazarus* F2
42 pieces, if] ~ : If F1–2
55 uppon't.] ~ , F1–2
57 go, if] ~ : If F1–2
58–59 Now...point.] *One line in* Ff
59–60 Why...hither?] *One line in* Ff
60–62 And...me?] *One line in* Ff
62 it!] ~ ? F1–2
67–68 Base by...base.] *One line in* Ff
69 know;] ~ , F1–2
78 go,] ~ ∧ F1; ~ ; F2
80 done,] F2; ~ . F1
82 *Exit* Gentleman.] *One half line earlier* F1–2
83–84 I...us.] *One line in* Ff
86 Gentleman,...Lorne,] F2; ~ ∧ ...~ ∧ F1
98 none.——] ~ , ∧ F1–2
103 attempting∧] F2; ~ ; F1
104 *Exit* Longavile] *A half line earlier in* Ff
107 footman;] ~ ∧ F1; ~ , F2
115 you∧] F2; ~ , F1
116 furnisht;] ~ , F1–2
122–124 *Jaques*...wife?] Ff *line* *Jaques*...brusht | And...wife?
123 home.——] ~ ; F1–2
126 Dutches] *Dutches* F1–2
128 me;] ~ ∧ F1–2
133 low.] F2; ~ ∧ F1
134 household;] ~ , F1–2
135 my] F2; My F1
138 mountye——] ~ , F1–2
160 time,] ~ . F1–2
179 it.] ~ , F1–2
183 fortune∧] ~ , F1–2
202–203 Seem...hope——] Ff *line*

Seem...foote, | For...hope—
209 peace,] ~ ∧ F1–2
210–214 Leave...spirit,] Ff *line* Leave...words, | Or...enjoyed, | And...by, | I'le... proceedings; | I...satisfied. | You...fit, | But...spirit,
216–217 No...strength.] *One line in* Ff.
217–219 You...me.] Ff *line* You ...wife; | I...a | Cratchet... me.
220–226 Follow...comfort?] Ff *line* Follow...counsell.—— | I ...Wife. | I...stooles. | No ...not | Stir...life. | I...that | And...comfort?
220 *Jaques*,] F2; *Jaq.* F1
221 counsell.——] ~ , ∧ F1–2
225 I,] F2; ~ ∧ F1
242–243 I...enter.] Ff *line* I... againe.—— | Duchesse... place,—— | And...enter.
242 againe.——] ~ , ∧ F1–2
243 place,——] ~ , ∧ F1–2
252 well.——] ~ ; ∧ F1–2
255 house] F2; honse F1
258 me.] ~ , F1–2
259 King.] ~ ∧ F1; ~ , F2
261 *Jaques*,] F2; *Ja.* F1
267 same,] ~ : F1–2
266 honour. Pronounced] ~ , pronounced F1–2
268 *February*] Feb. F1–2
269 novo.] ~ , F1–2
269 *Duke*] F2; *D.* F1
277 evills.——] ~ , ∧ F1–2
281 commands.——] ~ ; ∧ F1–2
298 steps (that∧] F2; ~ ∧ ~ (F1
302 dye.——] ~ . ∧ F1–2
308–309 Lye...gone.] *One line in* Ff
318 this !] ~ ? F1; ~ : F2

321–326 Looke...true,] Ff *line*
    Looke...rise; | This...it. |
    His...you. | I'le...*Jaques.* |
    Now...true,
322 rise;] ~ , F 1–2
324 again:] ~ , F 1–2
346–348 I...*Shattillion.*] I...duty,
    | Next...you. | I'le...*Shattil-
    lion.*
347–348 rise.——Fetch...chair.
    ——Sit] ~ , ∧ fetch...~ , ∧
    sit F 1–2
348 *Shatillion*] *Shat.* F 1–2
358 then.——] ~ . ∧ F 1–2
374 *Jaques, Jaques,*] F 2; Jaques,
    Jaq. F 1
374 yet?] F 2; ~ , F 1
375 asleep,] ~ ∧ F 1–2
391 Duchesse;] ~ , F 1–2

393 experience,] F 2; ~ ∧ F 1
406–407 Hark...Duke.] *One line in*
    Ff
407–410 Yes...Parliament.] Ff *line*
    Yes...caution, | That...selfe: |
    For...Parliament.
416–418 By...Duke.] Ff *line* By...
    state. | Well then...Duke.
431–434 Tell...own.] Ff *line* Tell
    ...own: | I...been, | Or...
    thing, | But...own.
438 *Lady.*] *Wife. her prefix here and
    at line 444*
445 Yet.——] ~ . ∧ F 1–2
446–448 Now...husbands,] Ff *line*
    Now...wish: | Let...have |
    Dull...husbands,
447 wish:] ~ , F 1–2

HISTORICAL COLLATION

[The following editions are collated: F1 (1647), F2 (1679), L (*Works*, 1711, ed. Gerard Langbaine the Younger), S (*Works*, 1750, ed. Theobald, Seward, and Sympson), C (*Works*, 1778, ed. George Colman the Younger), W (*Works* 1812, ed. Henry Weber), D (*Works*, 1843–6, ed. Alexander Dyce).]

Prologue

6 yeare] years Q49 *Thierry* F2+ (−D)

11 memory...name] memories... names Q49 *Thierry*
12 live] lives C, W, D

I.i

15 Tenants] Tenant's F2, L, S
35 Always] Or alwayes S
39 you] ye F2, L, S
46 preacht] preach F2+(−S)
52 these] those D
74 these pieces] those pieces D
77 lights...makes] light...make F2, S, C, W, D; like...make L
82 faire] faire too S
93 Sir] *om.* F2, L, S
107 will ∧ yet] ∼ , ∼ F2
107 the humour] this humour *or* the humouring S (*conj.*)

112 I,] I ∧ once S
129 you∧] ∼ ? F1–2, L; ∼ , S, C, W
136 wealthy] worthy F2, L, S, C
137 any] any one F2+
146 levied] levell'd S, C, W, D
147 ye] yet L
156 impute] upbraid F2, L
172 know] now C (*conj.*)
173 man] a man F2+
195 not, in] not ∧ in F2+(−D)
205 on't] of it S, C, W

I.ii

0.1 Her Servant] *the Servant* F1–2, L, S; Gentleman C, W; First Gentleman D *throughout the play*
1 hold] hold you S
3 We] Ye L, S, D
17 ye] he F2
22 looks] look F2+
22 upon...but] on...but are S

34 God] *om.* F1–2, L, S; Heaven C, W, D
39 eare] care F1–2, L; ears C, W
54 foole] tool L, S
60 The] 'To L; I'th' S
75 clapt] yclad S (*conj.*), C; and clapt D (*conj.*)
83 taske] taxe F2, L
90 neare] a near S
96 strong] strong'd L

I.iii

16 search it,] search it, search it, C
  (*conj.*)
49 pray] pray you S

78–79 with me | Heav'n save his
  Grace] with me F1–2, L
90 mine, till‸] mine ‸ still, F1

I.iv

12 *Tyrian*] trojan F1
12 sweet] *om.* F1–2, L, S, C; smell
  Seward (*conj.*), W, D
13 hung] flung or fling Seward
  (*conj.*); fling D

22 repriev'd] repriev'd else S (*conj.*)
25 will] can C
26 Has] H' as F2, L, S, D; He has C,
  W
36 her] *om.* C

II.i

8 and] an F1
12 happy] how happy S
36 hither? At] hither at F1–2
59 timely] mighty F2, L, S
60 call up] call F2, L
72 leades me] lead me L, S, D; lead
  W, C
90 idle for] for idle S, C, D
103 *Gentleman.*] *Lady.* C
108 I] that I S, C, W

109 were] are F2, L, S
111 came first] first came W
117 Why] Ay S
127 the full] full F1
130 *Gentleman.*] I *Gent.* F1
131 I am] am F1
133 made] mad F1
177 words] word S+
207 but if they will] if they will but
  (Mason), W, D

II.ii

15 home] whom F1
49 Gentlemen] Gentleman F1+
  (−D)
67 discourse] discovery F1–2, L, S
67 else held] held else S (*conj.*)
69 Have] Having L
87 to me] me L
89 ye] me S
96 and] an C, W, D
99 now he] he now W
114 ambitious] too ambitious S, D

120 commend] recommend S
142 durty] dirt-ty'd S (*conj.*)
156 answer] *om.* F1
162 henceforth] henceforward S
187 this] these S, C, W, D
200 helpt] help F1; help'd F2+
209 Foot, man] Foot-man F1+
  (−D)
216 to kisse] e'en to kiss S
229 you are] you F2

III.i

10 Fleamish] ſleamish F1; Fleemish F2
17 beufe] beef L, C, W; buff S, D
17–18 Is a Duke, | His] Is a Duke‸ |His F1–2 C; Is a Duke's L, S; He's a Duke, | His D

28 O] *om.* S
36 'For me,] 'for me‸ F2, L; For me‸ F1, S; For me, C, W
37 and] and that S
48 you] your C, W
68 up] *om.* F1–2, L, C

III.ii

0.1 Servant] Servants F1–2, L, S; Gentlemen C, W; First Gentleman D
31 stake] wake, F2, L
34 phrases] phrase S, C

54 *Groom.*] *om.* F1+(−D)
64 It] 'Thas S
92 with] *om.* S, C, W
125 of] o'th' S
147 Sir] Sir, I pray, S

III.iii

14 *Sound.*] Sound? F1–2, L, C, W *print as part of the dialogue;* S *conjectures that it is a stage direction; A Flourish* D
14 Give] *Jaques.* Give F1–2, L, S

21 Blesse] Heaven bless S, C
36 ingenious] ingenuous S, C, W
41.1 *fourth*] *a* F1+(−D)
43 faithfully] fairly S (*conj.*), C, W, D

III.iv

1 morn] morning S, C, W
7 mighty! God,] mighty‸ God? F1–2, L, S; ~ ‸ ~ , C
8 top-man] lope-man F1+
42–43 comming. | Go] coming‸ | To F1–2, L, | C
43 post horse] post-horses S, C'
49 good] *om.* F2, L
50 difference] deference S (*conj.*)
61 Is here] He's here L, S, D
65 babl] and babble S
66.1 Her Servant] Servant F1; Lady F2, L, S; Love C, W

86 That] The F2, L
93 I] and I S
98 *Clodion*] *Clodian* F1–2, L; *Clodius* S, C, W
98 *Merov*] *Meron* F1; *Meroveus* F2+
100 will] *om.* S
102 was‸ Sire] was, Sir F1; was, Sire F2
110 seventh] seventy F1
117 the] that the S
129 thy] the F2 +

IV.i

0.1 Cozen.] Cozen *and* F2+
3 *Man.*] Servant. L, S, C; *Anthony* W, D

4 this] these S, D
13 shall] *om.* S
13.1 *Exeunt.*] *om.* F2, L, S

IV.ii

5 Gentlmen] Gentlman F1
7 alove] alone F1–2, L; o' Love S+

26 o'th] i'th' L

IV.iii

6 house] horse F1
7 *Jaques.*] *om.* L
16 businesse] a businesse S, C, W, D
29 Tell] Tell it S
36 innumerall] innumerable F2+
36 to] of S, C, W, D
68 to] *om.* S, C, W
77 house; I hope∧] ~ , ~ , F2; ~ ∧ ~ , F1

85 No] Friend? No S
105 sword] *om.* F1
115 descend] defend F2, L, S, C
119 *Shattillion.*] *om.* F1–2, L
131 joyntes] joins L
137 the] thy F1
178 home] whom F1
180 spied] espied S, C, W; spred D
180 sitting? by this light∧] ~ ∧ ~ ? F1–2, L

IV.iv

11 is't] s't F1
24 to] o' S, C
43 Hate] And hate S
45.2 Maria.] Groom, *and* Maria. D
64 souse] S+; soule F1; feet F2, L
67 best] my best S
68 have you] you have F2, L, S
69 renounc'd] renounce F1
102 Farewell] Fare you well S
111 my] mine L, S

125 much may't do their good] much may do their good F1–2, L; much good may't do their S+
128 Had] Pray had S
135 full ∧ being,] F2; full, being ∧ F1
136 should] would F2, L S
138 made] mads F2
138 I] Now I S
143 I'll not] I F1–2, L

IV.v

5 heate] heats F2, L, S
40 have] or have S
45 you, it all∧] you ∧ all, it F1–2, L; you ∧ all ∧ S, C, W
48 and] as S

58 From this houre I…man] I… man from this houre S
61 thy] my F1+(−D)
68 Speake] Speake, speake S
75 for] from L
77 thankes] our thankes S

V.i

2 and the] the F2, L
47 confesse] do confesse S
55 undoings lyes] undoing lyes C; undoings lie D
56 there] there are L
61 those] these F2, L, S, C, W
68 Extreame] Extreamly S
79 Nor] Or F2+
86 Lorne] lorne F1; *Lorgue* F2, L, S
88 the] *om.* F2, L, S
103 our] your W
104.1 *Man] and* Servant L, S, C; Anthony, Maria *and* Groom W, D
118 laying on] buying one S (*conj.*); laying out Mason (*conj.*), W
125 royall] loyall S (*conj.*)
131 so] as S
133 hot] haut S (*conj.*)
134 down ᴧ my] down, my F2+
136 caroches] croches F1
138 Mountye, mountye...querry] Mountey, mountey...Querry F2, L; Montez, montez... Equerry S, C; Montez, montez ...querry W, D
146 for] for all S
151 proud] proud, proud S
164 Disgraced] Degraded F2+
167 to bring] bring S

170 God's my judge Gentlemen] *om.* F2, L
173 Antony] Here *Anthony* S
200 wave you to conceale] counsel you to wave S (*conj.*)
207 by heaven] *om.* F2, L, S
211 once enjoyed] enjoyed once S
219 Yet] And yet S
229 but] *om.* L, S
241 out a thing] a thing out S
245.1 *Sound Trumpet.*] Sound Trumpet. F1–2, L *print as part of Gentleman's speech*
290 for] for now S
300 doe] *om.* C, W
306 againe.——Servant,] ~ ᴧᴧ ~ . F1; ~ ,ᴧ ~ . F2, L
311 beare] do beare S
333 assures] assigns F1, S
350 pray] pray you S
351 paine] plain W
373 Jaques ᴧ *whistles.*] *Jaques, whistles?* F1–2 *print as part of dialogue*
400 know] now F1+ (−D)
402 such] *om.* S, C
434 art] art now S
436 merry] full merry S
438 say'e] saye F1
449 Learn by] Learn here by S

BEGGARS' BUSH

edited by

FREDSON BOWERS

TEXTUAL INTRODUCTION

Beggars Bush (Greg, no. 643) is twenty-fourth in the list of thirty plays entered 'To Mr Robinson. & M^r. Mozeley' on 4 September (or between 4 and 15 September) 1646 in preparation for the 1647 Folio. In a mass transfer of Beaumont and Fletcher titles from Humphry Robinson to John Martin and Henry Herringman on 30 January 1672/3 it is noted as 'Beggars Bush. halfe'. Finally, on 21 August 1683 it is included in a transfer from the widow of John Martin to Robert Scott.

Theatrical records indicate that it was popular at court. G. E. D. Bentley notes performances on 27 December 1622 at Whitehall; on 30 November it appears in a bill presented by the King's players for court performances in 1630 and 1630/1; on 19 November 1636 it was acted at Hampton Court before the King and Queen; and on 1 January 1638/9 it was billed for playing at court in Richmond on that New Year's Day. *Beggars Bush* was listed on 7 August 1641 among those of the King's Men's plays not to be printed without the company's consent. It was revived after the Restoration, but earlier a droll 'The Lame Common-Wealth' had been made from II.i, which was printed in *The Wits*.

The text is preserved in four early documents: (1) a private-transcript manuscript in the Lambarde volume preserved in the Folger Shakespeare Library;[1] (2) a text in the 1647 Folio; (3) a separate quarto reprint in 1661 (Greg, no. 643[b]*†) from this Folio without authority; (4) a text in the 1679 Folio reprinted from 1647 but with a few alterations that must derive from some authoritative source, probably the ancestor prompt-book. The Lambarde manuscript is in the hand of the scribe who wrote out a manuscript of Suckling's *Aglaura* for presentation to the King shortly before 7 February 1637/8. The manuscripts may be within a year or so in date, for an interest in *Beggars Bush* would have been stimulated by the court performance either of 1636 or of 1639. The recipient is unknown.

---

[1] Permission to collate and to utilize the manuscript for this edition is gratefully acknowledged.

The history of the date and composition of *Beggars Bush* is obscure. It has long been conjectured that more than one hand could be detected in the play. The most careful study, based on the linguistic evidence of contractions and forms like 'ye'–'you', 'hath'–'h'as'–'ha'–'have', and 'doth'–'does', assigns Acts I and V.ii.1–65 to Massinger, Acts II and V.i, ii.65–254 to Beaumont, and Acts III–IV to Fletcher.[1] Although difficulties to be mentioned are present in this assignment, on the whole it may serve as the basis for a working hypothesis.

The date of original composition is uncertain. If Massinger were an original contributor to the play and not a later reviser, the play could well represent Beaumont's last dramatic writing before his retirement and a date of 1612–14 might be assigned when Massinger was beginning to take over as Fletcher's collaborator. Bentley allows only that the play was probably not new when its first recorded performance was given in 1622.[2] On the other hand, if Massinger were a reviser, perhaps for the court performance in 1622, an original Beaumont and Fletcher play could be dated several years earlier. The evidence for the nature of Massinger's participation is conflicting. That the Folio of 1647 was set up from working papers and not from prompt-copy seems to be clear.[3] At one time evidence seemed to accumulate that the Folio printer's copy was a fair transcript made by Massinger, the evidence being the use of full stops for commas in some of the stage-directions in the manner of

[1] Cyrus Hoy, 'The Shares of Fletcher and his Collaborators in the Beaumont and Fletcher Canon (III)', *Studies in Bibliography*, XI (1958), 87–9, 100. The objections of J. H. Dorenkamp (ed.), *Fletcher and Massinger: Beggars Bush* (Mouton, 1967), pp. 33–7, to the presence of Beaumont are vitiated by his attempts to assign Hoy's Beaumont sections to Massinger, a transfer that can scarcely be defended on stylistic or linguistic evidence.

[2] For what it is worth, E. H. C. Oliphant argued that *Beggars Bush* was perhaps a Princess Elizabeth play transferred to the King's Men in 1616: *The Plays of Beaumont and Fletcher* (1927), pp. 257–9.

[3] Much of the evidence for the nature of the copy for the 1647 Folio and its relation to that of the Lambarde manuscript is discussed in detail in Bowers, '*Beggars Bush*: A Reconstructed Prompt-Book and its Copy', *Studies in Bibliography*, XXVII (1974), 113–36, and is only briefly summarized here. One caveat needs to be made, however. In this article I took the evidence of the full stops as demonstrating the fact of a Massingerean fair copy. For reasons given below, it now seems to me that the case is moot, and that these stops are an idiosyncrasy of the Compositor *B* who set this section of the Folio is as probable as that they reflect the printer's copy.

Massinger's holograph *Believe as You List.*[1] On the other hand, the fact that with only one exception these stops appear solely in the work of Compositor *B* gives one pause,[2] for whereas one could argue in *Beggars Bush* that *B* sporadically followed copy but *A* did not, the use of full stops is not confined to this one play. Compositors *A* and *B* appear throughout section 2 of the Folio, printed by W. Wilson, consisting of *The Custom of the Country, The Noble Gentleman, The Captain, Beggars Bush, The Coxcomb,* and *The False One.* In *The Custom of the Country* full stops appear in eleven stage-directions set by *B*, five times in *The Noble Gentleman,* once, possibly twice, in *The Captain,* four times in *The Coxcomb.* In *The Custom of the Country* Compositor *B* set these full stops often when Massinger's part was his copy but four times in Fletcher's part, whereas it is striking that in *Beggars Bush* these stops never appear in Massinger's share but once in Beaumont's and the rest in Fletcher's. Massinger is supposed to have had no share in *The Coxcomb* and his presence cannot be shown in *The Noble Gentleman.* Compositor *A* set a full stop in Massinger's part in *The False One,* but this may be an example of foul case. In short, if full stops in *B*'s typesetting are supposed to show Massinger's copy, whether his own composition or transcription, the evidence is against their presence in the copy and in favor of them, erratic as they are, as a trait of *B*'s. It is also curious that such full stops appear with some frequency in another section of the Folio by a different printer, in *The Mad Lover,* a straight Fletcher play seemingly printed from prompt-copy as a basis, where once more Massinger's hand would be difficult to trace. The anomaly in *Beggars Bush* is particularly marked in that the full stops do not appear in what seems to be typesetting from Massinger's own manuscript but instead chiefly in Fletcher's share, where the predominance of Fletcher's linguistic

---

[1] This evidence was first noticed by W. J. Lawrence, *Those Nutcracking Elizabethans* (1935), pp. 194ff. and was accepted by R. C. Bald in his *Bibliographical Studies in the Beaumont and Fletcher Folio of 1647* (1938), pp. 62–4.

[2] In Compositor *A*'s stint a full stop creeps in at III.i.61.1 in the direction '*Enter Prig. and Ferret.*' The first time that *B* sets a direction with full stops, at II.iii.0.1, he sets a full stop after *Enter* in the manner of Massinger, but otherwise the full stops are set only after names. The stopped directions in *B* occur at II.iii.0.1; III.iv.0.1, 97.1; IV.i.0.1, 41.1; IV.iii.0.1; V.i.98.1. In the direction at IV.i.0.1 one full stop appears among three commas.

characteristics would argue more for his own working papers than for a fair copy by Massinger. Thus despite *B*'s use once or twice in Wilson's section of a full stop in the Massingerean manner after *Enter*, and the difficulty of finding a rationale for his uneven use after names except the sporadic influence of copy, the linguistic evidence is against any hypothesis that the 1647 Folio was set from a fair copy made by Massinger instead of from the authors' own working papers: the appearance of full stops in section 2 thus seems to be compositorial.[1]

The appearance in the Lambarde manuscript of a number of prompter's added directions not found in the Folio[2] establishes without question that this manuscript was copied from a prompt-book. In turn, the various examples of common errors seem to establish that the prompt-book so copied had itself been made up directly from the very manuscript (conjecturally the authors' working papers) that was later to serve as printer's copy for the 1647 Folio.[3] It is an oddity, however, that the prompt-book does not seem to have been the original, given a date for the play as no later than 1612–14, if Beaumont's hand is indeed to be found in Act II and perhaps in Act V. The late R. C. Bald (*Bibliographical Studies*, pp. 62–4) remarked the liberal use of colons to punctuate

---

[1] Little or no evidence in this matter can be adduced from the Lambarde manuscript, the more especially since Knight's colons would have had a tendency to blot out any Massingerean full stops; and indeed the scribe of the MS often interposed his own commas instead of the colons presumed to have been present in his copy. For what it is worth, however, in Massinger's I.ii.0.1 a colon after 'Woolfort' is followed by what may be a full stop after 'Hubert', although a truncated comma is not an impossibility. In Fletcher's II.i.0.1 'Higgen' and 'Snap' are followed by colons and 'Ferret', 'Clause', 'Jaculine', and 'Gincks' by commas; but what looks very like a full stop comes after 'Prigg'. This slim evidence, if evidence it is, is certainly insufficient to support any conjecture that in these two isolated directions a Massingerean full stop has slipped past both Knight and the scribe of the manuscript.

[2] See Bowers, '*Beggars Bush*', pp. 120ff. For example, MS copies to the left of the opening direction for II.iii '*Table out:*'; as part of the centered direction for III.i MS adds '*A table kans, and stooles sett out*'; at IV.iii.14 MS adds to the right, braced, '*Drum, flourish | Peeces discharg | Enter saylors*'.

[3] The links between the copy for F1 and that for MS are discussed *ibid.*, pp. 115ff. One further interesting example may be added, where in II.ii.5–6 both F1 and MS agree in the faulty punctuation after 'thinke' and 'ships' in reading 'What should I thinke unlesse the Seas, and Sandes | Had swallow'd up my ships?' The correct reading must be 'What should I thinke? unlesse the Seas, and Sandes | Had swallow'd up my ships, or fire had spoyl'd | My ware-houses...'

stage-directions in the Lambarde manuscript and suggested that this idiosyncrasy betrayed in the prompt-book from which the manuscript had been copied the hand of the same scribe (whom he called 'Jhon') who wrote out the manuscript of *The Honest Mans Fortune* and who annotated Massinger's manuscript of *Believe as You List* to make it into prompt-copy. This scribe is now recognized as Edward Knight, who had connections with the King's Men in 1616 and is known in the early 1630s, and probably before, to have been their book-keeper. Indeed, since he heads the list of attendants of the King's Men in Herbert's protection order of 27 December 1624, the year of the copy of *The Honest Mans Fortune*, he may have been the book-keeper at this date and even earlier. However, it would seem an impossibility for him to have been in a position to transcribe the prompt-book of *Beggars Bush* in 1612–14, and it is tempting to speculate that he made up the book behind the Lambarde manuscript of *Beggars Bush* for a revival of the play at court on 27 December 1622. If this is so, one would need to assume that he went back to the preserved authorial working papers since the original prompt-book had been lost, and that the frequently casual treatment he gave to distinct anomalies in the text (as well as to erroneous stage-directions that should have revealed themselves in the acting) resulted because only the single performance was planned.[1] Of course, it may be impossible to pinpoint the writing of the second book so precisely, for a new book might have been needed for the performance at court in 1630 or 1631, or even for that in November 1636. All one can say with certainty is that the Lambarde manuscript (if it is to be dated near 1637–8) reflects the prompt-book used in the court performance on 19 November 1636.[2]

[1] For the details of his treatment of the working papers, see *ibid.*, pp. 118–23, 134–5.

[2] It would be idle speculation, quite without evidence of any weight, that Massinger appears as a collaborator because in 1622 he was called in to revise the play and that he rewrote the first act and added the exposition in V.ii.1–65 about Florez' past history narrated by Gerrard. It is true that his sudden interposition here, and for such lines, is a little odd; but if he had surveyed the original play when the various papers were assembled he could have inserted the lines then, even though they clash in the time these events would have needed with what he had written about the chronology of antecedent action in Act I. For an analysis of the highly irregular double time scheme of the play, and the futile efforts Knight made to improve it, see *ibid.*, pp. 125, 133–4.

Several disruptions in the text occur, most being readily ex-
plicable. At least two additions were made to the original papers
after they had been inscribed. The first of these occurs at III.iv.130
and concerns the position of Higgen's canting speech to Hubert. In
the Lambarde manuscript all is in order. The disguised Hubert
makes his offer to serve the beggars and is accepted by Gerrard
(lines 119–20), who orders the beggars to welcome him. Higgen
takes the duty upon himself, greets Hubert, and then at line 129 is
told by Gerrard, 'Now sweare him', after which appears the canting
oath (lines 130–142),[1] ending 'Y'are wellcome Brother' (line 143).
In F, on the other hand, Gerrard's 'Now sweare him' is followed by
line 143 'You are welcom Brother', after which comes the dialogue
of lines 144–56 including Hemskirk's being placed in Hubert's
charge. Immediately after the part-line 156 (Hubert's 'And ye play
tricks with me') occurs repeated line 129 'Now sweare him',
followed by the oath, after which the text picks up again with the
second half of line 156 (Gerrard's 'So, now come in'). Two points
are of concern: first, material of a special interest – the canting
oath – is misplaced in F; second, the misplaced oath is prefaced by
the cue-line of the text, repeated, Gerrard's 'Now sweare him.'
What seems to have happened is that the oath, an addition, was
written on a separate piece of paper with the cue-line 'Gerrard. Now
sweare him' prefixed as a key to its placement, but the position was
mistaken by the F compositor. It is worth notice that the 1679
Folio, set from 1647 but with some reference to theatrical copy,
places the oath correctly as in MS.

The second case is more difficult to assess. In MS at V.i.71.1
Bertha makes her entrance, is captured, and after Hemskirk and
Wolfort have congratulated themselves on discovering her,
Hubert hollos within as he approaches for the meeting. At this
point in MS Bertha speaks three lines (lines 84–6):

> *Ber.*   O I am miserablie lost, thus faln
>   into myne uncles hands from all my hopes
>   can I not thinke away my selfe, and die?

---

[1] It is noteworthy that in MS this oath is transcribed in an Italian hand like the
songs, with which it is perhaps confused.

after which Hubert enters with the disguised beggars. In F, on the other hand, the three lines of speech (84–6) are followed by a repetition of the first two lines with different spelling:

> *Ber.*   O I am miserably lost, thus falne
> Into my uncles hands from all my hopes,
> Can I not thinke away my selfe and dye?
> O I am miserably lost; thus fallen
> Into my Uncles hands, from all my hopes:

Then comes a continuation of her lamenting speech for twelve lines (86–97), absent in MS, before she concludes with a repetition of the third line of the MS speech,

> Can I not thinke away my selfe and dye?

after which Hubert and the beggars enter.

Once again the repetition of what appear to be the lines that key the speech in its proper place indicates that Bertha's brief three lines in the original manuscript were expanded by a dozen additional ones written on a separate sheet of paper with the cue. In this case, however, whether by accident or design, the prompt-book omitted these lines (followed again by 1679 in its treatment). Whether Knight overlooked the separate piece of paper on which they were written, or whether he rejected the expansion of the speech is not to be demonstrated. The point is that the omission of these lines in MS is not a theatrical cut of original material but either a cut or an error in treating an added passage.

Another difference between the two texts comes at III.i.42, where in F the MS song about the devil is omitted although the lines leading to it are preserved:

> *Hig.*   Will you heare a Song how the Divel was gelded?
> *3. Bo.*   I, I, lets heare the Divell roare, Sow-gelder.

These lines are followed not by the song but by the resumption of the dialogue after it at line 60. Although there is a good possibility that the indecency of the song led to its omission in the printing of F, the use in MS of an Italian hand for the song, as for the added canting oath, could suggest the contrary possibility – even though slight – that the play's songs were inserted in the original papers, written on separate sheets, the sheet for the devil-gelding song having been lost after transcription into the prompt-book.[1]

The Folio omits almost nothing from the MS text. The loss of Higgen's half-line 'I thanke your worshipps' at III.i.61 is certainly accidental. The omission at III.i.19 of 'Shees vengeance ranck o'th Man' in F, coming after 'Canst tell me a way now, how to cut off my wives Concupiscence?' is uncertain whether simply the dropping of the last line of a speech by accident or else an act of censorship. No very serious formal censorship of oaths is evident in either text, both of which join without variation in the usual quotas of *by the mass*, *slid*, and *faith*. On the other hand, at III.i.131 and 132 F prints dashes to substitute for some indecency in the speech of the Second Boor. It seems possible that these dashes are not independent F censorship but instead the representation of dashes found in the original manuscript, as indicated by the mildness of the MS substitutes, which in the first instance has 'Plague' and in the second, 'Pox'. Since one cannot imagine anybody deleting 'plague', or possibly 'pox', by a dash, it is reasonable to conjecture that Knight added what he thought was acceptable for the dashes he found in his copy. If so, it is likely some overseer substituted the dashes for an indecency he found in Fletcher's original text. When F has Hubert harangue Wolfort as 'A Prince, in nothing but your princely lusts' where MS has 'beastlie lusts', censorship may have operated although compositorial memorial contamination is as possible as compositorial censorship. Only one other possible case of censorship occurs – this in MS – where the line 'No impositions, taxes, grievances' (II.i.105) is omitted. This line might be taken as reflecting on the King; but another explanation for its omission is possible (see below).

In contrast to F, MS omits a number of lines. Various of these are cases of eyeskip, presumably by the MS scribe, such as the omission of 'to beleeve...dangerous' at I.ii.57–8, the half-line 'he...pur-veyers' (II.i.120), and the last line of two speeches (II.iii.18; IV.vi.72), 'It is not...from' (V.ii.89), and 'I speake...*Hemskirck*'

---

[1] Against such a hypothesis, however, is not only the specific reference in this case to the subject of the song, but also the case at III.i.96.1 in which the title 'Song' as a heading has been confused in F as part of the stage-direction, '*and a boy singing the Song*'.

(V.ii.133). Knight seems to have started by cutting what he considered to be repetitious parts of speeches. For instance, at I.ii.11–17 he may have felt that the sentiments in 'Who ever...prayers with' did not need the elaboration given them and removed the text as found in F. Similarly, later in the same scene he cut 'Despise them not...actions' in F I.ii.108–14 perhaps because he found the hypocrisy was too blatant for Hubert to have swallowed. These are the only clearcut examples of Knight's editing by deletion, and it would seem that he soon gave up his initial intention to tighten the dialogue by excisions. Two other cases seem to represent Knight's omissions but for other reasons. The first is the omission of the single line 'No...grievances' mentioned above as a possible case of censorship. However, if F's reading 'On', which needs emendation to 'No', stood in the copy by mistake, it may have been that Knight simply omitted the line when he could make no sense of it. This is the more possible as an explanation, because something of the same sort seems to have occurred at IV.vi.9–12 in the omission in MS of '*1. Merchant.* No doubt on't... *Vanlock.*' Here there was no reason to delete these lines, which in fact are useful to introduce a new character just making his entrance. However, signs of textual disruption in F suggest that the copy was not clear to Knight. F here omits the speech-prefix '*2. Merchant.*' present in MS for the first half of line 9 and prints as a separate line without speech-prefix what should have been the 1. Merchant's response (cut in MS) which started by completing line 9, followed by the remaining lines of the response. This double omission of speech-prefixes in F, connected with a passage omitted from MS, suggests a simple cut when Knight could not reconcile the text with the single prefix that was perhaps the only one present in his copy. The third example at IV.i.29–32 consisting of Florez' entire speech 'Is my misery...reproaches?' appears to have no reason behind its omission from MS. It usefully comes between two speeches to him by the Merchants and is not repetitious. That it was deliberately cut by Knight for such reasons as had moved him to cut in I.ii is difficult to believe. Whether there was some unknown form of textual disruption that caused him to omit it, or whether it was left out by mistake either by Knight or the scribe of MS is not to be known. This account of Knight's small attention to questions of text with especial reference to shortening the play, suggests that he omitted Bertha's expanded speech in V.i.86–97 more because he did not have the separate sheet of paper on which it was written than because he cut the passage. However, the case is uncertain.

On the whole the Folio speech-prefixes seem to be generally accurate. The difficulty due to copy in IV.vi.9–12 is repeated only a few lines later (although in this case not corrected by Knight) in the double error in F and MS of the prefix *3. Merchant* at IV.vi.17, which conflicts with the opening entrance direction specifying two Merchants. At II.i.194 F's assignment of the first stuttering speech to Higgen may just possibly be right if he immediately exits, for it would then be the change from his normal speech to the stutter that provoked Hubert's 'Slid they did all speak plain ev'n now me thought.' But since after this remark he addresses Snap, continuing, 'Do'st thou know this same Maid?', the MS assignment of line 194 to *Snap*, the only known stutterer, is very likely correct, and Hubert's wonder at the stuttering is natural enough if Snap answers. The correctness of F is not certain in several more cases of doubt. At III.i.95, 96 a pair of related variants appears, suggesting in itself more Knight's intervention than F's error, although the compositor may have overlooked the copy prefixes in this series of short speeches. At any rate, whether all the boors chorus in lines 94–5 'I, take it, take it, | And take some drinke too', or whether it is the second boor who adds 'And take some drinke too' as in MS, is uncertain. It is correspondingly uncertain whether in lines 95–6 it is Prig who has the whole speech in response 'Not a drop now | I thanke you; away, we are discover'd else', the latter an aside to Higgen, or whether as in MS it is Prig who answers the boor and Higgen who speaks the closing half-line to Prig as an aside. One would be inclined to rely on the aptness of the MS ascriptions and to treat the F assignments as oversights (difficult as double error may be here) were it not for a single clearcut case of Knight's sophistication of the text, encouraging a hypothesis for his intervention here. This sophistication comes in an entrance direction at V.ii.109.1 in F, which follows Gerrard's 'Insolent Devill!' addressed to Wolfort: he entrance is moved up a line so that Costin, who would be otherwise mute in this scene (and in the play), is given the ejaculation as his entrance line that should obviously be assigned to Gerrard. An earlier difference in speech-prefixes in this scene, the omission of Florez' prefix before 'Is this that Traitor *Woolfort?*' in line 73, seems to be a simple error in MS, not an attempt to assign Florez' line to the previous speaker Gerrard. In other differences, MS is pretty clearly wrong. In III.iv.5–6 the error involves giving Prig the last line of Higgen's speech by raising his prefix one line, doubtless a mechanical error perhaps by the MS scribe. At III.i.16 F's *1. B.* is correct and MS *3. Boor* in error as shown by the context before and the song. It is unlikely at III.i.68 that MS *1. 2. 3. Boors* for F *1. 2. B.* is correct, for all other choruses from the three are prefixed by *All Boors.* The omission of Higgen's prefix at III.iv.39 in MS is a simple error, whether Knight's or the scribe's, apparently caused by confusion between his speech beginning 'Brother' and Prig's preceding 'A shrew'd point Brother' as if 'Brother' had been repeated by the same speaker.

With the exception of the deliberate alteration in the position of the entrance direction at V.ii.109.1 already noted in order to transfer Gerrard's line to Costin, there is no indication that Knight altered the position of his copy's directions. However, the varying treatment given entrance directions by the MS scribe, sometimes centering them in a large hand, and at other times squeezing them in on a text line, indicates that as in *Believe as You List* Knight had placed some of the original centered directions in the margin. The position the MS scribe chose for them gives no indication that Knight had made them at all anticipatory.

Fletcher's Act III contains no more than the usual transmissional variation between MS and F, nor is there anything exceptional found in IV.i–ii. However, in IV.iii beginning at least as early as Van-dunck's speech at line 41, and perhaps a few lines earlier, abnormal substantive differences begin between the two texts in which, in general, the MS readings seem to be the superior although previously the F readings had ordinarily been preferable. These variants continue to the end of the scene and carry over into scene iv for at least the first twenty-two lines. This unique patch of serious variation constitutes a difficult problem, especially since any theory of revision behind the copy for MS causes more difficulties than it solves, and the nature of any hypothesized revision is as puzzling as its sudden beginning and ending. The dilemma appears to be solvable by bibliographical evidence, even though conjecturally applied. Scene iii of Act IV heads the first column on sig. Mm1; scene iv begins halfway down on the second column. The patch of variants, therefore, is confined to this bibliographical unit of the page set by Compositor B. After line 22 of scene iv Compositor A takes over on sig. Mm1^v, and the variants revert to normal with the preponderance of authority in F. Quire Mm was set, as usual, from the inside out divided between the two compositors. Thus typesetting for this gathering started (not necessarily at the same time) with Compositor A setting Mm2^v and B setting Mm3. Compositor A then moved backward, setting Mm2, column a and Mm1^v, while B (after setting Mm2, column b) moved forward, setting the complementary pages Mm3^v and Mm4. The play ends with twenty-seven lines of text on sig. Mm4^v set by B; but instead of A setting its forme-page Mm1, we find that B was the workman. In order to keep up with the press, therefore, B had to set the part-page Mm4^v and then the whole of Mm1, presumably in the time usually allotted for only one page. Thus one may conjecture that the unsatisfactory nature of the text on sig. Mm1 in scene iii and the start of iv resulted from this haste. Some corroboration may be found in the similar state of Mm4^v. Throughout V.ii when B is setting normally as A's partner, only the usual variants are present in the two texts up to the foot of sig. Mm4, or V.ii.234, and the F readings seem in general to be preferable. But beginning with line 241 on sig. Mm4^v, where B would have been aware that his time was limited, the proportion of corrupt F readings rises, with 'good' in F for MS 'gold' (line 241), 'nor' for 'and' (line 241), the omission of 'get' (line 243), the misreading 'Drunkards' for 'Drinkers' (line 246), the omission of 'And' (line 248), and the curious corruption 'Midwives' for MS 'widdowes' (line 249).[1] The corruption in-

---

[1] As against this list F is to be preferred to MS in the first few lines of the page with F 'ne'er' omitted in MS (line 238), F 'nor' for 'or' (line 240), and 'Gentlemen' for the curious MS false start 'wa'. After line 241 F seems correct in the plural 'Lawyers' for the MS singular (line 244), in printing 'of' omitted by MS (line 248), and in the plural 'we' for MS 'I' (line 252).

creases when *B* goes on to complete the forme with page Mm1.

The spelling of the names seems to differ both in MS and in F in considerable part by authors but also in F in part by compositors; very likely in MS both Knight and the scribe have worn away some of the original distinctions. So far as the MS is concerned, the spelling *Florez* is found only in Fletcher's Acts III and IV, where it is consistent. On the other hand the spelling *Floriz* is consistent in Acts I, II, and part of Act V (namely, at V.i.126, ii.o.1, and ii.71), whereas at V.ii.53, 85, 112, 115 the variant *Floris* is found. In F the spelling is almost wholly compositorial. *Floriz* is normal for Compositor *B* except for a curious patch of five *Florez* spellings on Mm3ᵛ in V.ii (V.ii.53, 71, 85, 112, 115), all of which are *Floris* in MS except for MS *Floriz* at V.ii.71. The first of these variants at V.ii.53 is in the Massinger passage but the rest in the work of the third playwright, assigned by Hoy as Beaumont. Actually, the *Floris* spellings must have started earlier in Act V than is indicated in MS, for at V.i.78, 126 Compositor *B* of F spells *Floris* (where MS is *Floriz*) although *Floriz* on the same Folio page occurs also at V.i.124 and V.ii.o.1.

The spelling *Hemskirk* occurs in MS in Acts I.ii; II.iii; III.ii, iii, iv; and V.i, ii. The variant *Hemskirke* although it appears once in MS in II.iii, iv; III.i; and IV.iv, clusters in Act V, both scenes, where it comes a few more times than the standard *Hemskirk*. The MS contains no other form. In the Folio Compositor *A* prefers *Hemskirke* but sets *Hemskirk* once. Compositor *B* allows *Hemskirk* once on Ll3ᵛ, but, curiously, on sig. Mm3ᵛ (already unusual for *B*'s *Florez* spellings) he sets *Hemskirk* once and *Hemskirke* five times, these contrasting with his invariable *Hemskirck* elsewhere. Not much can be told about *Woolfort*, the predominant form, versus the minority *Wolfort*, except that after only one appearance of *Wolfort* in I.i.15 and two in II.iii, MS spells the name *Woolfort* but beginning with V.ii.46 no less than ten *Wolfort* forms occur. In MS *Jaqueline* appears in I.ii and in V.ii, as against *Jaculin* once each in IV.ii and V.i, and *Jaculine* in II.i (twice) and IV.ii (once). This distinction is observed in the Folio except that *Jaculin* in MS is invariably *Jaculine* in F. *Vandunck* is the most common form in

MS in II.iii; IV.iii, v, vi; and V.ii, but it is hyphenated *Van-dunck* also in II.iii; IV.v; V.ii. The variant *Van-dunke* occurs only once, in II.iii. The Folio usually hyphenates the name but varies between *Van-dunck* and *Van-donck*. The spelling of Gertrude's name in the Folio is more variable than in the MS. In III.v.7, 23, 43 (Compositor *B*) she is *Jertred* and at III.v.33 *Gertred*, but *Gertrude* in MS. At II.iii.145 (Compositor *A*) she is *Gertrude* as in MS. Finally, in V.ii.88, 93 she is *Gertrude* but *Gertrud* in V.ii.77; MS has *Gertrude* throughout.

Dr Cyrus Hoy's analysis of the linguistic characteristics of *Beggars Bush* appears to be incontrovertible in assigning Acts III and IV to Fletcher as well as Act I and V.ii.1–65 to Massinger. The hypothesis that Beaumont wrote Act II and all of Act V except V.ii.1–65 is less certain, in some part because of the notorious difficulty of establishing Beaumont's linguistic characteristics and in some part because of the contrary evidence for the spelling of names in different ways that seems established in the original copy both for F and for MS in Act V. Yet a third hand does seem to appear in the play, one that differentiates itself from Massinger's Act I by its occasional use of 'ha" for 'have', and its admission of 'i'th(e)' and 'o'th(e)', all of which are wanting in Act I but present both in Acts II and V. These acts also contain a larger number of 'ye' forms for 'you' than Massinger favored. The problem, then, is in part whether the variants in the spellings of the names of the characters between Acts II and V is compatible with the general agreement of the linguistic evidence that the same author wrote both acts, and if so whether Beaumont is the author of both, or whether one must posit the appearance of four authors, one of whom is presumably Beaumont but the other unidentifiable. The case is complicated by doubts whether the authorial working papers that lie at the back of both the Folio and the Lambarde manuscript, although at different removes, represent the original play or the original play with some revision by another hand, possibly by Massinger. That is, so far as is known Beaumont retired as a dramatist in 1612 but Massinger did not begin to collaborate with Fletcher in original work until 1613–14.

The answer to these difficulties can be only speculative. The question of date may cause the least problem since Massinger may have joined Fletcher earlier than usually supposed, or Beaumont may have written later. Dr Hoy remains firm in his conviction that Beaumont wrote both Acts II and V, and the present editor is inclined to accept his peculiar expertise in this matter. Very conjecturally, however, the evidence of the names does suggest that if Beaumont is indeed the author of both acts, or if any other dramatist wrote both, either Act II or Act V must represent a fair copy by some other hand in order to explain the curious discrepancy in names. Since Massinger is known to have supplied (or to have rewritten) V.ii.1–65, he would be the natural candidate to have copied over the rest of the act, probably with some changes. But the forms of the names do not agree with those in Act I. No definite pronouncement can be made, but the tentative suggestion may be offered that on the evidence of Massinger's interposition in Act V he may have done some further working over of Beaumont's text of this act, sufficient to call for a scribal fair copy before the play was given to the company.

The status of the text of the Second Folio of 1679 presents another problem. Despite Sir Walter Greg's hurried estimate that the variation between F1 and F2 indicates that 1679 was set from an independent manuscript (*Bibliography*, II, 773), the facts are otherwise and the bibliographical links deriving from the characteristics of F1's Compositors *A* and *B* as reflected in F2 effectively demonstrate that the printer's copy for 1679 was an example of the 1647 Folio, although one that had been annotated occasionally by reference to some other source. In the preliminary statement of the 'Book-sellers to the Reader' the 1679 Folio asserts that

...to make a Second Impression, we were very desirous they might come forth as Correct as might be. And we were opportunely informed of a Copy which an ingenious and worthy Gentleman had taken pains (or rather the pleasure) to read over; wherein he had all along Corrected several faults (some very gross) which had crept in by the frequent imprinting of them. His Corrections were the more valued because he had an intimacy with both our Authors, and had been a Spectator of most of them when they were Acted in their life-time.

The language here implies that this corrected copy of the 1647 Folio had no more authority than the private knowledge of the

gentleman who had annotated it. Various of the Beaumont and
Fletcher plays illustrate this truth by the identification of the 1679
variants merely as educated guesses as to the meaning. A certain
number of such variant readings are also present in *Beggars Bush*,
very likely mixed in with compositorial sophistications; nevertheless, some appear to indicate that the gentleman in this case had had
access to the prompt-book itself and had made a hurried and incomplete collation of it with his copy. The prime evidence of this
consultation of the prompt-book is the manner in which F2 removes
the dozen lines of Bertha's speech in V.i wanting in the Lambarde
manuscript but present in F1.[1] On the other hand, the song of the
gelding of the devil in III.i is supplied although wanting in F1; the
song's text in F2, however, differs from that in MS in various
readings and seems to have been affected by some other tradition
although not one represented by the known separate texts. Yet, like
MS, it appears in a three-stanza form instead of the five-stanza
version of the popular tradition.

The gentleman seems to have made at least a partial collation of
the text since an occasional reading in which F2 follows MS as
against F1 seems to go beyond the realm of guesswork, such as
MS/F2 'haunch' for F1 'ham' at V.i.29, or the appearance of
'strange' at V.i.36 omitted in F1. Unique F2 variants like 'home'
for MS/F1 'him' (I.iii.48), 'calling' for 'call' (II.i.50), or 'practise'
for 'learne' (III.iv.127) seem to be sophistications, whether by the
annotator or the F2 compositor; others are clearly wrong, like F2
'here' for F1 'ye are' (MS 'yeare') at IV.iii.35. The origin of other
F2 readings is obscure. F2 agreement with MS in 'torne' versus
F1 'true' (II.i.134) may or may not represent more than intelligent
emendation, nor is MS/F2 'he' for F1 'she' at II.i.199, 'lost' for
'toss'd' (III.ii.16), or even 'blister'd' for 'baster'd' (IV.v.45)
necessarily the result of collation with authority. Such a reading as
F2 'bread' for MS 'breed' and F1 'end' in context may represent
only a good guess. No case exists where with any certainty F2 can
be said to copy a reading in the prompt-book later than the stage at
which it was transcribed for the Lambarde manuscript, or to own a

[1] The lines in I.i removed in the MS but present in F1 are repeated in F2, however,
and other MS lacunae are not observed.

reading in a positively authoritative purer state against MS/F1 agreement.[1] On the whole, the authority of the F2 variants is usually suspect, but enough genuine cases of MS/F2 agreement against F1 exist to indicate something other than intelligent guesswork. Thus F2/MS agreements against F1 must be taken seriously as at the minimum establishing the prompt-book reading, which would be authoritative if there is reason to suspect corruption in F1. The addition of several stage-directions, especially the reference to the wounding of Hemskirk by Florez (II.iii.137.1), seems to be drawn from the prompt-book although omitted by the scribe of the Lambarde manuscript.

As F1 is taken to derive immediately from the authorial manuscripts whereas the Lambarde manuscript derives from these papers through the intermediary transcription of the prompt-book, the 1647 Folio is the proper copy-text to select since in its transmission of the accidentals, at least, it is one step nearer to authority. On the other hand, the compositors of F1 seem to have been hurried in their work, and under pressure they not only misread their copy but on a number of occasions guessed at the meanings or substituted unauthoritative words when their overloaded memory failed. The level of accuracy is by no means reassuring. Under these circumstances the Lambarde manuscript must be elevated for the substantives to the position of an equal authority and can be freely drawn on to correct the supposed compositorial errors of F1. In this process of the selection of readings from the two radiating authorities no substitute exists for critically eclectic editing that takes into account on the one hand the observable levels of error of the two different compositors and on the other hand the opportunities for unauthoritative variation in the double transcription of MS. On a few occasions the suspect authority of F2 may prove decisive when it agrees with MS against F1. (Agreement of F2 with F1 is, of course, no guarantee of correctness, since F2 is not

---

[1] F2 'honour' at II.iii.109 for MS/F1 'errour' is tempting but likely a sophistication, as is the F2 addition 'Brother, I pray lead, You must, you must, Brother' (III.iv.161 +) although this last is less certain. The close pairing of F2 'shift' for MS/F1 'change' and of 'hide' for 'soule' at IV.v.47, 49 is curious because they are unnecessary changes, followed in line 56 by the characteristic 'horrible' for MS/F1 'monstrous', this latter, however, a clearer sophistication.

throughout an independent radiating authority as is MS.) Given the facts of transmission and the problem of working with radiating texts from a lost original, editorial judgment can be devoted only to an attempt by selection to recover as many substantives of the underlying authorial papers as seems possible on the bibliographical and stylistic evidence.

In the text and stage-directions the spelling of the names in the F1 copy-text has been retained because of the difficulty of determining in some cases the actual forms of the different authors, which on the evidence certainly varied within themselves. However, for uniformity arbitrary selections for the abbreviated speech-prefixes have been made. The standard spelling *Floriz* has been adopted since it bridges the work of two authors in Acts I, II, and V, and is in part confirmed by the Act V variant *Floris*. Similarly, *Hemskirk* on the total evidence seems more authoritative than the other forms, as do *Woolfort*, *Jaqueline*, and *Van-dunck*. In the text the treatment of 'ye'–'you' has had to be somewhat arbitrary owing to the conflicting evidence of F1 and MS and the problems in each document arising from contamination. However, any change from the copy-text has been recorded as an emendation, and all rejected variants in the early editions have been noted in the historical collation. On the other hand, it was found to be impracticable and of insufficient value to record variants in these two forms found in later edited texts.

The F1 text is badly typeset, with a number of literals that were never corrected. Indeed, nothing that can be called formal press-correction appears in the large number of collated copies although some exhibit different stages of types that did not ink, were pulled, or just possibly were raised or replaced by the pressmen. The modern editions collated are noticed in the headnote to the historical collation. Only the Dorenkamp edition of 1967 has been able, like the present edition, to avail itself of the Lambarde manuscript authority; the present edition, however, makes more extensive use of the manuscript readings and suggests a different hypothesis for the textual transmission.

The following is a breakdown of the F1 copy-text typesetting by compositors.

COMPOSITOR A: I.iii.11–II.ii.182; II.iii.31(|And)–III.ii.76; IV.iv.
23–IV.v.49; IV.v.50–IV.vi.30 (doubtful); IV.vi.78–V.i.66.
COMPOSITOR B: I.i.0.1–I.iii.10; II.ii.183–II.iii.31(still.|); III.ii.77–
IV.iv.22; IV.vi.31–77 (doubtful); V.i.67–V.ii.254.

[Dramatis Personæ

Wolfort, an usurper of the Earldom of Flanders
Gerrard, falsely called Clause, King of the Beggars, Father in Law to Florez
Hubert, an honest Lord, a friend to Gerrard
Florez, falsely called Goswin, a rich Merchant of Bruges
Hemskirk, a Captain under Wolfort
Herman, a Courtier ⎱ inhabitants of Flanders
A Merchant ⎰
Van-dunck, a drunken Burgomaster and Merchant friend to Gerrard, falsely called Father to Bertha
Van-lock, and ⎱ of Bruges
Four Merchants ⎰
Higgen, ⎱
Prig, ⎬ Three Knavish Beggars
Snap ⎰
Ferret ⎱ Two Gentlemen disguised under the names of Gerrard's
Ginks ⎰ party
Boors
Servants
Soldiers
A Sailor

Jaqueline, Daughter to Gerrard, beloved of Hubert, falsely called Minch
Bertha, called Gertrude, Daughter to the Duke of Brabant, Mistress to Florez
Margaret, Wife to Van-dunck
Mistress Frances, a frow, Daughter to Van-lock

The Scene Flanders.]

BEGGARS BUSH

Enter a Merchant, and Herman.

Merchant. Is he then taken?

Herman.   And brought back even now sir.

Merchant. He was not in disgrace?

Herman.   No man more lov'd,
Nor more deserv'd it, being the onely man
That durst be honest in this Court.

Merchant.   Indeed?
We have heard abroad sir, that the State hath suffered
A great change, since the countesse death.

Herman.   It hath sir.

Merchant. My ten yeares absence, hath kept me a stranger
So much to all the occurrents of my Country,
As you shall bind me for some short relation
To make me understand the present times.   10

Herman. I must begin then with a war was made
And seven yeares with all cruelty continued
Upon our *Flanders* by the Duke of *Brabant*,
The cause grew thus: during our Earles minority,
Woolfort, (who now usurps) was employed thither
To treat about a match betweene our Earle
And the daughter and Heire of *Brabant*: during which treaty
The *Brabander* pretends, this daughter was
Stolne from his Court, by practice of our State,
Though we are all confirm'd, 'twas a sought quarrell   20
To lay an unjust gripe upon this Earledome,
It being here beleev'd the Duke of *Brabant*
Had no such losse. This war upon't proclaim'd,
Our Earle, being then a Child, although his Father
Good *Gerrard* liv'd, yet in respect he was
Chosen by the Countesse favour for her Husband

*7 ten] MS; five F 1

And but a Gentleman, and *Floriz* holding
His right unto this Country from his Mother,
The State thought fit in this defensive war,
Woolfort being then the only man of marke,   30
To make him Generall.

Merchant.   Which place we have heard
He did discharge with honour.

Herman.   I, so long,
And with so blest successes, that the *Brabander*
Was forc't (his treasures wasted, and the choyce
Of his best men of Armes tyr'd, or cut off)
To leave the field, and sound a base retreat
Back to his Countrey: but so broken both
In minde and meanes, er'e to make head againe,
That hitherto he sitts downe by his losse,
Not daring or for honour, or revenge   40
Againe to tempt his fortune. But this Victory
More broke our State, and made a deeper hurt
In *Flanders*, then the greatest overthrow
She e're receiv'd: For *Woolfort*, now beholding
Himselfe, and actions in the flattering glasse
Of selfe-deservings, and that cherish't by
The strong assurance of his power, for then
All Captaines of the Army, were his creatures,
The common Souldier too at his devotion,
Made so by free indulgence to their rapines   50
And secret bounties, this strength too well knowne
And what it could effect, soone put in practice,
As furtherd by the child-hood of the Earle
And their improvidence, that might have peirc't
The heart of his designes, gave him occasion
To sieze the whole, and in that plight you find it.

Merchant.   Sir, I receive the knowledge of thus much
As a choyce favour from you.

Herman.   Onely I must add
Bruges holds out.

Merchant.   Whether sir, I am going
For there last night I had a ship put in,   60
And my horse waits me.   *Exit.*
Herman.   I wish you a good journey.

                                                   Exit.

        Enter Woolfort, Hubert, Hemskirk [*with guard*].   [I. ii]

Woolfort.   What *Hubert*, stealing from me? who disarm'd him,
It was more then I commanded; take your sword,
I am best guarded with it in your hand,
I have seene you use it nobly.
Hubert.   And will turne it
On mine owne bosom, ere it shall be drawne
Unworthily or idly.
Woolfort.   Would you leave me
Without a farewell *Hubert?* fly a friend
Unwearied in his study to advance you?
What have I ev'r possessed which was not yours?
Or rather did not court you to command it?   10
Who ever yet arriv'd to any grace,
Reward or trust from me, but his approaches
Were by your faire ieports of him prefer'd?
And what is more I made my selfe your Servant,
In making you the Master of those secrets
Which not the rack of conscience could draw from me.
Nor I, when I askt mercy, trust my prayers with;
Yet after these assurances of love,
These tyes and bonds of freindship, to forsake me,
Forsake me as an enemie? come you must   20
Give me a reason.
Hubert.   Sir, and so I will,
If I may do't in privat: and you heare it.

        *0.1 Hemskirk] MS; *omit* F1
        *1 What *Hubert*,] ~ ? ~ ∧ F1–2; ~ ∧ ~ ∧ MS
        *6 idly] MS; rudely F1   10 rather] MS; either F1

Woolfort. All leave the roome: [*Exeunt* Hemskirk *and guard.*]
                You have your will, sit downe
And use the liberty of our first friendship.
Hubert.   Friendship? when you prov'd Traitor first, that vanish'd
Nor do I owe you any thought, but hate;
I know my flight hath forfeited my head,
And so I may make you first to understand
What a strange monster you have made your selfe,
I welcome it.
Woolfort.   To me this is strange language.   30
Hubert.   To you? why what are you?
Woolfort.   Your Prince and Master,
The Earle of *Flaunders.*
Hubert.   By a proper title,
Rais'd to it by cunning circumvention, force,
Blood, and proscriptions.
Woolfort.   And in all this, wisedome;
Had I not reason? when by *Gerrards* plotts
I should have first been call'd to a strict accompt
How, and which way I had consum'd that masse
Of money, as they terme it, in the warr,
Who underhand, had by his Ministers
Detracted my great action, made my faith   40
And loyalty so suspected: in which failing
He sought my life by practice.
Hubert.   With what fore-head,
Do you speake this to me? who (as I know't)
Must, and will say 'tis false.
Woolfort.   My guard there.
Hubert.   Sir, you bad me sit, and promis'd you would heare
Which I now say you shall, not a sound more,
For I that am contemner of mine owne,
Am Master of your life then; heer's a Sword
Betweene you, and all aydes Sir. Though you blind

---

23 sit] MS; set F1   28 to] MS; *omit* F1
*33 cunning∧] *stet* F1, MS   *47 I that] *stet* F1-2
48 life∧ then;] MS (~ ∧ ~ ,); ~ ; ~ ∧ F1-2

The credulous beast, the multitude, you passe not   50
These grosse untruthes on me.

Woolfort.   How? grosse untruthes.

Hubert.   I, and it is favourable language,
They had bin in a meane man lyes, and foule ones.

Woolfort.   You take strange licence.

Hubert.   Yes, were not those rumours
Of being called unto your answer, spread
By your owne followers; and weake *Gerrard* wrought
(But by your cunning practise) to beleeve
That you were dangerous; yet not to be
Punish'd by any formall course of law,
But first to be made sure, and have your crimes   60
Layd open after, which your queint traine taking
You fled unto the Campe, and there crav'd humbly
Protection for your innocent life, and that,
Since you had scap'd the fury of the warr,
You might not fall by treason; and for proofe,
You did not for your owne ends make this danger,
Some that had been before, by you subornd,
Came forth and tooke their oathes they had been hir'd
By *Gerrard* to your murther. This once heard,
And easily beleev'd, th'inraged Souldier   70
Seeing no further then the outward man,
Snatch'd hastily his Armes, ran to the Court,
Kill'd all that made resistance, cut in pieces
Such as were Servants, or thought friends to *Gerrard*,
Vowing the like to him.

Woolfort.   Will you yet end?

Hubert.   Which he foreseeing, with his Sonne, the Earle,
Forsooke the Citty; and by secret wayes
As you give out, and we would gladly have it,
Escap'd their fury: though 'tis more then fear'd
They fell among the rest. Nor stand you there   80
To let us onely mourne, the impious meanes

55 answer] MS (answere); answers F1
*57–58 to beleeve] FK; to be beleeve F1; *omit* MS

By which you got it, but your cruelties since
So farr transcend your former bloody ills,
As if compar'd, they onely would appeare
Essayes of mischiefe; do not stop your eares,
More are behind yet.

Woolfort.   O repeat them not,
'Tis hell to heare them nam'd.

Hubert.   You should have thought,
That hell would be your punishment when you did them,
A Prince, in nothing but your beastly lusts,
And boundless rapines.

Woolfort.   No more I beseech you.   90

Hubert.   Who was the Lord of house or land, that stood
Within the prospect of your coveteous eye?

Woolfort.   You are in this to me a greater Tyrant,
Then ere I was to any.

Hubert.   I end thus
The generall griefe, now to my private wrong;
The losse of *Gerrards* daughter *Jaqueline*:
The hop'd for partner of my lawfull bed,
Your cruelty hath frighted from mine armes;
And her, I now was wandring to recover.
Thinke you that I had reason now to leave you,   100
When you are growne so justly odious,
That ev'n my stay here with your grace and favour,
Makes my life ircksome? here securely take it,   [*Gives sword.*]
And do me but this fruite of all your frendship,
That I may dye by you, and not your hang-man.

Woolfort.   Oh *Hubert*, these your wordes and reasons have
As well drawne drops of blood from my griev'd hart.
As these teares from mine eyes; Despise them not,
By all that's sacred, I am serious *Hubert*,
You now have made me sensible, what furyes,   110
Whips, hangmen, and tormentors a bad man
Do's ever beare about him: let the good

*89 beastly] MS (beastlie); princely F 1
*103 securely] MS (securelie); surely F 1

252

That you this day have done, be ever numberd,
The first of your best actions; Can you think,
Where *Floriz* is or *Gerrard*, or your love,
Or any else, or all that are proscrib'd?
I will resigne, what I usurpe, or have
Unjustly forc'd; the dayes I have to live
Are too too few to make them satisfaction
With any penitence: yet I vow to practise   120
All of a man.
Hubert.   O that your hart and tongue
Did not now differ!
Woolfort.   By my griefes they do not;
Take the good paines to search them out; 'tis worth it,
You have made cleane a Leper: trust me you have,
And made me once more fit for the society,
I hope of good men.
Hubert.   Sir, do not abuse
My aptnesse to beleeve.
Woolfort.   Suspect not you
A faith that's built upon so true a sorrow,
Make your owne safetyes: aske them all the ties
Humanity can give, *Hemskirck* too shall   130
Along with you to this so wish'd discovery,
And in my name profess all that you promise;
And I will give you this helpe to't: I have
Of late receiv'd certaine intelligence,
That some of them are in or about *Bruges*
To be found out: which I did then interpret,
The cause of that Townes standing out against me;
But now am glad, it may direct your purpose
Of giving them their safety, and mee peace.
Hubert.   Be constant to your goodnesse, and you have it.   140
                                             Exeunt.

Enter Three Marchants.   [I.] iii

1. Merchant.   'Tis much that you deliver of this *Goswin.*

2. Merchant.   But short of what I could, yet have the Country
Confirme it true, and by a generall oath,
And not a man hazard his credit in it:
He beares himselfe with such a confidence
As if he were the Master of the Sea,
And not a winde upon the Sailers compasse,
But from one part or other, was his factor,
To bring him in the best commodities,
Merchant e're venturd for.

1. Merchant.   'Tis strange.

2. Merchant.   And yet   10
This do's in him deserve the least of wonder,
Compared with other his peculiar fashions,
Which all admire: he's young, and rich, at least
Thus far reputed so, that since he liv'd
In *Bruges,* there was never brought to harbour
So rich a Bottome, but his bill would passe
Unquestion'd for her lading.

3. Merchant.   Yet he still
Continues a good man?

2. Merchant.   So good, that but
To doubt him, would be held an injury
Or rather malice, with the best that traffique;   20
But this is nothing, a great stocke, and fortune,
Crowning his judgement in his undertakings
May keep him upright that way: But that wealth
Should want the power to make him dote on it,
Or youth teach him to wrong it, best commends
His constant temper: for his outward habit
'Tis sutable to his present course of life:
His table furnish'd well, but not with dainties
That please the appetite only for their rarenesse,
Or the deare price: nor given to wine or women,   30

3 Confirme] MS; Confirmd F 1–2

Beyond his health, or warrant of a man,
I meane a good one: and so loves his state
He will not hazard it at play; nor lend
Upon the assurance of a well-pen'd Letter,
Although a challenge second the denyall
From such as make th'opinion of their valour
Their meanes of feeding.

1. Merchant.   These are wayes to thrive,
And the increase not curs'd.

2. Merchant.   What follows this,
Makes many Venturers with him, in their wishes,
For his prosperity: for when desert   40
Or reason leads him to be liberall,
His noble mind and ready hand contend
Which can add most to his free curtesies,
Or in their worth, or speed to make them so.
Is there a Virgin of good fame wants dowre?
He is a father to her; or a Souldier
That in his Countreyes service, from the warre
Hath brought him only scars, and want? his house
Receives him, and relieves him, with that care
As if what he posses'd had been laid up   50
For such good uses, and he steward of it.
But I should loose my selfe to speake him further
And stale in my relation, the much good
You may be witnesse of, if your remove
From *Brugis*, be not speedy.

1. Merchant.   This report
I do assure you will not hasten it,
Nor would I wish a better man to deale with
For what I am to part with.

3. Merchant.   Never doubt it,
He is your man and ours, only I wish
His too much forwardnesse to embrace all bargains   60
Sinke him not in the end.

*38 increase] MS; meanes F 1   61 Sinke] MS; Sucke F 1

2. Merchant.   Have better hopes,
For my part I am confident; here he comes.

         Enter Florez [*as* Goswin] *and the fourth Merchant.*

Floriʒ.   I take it at your own rates, your wine of *Cyprus*:
But for your *Candy* sugars, they have met
With such foule weather, and are priz'd so high
I cannot save in them.
4. Merchant.   I am unwilling
To seeke another Chap-man: make me offer
Of something near my price, that may assure me
You can deale for them.
Floriʒ.   I both can, and will,
But not with too much losse; your bill of lading   70
Speakes of two hundred chests, valued by you
At thirty thousand gilders. I will have them
At twenty-eight; so, in the payment of
Three thousand sterling, you fall only in
Two hundred pound.
4. Merchant.   You know, they so are cheape.——
Floriʒ.   Why looke you, I'le deale fairly; ther's in prison,
And at your suite, a Pirat, but unable
To make you satisfaction, and past hope
To live a weeke, if you should prosecute
What you can prove against him: set him free,   80
And you shall have your money to a Stiver,
And present payment.
4. Merchant.   This is above wonder,
A Merchant of your ranke, that have at Sea
So many Bottoms in the danger of
These water-Theeves, should be a meanes to save 'em,
It more importing you for your owne safety
To be at charge to scoure the Sea of them
Then stay the sword of Justice, that is ready
To fall on one so conscious of his guilt
That he dares not deny it.

Floriz.   You mistake me,   90
If you thinke I would cherish in this Captaine
The wrong he did to you, or any man;
I was lately with him, (having first, from others
True testimony been assured, a man
Of more desert never put from the shore)
I read his letters of Mart from this State granted
For the recovery of such losses, as
He had receiv'd in *Spain*, 'twas that he aim'd at,
Not at three tuns of wine, bisket, or beefe,
Which his necessity made him take from you.   100
If he had pillag'd you neare, or sunke your ship,
Or thrown your men o'r-boord, then he deserv'd
The Lawes extreamest rigour: But since want
Of what he could not live without, compel'd him
To that he did (which yet our State calls death)
I pitty his misfortune; and to worke you
To some compassion of them, I come up
To your own price: save him, the goods are mine;
If not, seeke else-where, I'le not deale for them.
4. Merchant.   Well, Sir, for your love, I will once be lead   110
To change my purpose.
Floriz [*aside*].   For your profit rather.
4. Merchant.   I'le presently make meanes for his discharge,
Till when, I leave you.   [*Exit.*]
2. Merchant.   What do you thinke of this?
1. Merchant.   As of a deed of noble pitty: guided
By a strong judgement.
2. Merchant.   Save you Master *Goswin*.
Floriz.   Good day to all.
2. Merchant.   We bring you the refusall
Of more Commodities.
Floriz.   Are you the owners
Of the ship that lastnight put into the Harbour?
1. Merchant.   Both of the Ship, and lading.
Floriz.   What's her fraught?

119 her] MS; the F1

257

1. Merchant.   *Indico*, *Quitchineel*, choise *Chyna* stuffs.   120

3. Merchant.   And cloath of Gold brought from *Camball*.

Floriz.   Rich lading,
For which I were your Chapman, but I am
Already out of cash.

1. Merchant.   I'le give you day
For the moiety of all.

Floriz.   How long?

3. Merchant.   Sixe moneths.

Floriz.   'Tis a faire offer: which (if we agree
About the prizes) I, with thanks accept of,
And will make present payment of the rest;
Some two hours hence I'le come aboord.

1. Merchant.   The Gunner
Shall speake you welcome.

Floriz.   I'le not faile.

3. Merchant.   Good morrow.

                          Exeunt Merchants.

Floriz.   Heaven grant my Ships a safe returne, before   130
The day of this great payment: as they are
Expected three moneths sooner: and my credite
Stands good with all the world.

              Enter Gerrard [*as* Clause].

Gerrard.   Blesse my good Master,
The prayers of your poor Beads-man ever shall
Be sent up for you.

Floriz.   God 'a mercy *Clause*,
Ther's something to put thee in minde hereafter
To thinke of me.

Gerrard.   May he that gave it you
Reward you for it, with encrease, good Master.

Floriz.   I thrive the better for thy prayers.

Gerrard.   I hope so.
This three yeares have I fed upon your bounties,   140
And by the fire of your blest charity warm'd me,
And yet, good Master, pardon me, that must,

258

Though I have now receiv'd your almes, presume
To make one sute more to you.

Floriz.   What is't *Clause*?

Gerrard.   Yet do not think me impudent I beseech you,
Since hitherto your charity hath prevented
My begging your reliefe, 'tis not for money
Nor cloaths (good Master) but your good word for me.

Floriz.   That thou shalt have, *Clause*, for I think thee honest.

Gerrard.   To morrow then (dear Master) take the trouble   150
Of walking early unto *Beggars Bush*,
And as you see me, among others (Brethren
In mine affliction) when you are demanded
Which you like best amongst us, point out me,
And then passe by, as if you knew me not.

Floriz.   But what will that advantage thee?

Gerrard.   O much Sir,
'Twill give me the preheminence of the rest,
Make me a King among them, and protect me,
From all abuse, such as are stronger, might
Offer my age; Sir, at your better leizure   160
I will informe you further of the good
It may do to me.

Floriz.   'Troth thou mak'st me wonder;
Have you a King and Common-wealth among you?

Gerrard.   We have, and there are States are governd worse.

Floriz.   Ambition among Beggars?

Gerrard.   Many great ones
Would part with halfe their States, to have the place,
And credit to beg in the first file, Master:
But shall I be so much bound to your furtherance
In my Petition?

Floriz.   That thou shalt not misse of,
Nor any worldly care make me forget it,   170
I will be early there.

Gerrard.   Heaven blesse my Master.

                                        Exeunt.

154 amongst] MS; among F1

259

Enter Higgen, Ferret, Prig, Clause,
Snap, Gynkes, *and other Beggars.*

Higgen.   Come Princes of the ragged regiment,
   You 'o the blood, *Prig* my most upright Lord,
   And these (what name or title, e're they beare)
   Jarkman, or *Patrico, Cranke*, or *Clapperdudgeon*,
   Frater, or *Abram-man*; I speake to all
   That stand in faire Election for the title
   Of King of *Beggars*, with the command adjoyning;
   Higgen, your Orator, in this Inter-regnum,
   That whilom was your Dommerer, doth beseech you
   All to stand faire, and put your selves in ranke,   10
   That the first Commer, may at his full view
   Make a free choise, to say upon the question.
Ferret, Prig.   'Tis done Lord *Higgen.*
Higgen.   Thankes to Prince *Prig,*
                                              Prince *Ferret.*

Ferret.   Well, pray my Masters all, *Ferret* be chosen,
   Ye'ar like to have a mercifull mild Prince a me.
Prig.   A very tyrant, I, an arrant tyrant
   If e're I come to reigne; therefore looke to't,
   Except ye do provide me hum enough
   And Lour to bouze with: I must have my Capons
   And Turkeys brought me in, with my green Geese,   20
   And Ducklings i'th season, fine fat cheats,
   Or if you chance where an eye of tame Phesants
   Or Partridges are kept, see they be mine,
   Or straight I seize on all your priviledges,
   Places, revenues, offices, as forfeit,
   Call in your crutches, wooden legs, false bellyes,
   Forc'd eyes and teeth, with your dead arms; not leave you
   A durty clout to beg with a your heads,

> 0.1 Clause,] Clause, Jaculine F1–2, MS
> 11 full] MS; first F1   12 upon] MS; up F1
> *21 cheats] MS (Cheates); chickens F1
> 24 priviledges] MS (Priviledges); priviledge F1

Or an old rag with Butter, Frankinsence,
Brimstone and Rozen, birdlime, blood, and creame,   30
To make you an old sore; not so much sope
As you may fome with i'th Falling-sicknesse;
The very bag you beare, and the brown dish
Shall be escheated. All your daintiest dells too
I will deflowr, and take your dearest Doxyes
From your warme sides; and then some one cold night
I'le watch you what olde barne you goe to roost in,
And there I'le smoother ye all i'th musty hay.
Higgen.   This is tyrant-like indeed: But what would *Ginkes*
Or *Clause* be here, if either of them should raigne?   40
Gerrard [*aside*].   Best aske an asse, if he were made a Camell,
What he would be; or a dog, and he were a Lyon.
Ginks.   I care not what you are, Sirs, I shall be
A Begger, still, I am sure, find my selfe there.

Enter Florez.

Snap.   O here a Judge comes.
Higgen.   Cry, a Judge, a Judge.
Floriz.   What aile you Sirs? what means this out-cry?
Higgen.   Master
A sort of poor soules met: Gods fools, good Master:
Have had some little variance 'mongst our selves
Who should be honestest of us; and which lives
Uprightest in his call: Now, 'cause we thought   50
We ne're should gree on't our selves, because indeed
'Tis hard to say: we all dissolv'd, to put it
To him that should come next, and that's your Mastership,
Who, I hope, will termine it as your mind serves you,
Right, and no otherwise we aske it: which?
Which does your Worship thinke is he? sweet Master
Looke ore us all, and tell us; we are seven of us,
Like to the seven wise Masters, or the Planets.
Floriz.   I should judge this the man with the grave beard,
And if he be not——

53 him] MS; whom F1

261

Gerrard. Blesse you, good Master, blesse you. 60

Floriȝ. I would he were: there's something too, amongst you
To keep you all honest. *Exit.*

Snap. King of heaven goe with you.

Omnes. Now good reward him, may he never want it,
To comfort still the poor, in a good houre.

Ferret. What is't? see: *Snap* ha's got it.

Snap. A good crown, marry.

Prig. A crown a gold.

Ferret. For our new King: good luck.

Ginks. To the common treasury with it; if't be gold,
Thither it must.

Prig. Spoke like a Patriot, *Ferret*——
King *Clause*, I bid God save thee first, first, *Clause*,
After this golden token of a crowne; 70
Wher's Oratour *Higgen* with his gratuling speech now,
In all our names?

Ferret. Here he is pumping for't.

Ginks. H'has cough'd the second time, 'tis but once more
And then it comes.

Ferret. So, out with all: expect now——

Higgen. That thou art chosen, venerable *Clause*,
Our King and Soveraign, Monarch o'th Maunders,
Thus we throw up our Nab-cheats, first for joy,
And then our filches; last, we clap our fambles,
Three subject signes: we do it without envy,
For who is he here did not wish thee chosen? 80
Now thou art chosen, aske 'em: all will say so,
Nay swear't: 'tis for the King, but let that passe;
When last in conference at the bouzing ken
This other day we sate about our dead Prince
Of famous memory: (rest, goe with his rags:)
And that I saw thee at the tables end,
Rise mov'd, and gravely leaning on one Crutch,

*68 *Ferret*] stet F1, MS
79 signes:...envy,] ~ ,...~ : F1–2; ~ ∧...~ ∧ MS
*80-81 chosen? ...chosen,] MS; ~∧...~? F1

Lift the other like a Scepter at my head,
I then presag'd thou shortly wouldst be King
And now thou art so: but what need presage   90
To us, that might have read it, in thy beard,
As well as he that chose thee? by that beard
Thou wert found out, and mark'd for Soveraignty.
Oh happy beard! but happier Prince, whose beard
Was so remark'd, as mark'd him out our Prince,
Not bating us a haire. Long may it grow,
And thick, and faire, that who lives under it,
May live as safe, as under *Beggars Bush*,
Of which this is the thing, that but the type.
Omnes.   Excellent, excellent oratour, forward good *Higgen.*   100
Gi' him leave to spit: the fine, well-spoken *Higgen.*
Higgen.   This is the beard, the bush, or bushy-beard,
Under whose gold and silver raigne 'twas said
So many ages since, we all should smile.
No impositions, taxes, grievances,
Knots in a State, and whips unto the Subject,
Lye lurking in this Beard, but all kem'd out:
If now, the Beard be such, what is the Prince
That owes the Beard? a Father; no, a Grandfather;
Nay the great Grand-father of you his people.   110
He will not force away your hens, your bacon,
When you have ventur'd hard for't, nor take from you
The fattest of your puddings: under him
Each man shall eate his own stolne eggs, and butter,
In his owne shade, or sun-shine, and enjoy
His owne deare Dell, Doxy, or Mort, at night
In his own straw, with his owne shirt, or sheet,
That he hath filch'd that day, I, and possesse
What he can purchase, backe, or belly-cheats
To his own prop: he will have no purveyers   120
For Pigs, and poultry.

95 him] MS; *omit* F 1   105 No] Seward; On F 1–2; *omit* MS
106 the Subject] MS; a Subject F 1   107 kem'd] MS; hem'd F 1
*120 he...purveyers]*stet* F 1

Gerrard.   That we must have, my learned Oratour,
It is our will, and every man to keep
In his own path and circuite.
Higgen.   Do you heare?
You must hereafter maund o' your own pads he saies.
Gerrard.   And what they get there, is their owne, besides
To give good words.
Higgen.   Do you marke? to cut bene whids,
That is the second Law.
Gerrard.   And keepe a-foote
The humble, and the common phrase of begging,
Lest men discover us.
Higgen.   Yes; and cry sometimes,   130
To move compassion: Sir, there is a table,
That doth command all these things, and enjoyns 'em
Be perfect in their crutches, their fain'd plaisters,
And their torne pas-ports, with the ways to stammer,
And to be dumb, and deafe, and blind, and lame,
There, all the halting paces are set downe,
I'th learned language.
Gerrard.   Thither I refer them,
Those, you at leisure shall interpret to them,
We love no heapes of lawes, where few will serve.
Omnes.   O gracious Prince, 'save, 'save the good King *Clause.*   140
Higgen.   A Song to crowne him.
Ferret.   Set a Centinell out first.
Snap.   The word?
Higgen.   *A Cove comes*, and *fumbumbis* to it.
                                        [*Exit* Snap.]
                                        Strike music. Song.

The SONG.

Cast our Caps and cares away,
This is Beggars Holli-day:

134 torne] MS; true F1
142.1 *Strike music. Song.*] MS (*musick*); *strike.* F1

264

At the Crowning of our King,
Thus we ever dance and sing.
In the world looke out and see:
Where so happy a Prince as he?
Where the Nation live so free,
And so merry as do we?　　　　　　　　　150
Be it peace, or be it war,
Here at liberty we are,
And enjoy our ease and rest;
To the field we are not prest;
Nor are called into the Towne,
To be troubled with the Gowne.
Hang all Officers we cry,
And the Magistrate too, by;
When the Subsidie's encreast,
We are not a penny ceast.　　　　　　　　160
Nor will any goe to law,
With the Beggar for a straw.
All which happinesse, he brags,
He doth owe unto his rags.

Enter Snap, [then] Hubert, and Hemskirke [disguised].

Snap.　　A Cove: Fumbumbis.
Prig.　　　　　　　　　To your postures; arme.
Hubert.　　Yonder's the Towne: I see it.
Hemskirk.　　　　　　　　　Ther's our danger
Indeed afore us, if our shadows save not.
Higgen.　　Blesse your good Worships——
Ferret.　　　　　　　　　　One small piece of
money——
Prig.　　Amongst us all poore wretches——
Gerrard.　　　　　　　　　Blinde, and lame——
Ginks.　　For his sake that gives all.
Higgen.　　　　　　　　Pittifull Worships——　170
Snap.　　One little doyt.

157 *Officers*] MS; *Offices* F 1
159 *Subsidie's*] FK; *Subsidies* F 1, MS

Enter Jaculine [*as* Minche].

Jaqueline.   King, by your leave, where are you?
Gerrard.   To buy a little bread——
Higgen.   To feed so many
  Mouths, as will ever pray for you.
Prig.   Here be seven of us.
Higgen.   Seven, good Master, ô remember seven,
  Seven blessings.
Ferret.   Remember, gentle Worship——
Higgen.   'Gainst seven deadly sins——
Prig.   And seven sleepers.
Higgen.   If they be hard of heart, and will give nothing——
  Alas, we had not a charity this three dayes.
Hubert.   Ther's amongst you all.
Ferret.   The King of Heaven reward you.
Prig.   Lord reward you.   180
Higgen.   The Prince of pitty blesse thee.
Hubert.   Do I see?
  Or is't my fancy that would have it so?
  Ha? 'tis her face: come hither Maid.
Jaqueline.   What, ha' you
  Bells for my squirrell? I ha' giv'n Bun meat,
  You do not love me, do you? catch me a butter fly,
  And I'le love you againe; when? can you tell?
  Peace, we go a birding: I shall have a fine thing.   [*Exit.*]
Hubert.   Her voyce too says the same; but for my head
  I would not that her manners were so chang'd.
  Heare me thou honest fellow; what's this Mayden,   190
  That lives amongst you here?
Ginks.   Ao, ao, ao, ao.
Hubert.   How? nothing but signes?
Ginks.   Ao, ao, ao, ao.
Hubert.   'Tis strange,
  I would faine have it her, but not her thus.

*180 The King of] MS; *omit* F1
192 'Tis] MS (tis); This F1

266

Higgen.   He is de-de-de-de-de-de-deafe, and du-du-du-du-dumb
                                                                Sir.
Hubert.   Slid they did all speak plain ev'n now me thought.
Do'st thou know this same Maid?
                              [*Beggars steal off, all but* Snap.]
Snap.   Whi-whi-whi-whi-which, gu-gu-
                                   gu-gu-Gods foole,
She was bo-bo-bo-bo-borne at the barne younder, by
                              be-be-be-be-Beggars bu-bu-Bush:
Her name is *Mi-Mi-Mi-Mi-Minche*; so was her Mo-mo-mo-
                                        Mothers too-too.
Hubert.   I understand no word he sayes; how long
Has she been here?
Snap.   Lo-lo-long enough to be ni-ni-nigled: 200
And she ha' go-go-go-good luck.
Hubert.   I must be better inform'd, then by this way.
Here was another face too, that I mark'd
O' the old mans: but they are vanish'd all
Most sodainly: I will come here againe,
O, that I were so happy, as to finde it,
What I yet hope it is, put on.
Hemskirk.   What meane you Sir,
To stay there with that stammerer?
Hubert.   Farewell friend——
                                        [*Exit* Snap.]
It will be worth returne, to search it: Come,
Protect us our disguize now, pre'thee *Hemskirck*   210
If we be taken, how do'st thou imagine
This Towne will use us, that hath stood so long
Out, against *Woolfort*?
Hemskirk.   Faith ev'n to hang us forth
Upon their walls a sunning, to make Crowes meate,
If I were not assur'd 'o the *Burgomaster*,

194 du-du-du-du-dumb] du-du-dude—dumb F1; du-du-du-dumbe MS
197 bu-bu-Bush] MS; Bush bo-bo-bo-Bush F1
198 *Minche*] MS; match F1   199 he] MS (hee); she F1
207 hope ∧ it is,] MS; ~ ? ~ ~ ∧ F1   209 it] MS; *omit* F1
213 Faith] MS; *omit* F1

And had a pretty skuys, to see a niece there,
I should scarce venture.
Hubert.   Come 'tis now too late
To looke back at the ports: good luck, and enter.

Exeunt.

Enter Floriz.   [II.]

Floriz.   Still blow'st thou there? and from all other parts,
Do all my Agents sleepe? that nothing comes?
Ther's a conspiracy of windes, and servants,
If not of Elements, to ha' me breake;
What should I thinke? unlesse the Seas, and Sandes
Had swallow'd up my ships, or fire had spoyl'd
My ware-houses, or death devour'd my Factors,
I must ha' had some returnes.

Enter [*First and Second*] *Merchants.*

1. Merchant.   'Save you Sir.
Floriz.   'Save you.
1. Merchant.   No newes, yet 'o your Ships?
Floriz.   Not any yet Sir.
1. Merchant.   'Tis strange.   *Exit* [*1. Merchant*].
Floriz.   'Tis true Sir:
                    What a voyce was here now? 10
This was one passing bell, a thousand ravens
Sung in that man now, to presage my ruines.
2. Merchant.   Goswin, good day, these winds are very constant.
Floriz.   They are so Sir; to hurt——
2. Merchant.   Ha' you had no letters,
Lately from *England*, nor from *Denmark*?
Floriz.   Neither.
2. Merchant.   This winde brings them; nor no newes over land,
Through *Spaine*, from the *Straights*?
Floriz.   Not any.
2. Merchant.   I am sorry Sir.
                              Exit [*2. Merchant*].

*8 returnes] stet F1   10, 17.1 Exit.] F2; omit F1, MS

Floriʒ.   They talke me downe: and as 'tis said of Vultures,
They sent a feild fought, and do smell the carkasses
By many hundred miles: So do these, my wracks   20
At greater distances: why thy will heaven
Come on, and be: yet if thou please preserve me
But in my one adventure, here at home,
Of my chast love, to keep me worthy of her,
It shall be put in scale 'gainst all ill fortunes:
I am not broken yet: nor should I fall,
Me thinkes with lesse then that, that ruines all.

                                                         Exit.

          Enter Van-dunck, Hubert, Hemskirck, *and*   [II. iii]
                    Margaret, *Boores.*

Van-dunck.   Captaine you are welcome, so is this your friend
Most safely welcome; though our Towne stand out
Against your Master, you shall finde good quarter:
The troth is, we not love him: *Margee*, some wine,
Let's talke a little treason, if we can
Talk treason, 'gainst the Traitor; by your leave, Gentlemen,
We here in *Brugis*, thinke he do's usurpe,
And therefore I am bold with him.
Hubert.   Sir, your boldnesse,
Happely becomes your mouth, but not our eares,
While we are his servants; And as we come here,   10
Not to aske questions, walke forth on your walls,
Visit your courtes of guard, view your Munition,
Aske of your corne-provisions, nor enquire
Into the least, as spies upon your strengthes,
So let's entreate, we may receive from you
Nothing in passage or discourse, but what
We may with gladnesse, and our honesties hear,
And that shall seale our welcome.
Van-dunck.   Good: let's drinke then,
Margee, fill out, I keep mine old pearle still Captaine.

---

23 one] MS; owne F1   *0.2 *Boores*] stet F1, MS
6 Traitor] MS (traytor); Traitors F1   17 hear] MS (heare); here F1

269

Margaret.   I hang fast, man.

Hemskirk.   Old Jewels, commend their keeper,
                                                                Sir. 20

Van-dunck.   Heer's to you with a hart, my Captaines friend,
With a good heart, and if this make us speake
Bold words, anon: 'tis all under the Rose
Forgotten: drowne all memory, when we drinke.

Hubert.   'Tis freely spoken noble *Burgomaster,*
I'le do you right.

Hemskirk.   Nay Sir, mine heire *Van-dunck,*
Is a true Statesman.

Van-dunck.   Fill my Captaines cup there,
O that your Master *Woolfort*
Had been an honest man.

Hubert.   Sir?

Van-dunck.   Under the Rose.

Hemskirk.   Heer's to you *Margee.*

Margaret.   Welcom; welcom Captaine.   30

Van-dunck.   Well said, my pearle still.

Hemskirk.   And how does my Niece?
Almost a woman; I thinke? This friend of mine,
I drew along with me, through so much hazard,
Only to see her: she was all my errand.

Van-dunck.   I, a kinde Uncle you are (fill him his glasse)
That in seven yeare, could not find leizure——

Hemskirk.   No,
It's not so much.

Van-dunck.   I'le bate you nev'r an houre on't,
It was before the *Brabander* gan his war,
For moone-shine, i'th water there, his daughter
That nev'r was lost: yet you could not finde time   40
To see a Kinswoman: But shee is worth the seeing Sir.
Now you are come, y'aske if she were a woman?
Shee is a woman Sir; fetch her forth *Margee.*   *Exit* Margaret.
And a fine woman, and has Suitors.

Hemskirk.   How?
What Suitors are they.
Van-dunck.   Bachellors: young Burgers:
And one, a gallant, the young Prince of Merchants,
We call him here, in *Bruges*.
Hemskirk.   How? a Merchant?
I thought *Van-doncke*, y'ad understood me better,
And my Niece too, so trusted to you by me:
Then t'admit of such in name of Suitors.   50
Van-dunck. Such? he is such a such, as were she mine
I'de give him thirty thousand crownes with her.
Hemskirk. But the same things Sir, fit not you and me.   *Exit.*
Van-dunck. Why, give's some wine, then; This will fit us all:
Here's to you still, my Captains friend: All out:
And still, would *Woolfort* were an honest man,
Under the Rose, I speake it: but this Merchant
Is a brave boy: he lives so, i'the town here,
We know not what to thinke on him: At sometimes
We feare he will be Bankrupt; he do's stretch   60
Tenter his credite so; embraces all,
And too't, the winds have been contrary, long.
But then, if he should have home all his returnes,
We thinke he would be a King, and are halfe sure on't.
Your Master is a Traytor, for all this,
Under the Rose (here's to you) and usurps
The Earldome from a better man.
Hubert.   I marry Sir,
Where is that man?
Van-dunck.   Nay soft: and I could tell you
'Tis ten to one I would not: here's my hand,
I love not *Woolfort*: sit you still, with that: 70
Here comes my Captaine againe, and his fine Niece,
And ther's my Merchant: view him well, fill wine here.

        Enter Hemskirke, Bertha [*as* Gertrude], *and* Florez.

Hemskirk. You must not only know me for your Uncle,

                63 home] MS; *omit* F 1

Now, but obey me; you, goe cast your selfe
Away, upon a dunghill here? a Merchant?
A petty fellow? one that makes his trade
With oathes and perjuries?

Floriz. What is that you say Sir?
If it be me you speake of; as your eye
Seems to direct: I wish you would speake to me, Sir.

Hemskirk. Sir, I do say, she is no Merchandize, 80
Will that suffice you?

Floriz. Merchandize good Sir:
Though you be Kinsman to her, take no leave thence
To use me with contempt, I ever thought
Your Niece above all price.

Hemskirk. And do so still, Sir,
I assure you, her rate's at more then you are worth.

Floriz. You do not know, what a Gentleman's worth sir,
Nor can you value him.

Hubert. Well said Merchant.

Van-dunck. Nay,
Let him alone, and ply your matter.

Hemskirk. A Gentleman?
What, a the wool-pack? or the Sugar-chest?
Or lists of Velvet? which is't? pound, or yard, 90
You vent your Gentry by?

Hubert. O *Hemskirke*, fye.

Van-dunck. Come, do not mind 'em; drink, he is no *Woolfort*,
Captaine, I advise you.

Hemskirk. Alas, my pretty man,
I think't be angry, by its looke: Come hither,
Turne this way, a little: if it were the blood
Of *Charlemaine*, as't may (for ought I know)
Be some good Botchers issue, here in *Bruges*.

Floriz. How?

Hemskirk. Nay: I'me not certaine of that; of this I am,
If it once buy, and sell, its Gentry's gone.

Floriz. Ha, ha.

76 his] MS; this F 1

272

Hemskirk.   You are angry, though you laugh.

Floriz.   No, now 'tis pitty 100
Of your poor argument. Do not you, the Lords
Of land (if you be any) sell the grasse,
The corne, the straw, the milke, the cheese?

Van-dunck.   And butter:
Remember butter; doe not leave out butter.

Floriz.   The Beefs and Muttons that your grounds are stock'd
    with?
Swine, with the very mast, beside the woods?

Hemskirk.   No, for those sordid uses, we have Tenants,
Or else our Bayliffs.

Floriz.   Have not we Sir, Chap-men,
And Factors, then to answer those? your errour
Fetch'd from the Heralds *A B C*, and said over   110
With your Court faces, once an houre, shall never
Make me mistake my selfe. Do not your Lawyers
Sell all their practise, as your Priests their prayers?
What is not bought, and sold? The company
That you had last, what had you for't, y'faith?

Hemskirk.   You now grow sawcy.

Floriz.   Sure I have been bred
Still, with my honest liberty, and must use it.

Hemskirk.   Upon your equals, then.

Floriz.   Sir, he that will
Provoke me first, doth make himselfe my equall.

Hemskirk.   Do you heare? no more.

Floriz.   Yes Sir, this little, I pray you, 120
And't shall be aside, then after, as you please.
You appeare the Uncle, sir, to her I love,
More then mine eyes; and I have heard your scorns
With so much suffering, and so much shame,
As each strive which is greater: But, beleeve me
I suck'd not in this patience with my milke.
Do not presume, because you see me young,

105 stock'd] MS; stor'd F1   109 those] MS; these F1
124 suffering] MS (suffring); scoffing F1

273

Or cast despights on my profession
For the civility and tamenesse of it.
A good man beares a contumely worse   130
Then he would do an injury. Proceed not
To my offence: wrong is not still successefull,
Indeed it is not: I would approach your Kins-woman
With all respect, due to your selfe and her.
Hemskirk.   Away Companion: handling her? take that.

                                        Strikes him.

Floriz.   Nay, I do love no blows, sir, there's exchange.
Hubert.   Hold sir,
Margaret.   O murther.
Bertha.   Help, my *Goswin.*
Margaret.   Man.

    He gets Hemskirk's *sword and cuts him on the head.*

Van-dunck.   Let 'em alone; my life for one.
Floriz.   Nay come
If you have will.
Hubert.   None to offend you, I, Sir.
Floriz.   He that had, thank himself: not hand her? yes Sir,   140
And claspe her, and embrace her; and (would she
Now goe with me) bear her through all her race,
Her Father, Brethren, and her Uncles, arm'd,
And all their Nephews, though they stood a wood
Of pikes, and wall of Canon: kisse me *Gertrude,*
Quake not, but kisse me.
Van-dunck.   Kisse him, girle, I bid you;
My Merchant royall; feare no Uncles: hang 'em,
Hang up all Uncles: Are we not in *Bruges?*
Under the Rose here?
Floriz.   In this circle, Love,
Thou art as safe, as in a towre of brasse;   150
Let such as do wrong, feare.

        134 due] MS; done F1
        *135.1 *Strikes him.*] F2; *omit* F1, FK, MS
        137.1 *He gets...head.*] F2; *omit* F1, FK, MS

Van-dunck.   I, that's good,
Let *Woolfort* looke to that.
Floriȝ.   Sir, here she stands,
Your Niece, and my beloved. One of these titles
She must apply to; if unto the last,
Not all the anger can be sent unto her,
In frowne, or voyce, or other act, shall force her,
Had *Hercules* a hand in't; Come, my Joy,
Say thou art mine, aloud Love, and professe it.
Van-dunck. Doe: and I drinke to it.
Floriȝ.   Prethee say so, Love.
Bertha. 'Twould take away the honour from my blushes: 160
Doe not you play the Tyrant, sweet: they speake it.
Hemskirk. I thanke you Niece.
Floriȝ.   Sir, thanke her for your life,
And fetch your sword within.
Hemskirk.   You insult too much
With your good fortune, Sir   *Exeunt* Florez *and* Bertha.
Hubert.   A brave cleare spirit;
Hemskirke, you were too blame: a civill habit
Oft covers a good man: and you may meete
In person of a Merchant, with a soule
As resolute, and free, and all wayes worthy,
As else in any file of man-kinde: pray you,
What meant you so to slight him?
Hemskirk.   'Tis done now,   170
Aske no more of it; I must suffer.   *Exit* Hemskirk.
Hubert.   This
Is still the punishment of rashnesse, sorrow;
Well; I must to the woods, for nothing here
Will be got out. There, I may chance to learne
Somewhat to help my enquiries further.
Van-dunck.   Ha?
A Looking-glasse?
Hubert.   How now, brave Burgo-master?
Van-dunck. I love no *Woolforts*, and my name's *Vanduncke*.

Hubert.   *Van-drunke* it's rather: Come, go sleep within.

Van-dunck.   Earle *Florez* is right heir, and this same *Woolfort*
Under the Rose I speake it——

Hubert.   Very hardly.   180

Van-dunck.   Usurpes: and a ranke Traitor, as ever breath'd,
And all that do uphold him. Let me goe,
No man shall hold up me, that upholds him;
Doe you uphold him?

Hubert.   No.

Van-dunck.   Then hold me up.

Exeunt.

Enter Florez *and* Hemskirke.   [II.

Hemskirk.   Sir, I presume, y'ave a sword of your owne,
That can so handle anothers.

Floriz.   Faith you may Sir.

Hemskirk.   And ye have made me have so much better thoughts of
        you
As I am bound to call you forth.

Floriz.   For what sir?

Hemskrik.   To the repairing of mine honour, and hurt here.

Floriz.   Expresse your way.

Hemskirk.   By fight, and speedily.

Floriz.   You have your will: Require you any more?

Hemskirk.   That you be secret: and come single.

Floriz.   I will.

Hemskirk.   As you are the Gentleman you would be thought.

Floriz.   Without the Conjuration: and I'le bring   10
Only my sword, which I will fit to yours,
I'le take his length within.

Hemskirk.   Your place now Sir?

Floriz.   By the Sand-hills.

Hemskirk.   Sir, nearer to the woods,
If you thought so, were fitter.

Floriz.   There, then.

183 up] MS; *omit* F 1

Hemskirk.   Good.
  Your time?
Floriz.   'Twixt seven and eight.
Hemskirk.   You'l give me Sir
  Cause to report you worthy of my Niece,
  If you come, like your promise.
Floriz.   If I do not
  Let no man think to call me unworthy first,
  I'le doe't my selfe: and justly wish to want her.

                                        Exeunt.

              Enter three or foure Boores.   III. i

1. Boore.   Come, *English* beer Hostess, *English* beer bi'th belly.
2. Boore.   Start beer boy, stout and strong beer: so, sit downe
    Lads,
And drinke me upsey-Dutch.
3. Boore.   Frollicke, and feare not.
                    Winde a Sowgelders horn within.

     Enter Higgen *like a Sow-gelder, singing: and Piper.*

Higgen.   *Have ye any worke for the Sow-gelder, hoa,*
            My horne goes too high too low, too high too low.
            Have ye any Piggs, Calves, or Colts,
            Have ye any Lambs in your holts
            To cut for the Stone,
            Here comes a cunning one.
            Have ye any braches to spade,   10
            Or e're a faire maide
            That would be a Nun,
            Come kisse me, 'tis done.
            Harke how my merry horne doth blow,
            Too high too low, too high too low.

1. Boore.   O excellent! two-pence a piece boyes, two-pence a piece:
Give the boys some drink there. Piper, wet your whistle.

---

3 *3. Boore.*] MS (*3. Boor.*); *omit* F1   3.1 *Winde...within.*] MS; *omit* F1
3.2 *and Piper*] MS; *omit* F1   *16 *1. Boore.*] *stet* F1

Canst tell me a way now, how to cut off my wives Concupiscence?
Shees vengeance ranck o'th Man.

Higgen.   I'le sing ye a Song for't.

The Song.

Take her, and hug her,   20
And turn her and tug her,
And turn her again boy, again boy, again.
Then if she mumble,
Or if her taile tumble,
Kisse her amain boy, amain boy, amain.
Do thy endeavour,
To take off her feaver,
Then her disease no longer will raign.

If nothing will serve her,
Then thus to preserve her,   30
Swinge her amain boy, amaine boy, amaine.
Give her cold jelly
To take up her belly,
And once a day swinge her again boy, again.
If she stand all these pains
Then knock out her brains,
And her disease no longer wil reign.

1. Boore.   More excellent, more excellent, sweet Sow-gelder.
2. Boore.   Three-pence a peice, three-pence a peice.
Higgen.   Will ye heare a Song how the Divel was gelded?   40
3. Boore.   I, I, lets heare the Divell roare, Sow-gelder.

Song.

I met with him first in the shape of a Ram,
And over and over the Sowgelder came;
I caught, and I haltred him fast by the horne,

19 Shees...Man.] MS; *omit* F1   22, 34 ²*boy, again.*] MS (*againe*); *omit* F1
25, 31 ²*boy, amain*] MS (*Boy, amaine*); *omit* F1
37 *And*] MS; *omit* F1   *41.1–59 *Song.*] MS; *omit* F1

I pluckt out his Stones, as you'd pick out a corne.
Baa quoth the Devill, and forth then hee slunck,
    And left us a carkas of Mutton that stunck.

By that I had ridd a good mile and a halfe,
I heard where he liv'd in disguise of a Calfe;
I bound, and I gelt him, ere hee did any Evill,   50
He was here att his best, but a sucking Devill.
Maa quoth the Calfe, and forth hee did steal,
    And this was sould after for excellent Veale.

Some halfe a yeare after in the forme of a Pigg,
I mett with the rogue and hee look'd very bigg;
I caught att his legg, laid him downe, on a Logg,
Ere a man could fart twice, I had made him a hogg.
Ugh: quoth the Devill, and forth gave a Jirck
    That a Jew was conuerted, and eate of the Pirck.

1. Boore.   Groats a piece, groats a piece, groats a piece,   60
There sweet Sow-gelder.
Higgen.   I thanke your Worships.

Enter Prig, *and* Ferret.

Prig.   Will ye see any feates of activity,
Some sleight of hand, leigerdemaine? hey passe,
Presto, be gone there?
2. Boore.   Sit downe Jugler.
Prig [*aside*].   Sirha, play you your art well; draw neer piper:
Looke you, my honest friends, you see my hands;
Plaine dealing is no Divel: lend me some money;
Twelve-pence a piece will serve.
1. 2. Boores.   There, there.
Prig.   I thanke ye,
Thanke ye heartily: when shall I pay ye?
All Boores.   Ha, ha, ha, by'th masse this was a fine trick.   70

46 *Baa*] F2; *Bay* MS
48–59] F2, PPM, MMS7; MS *has the order* 54–9 *followed by* 48–53
50 *ere*] F2; *where* MS
61 *Higgen.* I...Worships.] MS (worshipps); *omit* F1

Prig.   A merry sleight toy: but now I'le shew your Worships
A tricke indeed.

Higgen.   Marke him well now my Masters.

Prig.   Here are three balls, these balls shall be three bullets,
One, two, and three: *ascentibus malentibus.*
Presto, be gone: they are vanish'd: faire play Gentlemen,
Now these three, like three bullets, from your three noses
Will I plucke presently: feare not, no harme boyes,
Titere, tu patule——

1. Boore.   Oh, oh, oh.

Prig.   *Recubans sub tegmine fagi.*

2. Boore.   Ye pull too hard; ye pull too hard.

Prig.   Stand faire then: 80
Silvestramtrim-tram.

3. Boore.   Hold, hold, hold.

Prig.   Come aloft bullets three, with a whim-wham:
Have ye their moneys?   [*Aside.*]

Higgen.   Yes, yes.

1. Boore.   Oh rare Jugler.

2. Boore.   Oh admirable Jugler,

Prig.   One tricke more yet;
Hey, come aloft: *sa, sa, flim, flam, taradumbis?*
East, west, north, south, now flye like *Jacke* with a *bumbis.*
Now all your money's gone: pray search your pockets.

1. Boore.   Humh.

2. Boore.   Ha.

3. Boore.   The Divell a penny's here.

Prig.   This was a rare
                                           tricke.

1. Boore.   But 'twould be a far rarer to restore it.

Prig.   I'le doe ye that too: looke upon me earnestly,   90
And move not any wayes your eyes from this place,
This button here: pow, whir, whiss, shake your pockets.

1. Boore.   By'th masse 'tis here againe boyes.

79 *tegmine*] MS; *jermine* F 1
81 *Silvestramtrim*] MS (*Silvestnam*); *Silvertramtrim* F 1
85 *flam*] MS; *flum* F 1   88 Ha] MS; He F 1

Prig.   Rest ye merry;
  My first tricke has paid me.
All Boores.   I, take it, take it.
2. Boore.   And take some drinke too.
Prig.   Not a drop now I thanke
                                                          you.
Higgen.   Away, we are discover'd else.

                    Exeunt [Prig, Ferret *and* Higgen].

            Enter Gerrard *like a blinde Aquavitæ-man, and a
                    boy singing the Song.*

        Bring out your Cony-skins, faire maids to me,
        And hold 'em faire that I may see;
        Grey, blacke, and blew: for your smaller skins,
        I'le give ye looking-glasses, pins.   100
        And for your whole Coney, heer's ready ready money.
        Come gentle Jone, *do thou begin*
        With thy blacke, blacke, blacke Cony-skin.
        And Mary *then, and* Jane *will follow,*
        With their silver-hair'd skins, and their yellow.
        The white Cony-skin, I will not lay by,
        For though it be faint, 'tis faire to the eye,
        The grey it is warme, but yet for my money,
        Give me the bonny, bonny, blacke Coney.
        Come away faire maides, your skins will decay: 110
        Come, and take money maids, put your ware away.
        Cony-skins, Cony-skins, have ye any Cony-skins,
        I have fine brace-lets, and fine silver pins.

Gerrard.   Buy any brand wine, buy any brand wine?
Boy.   Have ye any Cony-skins?
2. Boore.   My fine Canary-bird, ther's a cake for thy worship.
1. Boore.   Come, fill, fill, fill, fill suddenly: let's see Sir,
  What's this?
Gerrard.   A penny Sir.

        95 *2. Boore.*] MS; *omit* F1   96 *Higgen.*] MS; *omit* F1

1. Boore.   Fill till't be six-pence,
And there's my pig.
Boy.   This is a counter Sir.
1. Boore.   A counter? stay ye bully, what are these then?   120
O execrable Jugler! ô damn'd Jugler!
Look in your hose, hoa: this comes of looking forward.
3. Boore.   Divell a Dunkirke! what a rogue's this Jugler,
This hey passe, repasse, h'as repast us sweetly.
2. Boore.   Doe ye call these tricks.

Enter Higgen.

Higgen.   Have ye any ends
Of gold or silver.
2. Boore.   This fellow comes to mock us;
Gold or silver? cry copper.
1. Boore.   Yes my good friend,
We have e'ne an end of all we have.
Higgen.   'Tis well Sir,
You have the lesse to care for: gold and silver.   *Exit.*

Enter Prig.

Prig.   Have he any old cloaks to sel, have ye any old clokes to sel.
                    Exit. 130
1. Boore.   Cloakes? looke about ye boyes: mine's gone.
2. Boore.   A pox juggle 'em!
Pox o' their Prestoes: mine's gone too.
3. Boore.   Here's mine yet.
1. Boore.   Come, come, let's drink then: more brand wine, boy.
Boy.   Here Sir.
1. Boore.   If e're I catch your Sow-gelder, by this hand I'le strip
him;
O were ever fooles so ferkt? we have a cloake yet,
And all our caps; the Divell take the flincher.
All Boores.   Yaw, yaw, yaw, yaw.

120 bully] MS; *omit* F1
131 A pox] Colman; A —— F1; A Plague MS
132 Pox o'] MS; —— o' F1   133 wine, boy] MS (~ ‸ ~); wine. F1
135 O] MS (ô); *omit* F1   135 a cloake] MS (cloke); two cloakes F1

Enter Hemskirke.

Hemskirk.   Good d'en my honest fellows,
  You are merry here I see.
3. Boore.   'Tis all we have left Sir.
Hemskirk.   What hast thou? Aquavitæ?
Boy.   Yes.
Hemskirk.   Fill out then,
  And give these honest fellows round.
All Boores.   We thanke ye.   140
Hemskirk.   May I speake a word in private to ye?
All Boores.   Yes Sir.
Hemskirk.   I have a businesse for ye, honest friends,
  If ye dare lend your help, shall get ye crownes.
Gerrard.   Ha? Lead me a little nearer, boy.
1. Boore.   What is't Sir?
  If it be any thing to purchase money,
  Which is our want, command us.
All Boores.   All, all, all Sir.
Hemskirk.   Ye know the young spruce Merchant here in *Brugis*.
2. Boore.   Who? Master *Goswin*?
Hemskirk.   That: he owes me money,
  And here in towne there is no stirring of him.
Gerrard.   Say ye so?
Hemskirk.   This day, upon a sure appointment,   150
  He meets me a mile hence, by the Chase side
  Under the row of Okes, do ye know it?
All Boores.   Yes Sir.
Hemskirk.   Give 'em more drinke: there if ye dare but venture
  When I shall give the word to seize upon him,
  Here's twenty pound.
3. Boore.   Beware the Jugler.
Hemskirk.   If he resist, downe with him, have no mercy.
1. Boore.   I warrant you: wee'l hamper him.
Hemskirk.   To discharge you,
  I have a warrant here about me.

147   here] MS; *omit* F 1

3. Boore.   Her's our warrant,
  This carries fire i'the tayle.
Hemskirk.   Away with me then,
  The time draws on;   160
  I must remove so insolent a Suitor,   [*Aside.*]
  And if he be so rich, make him pay ransome
  Ere he see *Bruges* towres againe: thus wise men
  Repaire the hurts they take by a disgrace,
  And piece the Lyons skyn with the Foxes case.
Gerrard.   I am glad I've heard this sport yet.
Hemskirk.   Ther's for thy drink; come pay the house within boyes,
  And loose no time.
Gerrard.   Away with all our hast too.

                                                           Exeunt.

                       Enter Florez.   [III.

Floriƶ.   No winde blow faire yet? no returne of moneys?
  Letters? nor any thing, to hold my hopes up?
  Why then 'tis destin'd, that I fall, fall miserably,
  My credite I was built on, sinking with me.
  Thou boystrous North-wind, blowing my mis-fortunes,
  And frosting all my hopes to cakes of coldnesse,
  Yet stay thy fury: give the gentle South
  Yet leave to court those sailes that bring me safety,
  And you auspicious fires, bright twins in heaven
  Daunce on the shrowds: he blows still, stubbornly,   10
  And on this boystrous racke rides my sad ruine;
  There is no help, there can be now no comfort,
  To morrow with the Sun-set sets my credite.
  Oh misery! thou curse of man, thou plague,
  How in the midst of all our strength thou strik'st us;
  My vertuous Love is lost too: all, what I have been,
  No more hereafter to be seen then shadow;
  To prison now? well, yet ther's this hope left me,
  I may sinke fairely under this dayes venture

        15 How] MS (Howe); *omit* F1   15 of] MS; *omit* F1
        16 lost] MS; toss'd F1

                              284

And so to morrow's cross'd, and all those curses:
Yet manly I'le invite my fate, base fortune
Shall never say, sh'as cut my throate in feare.
This is the place his challenge call'd me too,
And 'twas a happy one at this time for me,
For let me fall before my foe i'the field,
And not at Bar, before my Creditors.

Enter Hemskirke.

Ha's kept his word: now Sir, your swords tongue only
Loud as you dare, all other language——
Hemskirk.   Well Sir,
You shall not be long troubled: draw.
Floriʒ.   'Tis done Sir,
And now have at ye.
Hemskirk.   Now.

Enter Boores.

Floriʒ.   Betray'd to villains?   30
Slaves ye shall buy me bravely, and thou base coward.

Enter Gerrard *and Beggars* [*all disguised*].

Gerrard.   Now upon 'em bravely,
Conjure 'em soundly boyes.
Boores.   Hold, hold.
Gerrard.   Lay on still,
Down with that Gentleman rogue, swinge him to sirrup:
                              [*Exit* Hemskirk *running.*]
Retire Sir, and take breath: follow and take him,
Take all, 'tis lawfull prize.
Boores.   We yield.
Gerrard.   Downe with 'em,
Into the wood, and rifle 'em, tew 'em, swinge 'em,
Knocke me their braines into their breeches.
Boores.   Hold, hold.
                              Exeunt. [*Manet* Floriz.]

24 'twas] MS (twas); was F1

285

Floriz. What these men are I know not, nor for what cause
They should thus thrust 'emselves into my danger,   40
Can I imagine. But sure heavens hand was in't,
Nor why this coward knave should deale so basely
To eate me up with slaves: but heaven, I thanke thee,
I hope thou hast reserv'd me to an end
Fit for thy creature, and worthy of thine honour:
Would all my other dangers here had suffered,
With what a joyfull heart should I goe home then?
Wher now, heaven knows, like him that waits his sentence
Or heares his passing bell; but ther's my hope still.

Enter Gerrard [*as* Clause].

Gerrard. Blessing upon you Master.
Floriz.   Thanke ye: leave me,   50
For by my troth I've nothing now to give thee.
Gerrard. Indeed I do not aske Sir, only it grieves me
To see ye looke so sad; now goodnesse keepe ye
From troubles in your minde.
Floriz.   If I were troubled
What could thy comfort do? prethee *Clause*, leave me.
Gerrard. Good Master be not angry; for what I say
Is out of true love to ye.
Floriz.   I know thou lov'st me.
Gerrard. Good Master blame that love then, if I prove so sawcy
To aske ye why y'are sad.
Floriz.   Most true, I am so,
And such a sadnesse I have got will sinke me.   60
Gerrard. Heaven shield it, Sir.
Floriz.   Faith thou must loose thy Master.
Gerrard. I had rather loose my neck Sir: would I knew——
Floriz. What would the knowledge do thee good, so miserable,
Thou canst not help thy selfe? when all my ways
Nor all the friends I have——
Gerrard.   You do not know Sir,
What I can doe: cures sometimes, for mens cares
Flow, where they least expect 'em.

286

Floriz.   I know thou wouldst doe,
But fare-well *Clause*, and pray for thy poore Master.
Gerrard.   I will not leave ye.
Floriz.   How?
Gerrard.   I dare not leave ye,
And till ye beate me dead, I must not leave ye.   70
By what ye hold most pretious, by heavens goodnesse,
As your faire youth may prosper, good Sir tell me:
My minde beleeves yet something's in my power
May ease ye of this trouble.
Floriz.   I will tell thee,
For a hundred thousand crownes upon my credit,
Taken up of Merchants to supply my traffiques,
The windes and weather envying of my fortune,
And no returne to help me off yet shewing,
To morrow, *Clause*, to morrow, which must come,
In prison thou shalt finde me poore, and broken.   80
Gerrard.   I cannot blame your griefe Sir.
Floriz.   Now, what say'st thou?
Gerrard.   I say you should not shrinck, for he that gave ye,
Can give ye more; his power can bring ye off Sir,
When friends and all forsake ye, yet he sees ye.
Floriz.   That's all my hope.
Gerrard.   Hope still Sir, are ye tide
Within the compasse of a day, good Master,
To pay this masse of money?
Floriz.   Ev'n to morrow;
But why do I stand mocking of my misery?
Is't not enough that floods, and friends forget me?
Gerrard.   Will no lesse serve?
Floriz.   What if it would?
Gerrard.   Your patience,   90
I do not aske to mock ye: 'tis a great sum,
A sum for mighty men to start, and stick at;
But not for honest: have ye no friends left ye,
None that have felt your bounty? worth this duty?

Floriz.   Duty? thou know'st it not.

Gerrard.   It is a duty,
And as a duty, from those men have felt ye,
Should be return'd againe: I have gain'd by ye,
A daily almes these seven yeares you have showr'd me.
Will halfe supply your want?

Floriz.   Why do'st thou foole me?
Can'st thou worke miracles?

Gerrard.   To save my Master,   100
I can worke this.

Floriz.   Thou wilt make me angry with thee.

Gerrard.   For doing good?

Floriz.   What power hast thou?

Gerrard.   Enquire not:
So I can do it, to preserve my Master;
Nay if it be three parts.

Floriz.   O that I had it,
But good *Clause*, talke no more, I feele thy charity,
As thou hast felt mine: but alas!

Gerrard.   Distrust not.
'Tis that that quenches ye: pull up your spirit,
Your good, your honest, and your noble spirit;
For if the fortunes of ten thousand people
Can save ye, rest assur'd; ye have forgot Sir,   110
The good ye did, which was the power ye gave me;
Ye shall now know the King of Beggars treasure:
And let the windes blow as they please, the Seas roare,
Yet, here to morrow, you shall finde your harbour,
Here faile me not, for if I live I'le fit ye.

Floriz.   How faine I would believe thee.

Gerrard.   If I ly Master,
Believe no man hereafter.

Floriz.   I will trye thee,
But he knowes, that knowes all.

Gerrard.   Know me to morrow,
And if I know not how to cure ye, kill me;
So passe in peace, my best, my worthiest Master.   120

                                              Exeunt.

Enter Hubert *like a Huntesman.*   [III.] iii

Hubert. Thus have I stolne away disguiz'd from *Hemskirck*
 To try these people, for my heart yet tells me
 Some of these Beggars, are the men I looke for.
 Appearing like my selfe, they have no reason
 (Though my intent is faire, my maine end honest)
 But to avoyde me narrowly. That face too,
 That womans face, how neere it is: ô may it
 But prove the same, and fortune how I'le blesse thee;
 Thus, sure they cannot know me, or suspect me,
 If to my habit I but change my nature,   10
 As I must do; this is the wood they live in,
 A place fit for concealement: where, 'till fortune
 Crowne me with that I seeke, I'le live amongst 'em.

              Exit.

Enter Higgen, Prig, Ferret, Gynks, [III. iv]
and the rest with Boores.

Higgen. Come bring 'um out, for here we sit in justice:
 Give to each one a cudgell, a good cudgell:
 And now attend your sentence: that ye are rogues,
 And mischeivous base rascalls, (ther's the point now)
 I take it, is confess'd.
Prig. Deny it if you dare knaves.
Boores.   We are Rogues Sir.
Higgen. To amplify the matter then, Rogues as ye are,
 And lamb'd, ye shall be ere we leave ye——
Boores.   Yes Sir.
Higgen. And to the open handling of our justice,
 Why did ye this upon the proper person   10
 Of our good Master? were ye drunk when ye did it?
Boores. Yes indeed were we.
Prig.   Ye shall be beaten sober.
Higgen. Was it for want you undertooke it?

   0.2 *with*] MS; *of the* F1   *8 lamb'd] stet* F1, MS

Boores.   Yes Sir.

Higgen.   You shall be swing'd aboundantly.

Prig.   And yet for all that,
You shall be poore rogues still.

Higgen.   Has not the Gentleman,
Pray marke this point Brother *Prig*, that noble Gentleman
Reliev'd ye often, found ye meanes to live by,
By employing some at Sea, some here; some there;
According to your callings?

Boores.   'Tis most true sir.

Higgen.   Is not the man, an honest man?

Boores.   Yes truly.   20

Higgen.   A liberall Gentleman? and as ye are true rascalls
Tell me but this, have ye not been drunk, and often,
At his charge?

Boores.   Often, often.

Higgen.   Ther's the point then,
They have cast themselves, brother *Prig*.

Prig.   A shrew'd point Brother.

Higgen.   Brother, proceed you now; the cause is open,
I am some what weary.

Prig.   Can you do these things?
You most abhominable stincking Rascalls,
You turnip-eating Rogues.

Boores.   We are truly sorry.

Prig.   Knock at your hard harts Rogues, and presently
Give us a signe you feele compunction,   30
Every man up with's cudgell, and on his neighbour
Bestow such almes, 'till we shall say sufficient,
For there your sentence lyes: without partiality
Either of head, or hide, Rogues, without sparing,
Or we shall take the paines to beat ye dead else:
Ye know your doom.

Higgen.   One, two, and three about it.
                                        Beat one another.

36 know] MS; shall know F1
36.1 *Beat one another.*] F2; *omit* F1, FK, MS

Prig.   That fellow in the blew, has true compunction,
He beates his fellowes bravely, ah, well struck boyes.

Enter Gerrard.

Higgen.   Up with that blew breech, now playes he the Divell,
So get ye home, drink small beere, and be honest;   40

[*Exeunt Boores.*]

Call in the Gentleman.
Gerrard.   Do, bring him presently,
His cause I'le heare my selfe.

Enter Hemskirck [*in his shirt, guarded*].

Higgen, Prig.   With all due reverence,
We do resigne Sir.
Gerrard.   Now huffing Sir, what's your name?
Hemskirk.   What's that to you
Sir?

Gerrard.   It shall be ere we part.
Hemskirk.   My name is *Hemskirk*,
I follow the Earle, which you shall feele.
Gerrard.   No threatning,
For we shall coole ye Sir; why did'st thou basely
Attempt the murder of the Merchant *Goswin*?
Hemskirk.   What power hast thou to aske me?
Gerrard.   I will know it.
Or flea thee till thy paine discover it.   50
Hemskirk.   He did me wrong, base wrong.
Gerrard.   That cannot save ye,
Who sent ye hither? and what further villanies
Have ye in hand?
Hemskirk.   Why would'st thou know? what profit,
If I had any private way, could rise
Out of my knowledge, to do thee commodity?
Be sorry for what th'ast done, and make amends foole,
I'le talke no further to thee: nor these rascalls.
Gerrard.   Tye him to that tree.
Hemskirk.   I have told ye whom I follow.

Gerrard.   The Divell you should do, by your villanies,
Now he that has the best way, wring it from him.   60
Higgen.   I undertake it: turne him to the Sun boyes;
Give me a fine sharpe rush, will ye confesse yet?
Hemskirk.   Y'ave rob'd me already, now you'le murder me?
Higgen.   Murder your nose a little: does your head purge Sir?
To it againe, 'twill do ye good.
Hemskirk.   Oh,
I cannot tell ye any thing.
Gerrard.   Proceed then.
Higgen.   Ther's maggots in your nose, I'le fetch 'em out Sir.
Hemskirk.   O my head breakes.
Higgen.   The best thing for the rhewme
                                        Sir,
That falls into your worships eyes.
Hemskirk.   Hold, hold.
Gerrard.   Speake then.
Hemskirk.   I know not what.
Higgen.   It lyes in's braine yet,   70
In lumps it lyes, I'le fetch it out the finest;
What pretty faces the foole makes? heigh!
Hemskirk.   Hold,
Hold, and I'le tell ye all, looke in my doublet;
And there within the lining in a paper,
You shall finde all.
Gerrard.   Go fetch that paper hither,
And let him loose for this time.

                    [*Exeunt* Ferret *and others.*]

                Enter Hubert [*as Huntsman*].

Hubert.   Good ev'n my honest friends.
Gerrard.   Good ev'n good fellow.
Hubert.   May a poore huntsman, with a merry hart,
A voyce shall make the forrest ring about him,
Get leave to live amongst ye? true as steele, boyes?   80
That knowes all chases, and can watch all howres,
And with my quarter staffe, though the Divell bid stand,

Deale such an almes, shall make him roare again?
Prick ye the fearefull hare through crosse wayes, sheepe walkes,
And force the crafty Reynard climb the quiksetts;
Rouse ye the lofty Stag, and with my bell-horne,
Ring him a knell, that all the woods shall mourne him,
'Till in his funerall teares, he fall before me?
The *Polcat*, *Marterne*, and the rich skin'd *Lucerne*,
I know to chase, the Roe, the winde out-stripping;   90
Isgrim himselfe, in all his bloody anger
I can beate from the bay, and the wild Sounder
Single, and with my arm'd staffe, tew the Boare,
Spight of his fomy tushes, and thus strike him;
'Till he fall downe my feast.
Gerrard.   A goodly fellow.
Hubert [*aside*].   What mak'st thou here, ha?
Gerrard.   We accept thy
                                    fellowship.
Hubert [*aside*].   *Hemskirck*, thou art not right I feare, I feare thee.

         Enter Ferret [*and others*], *a letter.*

Ferret.   Here is the paper: and as he said we found it.
Gerrard.   Give me it, I shall make a shift yet, old as I am
To finde your knavery — you are sent here Sirra,   100
To discover certaine Gentlemen, a spy-knave,
And if ye finde 'em, if not by perswasion
To bring 'em back, by poyson to dispatch 'em.
Hubert [*aside*].   By poyson, ha?
Gerrard.   Here is an other, *Hubert*;
What is that *Hubert* Sir?
Hemskirk.   You may perceive there.
Gerrard.   I may perceive a villany and a ranke one,
Was he joyn'd partner of thy knavery?
Hemskirk.   No.
He had an honest end, would I had had so,

---

85 Reynard] MS; Reimald F1
90–91 -stripping;...anger ∧] ~ ∧...~ ; F1–2; ~ ∧...~ ∧ MS
*93 tew] MS; turne F1   108 had had] MS; have had F1

Which makes him scape such cut throates.

Gerrard.   So it seemes,
For here thou art commanded, when that *Hubert*   110
Has done his best and worthiest service this way
To cut his throat, for here he's set downe dangerous.

Hubert [*aside*].   This is most impious.

Gerrard.   I am glad we have found ye,
Is not this true?

Hemskirk.   Yes? what are you the better?

Gerrard.   You shall perceive Sir, ere you get your freedome:
Take him aside, and friend, we take thee to us,
Into our company, thou dar'st be true unto us?

Higgen.   I, and obedient too?

Hubert.   As you had bred me.

Gerrard.   Then take our hand: thou art now a servant to us,
Welcom him all.

Higgen.   Stand off, stand off: I'le do it,   120
We bid yee welcome three wayes; first for your person,
Which is a promising person, next for your quallity,
Which is a decent, and a gentle quality,
Last for the frequent meanes you have to feed us,
You can steale 'tis to be presum'd?

Hubert.   Yes, venson,
Or if I want——

Higgen.   'Tis well, you understand right,
And shall learne dayly: you can drink too?

Hubert.   Soundly.

Higgen.   And ye dare know a woman from a weathercock?

Hubert.   Yes, if I handle her.

Gerrard.   Now sweare him.

Higgen.   I crowne thy nab, with a gage of benbouse,   130
And stall thee by the salmon into the clowes,
To mand o' the pad, and strike all the cheates;
To mill from the Ruffmans, commission and slates,

---

*130–142 *Higgen.* I crowne...hang.] MS; F1 *places lines* 143–56 (...with me.)
after line 129, *and transfers lines* 130–142, *preceded by duplicated* 'Gerrard. Now sweare
him.' *after line* 143   130 gage] MS; gag F1

Twang dell's i'the stromell, and let the Quire Cuffin:
And Herman Becks trine, and trine to the Ruffin.
Gerrard.   Now interpret this unto him.
Higgen.   I powre on thy pate a pot of good ale,
And by the Rogues oth a Rogue thee install:
To beg on the way, to rob all thou meetes;
To steale from the hedge, both the shirt and the sheetes: 140
And lye with thy wench in the straw till she twang,
Let the Constable, Justice, and Divell go hang.
Y'are welcom Brother.
All.   Welcom, welcom, welcom, but who shall have
The keeping of this fellow?
Hubert.   Thank ye friends,
And I beseech ye, if ye dare but trust me;
For I have kept wilde doggs and beastes for wonder,
And made 'em tame too: give into my custody
This roaring rascall and I shall hamper him,
With all his knacks and knaveryes, and I feare me   150
Discover yet a further villany in him;
O he smells ranck 'oth rascall.
Gerrard.   Take him to thee,
But if he scape——
Hubert.   Let me be ev'n hang'd for him;
Come Sir, I'le tye ye to my leash.
Hemskirk.   A way Rascall.
Hubert.   Be not so stubborne: I shall swindge ye soundly,
And ye play tricks with me.
Gerrard.   So, now come in,
But ever have an eye Sir, to your prisoner.
Hubert.   He must blinde both mine eyes, if he get from me.
Gerrard.   Go, get some victualls, and some drink, some good drink,
For this day wee'le keep holly to good fortune,   160
Come and be frollick with us.
Higgen.   Ye are a stranger.
                                        Exeunt.

147 I] MS; if I F1   149 and] MS; *omit* F1
154 Come] MS; Roome F1   *161 stranger] MS (Stranger); stanger F1

Enter Floriz, *and* Bertha.   [III.]

Bertha.   Indeed y'are welcom: I have hard your scape,
And therefore give her leave, that onely loves you,
(Truely and dearely loves ye) give her joy leave,
To bid ye welcom: what is't makes ye sad man?
Here are noe enemyes, heres none that hates you.
Why do ye looke so wilde? is't I offend ye?
Be shrew my heart, not willingly.
Floriz.   No *Gertred.*
Bertha.   Is't the delay of that ye long have look'd for,
Our happy marriage? now I come to urge it:
Now when ye please to finish it.
Floriz [*aside*].   No newes yet?   10
Bertha.   Do you heare Sir?
Floriz.   Yes.
Bertha.   Do ye love me?
Floriz [*aside*].   Have I liv'd,
In all the happinesse fortune could seat me,
In all mens faire opinions——
Bertha.   I have provided
A Priest, that's ready for us.
Floriz [*aside*].   And can that Divell,
In one ten dayes, that Divell chance devour me?
Bertha.   Wee'le fly to what place ye please.
Floriz [*aside*].   No star prosperous?
All at a swoope?
Bertha.   You do not love me *Goswin*?
You will not looke upon me?
Floriz [*aside*].   Can mens prayers
Shot up to heaven, with such a zeale as mine are,
Fall back like lazy mists, and never prosper?   20
Geyves, I must weare, and cold must be my comfort;
Darknesse, and want of meat; alas she weepes too,
Which is the top of all my sorrowes: *Gertred*!

    5 Here...you.] MS; *omit* F1   9 Our] MS; A F1
    14 that] MS; the F1

Bertha.   No, no, you will not know me; my poore beauty,
  Which has been worth your eyes.
Floriʒ [*aside*].   The time growes on still:
  And like a tumbling wave, I see my ruine,
  Coming rolling over me.
Bertha.   Yet will ye know me?
Floriʒ [*aside*].   For a hundred thousand crownes.
Bertha.   Yet will ye love me?
  Tell me but how I have deserv'd this slighting.
Floriʒ [*aside*].   For a hundred thousand crownes?
Bertha.   Farewell
                    dissembler. 30
Floriʒ [*aside*].   Of which I have scarce ten: ô how it starts me.
Bertha.   And may the next you love, hearing my ruine——
Floriʒ.   I had forgot my selfe, ô my best *Gertred*,
  Crowne of my joyes, and comforts.
Bertha.   Sweet what ayle ye?
  I thought you had been vext with me.
Floriʒ.   My minde wench,
  My minde o're flow'n with sorrow, sunck my memory.
Bertha.   Am not I worthy of the knowledge of it?
  And cannot I as well affect your sorrowes,
  As your delights? you love no other woman?
Floriʒ.   No I protest.
Bertha.   You have no ships lost lately?
Floriʒ.   None that I know of.   40
Bertha.   I hope y'have spilt no blood: whose innocence
  May lay this on your conscience.
Floriʒ.   Cleare, by heaven.
Bertha.   Why should you be thus then?
Floriʒ.   Good *Gertred*, aske not,
  Ev'n by the love you beare me.
Bertha.   I am obedient.
Floriʒ.   Go in my faire; I will not be long from ye——

29 this] MS; your F1
36 flow'n] MS; flow'd F1
37 not I] MS; I not F1

Nor long I feare me with thee.——At my returne
Dispose me as ye please.
Bertha.   The good gods guide ye.   *Exit.*
Floriz.   Now for my last which is the least I hope for,
And when that failes, for mans worst fortune, pitty.

                                                          Exit.

Enter Floriz *and four Merchants.*   **IV.**

Floriz.   Why Gentlemen, 'tis but a week more I intreat you,
But seven short daies, I am not running from ye,
Nor, if ye give me patience, is it possible
All my adventures faile; you have ships abroad,
Endure the beating both of winde, and weather:
I'm sure 'twould vex your hearts, to be protested;
Ye are all faire Merchants.
1. Merchant.   Yes, and must have faire play;
There is no lyving here else, one howres failing
Failes us of all our friends, of all our credits:
For my part I would stay; but my wants tell me,   10
I must wrong others in't.
Floriz.   No mercy in ye?
2. Merchant.   'Tis foolish to depend on others mercy:
Keepe your selfe right, and even, cut your cloth Sir,
According to your calling: you have liv'd here
In Lordlike prodigality; high, and open,
And now ye finde what 'tis: the liberall spending
The summer of your youth, which you should gleane in,
And like the labouring Ant, make use and gaine of,
Has brought this bitter stormy winter on ye,
And now ye cry.
3. Merchant.   Alas before your poverty,   20
We were no men, of no marke, no endeavour;
You stood alone, tooke up all trade, all business,
Running through your hands, scarce a sayle at Sea,

*47 Dispose] MS; Despise F1   *48 last] MS; selfe F1
5 and] MS; or F1   8 lyving] MS; lying F1

But loaden with your goods: we poore weak pedlers,
When by your leave, and much intreaty to it,
We could have stoage for a little cloth,
Or a few wines, put of and thanke your worship.
Lord, how the world's chang'd with ye? now I hope Sir,
We shall have sea-roome.

Floriz.   Is my misery,
Become my scorne too? have ye no humanity,   30
No part of men left? are all the bountyes in me
To you, and to the Towne, turn'd my reproaches?

4. Merchant.   Well, get your monyes ready: 'tis but two howres,
We shall protest ye else, and sodainly.

Floriz.   But two dayes.

1. Merchant.   Not an howre, ye know the hazard.

                                                        Exeunt.

Floriz.   How soone's my light put out: hard harted *Bruges;*
Within thy walls, may never honest Merchant
Venture his fortunes more: ô my poore wench too.

                    Enter Gerrard.

Gerrard.   Good fortune Master.
Floriz.   Thou mistak'st me *Clause,*
I am not worth thy blessing.
Gerrard.   Stil a sad man?   40
No beliefe gentle Master? come bring it in then,

            Enter Higgen *and* Prig *like Porters.*

And now believe your Beadesman.
Floriz.   Is this certaine?
Or do'st thou work upon my troubled sence?
Gerrard.   'Tis gold Sir,
Take it and try it.
Floriz.   Certainely 'tis treasure,
Can there be yet this blessing?
Gerrard.   Cease your wonder,

---

*27 thanke] *stet* F 1   36 soone's my light] MS; soone my light's F 1
*41.1 *Porters*] FK; *Porter* F 1

You shall not sinke, for nev'r a sowst Flap-dragon,
For nere a pickell'd pilcher of 'em all Sir:
'Tis there your full summ, a hundred thousand crownes,
And good sweet Master, now be merry; pay 'em,
Pay the poore pelting knaves, that know no goodnesse: 50
And cheere your heart up handsomely.
Floriz.   Good *Clause*,
How cam'st thou by this mighty summ? if naughtily
I must not take it of thee, 'twill undo me.
Gerrard.   Feare not: ye have it by as honest meanes
As though your father gave it: Sir, you know not
To what a masse, the little we get dayly,
Mounts in seven yeares; we beg it for heavens charity,
And to the same good, we are bound to render it.
Floriz.   What great security?
Gerrard.   Away with that Sir,
Were not ye more then all the men in *Bruges*;   60
And all the money in my thoughts——
Floriz.   But good *Clause*,
I may dye presently.
Gerrard.   Then this dyes with ye——
Pay when ye can good Master, I'le no parchments,
Onely this charity I shall intreat ye,
Leave me this Ring.
Floriz.   Alas, it is to poore *Clause*.
Gerrard.   'Tis all I aske, and this withall, that when
I shall deliver this back, you shall grant me
Freely one poore petition.
Floriz.   There I confirme it,
And may my faith forsake mee when I shun it.
Gerrard.   Away, your time drawes on. Take up the money   70
And follow this young Gentleman.
Floriz.   Farewell *Clause*,
And may thy honest memory live ever.
Gerrard.   Heaven blesse ye and still keep ye, farewell Master.
Exeunt.

68 confirme] MS; confesse F1

300

Enter Hubert [*as Huntsman*].

Hubert. I have lockt my youth up close enough for gadding
In an olde tree, and set watch over him.

Enter Jaculine [*as* Minche].

Now for my Love, for sure this wench must be she,
She follows me; Come hither, pretty *Minche*.
Jaqueline.   No, no, you'l kisse me.
Hubert.   So I will.
Jaqueline.   Y'deed law?
How will ye kisse me, pray you?
Hubert.   Thus:——soft as my loves lips.
Jaqueline.   Oh!
Hubert.   What's your Fathers name?
Jaqueline.   He's gone to heaven.
Hubert.   Is it not *Gerrard*, sweet?
Jaqueline.   I'le stay no longer,
My mother's an olde woman, and my Brother
Was drown'd at sea, with catching Cockles.——O love: 10
O how my heart melts in me: how thou fir'st me!
Hubert. 'Tis certain she:——pray let me see your hand, sweet.
Jaqueline.   No, no, you'l bite it.
Hubert.   Sure I should know that Gymmall.
Jaqueline [*aside*].   'Tis certaine he: I had forgot my ring too.
O *Hubert, Hubert.*
Hubert.   Ha? me-thought she nam'd me——
Doe you know me, Chicke?
Jaqueline.   No indeed, I never saw ye,
But me-thinks ye kisse finely.
Hubert.   Kisse againe then;——
By heaven 'tis she.
Jaqueline [*aside*].   O what a joy he brings me.
Hubert.   You are not *Minche*?

5 me] MS (mee); *omit* F1

301

Jaqueline.   Yes pretty Gentleman,
And I must be married to morrow to a Capper.   20
Hubert.   Must ye my sweet, and doe's the Capper love ye?
Jaqueline.   Yes, yes, he'l give me pye, and looke in mine eys
   thus:——
Tis he: it is my deare Love; ô blest fortune.
Hubert.   How fain she would conceal her selfe? yet shew it:——
Will ye love me, and leave that man? I'le serve.
Jaqueline [*aside*].   O I shall loose my selfe.
Hubert.   I'le waite upon ye,
And make ye dainty Nose-gayes.
Jaqueline.   Where will ye sticke 'em?
Hubert.   Here in thy bosome, and make a crown of Lillies
For thy faire head.
Jaqueline.   And will ye love me, deed-law?
Hubert.   With all my heart.
Jaqueline.   Call me to morrow then,   30
And we'l have brave chear, and goe to Church together:
Give ye good ev'n Sir.
Hubert.   But one word faire *Minche.*
Jaqueline.   I must be gone a milking.
Hubert.   Ye shall presently.
Did ye never heare of a young Maid called *Jaculine?*
Jaqueline.   I am discovered: hark in your eare, I'le tell ye;
You must not know me: kisse and be constant ever.
Hubert.   Heaven curse me else; tis she, and now I'm certain
They are all here: now for my other project.——

                                        Exeunt.

Enter Floriz, *Four Merchants*, Higgen, *and* Prig [*as porters*].   [IV.]

1. Merchant.   Nay if 'twill do you courtesy.
Floriz.   None at all Sir;
Take it, 'tis yours: ther's your ten thousand for ye,
Give in my Bills: your sixteene.

27 Where] MS; And where F 1   28 thy] MS; *omit* F 1
29 thy] MS; your F 1   1 'twill] MS (twill); it would F 1

3. Merchant.　　　　　　　Pray be pleas'd Sir,
To make a further use.
Flori₹.　　　　　No.
3. Merchant.　　　　　　What I have Sir,
You may command; pray let me be your Servant.
Flori₹. Put your hatts on: I care not for your courtisies,
They're most untimely don, and no truth in 'em.
2. Merchant. I have a fraught of pepper.
Flori₹.　　　　　　　　　Rot your pepper,
Shall I trust you againe? ther's your seven thousand.
4. Merchant. Or if you want fine suger, 'tis but sending.　10
Flori₹. No, I can send to *Barbary*, those people
That never yet knew faith, have nobler freedoms:
These carry to *Vanlock*, and take my Bills in.
To *Peter Zuten* these: bring back my Jewells;
　　　　　　　　Drum, flourish: Peeces discharge.
Why are these peices?

　　　　　　　　Enter Saylor.

Saylor.　　　　　　Health to the noble merchant,
The *Susan* is return'd.
Flori₹.　　　　　Well?
Saylor.　　　　　　　Well, and rich Sir,
And now put in.
Flori₹.　　　　　Heaven thou hast heard my prayers.
Saylor. The brave *Rebecca* too: bound from the straights,
With the next tide is ready to put after.
Flori₹. What newes o'th' fly-boate?
Saylor.　　　　　　　　If this winde hold till
　　　　　　　　　　　　　　midnight, 20
She will be here, and wealthy, scap't fairely.
Flori₹. How, pre'thee Saylor?
Saylor.　　　　　　Thus Sir, sh'ad fight
Seven howers together, with six Turkish Gallyes,
And she fought bravely: but at length was borded:

14.1 Drum...discharge.] MS (*flourish* ∧ | *discharg*); *omit* F1
21 scap't] *query* she scap't

303

And over lai'd with strength: when presently
Comes boring up the winde Captaine *Van-noke*,
That valiant Gentleman, you redeem'd from prison;
He knew the Boate, set in: and fought it bravely:
Beate all the Gallies off; sunk three, redeem'd her,
And as a service to ye, sent her home Sir.   30

Floriz.   An honest noble Captaine, and a thankfull;
Ther's for thy new's: go drink the Merchants health, Saylor.

Saylor.   I thanke your bounty, and I'le do it to a doyt, Sir.

Exit Saylor.

1. Merchant.   What miracles are powr'd upon this fellow?

Floriz.   This yeare I hope my friends, I shall scape prison,
For all your cares to catch me.

2. Merchant.   You may please Sir
To think of your poor servants in displeasure,
Whose all we have, goods, monyes, all our service——

Floriz.   I thank ye, when I have need, I shall forget ye:
You are paid I hope.

All.   We joy in your good fortunes.   40

Exeunt Merchants.

Enter Van-donck.

Van-dunck.   Come, come Sir, take your ease, you must home
    with mee,
Yonder's one weepes and howles.

Floriz.   Alas how does she?

Van-dunck.   She will be better soone I hope.

Floriz.   Why soone sir?

Van-dunck.   When you have her in your armes, this night my
    blest boy
She is thy wife.

Floriz.   With all my hart I take her.

*38 we...all our service——] MS (service ʌ); they... are at your service. F1
*39 need,] MS; need of you ʌ F1
*41 Come, come ʌ Sir] MS; Come Sir, come F1
41 home] MS; go home F1   44 When] MS; Why when F1
44 blest] MS; *omit* F1

Van-dunck.   We have prepar'd, and all thy friends shall be there,
And all the Roomes shall reeke to see thee revell;
Thou hast been wrong'd and no more shall my service
Waite on the knave her Uncle, I have hard all,
All his baites for my Boy, but thou shalt have her;   50
Hast thou dispatch't thy businesse?
Floriz.   Most.
Van-dunck.   By the masse Boy,
Thou tumblest now in wealth, and I joy in it,
Thou art the best Boy, that *Bruges* ever nourish'd:
Thou hast been sad, I'le cheere thee up with Sack,
And when th'art lusty, fling thee to thy Mistris.
Shee'l hug thee, sirha.
Floriz.   I even long to see it,
I had forgot you: ther's for your rewards, friends: [*To* Higgen,
                                                      Prig.]

You have had heavy burthens, commend my love,
My best love, all the love I have indeed
To honest, honest *Clause*, shortly I'le thanke him.   *Exit* 60
Higgen.   By the masse a royall Merchant, gold by the handfulls,
Here will be sport soone, *Prig.*
Prig.   It partly seemes so,
And here will I be in a trice.
Higgen.   And I boy,
Away a pace, we are look'd for.
Prig.   Oh these bak'd meates,
Me thinkes I smell 'em hither.
Higgen.   Thy mouth waters.

                                                      Exeunt.

46 and] MS; *omit* F1   46 shall be] MS (shalbe); will be F1
47 the Roomes] MS; my Roomes F1   47 reeke] MS; smoake F1
47 thee] MS; the F1   55 lusty,] MS; lusty I'le F1
56 even] MS; *omit* F1   57 your rewards,] MS; you my F1
58 have had] MS; had but F1   59 My] MS; To my F1
59 indeed] MS; *omit* F1   60 honest, honest] MS; honest F1
60 him] MS; him better F1   61 handfulls] MS; handfull F1

Enter Hubert, *and* Hemskirck.

Hubert.   I must not.
Hemskirk.   Why? 'tis in thy power to do it,
And mine to recompence thee to thy wishes.
Hubert.   I dare not, nor I will not.
Hemskirk.   Gentle Huntsman,
  Though thou hast kept me hard: though in thy duty,
  Which is requir'd thou dost, th'hast used me stubbornly;
  I can forgive thee freely.
Hubert.   You the Earles servant?
Hemskirk.   I sweare I am neare as his owne thoughts to him;
  Able to doe thee——
Hubert.   Come, come, leave your prating.
Hemskirk.   If thou dar'st but try.
Hubert.   I thanke ye hartily,   10
  You'le be the first shall hang me, a sweet recompence;
  I could do, but I do not say I will,
  To any honest fellow that would thinke on't
  And know a benefit.
Hemskirk.   If it be not recompenc'd,
  And to thine owne desires, if within these ten dayes
  I do not make thee——
Hubert.   What, a false knave?
Hemskirk.   Prethee,
  Prethee conceive me rightly, any thing
  Of profit or of place that may advance thee.
Hubert.   Why what a Goosecap would'st thou make me, do not
  I know men in thy misery will promise any thing,
  More then their lives can reach at?
Hemskirk.   Beleeve it Huntsman,   20
  There shall not one short sillable come from me,

---

*2 mine...recompence] MS; in mine...reward F 1
5 thou dost] MS; to do it F 1   10 shall] MS; man that will F 1
13 know a benefit] MS (knowe a benefitt); be a benefactor F 1
19 men in thy] MS; that men in F 1   20 it] MS; me F 1
21 come] MS; That comes F 1

Passe without full performance.

Hubert.   Say ye so Sir?
Have ye e're a good place for my quality?

Hemskirk.   A thousand: Chases, Forrests, Parks: I'le make thee
Chiefe ranger over all the games.

Hubert.   When?

Hemskirk.   Presently.

Hubert.   This may provoke me: and yet to prove a knave too——

Hemskirk.   'Tis to prove honest: 'tis to do good service,
Service for him th'art sworn to, for thy Prince,
Then for thy selfe that good; what fool would live here,
Poore, and in misery, subject to all dangers
Law, and lewd people can inflict, when bravely   30
And to himselfe he may be law, and credit?

Hubert.   Shall I believe thee?

Hemskirk.   As that thou holdst most holy.

Hubert.   Ye may play tricks.

Hemskirk.   Then let me never live more.

Hubert.   Then you shall see Sir, I will do a service
That shall deserve indeed.

Hemskirk.   'Tis well said, hunts-man,
And thou shall be well thought of.

Hubert.   I will do it:
'Tis not your letting free, for that's meer nothing,
But such a service, if the Earl be noble,
He shall for ever love me.

Hemskirk.   What is't hunts-man?

Hubert.   Do you know any of these people live here?   40

Hemskirk.   No.

Hubert.   You are a foole then: here be those to have 'em,
I know the Earl so well, would make him caper.

Hemskirk.   Any of the old Lords that rebel'd?

Hubert.   Peace, all,
I know 'em every one, and can betray 'em.

Hemskirk.   But wilt thou doe this service?

Hubert.   If you'l keep

Your faith, and free word to me.

Hemskirk.   Wilt thou swear me?

Hubert.   No, no, I will beleeve ye: more then that too,
Here's the right heire.

Hemskirk.   O honest, honest hunts-man!

Hubert.   Now, how to get these Gallants, ther's the matter,   50
You will be constant, 'tis no work for me else.

Hemskirk.   Will the Sun shine agen?

Hubert.   The way to get 'em——

Hemskirk.   Propound it, and it shall be done.

Hubert.   No sleight;
(For they are Devillish crafty, it concerns 'em,)
Nor reconcilement, (for they dare not trust neither)
Must doe this tricke.

Hemskirk.   By force?

Hubert.   I, that must doe it.
And with the person of the Earl himselfe,
Authority (and mighty) must come on 'em:
Or else in vaine: and thus I'de have ye do it.
To morrow-night be here: a hundred men will bear 'em,   60
(So he be there, for he's both wise and valiant,
And with his terrour will strike dead their forces)
The houre be twelve a clock: now for a guide
To draw ye without danger on these persons,
The woods being thicke, and hard to hit, my selfe
With some few with me, made unto our purpose,
Beyond the wood, upon the plain, will wait ye
By the great Oke.

Hemskirk.   I know it: keep thy faith hunts-man,
And such a showr of wealth——

Hubert.   I warrant ye:
Misse nothing that I tell ye.

Hemskirk.   No.

Hubert.   Farewell;   70
You have your liberty, now use it wisely;

*62 And...forces] *stet* F 1

And keep your houre, goe close about the wood there,
For feare they spy ye.
Hemskirk.　　　　Well.
Hubert.　　　　　　　And bring no noyse with ye.
Hemskirk.　All shall be done to'th purpose: farewel hunts-man.
　　　　　　　　　　　　　　　　　　　Exeunt.

Enter Gerrard, Higgen, Prig, Ginks, Snap, Ferret.　　[IV. v]

Gerrard.　Now, what's the news in towne?
Ginks.　　　　　　　　　　No news, but joy Sir;
Every man wooing of the noble Merchant,
Who has his hearty commendations to ye.
Ferret.　Yes, this is news, this night he's to be married.
Ginks.　By'th masse that's true, he marryes *Vandoncks* daughter,
The dainty black-ey'd bell.
Higgen.　　　　　　　I would my clapper
Hung in his baldricke, what a peale could I ring?
Gerrard.　Marryed?
Ginks.　　　　　　　'Tis very true Sir, ô the pyes,
The piping-hot mince-pyes.
Prig.　　　　　　　　O the Plum-pottage.
Higgen.　For one leg of a goose now would I ventur a limb boys, 10
I love a fat goose, as I love allegiance,
And pox upon the Boors, too well they know it,
And therefore starve their powltry.
Gerrard [aside].　　　　　　To be married
To *Vandonks* daughter?
Higgen.　　　　　　　O this pretious Merchant:
What sport will he have? but hark ye brother *Prig*,
Shall we do nothing in this fore-said wedding?
Ther's money to be got, and meate I take it,
What thinke ye of a morise?
Prig.　　　　　　　No, by no meanes,

　　72 close] MS; closer F1
　　12, 44 pox] Colman; —— F1-2; plague MS
　　15 will he] MS (hee); he will F1　　　16 this] MS; the F1

That goes no further then the street, there leaves us,
Now we must think of something that must draw us   20
Into the bowels of it, into'th buttery,
Into the Kitchin, into the Cellar, something
That that old drunken Burgo-master loves,
What think ye of a wassell?
Higgen.   I think worthily.
Prig.   And very fit it should be, thou, and *Ferret,*
And *Ginks* to sing the Song: I for the structure,
Which is the bowle.
Higgen.   Which must be up-sey *English,*
Strong, lusty London beer; let's think more of it.
Gerrard [aside].   He must not marry.

Enter Hubert.

Hubert.   By your leave in private,
One word Sir, with ye; *Gerrard:* do not start; nay,   30
I know ye, and he knows ye, that best loves ye:
Hubert speakes to ye, and you must be *Gerrard,*
The time invites ye to it.
Gerrard.   Make no show then,
I am glad to see ye Sir; and I am *Gerrard.*
How stands affaires?
Hubert.   Faire, if ye dare now follow;
Hemskirke I have let goe, and these my causes,
I'le tell ye privately, and how I have wrought him,
And then to prove me honest to my friends,
Looke upon these directions; you have seen his.   [*Gives letter.*]
Higgen.   Then will I speak a speech, and a brave speech   40
In praise of Merchants; where's the Ape?
Prig.   Pox take him,
A gowty Beare-ward stole him t'other day.
Higgen.   May his Beares worry him, that Ape had paid it,
What dainty tricks? Pox o' that whorson Bear-ward:

30 start; nay,] MS (nay ∧); start ∧ me, F1
*41 Pox take] Colman; —— Take F1–2; plague take MS

In his french doublet, with his blister'd bullions,
In a long stock ty'd up; o how daintily
Would I have made him waite, and change a trencher,
Cary a cup of wine? ten thousand stinks
Waite on thy mangy soule, thou lowzy Bear-ward.

Gerrard. 'Tis passing well, I both beleeve and joy in't   50
And will be ready; keepe ye here the meane while,
And keepe this in.—— I must a while forsake ye,
Upon mine anger no man stir, this two houres.

Higgen.   Not to the wedding sir?

Gerrard.   Not any whither.

Higgen.   The wedding must be seene sir; we want meat too,
We be monstrous out of meat.

Prig.   Shall it be spoken,
Fatt Capons shak't their tailes at's in defiance,
And turkey toombs such honorable monuments?
Shall piggs, sir, that the Persons selfe would envy,
And deintie Ducks——

Gerrard.   Not a word more, obey me.   60

                              Exit Gerrard.

Higgen.   Why then come dolefull death, this is flat tyrany
And by this hand——

Hubert.   What?

Higgen.   Ile goe sleepe upon't.

                              Exit Higgen.

Prig.   Nay, and there be a wedding, and we wanting,
Farewell our happie daies: we doe obey sir.

                              Exeunt.

          Enter two young Merchants severallie.   [IV.] vi

1. Merchant.   Well met sir, you are for this lusty wedding?

2. Merchant.   I am so, so are you I take it.

1. Merchant.   Yes,
And it much glads me, that to doe him service

          45 blister'd] MS (blistred); baster'd F1
          57 Capons] MS; Capon F1

Who is the honour of our trade, and luster,
We meet thus happily.
2. Merchant.   He's a noble fellow,
And well becomes a bride of such a beauty.
1. Merchant.   She's passing faire indeed, long may their loves
Continue like their youths, in spring of sweetnesse.
2. Merchant.   All the young Merchants will be here.
1. Merchant.   No doubt
                            on't,
For he that comes not to attend this wedding   10
The curse of a most blind one fall upon him,
A lowd wife, and a lazie: here's *Vanlock.*

Enter Vanlock *and Mistris* Frances.

Vanlock.   Well overtaken gentlemen: save ye.
1. Merchant.   The same to you sir; save ye faire Mistris *Frances,*
I would this happie night might make you blush too.
Vanlock.   She dreames a pace,
Frances.   That's but a drowsie fortune.
2. Merchant.   Nay take us with ye too; we come to that end,
I am sure y'are for the wedding.
Vanlock.   Hand and heart man,
And what these feet can doe: I could a tript it
Before this whorson gout.

Enter Gerrard.

Gerrard.   Blesse ye Masters.   20
Vanlock.   *Clause?* how now Clause; th'art come to see thy Master,
(And a good master he is to all poore people)
In all his joy, 'tis honestly don of thee.
Gerrard.   Long may hee live sir, but my businesse now is
If you would please to doe it, and to him too.

---

9 *2. Merchant.*] MS; *omit* F1   9 *1. Merchant.*] Dorenkamp; *omit* F1
12.1 *Mistris* Frances] MS (M^rs); Francis F1–2
14 *et seq. Frances*] MS; *Francis* F1–2
17 *2. Merchant.*] FK; *3. Mer.* F1, MS
*19 these] MS (theis); their F1

312

Enter Florez.

Vanlock.   He's heere himselfe.

Floriz.   Stand at the doore my friends?
I pray walke in: welcome faire Mistris *Frances*,
See what the house affords, ther's a young Lady
Will bid ye welcome,

Vanlock.   We joy your happinesse.   *Exeunt.*

Floriz.   I hope it will be so: *Clause* nobly welcome,   30
My honest, my best friend, I have been carefull
To see thy monys——

Gerrard.   Sir, that brought not me,
Do you know this Ring againe?

Floriz.   Thou hadst it of me.

Gerrard.   And do ye well remember yet, the boone ye gave me
Upon returne of this?

Floriz.   Yes, and I grant it,
Be it what it will: aske what thou can'st, I'le do it;
Within my power.

Gerrard.   Ye are not married yet?

Floriz.   No.

Gerrard.   Faith I shall aske ye that that will disturb ye,
But I must put ye to your promise.

Floriz.   Do,
And if I faint or flinch in't——

Gerrard.   Well said Master,   40
And yet it grieves me too: and yet it must be.

Floriz.   Prethee distrust me not.

Gerrard.   You must not marry,
That's part of the power you gave me: which to make up,
You presently must depart, and follow me.

Floriz.   Not marry *Clause*?

Gerrard.   Not if you keep your promise,
And give me power to aske.

Floriz.   Pre'thee thinke better.
I will obey, by heaven.

Gerrard.   I've thought the best Sir.

40 or] MS; and F1   44 presently must] MS (presentlie); must presently F1

Flori. Give me thy reason, do'st thou feare her honesty?

Gerrard. Chaste as the yce, for any thing I know, Sir.

Flori. Why should'st thou light on that then? to what purpose? 50

Gerrard. I must not now discover.

Flori.   Must not marry?
Shall I breake now when my poore hart is pawn'd?
When all the preparation?

Gerrard.   Now or never.

Flori. Come, 'tis not that thou would'st: thou dost but fright me.

Gerrard. Upon my soule it is Sir, and I binde ye.

Flori. *Clause*, can'st thou be so cruell?

Gerrard.   You may breake Sir,
But never more in my thoughts, appeare honest.

Flori. Did'st ever see her?

Gerrard.   No.

Flori.   She is such a thing,
O *Clause*, she is such a wonder, such a mirror,
For beauty, and faire vertue, *Europe* has not: 60
Why hast thou made me happy, to undo me?
But looke upon her; then if thy heart relent not,
I'le quit her presently, who waites there?

Servant within.   Sir.

Flori. Bid my faire love come hither, and the company,
Pre'thee be good unto me; take a mans hart
And looke upon her truly: take a friends hart
And feele what misery must follow this.

Gerrard. Take you a noble hart and keep your promise;
I forsooke all I had, to make you happy.
Can that thing call'd a woman, stop your goodnesse?   70

Enter Bertha, Van-donck, *and the rest*, Merchants.

Flori. Looke there she is, deale with me as thou wilt now,
Did'st ever see a fayrer?

Gerrard.   She is most goodly.

Flori. Pray ye stand still.

Bertha.   What ayles my love?

Flori.   Did'st thou ever,

314

By the faire light of heaven, behold a sweeter?
O that thou knew'st but love, or ever felt him,
Looke well, looke narrowly upon her beauties.
1. Merchant.   Sure h'as some strange designe in hand, he starts so.
2. Merchant.   This Beggar has a strong power ore his pleasure.
Floriz.   View all her body.
Gerrard.   'Tis exact and excellent.
Floriz.   Is she a thing then to be lost thus lightly?   80
Her mind is ten times sweeter, ten times nobler,
And but to heare her speak, a Paradise,
And such a love she beares to me, a chaste love,
A vertuous, faire, and fruitfull love: 'tis now too
I am ready to enjoy it; the Priest ready *Clause*,
To say the holy words shall make us happy,
This is a cruelty beyond mans study,
All these are ready, all our joyes are ready,
And all the expectation of our friends,
'Twill be her death to do it.
Gerrard.   Let her dye then.   90
Floriz.   Thou canst not: 'tis impossible.
Gerrard.   It must be.
Floriz.   'Twill kil me too, 'twil murder me: by heaven *Clause*
I'le give thee halfe I have; come thou shalt save me.
Gerrard.   Then you must goe with me: I can stay no longer,
If ye be true, and noble——   [*Exit.*]
Floriz.   Hard heart, I'le follow:
Pray ye all goe in againe, and pray be merry,
I have a weighty businesse, give me my cloake there,

Enter Servant (with a Cloake).

Concerns my life, and state, (make no enquiry,)
This present houre befaln me: with the soonest
I shall be here againe: nay pray goe in Sir,   100
And take 'em with ye, tis but a night lost, Gentlemen.
Van-dunck.   Come, come in, we will not loose our meat yet,

97 me] Dorenkamp; *omit* F 1–2, MS

Nor our good mirth, he cannot stay long from her
I am sure ò' that.

Floriz.   I will not stay; beleeve Sir.   *Exeunt* [Van-dunck
                                                                and the rest].

Gertrud, a word with you.

Bertha.   Why is this stop, Sir?

Floriz. I have no more time left me, but to kisse thee,
And tell thee this, I am ever thine: farewell wench.   *Exit.*

Bertha. And is that all your ceremony? Is this a wedding?
Are all my hopes and prayers turnd to nothing?
Well, I will say no more, nor sigh, nor sorrow,   110
Till to thy face I prove thee false. Ah me!

                                                        Exit.

                    Enter Bertha, *and a Boore.*   V. i

Bertha. Lead, if you thinkst we are right: why dost thou make
These often stands? thou saidst thou knewst the way.

Boore. Fear nothing, I doe know it: would 'twere homeward.

Bertha. Wrought from me, by a Beggar? at the time
That most should tye him? 'Tis some other Love
That hath a more command on his affections,
And he that fetcht him, a disguised Agent,
Not what he personated; for his fashion
Was more familiar with him, and more powerfull
Then one that ask'd an almes: I must finde out
One, if not both: kind darknesse be my shrowd   10
And cover loves too curious search in me,
For yet, suspition, I would not name thee.

Boore. Mistris, it grows some-what pretty and dark.

Bertha. What then?

Boore.   Nay, nothing; do not thinke I am affeard,
Although perhaps you are.

Bertha.   I am not, forward.

Boore. Sure but you are: give me your hand, fear nothing.

*104 *Exeunt*] *Exit* F 1-2, MS
*110-111 sorrow, | Till...false. Ah me!] F 2; sorrow; oh me, | Till...false.
F 1-FK; sorrowe‸ | till...false: MS   15 affeard] MS; afraid F 1

There's one leg in the wood, do not pull backward:
What a sweate one a us are in, you or I?
Pray God it do not prove the plague; yet sure   20
It has infected me; for I sweat too,
It runs out at my knees, feele, feele, I pray you.
Bertha.   What ailes the fellow?
Boore.   Hark, hark I beseech you,
Doe you heare nothing?
Bertha.   No.
Boore.   Lyst: a wilde hog,
He grunts: now 'tis a beare: this wood's full of 'em,
And now, a wolfe Mistris, a wolfe a wolfe,
It is the howling of a wolfe.
Bertha.   The braying
Of an asse, is't not.
Boore.   Oh, now one has me;
Oh, my left haunch, farewell.
Bertha.   Looke to your shankes,
Your breech is safe enough, the wolfe's a Fern-brake.   30
Boore.   But see, see, see. There is a serpent in it,
'Tas eyes as broad as platters; it spits fire;
Now it creeps towards us, help me to say my prayers:
'Thath swallowed me almost, my breath is stopt,
I cannot speake; do I speake Mistris? tell me.
Bertha.   Why, thou strange timerous Sot, canst thou perceive
Any thing i'the bush, but a poore glo-worme?
Boore.   It may be 'tis but a glo-worm now, but 'twill
Grow to a fire-drake presently.
Bertha.   Come thou from it:
I have a pretious guide of you; and a courteous   40
That gives me leave to lead my selfe the way thus.
                                   Hubert, *hollowes within.*
Boore.   It thunders, you heare that now.
Bertha.   I heare one hollow.
Boore.   'Tis thunder, thunder: see, a flash of Lightning:

*29 haunch] MS, F2; ham F1   36 strange] MS, F2; omit F1
41.1 Hubert...within.] MS; omit F1-2

317

Are ye not blasted Mistris? pull your maske off,
'Tas plaid the barber with me here: I have lost
My beard, my beard, pray God you be not shaven,
'Twill spoile your marriage Mistris.

Bertha.   What strange wonders,
Feare fancies in a Coward?

Boore.   Now, the earth opens.

Bertha.   Prethee hold thy peace.

Boore.   Will ye goe on then?

Bertha.   Both love and jealousie have made me bold,   50
Where my fate leads me, I must goe.   *Exit.*

Boore.   God be wi' you then.

Enter Woolfort, Hemskirke, *Guard, and Attendants.*

Hemskirk.   It was the fellow sure, he that should guide me,
The hunts-man that did hollow us.

Woolfort.   Best make a stand
And listen to his next: ha?

Hemskirk.   Who goes there?

Boore.   Mistris, I am taken.

Hemskirk.   Mistris? look forth souldiers.
                              [*Exeunt guard.*]

Woolfort.   What are you sirha?

Boore.   Truly all is left
Of a poore Boore, by day-light, by night no body,
You might have spar'd your drum, and guns, and pikes too,
For I am none that will stand out Sir, I.
You may take me in with a walking sticke   60
Even when you please, and hold me with a pack-threed.

Hemskirk.   What woman was't you call'd to.

Boore.   Woman? none Sir.

Woolfort.   None? did not you name Mistris?

Boore.   Yes, but shee's
No woman yet! she should have been this night,
But that a Beggar stole away her Bridegroome,

Whom we were going to make hue and cry after;
I tell you true Sir, she should ha' bin maried to day,
And was the Bride, and all; but in came *Clause*,
The old lame Beggar, and whips up Master *Goswin*
Under his arme; away with him as a Kite,   70
Or an old Fox, would swoope a way a gosling.

Enter Bertha [*guarded*].

Hemskirk. 'Tis she, 'tis she, 'tis she, Niece?
Bertha.   Ha?
Hemskirk.   She Sir,
This was a notable entrance to your fortune,
That being on the point thus to be married,
Upon her venture here you should surprise her.
Woolfort. I begin *Hemskirck*, to believe my fate,
Works to my ends.
Hemskirk.   Yes Sir, and this adds trust,
Unto the fellow our guide, who assur'd me *Floris*,
Liv'd in some Merchants shape, as *Gerrard* did
In the old beggars, and that he would use   80
Him for the traine, to call the other forth,
All which we finde is done. — That's he againe——
                              Holla againe.
Woolfort. Good we sent out to meet him.
Hemskirk.   *Heer's the Oke.*
Bertha. O I am miserably lost, thus fallen
Into my Uncles hands, from all my hopes:
No matter now, where thou be false or no,
Goswin, whether thou love an other better;
Or me alone; or where thou keep thy vow,
And word, or that thou come, or stay: for I
To thee from henceforth, must be ever absent,   90

71.1 Enter Bertha.] MS; omit F 1–2   73 notable] MS; noble F 1
79 shape] MS, F 2; shop F 1
*84–85 F 1 *follows these lines* (lost,...falne...Uncles hands ʌ...hopes,) *with line*
98 (*as in* MS, FK, F 2) *but then adds*: 'O I am miserably lost; thus fallen | Into my
Uncles hands, from all my hopes:' *after which it inserts lines 86–97 and concludes with a
repetition of line 98*

319

And thou to me: no more shall we come neere,
To tell our selves, how bright each others eyes were,
How soft our language, and how sweet our kisses,
Whil'st we made one our food, th'other our feast,
Not mix our soules by sight, or by a letter
Hereafter, but as small relation have,
As two new gon to inhabiting a grave:
Can I not thinke away my selfe and dye?

Enter Hubert [*with*] Higgen, Prig, Ferret, Snap, Gincks, *like Boores.*

Hubert.   I like your habits well: they are safe, stand close.
Higgen.   But what's the action we are for now? ha?   100
Robbing a Ripper of his fish?
Prig.   Or taking
A poultrer prisoner, without ransome, Bullyes?
Higgen.   Or cutting off a convoy of butter?
Ferret.   Or surprising a Boores ken, for grunting cheates?
Prig.   Or cackling cheates?
Higgen.   Or mergery-praters, Rogers,
And Tibs o'the Buttry?
Prig.   O, I could drive a Regiment
Of geese afore me, such a night as this
Ten leagues with my hatt, and staff, and not a hisse
Heard, or a wing of my troopes disordered.
Higgen.   Tell us,
If it be milling of a lag of duds,   110
The fetching of a buck of clothes or so;
We are horribly out of linnen.
Hubert.   No such matter.
Higgens.   Let me alone for any Farmers dog,
If ye have a minde to the cheese-loft: 'tis but thus:
And he is a silenc'd Mastiff, during pleasure
Hubert.   Would it would please ye to be silent.
Higgen.   Mum.
Woolfort.   Who's there?

92 others] FK; other F1   104 grunting] MS; granting F1
111 buck] MS (bucke); back F1

320

Hubert.   A friend, the Huntsman.
Hemskirk.   O 'tis he.
Hubert.   I ha' kept touch Sir, which is the Earle of these?
  Will ye know a man now?
Hemskrik.   This my Lord's the friend,
  Hath undertooke the service.
Hubert.   If't be worth   120
  His Lordships thanks anon when it is done,
  Lording, I will looke for't, a rude woodman,
  I know how to pitch my toyles, drive in my game:
  And I have don't, both *Floriʒ* and his Father
  Old *Gerrard*, with Lord *Arnold* of *Benthuisen*,
  Costin, and *Jaqueline*, young *Floris* Sister;
  I have 'em all.
Woolfort.   Thou speak'st too much, too happy,
  To carry faith with it.
Hubert.   I can bring you
  Where you shall see, and finde 'em.
Woolfort.   We will double,
  What ever *Hemskirck* then hath promis'd thee.   130
Hubert.   And I'le deserve it treble; what horse ha' ye?
Woolfort.   A hundred.
Hubert.   That's well: ready to take
  Upon surprise of 'em?
Hemskirk.   Yes.
Hubert.   Devide then,
  Your force into five Squadrons; for there are
  So many outlets, wayes, thorough the wood,
  That issue from the place where they are lodg'd;
  Five severall wayes, of all which passages
  We must posses our selves, to round 'em in,
  For by one starting hole, they'll all escape else;
  I and four Boores, here to me, will be guides,   140
  The Squadron, where you are, my selfe will lead:
  And that they may be more secure, I'le use
  My wonted whoopes, and hollowes, as I were

121 it is] Weber; 'tis F1-2, MS   122 I will] I'le F1-2; I MS

321

A hunting for 'em; which will make 'em rest,
Careles of any noyse, and be a direction
To the other guides, how we approch 'em still.
Woolfort.   'Tis order'd well, and relisheth the Souldier,
Make the division *Hemskirck*: you are my charge
Faire one, I'le looke to you.   [*To* Bertha.]
Boore.   Shall no body need
To looke to me, I'le looke unto my selfe.   [*Exit.*] 150

Hubert.   'Tis but this, remember.
Higgen.   Say 'tis don boy.
                                        Exeunt.

Enter Gerrard *and* Floriz.   [V.] ii

Gerrard.   By this time Sir I hope you want no reasons
Why I broke off your marriage, for though I
Should as a Subject study you my Prince
In things indifferent, it will not therefore
Discredit you, to acknowledge me your Father,
By harkning to my necessary counsells.
Floriz.   Acknowledge you my Father? Sir I do.
And may impiety, conspiring with
My other Sinnes, sinck me, and sodainly
When I forget to pay you a Sonnes duty   10
In my obedience, and that help'd forth
With all the cheerefullnesse——
Gerrard.   I pray you rise,
And may those powers that see and love this in you,
Reward you for it: Taught by your example,
Having receiv'd the rights due to a Father,
I tender you th'allegance of a Subject:
Which as my Prince accept of.
Floriz.   Kneele to me?
May mountaines first fall down beneath their valleys,
And fire no more mount upwards, when I suffer
An act in nature so preposterous;   20

322

I must o'recome in this, in all things else
The victory be yours: could you here read me,
You should perceive how all my faculties
Triumph in my blest fate, to be found yours;
I am your son, your son Sir, and am prouder
To be so, to the Father, to such goodnesse
(Which heaven be pleas'd, I may inherit from you)
Then I shall ever of those specious titles
That plead for my succession in the Earldome
(Did I possesse it now) left by my mother.   30
Gerrard.   I do beleeve it: but——
Floriz.   O my lov'd Father,
Before I knew you were so, by instinct,
Nature had taught me, to look on your wants,
Not as a strangers: and I know not how,
What you call'd charity, I thought the payment
Of some religious debt, nature stood bound for;
And last of all, when your magnificent bounty
In my low ebb of fortune, had brought in
A flood of blessings, though my threatning wants
And feare of their effects, still kept me stupid,   40
I soone found out, it was no common pitty
That lead you to it.
Gerrard.   Thinke of this hereafter
When we with joy may call it to remembrance,
There will be a time, more opportune, then now
To end your story, with all circumstances;
I add this only: when we fled from *Woolfort*
I sent you into *England,* and there placed you
With a brave *Flanders* Merchant, call'd rich *Goswin,*
A man supplyed by me unto that purpose,
As bound by oath never to discover you,   50
Who dying, left his name and wealth unto you
As his reputed Son, and yet receiv'd so;
But now, as *Florez,* and a Prince, remember
The countreys, and the subjects generall good
Must challenge the first part in your affection:

The faire maid, whom you chose to be your wife,
Being so far beneath you, that your love
Must grant shee's not your equall——
Floriẓ.   In discent
Or borrowed glories, from dead Ancestors,
But for her beauty, chastity, and all vertues   60
Ever remembred in the best of women,
A Monarch might receive from her, not give,
Though she were his Crownes purchase; In this only
Be an indulgent Father: in all else,
Use my authority.

> *Enter* Hubert, Hemskirke, Woolfort, Bertha
> *and Souldiers.*

Hubert.   Sir, here be two of 'em,
The Father and the Son, the rest you shall have
As fast as I can rouze 'em.   [*Exeunt* Hubert, Hemskirke.]
Gerrard.   Who's this? *Woolfort?*
Woolfort.   I Criple, your faigned crutches wil not help you,
Nor patch'd disguise that hath so long conceal'd you,
It's now no halting: I must here finde *Gerrard*,   70
And in this Merchants habit, one called *Floreẓ*
Who would be Earl.
Gerrard.   And is, wert thou a subject.
Floriẓ.   Is this that Traitor *Woolfort?*
Woolfort.   Yes, but you
Are they that are betraid: *Hemskirke*——
Bertha.   My *Goswin*
Turn'd Prince? ô I am poorer by this greatnesse,
Then all my former jealousies or misfortunes.
Floriẓ.   *Gertrud?*
Woolfort.   Stay Sir, you were to day too neare her,
You must no more ayme at those easy accesses,
Lesse you can do't in aire, without a head,
Which shall be sodainly tri'de.
Bertha.   O take my heart, first,   80

72 Earl] MS (Earle); an Earl F1

And since I cannot hope now to enjoy him,
Let me but fall a part of his glad ransome.
Woolfort.　　You know not your own value, that entreat——
Gerrard.　　So proud a fiend as *Woolfort*——
Woolfort.　　　　　　　　　　　　For so lost
A thing as *Flore*ꝫ.
Floriꝫ.　　　　　　　And that would be so
Rather then she should stoop againe to thee;
There is no death, but's sweeter then all life,
When *Woolfort* is to give it: O my *Gertrude*,
It is not that, nor Prince-dome that I goe from,
It is from thee, that losse includeth all.　　　　　　　90
Woolfort.　　I, if my young Prince knew his losse, hee'd say so,
Which that he yet may chew on, I will tell him
This is no *Gertrude*, nor no *Hemskirks* Niece,
Nor *Vandoncks* daughter; this is *Bertha, Bertha,*
The heir of *Brabant*, she that caus'd the warr,
Whom I did steale, during my treaty there,
For your minority, to raise my selfe;
I then fore-seeing 'twould beget a quarrell,
That, a necessity of my employment,
The same employment, make me master of strength,　　　100
That strength, the Lord of *Flanders*, so of *Brabant*,
By marrying her: which had not been to doe Sir,
She come of years, but that the expectation
First of her Fathers death, retarded it,
And since the standing out of *Bruges*, where
Hemskirke had hid her, till she was neer lost:
But Sir, we have recover'd her: your Merchantship
May breake, for this was one a your best bottoms
I thinke.
Gerrard.　　Insolent Devill!

Enter Hubert, [Hemskirk,] *with* Jaqueline, Gynks *and* Costin.

Woolfort.　　　　　　Who are these, *Hemskirke?*
Hemskirk.　　More, more, Sir.
Floriꝫ.　　　　　　How they triumph in their treachery?　110

Hemskirk. Lord *Arnold* of *Benthuisen*, this Lord *Costin*,
This *Jaqueline* the sister unto *Florez*.
Woolfort. All found? why here's brave game, this was sport-
    royall,
And puts me in thought of a new kind of death for 'em.
Hunts-man, your horn: first wind me *Florez* fall,
Next *Gerrards*, then his daughter *Jaquelins*,
Those rascalls, they shall dye without their rights:
Hang 'em *Hemskirke* on these trees; I'le take
The assay of these my selfe.
Hubert.   Not here my Lord,
Let 'em be broken up, upon a scaffold,   120
'Twill shew the better when their arbour's made.
Gerrard. Wretch art thou not content thou has betraid us
But mocke us too?
Ginks.   False *Hubert*, this is monstrous.
Woolfort. *Hubert*?
Hemskirk.   Who, this?
Gerrard.   Yes, this is *Hubert*, *Woolfort*,
I hope he ha's helpt himselfe to a tree.
Woolfort.   The first,
The first of any, and most glad I have you Sir,
I let you goe before, but for a traine;
Is't you have done this service?
Hubert.   As your Hunts-man;
But now as *Hubert*, save your selves, I will,
The *Woolf's* a foote, let slip; kill, kill, kill, kill.   130

        Enter with a drum Van-donck, *Merchants*, Higgen, Prig,
                        Ferret, Snap.

Woolfort. Betray'd?
Hubert.   No, but well catch'd: and I the Huntsman.
Van-dunck. How do you *Woolfort*? Rascall, good knave *Woolfort*.
I speake it now without the Rose, and *Hemskirck*,
Rogue *Hemskirck*, you that have no neice, this Lady
Was stolen by you, and tane by you, and now

                        326

Resign'd by me, to the right owner here:
Take her my Prince.

Flori₹.   Can this be possible,
Welcom my love, my sweet, my worthy love.

Van-dunck.   I ha' giv'n you her twice: now keep her better and
    thanke
Lord *Hubert*, that came to me in *Gerrards* name,   140
And got me out, with my brave Boyes, to march
Like *Cæsar*, when he bred his Comentaryes,
So I, to breed my Chronicle, came forth
Cæsar Van-donck, et veni, vidi, vici:
Give me my Bottle, and set downe the drum;
You had your tricks Sir, had you? we ha' tricks too,
You stole the Lady?

Higgen.   And we led your Squadrons
Where they ha' scratch'd their leggs a little, with brambles,
If not their faces.

Prig.   Yes, and run their heads
Against trees.

Higgen.   'Tis Captaine *Prig*, Sir.

Prig.   And Coronell *Higgen*.   150

Higgen.   We have fill'd a pitt with your people, some with leggs
Some with armes broken, and a neck, or two
I think be loose.

Prig.   The rest too, that escap'd,
Are not yet out o'the briars,

Higgen.   And your horses, Sir,
Are well set up in *Bruges* all by this time:
You looke as you were not well Sir, and would be
Shortly let blood; do you want a scarfe?

Van-dunck.   A halter.

Gerrard.   'Twas like your selfe, honest, and noble *Hubert*:
Can'st thou behold these mirrors altogether,   [*To* Woolfort.]
Of thy long, false, and bloody usurpation?   160
Thy tyrranous proscription, and fresh treason:
And not so see thy selfe, as to fall downe

143 breed] MS; end F1

327

And sincking, force a grave, with thine owne guilt,
As deep as hell, to couer thee and it?
Woolfort.   No, I can stand: and praise the toyles that tooke me
And laughing in them dye, they were brave snares.
Floriz.   'Twer truer valour, if thou durst repent
The wrongs th'hast don, and live.
Woolfort.   Who, I repent?
And say I am sorry? yes, 'tis the fooles language
And not for *Woolfort.*
Van-dunck.   *Woolfort* thou art a Divell,   170
And speaks his language, oh that I had my longing
Under this row of trees now would I hang him.
Floriz.   No let him live, untill he can repent,
But banish'd from our State, that is thy doome.
Van-dunck.   Then hang his worthy Captaine here, this *Hemskirck,*
For profit of th'example,
Floriz.   No let him
Enjoy his shame too, with his conscious life,
To shew how much our innocence contemnes
All practise from the guiltiest, to molest us.
Van-dunck.   A noble prince.
Gerrard.   Sir, you must helpe to joyne   180
A paire of hands, as they have don their heartes here,
And to their loves wish joy.
Floriz.   As to mine owne,
My gratious Sister, worthiest Brother: take her.
Van-dunck.   I'le go afore, and have the first bon-fire made,
My fire-workes, and flap dragons, and good backrack,
With a peck of little fishes, to drink downe
In healthes to this day.
Higgen.   Slight, here be changes,
The Bells ha' not so many, nor a dance, *Prig.*
Prig.   Our Company's growne horrible thin by it,
What think you *Ferret?*
Ferret.   Marry I do thinke,   190

182 wish] MS; with F1   183 take her] MS; *omit* F1
184 first] MS; *omit* F1

That we might all be Lords now, if we would stand for't.
Higgen.   Not I if they should offer it: I'le dislodge first,
Remove the Bush first to another climat.
Gerrard.   Sir, you must thanke this worthy *Burgomaster*,
Here be friends aske to be look'd on too,
And thank'd, who though their trade, and course of life
Be not so perfect, but it may be betterd,
Have yet us'd me with curtesy, and bin true
Subjects unto me, while I was their King,
A place I know not well, how to resigne   200
Nor unto whom: But this I will entreat
Your grace, command them, follow you to *Bruges*;
Where I will take the care on me, to finde
Some manly, and more profitable course
To fit them, as a part of the Republique.
Floriȝ.   Do ye heare Sirs? do so.
Higgen.   Thankes to your good grace.
Prig.   To your good Lordship.
Ferret.   May ye both live long.
Gerrard.   Attend me at *Van-doncks*, the Burgomasters.
                                        Exeunt all but Beggars.
Higgen.   Yes, to beat hemp, and be whipt twice a weeke,
Or turne the wheele, for *Crab* the Rope-maker: 210
Or learne to go along with him, his course;
That's a fine course now, i'the Common-wealth, *Prig*,
What say you to it?
Prig.   It is the backwardst course,
I know i'the world.
Higgen.   Then *Higgen* will scarce thrive by it,
You do conclude?
Prig.   'Faith hardly, very hardly.
Higgen.   Troth I am partly of your minde, Prince *Prig*;
And therefore farewell *Flanders*, *Higgen* will seek
Some safer shelter, in some other Clymat
With this his tatterd Colony: Let me see,

191 would] MS; could F1   193 first] MS; *omit* F1
*202 you] MS, F2; me F1

Snap, *Ferret*, *Prig*, and *Higgen*, all are left   220
O'the true blood: what? shall we into *England*?
Prig.   Agreed.
Higgen.   Then beare up bravely with your Brute my lads;
   Higgen hath prig'd the prancers in his dayes,
   And sold good peny-worthes; we will have a course,
   The spirit of *Bottom*, is growne bottomlesse.
Prig. I'le mand no more, nor cant.
Higgen.   Yes, your sixpenyworth
   In private, brother, sixpence is a summ,
   I'le steale you any mans dogg for.
Prig.   For Sixpence more,
   You'l tell the owner where he is.
Higgen.   'Tis right,
   Higgen must practise, so must *Prig* to eat;   230
   And write the Letter; and gi' the word. But now
   No more, as either of these——
Prig.   But as true Beggars,
   As ere we were——
Higgen.   We stand here, for an Epilogue;
   Ladyes, your bountyes first; the rest will follow,
   For womens favours, are a leading almes,
   If you be pleas'd look cheerely, throw your eyes
   Out at your maskes.
Prig.   And let your beauties sparkle.
Higgen.   So may you ne'er want dressings, Jewells, gownes
   Still i'the fashion.
Prig.   Nor the men you love,
   Wealth nor discourse to please you.
Higgen.   May you Gentlemen,   240
   Never want gold, fresh suites and liberty.
Prig. May every Merchant here see safe his ventures.
Higgen. And every honest Citizen get his debts in.
Prig. The Lawyers gaine good Clyents.

241 gold,] MS; good ∧ F1   241 and] MS; nor F1
243 get] MS; *omit* F1

Higgen.   And the Clyents
    Good Councell.
Prig.   All the Gamesters here good fortune.
Higgen.   The Drinkers too, good wine.
Prig.   The eaters meate
    Fit for their tasts and pallats.
Higgen.   The good wives
    Kind Husbands.
Prig.   And the young maides choyce of Sutors.
Higgen.   The Widdowes, merry hearts.
Prig.   And all good cheere.
Higgen.   As you are kinde unto us and our Bush,   250
    We are the Beggars and your dayly Beadsmen,
    And have your money, but the Almes we aske
    And live by, is your Grace, give that and then
    Wee'l boldly say our word is, *Come agen.*

                                                  [*Exeunt.*]

*246 Drinkers] MS; Drunkards F1   248 And] MS; *omit* F1
249 Widdowes,] MS (widdowes); Midwives ∧ F1

TEXTUAL NOTES

I.i

7 ten yeares] F 1–2 read 'five yeares' but in the preparation of the prompt-book Knight seems to have adjusted the time to 'ten', a desirable change although one that by no means solved the problems of the play's time-scheme.

I.ii

0.1 Hemskirk] The theatrical version, represented by MS, properly includes Hemskirk in this scene even though he is a mute. As Wolfort's trusted henchman he would have been in charge of the guard which intercepted Hubert. It is a fault that MS follows the original papers, apparently, as represented by F 1 and does not provide for Hemskirk's exit and that of the guard at line 23.

1 What *Hubert*,] Since it is clear that Wolfort has given orders for Hubert's capture, it is not likely that F 1 'What? *Hubert* ʌ' represents his mock surprise at the information just given him off-stage. This interpretation would not jibe with 'It was more then I commanded', which indicates beyond question the order of events. As emended here, *Hubert* is a vocative as it may be in MS.

6 idly] Either F 1 'rudely' or MS 'idly' makes sense. The words are so close in their letter formation that the odds favor a handwriting mistake instead of a revision. Although 'rudely' may seem to be the better antithesis to 'nobly' of line 4, Compositor *B*'s frequent misreadings suggest that the odds may here favor the MS word.

33 cunning ʌ] The agreement of F 1 and MS in no pointing after 'cunning' appears to indicate the reading of the underlying lost manuscript. In turn, whether it was right or whether 'cunning' is a noun in the series is not to be demonstrated.

47 I that] It is an easy temptation to suggest that MS 'that I' has been sophisticated by the F 1 compositor and to associate the change of the syntax involving 'then' in line 48 with this sophistication. It may be that the MS meaning *Because I am contemner of my own, I am then master of your life* is the right one, for it is difficult to account for the inversion in MS. Yet the MS syntax is so contorted as to be uncharacteristic of the easy Massingerean style. Emendation of the punctuation to associate 'then' with the first, not the second, clause seems to be all that is strictly required of an editor: it is otiose to make two such independent statements as (1) *Because*

I wear a sword I am master of your life; (2) *I hold my sword between you and all aid*. Regardless of the inversion of F1 'I that', the MS placing of 'then' seems preferable.

57–8 to beleeve]　The cut in MS between 'to beleeve . . . dangerous;' is not at all likely to be theatrical but instead is probably a scribal eyeskip or a failure to copy altered material in the underlying manuscript. The F1 'to beleeve' may be a form of dittography but might faithfully copy some manuscript alteration not entirely deleted.

89 beastly lusts]　The MS reading 'beastlie Lusts' suggests that the F1 compositor in 'princely' was censoring the language of the original for fear of offence.

103 securely]　The metre indicates that F1 'surely' is a misreading and MS 'securelie' is correct.

I.iii

38 increase]　F1's Compositor *A* seems to have picked up 'meanes' from line 37; 'increase' is metrically correct.

74 fall]　Agreement of F1 and MS in 'fall' prevents any strong temptation to emend to 'fail'. The meaning probably is *fall short only by*.

75 so are]　F1's 'they are so cheape' has no great deal of meaning in context, whereas MS says, in effect: *You know that at that price they are cheap*. This is a mild protest, implying that the offer is not wholly 'something near my price' (line 68) and in a sense appealing to Goswin to be more generous, for he will have a good profit at the price.

II.i

21 cheats]　F1 'chickens' is almost certainly a sophistication since MS 'Cheates' is canting language for 'things' (see II.i.119) and so refers to the capons, turkeys, geese, and ducklings. Compositor *A* is likely the source of the F1 corruption since he set a colon after 'season' to associate the chickens with the pheasants next mentioned. MS, instead, has a comma, which makes 'fine fat Cheates' parenthetical. Although MS capitalizes 'Cheates', it may be significant that alone among the other fowl mentioned in F1, 'chickens' is in lower case.

68 *Ferret*]　Seward's emendation to 'Ginks', adopted by the Variorum, is tempting since the patriotic remark is applied most naturally not only to the last speeches but also to Ginks' sentiments. But agreement of F1 and MS demonstrates that '*Ferret*' was the reading of the underlying manuscript, whether or not a slip. Perhaps it can be justified. If Prig disapproves of Ginks' suggestion but approves of Ferret's, he would be justified in calling Ferret the patriot.

80–1 chosen?...chosen,] The MS punctuation for F1 'chosen ‸...
chosen?' adds an ironic touch that alone explains "'tis for the King, but let
that passe' in the next line. The F1 reading seems to represent Compositor
A's misunderstanding of the sense in a more conventional manner.

120 he...purveyers] Some disruption or revision in the underlying manuscript seems indicated here. If 'For Pigs, and poultry' in F1 is a part line,
it is one of the rare cases in which such a line is not completed by the next
speech to form a pentameter. Moreover, Gerrard's agreement 'That we
must have' goes back to Higgen's 'and possesse | What he can purchase'
and comes inappositely in reference to 'he will have no purveyers'. Yet the
MS line 'to his owne proper, for Piggs, and Poultrey' is unmetrical and
doubtless corrupt. It is possible that some such word as 'use' has dropped
out after 'proper'; certainly, F1 'prop' is a difficult reading. Of course, if
'To his own prop' were removed, 'He will...poultry' would be an excellent pentameter, and the full pentameter of line 121 would be justified.
It would seem impossible here to recover the true text.

180 The King of] The addition of these words from MS may seem to be
justified on the basis of Snap's 'King of heaven goe with you' in line 62.
The change somewhat alters the metrics. Without the MS phrase editors
assign 'Heaven reward you' to complete a pentameter with 'Ther's
amongst you all', and 'The Prince of pitty blesse thee' to complete 'Lord
reward you'. However, this leaves 'Do I see? Or is't...so?' as one hypermetrical line both in F1 and MS. Although 'Do I see?' as an exclamation
might stand alone as a short line, the present arrangement enables it to
complete the pentameter with 'The Prince...thee', leaving only Hubert's
original 'Ther's amongst you all' as a detached short line.

II.ii

8 returnes] For the correctness of F1 plural here versus MS singular, see
II.iii.63, 'But then, if he should have home all his returnes'.

II.iii

0.2 *Boores*] Dyce thought that this part of the stage-direction was a
mistake and omitted it. However, both F1 and MS attest to its presence in
the original. Possibly at lines 4, 19 Margaret pours the wine and the
servants take it to the various persons.

135.1 *Strikes him.*] This stage-direction, like that at 137.1, derives from F2
and ordinarily would appear to have no authority. However, the specification in the direction at 137.1 is curious since it does not depend upon the
text as does that at 135.1. In MS (which on occasion omits such directions
for action) it is also a little odd that both lines 134 and 135 end with dashes,

a mark customarily employed by the scribe when a direction follows the line, and one less often used for broken-off speech. The present editor takes these dashes seriously enough to speculate that they may represent directions added in the preparation of the prompt-copy but omitted by the scribe of MS, in which case F2 serves as well as anything as a possible jotting from the prompt-book. The F2 direction at 137.1, however, does not appear to represent the possible lost direction at 135.1; instead, the action seems to call for a blow and its return, followed by a scuffle during which Goswin secures the sword and wounds Hemskirk at about the point represented in the F2 text.

<h2 style="text-align:center">III.i</h2>

16 *1. Boore.*] F1's assignment of this speech to *1. Boore* instead of MS *3. Boore* seems justified not only by the oddity in MS of the same Boor speaking in succession but also by line 38 where the *1. Boore* seems to repeat his approbation of line 16.

41.1–59 *Song.*]   The gentleman who owned the copy of F1 used to 'correct' F2 knew about this song, probably from the prompt-book, although it is omitted from F1 very likely owing to censorship. The version in F2 has a closer verbal connection with the theatrical copy as transmitted through MS than with popular tradition, since it consists of the three stanzas found in MS (although transposing MS stanzas 2 and 3), not greatly altered, even though some other source was also consulted. The order of F2 stanzas 2 and 3 coincides with that in the five- and six-stanza popular texts and seems to be the correct one, in part because of the more natural sequence of line 48 following line 47 but also because of the superior climax of line 59. *Pills to Purge Melancholy* adds a fourth stanza continuing the theme to a punk and a fifth stanza concluding with a meeting with a friar. The MMS[7] adds a sixth stanza not present in *Pills*:

> My Ram Calfe my Porker my puncke & my fryer
> I have left them unfurnisht of theire best Lady-ware
> And now he runs rovinge from Ale howse to taverne
> And sweares he'el turne sutor to the swaggeringe gallant
> But if I catch him Ile serve him noe worse
> [Ile] for Ile libe him and leave him not a peny in his purse
> Finis

<h2 style="text-align:center">III.iv</h2>

8 lamb'd] *O.E.D.* indicates that this is acceptable for *beaten soundly*. The problem might seem to come, in fact, in the syntax, but no problem exists if 'And to the open handling of our justice (line 9) is seen as the continua-

tion of 'To amplify the matter then', and if 'rogues...leave ye' is parenthetical, with a repeated 'as' to be understood before 'ye shall be'. An
editorial dash helps to clarify the suspension in line 8.

93 tew] F 1 'turne' appears to be a misreading. The correctness of MS
'tew' would seem to be established by III.ii.37, 'tew 'em, swinge 'em'.

129–43 *Gerrard*. Now...hang.] This passage appears to have been written
in the original on a separate sheet, the position of which was mistaken by
the printer of F 1. Moreover, it is pretty clearly an addition: Higgen's
'Y'are welcom Brother' of line 143 completes the pentameter with Hubert's
'Yes, if I handle her' of line 129. Moreover, a note '*Ger*. Now sweare him.'
must have been written in the working papers as a cue for the first line of
the new material on the added sheet since F 1 repeats it, first where the
added passage should come at line 129 but then also heading the misplaced
added passage after the first half of line 156. It should be observed that
the addition consists of canting speech.

161 stranger] This abrupt ending appears to be confirmed by its appearance
in both F 1 and MS. The F 2 addition 'Brother, pray | You must, you must,
Brother.' may derive from the prompt-book (although its absence from MS
is then strange) but it is more likely a sophistication by the gentleman who
annotated the printer's copy for F 2 since it attempts verbally to explain
Higgen's remark (presumably dealt with by the actor's gesture for Hubert
to follow him, instead of taking precedence, on the grounds that Hubert is a
stranger and so needs to be led).

III.v

47 Dispose] F 1 'Despise' appears to be a misreading, or at least a misunderstanding of correct MS 'Dispose'. The question is, of course, the
length of the aside. In this connection it is perhaps significant that F 1
begins 'At' with a capital although preceded by a comma after 'thee'. The
sense of the simple aside 'Nor long I feare with thee' is superior, since
Florez has no reason to believe that Bertha will reject him in his downfall.
'Dispose me as you please' means *I will agree to any arrangements you wish
to make*. It is partly ironic, although Bertha cannot, of course, recognize the
double meaning.

48 last] MS 'last' seems required here, partly in order to make the word-
play with 'least' which is wanting in F 1 'selfe'. The F 1 reading makes
little sense as the subject of 'which is the least I hope for', whereas the last
chance is Clause's promise, which is something Goswin trusts least and
expects to fail, leaving him only pity.

IV.i

27 put of and thanke]   Both F1 and MS agree in the spelling of 'of' for *off* but F1 reads 'thanke' and MS 'thankt'. The sense is not entirely clear, perhaps, but it would seem that to 'put of' is to *put off from shore*, to *set out on a voyage*, as 'put in' (see IV.iii.17) is to *enter the harbor after a voyage*. If this is so, then F1 'thanke' is correct. The merchant's sarcasm is apparent: it took much pleading for us to get space for our wares aboard your ships sent out trading, and thank your worship for the privilege. See also 'put after' at IV.iii.19.

41.1 Porters]   It is possible that F1 '*Porter*' is a sophistication, but it is more probable, perhaps, that MS '*Boores*' represented the staging and '*Porters*' the original working-papers designation. The same disguises later used in Act V could do service here on the stage.

IV.iii

38 we...all our service——]   The variants between the two texts can be put down only to sophistication by one or the other. Under these conditions it seems probable that Compositor *B* of F1 did not understand the suspension (emphasized in this edition by the editorial dash after 'service') and thus altered the line to form a conventional statement.

39 need,]   The differences in the text continue in the next line. F1 reads with a short line, 'I thanke you, | When I have need of you I shall forget you:', but MS is more regular by omitting the need for the short line. The authority is in doubt, but it is possible that 'need of you' is a compositorial sophistication since simple 'need' makes better sense; i.e., *when I need something I shall not remember you*. However, the possibility of some revision in this area (probably unauthoritative) when the prompt-book was made up cannot be discounted, for the metrical difficulties in F1 persist in Van-dunck's first speech. On the other hand, see the Textual Introduction for the bibliographical explanation that Compositor *B* set the text on this page with extra haste and thus that the fault may be his.

41 Come, come Sir,]   Consistency requires the acceptance of this form of the line from MS, in view of the acceptance of MS in the lines immediately above. In some respects F1 'come take your ease' is clearer as an invitation than in MS, but the sense remains the same. The disruption in this area of the text of the working papers is difficult to explain, but that the F1 text is faulty is indicated by the wrong lining and metrics. See the Textual Introduction for the hypothesis that the defects were caused by compositorial haste.

IV.iv

2 recompence]   It is interesting to see that this MS word for F1 'reward' is echoed ironically in line 10 and again in line 14.

62 And...forces]   It may be suspicious that the omission of this line in MS is accompanied by the misplacement in F1 of its closing round bracket after line 61 where it would have rested if line 62 had been deleted in the original manuscript but copied nevertheless by Compositor *A*.

IV.v

41 Pox take]   The fact that F1 capitalizes 'Take' after a dash substituting for 'Pox' seems to indicate that the dash stood in its copy and Compositor *A* mistook its meaning. MS 'plague' for the dash is, of course, prompt-book substitution.

IV.vi

19 these feet]   MS 'these' for F1 'their' makes good sense. It is odd, however, that the spelling is 'these' in MS instead of the usual 'theis', which indicates the slight possibility that double misreading has occurred and the underlying manuscript could have had 'there'. On the other hand, the F1 spelling 'their' – although not unknown for *there* – could be explained as a misreading of *theis* if that were the copy-spelling. In this stand-off the MS reading seems more acceptable than a normalization of 'their' to 'there'. Dorenkamp is mistaken in noting the MS reading as 'there'.

104 *Exeunt*]   F1 '*Exit.*' is manifestly wrong as applying to Florez but could be a simple mistake for *Exeunt*. On the other hand, MS reads '*Exit Gerr:*', which must be equally wrong. Florez' promise in line 104 not to stay is addressed not to Gerrard but to Van-dunck; Gerrard's exit, although unmarked in F1 and MS, must be placed after his suspended line 95, with Florez' promise to follow. We cannot know whether the MS attribution of the exit to Gerrard was a scribal mistake or whether the error originated in the prompt-book's misunderstanding of the original manuscript's direction, which could have read simply '*Ex.*'

111 Ah me!]   The position of this anomaly in F2 may well have agreed with that in the prompt-book consulted. The tacking of 'oh me' on at the end of line 110 as in F1 is not encouraged by MS; and indeed it is simpler to conjecture that the scribe of MS omitted a final phrase in line 111 than a misplaced phrase in the original manuscript. The occasional authority of F2 ⸱oins with the irregularity in MS to discredit F1 here.

V.i

29 haunch] The correctness of MS 'haunch' is most interestingly suggested not alone by the reference to 'breech' in line 30 but by F 2's alteration of F 1 'ham' to 'haunch', apparently by consultation of the prompt-book. Of course, logically the F 2, MS agreement shows only the reading of the prompt-copy, which could have varied from the original manuscript faithfully transmitted as 'ham' in F 1, but given the compositors' carelessness the odds may favor corruption in F 1 in this reading. For another example of F 2, MS agreement, see the appearance of 'strange' in line 36, omitted by F 1.

71.1 *Enter* Bertha.] The direction in MS gives no indication that Bertha has been captured or has done anything but inadvertently wander into the group, and her 'Ha?' of surprise might suggest this staging. On the other hand, at line 55 soldiers were ordered to search about, and presumably left the stage to execute the order. It would be only appropriate for them to have executed it and to have found Bertha. Her 'Ha?' need be no more than an exclamation at seeing Hemskirk.

84 O I am miserably lost] One would ordinarily take it that the omission of lines 86–97 in MS confirmed by their absence also in F 2, was a theatrical cut. But the appearance in F 1 first of the short version, lines 84–5, 98, and then of the long version 84–98 indicates that an addition was made in the working papers on a separate sheet in order to expand Bertha's speech. Just such another cue for an added speech was found at III.iv.130 for the canting swearing-in of Hubert (see the Textual Note). It would seem, then, that the scribe of the prompt-book either ignored the added sheet or by some error did not notice it.

V.ii

202 you] The agreement of F 2 with MS in 'you' establishes the reading of the prompt-book. It may be that the working papers underlying F 1 are correct in 'me'; but the odds favor 'you' since (a) Gerrard as King of the Beggars is perfectly capable of commanding them to follow him but defers to Florez in courtesy; (b) the 'me' of line 203 probably has contaminated the F 1 reading by compositorial error.

246 Drinkers] Since all the other addresses are complimentary, it is likely that F 1 'Drunkards' is a slip by Compositor *B* and that MS 'Drinkers' is correct. In other key readings in this epilogue MS seems to be generally superior to F 1 for reasons conjecturally explained in the Textual Introduction as unusual compositorial haste in typesetting.

EMENDATIONS OF ACCIDENTALS

[NOTE: In order to reduce the number of the alterations recorded in the footnotes, emendations of full by contracted forms like 'y'have' for 'you have' have been placed in the present list; also included are such variant forms as 'ye' for 'you' and 'mine' for 'my', and the reverse. The usual manuscript spelling 'yee' has not been specifically noted when F 1 'you' is emended from MS to 'ye'.]

I.i

0 I.i] *Actus Primus, Scæna Prima.*
  F 1–2 ±; *Actus primus: Scæna*
  j^a MS
3 man_∧] MS; ~ . F 1
4 Indeed?] MS (*unrevised*); ~ _∧
  F 1; ~ ! MS (*revised*)

5 suffered_∧] MS; ~ , F 1
26 favour_∧] MS; ~ , F 1
40 daring_∧] MS; ~ , F 1
44 e're] MS; ever F 1
61.1 ²*Exit.*] MS; *omit* F 1

I.ii

23 You] you F 1–2, MS
26 hate;] FK; ~ , F 1; ~ _∧ MS
27 head,] ~ ; F 1–2; ~ _∧ MS
34 this,] ~ _∧ F 1–2; theis _∧ MS
36 accompt] MS; accop F 1
38 it,] MS; ~ _∧ F 1
49 Sir. Though] MS; ~ , though
  F 1, 2; ~ ; though FK
57 cunning] MS; cunnig F 1
65 treason;] FK; ~ , F 1, MS
66 danger,] FK; ~ ; F 1; ~ _∧ MS
76 Earle] MS; *Earle* F 1

80 rest.] ~ ; F 1, 2, MS; ~ : FK
108 F 1–2 *line:* eyes; | Despise...
  not (*omit* MS)
108 not,] ~ _∧ F 1; ~ ; FK; ~ : F 2
  (*omit* MS)
114 F 1–2 *line:* actions; | Can you
  think, (MS | Can)
122 not;] FK; ~ _∧ F 1, MS; ~ . F 2
123 Take] MS; Nake F 1
130 *Hemskirck*] *Hemskiricke* F 1–FK;
  Hemskirk MS, F 2

I.iii

0 I.iii] *Scæna Secunda.* F 1–2 ±;
  omit MS
0.1 *Three*] MS; 3. F 1
1 'Tis] FK; T'is F 1; _∧ Tis MS
10 yet_∧] MS; ~ ; F 1
18 man?] MS; ~ . F 1
26 temper:] ~ ; F 1–2

63 rates,... *Cyprus:*] ~ :...~ ,
  F 1; ~ ,...~ ; FK; ~ ,...~ ,
  F 2; ~ ,...~ _∧ MS
76 you,] MS; ~ ; F 1
76 fairly;] ~ , F 1–2, MS
85 'em,] FK (them,); ~ _∧ F 1, MS

340

128–129 The Gunner...welcome.]
  one line in F1–2, MS
129.1 *Exeunt*] MS; *Exit* F1

150 Master] MS; M^r. F1
153 mine] MS; my F1
158 them] MS; 'em F1

II.i

0 II.i] Actus Secundus, Scæna
  Prima. F1–2±; *Actus Secundus*
  MS
4 *Clapperdudgeon*,] MS; ~ . F1
7 adjoyning;] FK; ~ , F1; ~ ‸
  MS
14 chosen,] FK; ~ ‸ F1, MS
15 a me] MS; of me F1
16 tyrant‸] MS; ~ . F1
18, 38 ye] MS; you F1
21 season,] MS; ~ : F1
28 a] MS; o' F1
47 Master:] ~ , F1–2; ~ ‸ MS
48 'mongst] MS (mongst); amongst
  F1
51–52 We...it] F1–2, MS *line*: We
  ...because | Indeed...it
57 ore] MS; over F1
63–64 Now...houre.] F1–2, MS
  line: Now...him, | May...
  houre.
65 marry.] FK (marrie); ~ : F1;
  ~ ‸ MS
66 a] MS; of F1
72 for't] MS; for it F1
76 Soveraign,] FK; ~ ; F1; ~ ‸
  MS
76 Maunders,] F2; ~ . F1, FK;
  ~ ‸ MS
90 presage‸] MS; ~ , F1
92 well‸] MS; ~ , F1
94 beard‸] MS; ~ , F1
100 *Higgen*.] MS; ~ ‸ F1
101 Gi'] MS (Gy'); Give F1
104 smile.] ~ ‸ F1–2, MS
125 o'] MS (ô); on F1
132 'em‸] MS; ~ ; F1

133 crutches,] MS; ~ : F1
140 King] MS; K. F1
142 *A   Cove   comes...fumbumbis*]
  MS; *roman in* F1
143–164 *Lining from* MS; F1–2 *line
  as*: Cast...Holli-day | At...
  sing. etc.
143 away,] FK; ~ : F1; ~ ‸ MS
144 *Holli-day*:] ~ , F1, 2, MS; ~ ;
  FK
168 Worships——...money——]
  ~ :...~ . F1; ~ ...~ ‸ FK;
  ~ ....~ . F2; ~ !...~ ! MS
169 wretches——...lame——] ~ :
  ...~ , F1; ~ ...~ . FK–
  F2; ~ ‸...~ ‸ MS
170 Worships——] ~ ; F1; ~ .
  FK–F2; ~ ! MS
172 bread——] ~ , F1–FK; ~ .
  F2; ~ ‸ MS
175 Worship——] ~ . F1–2; ~ !
  MS
176 sins——] ~ , F1–FK; ~ .
  F2; ~ ‸ MS
179 all.] F2; ~ ? F1–FK; ~ ‸ MS
180 Lord‸] MS; ~ , F1
180 ² you.] FK; ~ ? F1; ~ ‸ MS
181–182 Do...so?] *one line in* F1–2,
  MS (see ? or)
183 What, ha'] ~ ‸ ~ , F1; ~ ‸ ~ ‸
  FK–F2; ~ ‸ ~ – MS
187 *Exit*.] F2; *omit* F1–FK, MS
189 manners‸] FK; ~ , F1, MS
189 chang'd.] F2; ~ , F1; ~ :
  FK; ~ ‸ MS
195 thought.] F2; ~ ‸ F1, MS;
  ~ ; FK

196 Whi-whi-whi-whi-] MS (*3 times*); Why, why, why, why, F1
196 gu-gu-gu-gu-] MS (*3 times*); ∼ , ∼ , ∼ , ∼ , F1
196 foole,] FK; ∼ ‸ F1; ∼ ? MS
197 She...Bush:] MS; F1–2 *line*: younder, | By
197 by‸] MS; ∼ – F1

197 Bush:] MS; ∼ ‸ F1
198 *Mi-Mi-Mi-Mi*-] MS (*2 times*); My-my-my-my- F1
200–201 Lo-...luck.] *one line in* F1–2, MS
201 luck.] MS; ∼ , F1
204 O'] MS; O ‸ F1
208 friend——] ∼ , ——F1, 2; ∼ ; ——FK; ∼ ‸ MS

II.ii

0 II.ii] *Scæna Secunda.* F1–2±; *omit* MS
3 servants,] FK; ∼ : F1; ∼ ‸ MS
5 thinke?] ∼ ‸ F1, 2, MS; ∼ , FK
6 ships,] ∼ ? F1–2, MS
7 ware-houses,] MS; ∼ ? F1
7 Factors,] Facto ‸ F1; Factors? FK, F2; Factors ‸ MS

8 returnes.] FK; ∼ ; F1; ∼ : MS
13 winds‸] MS (windes); ∼ , F1
14 Ha'‸] MS; Ha? F1
18 said‸] MS; ∼ , F1
18 Vultures,] FK; ∼ ‸ F1, MS
22 please ‸...me‸] MS; ∼ , ... ∼ ; F1
25 'gainst] MS; against F1

II.iii

0 II.iii] Scæna Tertia. F1–2±; *omit* MS
1 welcome,] MS; ∼ ; F1
2 welcome;] FK; ∼ , F1, MS
3 Master,] MS; ∼ ; F1
4 *Margee,*] MS; *Meg*: F1
5 if] MS; If F1
6 'gainst] MS; gain' F1
6 Gentlemen,] FK; ∼ ‸ F1, MS
11 walls,] FK; ∼ ; F1; ∼ ‸ MS
19 *Margee,*] MS; *Mage*: F1
20 fast,] ∼ ‸ F1–2, MS
26 Sir,] MS; ∼ ‸ F1
27–28 Fill...*Woolfort*] *one line in* F1–2, MS
28 *Woolfort*‸] MS; ∼ . F1
30 *Margee*] MS; *Marget* F1
31 said,] F1 (*in repeated line*); ∼ ‸ F1 *original line*
36 leizure——] F2; ∼ . ——F1– FK; ∼ ‸ MS

40 nev'r] MS (nere); never F1
42 y'aske] MS you aske F1
47, ¹48 *Bruges*] FK; Bruges F1, MS
48 y'ad] MS (ya'd); you had F1
65 this,] FK; ∼ ‸ F1, MS
66 Rose (here's...you)] MS; ∼ : ∼ ...∼ ; F1
69 'Tis] FK; ‸ Tis F1, MS
81 Sir:] ∼ , F1; ∼ ! MS, FK; ∼ ? F2
82, ²100, ¹120 you] MS; ye F1
82 her,] MS; ∼ : F1
88 Gentleman] MS (gentleman); Genntleman F1
89 a] MS; o' F1
99 Gentry's] MS (gentryes); Gentry is F1
101 Lords‸] MS; ∼ , F1
110 *C*,] MS; ∼ . F1
115 for't] FK; fort F1, MS

120 ᵗyou] MS; ye F1
121 please.] FK; ~ , F1; ~ ˄ MS
122 sir] MS; siir F1
143 arm'd] MS; arme'd F1
164 *Exeunt*] F2; *Exit* F1–FK, MS

164 *and* Bertha] F2 (*and* Ger.);
    omit F1–FK, MS
171 This˄] MS; ~ , F1
177 *Vanduncke*] MS (*Vandunk*);
    Vandoncke F1
180 it——] MS; ~ .——F1

II.iv

1 y'ave] MS; you have F1

19 her.] FK; ~ .——F1; ~ :——
   MS

III.i

0 III.i] Actus Tertius, Scæna
  Prima. F1–2±; *Actus tertius*
  MS
5 *too...too...too...too*] MS; *to*
  ...to...to...to F1
8 *Stone,*] F2; ~ ˄ F1, MS; ~ ?
  FK
16 pence a] MS; pencea F1
22 *again.*] ~ , F1–2; ~ ˄ MS
34 *again.*] FK; ~ ˄ F1, MS
40, 68 ye] MS; you F1
42 *Ram,*] F2; ~ ˄ MS
43 *And*] F2; *and* MS
43 *came;*] F2; ~ ˄ MS
44 *horne,*] F2; ~ ˄ MS
45 *corne.*] F2; ~ ˄ MS
46 *slunck,*] F2; ~ ˄ MS
48 *halfe,*] F2; ~ ˄ MS
49 *Calfe;*] F2; ~ ˄ MS
50 *Evill,*] ~ ˄ MS; ~ ; F2
51 *Devill.*] F2; ~ ˄ MS
52 *steal,*] F2; ~ ˄ MS
54 *Pigg,*] F2; ~ ˄ MS
55 *bigg;*] F2; ~ ˄ MS
56 *Logg,*] F2; ~ ˄ MS
57 *hogg.*] F2; ~ ˄ MS

73 Here...bullets] F1–2, MS *line*:
   balls, | These
76 three bullets] MS; 3. bullets F1
78 *patule*——] MS; ~ . F1
79 *fagi*——] MS (~ .——); ~ .
   F1
96 *Exeunt*] *Exit.* F1–2; omit MS
107 'tis] FK; ˄ ~ F1, MS
115 -skins?] MS; ~ . F1
125–126 Have...silver.] *one line in*
   F1–2, MS
126–127 This...copper.] *one line in*
   F1–2, MS
128 'Tis] MS (Tis); 'Ts F1
131 'em!] ~ ? F1–2; ~ ˄ MS
137 d'en] MS; do'n F1
142–143 (*twice*), 147, 152, 153 ye]
   MS; you F1
144 Ha?...boy.] F1–2, MS *line*:
   Ha? | Lead
155, 158 *3. Boore.*] MS (*3. Bo:*); 3
   Boy F1
157 *1. Boore.*] MS (*1. Bo:*); 1 *Boy*.
   F1
166 I've] MS; I have F1

343

III.ii

0 III.ii] *Scæna Secunda.* F 1–2±;
omit MS
22 sh'as] MS; she has F 1
26 Creditors.] MS; ~ , F 1
26.1 *Enter* Hemskirke.] MS (Hemskirk); F 1–2 *place as line* 28.1
31 F 1–2, MS *line*: bravely, | And
36 lawfull] MS; lawfell F 1
36 'em,] ~ ᴀ F 1–2, MS
37 rifle] MS; rifle F 1
38 hold. *Exeunt.*] MS; F 1 places
Exeunt after breeches
40 should] MS; should F 1
40 'emselves] MS; themselves F 1
51 I've] MS; I have F 1
58 Master] MS (master); Mr. F 1

59 y'are] MS (yare); ye are F 1
63 knowledge] MS; knowledg (|)
F 1
74, 85, ²110, ²111 ye] MS; you F 1
74 thee,] MS (*doubtful*), FK; ~ ᴀ
F 1
78 off ᴀ yet shewing,] ~ , ~ ~ ᴀ
F 1, 2, MS; ~ , ~ ~ , FK
79 *Clause*] MS; Clause F 1
79 come,] F 2; ~ ᴀ F 1–FK, MS
83 ¹ye] MS; you F 1
84 ²ye] MS; you F 1
98 yeares] MS; yearess F 1
98 me.] ~ , F 1–2; ~ ᴀ MS
99 want?] MS; ~ . F 1
106 hast] MS; has F 1

III.iii

0 III.iii] *Scnæa Tertia.* F 1–2±;
omit MS
3 for.] ~ ᴀ F 1, MS; ~ ; FK, F 2

6 narrowly. That] MS; ~ , that
F 1
10 nature,] FK; ~ ; F 1; ~ ᴀ MS

III.iv

1 'um] MS; 'em F 1
3 sentence:] MS; ~ , F 1
3, 11 (*twice*), 12, 35, 36, 47, 58, 66
ye] MS; you F 1
7 then,] F 2; ~ ᴀ F 1–FK, MS
7 Rogues] MS; rogues F 1
8 ye——] ~ . F 1–2, MS
33 lyes:...partialityᴀ] MS; ~ ᴀ
...~ ; F 1
38 ah] MS; oh F 1
56 th'ast] MS (tha'st); thou hast F 1
56 foole,] FK; ~ ᴀ F 1, MS
63 Y'ave] MS; Ye have F 1
63 me?] ~ ᴀ F 1, MS; ~ . FK, F 2
67 'em] MS; ᴀ ~ F 1
77 friends] MS (freinds); feiends F 1

84 walkes,] F 2; ~ ᴀ F 1, MS; ~ ;
FK
91 *Isgrim*] MS; *Isgrin* F 1
100 knavery——] MS; ~ : F 1
100 here ᴀ Sirra,] MS; ~ , ~ ᴀ F 1
101 -knave,] F 2; ~ ᴀ F 1, MS; ~ :
FK
102 if] MS; If F 1
103 dispatch] MS; dispateh F 1
111 serviceᴀ] MS; ~ , F 1
114 better?] MS; ~ ; F 1
115 freedome] MS; fredome | F 1
125 presum'd?] MS; ~ . F 1
126 well,] ~ ᴀ F 1–2, MS
132 o'] MS; on F 1
134 stromell] MS; stiromell F 1

135 Herman Becks trine] Herman
   Beck strine F1–2; harmon, beck
   trim MS
143 Y'are] MS (yare); You are F1

144–145 F1–2, MS *line*: Welcom...
   keeping | Of...fellow?
146 ye dare] MS; you dare F1
153 him;] FK; ~ , F1; ~ ₄ MS
159 ²drink,] FK; ~ ₄ | F1, MS

III.v

0 III.v] *Scæna quarta.* F1–2±;
   omit MS
0.1 *Bertha*] MS; *Bereha* F1
1 y'are] MS (yare); yae'r F1; ye
   are FK; you're F2
2 you,] FK; ~ ; F1; ~ ₄ MS
4 what is't] MS; what'ist F1
4, 11, 16 ²ye] MS; you F1
5 you.] ~ ₄ MS
6, 47 ¹ye] MS; you F1
7, 23, 43 *Gertred*] *Jertred* F1–FK.
   Gertrude MS, F2

8 ye] MS; ye' F1
13 opinions——] ~ ? F1–2, MS
23 sorrowes: *Gertred*!] MS (*Ger-*
   trude!); ~ , ~ . F1
32 ruine——] ~ . F1–2; ~ ₄ MS
36 flow'n] MS (flowne); flow'd F1
41 y'have] MS; you have F1
44 by] MS; By F1
45 ye——] ~ , F1–2; ~ ₄ MS
46 thee.——] ~ , F1–2, MS

IV.i

0 IV.i] Actus Quartus Scæna
   prima. F1–2±; Actus quartus:
   MS
0.1 *four*] FK; 4. F1, MS
1 you,] FK; ~ ₄ | F1, MS
2 seven] MS (seavn); 7. F1
2 running] MS; runnig F1
3, 20, 54, 63 ye] MS; you F1
6 I'm] MS; I am F1
6 protested;] FK; ~ ₄ F1, MS
25 it,] FK; ~ : F1; ~ ₄ MS
27 worship.] FK; ~ ₄ F1, MS
32 Towne,] FK; ~ ; F1

33 two] MS; 2. F1
33 howres,] FK; ~ ₄ | F1, MS
35.1 *Exeunt*] MS; *Exit* F1
41.1 *Enter*] MS; F1 *places as line*
   40.1
41.1 *Porters*] FK; *Porter* F1;
   Boores MS
46–47 -dragon,...Sir:] FK (~ ,
   ...~ ;); ~ :...~ , F1; ~ ₄
   ...~ ₄ MS
49 be] MS; Be F1
49 'em,] FK; ~ ₄ F1, MS
66 withall] MS; with all F1

IV.ii

0 IV.ii] *Scæna Secunda.* F1–2±;
   omit MS
4, 32 *Minche*] FK; Minche F1, MS
5 Y'deed] MS; Y'ded F1

6 Thus:——] ~ : ₄ F1–2; ~ ₄
   MS
10 Cockles.——] ~ . ₄ F1–2, MS
12 she:——] ~ : ₄ F1–2; ~ , ₄ MS
17, 32, 34 ye] MS; you F1

17 then;——] ~ ;ᴧ F1–2; ~ ᴧ
MS
22 thus:——] ~ :ᴧ F1–2; ~ ᴧ MS
23 it is] MS; 'tis F1

24 it:——] ~ ,ᴧ F1–FK . ~ !ᴧ
F2; ~ ᴧ MS
37 I'm] MS (Ime); I am F1

IV.iii

0 IV.iii] *Scæna Tertia.* F1–2±;
omit MS
2 it,] FK; ~ ᴧ F1, MS
7 They're] MS (They'r); They
are F1
8 fraught] MS; frought F1
13 in.] ~ ᴧ F1, MS; ~ , F2
22, 32 Saylor] MS; *Saylor* F1
22 sh'ad] MS (shad); she had F1
35 yeare] MS; ye are F1
39 I...ye:] MS; you. | When F1–2
39 ye...ye] MS; you...you F1
40.1 *Exeunt Merchants.*] MS; *omit*
F1
41–42 Come...me, | Yonder's]
MS; Come...home | With...
howles. F1–2
41 ease,] MS; ~ ᴧ F1

42 Yonder's] MS (Yonders); Yonder is F1
44–45 When...wife.] MS; Why
when...night, | My boy...
wife, F1–2
44 nightᴧ] MS; ~ , F1
48 serviceᴧ] MS; ~ , F1
53 *Bruges*] FK; Bruges F1, MS
53 nourished:] FK; ~ ᴧ F1, MS
55 th'art] MS; thou art F1
55 lusty,] MS; ~ ᴧ F1
58 love,] ~ ᴧ F1–2, MS
60 I'le] MS (Ile); I will F1
61–63 By...trice.] MS; By...
Merchant, | Gold...*Prig.* | It
...trice. F1–2
62 sport ᴧ soone,] MS; ~ , ~ ᴧ F1
64 pace,] F2; ~ ᴧ F1–FK, MS
65 'em] MS; them F1

IV.iv

0 IV.iv] *Scæna Quarta.* F1–2±;
omit MS
1–2 Why...wishes.] MS; Why
...mine | To...wishes. F1–2
6 servant?] FK; ~ . F1; ~ ᴧ MS
9–10 I...recompence;] MS; I...
be | The...recompence, F1–2
9, 22 ye] MS; you F1
10 You'le] MS (Youl); you will F1
10 recompence;] FK; ~ , F1;
~ ᴧ MS
12 on'tᴧ] MS; ~ : F1
13–15 If...thee——] MS; If...
desires, | If...thee——F1–2

14 thine] MS; thy F1
15–16 Prethee...thing] MS; *one
line in* F1–2
18–19 Why...not | I...thing,]
MS; Why...me, | Do...
promise | Any F1–2
20–22 More...performance.] MS;
Any thing, more...at? | Beleeve
me Huntsman, | There...
sillable | That...passe | With-
out...performance. F1–2
23 quality?] FK; ~ . F1; ~ ᴧ MS
24 thousand:] MS; ~ ᴧ F1
26 too——] MS; ~ . F1

28 th'art] MS; thou art F1
30 dangers‸] FK; ~ , F1; ~ ?
   MS
37–38 I…nothing,] *one line in*
   F1–2, MS
52 'em——] MS; ~ . F1

59 I'de] MS; I would F1
61–62 valiant,…forces)] FK; ~)
   …~ , F1
63 clock:] MS; ~ , F1
73 ¹ye] MS; you F1
74.1 *Exeunt.*] *Exit.* F1–2; *Exᵗ* MS

IV.v

5 daughter,] MS; ~ ‸ F1
33, 34, 51 ye] MS; you F1
35 follow;] FK; ~ , F1; ~ ‸ MS
41 Merchants;…Ape?] MS; ~ ,
   …~ ‸ F1
42 t'other] MS (tother); the other
   F1

50 'Tis] FK; ‸ ~ F1, MS
57–58 defiance,…monuments?]
   FK; ~ ?…~ , F1; ~ ‸…‸
   MS
60 Ducks——] F2; ~ ? F1; ~ ?
   ——FK; ~ ‸ MS
63 wanting,] FK; ~ ‸ F1, MS

IV.vi

0 IV.vi] *Scæna Quinta.* F1–2±;
   omit MS
0.1 *severallie*] MS; *omit* F1
1 wedding?] ~ . F1–2; ~ ‸ MS
7 She's] MS (Shees); She is F1
18 y'are] MS (yare); ye are F1
18–19 man,…doe:] FK (~ ,…
   ~ ;); ~ :…~ , F1, MS
19 could a] MS (coo'd a'); could
   have F1
21 th'art] MS (thart); thou art F1
23 'tis] FK; ‸ ~ F1, MS
25 please] MS; plase F1
29, 34 (*twice*), ¹38 ye] MS; you F1
29 *Exeunt.*] MS; *Exit.* F1
37 yet?] FK; ~ ‸ F1, MS
47 I've] MS; I have F1
70.1 *Enter*] MS; F1 *places as line*
   69.1

70.1 *rest,*] ~ ‸ F1–2
71 now,] F2; ~ ‸ F1–FK, MS
78 ore] MS; over F1
85 ready‸] MS; ~ : F1
90 'Twill] FK; T will F1; Twill
   MS
92 *Clause*] MS; *Claus* | F1
94 longer,] FK; ~ ‸ F1, MS
95 noble——] ~ . F1–2; ~ : MS
97 there,] FK; ~ . F1; ~ ‸ MS
98 state, (make…enquiry,)] F2;
   ~ ;‸ ~ …~ , F1–FK; ~ ,‸
   ~ …~ ‸ MS
101 'em…ye] MS; them…you F1
104 o'] MS; of F1
104 *Exeunt*] Exit F1–2; *Exᵗ. Gerr:*
   MS

V.i

0 V.i] *Actus Quintus, Scæna Prima.*
   F1–2±; Actus quintus: MS
3 Fear] MS (feare); Fsar F1

3 'twere] FK; twere F1; it were
   MS
5, 38 'Tis] FK; ‸ ~ F1, MS

19 a us] MS; on's F1
23 beseech] MS (beseeche); besech
 F1
25 wood's] MS (woods); wood is
 F1
27–28 The...not.] *one line in*
 F1–2, MS
28 is't] MS; is it F1
32, 45 'Tas] MS; It has F1
34 'Thath] MS; It hath F1
43 'Tis...Lightning.] MS; thun-
 der: | See, F1–2
44, 49 ye] MS; you F1
51 wi'] MS (wi); with F1
58 too,] ~ ₐ F1–2, MS
69 Master] Mʳ. F1–2, MS
69 *Goswin*ₐ] MS; ~ ; F1
74 married,] FK; ~ : F1; ~ ₐ MS
75 hereₐ] MS; ~ : F1
79 didₐ] MS; ~ : F1
80 In the] MS; I'the F1
82 done.] ~ ₐ F1–2; ~ : MS

97 inhabiting] FK; in habiting F1
101 takingₐ] MS; ~ , F1
106 o'the] MS; o'th the F1–FK
106 O,] O' F1–FK; O ₐ F2; ô MS
114, 116, 131 ye] MS; you F1
118 ha'] MS (ha); have F1
121 anonₐ] MS; ~ , F1
121 done,] ~ ₐ F1–2, MS
124 don't,] MS; ~ . F1
126 *Costin*] *Coʒin* F1–2; *Cosein* MS
134 Squadrons] MS (squadrons);
 Squadrous F1
135 outlets] MS (outletts); out lets
 F1
136 placeₐ] MS; ~ : F1
140 four] MS (foure); 4. F1
140 Boores, here to me,] MS; ~ ₐ
 ~ , ~ ~ ₐ F1
144 ²'em] MS; them F1
147 order'd] F2; orderd F1;
 ordered MS, FK
150 me,] MS; ~ ? F1

V.ii

0 V.ii] *Scæna Secunda.* F1–2±;
 omit MS
12 cheerefullnesse——] ~ . F1–2,
 MS
14 example,] MS; ~ ₐ F1
45 circumstances;] ~ , F1–2; ~ ₐ
 MS
58 equall——] ~ . F1–2; ~ ₐ MS
67 'em] MS; them F1
74 *Hemskirke*——] ~ ; F1–FK;
 ~ . F2; ~ ₐ MS
83 entreat——] ~ ₐ F1–FK, MS;
 ~ . F2
84 *Woolfort*——] ~ . F1–2; ~ ₐ
 MS
91 hee'd] MS (he'ed); hee would F1
98 quarrell,] F2; ~ . F1–FK; ~ ₐ
 MS
108 a] MS; of F1

111 *Benthuisen*] MS; *Benthusin* F1
121 'Twill] FK; ₐ ~ F1, MS
128–129 Hunts-man;...*Hubert*,] ~ ,
 ...~ ; F1–2; ~ ₐ...~ , MS
132 *Woolfort*.] FK; ~ ₐ MS; *Wool:*
 F1
144 *Van-donck*,] MS; ~ ₐ F1
144 *et*] MS; & F1
144 *vici*:] ~ , F1–2; ~ ₐ MS
151 people,] FK; ~ ₐ F1; *omit* MS
172 row] MS; rew F1
175 *Hemskirck*,] MS; ~ ₐ F1
176 himₐ] MS; ~ , F1
177, 195 too,] MS; ~ : F1
178 contemneₐ] MS (contemneₐ);
 ~ ; F1
200 resigneₐ] MS; ~ . F1
206, 207 ye] MS; you F1
210 *Crab*] Crab F1–2, MS

218 Clymat‸] MS; ~ : F1
219 see,] FK; ~ ‸ F1, MS
221 O'] F2; O ‸ F1; Of FK, MS
222 lads;] F2; ~ ‸ F1–FK, MS
230 Letter;] ~ : F1–2; ~ ‸ MS
231 word.] F2; ~ , F1, FK; ~ ;
    MS
232 these——] ~ . F1–2; ~ ‸ MS
233 were——] ~ . F1–2; ~ : MS

236 cheerely,...eyes‸] MS; ~ ‸...
    ~ : F1
244–245 And...Councell.] *one line*
    in F1–2, MS
247 too,] MS; ~ ‸ F1
247–248 The good...Husbands.]
    one line in F1–2, MS
254 Wee'l] FK; W'eel F1; weel MS

349

HISTORICAL COLLATION

[NOTE: Only rejected substantive readings are recorded here joined by a few accidentals that have substantive import. For simplicity, the record of 'ye'– 'you' variants is confined to the early editions ending with F2; moreover, the historical collation does not record such variants where they appear as emendations. Editions collated are: F1 (Folio of 1647), MS (Lambarde manuscript), FK (Quarto of 1661), F2 (Folio of 1679), and the edited texts of (L) Langbaine (1711), (S) Seward (1750), (C) Coleman (1778), (W) Weber (1812), (D) Dyce (1845), (V) Variorum (1905), and (Dp) Dorenkamp (1967) Texts of the songs have been collated in MMS[1] (Bodleian MS Mus.b.1, fols. 45–45^v, with music); MMS[2] (Bodleian MS Douce. c. 57, fols. 75^v, 139^v, with music); MMS[3] (Edinburgh University Library MS Dc1, 69, fol. 154, with music); MMS[4] (New York Public Library MS Drexel 4041, no. 7, fols. 81^v– 82^v, with music); MMS[5] (Folger Shakespeare Library MS V.a.308, fol. 7, no music); MMS[6] (British Museum Harleian MS 3991, fol. 141, no music); MMS[7] (New York Public Library Drexel 4257, fol. 67, music); CA (*Cheerfuι Ayres* (1660), ed., John Wilson, pp. 22–3, with music); PPM (*Pills to Purge Melancholy* (1707), ed. Thomas D'Urfey), pp. 115–16, music).]

I.i

7 ten] five F1–2, L–V
18 this] his MS
40 Not] Nor L–S

42 made] make L
50 free] full F1–2, L+

I.ii

0.1 Hemskirk] *omit* F1–2, L+
2 It was] twas MS
6 idly] rudely F1–2, L+
10 rather] either F1–2, L+ (–C, D)
11–17 Who...with;] *omit* MS
13 Were] Where L
17 askt] ask Dp
23 sit] set F1, FK
28 to] *omit* F1–2, L–V
34 proscriptions] prescriptions MS
34 this] theis MS, Dp

34 wisedome;] ~ ‸ MS
40 action] actions L–D
41 so] *omit* MS, F2, L–D
47 I that] that I MS
48 life ‸ then;] ~ ; ~ ‸ L–D
51 These] This MS
52 it is] tis a MS; it is a S
55 answer] answers F1, FK
57–58 to...dangerous;] *omit* MS
71 further] farther MS
75 Vowing] Vow'd L–S
89 beastly] princely F1–2, L+

350

100 now] not Dp
103 securely] surely F1–2, L, C–D,
    Dp; Sir, freely S
108–114 Despise...actions;] *omit*
    MS
115 *Floriz*] *Goswin* F2, L–S
116 proscrib'd] prescrib'd MS

124 you] yee MS
126 good men] goodmen MS
126–127 Sir...beleeve.] *one line in*
    MS
129 them] thee S
140 you] you'll S
140.1 *Exeunt.*] *Ex.* F1; *Exit.* FK

I.iii

3 Confirme] Confirmd F1–2, L–S
4 in it] in't MS
8 was] has MS
17 Unquestion'd] Questionlesse FK
18 Continues] Continue MS
27 sutable] suited S
30 the] their F2, L–D
30 nor] Not S
38 And the increase] And the
    measures F1–2; And the means
    L; Yet the means S, C
38 follows this,] follows, this ᴧ F2,
    L, W; follows? | *2. Merch.* This
    S
45 dowre] Dowrie MS
48 him] home F2, L–D
58 am] want MS
59 only] and only Dp
60 His] Hees MS
61 Sinke] Sucke F1, FK
62.1 *et seq.* Florez] *Goswin* F2,
    L–D
62.1 and] *omit* MS
68 my] *omit* F2, L; the S
75 so are] are so F1–2, L+
76 you] yee MS
85 'em] them FK
100 necessity] necessities MS

106 misfortune] misfortunes MS,
    S–D
109 for] with MS
118 lastnight] last MS; last night
    FK+
119 her] the F1–2, L+
119 fraught] fraight L–S; freight
    C–W
121 Rich lading,] *omit* MS
127 will] I will Dp
129 you] yᵉʳ MS ('r' *probably
    added*)
129 *3 Merchant.*] *Merchants.* D
    (*qy*)
133 Stands] Stand MS
135 'a] o' F2, L–C, V
140 This] theis MS
140 three] seavne MS, Dp
140 have I] I have MS
144 sute more] more suite MS
153 mine] my F1–2, L+
154 best] the best L
154 amongst] among F1–2, L+
158 them] 'em F1–2, L+
159 are] oure MS
167 beg in] begin MS
170 worldly] wordly Dp

II.i

0.1 Clause,] Clause, Jaculine F1–
    2, MS, L–W, Dp
4 *Patrico*] Patrin MS

11 full] first F1–2, L–V
12 say upon the] say up the F1–2,
    L, C–V; save us further S

15 a me] of me F 1–2, L+
21 cheats] chickens F 1–2, L+
24 priviledges] priviledge F 1–2,
      L+
27 teeth] tongues S, C
27 you] *omit* MS
28 a] o' F 1–2, L+
33 The] They Dp
37 roost] roose Dp
38 musty] misty MS
42 and he were] were hee MS
44 I am] Ime MS, Dp
44 find] findeing MS; I find L–V
48 'mongst] amongst F 1–2, L+
50 call] calling F 1, L–C, Dp
51 ne're] never MS
52 hard] heard MS
52 dissolv'd] resolv'd S
53 him] whom F 1–2, V
57 ore] over F 1–2, L–D
57 of] on MS
59 the man] man FK
61 you] yee MS
66 a] of F 1–2, L+
68 *Ferret*] Ginks S, C–V
71 gratuling] gratulating FK, S, C
73 H'has] has MS; He has W, Dp
74 it] hee MS
75 That thou] Thou that FK
76 o'th] of the MS
79 signes:...envy,] ~ ,...~ :
      F 1–2, L–D
80 thee] the MS
80–81 chosen?...chosen,] ~ ₄...
      ~ ? F 1–2, L+
84 about] 'bout MS
88 the other] thother MS; t'other
      S, C
95 him] *omit* F 1–2, L+
101 Gi?] Give F 1–2, L+
105 No] On F 1–2
105 No...grievances,] *omit* MS
106 the] a F 1–2, L+
107 kem'd] hem'd F 1–FK

110 you] yee MS
120 prop] proper MS
120 he...purveyers] *omit* MS
125 o'] ô MS; on F 1–2, L+
133 in] *omit* MS
134 torne] true F 1, FK
142 *Higgen.*] *omit* MS
142.1 *Strike music. Song.*] *strike*
      F 1–2, L+
142.2 *The SONG.*] *Song.* MS
143 *our*] your MMS²⁻⁶, Cᵃ
144 *This is*] Each day's MMS⁵
144 *Beggars*] the beggers MMS¹⁻⁴, ⁶,
      Cᵃ
145–146, 148–150 *omit* MMS⁵
146 *ever...sing*] Dance and thus we
      Sing MMS⁶
148 *Where*] wher's F 2, MMS³, L;
      where is MMS⁴
148 *Prince*] king MMS¹⁻⁴, ⁶, Cᵃ
149 *Where*] wheres MMS⁴
149 *the Nation*] that nation MMS⁴; a
      Nation MMS⁵; the Nations L, S
149 *live*] *lives* MS, MMS ¹⁻⁴, ⁵, C–W
150 *merry*] happy MMS²; merily
      MMS⁴
153 *And*] we MMS⁵
155 *are*] or MS
156 *the Gowne*] a Gowne MMS²⁻⁴, ⁶,
      Cᵃ, Dp
157 *Hang all*] Hang up the MMS⁶
157 *Officers*] *Offices* F–FK, MMS⁵,
      C–D
158 *the Magistrate*] your Masters
      MMS⁶
158 *by*] buy MMS⁴
159 *When*] Where MMS⁴
159 *Subsidie's*] *Subsidies* F 1, MS;
      subsitties are MMS⁴; Subsity
      dayes MMS⁶
160 *are*] were MS
162 *the Beggar*] a Beggar MMS²⁻⁴, Cᵃ
164.1 *Enter...Hemskirke.*] *omit*
      MS

165 Cove] Cove comes F2, L–S
166 see it] see't MS
168 *Ferret.*] *Prig.* FK; *Per.* L
171 by] be MS
172 *Gerrard.*] *Fer.* F2, L–D
175 Remember] O Remember S
178 this] theis MS, L–W
180 The King of] *omit* F1–2, L+
192 'Tis] This F1, FK; This is F2, L–V
194 *Higgen.*] *Snap.* MS
194 de-] *five times* MS; *seven times* D
194 du-du-du-du-dumb] du-du-dude–dumb F1–2, L; du-du-du-dumbe MS
196 gu-gu-gu-gu-] gu-gu-gu MS
196 foole,] ~ ? MS, F1–2, L–V

197 bu-bu-Bush] Bush bo-bo-bo-Bush F1–2, L+
198 *Mi-Mi-Mi-Mi-*] *Mi-Mi-* MS
198 *Minche*] match F1–2, L
199 he] she F1, FK
200 ni-ni-nigled] in-in-ingled MS
201 ha'] had MS
201 go-go-go] go-go- MS
204 O'] Of F2, L–W; Oh D
205 I will] but Ile MS
207 hope ‸ it is,] ~ ? ~ ~ ‸ F1; ~ ‸ ~ ~ ‸ FK; ~ : ~ ~ ‸ F2, L–C
209 it] *omit* F1–2, L+
213 Faith] *omit* F1–2, L+
214 sunning] succing MS
215 the] thee MS
216 skuys] excuse F2, L–V (–D)

II.ii

8 ha'] a MS
8 returnes] returne MS
10, 17.1 *Exit.*] *omit* F1–2, MS
12 ruines] ruine FK
14 hurt] heart MS
17 Not any] Neither MS

21–22 MS *lines:* heaven come on | And
23 my] mine FK
23 one] owne F1–2, L–V
25 'gainst] against F1–FK
25 ill fortunes] misfortunes MS
27 Me] My MS

II.iii

0.1 *Enter*] *Table out. Enter* MS
0.2 *Boores*] *and Boores* MS, L
4 *Margee*] *Meg* F1–FK, C–D; *Margaret* F2, L–S
6 'gainst] 'gain F1, D
6 Traitor] Traitors F1–2, L+
6 Gentlemen] MS gentlemen *altered from* gentleman
17 hear] here F1–2
18 And...welcome] *omit* MS
19 *Margee,*] *Mage:* F1–FK; *omit* F2, L–S; *Madge* C–V
27 Statesman] Statesmen F1

30 *Margee*] *Margret* F1–FK; *Margaret* F2, L–S; *Marget* C–D
31 *Van.* Well...still.] *set by Comp. B foot of 2K4ᵛ and repeated by Comp. A head of 2L1 as Van.* Well said, my pearly still, *after catchword* And
33 through] though Dp
34 all] *omit* F1–2, L+
34 errand] errand here S
36 yeare] yeares F1–2, L+
38 It] I F1–FK
42 y'aske] you aske F1–2, L+

43 *Margee*] *Marget* FK, F2; *Margaret* L, S
43 *Exit* Margaret.] *omit* MS
48 y'ad] you had F1–2, L+
50 t'] to FK
63 home] *omit* F1–2, L+
72 here] *omit* MS
72.1 MS *places s.d. as* 71.1
74–75 your selfe | Away] away | Your selfe MS
76 petty] pretty L–S
76 his] this F1, FK, Dp
82 you] ye F1–2
85 at] are F2, L–S
92 he is] he's Dp
93 Captaine] *Gos.* Captain S
93 Alas] 'las MS
94 looke] lookes MS
97 issue, here in *Bruges*] sonne in *Bruges* here MS
99 Gentry's] Gentry is F1–2, L–V
100–103 No...cheese?] MS *lines:* Noe...Argument | Doe... any! | Sell...Cheese?
105 stock'd] stor'd F1–2, L–V
106 woods] wood V (*qy*)
108–109 Chap-men...Factors] Factors...Chapmen MS

109 those] these F1–2, L+
109 errour] honour F2, L–V
116 Sure] Sir S
120 ¹you] ye F1–2, L
121 after] oft MS
124 suffering] scoffing F1–2, L–V
124 and] and with S, C, D, V
125 strive] strives D, V
132 my] myne MS
134 respect] respects MS
134 due] done F1–2, L–D
135.1 *Strikes him.*] *omit* F1–FK, MS
137.1 *He...head.*] *omit* F1–FK, MS
139 I] *omit* MS
144 they] theire MS
148 we not] not we F2, L–S
149 circle] circle here MS
156 act] art F1–2, L, Dp
158 aloud Love,] ~ : love ∧ V (*qy*)
161 you] *omit* FK
168 all wayes] alwayes FK
171 *Exit* Hemskirk.] *Exit.* MS
171–172 This | Is] *one line in* MS
175 further] farther MS
181 and] and's S
183 up] *omit* F1–2, L; me up S–V
183 me] he L

II.iv

1 y'ave] you have F1–2, L+
3 ye have] you have MS, D; ye've S; you've C

9 thought] thought to bee MS
12 his] its S–C

III.i

0.1 Boores.] *Boores* | *A table kans, and stooles* | *sett out* MS
1 belly] barrel S, C, W
2 Start] Stark F2, L–D, Dp
3 *3. Boore.*] *omit* F1–2, L–V
3.1 *Winde...within.*] *omit* F1–2, L+

3.2 *and Piper*] *omit* F1–2, L+
3.3 *omit*] *Song.* MS
4, 6, 7, 10 *ye*] you MMS³, CA
10 *braches*] Branches FK; *Brauches* MMS³, CA
16 *1. Boore.*] *3. Boor.* MS
17 boys] boy S–V

17 wet] whet L–W
19 Shees...Man.] *omit* F1–2, L–V
19.1 *The Song.*] *Song.* MS
22 *her*] *omit* MS
22, 34 *again boy, again.*] *again.*
   F1–2, L–V
25, 31 *amain boy, amain.*] *amain.*
   F1–2, L–V
28 *Then*] *And then* MS
37 *And*] *omit* F1–2, L+
40 ye] you F1–2, L+
41 I, I] I, MS
41.1–59 *Song. omit* F1–FK
42 *I met with him first*] *He ran at me
   first* F2, L–V; *I met with the
   Devil* PPM
43 *And*] *omit* MMS[7]
44 *I caught*] *I rise* F2, S–V; *I tooke
   him* MMS[7]; *I rose* PPM, L
44 *I haltred*] *haltered* MMS[7], PPM
44 horne] horne MMS[7] (*interlined
   above deleted* 'legg')
45 *pluckt*] *pickt* MMS[7], PPM
45 *you'd*] *you would* MS, PPM, Dp
45 *a corne*] *Corns* PPM
46 *Baa*] *Bay* MS, Dp; *Oh* MMS[7]
46 *then*] *omit* F2, L–V
48–53 MS *inscribes as stanza* 3
48 *By...ridd*] *The next time I rode*
   F2, L–V
49 *I... liv'd*] *Where I heard he did
   live* F2, L–V
50 *ere*] *where* MS
51 *sucking*] *young sucking* PPM, S, C
52 *Maa*] *Baa* MS
52 *quoth the Calfe*] *yet he cry'd* F2,
   L–V
54–59 MS *inscribes as stanza* 2
54 *the*] *omit* S, C
56 *caught*] *catch'd* F2, L–V
60–61 *1. Boore.* Groats...-gelder.]
   omit W
61 *Higgen.* I...Worships.] *omit*
   F1–2, L–V

63 sleight] sleightes MS
65 art] part V (*qy*)
66 you see my hands;] *omit* MS
68 *1. 2. Boores.*] *1. 2. 3. Boors.* MS
68 ye] you F1–2, L+
74 *ascentibus*] ascenti-bub- MS
76 Now] How Dp
77 Will...boyes.] *omit* MS
79 *tegmine*] jermine F1–2, L–V
81 *Silvestramtrim-tram*] Silvestnam
   trim tram—— MS; *Silvertram-
   trim-tram* F1–2, L+; *Silvestram
   trim tram* FK
85 *flam*] flum F1–2, L+
86 *bumbis*] oumbis FK
88 Ha] He F1–2, L+
89 far] *omit* MS
91 move] turne MS
92 whiss] whig MS
92 shake] snake F2
92 pockets] pockett MS
93 boyes] *omit* MS; boye FK
95 *2. Boore.*] *omit* F1–2, L+
96 *Higgen.*] *omit* F1–2, L+
96 *Exeunt.*] *omit* MS
96.2 *singing the Song.*] *Singing:* |
   Song MS
97 *faire maids*] bring out your
   Cunny Skins Maids VS
98 *'em*] them VS
99 *your*] the VS
100 *ye looking-glasses*] you Bracelets,
   Laces VS
103 *blacke, blacke, blacke*] black VS
104 Mary] Marie MS
104 *then*] *omit* VS
104 Jane] Jone VS
105 *skins*] skin MS
108 *warme*] worn VS
111 *ware*] wares VS
112–113 *Cony-...pins.*] ha'ye any
   Cunny Skins, ha'ye any Cunny
   Skins, ha'ye any Cunny Skins
   here to sell. VS

113 *and fine*] *Rings, and I have* MS
117 fill . . . fill] fill, fill, fill FK
120 bully] *omit* F 1–2, L+
125 (twice), 126 ye] you MS
128 e'ne] even MS
131 ye] *omit* MS
131 A pox] A——F 1–2, L–S; A plague MS, Dp
132 Pox o']——o' F 1–2, L–S
132 their] they're F 2, L–S
133 then:] ~ ∧ F 2, L–S
133 boy] *omit* F 1–2, L+
134 your] yee MS
134 strip] stick MS
135 O] *omit* F 1–2, L+
135 a cloake] two cloakes F 1–2, L–V

137 *Enter* Hemskirke.] MS *places after* Here Sir *in line* 133
137 d'en] d'on F 1–2, L; Ev'n S
141 ye] 'ee MS
142, 143 (twice), 147, 152, 153 ye] you F 1–2, L+
144 nearer] neer MS
146 command] commands F 2
147 here] *omit* F 1–2, L–V
148 That:] ~ ∧ F 2, L–S
148 me] the V
151 a] *omit* FK
152 Okes] oak V
155 Jugler] Jugler, Lads S
156 resist] resists Dp
157–158 To . . . me.] *one line in* MS
166 I've] I have F 1–2, L+

III.ii

3 fall, fall] fall MS
6 cakes] capes Dp
10 on] ore MS
13 Sun-set] suns sett MS
15 How] *omit* F 1–2, L–V
15 of] *omit* F 1–FK
15 strength] strengths MS
16 lost] toss'd F 1–FK
20 cross'd] crosse MS
24 twas] was F 1–2, L–V
30 ye] you MS
32, 33 'em] them MS
34 that] th' S
37 rifle] riffle F 1; riffle Dp
37 tew 'em] tew 'm Dp
40 'emselves] themselves F 1–2, L+
41 in't] in it MS
45 thine] thy FK
46 my] mine MS
48 heaven knows] [*like deleted*] heavns knowe MS
51 I've] I have F 1–2, L+
53 see ye] see you FK
53 keepe ye] keep 'ee MS

57 ye] you MS
59 ¹ye] 'ee MS
59 y'are] your MS
69 ²ye,] you MS; ye, Sir, I must not leave ye, F 2, L–V
70 (twice), 71 ye] you MS
70 must] will F 2, L–V
73 something's] something MS
75 a] an MS
80 prison] spron F 1–FK
85 That's] There's F 2, L–V
89 that] the F 1–2, L+
92 stick] kick FK
96 have] that have FK
98 you have] have ye FK
98 me] on me F 2, L–V
106 hast] has F 1–2, L
110 Sir] *omit* MS
111 me] *omit* MS
113 please] list F 2, L–V
113 the Seas] Seas MS
116–117 If . . . hereafter.] *one line in* MS
119 ye] you MS

III.iii

6 That] the Dp

III.iv

0.2 with] *of the* F1–2, L–C
1 'um] 'em F1–2, L+
3 your] our S
5 I] *Prig*: I MS
6 *Prig.*] *omit* MS
6 knaves] Rascalls MS
7 then] *omit* S
7 as] *omit* S–W
25 cause] Case MS
31 with's] with his FK
33 lyes] is MS
36 Ye know] You shall know F1–2, L–S, W
38 fellowes] fellow S–D
38 ah] oh F1–2, L+
38.1 *Enter* Gerrard.] *omit* MS
39 *Higgen.*] *omit* MS
46 Earle] Earles MS
51, 52, 65 ye] you MS
65 Oh] *omit* MS
69 eyes] eye Dp
85 Reynard] Reimald F1
86 lofty] lusty MS
90–91 -stripping;...anger₍ₐ₎] ~ ₍ₐ₎
~ ; F1–2, MS±, L–S, Dp
93 tew] turne F1–2, L+
96 thou] thee L–S
97 I feare,] *omit* V
97.1 *a letter*] *with the Paper* MS
101 Gentlemen] Gentleman Dp
104 an other] another Dp
108 had had] have had F1
109 makes] make MS
117 unto] to S
121 yee] you FK
123 and a] and FK
123 gentle] gentile MS
126 Or if I] And if you F2, L–S
127 learne] practise F2, L–V

128 ye] you MS
129 Yes] omit F2, L
130–142 *Higgen. I crowne...hang.*] F1–2, L–V *place lines* 143–56 *after line* 129, *and transfer lines* 130–42, *preceded by repeated* 'Gerrard. Now sweare him.' *after line* 143
130–135, 137–142 MS *inscribes in Italian hand*
130 gage] gag F1–2, L–S
133 Ruffmans] Fuffmans MS
133 commission] and Commission L–S
134 dell's] dell MS
134 stromell] stiromell F1–2, L–S
135 Herman Becks trine] Herman Beck strine F1–2, L; Herman-Becktrine S; harman, beck trim MS
135 trine to] trim to MS
141 And] To MS
145 Thank ye friends,] omit F2, L–S
146 And I beseech ye] omit F2, L–S; I do beseech C
146 if] Sir, if F2, L–S
147 I] if I F1–2, L, Dp
149 and] omit F1–2, L+
150 knaveryes] knavery FK
151 villany] villaine MS
153 be ev'n hang'd] even hang MS
154 Come] Roome F1–FK
154 my] the L–S
158 me] hee MS
161 be] omit Dp
161 stranger.] Stranger, Brother, I pray lead, | You must, you must, Brother. F2, L+

III.v

4 makes] that makes MS
5 Here...you.] *omit* F1–2, L–V
5 heres] here Dp
6 ²ye] you MS
9 Our] A F1–2, L+
10 ye] you FK
14 that] the F1–2, L–V
22 meat; alas‸] ~ , ~ ! MS
27, 28 ye] you MS
29 this] your F1–2, L+

33 my] by my MS
34 ayle] ails F2, L–W
36 flow'n] flow'd F1–2, L+
37 not I] I not F1–2, L+
38 your] you Dp
46 me] *omit* W
47 Dispose] Despise F1–2, L+
47 gods guide] god guides MS
48 last] selfe F1–2, L+
49 pitty] pitty mee MS

IV.i

5 Endure...of] Upon the beating of, by MS
5 both of] of both V
5 and] or F1–FK
8 lyving] lying F1–FK
9 of all our friends,] *omit* MS
11 No] *preceded in* MS *by deleted* tis
21 endeavour] endeavours Dp
24 loaden] laden MS
27 thanke] thankt MS, S–V
29–32 *Floriȝ.* Is...reproaches?] *omit* MS

36 soone's my light] soone my light's F1–2, L+
41.1 *Porters*] *Porter* F1; *Boores* MS
47 'em] them MS
60, 62 ye] you MS
68 confirme] confesse F1–FK
70 drawes] growes MS
72 ever] for ever F2, L–S
73 ye...ye] you...you F2

IV.ii

4 *Minche*] Menche MS
5 me] *omit* F1–2, L+
19 are] be MS
19 pretty] indeed fine MS
20, 21 Capper] Cupper MS
24 shew] shews S–V
25 ye] you MS, F2
25 serve] serve you S, C
27 Where] And where F1–2, L+

27 ye...ye] you...you F2
28 thy] *omit* F1–FK; my F2
28 bosome,] bosom, Sweet F2, L–W
29 thy] your F1–2, L–V
29 deed] *preceded in* MS *by deleted start of* y
35 I] *preceded in* MS *by deleted* h
37 else;] ~ ‸ Dp

IV.iii

1 if 'twill] if it would F1–FK; if 'twould F2, L–V; if't twill MS
4–5 What...Servant.] *one line in* MS

6 courtisies] courtesie MS
7 'em] them MS
8 fraught] freight C–W
13 These] This MS

358

14 back] *omit* MS
15 *Saylor*] saylors MS
19 tide] *omit* MS
20 this] *omit* MS
21 scap't] she scaped S–W; escap'd
    D
33.1 *Saylor.*] *omit* MS
35 yeare] ye are F1; here F2, L
36 cares] care L+
38 we...all our] they...are at
    your F1–2, L+
39 need,] need of you F1–2, L+
41 Come, come Sir] Come Sir,
    come F1–2, L+
44 When] Why when F1–2, L+
44 blest] *omit* F1–2, L+
46 and] *omit* F1–2, L–V
46 shall] will F1–2, L+

47 the Roomes] my Roomes F1–2,
    L+
47 reeke] smoake F1–2, L+
47 thee] the F1–2, L+
55 lusty,] lusty I'le F1–2, L+
56 even] *omit* F1–2, L+
57 your rewards] you my F1–2,
    L+
58 have had] had but F1–2, L+
59 My] To my F1–2, L; Commend
    my best Love S; To my best
    friend, my best love C; To
    Clause my best love D, V
59 indeed] *omit* F1–2, L–V
60 honest, honest] honest F1–2,
    L+
60 him.] him better. F1–2, L+
61 handfulls] handfull F1–2, L+

IV.iv

1 'tis] it is MS
2 mine...recompence] in mine
    ... reward F1–2, L+
5 thou dost] to do it F1–2, L+
10 shall] man that will F1–2, L+
11 do] do't S–D
13 know a benefit] be a benefactor
    F1–2, L+
13 If it be not] Not Dp
14 if...dayes] Within these ten
    days if S
15–16 Prethee, prethee] Prithee S,
    C
19 men in thy] that men in F1–2,
    L+

20 it] me F1–2, L+
21 come] that comes F1–2, L+
    (–S); that now | Comes S
22 full] it's full F1–2, L+
38 letting] setting F2, L–V
42 'em] them MS
48 ye] you F2
49 honest, honest] honest MS
50 *Hubert....matter,*] *omit* Dp
62 And...forces] *omit* MS
63 be] by MS
64 these] those C–W
69 showr] show MS
72 close] closer F1–2, L–V

IV.v

3 has] sends S
4 to be] *omit* MS
6 bell] Dell S, D, V
7 what] a what F2; ah what L–W
9 mince-] minc'd MS

9 -pottage] -porridge MS
10 boys] *omit* MS
12, 41, 44 pox] plague MS;——
    F1–2, L–S
15 will he] he will F1–2, L+

16 this] the F 1–2, L+
20 ²must] may S–W
26 structure] *preceded in* MS *by deleted* bowle
29 Hubert.] *Hubert, a letter* MS
30 start; nay] start me, F 1–2, L, C–V; start Man S
35 stands] stand F 2, L–V
40 and] *omit* MS
42 Beare-ward] beareheard MS
44 whorson] burson F 2; bursen L–S
45 blister'd] baster'd F 1–FK; bastard W

46 o] *omit* MS
47 change] shift F 2, L–S
48 stinks] sinckes MS
49 soule] hide F 2, L–V
52 this] theres MS; *omit* F 2, L; you S
53 this] theis MS
56–57 Shall. . .defiance,] *one line in* MS
56 be] are MS, F 2, L–V
56 monstrous] horrible F 2, L–W
57 Capons] Capon F 1

IV.vi

4 luster] lustie MS
9 *2. Merchant.] omit* F 1–2, L–V
9–12 *1. Merchant. No . . . Vanlock.] omit* MS
9 *1. Merchant.] omit* F 1–2, L–V
17 *2. Merchant.] 3. Merchant.* F 1–2, MS
17, 39 ye] you MS
19 these] their F 1–2, L–W
19 a] have F 1–2, L+
20 Masters] Master Dp
35 Upon] Upon the FK–F 2, L; On the S
40 I] *omit* L–S
40 or] and F 1–2, L–V
44 presently must] must presently F 1–2, L+
63 *within] omit* MS
70.1 *and . . . Merchants] &c* MS

72 Did'st. . .fayrer?] *omit* MS
73 Pray ye] Prithee MS; Pray thee L–S
76 beauties] beautie FK
78 pleasure] Pleasures MS
85 Priest] Priest is FK
92 'twil] 'till FK
92 me: . . . *Clause]* ~ ∧ . . . ~ , MS
92 by] *omit* Dp
97 me] *omit* F 1–2, MS; L–V
97.1 *Enter . . . Cloake.] omit* MS
104 *Exeunt] Exit.* F 1–2; *Exᵗ Gerr:* MS
107 *Exit.] omit* Dp
110 sorrow,] sorrow; oh me F 1–FK, Dp
111 Till] Oh me, till W–Dp
111 Ah me!] *omit* F 1–FK, MS

V.i

3 'twere] it were MS
12 And] To MS
15 affeard] afraid F 1–2, L+
18 pull] pull me F 2, L–S
25 grunts] grins MS

26 And] A MS
29 haunch] ham F 1, Dp; arm FK
36 strange] *omit* F 1–FK, W, Dp
39 to] to be MS
41 gives] give MS

47 'Twill] It will FK
49 goe] omit F 1–2, L+
51 God] Good MS
51.1 Attendants] Guard and Attendants MS, Dp
52 he] omit MS
52 me] us MS
53–54 Best...ha?] one line in MS
56 sirha?] sir: ha? MS
63 not you] you not F 1–2, L+
65 that] omit Dp
67 Sir] omit MS
69 whips] whipt FK, D, V
69 Master] omit Dp
71 swoope] sweep MS
72 'Tis...she] 'Tis shee, 'tis shee FK
73 notable] noble F 1–2, L–V
79 shape] shop F 1–FK
80 In the] I'the F 1–2; I'th the FK
82 againe] omit MS
84–85 F 1–FK print lines 84–5, 98 and then follow with 84–98
84 O] omit F 2, L–S
85 my] mine MS
86–97 No...grave:] omit MS, F 2, L–C
92 others] other F 1
101–102 Or...Bullyes?] one line in MS

102 poultrer] Powlter MS
103 convoy] Convey MS
104 grunting] granting F 1–2, L
105 mergery-] margerie MS
109 or] nor F 2, L–S
109 my] all my S
111 buck] back F 1–2, L, Dp
113 for any] with the F 2, L–S
119 ye] he F 2, L–D
120 Hath] That MS
120 If't] If it MS
121 it is] 'tis F 1–2, MS; L–C, Dp
122 I will] I'le F 1–2; L+; I MS
122–123 woodman, | I know] MS lines: woodman, I | know
125 Benthuisen] Benchursen MS
128–129 I...'em.] one line in MS
129–130 We...thee.] one line in MS
130 ever] ere MS
130 then] omit MS
132–133 That's...'em?] one line in MS
132 Hubert.] omit F 2, L–S
132 That's well] omit MS
133 'em] them. | Tis well MS
135 thorough] through MS
135 wood] woodes MS
140 me] ye FK
148 division] divisions MS

V.ii

0.1 and] omit MS
1 reasons] reason MS
5 you] omit MS
11 help'd] too held S
17 my] a MS
24 blest] best MS
28 specious] speciall FK
40 effects] offers MS
40 stupid] preceded in MS by deleted backe
45 your] our MS, L–S

50 never] nere MS
63 only] one MS
65 my] your FK, F 2, L–V
65 Hemskirke, Woolfort] Wolfort, Hemsk: MS
65 'em] them MS
72 Earl] an Earl F 1–2, L+
73 Floriz,] omit MS
75 Turn'd] Turne MS
84 Gerrard.] Florez. V (qy)
84 fiend] frend MS

89 It...from] *omit* MS
91 knew] MS *doubtfully* know
97 For] In F2, L–V
109 *Gerrard*.] *Costin* MS; *Florez*
   V (*qy*)
109 *Enter*...] MS *places after* thinke
109 with] *omit* MS
109 these] those MS
118 'em] 'em up S
122 betraid] betray S
123 mocke] mockst MS, D
125 helpt] helpe MS
130.1 *a drum*] *Drum* MS
133 I...*Hemskirck*,] *omit* MS
135 Was...now] *omit* Dp
143 breed] end F1–FK; bread F2
144 *vici*] *visi* MS
150 And] *omit* MS
151 have] *omit* FK
151 with your people] *omit* MS
153 loose] lost MS
157 want] lacke MS
161 proscription] prescription MS
162 so] to MS
166 laughing] tangling MS
168 live] evil V
170–171 MS *lines*: *Wolferts*...lan-
   guage | ô...longing
170 *Woolfort* thou art] Wolferts MS
176–177 No....life,] *one line in* MS
178 contemnes] can contemne MS
181 their] of L–W
181 here] there MS
182 wish] with F1–2, L
183 take her] *omit* F1–2, L+
184 first] *omit* F1–2, L+
188 ha'] have MS
190 you] ye MS

191 would] could F1–2, L+ (–S);
   we'd S
192 Not I if] Not if L; No not if S
193 first] *omit* F1–2, L+
193 to] unto S; into C
194 worthy] *omit* MS
195 friends] more friends S
202 you] me F1–FK, L+
212 i'the] in the MS
217 *Flanders*] banish *Flanders* MS
221 O'] Of FK, MS
222 my lads] *omit* MS
224 peny-worthes] pen-worthes MS
224 will] *omit* L–S
226 Yes] *omit* FK
226 sixpenyworth] six pence worth
   MS
228 For] *omit* MS
232 these] theires MS
233 an] old MS
236 throw] through FK
238 ne'er] *omit* MS
239 you] yee MS
240 nor] or MS
240 Gentlemen] wa MS
241 gold,] good ⌄ F1–2, L+
241 and] nor F1–2, L+
243 get] *omit* F1–2, L+
244 Lawyers] Lawyer MS
246 Drinkers] Drunkards F1–2, L+
246–247 The eaters...pallats.] *one
   line in* MS
248 And] *omit* F1–2, L+
248 of] *omit* MS
249 Widdowes] Midwives F1–2,
   L–V
252 we] I MS

THE TRAGEDY OF
THIERRY AND THEODORET

edited by

ROBERT K. TURNER, JNR

TEXTUAL INTRODUCTION

According to Dr Hoy's study of authorship, *The Tragedy of Thierry and Theodoret* (Greg, *Bibliography*, no. 368) was a three-fold collaboration: Beaumont wrote III and V.i; Fletcher I.i, II.ii–iii, IV.i, and V.ii; and Massinger I.ii, II.i and iv, and IV.ii. The contrasting linguistic preferences of the writers are distinct in their shares, the most notable peculiarity of the evidence being the appearance in Fletcher's of the pronominal contraction ''um' instead of the more usual ''em', according to the following distribution:

	''um'	''em'	'them'
Fletcher	18	3	1
Beaumont	0	6	6
Massinger	0	2	18

Because it is also found in *Rule a Wife* and in the *Bonduca* manuscript as well as in Fletcher's parts of *Cupid's Revenge*, *The Scornful Lady*, and *The Woman Hater*, there is reason to suppose the form distinctive of Fletcher, yet it occurs in *A King and No King* and in *Philaster* in Beaumont's as well as in Fletcher's shares. Whether this anomaly arises from the various responses to copy of various compositors or whether the explanation lies elsewhere is not clear, but in *Thierry* ''um's' appear validly to set Fletcher's work apart from that of his collaborators.[1]

There is virtually no evidence bearing directly on the play's date of composition. The claims of Fleay (*ca.* 1617) and Thorndike (1607) are reviewed and dismissed by Chambers, who declines to assign any date at all.[2] Harbage sets the limits as 1607 and 1621, which is as much as to say that the play may have been composed at any time between the beginning of Beaumont's and Fletcher's careers (assuming Massinger to have been a reviser) and the date of

[1] Cyrus Hoy, 'The Shares of Fletcher and His Collaborators in the Beaumont and Fletcher Canon (III)', *Studies in Bibliography*, 11 (1958), 97–8, 105.

[2] E. K. Chambers, *The Elizabethan Stage* (1923), III, 230.

publication of Q 1.[1] However, as Hoy's attribution of several scenes to Massinger implies that he had a hand in the play from its inception, the limits may be narrowed tentatively, for Massinger did not make a definite appearance as a dramatist until about 1613.[2]

Without having been entered in the Stationers' Register and without indication of its authorship, *Thierry* was published in 1621 by Thomas Walkley, who had brought out *A King and No King* in 1619 and *Philaster* in 1620. The printer is not named in the imprint, but the title-page bears the device of Nicholas Okes, in whose shop *The Knight of the Burning Pestle* Q1 (1613), *The Maid's Tragedy* Q1 (1619) and *Philaster* Q1 and Q2 (1620 and 1622) were also manufactured. *Thierry* Q1, which collates A^2 B–K^4, appears to have been set by two compositors: *A* (who preferred 'honour', 'doe', 'lye', 'onely', either terminal '-ie' or '-y', either '-e' or '-ee' in such words as 'hee', 'shee', and 'bee', and for the character Bawdber speech-prefixes in the form *Bawd.* or *Baw.*) composed sigs. B 1 through B 4; *B* (who preferred 'honor', 'do', 'lie', 'only', terminal '-y', single '-e' and *Bawdb.*) composed the rest.

Two skeleton-formes were employed to print the volume, Skeleton I imposing B(i), C(o), D(i, o) and II imposing B(o), C(i), E(i, o) and all subsequent formes. The composition of Sheet B (I.i.1–I.ii.65) cannot be reconstructed with any certainty, but it is clear that after he set B1–B4 (to I.ii.29) Compositor *A* left B4^v to his partner and that, since types from both formes of B reappear in both formes of C, printing was suspended for a time between the last forme of B to be machined and the first forme of C. After that, Compositor *B* carried on alone, apparently setting by formes, outer first, through H(i).[3] In Sheet I, however, the inner forme seems to

[1] Alfred Harbage, *Annals of English Drama 975–1700*, rev. S. Schoenbaum (Philadelphia, 1964), p. 106.

[2] T. A. Dunn, *Philip Massinger* (London, 1957), pp. 15–17. Massinger's earliest datable contribution to the Beaumont and Fletcher canon seems to have been his share of *The Honest Man's Fortune* of 1613 (see Hoy, 'Fletcher (IV)', *Studies in Bibliography*, 12 (1959), 100–8).

[3] The inference is based upon type recurrence data: with only one unimportant exception, types from the outer forme of each sheet are found throughout the sheet following, whereas types from the inner forme reappear only in the inner forme of the sheet following. This order of composition accords with what can be demonstrated about the order of printing: (1) The running-title *The Tragedy of* appears undamaged

have been the first composed. Toward the end of the book the workman began wherever possible to set short one-line speeches in the same line of type as the concluding line of preceding speeches and to increase the number of lines per page, in Sheet K to thirty-nine or forty rather than the thirty-seven usual earlier. His object evidently was to get the conclusion of the text into K4^v so that an additional sheet would not be required. In Sheet I he may have set the inner forme before the outer to guard against an error in casting off, for I3^v and I4 are solid prose whereas I1, I2^v, and I3 are mostly verse and I3 contains an act-head around which a certain amount of space could be saved or wasted as necessity required. Even so, the text allotted to I3 got in only because the last speech on the page was set in the white space in the type line left by the conclusion of the speech immediately before.[1] If for this reason the workman did reverse his usual procedure in composing Sheet I, it is surprising that he did not also set K(i) before K(o), particularly as K4^v ends with a rather large *FINIS* that could have been omitted or set smaller if space were needed, but typographical evidence suggests that in the last sheet the outer forme preceded.[2]

From Sheet E on the printing was carried out in only one skeleton-forme and also from Sheet E on there is no further evidence of the shortage of W types which is apparent earlier. Both these details suggest that other material was being worked simultaneously with *Thierry*, its types being returned from time to time to the cases from which *Thierry* was being composed. Yet there is no indication that

on B1^v, C4^v, and D4^v, but at D3^v and subsequently the top of the *f* is broken off. Thus D(o) was machined before D(i). (2) The running-title *Thierry and Theoderet* appears with the mis-spelling on C4, on E3, and, in some copies, on E4, but in other copies its E4 manifestation has been corrected to *Theodoret*. E(o) therefore preceded E(i).

[1] This phenomenon occurs earlier on B2, C1^v, C3^v, D2^v, D4, E4, and F3 – that is, usually, but not exclusively, in the second forme. In these instances it looks as though the workmen may have been following copy if they were not merely seizing occasional opportunities to save space, but in Sheet K the practice is much more frequent.

[2] Eight types from I(i) have been found in K, one on K2^v, six on K3, and one on K2. Unfortunately, only two types from I(o) have been discovered, both on K2. The pattern is thin, but what evidence there is implies the prior composition of K(o). An assumption of *seriatim* setting would be discouraged by the too-early distribution of I(o).

either compositor was unduly hampered by any of the circumstances attending the printing. Press-variants in surviving copies (including those resulting from a reader's scrutiny of the proofsheet of sig. C1 preserved in the Boston Public copy) are quite routine and certainly do not betoken any special incompetence on the part of the workmen.[1]

Nor is there any indication in the text of Q1 that the copy from which it was set was illegible enough to cause more than occasional difficulties, although there are a few tangles (e.g., in the Second Soldier's speech at V.i.92 and errors apparently of misreading sporadically throughout) which show that the compositors sometimes had trouble in making out the handwriting. The text generally, however, seems too clean to have derived directly from foul papers. Prompt-copy as well is argued against by the absence of 'professional' stage-directions and the appearance in their stead of directions calling for an indefinite number of characters (e.g., at II.i.33; III.ii.91.1 [III.ii.42.1 in Q1]; IV.ii.36.1; V.ii.27, and V.ii.67) and of directions employing the formula &c., which indicates that although the scene begins with the characters specified, others enter later (I.ii.0.1; II.i.0.1, and II.iv.0.2 – all Massinger's scenes). There is also some small variation in the designation of characters. The honest soldier is both 'Vitry' and 'Devitry' and the astrologer who is impersonated by Lecure both 'Forte' and 'Leforte'. Casual treatment of such foreign names, however, is not unusual; it may be more to the point that whereas the stage-direction at II.iii.0.1 designates 'Huntsmen', these characters are subsequently in another stage-direction and in the text called 'Keepers'.

These features of Q1 and its unblurred preservation of the three sets of linguistic characteristics suggest that the underlying manuscript consisted of the authors' papers, possibly fair copies by each. Particularly striking is the frequent use of parentheses in Massinger's

[1] A more detailed examination of the printing of Q1 may be found in 'Notes on the Text of *Thierry and Theodoret* Q1', *Studies in Bibliography*, 14 (1961), 218–25. This investigation, however, has been extended by Mr James Hammersmith, who found the evidence which allows the attribution of B4^v to Compositor *B* and that which indicates that I(i) was set before I(o). Mr Hammersmith also noticed several details which convinced me that the Q1 copy probably was a transcript rather than authorial fair copy as I previously thought most likely.

scenes to punctuate nominatives of address, non-restrictive modifiers, and asides. No parentheses whatever appear in the rest of the play, and, since they abound in the early editions of Massinger's unaided works and are employed profusely in the autograph manuscript of *Believe as you List*, they are considered a distinctive characteristic of his.[1] Thus for the Massinger scenes, and it might follow for the rest as well, it would seem that the print stands at no great distance from holograph.

Yet there are difficulties in the way of assuming the manuscripts of the authors themselves to have been sent to the printer. To begin with, although the overall incidence of misreading error is low, it is reasonably uniform. Moreover, there is consistency in the form of certain speech-prefixes: Theodoret is *Theod.* and Brunhalt is *Brun.* in the work of both compositors and all three authors; *Ordella* and *Lecure* are never abbreviated, although they appear in various authorial shares. Similarly, when Martell enters at II.iii.11.1 and Protaldye at II.iv.53 Q1 omits the prefix for their immediately following speeches (although elsewhere in the same situation prefixes are provided); the former scene is Fletcher's and the latter Massinger's. These features indicate that the manuscript was in a single hand. Because authorial characteristics do not overlap, it seems unlikely that one of the writers copied out the work of the other two, and if that was not the case we are left with a scribal transcript that preserved certain features of its underlying copy with considerable fidelity.

If a scribe had a hand in the transmission of the text, several of its anomalies are a bit easier to explain, although responsibility for most is finally uncertain. A very mysterious error is found at IV.i.159 (Q1: H1ᵛ), Fletcher's scene, where in the midst of dialogue between Ordella and Martell a speech clearly belonging to the latter is assigned to *Deui*. Since the single incorrect prefix is found some

---

[1] Massinger himself probably inserted parentheses in the printed copies of *The Bondman, The Renegado, The Emperor of the East, The Roman Actor*, and parts of *The Picture*. See W. W. Greg, 'More Massinger Corrections', *The Library*, 4th ser., 5 (1925), 64–71, and also J. E. Gray, 'Still More Massinger Corrections', *The Library*, 5th ser., 5 (1950), 132–9 and A. K. McIlwraith, 'The Manuscript Corrections in Massinger's Plays', *The Library*, 5th ser., 6 (1951), 213–16, where the authenticity of some of the corrections is discussed.

ten quarto pages after Devitry's last speech and some ten before his next, it seems nearly impossible that the mistake was the compositor's. Since he does not employ Devitry until V.ii, it is equally improbable that Fletcher wrote the prefix, at least as a part of the original composition. It perhaps could have made its way into the text through an authorial lapse during revision or final touching up, but it may be as likely that a scribe went rather strangely awry during his copying. At III.ii.42.1 (F3ᵛ), Beaumont's scene, Protaldye and a lady correctly enter to Bawdber and Devitry, but the Q1 stage-direction also brings on revellers who are not required for some time. The text is explicit on this point: at III.ii.90 (F4) Thierry, who has since entered, orders, 'Command the Revellers in.' It is difficult to see how the compositor could have been guilty of placing a direction forty lines early, and one doubts that Beaumont, whose mind must have been on working out the comic discomfiture of Protaldye, would have introduced the revellers in the wrong place. Again, an authorial error during revision is possible, but so is a scribal rationalization of a marginal direction whose exact location was unclear. Finally, it may be significant that the Massinger formula *Exeunt omnes, præter*...(as at II.i.253.1)[1] is transformed at II.iv.131.1 (E3ᵛ), Massinger's scene, into the more ordinary *Exeunt all, but*..., which is the phraseology of the stage-direction at III.i.131.1 (F2), Beaumont's scene.

Collateral support for scribal copy may be found in the strong probability that Q1's publisher, Walkley, had *A King and No King* Q1 (1619) printed from a private transcript or at least a transcript obtained from a private source; he may also have acquired similar copy for *Othello* Q1 (1622).[2] The quarto of *Thierry* unfortunately lacks a preface in which Walkley might have tipped his hand as he did in *A King and No King*, but the text does contain what could be traces of other manuscript than the scribe's. Three stage-directions ('Reades' [II.i.231.1 (D1ᵛ)], 'aside' [II.iv.22 (E1ᵛ)], and

---

[1] It is found in *The Bondman* (1624) K4, *The City Madam* (1659) C2, *The Roman Actor* (1629) B1ᵛ, and *The Picture* (1630) E1ᵛ, as well as in collaborations like *The Fatal Dowry*.

[2] For *A King and No King* see George Walton Williams in vol. II of this series, pp. 169–70. For *Othello* see W. W. Greg, *The Shakespeare First Folio* (Oxford, 1955), pp. 357–71.

'aside' [II.iv.28 (E 1ᵛ)]) are printed in roman rather than italic type, implying that they were written in secretary rather than Italian script. Since that style, as far as one can tell, was neither authorial nor scribal, the directions could be later additions. There is some possibility, therefore, that the scribal copy was given at least cursory attention by a theatrical person as a preliminary to the preparation of a prompt-book, but it must be admitted that none of the presumably added directions is beyond the capacity of an attentive non-theatrical reader.

Although the Q 1 text is fairly clean substantively, it is rather badly punctuated. For the play's more serious and emotional scenes, the authors seem to have conspired to force their styles to a height through obliquity of expression, ellipsis, and a syntax sometimes based on association rather than logic. The result was occasional obscurity, and the defects in punctuation suggest that neither the scribe nor the compositor always penetrated the authors' meaning. Whether the faults were primarily the scribe's or the compositors' it is impossible to tell, but the fact that the scribe retained so many mechanical features of the authors' manuscript leads one to think him a rather literal-minded fellow (perhaps because he was directed to be so) and suggests that Compositor B primarily was left to handle punctuation as best he could.

The lineation of the verse of Q 1 sometimes requires repair, evidently because the scribe did not always grasp the authors' intention or because the manuscripts from which he copied did not always make their intentions clear. The incidence of mislining varies. In Fletcher's scenes either there is no mislining at all (I.i and IV.i) or it is sparse, caused chiefly by the misconstruction of pentameters in series shared by two or more speakers (as at II.ii.10–12; II.iii.51–5, and V.ii.178–82). Massinger's scenes too are generally correct. Again there are sometimes problems with linked speeches (as at II.i.154–6 and IV.ii.258–61), and either the scribe did not understand or Massinger did not indicate that an apparently extra-metrical word beginning a speech may actually be the concluding syllable of the speech preceding (as at I.ii.14–15; II.i.193–4; II.iv.102–3, and IV. ii.173–4). Beaumont's scenes are another story; V.i is entirely prose and so lined, but in the prose parts of III.ii

(through line 88) and III.iii (through line 14) false verse lines
intrude. Like his partners, Beaumont often shares pentameters
between speakers (as at III.i.125–8, where a false linkage threw the
scribe off for several lines; III.ii.176–7, and III.iii.32–5), and he is
more apt to write short lines, of which the scribe tried unsuccess-
fully to make full pentameters (as at III.i.49–50, 88–9, 132; III.ii.
128–30, etc.). In his scenes the lining several times goes unaccount-
ably wrong (III.i.120–1; III.ii.170–1; III.iii.57–8), and one passage
seems to have been left in metrical disrepair (III.i.96–9). The impression given is that Beaumont was the most freewheeling of the
dramatists and perhaps the most careless.

Seventeenth-century editions subsequent to Q1 have little
textual significance. On 22 February 1647/8 the copy was transferred to Humphrey Moseley,[1] who brought out Q2 in a double-
columned layout like that of *The Woman Hater* Q2 (cf. vol. 1,
pp. 147–8). The presumed first issue collates A–E⁴; its title-page,
A1, ascribes the play to Fletcher alone and gives the date of publication as 1648. The text begins on A2 (A1ᵛ is blank). The second
issue, collating A⁴ ($-A1 + \pi^2$) B–E⁴, replaces A1 with a two-leaf
cancel. A new title-page ($\pi1$, $\pi1^v$ blank), reset with the same type
used to print A1, ascribes the play to Beaumont and Fletcher and
changes the date of publication to 1649. Subsequent pages of the
cancel add the following material:

[$\pi2$]　　The Prologue to *Thierry* and *Theodoret*.
　　　Wit is become an Antick; and puts on
　　　As many shapes of variation,
　　　To court the times applause, as the times dare
　　　Change severall fashions; nothing is thought rare
　　　Which is not new and follow'd; yet we know
　　　That what was worne some twenty yeares agoe
　　　Comes into grace againe, and we pursue
　　　That custome, by presenting to your view
　　　A Play in fashion then, not doubting now
　　　But 'twill appeare the same, if you allow
　　　Worth to their noble memories, whose names
　　　Beyond all power of death live in their fames.

[1] *A Transcript of the Registers of the Worshipful Company of Stationers 1640–
1708 A.D.* (London: Privately Printed, 1875–94), I, 290.

[π2ᵛ]   The Epilogue.

Our Poet knowes you will be just; but we
Appeale to mercy: he desires that ye
Would not distast his Muse, because of late
Transplanted; which would grow here if no fate
Have an unluckie bode: opinion
Comes hither but on crutches yet, the sun
Hath lent no beame to warme us; if this play
Proceed more fortunate, wee'll crowne the day
And Love that brought you hither: 'tis in you
To make A Little Sprig of Lawrell grow,
And spread into a Grove, where you may sit
And here soft Stories, when by blasting it
You gain no honour, though our ruines Lye
To tell the spoyles of your offended eye:
If not for what we are, (for alas, here
No Roscius *moves to charme your eyes or ear)*
Yet as you hope hereafter to see Playes,
Incourage us, and give our Poet Bayes.

The dramatis personæ which follows on π2ᵛ has served as copy-text
for the dramatis personæ of this edition. Q 2's prologue and epilogue,
however, are so much dramatic flotsam: as Fleay pointed out, the
former had appeared in the Folio of 1647 before *The Noble Gentle-*
man and the latter had been appended to the 1632 edition of James
Shirley's *Changes.*[1] The text of Q 2 derives from that of Q 1 without
additional authority. The Folio of 1679, in which *Thierry* appeared
for the last time in the seventeenth century, reprints Q 2, but omits
the portion of its text running from 'drench', V.ii.10, to '*Enter*
Messenger.', V.ii.127.1. Since 'drench', the last word of F2 3N 2,
is followed by the correct catchword 'As' and since '*Enter Mes-*
senger.' heads 3N 2ᵛ, the error appears to have arisen from a fault in
the printing rather than a defect in the copy.

Except for the dramatis personæ, Q 1 provided the copy-text for
this edition. Q 1's punctuation, since it stands at two removes from
the authors', has been emended when the original obscured or
falsified syntax. It seemed particularly necessary to mark elaborate
parentheses although the authors, Massinger excepted, did not do
so. Variations in the rendition of proper names have been allowed

---

[1] F. G. Fleay, *A Biographical Chronicle of the English Drama 1559–1642* (London,
1891; rpt. New York, n.d.), I, 205. See also Greg, *Bibliography*, II, 519–20.

to stand. Thus Theodoret's principality is *Austrachia* at II.i.111 and IV.ii.264, Massinger's scenes, but *Austracia* at III.ii.170, Beaumont's scene. Devitry is variously *Devitry* and *Vitry* and Theodoret *Theodoret* and *Theoderet*, although speech-prefix abbreviations are uniformly expanded to *Theodoret*. The name of the queen's paramour, however, spelled *Protaldie* and *Protaldy(e)*, has been standardized as *Protaldye*, the variation between *-y* and *-i* seeming without significance. Sixteen copies of Q1 and a fragmentary single leaf have been collated (see under 'Press-Variants in Q1', p. 460), and readings from the following editions have been recorded in the Historical Collation: Quarto 1621 (Q1), Quarto 1648–9 (Q2), Folio 1679 (F2), Langbaine 1711 (L), Seward 1750 (S), Colman 1778 (C), Weber 1812 (W), Dyce 1843 (D), and Strachey, *Mermaid Series* 1904 (M). Also noted are the substantive readings preferred by Mason 1798, Mitford 1856, and Deighton 1896.

Thierry, King of France.
Theodoret, his Brother Prince of Austrachia.
Martell, their noble Kinsman.
Devitry, an honest Souldier of fortune.
Protaldye,⎫
Bawdber, ⎬ Cowardly Pandars.
Lecure, ⎭
A Priest.
A Post.
Huntsmen.   10
Souldiers.
Doctors.
[Revellers, Gentleman.]

Brunhalt, Mother to the Princes.
Ordella, the matchlesse wife of Thierry.
Memberge, Daughter of Theodoret.
[Ladies.]
                         The Scene *France.*

0.1 *Dramatis Personæ] from* Q2 (*second ssue*); *om.* Q1–Q2 (*first issue*)
*3 their...Kinsman] *stet* Q2

THE TRAGEDIE OF
THIERRIE AND
THEODORET

Enter Theodoret, Brunhalt, Bawdber [*with her*]. I. i

Brunhalt. Taxe me with these hot tainters?

Theodoret. You are too sudaine;
I doe but gently tell you what becomes you,
And what may bend your honor! how these courses
Of loose and lazie pleasures, not suspected
But done and knowne, your minde that grants no limit
(And all your Actions) followes, which loose people
That see but through a mist of circumstance
Dare tearme ambitious; all your wayes hide sores
Opening in the end to nothing but ulcers.
Your instruments like these may call the world, 10
And with a fearefull clamour, to examine
Why, and to what wee governe. From example
If not for vertues sake yee may be honest:
There have beene great ones, good ones, and 'tis necessary
Because you are your selfe, and by your selfe
A selfe-peece from the touch of power and Justice,
You should commaund your selfe. You may imagine
(Which cozens all the world, but chiefly women)
The name of greatnesse glorifies your actions
And strong power like a pent-house, promises 20
To shade you from opinion; take heede mother,
And let us all take heede, these most abuse us.
The sinnes we doe, people behold through opticks,
Which shewes um ten times more then common vices,

0.1 I.i] *Act.* I. *Scœ.* I. Q1 *1 tainters] Q1(u); tainturs Q1(c)
*6 (And...Actions)] ∧ ~ ... ~ ∧ Q1–2, F2
22 take] Q1(c); rake Q1(u)

And often multiplyes um: then what justice
Dare we inflict upon the weake offenders
When we are theeves our selves?

Brunhalt.   This is *Martell*,
Studied and pend unto you, whose base person
I charge you by the love you owe a mother
And as you hope for blessings from her prayers,   30
Neither to give beliefe to, nor allowance.
Next I tell you Sir, you from whom obedience
Is so farre fled, that you dare taxe a mother,
Nay further, brand her honour with your slanders,
And breake into the treasures of her credit,
Your easinesse is abused, your faith fraited
With lyes, malitious lyes, your merchant mischiefe,
He that never knew more trade then Tales, and tumbling
Suspitions into honest harts; what you or hee,
Or all the world dare lay upon my worth,   40
This for your poore opinions: I am shee,
And so will beare my selfe, whose trueth and whitenesse
Shall ever stand as far from these detections
As you from dutie; get you better servants,
People of honest actions without ends,
And whip these knaves away, they eate your favours,
And turne em unto poysons: my knowne credite,
Whom all the Courts a this side *Nile* have envied,
And happy shee could site mee, brought in question
Now in my houres of age and reverence,   50
When rather superstition should be rendered,
And by a Rush that one dayes warmth
Hath shot up to this swelling; give me justice,
Which is his life.

Theodoret.   This is an impudence,
(And he must tell you, that till now mother
Brought yee a sonnes obedience, and now breakes it)
Above the sufferance of a sonne.

39 Suspitions] Langbaine; Suspitious Q1-2, F2
*52 And...warmth] *stet* Q1-2, F2

Bawdber [*aside*].   Blesse us!
 For I doe now begin to feele my selfe
 Turning into a halter, and the ladder
 Turning from me, one pulling at my legs too.   60
Theodoret.   These trueths are no mans tales, but all mens trobles,
 They are, though your strange greatnesse would out stare u'm:
 Witnesse the daily Libels, almost Ballads,
 In every place, almost in every Province,
 Are made upon your lust, Taverne discourses,
 Crowds cram'd with whisperes; Nay, the holy Temples
 Are not without your curses: Now you would blush,
 But your blacke tainted blood dare not appeare
 For feare I should fright that too.
Brunhalt.   O yee gods!
Theodoret.   Doe not abuse their names: they see your actions,   70
 And your conceald sinnes, though you worke like Moles,
 Lyes levell to their justice.
Brunhalt.   Art thou a sonne?
Theodoret.   The more my shame is of so bad a mother,
 And more your wretchednesse you let me bee so;
 But woman, for a mothers name hath left me
 Since you have left your honour, mend these ruines,
 And build againe that broken fame, and fairely,
 Your most intemperate fiers have burnt, and quickly
 Within these ten dayes take a Monasterie,
 A most strickt house, a house where none may whisper,   80
 Where no more light is knowne but what may make yee
 Beleeve there is a day, where no hope dwels,
 Nor comfort but in teares.
Brunhalt.   O miserie!
Theodoret.   And there to cold repentance, and starv'd penance
 Tye your succeeding dayes; or curse me heaven
 If all your guilded knaves, brokers, and bedders,
 Even he you built from nothing, strong *Protaldye*,
 Be not made ambling Geldings; all your maydes,
 If that name doe not shame um, fed with spunges
 To sucke away their rancknesse; and your selfe   90

Onely to emptie Pictures and dead Arras
Offer your olde desires.
Brunhalt.   I will not curse you,
Nor lay a prophesie upon your pride,
Though heaven might grant me both: unthankefull, no;
I nourishd yee, twas I, poore I groand for you,
Twas I felt what you sufferd, I lamented
When sicknesse or sad houres held back your sweetnes;
Twas I payd for your sleepes, I watchd your wakings;
My dayly cares and feares, that rid, plaid, walkt,
Discoursd, discoverd, fed and fashiond you   100
To what you are, and am I thus rewarded?
Theodoret.   But that I know these teares I could dote on em,
And kneele to catch um as they fall, then knit um
Into an Armlet, ever to be honoured;
But woman, they are dangerous drops, deceitfull,
Full of the weepers anger, and ill nature.
Brunhalt.   In my last houres despis'd.
Theodoret.   That Text should tell,
How ugly it becomes you to erre thus;
Your flames are spent, nothing but smoake maintaines ye;
And those your favour and your bounty suffers   110
Lye not with you, they doe but lay lust on you,
And then imbrace you as they caught a palsie;
Your power they may love, and like spanish Jennetts
Commit with such a gust.
Bawdber [*aside*].   I would take whipping,
And pay a Fine now.   *Exit* Bawdber.
Theodoret.   But were yee once disgraced,
Or fallen in wealth, like leaves they would flie from you,
And become browse for every beast; you will'd me
To stocke my selfe with better friends, and servants;
With what face dare you see mee, or any mankind,
That keepe a race of such unheard of relicks,   120
Bawds, Letchers, Leaches, femall fornications,

98 watchd] F2; watch Q1-2   *106 weepers∧] weeper, Q1-2, F2
121 Letchers, Leaches] Q1(c); Leachers, Letches Q1(u)

And children in their rudiments to vices,
Old men to shew examples and (lest Art
Should loose her selfe in act) to call backe custome:
Leave these, and live like *Niobe*. I told you how,
And when your eyes have dropt away remembrance
Of what you were, I am your sonne! performe it.   [*Exit.*]
Brunhalt.   Am I a woman, and no more power in me,
To tie this Tyger up? a soule to no end?
Have I got shame and lost my will? *Brunhalt*   130
From this accursed houre, forget thou bor'st him,
Or any part of thy blood gave him living;
Let him be to thee, an Antipathy,
A thing thy nature sweates at, and turnes backward:
Throw all the mischiefes on him that thy selfe
Or women worse then thou art, have invented,
And kill him drunke, or doubtfull.

> *Enter* Bawdber, Protaldye, Lecure.

Bawdber [*aside*].   Such a sweate,
I never was in yet, clipt of my minstrells,
My toyes to pricke up wenches withall; uphold me,
It runnes like snowballs through me.
Brunhalt.   Now my varlets,   140
My slaves, my running thoughts, my executions——
Bawdber [*aside*].   Lord how shee lookes!
Brunhalt.   Hell take yee all.
Bawdber [*aside*].   Wee shall bee gelt.
Brunhalt.   Your Mistresse,
Your old and honord Mistresse, you tyr'd curtalls,
Suffers for your base sinnes; I must be cloyster'd,
Mew'd up to make me vertuous: who can helpe this?
Now you stand still like Statues; come *Protaldye*,
One kisse before I perish, kisse me strongly,
                       [*Protaldye kisses her.*]
Another, and a third.
Lecure [*aside*].   I feare not gelding
As long as she holds this way.

381

Brunhalt. The young courser, 150
That unlickt lumpe of mine, will win thy Mistris,——
Must I be chast *Protaldye?*
Protaldye. Thus and thus Lady. [*Kisses her.*]
Brunhalt. It shall be so, let him seeke fooles for Vestalls,
Here is my cloister.
Lecure. But what safety Madam
Finde you in staying here?
Brunhalt. Thou hast hit my meaning,
I will to *Thierry* sonne of my blessings,
And there complaine me, tell my tale so subtilly
That the cold stones shall sweat, and statues mourne;
And thou shalt weepe *Protaldye* in my witnesse,
And there forsweare.
Protaldye. Yes, any thing but gelding; 160
I am not yet in quiet Noble Lady,
Let it be done to night, for without doubt
To morrow we are capons.
Brunhalt. Sleepe shall not sease me,
Nor any foode befriend me but thy kisses,
E're I forsake this desart; I live honest?
He may as well bid dead men walke; I humbled
Or bent below my power? let night dogs teare me,
And goblines ride me in my sleepe to Jelly,
Ere I forsake my spheare.
Lecure. This place you will.
Brunhalt. What's that to you, or any, 170
Yee dosse, you powdered pigsbones, rubarbe glister?
Must you know my designes? a colledge on you,
The proverbe makes but fooles.
Protaldye. But Noble Lady——
Brunhalt. You are a sawsie asse too; off I will not,
If you but anger me, tell a sowgelder
Have cut you all like colts; hold me and kisse me,

160 *Protaldye.*] Dyce; *Bawd.* Q 1–2, F 2
172 on] *i.e.* of   174 are] Seward; *om.* Q 1–2, F 2
175 tell] *i.e.* till

382

For I am too much troubled; make up my treasure,
And get me horses private; come, about it.

Exeunt.

Enter Theodoret, Martell. *&c.*   I. ii

Theodoret.   Though I assure my selfe (*Martell*) your counsell
Had no end but alleagance and my honour,
Yet I am Jealous, I have pass'd the bounds
Of a sonnes duty; for suppose her worse
Then your report, not by bare circumstance
But evident proofe confirmd, ha's given her out:
Yet since all weakenesses in a kingdome, are
No more to be severely punished, then
The faults of Kings are by the Thunderer
As oft as they offend, to be reveng'd: 10
If not for piety, yet for policy,
Since some are of necessity to be spar'd,
I might, and now I wish I had not look'd
With such strict eyes into her follies.
Martell.   Sir,
A duety well discharg'd is never follow'd
By sad repentance, nor did your Highnesse ever
Make payment of the debt you ow'd her, better
Then in your late reproofes, not of her, but
Those crimes that made her worthy of reproofe.
The most remarkeable point in which kings differ   20
From private men, is, that they not alone
Stand bound to be in themselves innocent,
But that all such as are allide to them
In neerenesse, or dependance, by their care
Should be free from suspition of all crime;
And you have reap'd a double benefit
From this last great act: first in the restraint
Of her lost pleasures, you remove th'example

0.1 I.ii] *Act.* I. *Scœ.* 2. Q1   1 Though] Q2; Thought Q1
*5 your] Seward; you Q1–2, F2

383

From others of the like licentiousnesse;
Then when 'tis knowne that your severitie 30
Extended to your mother, who dares hope for
The least Indulgence or connivence in
The easiest slips that may prove dangerous
To you or to the kingdome?

Theodoret. I must grant
Your reasons good (*Martell*) if as she is
My Mother, she had bene my subject, or
That only here she could make challenge to
A place of beeing; but I know her temper,
And feare (if such a word become a king,)
That in discovering her, I have let loose 04
A Tigres, whose rage being shut up in darkenesse,
Was grievous only to her selfe; which brought
Into the view of light, (her cruelty
Provok'd by her owne shame,) will turne on him
That foolishly presum'd to let her see
The loth'd shape of her owne deformity.

Martell. Beasts of that nature, when rebellious threats
Begin to appeare only in their eies,
Or any motion that may give suspition
Of the least violence, should be chaind up; 50
Their fanges and teeth, and all their meanes of hurt,
Par'd of, and knock'd out, and so made unable
To do ill, they would soone begin to loath it.
I'le apply nothing, but had your grace done,
Or would do yet, what your lesse forward zeale
In words did only threaten, far lesse danger
Would grow from acting it on her, then may
Perhaps have being from her apprehension
Of what may once be practis'd: for beleeve it,
Who, confident of his owne power, presumes 60
To spend threates on an enimy, that hath meanes
To shun the worst they can effect, gives armor

52 of] *i.e.* off   54 your] Q2; you Q1
61 an enimy] Q1(c); an nimy Q1(u)

To keepe off his owne strength; nay more, disarmes
Himselfe, and lies ungarded gainst all harmes
Or doubt, or malice may produce.
Theodoret.   'Tis true,
And such a desperate cure I would have us'd,
If the intemperate patient had not bene
So neere me as a mother; but to her,
And from me, gentle unguents only were
To be appli'd: and as phisitians   70
When they are sicke of fevers, eate themselves
Such viands as by their directions are
Forbid to others, though alike diseas'd,
So she considering what she is, may challenge
Those cordialls to restore her, by her birth,
And priviledge, which at no suite must be
Granted to others.
Martell.   May your pious care
Effect but what it aimde at, I am silent.

                    Enter Devitry.

Theodoret.   What laught you at Sir?
Vitry.   I have some occasion,
I should not else; and the same cause perhaps   80
That makes me do so, may beget in you
A contrary effect.
Theodoret.   Why, what's the matter?
Vitry.   I see and joy to see that sometimes poore men,
(And most of such are good) stand more indebted
For meanes to breathe to such as are held vitious,
Then those that weare like Hypocrites on their foreheads,
Th'ambitious titles of just men and vertuous.
Martell.   Speake to the purpose.
Vitry.   Who would e're have thought
The good old Queene, your Highnesse reverend mother,
Into whose house (which was an Academ,   90
In which all principles of lust were practis'd,)
No souldier might presume to set his foote;

                    385

At whose most blessed intercession
All offices in the state, were charitably
Confer'd on panders, o're-worne chamber wrastlers,
And such phisitions as knew how to kill
With safety under the pretence of saving,
And such like children of a monstrous peace,
That she I say should at the length provide
That men of warre and honest younger brothers,   100
That wold not owe their feeding to their cod-peece,
Should be esteem'd of more then mothes, or drones,
Or idle vagabonds.

Theodoret.   I am glad to heare it,
Prethee what course takes she to do this?

Vitry.   One
That cannot faile, she and her vertuous traine
With her Jewells and all that was worthy the carrying,
The last night left the court; and as 'tis more
Then sayd, for 'tis confirm'd by such as met her,
She's fled unto your brother.

Theodoret.   How?

Vitry.   Nay storme not,
For if that wicked tonge of hers hath not   110
Forgot its pace, and *Thierry* be a Prince
Of such a fiery temper, as report
Has given him out for; you shall have cause to use
Such poore men as my selfe; and thanke us too
For comming to you, and without petitions;
Pray heaven reward the good old woman for't.

Martell. I foresaw this.

Theodoret.   I heare a tempest comming,
That sings mine and my kingdomes ruine; hast,
And cause a troope of horse to fetch her backe:
Yet stay, why should I use meanes to bring in   120
A plague that of her selfe hath left me? Muster

---

*102 mothes] Seward; mothers Q1-2, F2
105 and...traine] F2 (virtuous train); and vertuous traine Q1(c)-2; and vertuous
traine traine Q1(u)

Our souldiers up, we'ele stand upon our gard,
For we shall be attempted: yet forbeare,
The inequality of our powers will yeeld me
Nothing but losse in their defeature: something
Must be done, and done suddainely: save your labor,
In this i'le use no counsell but mine owne.
That course though dangerous is best. Command
Our daughter be in readinesse to attend us:
Martell, your company,——and honest *Vitry*,   130
Thou wilt along with me?
Vitry.   Yes any where,
To be worse then I am here, is past my feare.

                                                    Exeunt.

          Enter Thierry, Brunhalt, Bawdber, Lecure. *&c.*   II.

Thierry.   You are here in a sanctuary; and that viper
(Who since he hath forgot to be a sonne,
I much disdaine to thinke of as a brother)
Had better in despight of all the gods,
To have razed their Temples, and spurn'd downe their altars,
Then in his impious abuse of you,
To have called on my just anger.
Brunhalt.   Princely sonne;
And in this worthy of so neere a name,
I have in the relation of my wrongs
Bene modest, and no word my tonge delivered   10
T'expresse my insupportable injuries,
But gave my hart a wound: nor has my griefe
Being from what I suffer; but that he,
Degenerate as he is, should be the actor
Of my extreames; and force me to devide
The fires of brotherly affection,
Which should make but one flame.
Thierry.   That part of his
As it deserves shall burne no more, if or

   0.1 II.i] *Act.* 2. *Scœ.* 1. Q1   *8 so neere a] Dyce (*qy*); a neere Q1-2, F2

The teares of Orphans, widdows, or all such
As dare acknowledge him to be their Lord,   20
Joyned to your wrongs, with his hart blood have powre
To put it out: and you, and these your servants,
Who in our favours shall finde cause to know
In that they left not you, how deere we hold them,
Shall give *Theodoret* to understand,
His ignorance of the prizelesse Jewell, which
He did possesse in you, mother in you,
Of which I am more proud to bee the owner,
Then if the absolute rule of all the world
Were offer'd to this hand; once more you are wellcome,   30
Which with all ceremonie due to greatnesse
I would make knowne, but that our just revenge
Admitts not of delay.

        Enter Protaldye, *with souldiers.*

        Your hand Lord Generall.
Brunhalt.   Your favour and his merrit I may say
Have made him such, but I am jealious how
Your subjects will receive it.
Thierry.   How, my subjects?
What do you make of me? Oh heaven! my subjects!
How base should I esteeme the name of Prince,
If that poore dust, were any thing before
The whirlewind of my absolute command?   40
Let them be happy, and rest so contented,
They pay the tribute of their harts and knees,
To such a Prince that not alone h'as power,
To keepe his owne but to increase it; that
Although he hath a body may adde to
The fam'd night labour of strong *Hercules,*
Yet is the maister of a continence
That so can temper it, that I forebeare
Their daughters, and their wives; whose hands though strong,
As yet have never drawne by unjust meane   50

28 owner] Seward; doner Q 1–2; donor F 2

388

Their proper wealth into my treasury.
(But I grow glorious,) and let them beware
That in their least repining at my pleasures,
They change not a mild Prince, (for if provok'd
I dare and will be so) into a Tyrant.
Brunhalt.   You see there's hope that we shall rule againe,   [*Apart.*]
And your falne fortunes rise.
Bawdber.   I hope your Highnesse
Is pleas'd that I shall still hold my place with you,
For I have bene so long us'd to provide you
Fresh bits of flesh since mine grew stale, that surely   60
If cashir'd now, I shall prove a bad Cator
In the Fishmarket of cold chastity.
Lecure.   For me I am your owne, nor since I first
Knew what it was to serve you, have remembred
I had a soule, but such a one whose essence
Depended wholy on your Highnesse pleasure,
And therefore Madam——
Brunhalt.   Rest assur'd you are,
Such instruments we must not lose.
Lecure. Bawdber.   Our service.
Thierry.   You have view'd them then, what's your opinion of em?
In this dull time of peace, we have prepar'd em   70
Apt for the war, ha?
Protaldye.   Sir, they have limbes
That promise strength sufficient, and rich armors,
The souldiers best lov'd wealth: more, it appeares
They have beene drill'd, nay very prettily drill'd,
For many of them can discharge their muskets
Without the danger of throwing off their heads,
Or being offensive to the standers by,
By sweating too much backwards; nay I find
They know the right, and left hand file, and may
With some impulsion no doubt be brought   80
To passe the *A, B, C,* of war, and come
Unto the Horne-booke.

Thierry.   Well, that care is yours;
And see that you effect it.

Protaldye.   I am slow
To promise much; but if within ten dayes,
By precepts and examples, not drawne from
Worme eaten presidents of the *Roman* wars,
But from mine owne, I make them not transcend
All that e're yet bore armes, let it be sayd,
Protaldye bragges, which would be unto me
As hatefull as to be esteemde a coward: 90
For Sir, few Captaines know the way to win em,
And make the souldiers valiant. You shall see me
Lie with them in their trenches, talke, and drinke,
And be together drunke; and what seemes stranger,
We'ele sometimes wench together, which once practisde
And with some other rare and hidden arts,
They being all made mine, i'le breathe into them
Such fearelesse resolution and such fervor,
That though I brought them to beseege a fort,
Whose walls were steeple high, and cannon proofe,   100
Not to be undermind, they should fly up,
Like swallowes; and the parapet once wonne,
For proofe of their obedience, if I willed them
They should leape downe againe; and what is more,
By some directions they should have from me,
Not breake their neckes.

Thierry.   This is above beleefe.

Brunhalt.   Sir, on my knowledge though hee hath spoke much,
He's able to do more.

Lecure [aside].   She meanes on her.

Brunhalt.   And howsoever, in his thankefulnesse
For some few favors done him by my selfe,   110
He left *Austrachia*; not *Theoderet*,
Though hee was chiefely aimde at, could have layd
With all his Dukedomes power, that shame upon him,

91 em] F 2 ('em); him Q 1–2   92 see me] Seward; seeme Q 1–2, F 2
*96 rare...arts] Seward; care...acts Q 1–2, F 2

Which in his barbarous malice to my honor,
He swore with threats to effect.
Thierry.   I cannot but
Beleeve you Madam,——thou art one degree
Growne neerer to my hart, and I am proud
To have in thee so glorious a plant
Transported hither; in thy conduct, we
Go on assurde of conquest, our remove   120
Shall be with the next sunne.

Enter Theoderet, Memberge, Martell, Devitry.

Lecure.   Amazement leave me,   [*Apart.*]
'Tis hee.
Bawdber. We are againe undone.
Protaldye.   Our guilt
Hath no assurance nor defence.
Bawdber.   If now
Your ever ready wit faile to protect us,
We shall be all discoverde.
Brunhalt.   Be not so
In your amazement and your foolish feares,
I am prepared for't.
Theodoret.   How? Not one poore welcome,
In answere of so long a jorney made
Only to see you, brother?
Thierry.   I have stood
Silent thus long, and am yet unresolvde   130
Whether to entertaine thee on my sword,
As fits a parricide of a mothers honor;
Or whether being a Prince, I yet stand bound
(Though thou art here condemnde) to give thee hearing
Before I execute. What foolish hope,
(Nay pray you forbeare) or desperate madnesse rather,
(Unlesse thou comest assurde, I stand in debt
As far to all impiety as thy selfe)
Has made thee bring thy necke unto the axe?

129 you,] Seward; your~A~ Q1-2, F2

Since looking only here, it cannot but   140
Draw fresh blood from thy searde up conscience,
To make thee sensible of that horror, which
They ever beare about them, that like *Nero*——
Like sayd I? thou art worse: since thou darest strive
In her defame to murther thine alive.

Theodoret.   That she that long since had the boldnes to
Be a bad woman, (though I wish some other
Should so report her) could not want the cunning,
(Since they go hand in hand) to lay faire colours
On her blacke crimes, I was resolvde before,   150
Nor make I doubt but that shee hath impoysonde
Your good opinion of me, and so far
Incensde your rage against me, that too late
I come to plead my innocence.

Brunhalt.   To excuse
Thy impious scandalls rather.

Protaldye.   Rather forc'd
With feare to be compelde to come.

Thierry.   Forbeare.

Theodoret.   This moves not mee, and yet had I not beene
Transported on my owne integrity,
I neither am so odious to my subjects,
Nor yet so barren of defence, but that   160
By force I could have justified my guilt,
Had I bene faulty: but since innocence
Is to it selfe an hundred thousand gardes,
And that there is no sonne, but though he owe
That name to an ill mother, but stands bound
Rather to take away with his owne danger
From the number of her faults, then for his owne
Security, to adde unto them. This,
This hath made me to prevent th'expence
Of bloud on both sides, the injuries, the rapes,   170
(Pages, that ever waite upon the war:)
The accompt of all which, since you are the cause,

144 art] F2; are Q1-2

Beleeve it, would have bene required from you;
Rather I say to offer up my daughter,
Who living only could revenge my death,
With my hart blood, a sacrifice to your anger,
Then that you shold draw on your head more curses
Then yet you have deserved.

Thierry [*aside*].   I do begin
To feele an alteration in my nature,
And in his full sailde confidence, a showre   180
Of gentle raine, that falling on the fire
Of my hot rage hath quenched it; ha! I would
Once more speake roughly to him, and I will;
Yet there is something whispers to me, that
I have sayd too much.——How is my heart devided
Betweene the duty of a sonne, and love
Due to a brother! yet I am swayed heere,
And must aske of you, how tis possible
You can affect me, that have learned to hate
Where you should pay all love?

Theodoret.   Which joynde with duty,   190
Upon my knees I should be proud to tender,
Had she not us'd her selfe so many swords
To cut those bonds that tide me to it.

Thierry.   Fie,
No more of that.

Theodoret.   Alas it is a theame,
I take no pleasure to discourse of; would
It could assoone be buried to the world,
As it should die to me: nay more, I wish
(Next to my part of heaven) that shee would spend
The last part of her life so here, that all
Indifferent Judges might condemne me, for   200
A most malicious slanderer: nay texte it
Upon my forehead,——if you hate me mother,
Put me to such a shame, pray you do; beleeve it
There is no glory that may fall upon me,

201 texte] Colman; texde Q 1–2, F 2

Can equall the delight I should receive
In that disgrace; provided the repeale
Of your long banishde vertues, and good name,
Usher'd me to it.
Thierry.   See, she shewes her selfe
An easie mother, which her teares confirme.
Theodoret.   Tis a good signe, the comfortablest raine   210
I ever saw.
Thierry.   Embrace: why this is well,
May never more but love in you, and duty
On your part rise betweene you.
Bawdber.   Do you heare Lord Generall,   [*Apart.*]
Does not your new stampde honor on the suddaine
Begin to grow sicke?
Protaldye.   Yes I finde it fit,
That putting off my armor, I should thinke of
Some honest hospitall to retire to.
Bawdber.   Sure
Although I am a bawd, yet being a Lord
They cannot whip me for't, what's your opinion?   220
Lecure.   The beadle will resolve you, for I cannot:
There is something that more neere concernes my selfe,
That calls upon me.
Martell.   Note but yonder scarabes,   [*Apart.*]
That livde upon the dunge of her base pleasures,
How from the feare that she may yet prove honest,
Hang downe their wicked heads.
Vitry.   What is that to me?
Though they and all the polecats of the Court,
Were trustde together, I perceive not how
It can advantage me a cardekue,
To helpe to keepe me honest.   *A horne.*

                Enter *a* Post.

Thierry.   How, from whence?   230
Post.   These letters will resolve your grace.

                394

Thierry.   What speake they?
                                               Reades.

How all things meete to make me this day happy?
See mother, brother, to your reconcilement
Another blessing almost equall to it,
Is comming towards me; my contracted wife,
Ordella daughter of wise *Dataricke*
The King of *Aragon*, is on our confines;
Then to arrive at such a time, when you
Are happily heere to honor with your presence
Our long deferde, but much wished nuptiall,   240
Falls out above expression; heaven be pleasde
That I may use these blessings powrde on me
With moderation.
Brunhalt [aside].   Hell and furies ayde me,
That I may have power to avert the plagues
That presse upon me.
Thierry.   Two dayes journy sayest thou?
We will set forth to meete her, in the meane time
See all things be preparde to entertaine her:
Nay let me have your companies; there's a Forrest
In the midway shall yeeld us hunting sport,
To ease our travaile: ile not have a brow   250
But shall weare mirth upon it, therefore cleere them.
We'ele wash a way all sorrow in glad feasts,
And the war we meant to men, we'ele make on beasts.

    Exeunt omnes, præter Brunhalt, Bawdber, Protaldye, Lecure.

Brunhalt.   Oh that I had the Magicke to transform you
Into the shape of such, that your owne hounds
Might teare you peece-meale;——are you so stupid?
No word of comfort? Have I fed you mothes
From my excesse of moysture, with such cost,
And can you yeeld no other retribution,
But to devoure your maker? pandar, sponge,   260
Impoysner, all growne barren?

242 blessings] Q2; blessing Q1   253 meant] Langbaine; meane Q1-2, F2
257 mothes] Dyce; mothers Q1-2, F2

Protaldye.   You your selfe
That are our mover, and for whom alone
We live, have failde your selfe in giving way
To the reconcilement of your sonnes.
Lecure.   Which if
You had prevented, or would teach us how
They might againe be severde, we could easily
Remove all other hindrances, that stop
The passage of your pleasures.
Bawdber.   And for me,
If I faile in my office to provide you
Fresh delicates, hang me.   270
Brunhalt.   Oh you are dull, and finde not
The cause of my vexation; their reconcilement
Is a mocke-castle built upon the sand
By children, which when I am pleasde to o'rethrow,
I can with ease spurne downe.
Lecure.   If so, from whence
Growes your affliction?
Brunhalt.   My griefe comes along
With the new Queene, in whose grace all my powre
Must suffer shipwracke: for me now,
That hitherto have kept the first, to know
A second place, or yeeld the least precedence   280
To any others, death; to have my sleepes
Lesse inquirde after, or my rising up
Saluted with lesse reverence, or my gates
Empty of suitors; or the Kings great favours
To passe through any hand but mine, or hee
Himselfe to be directed by another,
Would be to me——do you understand me yet?
No meanes to prevent this?
Protaldye.   Fame gives her out
To be a woman of a chastity
Not to be wrought upon, and therefore Madam   290

281 others] *i.e.* other is

396

For me, though I have pleasde you, to attempt her
Were to no purpose.
Brunhalt.   Tush, some other way.
Bawdber.   Faith I know none else, all my bringing up
Aimde at no other learning.
Lecure.   Give me leave,
If my art faile me not, I have thought on
A speeding project.
Brunhalt.   What ist? but effect it,
And thou shalt be my *Æsculapius*,
Thy image shall be set up in pure gold,
To which i'le fall downe and worship it.
Lecure.   The Lady is faire?
Brunhalt.   Exceeding faire.
Lecure.   And young?   300
Brunhalt.   Some fifteene at the most.
Lecure.   And loves the King
With equall ardor?
Brunhalt.   More, she dotes on him.
Lecure.   Well then, what thinke you if I make a drinke
Which given unto him on the bridall night,
Shall for five dayes so rob his faculties
Of all ability to pay that duty,
Which new made wives expect, that she shall sweare
She is not matchde to a man?
Protaldye.   'T were rare.
Lecure.   And then
If she have any part of woman in her,
She'le or fly out, or at least give occasion   310
Of such a breach which nere can be made up,
Since he that to all else did never faile
Of as much as could be performde by man,
Proves only ice to her.
Brunhalt.   Tis excellent.
Bawdber [*aside*].   The Physitian
Helps ever at a dead lift; a fine calling,
That can both raise, and take downe, out upon thee.

Brunhalt. For this one service I am ever thine;
Prepare it, ile give it him my selfe.——For you *Protaldye*,
By this kisse, and our promisde sport at night, 320
I do conjure you to beare up; not minding
The opposition of *Theodoret*,
Or any of his followers; what so ere
You are, yet appeare valiant, and make good
The opinion that is had of you: for my selfe
In the new Queenes remove, being made secure,
Feare not, ile make the future building sure.

Exeunt.

Wind hornes. Enter Theodoret, Thierry. [II. ii]

Theodoret. This Stag stood well, and cunningly.
Thierry. My horse
I am sure, has found it, for her sides are blooded
From flanke to shoulder, wheres the troope?

Enter Martell.

Theodoret. Past home-ward,
Weary and tirde as we are,——Now *Martell*,
Have you remembred what we thought of?
Martell. Yes Sir, I have snigled him, and if there be
Any desert in his blood, beside the itche,
Or manly heate, but what decoctions
Leaches, and callises have cramde into him,
Your Lordship shall know perfect.
Thierry. Whats that, 10
May not I know too?
Theodoret. Yes Sir, to that end,
We cast the project.
Thierry. What ist?
Martell. A desire Sir,
Upon the gilded flag your graces favour

321 I] Seward; *om.* Q1–2, F2 (*pulled type in* Q1?)
5 thought] Q2; though Q1

398

Has stuck up for a Generall, and to informe you,
(For this houre hee shall passe the test,) what valour,
Stayd judgement, soule, or safe discretion
Your mothers wandring eyes, and your obedience
Have flung upon us; to assure your knowledge,
He can bee, dare be, shall be, must be nothing,
(Loade him with piles of honors; set him off   20
With all the cunning foyles that may deceive us:)
But a poore, cold, unspirited, unmannerde,
Unhonest, unaffected, undone, foole,
And most unheard of coward, a meere lumpe
Made to loade beds withall, and like a nightmare
Ride Ladies, that forget to say their prayers;
One that dares only be diseased, and in debt,
Whose body mewes more plaisters every month,
Then women do old faces.
Thierry.   No more, I know him,
I now repent my error, take your time   30
And try him home, ever thus far reserv'd,
You tie your anger up.
Martell.   I lost it else Sir.
Thierry.   Bring me his sword faire taken, without violence,
For that will best declare him.
Theodoret.   That's the thing.
Thierry.   And my best horse is thine.
Martell.   Your graces servant.   *Exit.*
Theodoret.   You'le hunt no more Sir?
Thierry.   Not today, the weather
Is growne too warme, besides, the dogges are spent,
We'ele take a cooler morning, let's to horse,
And hollow in the troope.
                                   Exeunt. Wind hornes.

16 Stayd] *i.e.* staid

Enter two Huntsmen.

1. Huntsman.   I, marry *Twainer,*
This woman gives indeed, these are the Angells
That are the keepers saints.
2. Huntsman.   I like a woman
That handles the deeres dowsets with discretion;
And payes us by proportion.
1. Huntsman.   'Tis no treason
To think this good old Lady has a stumpe yet
That may require a currall.
2. Huntsman.   And the bells too,

Enter Protaldye.

She has lost a friend of me else, but here's the clarke,
No more for feare ath bell ropes.
Protaldye.   How now Keepers,
Saw you the King?
1. Huntsman.   Yes Sir, he's newly mounted,   10
And as we take it ridden home.
Protaldye.   Farewell then. *Exeunt* Keepers.

Enter Martell [*disguised*].

Martell.   My honord Lord, Fortune has made me happy
To meete with such a man of men to side me.
Protaldye.   How Sir?
I know ye not, nor what your fortune meanes.
Martell.   Few words shall serve, I am betraide Sir;
Innocent and honest, malice, and violence
Are both against me, basely and fowly layd for,
For my life Sir; danger is now about mee,
Now in my throate Sir.
Protaldye.   Where Sir?
Martell.   Nay I feare not,   20
And let it now powre downe in stormes upon me,
I have met a noble guard.

12 *Martell.*] Langbaine; *om.* Q1-2, F2

400

Protaldye.   Your meaning Sir,
For I have present businesse.
Martell.   O my Lord,
Your honour cannot leave a gentleman,
(At least a faire designe of this brave nature,
To which your worth is wedded, your profession
Hatcht in, and made one peece,) in such a perill;
There are but six my Lord.
Protaldye.   What six?
Martell.   Six villaines,
Sworne and in pay to kill mee.
Protaldye.   Six?
Martell.   Alas Sir,
What can sixe do, or six score now you are present?   30
Your name will blow em off, say they have shot too,
Who dare present a peece? your valour's proofe Sir.
Protaldye.   No, i'le assure you Sir, nor my discretion,
Against a multitude; 'tis true I dare fight,
Enough, and well enough, and long enough:
But wisedome Sir, and weight of what is on me,
In which I am no more mine owne, nor yours Sir,
Nor as I take it, any single danger,
But what concernes my place, tells me directly;
Beside my person, my faire reputation,   40
If I thrust into crowds, and seeke occasions,
Suffers opinion. Six? Why *Hercules*
Avoyded two, man: yet not to give example,
But only for your present dangers sake Sir,
Were there but foure Sir, I car'd not if I killd um,
They will serve to set my sword.
Martell.   There are but foure Sir,
I did mistake um, but foure such as *Europe*
Excepting your great valour——
Protaldye.   Well considerde,
I will not medle with um, foure in honor,

43 two, man] Colman; two‸ man Q1; two‸ men Q2, F2

Are equall with fourescore, besides they are people   50
Only directed by their fury.
Martell.   So much nobler
Shall be your way of Justice.
Protaldye.   That I find not.
Martell.   You will not leave me thus?
Protaldye.   I would not leave you;
But looke you Sir, men of my place, and busines,
Must not be questioned thus.
Martell.   You cannot passe Sir,
Now they have seene me with you, without danger,
They are heere Sir, within hearing, take but two.
Protaldye.   Let the Law take um, take a tree Sir,
(Ile take my horse,) that you may keepe with safety,
If they have brought no hand-sawes: within this houre   60
Ile send you rescue, and a toyle to take um.
Martell.   You shall not go so poorely; stay, but one Sir.
Protaldye.   I have bene so hamperde with these rescues,
So hewde and torturde, that the truth is Sir,
I have mainly vowde against um, yet for your sake,
If as you say there be but one, ile stay,
And see faire play a both sides.
Martell.   There is no more Sir,
And as I doubt a base one too.
Protaldye.   Fie on him,
Go lug him out by the eares.
Martell.   Yes: this is he Sir,   [*Seizes him.*]
The basest in the kingdome.
Protaldye.   Do you know me?   70
Martell.   Yes for a generall foole, a knave, a coward,
And upstart stallion bawd, beast, barking puppy,
That dares not bite.
Protaldye.   The best man best knowes patience.
Martell.   Yes, this way Sir: [*Kickes him.*]
                    Now draw your sword, and right you,
Or render it to me, for one you shall do.

68 too] Q2; two Q1   74 your] Q2; you Q1

402

Protaldye. If wearing it may do you any honor,
I shall be glad to grace you, there it is Sir.
Martell. Now get you home, and tel your Lady Mistresse
She has shot up a sweete mushrump; quit your place too,
And say you are counselde well; thou wilt be beaten else   80
By thine owne lanceprisadoes, when they know thee,
That tunes of oyle of roses wil not cure thee;
Go get you to your foyning worke at Court,
And learne to sweate agen, and eate dry mutton;
An armor like a frost will search your bones,
And make you rore you rogue; not a reply,
For if you do your eares go off.
Protaldye.   Still patience.

                                              Exeunt.

              Loude Musicke, a Banquet set out.   [II. iv]
Enter Thierry, Ordella, Brunhalt, Theodoret, Lecure, Bawdber. *&c.*

Thierry. It is your place, and though in all things else
You may and ever shall command me, yet
In this ile be obeyde.
Ordella.   Sir, the consent
That made me yours, shall never teach me to
Repent I am so, yet be you but pleasde
To give me leave to say so much; the honor
You offer me were better given to her,
To whom you owe the power of giving.
Thierry.   Mother,
You heare this and rejoyce in such a blessing
That payes to you so large a share of duty,——   10
But fie no more, for as you hold a place
Neerer my heart then she, you must sit neerest
To all those graces, that are in the power
Of Majesty to bestow.
Brunhalt [*aside*].   Which i'le provide,
Shall be short livde,——*Lecure.*

                82 tunes] *i.e.* tuns

Lecure [*apart to her*].   I have it ready.
Brunhalt [*to him*]. 'Tis well,——waite on our cup.
Lecure.   You honor me.
Thierry.   We are dull, no object to provoke mirth?
Theodoret.   *Martell*,
  If you remember Sir, will grace your feast
  With something that will yeeld matter of mirth,   20
  Fit for no common view.
Thierry.   Touching *Protaldye*?
Theodoret.   You have it.
Brunhalt (*aside*).   What of him? I feare his basenesse
  In spight of all the titles that my favors
  Have clothde him with, will make discovery
  Of what is yet concealde.

                    Enter Martell.

Theodoret.   Looke Sir, he has it,
  Nay wee shall have peace when so great a souldier
  As the renoumde *Protaldye*, will give up
  His sword rather then use it.
Brunhalt (*aside*).   'Twas thy plot,
  Which I will turne on thy owne head.
Thierry.   Pray you speake,
  How wonne you him to part from't?
Martell.   Wonne him Sir?   30
  He would have yeelded it upon his knees
  Before he would have hazarded the exchange
  Of a phillip of the forehead: had you willde me,
  I durst have undertooke he should have sent you
  His nose, provided that the losse of it
  Might have sav'd the rest of his face; he is Sir
  The most unutterable coward, that ere nature
  Blest with hard shoulders, which were only given him,
  To the ruine of bastinados.
Thierry.   Possible?
Theodoret.   Observe but how she frets.

        24 him‸ with,] Seward; him, which‸ Q 1–2, F 2
                            404

Martell.   Why beleeve it: 40
But that I know the shame of this disgrace,
Will make the beast to live with such, and never
Presume to come more among men, i'le hazard
My life upon it, that a boy of twelve
Should scourge him hither like a parish top,
And make him dance before you.
Brunhalt.   Slave thou liest,
Thou dar'st aswell speake treason in the hearing
Of those that have the power to punish it,
As the least sillable of this before him,
But 'tis thy hate to me.
Martell.   Nay, pray you Madam,   50
I have no eares too heare you, though a foote
To let you understand what he is.
Brunhalt.   Villaine.
Theodoret.   You are to violent.

                    Enter Protaldye.

Protaldye [*aside*].   The worst that can come
Is blanketting; for beating, and such vertues
I have bene long acquainted with.
Martell.   Oh strange!
Bawdber.   Behold the man you talke of.
Brunhalt.   Give me leave,——
Or free thy selfe (thinke in what place you are)
From the foule imputation that is layd
Upon thy valour (be bold, i'le protect you)
Or heere I vow (deny it or forsweare it)   60
These honors which thou wearest unworthily,
(Which be but impudent enough and keepe them)
Shall be torne from thee with thy eyes.
Protaldye [*aside*].   I have it,——
My valour! is there any here beneath
The stile of king, dares question it?

        53 *Protaldye.*] Langbaine; *om.* Q1–2, F2
        56 you] Q2; yon Q1

                    405

Thierry.   This is rare.
Protaldye.   Which of my actions, which have still bene noble,
  Has rendred me suspected?
Thierry.   Nay *Martell*,
  You must not fall off.
Martell.   Oh Sir, feare it not,——
  Do you know this sword?
Protaldye.   Yes.
Martell.   Pray you on what termes
  Did you part with it?
Protaldye.   Part with it say you?   70
Martell. So.
Thierry.   Nay study not an answere, confesse freely.
Protaldye.   Oh I remember't now, at the stags fall,
  As we to day were hunting, a poore fellow,
  (And now I view you better, I may say
  Much of your pitch:) this silly wretch I spoke of,
  With his petition falling at my feete,
  (Which much against my will he kisde,) desirde
  That as a speciall meanes for his preferment,
  I would vouchsafe to let him use my sword,   80
  To cut off the stags head.
Brunhalt.   Will you heare that?
Bawdber.   This lie beares a similitude of truth.
Protaldye.   I ever courteous, (a great weakenes in me)
  Granted his humble suite.
Martell.   Oh impudence!
Thierry.   This change is excellent.
Martell.   A word with you:
  Denie it not, I was that man disguisde,
  You know my temper, and as you respect
  A dayly cudgelling for one whole yeare,
  Without a second pulling by the eares,
  Or tweakes by the nose, or the most pretious balme   90
  You usde of patience, (patience do you marke me?)

65 rare] Q1(c); care Q1(u)
73 fall] Langbaine; falls Q1–2, F2

406

Confesse before these kings with what base feare
Thou didst deliver it.
Protaldye.   Oh! I shall burst,
And if I have not instant liberty
To teare this fellow limbe by limbe, the wrong
Will breake my hart, although *Herculean,*
And somewhat bigger; there's my gage, pray you here
Let me redeme my credit.
Thierry.   Ha, ha, forbeare.
Martell. Pray you let me take it up, and if I do not
Against all ods of armor and of weapons,   100
With this make him confesse it on his knees,
Cut off my head.
Protaldye.   No, that is my office.
Bawdber.   Fie,
You take the hangmans place.
Ordella.   Nay good my Lord
Let me attone this difference, do not suffer
Our bridall night to be the Centaures feast,——
You are a Knight and bound by oath to grant
All just suits unto Ladies; for my sake
Forget your supposde wrong.
Protaldye.   Well, let him thanke you,
For your sake he shall live, perhaps a day,
And may be, on submission longer.
Theodoret.   Nay,   110
Martell, you must bee patient.
Martell.   I am yours,
And this slave shall be once more mine.
Thierry.   Sit all;
One health, and so to bed, for I too long
Deferre my choisest delicates.
Brunhalt [aside].   Which if poyson
Have any power, thou shalt like *Tantalus*
Behold and never taste;——[to Lecure] be carefull.
Lecure [to her].   Feare not.

101 this] *i.e.* the sword   108 you] Q2; yon Q1

Brunhalt.   Though it be rare in our sex, yet for once
I will begin a health.
Thierry.   Let it come freely.
Brunhalt.   *Lecure*, the cup;——heere, to the sonne we hope
This night shall be an Embrion.   [*Drinks.*]
Thierry.   You have namde   120
A blessing that I most desirde, I pledge you,——
Give me a larger cup, that is too little
Unto so great a good.
Brunhalt.   Nay, then you wrong me,
Follow as I began.
Thierry.   Well as you please.   [*Drinks.*]
Brunhalt [*to* Lecure].   Ist done?
Lecure [*to her*].   Unto your wish, I warrant you,
For this night I durst trust him with my mother.
Thierry.   So, 'tis gone round,——lights.
Brunhalt.   Pray you use my service.
Ordella.   'Tis that which I shall ever owe you Madam,
And must have none from you, pray you pardon me.
Thierry.   Good rest to all.
Theodoret.   And to you pleasant labour.——   130
Martell your company,——Madam good night.
          Exeunt all, but Brunhalt, Protaldye, Lecure, Bawdber.
Brunhalt.   Nay you have cause to blush, but I will hide it,
And what's more I forgive you; ist not pitty
That thou that art the first to enter combat
With any woman, and what is more, orecome her,
(In which she is best pleasde,) should be so fearefull
To meete a man?
Protaldye.   Why, would you have me lose
That blood that is dedicated to your service,
In any other quarrell?
Brunhalt.   No, reserve it
As I will study to preserve thy credit.——   140
You sirha; be't your care to finde out one
That is poore though valiant, that at any rate

          123 good] Seward; god Q1–2, F2

          408

Will, to redeeme my servants reputation,
Receave a publike baffling.
Bawdber.   Would your highnesse
Were pleas'd to informe me better of your purpose.
Brunhalt.   Why one Sir, that would thus be boxde, or kickde;
                                        [*Strikes him.*]
Do you apprehend me now?
Bawdber.   I feele you Madam,
The man that shall receive this from my Lord,
Shall have a thousand crownes.
Brunhalt.   Hee shall.
Bawdber.   Besides
His day of bastinadoing past ore,   150
He shall not lose your grace, nor your good favor.
Brunhalt.   That shall make way to it.
Bawdber.   It must be a man
Of credit in the Court, that is to be
The foyle unto your valour.
Protaldye.   True, it should.
Bawdber.   And if he have place there, 'tis not the worse.
Brunhalt.   'Tis much the better.
Bawdber.   If he be a Lord,
'Twill be the greater grace.
Brunhalt.   Thou art in the right.
Bawdber.   Why then behold that valiant man and Lord,
That for your sake will take a cudgelling,
For be assurde when it is spread abroad   160
That you have dealt with me, the'ile give you out
For one of the nine Worthies.
Brunhalt.   Out you pandar,
Why to beate thee is only exercise
For such as do affect it, lose not time
In vaine replies, but do it:——come my sollace,
Let us to bed, and our desires once quenchde,
We'ele there determine of *Theodorets* death,
For he's the engin usde to ruine us:——

149 *Brunhalt.*] Seward; *Prot.* Q1–2, F2

27   409   B D W

Yet one worde more, *Lecure*; art thou assurde
The potion will worke?
Lecure.   My life upon it.   170
Brunhalt.   Come my *Protaldye*, then glut me with
Those best delights of man, that are denide
To her that does expect them, being a bride.

                                        Exeunt.

Enter Thierry, *and* Ordella, *as from bed.*   **III. i**

Thierry.   Sure I have drunke the blood of Elephants;
The teares of mandrake and the marble dew,
Mixt in my draught, have quencht my natural heate,
And left no sparke of fire but in mine eyes,
With which I may behold my miseries:
Ye wretched flames which play upon my sight,
Turne inward, make me all one peece, though earth;
My teares shall overwhelme you else too.
Ordella.   What moves my Lord to this strange sadnes?
If any late discerned want in me,   10
Give cause to your repentance, care and duty
Shall finde a painefull way to recompence.
Thierry.   Are you yet frozen, veines? feele you a breath,
Whose temperate heate would make the North star reele,
Her icie pillers thaw'd, and do you not melt?
Draw neerer, yet neerer,
That from my barren kisse thou maist confesse
I have not heate enough to make a blush.
Ordella.   Speake nearer to my understanding, like a husband.
Thierry.   How should he speake the language of a husband,   20
Who wants the tongue and organs of his voyce?
Ordella.   It is a phrase will part with the same ease
From you with that you now deliver.
Thierry.   Bind not
His eares up with so dull a charme, who hath
No other sence left open; why should thy words

---

169 worde] Langbaine; worke Q1–2, F2   173.1 *Exeunt.*] Q1(c); *om.* Q1(u)
0.1 III.i] *Act.* 3. *Scœ.* 1. Q1   *17 my] thy Q1–2, F2

410

Find more restraint then thy free speaking actions,
Thy close embraces and thy mid-night sighes,
The silent orators to slow desire?
Ordella.   Strive not to win content from ignorance
  Which must be lost in knowledge: heaven can witnesse   30
  My farthest hope of good reacht at your pleasure,
  Which seeing alone may in your looke be read:
  Adde not a doubtfull comment to a text
  That in it selfe's direct and easie.
Thierry.   Oh thou hast drunk the juice of hemlock too,
  Or did upbraided nature make this paire
  To shew she had not quite forgot her first
  Justly praisde workmanship, the first chast couple,
  Before the want of joy taught guilty sight
  A way through shame and sorrow to delight?   40
  Say, may we mixe as in their innocence
  When turtles kist, to confirme happinesse,
  Not to beget it?
Ordella.   I know no bar.
Thierry.   Should I beleeve thee? yet thy pulse beates woman;
  And sayes the name of wife did promise thee
  The blest reward of duty to thy mother,
  Who gave so often witnes of her joy,
  When she did boast thy likenes to her husband.
Ordella.   'Tis true,
  That to bring forth a second to your selfe,   50
  Was only worthy of my Virgin losse;
  And should I prize you lesse unpatternde Sir,
  Then being exemplified? ist not more honor
  To be possessor of unequalde vertue,
  Then what is paralelde? give me beleefe,
  The name of mother knowes no way of good,
  More then the end in me: who weds for lust
  Is oft a widdow; when I married you,
  I lost the name of maid to gaine a title
  Above the wish of change, which that part can   60

32 your] Q1(c); you Q1(u)

Only maintaine, is still the same in man,
His vertue and his calme society,
Which no gray haires can threaten to dissolve,
Nor wrinkles bury.

Thierry. Confine thy selfe to silence, lest thou take
That part of reason from me is only left
To give perswasion to me, I am a man:
Or say thou hast never seene the rivers haste
With glad-some speede to meete the amorous sea.

Ordella. Nere but to praise the coolenes of their streames. 70

Thierry. Nor viewde the kids taught by their lustfull fires,
Pursue each other through the wanton lawnes,
And likt the sport.

Ordella. As it made way unto their envied rest,
With weary knots binding their harmeles eyes.

Thierry. Nor do you know the reason why the dove,
One of the paire your hands wont hourely feede,
So often clipt and kist her happy mate?

Ordella. Unlesse it were to welcome his wisht sight,
Whose absence only gave her mourning voyce. 80

Thierry. And you could dovelike to a single object
Bind your loose spirits? to one, nay such a one
Whom only eyes and eares must flatter good,
Your surer sence made uselesse? nay my selfe,
As in my all of good already knowne?

Ordella. Let proofe plead for me, let me be mewde up
Where never eye may reach me but your owne;
And when I shall repent, but in my lookes,
If sigh,——

Thierry. Or shed a teare that's warme?

Ordella.   But in your sadnesse—— 90

Thierry. Or when you heare the birds call for their mates,
Aske if it be *St. Valentine*, their coopling day?

Ordella. If any thing may make a thought suspected,

70 Nere] Dyce; We are Q1-2, F2
84 nay my selfe,] Seward; my selfe, nay Q1-2, F2
93 thought] Q2; though Q1

412

Of knowing any happines but you,
Divorse me by the title of most falshood.
Thierry.   Oh who would know a wife,
 That might have such a friend? posterity
Henceforth lose the name of blessing, and leave
The earth inhabited to people heaven.

Enter Theodoret, Brunhalt, Martell, Protaldye.

Martell.   All happines to *Thierry*, and *Ordella*.   100
Thierry.   'Tis a desire but borrowde from me, my happines
 Shall be the period of all good mens wishes,
 Which friends, nay dying fathers shall bequeath,
 And in my one give all: is there a duty
 Belongs to any power of mine, or love
 To any vertue I have right to? here, place it here,
 Ordellas name shall only beare command,
 Rule, title, soveraity.
Brunhalt.   What passion swaies my son?
Thierry.   O mother, she has doubled every good
 The travaile of your blood made possible   110
 To my glad being.
Protaldye [*aside*].   He should have done
 Little to her, he is so light harted.
Thierry.   Brother, friends, if honor unto shame,
 If wealth to want inlarge the present sence,
 My joyes are unbounded; instead of question
 Let it be envy, not to bring a present
 To the high offering of our mirth; banquets, and maskes,
 Keepe waking our delights, mocking nights malice,
 Whose darke brow would fright pleasure from us; our court   120
 Be but one stage of Revells, and each eye
 The sceane where our content moves.
Theodoret.   There shall want
 Nothing to expresse our shares in your delight Sir.

*95 most falshood] *stet* Q1–2, F2   99 inhabited] *i.e.* uninhabited
117 to] Seward; *om.* Q1–2, F2

413

Martell. Till now I ne're repented the estate
Of widdower.
Thierry.   Musique, why art thou so
Slow voycte? it staies thy presence my *Ordella*,
This chamber is a spheare too narrow for
Thy al-moving vertue. Make way, free way I say;
Who must alone, her sexes want supply,
Had need to have a roome both large and high.   130
Martell. This passion's above utterance.   [*Apart.*]
Theodoret.   Nay credulity.
                    Exeunt all but Thierry, Brunhalt.
Brunhalt. Why son what meane you,
Are you a man?
Thierry.   No mother I am no man,
Were I a man, how could I be thus happy?
Brunhalt. How can a wife be author of this joy then?
Thierry. That being no man, I am married to no woman;
The best of men in full ability,
Can only hope to satisfie a wife,
And for that hope ridiculous; I in my want
And such defective poverty, that to her bed   140
From my first cradell brought no strength but thought,
Have met a temperance beyond hers that rockt me,
Necessity being her bar; where this
Is so much sencelesse of my depriv'd fire,
She knowes it not a losse by her desire.
Brunhalt. It is beyond my admiration.
Thierry. Beyond your sexes faith,
The unripe virgins of our age to hear't
Will dreame themselves to women, and convert
The example to a miracle.   150
Brunhalt. Alas 'tis your defect moves my amazement,
But what ill can be separate from ambition?
Cruell *Theodoret.*
Thierry.   What of my brother?
Brunhalt. That to his name your barrennesse adds rule;
Who loving the effect, would not be strange

In favouring the cause; looke on the profit,
And gaine will quickly point the mischiefe out.
Thierry.   The name of father to what I possesse
Is shame and care.
Brunhalt.   Were we begot to single happinesse   160
I grant you; but from such a wife, such virtue,
To get an heire, what Hermit would not find
Deserving argument to breake his vow,
Even in his age, of chastity?
Thierry.   You teach a deafe man language.
Brunhalt.   The cause found out, the malady may cease,
Have you heard of one *Forte*?
Thierry.   A learnde Astronomer, great Magician,
Who lives hard-by retirde.
Brunhalt.   Repaire to him, with the just houre and place   170
Of your nativity; fooles are amaz'd at fate,
Griefes but concealde are never desperate.
Thierry.   You have timely wakende me, nor shall I sleepe
Without the satisfaction of his art.
Brunhalt.   Wisedome prepares you to't.   *Exit* Thierry.

Enter Lecure.

                                   Lecure, met happily.
Lecure.   The ground answeres your purpose, the conveiance
Being secure and easie, falling just
Behind the state set for *Theodoret.*
Brunhalt.   'Tis well;
Your trust invites you to a second charge,   180
You know *Lefortes* cell?
Lecure.   Who constellated your faire birth.
Brunhalt.   Enough, I see thou knowst him, where's *Bawdber*?
Lecure.   I left him carefull of the project cast,
To raise *Protaldyes* credit.
Brunhalt.   A sore that must be plasterde, in whose wound
Others shall find their graves, thinke themselves sound,
Your eare, and quickest apprehension.

                                                        Exeunt.

167 *Forte*] Seward (*Leforte*); Forts Q1-2, F2

415

Enter Bawdber, *and a* Servant. [III.

Bawdber. This man of war will advance.

Servant. His houres upon the stroake.

Bawdber. Wind him backe as you favor my eares, I love no noyse in my head, my braines have hitherto bin imployde in silent businesses.

Enter Devitry.

Servant. The gentleman is within your reach Sir.

Bawdber. Give ground whilst I drill my wits to the encounter.

Exit [Servant].

Devitry, I take it.

Devitry. All that's left of him.

Bawdber. Is there another parcell of you? if it be at pawne I will 10 gladly redeeme it to make you wholy mine.

Vitry. You seeke too hard a penyworth.

Bawdber. You do ill to keepe such distance, your parts have bin long knowne to me, howsoever you please to forget acquaintance.

Vitry. I must confesse I have bin subject to lewd company.

Bawdber. Thankes for your good remembrance; you have bin a souldier *Devitry*, and borne armes?

Vitry. A couple of unprofitable ones, that have only serv'd to get me a stomacke to my dinner.

Bawdber. Much good may it do you Sir. 20

Vitry. You should have heard me say I had din'd first, I have built on an unwholesome ground, rais'd up a house before I knew a Tenant, marcht to meete wearines, fought to find want and hunger.

Bawdber. It is time you put up your sword, and run away for meate sir; nay if I had not withdrawne ere now, I might have kept the fast with you: but since the way to thrive is never late, what is the neerest course to profit thinke you?

2, 6 *Servant.*] Dyce; *Lecure.* Q1–2, F2±
7.1 *Exit.*] Dyce; *following line 6* Q1–2, F2
13 do] Seward; to Q1–2; too F2   23 marcht] Seward; matcht Q1–2, F2
25 away] Q2; a way Q1

Vitry.   It may be your worship will say bawdry.

Bawdber.   True sence, bawdry.   30

Vitry.   Why is their five kinds of em? I never knew but one.

Bawdber.   Ile shew you a new way of prostitution, fall backe,
further yet, further; there is fifty crownes, do but as much to
Protaldye the Queenes favoret, they are doubled.

Vitry.   But thus much?

Bawdber.   Give him but an affront as he comes to the presence,
and in his drawing make way like a true bawde to his valour,
the sum's thy owne; if you take a scratch in the arme or so, every
drop of blood weighes downe a ducket.

Vitry.   After that rate, I and my friends would begger the king-   40
dome. Sir you have made me blush to see my want, whose cure is
such a cheape and easie purchase; this is male bawdery belike.

Enter Protaldye, *and a* Lady.

Bawdber.   See, you shall not be long earning your wages, your
worke's before your eyes.

Vitry.   Leave it to my handling, ile fall upon't instantly.

Bawdber [*aside.*]   What opinion will the managing of this affaire
bring to my wisedome? my invention tickles with apprehension
on't.

Protaldye.   These are the joyes of marriage Lady, whose sights
Are able to dissolve virginity.   50
Speake freely,
Do you not envy the brides felicity?

Lady.   How should I, being partner of't?

Protaldye.   What you
Enjoy is but the banquets view, the taste
Stands from your pallat; if he impart by day
So much of his content, thinke what night gave?

Vitry.   Will you have a rellish of wit Lady?

Bawdber [*to* Protaldye].   This is the man.

Lady.   If it be not deare Sir.

38 sum's] Langbaine; son's Q1–2, F2
42.1 *Enter...*Lady] Dyce; *Enter Protaldy, a Lady, and Revellers* Q1–2, F2
43 be long] F2; belong Q1–2

417

Vitry. If you affect cheapenes, how can you prize this sullied 60
ware so much? mine is fresh, my owne, not retailde.
Protaldye. You are sawcy sirra.
Vitry. The fitter to be in the dish with such dry stockfish as
you are. [*Protaldye strikes him.*] How, strike?
Bawdber [*to* Vitry]. Remember the condition as you looke for
payment.
Vitry. That boxe was left out of the bargaine. [*Strikes* Protaldye.]
Protaldye. Helpe, helpe, helpe.
Bawdber. Plague of the scrivners running hand, what a blow is
this to my reputation? 70

Enter Thierry, Theodoret, Brunhalt, Ordella, Memberge, Martell,
[*Guards*].

Thierry. What villaine dares this outrage?
Devitry. Heere mee Sir, this creature hir'de mee with fifty crownes
in hand, to let *Protaldye* have the better of mee at single rapier on a
made quarrell; he mistaking the weapon, layes mee over the chops
with his clubfist, for which I was bold to teach him the art of
memory.
Omnes. Ha, ha, ha, ha.
Theodoret. Your Generall, mother, will display himselfe
Spight of our peace I see.
Thierry. Forbeare these civill jarres, fie *Protaldye,* 80
So open in your projects?——avoyde our presence sirra.
Devitry. Willingly,——if you have any more wages to earne,
you see I can take paines.
Theodoret. There's somewhat for thy labor, more then was
promis'd; ha, ha, ha. [*Exit* Devitry.]
Bawdber [*aside*]. Where could I wish my selfe now? in the Ile of
dogs, so I might scape scratching, for I see by her cats eyes I shall
be claw'd fearefully.
Thierry. Weele heare no more on't,—musique drowne al sadnes;
Soft musique.

Command the Revellers in.

                       [*Aside*] At what a rate ide purchase   90
My mothers absence, to give my spleene full liberty.

                  Enter Revellers.

Brunhalt.   Speake not a thoughts delay, it names thy ruine. [*Apart.*]
Protaldye. I had thought my life had borne more valew with you.
Brunhalt. Thy losse carries mine with't, let that secure thee;
The vault is ready, and the dore convyes too't
Falls just behind his chaire; the blow once given,
Thou art unseene.
Protaldye. I cannot feele more then I feare, ime sure.
Brunhalt. Be gone, and let them laugh their owne destruction.
                       [*Protaldye*] *withdrawes.*
Thierry. You will adde unto her rage.   [*Apart.*]
Theodoret.   Foote I shall burst   100
Unlesse I vent my selfe, ha, ha, ha.
Brunhalt [*to 1. Reveller*].   Me Sir?
You never could have found a time to invite
More willingnesse in my dispose to pleasure.
Memberge. Would you would please to make some other choice.
[2.] *Reveller.* 'Tis a disgrace would dwell upon me Lady,
Should you refuse.
Memberge. Your reason conquers;——[*aside*] my grandmothers
    lookes
Have turn'd all ayre to earth in me, they sit
Upon my heart like night charmes, black and heavy.

                  The Dance.

Thierry. You are too much libertine.   110
Theodoret. The fortune of the foole perswades my laughter
More then his cowardice; was ever ratte
Tane by the taile thus? ha, ha, ha.
Thierry. Forbeare I say.

      90 ide] Weber (I would *after* Mason); I do Q1-2, F2
      91.1 *Enter* Revellers.] Dyce; *at line* 42.1 *in* Q1-2, F2

Protaldye (behind the state).   No eie lookes this way, I will wink and
   strike,
                        Lest I betray my selfe.   *Stabs* Theodoret. [*Exit.*]
Theodoret.   Ha, did you not see one neere me?
Thierry.   How, neere you? why do you looke so pale brother?——
   Treason, treason.
Memberge.   Oh my presage!——Father.
Ordella.   Brother.   120
Martell.   Prince, noble Prince.
Thierry.   Make the gates sure, search into every angle
   And corner of the court; oh my shame! ——mother,
   Your son is slaine, *Theodoret,* noble *Theodoret,*
   Here in my armes, too weake a sanctuary
   'Gainst treachery and murther,——say is the traytor taken?
1. Guard.   No man has past the chamber on my life Sir.
Thierry.   Set present fire unto the palace,
   That all unseene may perish in this mischiefe;
   Who moves slow to't shall adde unto the flame.   130
Brunhalt.   What meane you? give me your private hearing.
Thierry.   Perswasion is a partner in the crime,
   I will renounce my claime unto a mother,
   If you make offer on't.
Brunhalt.   Ere a torch can take flame, I will produce
   The author of the fact.
Thierry.   Withdraw but for your lights.
Memberge.   Oh my too true suspition?
Exeunt Martell, Memberge [*and others. Manent* Thierry, Brunhalt].
Thierry.   Speake, where's the engin to this horrid act?
Brunhalt.   Here, you do behold her, upon whom   140
   Make good your causles rage; the deed was done
   By my incitement, not yet repented.
Thierry.   Whither did nature start, when you conceivde
   A birth so unlike woman? say, what part
   Did not consent to make a son of him,
   Reserv'd it selfe within you to his ruine.
Brunhalt.   Ha, ha, a son of mine! do not dissever

*128 palace] place Q1–2, F2

420

Thy fathers dust, shaking his quiet urne,
To which thy breath would send so foule an issue.
My son, thy brother?   150
Thierry. Was not *Theodoret* my brother, or is thy tongue
Confederate with thy hart, to speake and do
Only things monstrous?
Brunhalt. Heare me, and thou shalt make thine owne beleefe:
Thy still with sorrow mentionde father livde
Three carefull yeares in hope of wished heires,
When I conceivde: being from his jealious feare
Enjoynde to quiet home, one fatall day,
Transported with my pleasure to the chase,
I forc't command, and in pursuite of game   160
Fell from my horse, lost both my child and hopes.
Despaire which only in his love saw life
Worthy of being, from a gardners armes
Snatcht this unlucky brat, and call'd it mine,
When the next yeare repaide my losse with thee:
But in thy wrongs preserv'd my misery,
Which that I might diminish though not end,
My sighes and wet eyes, from thy fathers will,
Bequeathd this largest part of his dominions
Of *France* unto thee, and only left *Austracia*   170
Unto that changeling, whose life affoords
Too much of ill 'gainst me to prove my words
And call him stranger.
Thierry. Come, do not weepe, I must, nay, do beleeve you,
And in my fathers satisfaction count it
Merit, not wrong, or losse.
Brunhalt.   You do but flatter,
There's anger yet flames in your eyes.
Thierry. See, I will quench it, and confesse that you
Have suffer'd double travaile for me.   180
Brunhalt. You will not fire the house then?
Thierry. Rather reward the author, who gave cause
Of knowing such a secret; my oath and duty
Shall be assurance on't.

190 Bequeathd] Weber (Bequeathed *after* Mason); Bequeathe Q 1–2, F 2

421

Brunhalt.   *Protaldye*, rise good faithfull servant,——heaven
knowes
How hardly he was drawne to this attempt.

Enter Protaldye.

Thierry [*aside*].   *Protaldye?*
He had a gardners fate i'le sweare fell by thy hand;——
Sir, we do owe unto you for this service.
Brunhalt.   Why lookest thou so dejected?
Protaldye.   I want a little shift Lady, nothing else.   190

Enter Martell [*attended*].

Martell.   The fires are ready; please it your grace withdraw,
Whilst we performe your pleasure.
Thierry.   Reserve them for the body;
Since he had the fate to live and die a Prince,
He shall not lose the title in his funerall.   *Exit.*
Martell.   His fate to live a Prince?——
Thou old impiety, made up by lust and mischiefe.——[*Aside.*]
Take up the body.

Exeunt with the body of Theodoret.

Enter Lecure [*disguised*], *and a* Servant.   [III. iii

Lecure.   Doest thinke *Lefortes* sure enough?
Servant.   As bonds can make him, I have turn'd his eyes to the
east, and left him gaping after the morning starre; his head is a
meere Astrolobe, his eyes stand for the poles; the gag in his mouth
being the coachman, his five teeth have the neerest resemblance to
Charles Waine.
Lecure.   Thou hast cast a figure which shall raise thee; direct my
haire a little, and in my likenes to him reade a fortune suiting thy
largest hopes.
Servant.   You are so far 'bove likenesse you are the same: if you   10
love mirth, perswade him from himselfe; 'tis but an Astronomer
out of the way, and lying will beare the better place for't.

190.1 *Enter* Martell.] Weber; *following line* 189 Q1–2, F2
422

Lecure.   I have profitabler use in hand; hast to the Queene, and
tell her how you left me chang'd.   *Exit* Servant.
Who would not serve this vertuous active Queene?
She that loves mischiefe 'bove the man that does it,
And him above her pleasure, yet knowes no heaven else.

Enter Thierry.

Thierry [aside].   How well this loanes suits the art I seeke,
Discovering secret and succeeding fate,
Knowledge that puts all lower happines on,   20
With a remisse and carelesse hand,——
Faire peace unto your meditations father.
Lecure.   The same to you, you bring Sir.
Thierry.   Drawne by your much fam'd skill, I come to know
Whether the man who owes this character,
Shall ere have issue.   *[Gives scroll.]*
Lecure.   A resolution falling with most ease
Of any doubt you could have named, he is a Prince
Whose fortune you enquire.
Thierry.   He is nobly borne.
Lecure.   He had a dukedome lately falne unto him   30
By one call'd brother, who has left a daughter.
Thierry.   The question is of heires, not lands.
Lecure.   Heires? yes
He shall have heires.
Thierry.   Begotten of his body?
Why look'st thou pale? Thou canst not suffer in
His want.
Lecure.   Nor thou, I neither can nor will
Give farther knowledge to thee.
Thierry.   Thou must, I am the man my selfe,
Thy soveraigne, who must owe unto thy wisedome
In the concealing of my barren shame.
Lecure.   Your grace doth wrong your stars; if this be yours,   40
You may have children.
Thierry.   Speake it againe.

18 loanes] i.e. loneness   23 you, you] *i.e.* you that you

423

Lecure.   You may have fruitefull issue.
Thierry.   By whom? when? how?
Lecure.   It was the fatall meanes first strooke my bloud
With the cold hand of wonder, when I read it,
Printed upon your birth.
Thierry.   Can there be any
Way unsmooth, has end so faire and good?
Lecure.   We that behold the sad aspects of heaven,
Leading sence blinded men, feele griefe enough
To know, though not to speake their miseries.   50
Thierry.   Sorrow must lose a name, where mine finds life;
If not in thee, at least ease paine with speede,
Which must know no cure else.
Lecure.   Then thus,
The first of femalls which your eye shall meete
Before the sun next rise, comming from out
The Temple of *Diana*, being slaine,
You live father of many sonnes.
Thierry.   Callst thou this sadnes? can I beget a son
Deserving lesse then to give recompence   60
Unto so poore a losse? what eare thou art,
Rest peaceable blest creature, borne to be
Mother of Princes, whose grave shall be more fruitefull
                                        [*Exit* Lecure.]
Then others marriage beds: me thinkes his art
Should give her forme and happy figure to me,
I long to see my happines; he is gone:
As I remember he named my brothers daughter;
Were it my mother, 'twere a gainfull death
Could give *Ordellas* virtue living breath.

                                        Exit.

69.1 *Exit*] Colman; *Exeunt* Q 1–2, F 2

Enter Thierry, *and* Martell.   IV. i

Martell.   Your grace is early stirring.
Thierry.   How can he sleepe,
Whose happinesse is lay'd up in an houre,
Hee knowes comes stealing toward him? o *Martell!*
I'st possible the longing bride, whose wishes
Outrunne her feares, can on that day she is married
Consume in slumbers, or his armes rust in ease,
That heares the charge, and sees the honor'd purchase
Ready to gild his valor? Mine is more
A power above these passions; this day *France,*
(*France* that in want of issue withers with us;   10
And like an aged river runnes his head
Into forgotten wayes,) againe I ransome,
And his faire course turne right: this day, *Thierry,*
The son of *France,* whose manly powers like prisoners
Have bin tyed up, and fetter'd, by one death
Gives life to thousand ages; this day beauty
The envy of the world, pleasure the glory,
Content above the world, desire beyond it
Are made mine owne and usefull.
Martell.   Happy woman
That dies to do these things.
Thierry.   But ten times happier   20
That lives to do the greater; o *Martell,*
The gods have hard me now, and those that scorn'd me,
Mothers of many children, and blest fathers
That see their issues like the stars unnumber'd,
(Their comfort more then them,) shall in my prayses
Now teach their infants songs; and tell their ages
From such a son of mine, or such a queene,
That chast *Ordella* brings me: blessed marriage,
The chaine that linkes two holy loves together,

0.1 IV.i] *Act.* 4. *Scœ.* 1. Q1
*5 Outrunne] Langbaine; Outrunnes Q1–2, F2
16 Gives] Langbaine; Give Q1–2, F2   22 hard] *i.e.* heard

And in thee marriage, more then blest *Ordella*,   30
That comes so ne're the sacrament it selfe,
The Preists doubt whether purer.
Martell.   Sir, year'lost.
Thierry.   I prithee let me be so.
Martell.   The day weares;
And those that have bin offering earely prayers,
Are now retiring homeward.
Thierry.   Stand and marke then.
Martell.   Is it the first must suffer?
Thierry.   The first woman.
Martell.   What hand shall do it Sir?
Thierry.   This hand *Martell*,
For who lesse dare presume to give the gods
An incense of this offering?
Martell.   Would I were she,
For such a way to die, and such a blessing   40
Can never crowne my parting.

Enter two men passing over.

Thierry.   What are those?
Martell.   Men, men Sir, men.
Thierry.   The plagues of men light on um,
They crosse my hopes like hares.

Enter a Priest [passing over].

                    Who's that?
Martell.   A Priest Sir.
Thierry.   Would he were gelt.
Martell.   May not these rascalls serve Sir,
Well hang'd and quarter'd?
Thierry.   No.
Martell.   Here comes a woman.

Enter Ordella, *vail'd.*

Thierry.   Stand and behold her then.
Martell.   I thinke a faire one.

426

Thierry.   Move not whilst I prepare her: may her peace
  (Like his whose innocence the gods are pleas'd with,
  And offering at their altars, gives his soule
  Far purer then those fires;) pull heaven upon her;   50
  You holy powers, no humane spot dwell in her;
  No love of any thing but you and goodnes
  Tie her to earth, feare be a stranger to her,
  And all weake bloods affections but thy hope
  Let her bequeath to women: heare me heaven,
  Give her a spirrit masculine, and noble,
  Fit for your selfes to aske, and mee to offer.
  O let her meete my blow, doate on her death;
  And as a wanton vine bowes to the pruner,
  That by his cutting off more may encrease,   60
  So let her fall to raise me fruite;——haile woman,
  The happiest, and the best (if thy dull wil
  Do not abuse thy fortune) *France* ere found yet.
Ordella.   She is more then dull Sir, lesse and worse then woman,
  That may inherit such an infinite
  As you propound, a greatnesse so neare goodnesse,
  And brings a will to rob her.
Thierry.   Tell me this then,
  Was there ere woman yet, or may be found,
  That for faire fame, unspotted memory,
  For vertues sake, and only for it selfe sake   70
  Has, or dare make a story?
Ordella.   Many dead Sir,
  Living I thinke as many.
Thierry.   Say, the kingdome
  May from a womans will receive a blessing,
  The king and kingdome, not a private safety,
  A generall blessing Lady?
Ordella.   A generall curse
  Light on her hart denies it.
Thierry.   Full of honor;
  And such examples as the former ages
  Were but dim shadowes of, and empty figures.

Ordella.   You strangely stir me Sir, and were my weaknes
In any other flesh but modest womans,   80
You should not aske more questions, may I do it?
Thierry.   You may, and which is more, you must.
Ordella.   I joy in't,
Above a moderate gladnesse; Sir, you promise
It shall be honest?
Thierry.   As ever time discover'd.
Ordella.   Let it be what it may then, what it dare,
I have a mind will hazarde it.
Thierry.   But harke yee,
What may that woman merit, makes this blessing?
Ordella.   Only her duty Sir.
Thierry.   'Tis terrible.
Ordella.   'Tis so much the more noble.
Thierry.   'Tis full of fearefull shaddowes.
Ordella.   So is sleepe Sir,   90
Or any thing that's meerely ours and mortall,
We were begotten gods else; but those feares
Feeling but once the fires of nobler thoughts,
Fly, like the shapes of clouds we forme, to nothing.
Thierry.   Suppose it death.
Ordella.   I do.
Thierry.   And endlesse parting
With all we can call ours, with all our sweetenes,
With youth, strength, pleasure, people, time, nay reason:
For in the silent grave, no conversation,
No joyfull tread of friends, no voyce of lovers,
No careful fathers counsell, nothing's hard,   100
Nor nothing is, but all oblivion,
Dust, and an endlesse darknesse; and dare you woman
Desire this place?
Ordella.   'Tis of all sleepes the sweetest,
Children begin it to us, strong men seeke it,
And, kings from heigth of all their painted glories

96 with all] Q1(c); withall Q1(u)
100 hard] *i.e.* heard

428

Fall, like spent exhalations, to this center;
And those are fooles that feare it, or imagine
A few unhandsome pleasures, or lifes profits
Can recompence this place; and mad that staies it,
Till age blow out their lights, or rotten humors   110
Bring um despers'd to the earth.
Thierry.   Then you can suffer?
Ordella.   As willingly as say it.
Thierry.   *Martell*, a wonder,
Here is a woman that dares die,——yet tel me,
Are you a wife?
Ordella.   I am Sir.
Thierry.   And have children?——
She sighes, and weepes.
Ordella.   O none Sir.
Thierry.   Dare you venter,
For a poore barren praise you ne're shall heare,
To part with these sweete hopes?
Ordella.   With all but heaven,
And yet die ful of children; he that reades me
When I am ashes, is my son in wishes,
And those chast dames that keepe my memory,   120
Singing my yearely requiems, are my daughters.
Thierry.   Then there is nothing wanting but my knowledge;
And what I must do Lady.
Ordella.   You are the king Sir,
And what you do i'le suffer, and that blessing
That you desire the gods showre on the kingdome.
Thierry.   Thus much before I strike then, for I must kill you,
The gods have will'd it so; thou'rt made the blessing
Must make *France* young agen, and me a man:
Keepe up your strength still nobly.
Ordella.   Feare me not.
Thierry.   And meete death like a measure.
Ordella.   I am stedfast.   130
Thierry.   Thou shalt be sainted woman, and thy tombe

127 thou'rt] Seward; they'r Q 1-2, F 2

429

Cut out in Cristall, pure and good as thou art;
And on it shall be graven every age,
Succeeding peeres of *France* that rise by thy fall,
Tell thou liest there like old and fruitefull nature.
Darest thou behold thy happinesse?

Ordella.   I dare Sir.

Thierry.   Ha?   *Pulls off her vaile, lets fall his sword.*

Martell.   O Sir, you must not do it.

Thierry.   No, I dare not,
There is an Angell keepes that paradice,
A fiery angell, friend; o vertue, vertue,   140
Ever and endlesse vertue.

Ordella.   Strike Sir, strike;   [*Kneels.*]
And if in my poore death faire *France* may merit,
Give me a thousand blowes, be killing me
A thousand dayes.

Thierry.   First let the earth be barren,
And man no more remembred; rise *Ordella*,   [*She rises.*]
The nearest to thy maker, and the purest
That ever dull flesh shewed us,——o my hart-strings.   *Exit.*

Martell.   I see you full of wonder, therefore noblest
And truest amongst women, I will tell you
The end of this strange accident.

Ordella.   Amazement   150
Has so much won upon my hart, that truely
I feele my selfe unfit to heare; o Sir,
My Lord has slighted me.

Martell.   O no sweete Lady.

Ordella.   Robd me of such a glory by his pitty
And most unprovident respect——

Martell.   Deare Lady,
It was not meant to you.

Ordella.   Else where the day is,
And houres distinguish time, time runnes to ages,
And ages end the world, I had bin spoken.

135 Tell] *i.e.* till
151 won] Colman; woue Q1; wove Q2, F2

Martell.   I'le tell you what it was, if but your patience
Will give me hearing.

Ordella.   If I have transgrest,   160
Forgive me Sir.

Martell.   Your noble Lord was counsell'd,
(Grieving the barrennesse betweene you both,
And all the kingdome with him,) to seeke out
A man that knew the secrets of the gods:
He went, found such a one, and had this answere,
That if he woo'd have issue, on this morning
(For this houre was prefixt him,) he should kill
The first he met being female, from the Temple;
And then he should have children. The mistake
Is now to perfect Lady.

Ordella.   Still 'tis I Sir,   170
For may this worke be done by common women?
Durst any but my selfe, that knew the blessing
And felt the benefit, assume this dying?
In any other, t'ad bin lost, and nothing,
A curse, and not a blessing; I was figur'd;
And shall a little fondnesse barre my purchase?

Martell.   Where should he then seeke children?

Ordella.   Where they are:
In wombes ordainde for issues, in those beauties
That blesse a marriage bed, and makes it proceede
With kisses that conceive, and fruitefull pleasures;   180
Mine like a grave, buries those loyall hopes,
And to a grave it covets.

Martell.   You are too good,
Too excellent, too honest; robbe not us
And those that shall hereafter seeke example,
Of such inestimable worthines in woman,
Your Lord of such obedience, all of honor,
In coveting a cruelty is not yours,
A will short of your wisedome; make not error

---

159 *Martell.*] Langbaine; *Deui.* Q1–2, F2   170 to] *i.e.* too
*179 proceede] *stet* Q1   *185 worthines] worthies Q1–2, F2

431

A tombestone of your vertues, whose faire life
Deserves a constellation: your Lord dare not,   190
He cannot, ought not, must not run this hazard,
He makes a separation nature shakes at,
The gods deny, and everlasting justice
Shrinkes backe and sheathes her sword at.

Ordella.   All's but talke Sir,
I find to what I am reserv'd, and needefull,
And though my Lords compassion makes me poore
And leaves me in my best use, yet a strength
Above mine owne, or his dull fondnesse, finds mee;
The gods have given it to me.   *Drawes a knife.*

Martell.   Selfe destruction?
Now all good angells blesse thee, o sweete Lady   200
You are abus'd, this is a way to shame you,
And with you al that knowes you, al that loves you,
To ruine all you build; would you be famous,
Is that your end?

Ordella.   I would be what I should be.

Martell.   Live, and confirme the gods then, live and be loaden
With more then olives beare, or fruitefull Autum;
This way you kill your merit, kill your cause,
And him you would raise life to; where, or how
Got you these bloody thoughts? what divell durst
Looke on that Angell face, and tempt? do you know   210
What 'tis to die thus, how you strike the stars,
And all good things above? do you feele
What followes a selfe blood, whither you venter,
And to what punishment? excellent Lady,
Be not thus cozen'd, do not foole your selfe,
The priest was never his owne sacrifice,
But he that thought his hell here.

Ordella.   I am counsell'd.

Martell.   And I am glad on't, lie I know you dare not.

Ordella.   I never have done yet.

Martell.   Pray take my comfort,——
Was this a soule to lose? two more such women   220

432

Would save their sex; see, she repents and prayes,
O heare her, heare her, if there be a faith
Able to reach your mercies, she hath sent it.
Ordella.   Now good *Martell* confirme me.
Martell.   I will Lady,
And every houre advise you, for I doubt
Whether this plot be heavens, or hells your mother;
And I will find it, if it be in mankind
To search the center of it: in the meane time
I'le give you out for dead, and by your selfe,
And shew the instrument; so shall I find   230
A joy that will betray her.
Ordella.   Do what's fittest;
And I will follow you.
Martell.   Then ever live
Both able to ingrosse all love, and give.

                                                        Exeunt.

                    Enter Brunhalt, Protaldye.   [IV. ii]

Brunhalt.   I am in labour
To be deliverde of that burthenous project
I have so long gone with;

                         Enter Lecure.

                    ha? here's the mid-wife,——
Or life, or death?
Lecure.   If in the supposition
Of her death in whose life you die, you aske me,
I thinke you are safe.
Brunhalt.   Is she dead?
Lecure.   I have usde
All meanes to make her so, I saw him waiting
At the Temple doore, and usde such art within,
That only she of all her sexe, was first
Given up unto his fury.

228 hells ˄...mother;] Colman (~ ˄...~ !); ~;...~ ˄ Q1–2, F2
3 *Enter* Lecure.] Dyce (*following* mid-wife, *line* 3); *following* death, *line* 4 Q1–2, F2

Brunhalt.   Which if love   10
Or feare made him forbeare to execute
The vengeance he determine, his fond pitty
Shall draw it on himselfe: for were there left
Not any man but he to serve my pleasures,
Or from me to receive commands, (which are
The joyes for which I love life;) he should be
Removde, and I alone left to be Queene
O're any part of goodnesse that's left in me.
Lecure.   If you are so resolvde, I have provided
A meanes to ship him hence: looke upon this,   20

                     [Shewing a handkerchief.]

But touch it sparingly, for this once usde,
Say but to drie a teare, will keepe the eyelidde
From closing, untill death performe that office.
Brunhalt.   Give't me, I may have use of't, and on you
I'le make the first experiment if one sigh
Or heavy looke beget the least suspition,
Childish compassion can thaw the ice
Of your so long congealde and flinty hardnesse.
Slight, go on constant, or I shall.
Protaldye.   Best Lady,
We have no faculties which are not yours.
Lecure.   Nor will be any thing without you.   30
Brunhalt.   Be so,
And we will stand or fall together, for
Since we have gone so far, that death must stay
The journey which we wish should never end,
And innocent, or guilty we must die,
When we do so, let's know the reason why.

            Enter Thierry, *and Courtiers.*

Lecure.   The King.
Thierry.   We'le be alone.   *[Exeunt Courtiers.]*
Protaldye.   I would I had
A convoy too, to bring me safe off,
For rage although it be allaide with sorrow,

Appeares so dreadfull in him, that I shake   40
  To looke upon it.
Brunhalt.   Coward, I will meete it
And know from whence t'as birth:——sonne, kingly *Thierry*.
Thierry.   Is cheating growne so common among men,
  And thrives so well heere, that the gods endeavour
  To practice it above?
Brunhalt.   Your mother.
Thierry.   Ha!——
  Or are they only carefull to revenge,
  Not to reward? or when for our offences
  We study satisfaction, must the cure
  Be worse then the disease?
Brunhalt.   Will you not heare me?
Thierry.   To lose th'ability to performe those duties   50
  For which I entertainde the name of husband,
  Askde more then common sorrow; but t'impose
  For the redresse of that defect, a torture
  In marking her to death, for whom alone
  I felt that weakenesse as a want, requires
  More then the making the head bald, or falling
                    [*Teares his hair and falls.*]
  Thus flat upon the earth, or cursing that way,
  Or praying this: oh such a sceane of griefe,
  And so set downe, (the world the stage to act on)
  May challenge a Tragedian better practisde   60
  Then I am to expresse it; for my cause
  Of passion is so strong, and my performance
  So weake, that though the part be good, I feare
  Th'ill acting of it, will defraude it of
  The poore reward it may deserve, mens pitty.
Brunhalt.   I have given you way thus long: a King, and what
  Is more, my sonne, and yet a slave to that
  Which only triumphs over cowards, sorrow?
  For shame looke up.
Thierry.   I'st you? looke downe on me;

And if that you are capable to receive it,   70
Let that returne to you, that have brought forth
One markde out only for it: what are these?
Come they upon your priveledge, to tread on
The tombe of my afflictions?
Protaldye.   No not we Sir.
Thierry.   How dare you then omit the ceremony
Due to the funerall of all my hopes,
Or come unto the marriage of my sorrowes,
But in such colours as may sort with them?
Protaldye.   Alas, we will weare any thing.
Brunhalt.   This is madnesse,
Take but my counsell.
Thierry.   Yours? dare you againe   80
Though armde with the authority of a mother,
Attempt the danger, that will fall on you
If such another sillable awake it?
Go, and with yours be safe; I have such cause
Of griefe, (nay more, to love it,) that I will not
Have such as these be sharers in it.
Lecure.   Madam——   [*Apart.*]
Protaldye.   Another time were better.
Brunhalt.   Doe not stir,
For I must be resolvde and will, be statues.

Enter Martell.

Thierry.   I, thou art welcome, and upon my soule
Thou art an honest man;——do you see? he has teares   90
To lend to him whom prodigall expence
Of sorrow has made bankerout of such treasure,——
Nay thou doest well.
Martell.   I would it might excuse
The ill I bring along.
Thierry.   Thou makest me smile
In the height of my calamities, as if
There could be the addition of an Atome
To the gyant body of my miseries.

436

But try, for I will heare thee;——all sit downe, 'tis death
To any that shall dare to interrupt him
In looke, gesture, or word.

Martell.   And such attention   100
As is due to the last, and the best story
That ever was deliverde, will become you.
The grievde *Ordella*, (for all other titles
But take away from that) having from me,
Prompted by your last parting grone, enquirde
What drew it from you, and the cause soone learn'd:
(For she whom barbarisme could deny nothing,
With such prevailing earnestnesse desirde it,
'Twas not in me though it had bin my death,
To hide it from her;) she I say, in whom   110
All was, that *Athens*, *Rome*, or warlike *Sparta*,
Have registred for good in their best women,
But nothing of their ill, knowing herselfe
Markde out (I know not by what powre, but sure
A cruell one) to die, to give you children;
Having first with a setled countenance
Look'd up to heaven, and then upon her selfe
(It being the next best object) and then smilde,
As if her joy in death to do you service,
Would breake forth in despite of the much sorrow   120
She showde she had to leave you: and then taking
Me by the hand, (this hand which I must ever
Love better then I have done, since she touch'd it,)
Go, sayd she, to my Lord, (and to go to him
Is such a happinesse I must not hope for,)
And tell him that he too much prizde a trifle
Made only worthy in his love, and her
Thankfull acceptance, for her sake to robbe
The Orphan kingdome of such gardians, as
Must of necessity descend from him;   130
And therefore in some part of recompence
Of his much love, and to shew to the world
That 'twas not her fault only, but her fate,

437

That did deny to let her be the mother
Of such most certaine blessings; yet for proofe,
She did not envy her, that happy her,
That is appointed to them, her quicke end
Should make way for her: which no sooner spoke,
But in a moment this too ready engin   [*Shewes a dagger.*]
Made such a battery in the choicest castle   140
That ever nature made to defend life,
That straite it shooke, and sunke.
Thierry.   Stay, dares any
Presume to shed a teare before me? or
Ascribe that worth unto themselves to merit
To do so for her? I have done, now on.
Martell.   Falne thus, once more she smilde, as if that death
For her had studied a new way to sever
The soule and body, without sence of paine;
And then, tell him (quoth she) what you have seene,
And with what willingnesse 'twas done: for which   150
My last request unto him is, that he
Would instantly make choice of one (most happy
In being so chosen) to supply my place,
By whom if heaven blesse him with a daughter,
In my remembrance let it beare my name:
Which sayd she dide.
Thierry.   I heare this, and yet live,
Hart art thou thunder proofe, will nothing breake thee?
She's dead, and what her entertainement may be
In th'other world without me is uncertaine,
And dare I stay heere unresolvde?
                    [*Rises and drawes.* Martell *holds him.*]
Martell.   Oh Sir!   160
Brunhalt.   Deare son.   [*They rise.*]
Protaldye.   Great King.
Thierry.   Unhand me, am I falne
So low, that I have lost the powre to be
Disposer of my owne life?
Martell.   Be but pleasde

To borrow so much time of sorrow, as
To call to mind her last request, for whom
(I must confesse a losse beyond expression)
You turne your hand upon your selfe; 'twas hers,
And dying hers, that you should live and happy
In seeing little models of your selfe,
By matching with another, and will you   170
Leave any thing that she desirde ungranted?
And suffer such a life, that was layd downe
For your sake only, to be fruitelesse?
Thierry.   Oh
Thou doest throw charmes upon me, against which
I cannot stop my eares;——beare witnesse heaven
That not desire of life, nor love of pleasures
Nor any future comforts, but to give
Peace to her blessed spirit in satisfying
Her last demand, makes me defer our meeting,
Which in my choice, and suddaine choice shall be   180
To all apparant.
Brunhalt [aside]. How? do I remove one mischiefe
To draw upon my head a greater?
Thierry.   Go,
Thou only good man, to whom for her selfe
Goodnesse is deare, and prepare to interre it
In her that was (o my hart!) my *Ordella*,
A monument worthy to be the casket
Of such a jewell.
Martell.   Your command that makes way
Unto my absence is a welcome one,
For but your selfe there's nothing here *Martell*
Can take delight to looke on; yet some comfort   190
Goes backe with me, to her, who though she want it,
Deserves all blessings.   *Exit.*
Brunhalt.   So soone to forget
The losse of such a wife, beleeve it, will
Be censurde in the world.
Thierry.   Pray you no more,

439

There is no argument you can use to crosse it,
But does increase in me such a suspition
I would not cherish,——who's that?

Enter Memberge.

Memberge. One, no guarde
Can put backe from accesse, whose tongue no threats
Nor praiers can silence, a bould suitor and
For that which if you are your selfe, a King, 200
You were made so to grant it: Justice, Justice.
Thierry. With what assurance dare you hope for that
Which is denide to me? or how can I
Stand bound to be just, unto such as are
Beneath me, that find none from those that are
Above me?
Memberge. Their is justice; 'twere unfit
That any thing but vengeance should fall on him,
That by his giving way to more then murther,
(For my deare fathers death was parricide)
Makes it his owne.
Brunhalt. I charge you heare her not. 210
Memberge. Hell cannot stoppe just prayers from entring heaven,
I must and will be heard, Sir; but remember
That he that by her plot fell, was your brother,
And the place where, your pallace, against all
Th'inviolable rites of hospitality,
Your word, a kings word, given up for his safety,
His innocence, his protection, and the gods
Bound to revenge the impious breach of such
So great and sacred bonds; and can you wonder,
(That in not punishing such a horrid murther, 220
You did it) that heavens favour is gone from you?
Which never will returne untill his bloud
Be washde away in hers.
Brunhalt. Drag hence the wretch.
[*They offer to seize her.*]
Thierry. Forbeare:——with what variety

440

Of torments do I meete? oh thou hast opende
A booke in which writ downe in bloudy letters,
My conscience finds that I am worthy of
More then I undergo, but i'le begin
For my *Ordellas* sake, and for thine owne,
To make lesse heavens great anger: thou hast lost   230
A father, I to thee am so; the hope
Of a good husband, in mee have one; nor
Be fearefull I am still no man, already
That weakenesse is gone from me.
Brunhalt (aside).   That it might
Have ever growne inseparably upon thee,——
What will you do? is such a thing as this
Worthy the lov'd *Ordellas* place? the daughter
Of a poore gardiner?
Memberge.   Your sonne!
Thierry.   The powre
To take away that lownesse is in me.
Brunhalt.   Stay yet, for rather then that thou shalt adde   240
Incest unto thy other sins, I will
With hazard of my owne life utter all.
Theodoret was thy brother.
Thierry.   You denide it
Upon your oth, nor will I now beleeve you,
Your Protean turnings cannot change my purpose.
Memberge.   And for me, be assurde the meanes to be
Reveng'd on thee vile hag, admitts no thought,
But what tends to it.   [*Exit.*]
Brunhalt [*aside*].   Is it come to that?
Then have at the last refuge;——art thou growne
Insensible in ill, that thou goest on   250
Without the least compunction? there, take that
                              [*Gives him the handkerchief.*]
To witnesse that thou hadst a mother, which
Foresaw thy cause of griefe, and sad repentance,
That so soone after blest *Ordellas* death

247 Reveng'd] F2; Revenge Q1–2

Without a teare thou canst embrace another,
Forgetfull man.
Thierry.   Mine eyes when she is namde
Cannot forget their tribute, and your guift
Is not unuseful now.   [*Wipes his eyes.*]
Lecure [*aside*].   He's past all cure,
That only touch is death.
Thierry.   This night i'le keepe it,
To morrow I will send it you, and full   260
Of my affliction.   *Exit* Thierry.
Brunhalt.   Is the poyson mortall?
Lecure.   Above the helpe of phisicke.
Brunhalt.   To my wish.
Now for our owne security, you *Protaldye*
Shall this night post towards *Austrachia*,
With letters to *Theodorets* bastard sonne,
In which we will make knowne what for his rising
We have done to *Thierry*: no deniall,
Nor no excuse in such acts must be thought of,
Which all dislike, and all againe commend,
When they are brought unto a happy end.   270
                              Exeunt.

Enter Devitry, *and four* Souldiers.   V. i

Devitry.   No war, no mony, no master; banisht the Court, not trusted in the citty, whipt out of the country, in what a triangle runnes our misery: let me heare which of you has the best voice to beg in, for other hopes or fortunes I see you have not; bee not nice, nature provided you with tonges for the purpose, the peoples charity was your heritage, and I would see which of you deserves his birth-right.
Omnes.   We understand you not Captaine.
Devitry.   You see this cardicue, the last and the only quintessence of fifty crownes, distill'd in the lembicke of your gardage, of which 10
happy piece thou shalt be treasorer [*gives it to* First Souldier]:

now hee that can soonest perswade him to part with't, enjoyes it,
possesses it, and with it, mee and my future countenance.
1. Souldier.   If they want art to perswade it, ile keepe it my selfe.
Devitry.   So you be not a partiall judge in your owne cause, you
shall.
Omnes.   A match.
2. Souldier.   I'le begin to you; brave Sir, bee proud to make him
happy by your liberality, whose tongue vouchsafes now to petition
was never heard before lesse then to command: I am a souldier by 20
profession, a gentleman by birth, and an officer by place, whose
poverty blushes to be the cause that so high a vertue should
descend to the pitty of your charity.
1. Souldier.   In any case keepe your high stile; it is not charity to
shame any man, much lesse a vertue of your eminence, wherefore
preserve your worth, and i'le preserve my mony.
3. Souldier.   You perswade? you are shallow, give way to merit,
——ah by the bread of god man, thou hast a bonny countenance
and a blith, promising mickle good to a sicker wombe, that has
trod a long and a soare ground to meete with friends that wil owe 30
much to thy reverence, when they shall heare a thy courtesie to
their wandring countriman.
1. Souldier.   You that will use your friends so hardly to bring
them in debt Sir, will deserve worse of a strainger, wherefore
pead on, pead on I say.
4. Souldier.   It is the welch must doo't I see,——comrade man of
urship, *St. Tavy* bee her patron, the gods of the mountaines keepe
her cow and her cupboord, may shee never want the greene of the
leeke, nor the fat of the onion, if she part with her bounties to him
that is a great deale away from her cozines, and has too big suites 40
in law to recover her heritage.
1. Souldier.   Pardon me Sir, I will have nothing to do with your
suites, it comes within the statute of maintenance: home to your
cozines and sowe garlicke and hempeseede, the one will stop your

12 part] Q1(c); *om.* Q1(u)
28 of god] Colman; of good Q1–2; of a good F2
35 on, pead] Q2; one, pead Q1 (|)   40 cozines] *i.e.* cousins

hunger, the other end your suites. *Gammawash* comrade, *gamma-wash*.

4. Souldier. Foote, he'le hoord all for himselfe.

Vitry. Yes, let him; now comes my turne. I'le see if hee can answere me:——save you Sir, they say you have that I want, mony.   50

1. Souldier. And that you are like to want, for ought I perceave yet.

Vitry. Stand, deliver.

1. Souldier. Foote, what meane you, you will not robbe the Excheckor?

Vitry. Do you prate?   [*Threatens him.*]

1. Souldier. Hold, hold, here captaine.   [*Gives the cardicue.*]

2. Souldier. Why I could have done this before you.

3. Souldier. And I.

4. Souldier. And I.   60

Vitry. You have done this? brave man be proud to make him happy; by the bread of god man thou hast a bonny countenance; comrade man of urship, *St. Tavy* be her patron. Out upon you, you uncurried colts, walking cans that have no soules in you, but a little rosin, to keepe your ribs sweete, and hold in liquor.

Omnes. Why, what would you have us to do Captaine?

Devitry. Beg, beg, and keepe Constables waking, weare out stockes and whipcord, mander for butter milke, die of the jandize, yet have the cure about you, lice, large lice, begot of your owne dust, and the heate of the bricke-kills; may you starve, and feare 70 of the gallowes (which is a gentle consumption too't,) only preferre it; or may you fall upon your feare, and bee hanged for selling those purses to keepe you from famine whose monies my valour empties, and bee cast without other evidence: here is my fort, my castle of defence, who comes by shall pay me tolle, the first purse is your mittimus slaves.

2. Souldier. The purse! foote, we'le share in the mony Captaine, if any come within a furlong of our fingers.

4. Souldier. Did you doubt but wee could steale as well as your selfe? did not I speake welch?   80

68 mander] *i.e.* maunder   *72 preferre] *stet* Q 1

444

3. Souldier.   We are theeves from our cradells, and will die so.

Vitry.   Then you will not beg againe?

Omnes.   Yes, as you did: stand, and deliver.

2. Souldier.   Harke, here comes handsell, 'tis a trade quickly set up, and as soone cast downe.

Devitry.   Have goodnesse in your minds varlets, and too't like men; he that has more mony then we, cannot be our friend, and I hope there is no law for spoyling the enemy.

3. Souldier.   You need not instruct us farther, your example pleads enough.   90

Devitry.   Disperse your selves, and as their company is, fall on.

2. Souldier.   Come there a band of em, i'le charge single.

       Exeunt Souldiers. [Devitry *withdrawes.*]

      Enter Protaldye.

Protaldye.   'Tis wonderfull darke, I have lost my man, and dare not call for him, lest I should have more followers then I would pay wages too; what throws am I in, in this travaile? these bee honorable adventures; had I that honest blood in my veines againe Queene, that your feates and these frights have draind from me, honor should pull hard ere it drew mee into these brakes.

Devitry.   Who goes there?

Protaldye [*aside*].   Hey ho, here's a pang of preferment.   100

Devitry.   Hart, who goes there?

Protaldye [*aside*].   He that has no hart to your acquaintance, what shall I do with my jewells, and my letters? my cod-peece, that's to loose, good, my boots,——who ist that spoke to me? here's a friend.

Devitry.   We shal find that presently; stand, as you love safety stand.

Protaldye.   That unlucky word of standing, has brought mee to all this,——hold or I shall never stand you.

Devitry [*aside*].   I should know that voice,——deliver.   110

      Enter Souldiers.

  92 Come...a] Dyce (Mason); Come, there are a Q1–2, F2
  103 letters] Dyce; letter Q1–2, F2

Protaldye.   All that I have is at your service gentlemen, and much good may it do you.

Devitry.   Zones, downe with him,——do you prate?

Protaldye.   Keepe your first word as you are gentlemen, and let me stand, alas what do you meane?

2. Souldier.   To tie you to us Sir, bind you in the knot of friend- ship.   [*They bind him.*]

Protaldye.   Alas Sir, all the physicke in *Europe* cannot bind me.

Devitry.   You shold have jewels about you, stones, precious stones.   120

1. Souldier.   Captaine away, there's company within hearing, if you stay longer we are surpris'd.

Devitry.   Let the divell come, i'le pillage this frigot a little better yet.

2. Souldier.   Foote, we are lost, they are upon us.

Devitry.   Ha, upon us?——make the least noyse, 'tis thy parting gaspe.

3. Souldier.   Which way shall we make Sir?

Devitry.   Every man his owne;——[*apart to* Souldiers] do you heare, only bind mee before you go, and when the companie's 130 past, make to this place againe, this karvell should have better lading in him: you are slow, why do you not tie harder?

                                        [*They bind* Devitry.]

1. Souldier.   You are sure enough I warrant you Sir.

Devitry.   Darknesse befriend you, away.   *Exeunt* Souldiers.

Protaldye.   What Tyrants have I met with? they leave mee alone in the darke, yet would not have me cry. I shall grow wondrous melancholy if I stay long here without company; I was wont to get a nap with saying my prayers, i'le see if they will worke upon me now; but then if I should talke in my sleepe, and they heare me, they would make a recorder of my windpipe, slit my throate: 140 heaven be prais'd, I heare some noyse, it may bee new purchase, and then I shall have fellows.

Devitry [*aside*].   They are gone past hearing, now to taske *Devitry*, ——helpe, helpe, as you are men helpe, some charitable hand,

releeve a poore distressed miserable wretch; theeves, wicked
theeves have rob'd me, bound me.

Protaldye. Foote, would they had gag'd you too, your noyse will
betray us, and fetch em againe.

Devitry. What blessed tongue spake to mee? where, where are
you Sir?   150

Protaldye. A plague of your bawling throate, we are well enough,
if you have the grace to be thankefull for't; do but snore to mee,
and 'tis as much as I desire, to passe away time with till morning,
then talke as loude as you please Sir; I am bound not to stirre,
wherefore lie still and snore I say.

Devitry. Then you have met with theeves too I see?

Protaldye. And desire to meete with no more of em.

Devitry. Alas what can we suffer more? they are far enough by
this time; have they not all, all that we have Sir?

Protaldye. No by my faith have they not Sir, I gave em one tricke   160
to boote, for their learning: my bootes Sir, my bootes; I have
sav'd my stocke, and my jewells in them, and therefore desire to
heare no more of them.

Devitry. Now blessing on your wit Sir, what a dull slave was I,
dreampt not of your conveiance? helpe to unbind me Sir, and i'le
undo you; my life for yours no worse theefe then my selfe meetes
you againe this night.

Protaldye. Reach me thy hands.

Devitry. Here Sir, here, [*Protaldye unbinds him*] I could beate
my braines out, that could not thinke of bootes, bootes Sir, wide   170
top bootes, I shall love em the better whilst I live; but are you sure
your jewells are here Sir?

Protaldye. Sure saist thou? ha, ha, ha.

Devitry. So ho, illo ho.

Souldiers (within). Here Captaine, here.

Protaldye. Foote, what do you meane Sir?

Enter Souldiers.

Devitry. A tricke to boote, say you; [*takes jewells from* Protaldyes
bootes] heere you dull slaves, purchase, purchase, the soule of the
rocke, diamonds, sparkling diamonds.

Protaldye [*aside*].   I am betraide, lost, past recovery lost.——As 180
you are men——

Devitry.   Nay Rooke, since you will be prating, we'le share your
carion with you; have you any other conveiance now Sir?

1. Souldier. [*Takes letters from bootes.*]   Foote, here are letters,
epistles, familiar epistles; we'le see what treasure is in them, they
are seal'd sure.

Protaldye.   Gentlemen, as you are gentlemen spare my letters, and
take all willingly, all: ile give you a release, a generall release, and
meete you here to morrow with as much more.

Devitry.   Nay, since you have your trickes, and your conveiances, 190
we will not leave a wrinckle of you unsearcht.

Protaldye.   Harke, there comes company, you will be betraide; as
you love your safeties beate out my braines, I shall betray you
else.   [*Devitry reades letters*].

Devitry.   Treason, unheard of treason, monstrous, monstrous
villanies.

Protaldye.   I confesse my selfe a traytor, shew your selves good
subjects, and hang me up for't.

1. Souldier.   If it be treason, the discovery will get our pardon
Captaine.   200

Devitry.   Would we were all lost, hang'd, quarter'd, to save this
one, one innocent prince; *Thierry*'s poyson'd, by his mother
poyson'd, the Mistris to this stallion, who by that poyson ne're
shall sleepe againe.

2. Souldier.   Foote, let us mince him by piecemeale, tell he eate
himselfe uppe.

3. Souldier.   Let us dig out his heart with needles, and halfe broile
him, like a mussell.

Protaldye.   Such another and I prevent you, my blood's setled
already.   210

Devitry.   Here's that shall remove it, toade, viper;——drag
him unto *Martell*,——unnaturall parricide, cruell, bloody
woman.

Omnes.   On you dogfish, leech, caterpiller.

Devitry.   A longer sight of him will make my rage turne pitty, and
with his suddaine end prevent revenge, and torture,——wicked,
wicked *Brunhalt.*

Exeunt.

Enter Bawdber, *and three* Courtiers.   [V. ii]

1. Courtier.   Not sleepe at all, no meanes?

2. Courtier.   No art can do it?

Bawdber.   I will assure you he can sleepe no more
  Then a hooded hawke; a centinell to him,
  Or one of the citty Constables are tops.

3. Courtier.   How came he so?

Bawdber.   They are too wise that dare know:
  Somethings amisse, heaven helpe all.

1. Courtier.   What cures has he?

Bawdber.   Armies of those we call phisitians,
  Some with glisters, some with lettice caps,
  Some posset drinkes, some pills, twenty consulting here
  About a drench, as many here to blood him;   10
  Then comes a Don of *Spaine*, and he prescribes
  More cooling opium then would kill a turke,
  Or quench a whore ith dogdayes; after him
  A wise Italian, and he cries, tie unto him
  A woman of fourscore, whose bones are marble,
  Whose bloud snow water, not so much heate about her
  As may conceive a prayer: after him
  An English Doctor, with a bunch of pot hearbes;
  And he cries out, Endiffe and suckery,
  With a few mallow rootes and butter milke,   20
  And talkes of oyle made of a churchmans charity,
  Yet still he wakes.

1. Courtier.   But your good honor has a prayer in store
  If all should faile?

Bawdber.   I could have prayed, and handsomely,
  But age and an ill memory——

23 prayer] Q2; prayers Q1

449

3. Courtier.   Has spoyl'd your primmer.

Bawdber.   Yet if there be a man of faith i'the Court,
And can pray for a pension——

Enter Thierry, *on a bed, with* Doctors *and attendants.*

2. Courtier.   Here's the King Sir,
And those that will pray without pay.

Bawdber.   Then pray for me too.

1. Doctor.   How does your grace now feele your selfe?

Thierry.   What's that?

1. Doctor.   Nothing at all Sir, but your fancy.

Thierry.   Tell me,   30
Can ever these eyes more shut up in slumbers,
Assure my soule there is sleepe? is there night
And rest for humane labors? do not you
And all the world as I do, out stare time,
And live like funerall lampes never extinguisht?
Is there a grave, (and do not flatter me,
Nor feare to tell me truth;) and in that grave
Is there a hope I shall sleepe? can I die,
Are not my miseries immortall? o
The happinesse of him that drinkes his water   40
After his weary day, and sleepes for ever:
Why do you crucifie me thus with faces,
And gaping strangely upon one another?
When shall I rest?

2. Doctor.   O Sir, be patient.

Thierry.   Am I not patient? have I not endur'd
More then a maingy dog among your dosses?
Am I not now your patient? yee can make
Unholesome fooles sleepe for a garded foote-cloth;
Whores for a hot sin offering; yet I must crave
That feede ye, and protect ye, and proclame ye: 50
Because my powre is far above your searching,
Are my diseases so? can ye cure none
But those of equall ignorance? dare ye kill me?

1. Doctor.   We do beseech your grace be more recalm'd,
This talke doth but distemper you.
Thierry.   Well, I will die
In spight of all your potions; one of you sleepe,
Lie downe and sleepe here, that I may behold
What blessed rest it is my eyes are robde of: [*One lies downe.*]
See, he can sleepe, sleepe any where, sleepe now,
When he that wakes for him can never slumber;   60
I'st not a dainty ease?
2. Doctor.   Your grace shall feele it.
Thierry.   O never I, never; the eyes of heaven
See but their certaine motions, and then sleepe,
The rages of the *Ocean* have their slumbers,
And quiet silver calmes; each violence
Crownes in his end a peace, but my fixt fires
Shall never, never set,——who's that?

                Enter Martell, Brunhalt, Devitry, Souldiers.

Martell.   No, woman,
Mother of mischiefe, no, the day shall die first,
And all good things live in a worse then thou art,
Ere thou shalt sleepe, doest thou see him?   70
Brunhalt.   Yes, and curse him,
And all that love him, foole, and all live by him.
Martell.   Why art thou such a monster?
Brunhalt.   Why art thou
So tame a knave to aske me?
Martell.   Hope of hell,
By this faire holy light, and all his wrongs,
Which are above thy yeares, almost thy vices,
Thou shalt not rest, not feele more what is pitty,
Know nothing necessary, meete no society,
But what shall curse and crucifie thee, feele in thy selfe
Nothing but what thou art, bane and bad conscience,   80
Till this man rest; but for whose reverence
Because thou art his mother, I would say

*54 recalm'd] reclam'd Q1; reclaim'd Q2; *om.* F2

Whore, this shall be: do ye nod? ile waken ye
With my swords point.

Brunhalt.   I wish no more of heaven,
Nor hope no more, but a sufficient anger
To torture thee.

Martell.   See, she that makes you see Sir,
And to your misery still see, your mother,
The mother of your woes Sir, of your waking,
The mother of your peoples cries, and curses,
Your murdering mother, your malicious mother.   90

Thierry. Phisitians, halfe my state to sleepe an houre now;——
Is it so mother?

Brunhalt.   Yes it is so sonne;
And were it yet againe to do, it should be.

Martell. She nods againe, swing her.

Thierry.   But mother,
(For yet I love that reverence, and to death
Dare not forget you have bin so;) was this,
This endlesse misery, this curelesse malice,
This snatching from me all my youth together,
All that you made me for, and happy mothers
Crownde with eternall time are proud to finish,   100
Done by your will?

Brunhalt.   It was, and by that will——

Thierry. O mother, do not lose your name, forget not
The touch of nature in you, tendernes,
'Tis all the soule of woman, all the sweetenesse;
Forget not I beseech you what are children,
Nor how you have gron'd for um, to what love
They are borne inheritors, with what care kept,
And as they rise to ripenesse still remember
How they impe out your age; and when time calls you,
That as an Autum flower you fall, forget not   110
How round about your hearse they hang like penons.

Brunhalt. Holy foole,
Whose patience to prevent my wrongs has kill'd thee,

106 have] Q2; are Q1

Preach not to me of punishments, or feares,
Or what I ought to be, but what I am,
A woman in her liberall will defeated,
In all her greatnesse crost, in pleasure blasted;
My angers have bin laught at, my ends slighted,
And all those glories that had crownd my fortunes,
Suffer'd by blasted vertue to be scatter'd: 120
I am the fruitefull mother of these angers,
And what such have done, reade, and know thy ruine.
Thierry.   Heaven forgive you.
Martell.   She tells you true, for milions of her mischiefes
Are now apparent: *Protaldye*, we have taken,
An equall agent with her, to whose care
After the damnde defeate on you, she trusted

Enter Messenger.

The bringing in of *Leonor* the bastard
Sonne to your murder'd brother; her phisitian
By this time is attacht to, that dam'd divell.   130
Messenger.   'Tis like he will be so, for ere we came,
Fearing an equall justice for his mischiefes,
He drench't himselfe.
Brunhalt.   Hee did like one of mine then.
Thierry.   Must I still see these miseries? no night
To hide me from their horrors? that *Protaldye*
See justice fall upon.
Brunhalt.   Now I could sleepe too.
Martell.   Ile give you yet more poppy,——bring the Lady
And heaven in her embraces give him quiet;

Enter [one with] Ordella *[vailed]*.

Madam, unvaile your selfe.
Ordella.   I do forgive you,   [*Unvailes.*]
And though you sought my blood, yet ile pray for you.   140

130 to, that] Weber (Mason); ~ ‸ ~ Q1–2, F2 (to = too)
133 then] Q2; thine Q1
138.1 *Enter* Ordella.] Weber; *following line* 136 Q1–2, F2

Brunhalt.   Art thou alive?
Martell.   Now could you sleepe?
Brunhalt.   For ever.
Martell.   Go carry her without winke of sleepe, or quiet,
Where her strong knave *Protaldye's* broke oth wheele,
And let his cries and rores be musicke to her,
I meane to waken her.
Thierry.   Do her no wrong.
Martell.   No, right as you love justice.
Brunhalt.   I will thinke,
And if there be new curses in old nature,
I have a soule dare send um.
Martell.   Keepe her waking.

> *Exit* Brunhalt [*guarded*].

Thierry.   What's that appeares so sweetely there? that face——
Martell.   Be moderate Lady.
Thierry.   That angells face——
Martell.   Go nearer.   150
Thierry.   *Martell*, I cannot last long, see the soule,
(I see it perfectly) of my *Ordella*,
The heavenly figure of her sweetenes there:
Forgive me gods, it comes! divinest substance!
Kneele, kneele, kneele every one,——Saint of thy sexe,
If it be for my cruelty thou comest——
Do ye see her, hoe?
Martell.   Yes sir, and you shall know her.
Thierry.   Downe, downe againe,——to be reveng'd for blood,
Sweete spirit I am ready,——she smiles on me,
O blessed signe of peace.
Martell.   Go neerer Lady.   160
Ordella.   I come to make you happy.
Thierry.   Heare you that sirs?
She comes to crowne my soule: away, get sacrifice
Whilst I with holy honors——

146 No,] Weber; Nor ∧ Q 1–2, F 2
149 sweetely there?] Dyce (*qy citing* Heath, *MS. Notes*); sweetely? there's
Q 1–2, F 2

Martell.   She's alive Sir.
Thierry.   In everlasting life I know it, friend;
O happy, happy soule.
Ordella.   Alas I live Sir
A mortall woman still.
Thierry.   Can spirits weepe too?
Martell.   She is no spirit Sir, pray kisse her;——Lady,
Be very gentle to him.   [*She kisses him.*]
Thierry.   Stay, she is warme,
And by my life the same lips——tell me, brightnesse,
Are you the same *Ordella* still?
Ordella.   The same Sir,   170
Whom heavens and my good angell staid from ruine.
Thierry.   Kisse me agen.
Ordella.   The same still, still your servant.
                                       [*Kisses him.*]
Thierry.   'Tis she, I know her now *Martell*;—— sit down sweete.
O blest and happiest woman, a dead slumber
Begins to creepe upon me; o my jewell!
Ordella.   O sleepe my Lord.
Thierry.   My joyes are too much for me.

                Enter Messenger, *and* Memberge.

Messenger.   *Brunhalt* impatient of her constraint to see
Protaldye tortur'd, has chokt her selfe.
Martell.   No more,
Her sinnes go with her.
Thierry.   Love I must die, I faint,
Close up my glasses.
1. Doctor.   The Queene faints too, and deadly.   180
Thierry.   One dying kisse.
Ordella.   My last Sir, and my dearest,
                                       [*Kisses him.*]
And now close my eyes too.
Thierry.   Thou perfect woman,——

169 me] Q1(c); *om.* Q1(u)   170 *Ordella.*] Dyce; *Mart.* Q1–2, F2
176.1 *Enter*...Memberge.] Dyce; *following line* 175 Q1–2, F2

Martell, the kingdome's yours, take *Memberge* to you,
And keepe my line alive;——nay weepe not Lady,——
Take me, I go.
Ordella.   Take me too, farwell honor.   *Dies both.*
2. Doctor.   They are gone for ever.
Martell.   The peace of happy soules go after um,
Beare um unto their last beds, whilst I study
A tombe to speake their loves, whilst old Time lasteth;
I am your King in sorrowes.
Omnes.   We your subjects.   190
Martell.   *Devitry*, for your service be neere us:
Whip out these instruments of this mad mother
From Court, and all good people; and because
She was borne noble, let that title find her
A private grave, but neither tonge, nor honor:
And now leade on. They that shall read this story,
Shall find that vertue lives in good, not glory.

                                        Exeunt omnes.

                    FINIS

TEXTUAL NOTES

Dramatis Personæ

3 their...Kinsman]   As Dyce points out, Brunhalt at I.i.28 speaks of Martell as base, yet the fact that Thierry leaves him the kingdom implies that this description is inappropriate.

I.i

1 tainters]   The proof-reader probably directed a change to the more conventional 'taintures' and the compositor miscorrected to 'tainturs'. 'Tainters', however, is probably right; compare the Shakespeare Folio's 'rounder' for 'roundure', *King John* Through Line Number 565, and 'wafter' for 'wafture', *Julius Caesar* TLN 887. 'Tainture' is found in *Valentinian*, I.iii, but that text, like *Thierry*, seems to have been set from a scribal transcript, so the spelling may not be Fletcher's.

6 (And...Actions)]   The syntax of lines 3–8 is very knotty. Modern editors have agreed with Seward's alteration of 'followes' (line 6) to 'follow', apparently believing 'Actions' to be the subject of this verb. Weber *et seq.* in fact read 'And all your Actions follow' as parenthetical, an attempted improvement which if anything makes matters worse. Yet other alternatives are open. Theodoret may be saying, essentially, 'I do but gently tell you how these courses your mind (that grants no limit) and your actions follow...', in which case we have 'minde' and 'Actions' as a compound subject and in the verb a simple lack of concord, as probably in 'shewes' (line 23) and in 'Lyes' (line 72). More straightforward rhetorically and grammatically more consistent, however, is to consider 'And all your Actions' as the parenthesis: 'I tell you how these courses your mind that grants no limit (as well as all your actions) follows...'.

52 And...warmth]   Dyce notes, 'An epithet to "rush" or to "warmth" has drop out.'

106 weepers_A]   Compare the omission of terminal letters by Q1 at I.ii.54; II.i.242; II.ii.5; II.iii.74; III.i.32 (press corrected), 93; IV.i.16; V.i.103. Because the present reading is in the work of Compositor *A* and the rest in that of Compositor *B*, it seems likely that occasional obscurity in the representation of terminals was a characteristic of the manuscript.

I.ii

5 your] Although the Q1 reading can pass, Seward's emendation is encouraged not only by 'your counsell' (line 1) but also by the other omissions of terminal letters in Q1. See the note on I.i.106.

102 mothes] For the same misreading error, see II.i.257.

II.i

8 so neere a] The old editions read 'a neere', which modern editors emend to 'a nearer'. But Dyce, who invites comparison with I.ii.68, asks, 'What *name* could be *nearer* than that of *son*?'

96 rare...arts] Editors since Seward have agreed that Q1's 'acts' is a mistake for 'arts', but Colman declined to accept 'rare' for 'care', noting that 'the old reading, being sense, should stand'. Another instance of 'care' for 'rare', however, occurs at II.iv.65.

III.i

17 my] All editions follow Q1's 'thy', in accordance with which Ordella's kiss would be barren, presumably because it would awaken no answering warmth in Thierry's. Yet Thierry is the cold one, and his kiss, not really Ordella's, is barren. Q1's 'thy' could have arisen from misreading or confusion with the immediately following 'thou'.

95 most falshood] Beaumont's response to the emotional demands of this scene is a hyperbolic high style which, even though it edges toward obscurity in places (as at lines 29–32) is not often grammatically unconventional. This expression thus seems odd and may be a mistake for 'most false', 'most falsest', or something similar. An emendation, however, would be merely a guess; moreover, the fact that the metre of lines 96–9 goes haywire suggests that the scribe was here wrestling with a revision in the original manuscript that was so incomplete or unclear that the intended reading is unrecoverable.

III.ii

128 palace] Q1's 'place' has formerly been found acceptable, although in the context it would probably signify the state chamber. That Thierry means the entire building is evident from line 180.

IV.i

5 Outrunne]   Compare II.iv.73, where an 's' on a word preceding seems
in another instance to have induced an addition of 's' to the word following.

179 proceede]   Editors have found difficulty with the reading, but 'proceede' is acceptable as meaning 'prosper' (*OED*.3.*d*) or 'give rise to'
(compare 7.*b*).

185 worthines]   Perhaps because of the twelfth syllable it creates, editors
have altered Q1's 'worthies' to 'worth' or 'worths', emendations which
bring the line to an acceptable eleven syllables. In spite of the other terminal
misreadings in Q1, however, neither substitution is very plausible because
both ignore too many letters of the original reading. 'Worthies' (things of
value) makes sense, but because it throws a false accent on 'woman'
emendation to 'worthines' seems preferable. The line is thus a hexameter
or a pentameter in which the first three syllables are slurred.

V.i

72 preferre]   Although variously emended, 'preferre' is all right here, in
the sense of 'recommend' (*OED*.11.4). Starving will be recommended to
the soldiers only by their fear of hanging, which, says Devitry, is really the
easier death (consumption = destruction).

V.ii

54 recalm'd]   Q2's 'reclaim'd' (of which Mason notes, 'The expression is
taken from falconry. To *reclaim* a hawk is to make him tame') is the reading
of all modern editions. But 'reclaim'd' obviously proceeded from Q1's
'reclam'd', which may be only a transposition error for 'recalm'd'. There
is, however, no listing in the *OED* for *recalm*. It may be a neologism
(= resume one's previous state of calm) or possibly a word from the
vocabulary of medicine unnoticed by the *OED*.

PRESS-VARIANTS IN Q1

[Copies collated (all extant): BM¹ (British Museum, 644.d.5), BM² (British Museum, 841.b.1), BM³ (British Museum, Ashley 83), Bodl¹ (Bodleian Library, 4° P2 [5] Art BS), Bodl² (Bodleian Library, Malone 243 [1]), Dyce (Victoria and Albert Museum), NLS (National Library of Scotland), NLSB (National Library of Scotland, Bute Collection), TCC (Trinity College Library, Cambridge), CSmH (Henry E. Huntington Library), DFo (Folger Shakespeare Library), EC (Elizabethan Club, Yale University), MB (Boston Public Library), C1 (disjunct leaf C1 inserted in MB), MWiW-C (Chapin Library, Williams College), Pforz (The Carl H. Pforzheimer Library), and TxU (University of Texas Library).]

Notes

BM² is trimmed at the foot in Sheet K, which affects the last one or two lines on each page.

BM³ (Wise) leaves B2, C1, D1, E2, H3, H4, and I1 have been exchanged with the corresponding leaves in TxU (Wrenn). See D. F. Foxon, *Thomas J. Wise and the Pre-Restoration Drama* (London, 1959), p. 37, and D. F. Foxon and W. B. Todd, '*Thomas J. Wise and the Pre-Restoration Drama*: A Supplement', *The Library*, 5th ser., 16 (1961), 292. In BM³ leaves K2 and K3 have been cropped at the head and repaired in a such a way that the appearance of the running-titles is affected (for which information the editor is obliged to Mr Foxon).

Bodl² reads 'felf' at I.i.135 and 'inuentec' at I.i.136 evidently because of type damage or faulty impression, and omits 'h'example' at I.ii.28 probably because of faulty impression.

CSmH reads 'life pon' at II.iv.170 probably because of a pulled type. Some apparent variants on K4 and K4ᵛ in this copy are caused by the restoration of the leaf.

MB reads '*unhalt*' at I.i.o.1 because of faulty impression or a defect in the paper.

NLS lacks the bottom half of leaf K4, which prevents determination of whether K(i) in that copy is in the first or the second corrected state.

In several copies marks are found on B1 around the headpiece and head-title; they seem to have been caused by furniture working up during the printing. Because their appearance and disappearance does not accord with the stages of press-correction suggested by alterations in the readings of B(o), it appears that the offending pieces were noticed and driven down, but then worked up again.

In several copies the spacing of 'maydes', 'fpunges', and 'felfe' at I.i.88–90 is affected by an apparent failure to justify the lines or properly to lock up the type.

That 'defcend' (V.i.23) is the corrected reading can be proved on the evidence of a space type between 'i'le' and 'preferue' (V.i.26), the foot of which printed in some copies. It appears in no copies reading 'deffend'; it appears in all copies reading 'defcend' except BM³ and Bodl¹. Thus instead of the space being set high and later driven down, it evidently worked up during the course of printing. The reading associated with its appearance must, therefore, be the later reading.

SHEET B (*outer forme*)

Uncorrected: BM³ (*containing leaf B2 from TxU, fully corrected*), NLSB
1st stage corrected: BM², Bodl¹

Sig. B1
I.i.14 'tis neceffary] 'tis | neceffary
Sig. B4ᵛ
I.ii.37 here fhe] here Ifhe
61 an enimy] an nimy

2nd stage corrected: BM¹, Bodl², CSmH, DFo, Dyce, EC, MB, MWiW-C, NLS, Pforz, TCC, TxU (*containing leaf B2 from BM³, uncorrected*)

Sig. B1
head-title THE] ᴛHE
I.i.1 tainturs] tainters
Sig. B2ᵛ
I.i.84 ftaru'd] ftarud
107 defpif'd] defpifd
Sig. B3
I.i.121 Letchers, Leaches] Leachers, Letchecs
Sig. B4ᵛ
I.ii.52 Par'd] Pard
64 Himfelfe] himfelfe

SHEET B (*inner forme*)

Corrected: BM¹⁻², Bodl¹⁻², CSmH, DFo, Dyce, EC, MB, MWiW-C, NLS, Pforz, TCC, TxU
Uncorrected: BM³, NLSB

Sig. B1ᵛ
I.i.22 take] rake

SHEET C (*inner forme*)

Corrected: BM[1–3], Bodl[1–2], CSmH, DFo, Dyce, EC, MB, MWiW-C, NLS, NLSB, Pforz, TCC, TxU

Uncorrected: C1

Sig. C1[v]

I.ii.105 vertuous traine] vertuous traine traine
  119 a troope] a | troope (?)
  121 Mufter] Murfter (?)
  130 *Martell,*] *Martell*

SHEET E (*outer forme*)

Corrected: BM[1–3], CSmH, DFo, Dyce, EC, MB, MWiW-C, NLSB, Pforz, TxU

Uncorrected: Bodl[1–2], NLS, TCC

Sig. E2[v]

II.iv.65 rare] care

Sig. E4[v]

III.i.32 your] you
  35 iuice] iuce

SHEET E (*inner forme*)

Corrected: BM[1], CSmH, DFo, Dyce, EC, MB, MWiW-C, Pforz, TxU

Uncorrected: BM[2–3], Bodl[1–2], NLS, NLSB, TCC

Sig. E4

Running-title *Theodoret*] *Theoderet*
II.iv.173.1 *Exeunt:*] *om.*

SHEET G (*outer forme*)

Corrected: BM[1–3], Bodl[1–2], DFo, Dyce, EC, MB, MWiW-C, NLS, NLSB, Pforz, TCC

Uncorrected: CSmH, TxU

Sig. G4[v]

IV.i.96 with all] withall

462

SHEET H (*inner forme*)

Corrected: BM¹, Dyce, EC, MWiW-C
Uncorrected: BM²⁻³, Bodl¹⁻², CSmH, DFo, MB, NLS,
    NLSB, Pforz, TCC, TxU

Sig. H1ᵛ
IV.i.162 barrenneſſe,] barrenneſſe

SHEET I (*outer forme*)

Corrected: BM²⁻³, Bodl¹⁻², CSmH, DFo, Dyce, EC, MB,
    MWiW-C, NLS, NLSB, Pforz, TCC, TxU
Uncorrected: BM¹

Sig. I3
V.i.12 to part with't] to   with't

SHEET I (*inner forme*)

Corrected: BM¹, ³, Bodl¹⁻², CSmH, MB, MWiW-C, NLSB
Uncorrected: BM², DFo, Dyce, EC, NLS, Pforz, TCC, TxU

Sig. I3ᵛ
V.i.23 de-|ſcend] deſ-|ſend

SHEET K (*inner forme*)

Uncorrected: TxU
1st stage corrected: Bodl¹⁻², MB, NLS (?), TCC

Sig. K4
V.ii.169 tell me brightneſſe] tell brightneſſe

    2nd stage corrected: BM¹⁻³, CSmH, DFo, Dyce, EC, MWiW-C,
        Pforz, NLSB

Sig. K3ᵛ
V.ii.116 defeated] defeeaed

Sig. K4
V.ii.143 wheele] wheee

EMENDATIONS OF ACCIDENTALS

[Note: The formula 'Q1+' indicates the agreement of Q2 and F2 with Q1.]

Dramatis Personæ

5 Protaldye] *Protuldy* Q2   15 Memberge] *Memburges* Q2

I.i

4 pleasures,] ~ ; Q1+	125 how,] ~ ∧ Q1+
10 world,] ~ ∧ Q1+	127 were,] ~ . Q1+
17 selfe. You] ~ , you Q1+	129 up?] ~ , Q1+
18 (Which...women)]∧ ~ ...~ .	129 end?] ~ , Q1+
Q1+	130 will?] F2; ~ ; Q1–2
22 us.] ~ ∧ Q1+	132 living;] ~ , Q1+
27 is∧] ~ , Q1+	141 executions——] ~ . Q1+
33 mother,] ~ ; Q1+	144 curtalls,] ~ ∧ Q1+
45 without] Q2; withour Q1	146 vertuous:] ~ , Q1; ~ ∧ Q2, F2
47 credite,] ~ ∧ Q1+	146 this?] F2; ~ , Q1–2
55–56 (And...it)] ∧ ~ ...~ ∧	151 Mistris,——] ~ , ∧ Q1–2, F2±
Q1+	158 sweat,...mourne;] ~ ;...~ ,
63 Ballads,] ~ ∧ Q1+	Q1+
76 honour,] ~ ; Q1+	159 *Protaldye*] Q2; *Protaldie* Q1
77 fairely,] ~ ; Q1+	160 gelding;] ~ , Q1+
82 day,] ~ ∧ Q1+	164 kisses,] ~ . Q1+
87 *Protaldye*]*Portalyde* Q1–2; *Pro-*	165 desart;] ~ , Q1+
talyde F2	166 walke;] ~ , Q1+
94 no;] ~ , Q1+	172 designes?] F2; ~ , Q1–2
98 wakings;] ~ : Q1+	173 Lady——] ~ . Q1+
105 deceitfull] Q2; deceitfuil Q1	174 too;] ~ , Q1+
123 examples∧] ~ : Q1+	176 colts;] ~ , Q1+
123–124 (lest...act)]∧ ~ ...~ ,	177 troubled;] Q2; ~ ∧ Q1
Q1+	178 private;] ~ , Q1+
124 custome:] ~ , Q1+	178 come,] ~ ∧ Q1+

I.ii

2 honour,] ~ : Q1+	18 reproofes,] ~ ∧ Q1+
6 confirmd,] ~ ∧ Q1+	29 licentiousnesse;] ~ , Q1+
14–15 Sir...follow'd] *one line in*	38 temper,] ~ ∧ Q1+
Q1+	

464

43–44 (her...shame,)] ∧~ ...~ ,
  ∧ Q1+
47 nature,] Q2; ~ ∧ Q1
53 ill,] ~ ; Q1+
60 Who,] ~ ∧ Q1+
69 me,] ~ ∧ Q1+
90–91 Academ, ∧...practis'd,)] ~
  ,)...~ , ∧ Q1–2, F2±
96 kill∧] Q2; ~ , Q1

104–105 One...traine] *one line in*
  Q1+
123 attempted:...forbeare,] ~ ;...
  ~ ∧ Q1+
126 suddainely:] ~ , Q1+
127 owne.] ~ , Q1+
129 readinesse∧] ~ , Q1+
130 company,——] ~ , ∧ Q1+
131 me?] ~ . Q1+

II.i

5 Temples,] Q2; ~ ; Q1
13 he,] F2; ~ ∧ Q1–2
24 them,] ~ ; Q1+
30 wellcome] well- | come Q1
33 delay. | *Enter* Protaldye... |
  Your...Generall.] delay; your
  ...Generall. | *Enter Protaldie*
  ...Q1–2, F2±
41 contented,] ~ : Q1, F2; ~ ?
  Q2
46 *Hercules*,] ~ : Q1+
49 wives;] ~ , Q1+
52 (But...glorious,)] ∧ ~ ...~ , ∧
  Q1+
71 war, ha] war. Ha Q1+
72 armors,] ~ ∧ Q1+
102 swallowes;...wonne,] ~ ,...
  ~ ; Q1–2; ~ :...~ , F2
109 howsoever,...thankefulnesse∧]
  ~ ∧...~ , Q1+
111 Austrachia;] ~ , Q1+
116 Madam,——] ~ , ∧ Q1+
121–124 Amazement...us] Q1+
  line Amazement...hee. | We
  ...undone. | Our...defence. |
  If...us
129 brother?] ~ . Q1+
143 *Nero*——] ~ , Q1–2, F2±
154–156 To...come] Q1+ *line* To
  ...rather. | Rather...come
176 blood,] ~ ∧ Q1+
182 it;] ~ , Q1+

185 much.——] ~ . ∧ Q1+
189 me,...hate∧] ~ ∧...~ , Q1+
193–194 Fie...that] *one line in* Q1+
202 forehead,——] ~ , ∧ Q1+
203 do;] ~ , Q1+
218–219 Sure...Lord] *one line in*
  Q1+
221 cannot:] ~ , Q1+
237 *Aragon*,] ~ ∧ Q1+
245 thou?] ~ , Q1+
248 companies;] ~ , Q1+
250 travaile:] ~ , Q1+
251 them.] Q2; ~ , Q1
253.1 Brunhalt,...Protaldye] *Brun.*
  ...*Portaldy* Q1+
256 peece-meale;——] ~ ; ∧ Q1+
260 maker?] ~ , Q1+
287 me——] ~ : Q1+
287 me ∧ yet?] ~ , ~ ∧ Q1+
288 this?] ~ . Q1+
300 faire?...young?] ~...~ .
  Q1+
301–302 And...ardor] *one line in*
  Q1+
302 ardor?] ~ . Q1+
308 man?] ~ . Q1+
318–319 thine;...it,] ~ ,...~ ;
  Q1+
319 selfe.——] ~ , ∧ Q1+
321 ∧ I...you∧] F2; (~ ...~) Q1;
  (~ ...~ ∧ Q2

II.ii

0.1 Thierry] Q2; *Trierry* Q1
2–5 are...of] Q1+ *line* are |
Blooded...troope? | *Enter
Martell.* | Past...are, | Now...
of
4 are,——] ~ , ∧ Q1+
10–12 Whats...project] Q1+ *line*
Whats...too? | Yes Sir, | To
...project

15 (For...test,)] ∧ ~ ...~ , ∧
Q1+
18 us;] ~ , Q1+
20–21 (Loade...us:)] ∧ ~ ...~ : ∧
Q1+
26 prayers;] ~ , Q1+
36 Sir?] ~ , Q1–2, F2±

II.iii

In this scene prefixes for the Huntsmen *are simple numerals in* Q1+.

1 I,] ~ ∧ Q1+
7.1 Protaldye] Q2; *Protaldie* Q1
11 *Exeunt*] *Exit* Q1+
14–15 How...meanes] Q1+ *line*
How...not, | Nor...meanes
16–17 Sir;...honest,] ~ ,...~ ;
Q1; ~ :...~ ; Q2, F2
18–19 for,...Sir;] ~ ;...~ ,
Q1+
24 gentleman,] ~ ∧ Q1+
25–27 (At...peece,)] ∧ ~ ...~ , ∧
Q1–2, F2±
27 perrill;] ~ , Q1+
28–30 Six...present] Q1+ *line*
Six...mee. | Six? | Alas...
present
28–29 villaines, | Sworne ∧] ~ ∧ ~ ,
Q1+
30 present?] F2; ~ , Q1–2
33 discretion,] ~ ∧ Q1+
39 directly;] ~ , Q1+
41 occasions,] ~ ∧ Q1+
42 opinion. Six] ~ , six Q1+
43 man:...example,] ~ ,...~ :
Q1–2, F2±
48 valour——] ~ . Q1+

51–52 So...Justice] *one line in*
Q1+
53–55 I...thus] Q1+ *line* I...
Sir, | Men...not | Be...thus
59 (Ile...horse,)] ∧ ~ ...~ , ∧
Q1+
59–60 safety,...hand-sawes:] ~ :
...~ , Q1; ~ ,...~ , Q2, F2
62 poorely; stay,] ~ ,...~ ∧
Q1+
67–70 There...kingdome] Q1+
line There is no | More...too. |
Fie...eares. | Yes: | This...
kingdome
71–73 Yes...bite] Q1+ *line* Yes
...foole, | A...bawd, | Beast
...bite
74 Yes...you] Q1+ *line* Yes, |
This...you
74 Sir:] ~ , Q1+
78 Mistresse] Mis. Q1; Mistris Q2,
F2
79 mushrump;] F2; ~ , Q1–2
80 well;] ~ , Q1+
81 lanceprisadoes,] ~ ; Q1+

II.iv

0.2 Thierry] F2; *Trierry* Q1–2
10 duty,——] ~ ,ᴧ Q1+
15 livde,——] ~ ,ᴧ Q1–2, F2±
16 well,——] ~ ,ᴧ Q1+
17 We...mirth] Q1+ *line* We are dull, | No...mirth
17 mirth?] ~ . Q1+
21 *Protaldye*?] ~ . Q1+
30 Sir?] ~ , Q1+
39 Possible?] F2; ~ . Q1–2
43 men,] ~ ; Q1+
56 leave,——] ~ ,ᴧ Q1+
62 (Which...them)] ᴧ ~ ...~ , Q1+
63 it,——] ~ ,ᴧ Q1+
64 beneathᴧ] ~ , Q1+
68 not,——] ~ ,ᴧ Q1+
75–76 (And...pitch:)] ᴧ ~ ...~ :ᴧ Q1+
85 you:] ~ , Q1+
91 (patience...me?)]ᴧ ~ ...~ ,ᴧ Q1+

102–103 Fie...place] *one line in* Q1+
105 feast,——] ~ ,ᴧ Q1–2, F2±
110–111 Nay...patient] *one line in* Q1+
116 taste;——] ~ ;ᴧ Q1–2, F2±
119 cup;——] ~ ;ᴧ Q1+
119 heere,] ~ ᴧ Q1+
121 you,——] ~ ,ᴧ Q1–2, F2±
127 round,——] ~ ,ᴧ Q1+
130 labour.——] ~ .ᴧ Q1+
131 company,——] ~ ,ᴧ Q1+
131.1 Protaldye,] F2 (Protal,); *Protal.* Q1–2±
137 man?] ~ . Q1+
137 Why,] ~ ᴧ Q1+
140 credit.——] ~ .ᴧ Q1–2, F2±
146–147 Why...now] Q1+ *line* Why...boxde, | Or...now
165 it:——] ~ :ᴧ Q1+
168 us:——] ~ :ᴧ Q1–2, F2±
169 *Lecure*;] ~ , Q1+

III.i

1 Elephants;] ~ , Q1; ~ . Q2; ~ : F2
13 frozen, veines?] ~ ᴧ ~ , Q1+
23–25 Bind...words] Q1+ *line* Bind...charme, | Who... words
38–39 couple,...joyᴧ] ~ ᴧ...~ , Q1+
40 delight?] ~ : Q1+
44 thee?] ~ , Q1+
49–50 'Tis...selfe] *one line in* Q1+
53 beingᴧ exemplified?] ~ , ~ , Q1; ~ ᴧ ~ , Q2, F2
78 mate?] ~ . Q1–2, F2±
82 spirits?] ~ ᴧ Q1+

84 uselesse?] ~ , Q1+
85 knowne?] ~ . Q1+
88–89 And ...sigh] *one line in* Q1+
89 sigh,——] ~ ,ᴧ Q1–2, F2±
90 warme?] ~ . Q1+
90 sadnesse——] ~ . Q1+
92 day?] ~ . Q1+
96–99 Oh...heaven] Q1+ *line* Oh ...friend? | Posterity...blessing, | And...heaven
116 unbounded;] ~ , Q1+
118 mirth;...maskes,] ~ ,...~ ; Q1+
120–121 Whose...eye] Q1+ *line* Whose...us, | Our...eye

120 us;] ~ , Q1+
125–128 Musique...say] Q1+ *line*
Musique...presence | My...
spheare | Too...vertue. | Make
...say
131.1 *Exeunt*] *Exit* Q1+
131.1 Thierry,] Q2; ~ . Q1
132–134 Why...happy] Q1+ *line*
Why...man? | No...man, |
How...happy
139 ridiculous;] ~ , Q1+
161 virtue,] ~ ₐ Q1+

163–164 vow,...age,] ~ ₐ...~ ₐ
Q1+
174–175 Without...happily] Q1+
line Without...art. *Exit*
Thierry. | *Enter Lecure.* |
Wisedome...happily
175 to't.] ~ , Q1+
179 well;] ~ , Q1+
179–180 'Tis...charge] *one line in*
Q1+
181 cell?] ~ . Q1+
185 *Protaldyes*] *Protaldies* Q1+

III.ii

3–5 Wind...businesses] Q1+
line Wind...eares, | I...
hitherto | Bin...businesses
7 encounter.] ~ , Q1+
10–11 Is...mine] Q1+ *line* Is...
pawne | I...mine
10 you?] ~ , Q1+
12 penyworth] Q2; penywoth Q1
13–14 You...acquaintance] Q1+
line You...knowne | To...
acquaintance
16–17 Thankes...armes] Q1+
line Thankes...remembrance, |
You...armes
16 remembrance;] ~ , Q1+
17 armes?] ~ . Q1+
18–19 A...dinner] Q2; Q1 *lines*
A...only | serv'd...dinner
26 sir;] ~ , Q1+
27 the ₐ fast] ~ ; ~ Q1+
31 em?] ~ , Q1+
33 further;] ~ , Q1+
35 much?] ~ . Q1+
40–41 king- | dome] kingdome Q1
42 purchase;] ~ , Q1+
42.1 Protaldye] *Protaldy* Q1+
46–48 What...on't] Q1+ *line*
What...affaire | Bring...
tickles | With...on't

49–52 These...felicity] Q1+ *line*
These...Lady, | Whose...
virginity. | Speake...felicity
53–56 What...gave] Q1+ *line*
What...view, | The...impart
| By...gave
63–64 The...strike] Q2; Q1 *lines*
The...you | Are...strike
64 are. How] ~ , how Q1+
64 How,] F2; ~ ₐ Q1–2
69–70 Plague...reputation] Q1+
line Plague...hand, | What...
reputation
69 scrivners] scrviners Q1;
scriveners Q2, F2
81 projects?——] ~ , ₐ Q1+
82–83 Willingly...paines] Q1+
line Willingly... earne, | You
...paines
82 Willingly,——] ~ , ₐ Q1–2,
F2±
85 promis'd;] ~ , Q1+
86–88 Where...fearefully] Q1+
line Where...dogs, | So...
eyes | I...fearefully
89 on't,——] ~ , ₐ Q1+
90 in.] ~ , Q1+
94 thee;] ~ , Q1; ~ . Q2, F2
95 too't ₐ] F2; ~ , Q1–2

96 chaire;] ~ , Q1+
99.1 *withdrawes.*] *following line* 98
    in Q1+
100–101 Foote...ha, ha, ha] *one*
    line in Q1+
101–103 Me...pleasure] Q1+ *line*
    Me...could | Have...willing-
    nesse, | In...pleasure
101 Sir?] ~ , Q1+
103 willingnesse∧] Q2; ~ , Q1
107 conquers;——] ~ ;∧ Q1+
118 How,...you?] ~ ∧...~ ,
    Q1+
118 brother?——] ~ ?∧ Q1+
119 presage!——] ~ !∧ Q1+
123 shame!——] ~ !∧ Q1+
126 murther,——] ~ ,∧ Q1+
126 taken?] Q2; ~ . Q1
128–130 Set...flame] Q1+ *line* Set
    ...unseene | May...to't, |
    Shall...flame Q1+
129 mischiefe;] ~ , Q1+
130 to't∧] ~ , Q1–2; ~ . F2
140–142 Here...repented] Q1+

line Here...good | Your...
    incitement, | Not...repented
149 issue.] Q2; ~ , Q1
154 beleefe:] ~ , Q1+
155 mentionde∧] ~ , Q1+
157 conceivde:] ~ , Q1+
158 day,] ~ : Q1+
170–171 Of...affoords] Q1+ *line*
    Of...left | *Austracia*...
    affoords
176–177 You...eyes] Q1+ *line*
    You...flames | In your eyes
182 secret;] ~ , Q1+
184 servant,——] ~ ,∧ Q1+
186–188 *Protaldye*...service] Q1+
    line Protaldye...sweare | Fell
    ...service
187 hand;——] ~ ,∧ Q1+
191 ready;] ~ , Q1+
193–195 Reserve...funerall] Q1+
    line Reserve...fate | To...lose
    | The...funerall
196 Prince?——] ~ ,∧ Q1+
197 mischiefe.——] ~ ,∧ Q1+

III.iii

3 east,...starre;] ~ ;...~ ,
    Q1+
4 poles;] ~ , Q1+
7–8 thee;...little,] ~ ,...~ ;
    Q1–2, F2±
10–14 You...chang'd] Q1+ *line*
    You...same, | If...himselfe, |
    'Tis...way, | And...for't. | I
    ...Queene, | And...chang'd
10 same:] ~ , Q1+
11 himselfe;] ~ , Q1; ~ . Q2, F2
13 hand;] ~ , Q1+
19 Discovering] Q2; Discoveting
    Q1
21 hand,——] ~ ,∧ Q1+

32 of heires] Q2; ofheires Q1
32–35 Heires...want] Q1+ *line*
    Heires...heires. | Begotten...
    pale? | Thou...want
32 Heires?] ~ , Q1+
33 body?] ~ , Q1+
46–47 Can...good] Q1+ *line* Can
    ...end | So...good
49 blinded ∧ men,] ~ , ~ ∧ Q1+
51 life;] Q2; ~ , Q1
57–58 The...sonnes] Q1+ *line*
    The...live | Father...sonnes
59 sadnes?] ~ , Q1+
66 gone:] ~ , Q1+
67 daughter;] ~ , Q1+

IV.i

2 houre,] ~ . Q1+
3 him?] ~ , Q1+
10–12 (France...wayes,)] ∧ ~ ...
～ , ∧ Q1+
22 me,] F2; ~ ∧ Q1–2
25 (Their...them,)] ∧ ~ ...~ , ∧
Q1+
28 me:] ~ ∧ Q1+
36 suffer?] ~ . Q1+
43 hares. Who's] ~ , who's Q1+
43 *Enter a Priest.*] *following* that?
in Q1+
48–50 (Like...fires;)] ∧ ~ ...~ ;∧
Q1+
50 her;] ~ , Q1+
51 her;] ~ , Q1+
52 goodnes∧] ~ , Q1+
54 affections∧] ~ , Q1+
61 fruite;——] ~ ;∧ Q1+
66 goodnesse,] ~ ; Q1+
69 memory] Q2; memoty Q1
74 safety,] ~ . Q1+
75 Lady?] ~ . Q1+
83 gladnesse;] ~ , Q1+
84 honest?] ~ . Q1+
94 Fly,...forme,] F2; ~ ∧...~ ∧
Q1–2
110 humors∧] ~ , Q1; ~ . Q2, F2

111 suffer?] F2; ~ . Q1–2
113 die,——] ~ , ∧ Q1+
114 children?] F2; ~ , Q1–2
117 heaven,] F2; ~ ; Q1–2
128 man:] ~ , Q1+
140 angell,] ~ ∧ Q1+
152 heare;] ~ , Q1+
155 respect——] ~ . Q1+
162–163 (Grieving...him,)] ∧ ~
...~ , ∧ Q1+
162 barrennesse∧] Q1(u); ~ , Q1(c)
164 gods:] ~ , Q1+
167 (For...him,)] ∧ ~ ...~ , ∧
Q1+
169 children. The] ~ , the Q1+
171 women?] F2; ~ , Q1–2
172 selfe,...blessing∧] ~ ∧...~ ,
Q1+
173 dying?] ~ , Q1; ~ ∧ Q2, F2
177 are:] ~ ∧ Q1+
186 honor,] ~ ∧ Q1+
198 fondnesse,] ~ ∧ Q1+
198 mee;] F2; ~ , Q1–2
199 destruction?] ~ , Q1–2; ~ ! F2
203 build;] ~ , Q1+
219 comfort,——] ~ , ∧ Q1+
230 instrument;] ~ , Q1+

IV.ii

3 mid-wife,——] ~ , ∧ Q1+
4 death?] ~ . Q1+
12 pitty∧] Q2; ~ , Q1
15–16 (which...life;)] ∧ ~ ...
～ ;∧ Q1–2, F2±
25 experiment∧] ~ : Q1+
36 why.] Q2; ~ ? Q1
42 birth:——] ~ :∧ Q1+
45 above?] Q2; ~ ! Q1
45 Ha!——] ~ !∧ Q1+

45–46 Ha...revenge] *one line* n
Q1+
56 bald,] ~ ? Q1–2; ~ : F2
58 this:] ~ , Q1+
66 long:] ~ , Q1+
68 cowards, sorrow?] ~ ∧ ~ ∧ Q1–
2; ~ ∧ ~ , F2
69 you?] ~ , Q1+
84 safe;] ~ , Q1+
85 (nay...it,)] ∧ ~ ...~ , ∧ Q1+

86 Madam——] ~ . Q1+
90 man;——] ~ ;ᴧ Q1-2, F2±
90 see?] ~ , Q1+
92 treasure,——] ~ ,ᴧ Q1+
98 thee;——] ~ ;ᴧ Q1-2, F2±
104 me,] ~ ᴧ Q1+
107-110 (For...her;)]ᴧ ~ ...~ ;ᴧ
　　Q1-2, F2±
112 women,] ~ : Q1+
122-123 (this...it,)]ᴧ ~ ...~ ,ᴧ
　　Q1+
135 blessings;] ~ : Q1+
138 her:] ~ ; Q1-2; ~ , F2
149 then,] ~ ᴧ Q1+
149 (quoth she)] F2;ᴧ ~ ~ ᴧ Q1-2
155 name:] ~ , Q1; ~ ᴧ Q2, F2
167 selfe;] ~ , Q1+
167 hers,] ~ ᴧ Q1+
172-173 life,...only,] ~ ᴧ...~ ᴧ
　　Q1+

173-174 Oh...which] *one line in*
　　Q1+
175 eares;——] ~ ;ᴧ Q1-2, F2±
182-183 Go...selfe] *one line in* Q1+
185 was ᴧ (o...hart!)] ~ ; ᴧ ~ ...
　　~ !ᴧ Q1+
193 it,] ~ ᴧ Q1+
201 it:] ~ , Q1+
206 justice;] ~ , Q1+
224 Forbeare:——] ~ :ᴧ Q1-2,
　　F2±
235 thee,——] ~ ,ᴧ Q1+
237 place?] ~ , Q1+
238 sonne!] ~ , Q1; ~ . Q2, F2
249 refuge;——] ~ ;ᴧ Q1-2, F2±
258-261 He's...affliction] Q1+
　　line He's...death. | This...it, |
　　To...affliction Q1+

V.i

In this scene prefixes for the Souldiers *are simple numerals in* Q1+.

0.1 *four*] F2; 4 Q1-2
10 fifty] 50 Q1+
12 soonest] Q2; sonest (|) Q1
18 you;...Sir,] ~ ,...~ ; Q1+
24 stile;] ~ , Q1+
27 perswade?] Q2; ~ , Q1
27-28 merit,——] ~ ,ᴧ Q1-2,
　　F2±
31 courtesie] Q2; tourtesie Q1
36 see,——] ~ ,ᴧ Q1+
44 cozines] Q2; coznes Q1
47 Foote,] ~ ᴧ Q1+
49 me:——] ~ :ᴧ Q1+
54 Foote,] ~ ᴧ Q1+
54 you,] Q2; ~ ᴧ Q1 (?)
61 this?] ~ , Q1+
62 happy;] ~ , Q1+
62 bonny] Q2; bony (|) Q1
62 countenance;] ~ , Q1+

63 patron.] ~ , Q1+
71 gallowes ᴧ (which...too't,)] ~
　　ᴧ ~ ...~ ,ᴧ Q1; ~ , ~ ...
　　~ ,ᴧ Q2, F2
74 evidence:] ~ ; Q1+
77 purse!] ~ , Q1+
77 foote,] ~ ᴧ Q1+
80 selfe?] ~ , Q1+
82 againe?] ~ . Q1+
83 did:] ~ , Q1+
92.1 *Exeunt*] *Exit* Q1+
103 letters?] ~ , Q1+
104 boots,——] ~ , Q1+
104-105 me?...friend.] Q2; ~ ,
　　...~ ? Q1
106 presently;] ~ , Q1+
109 this,——] ~ ,ᴧ Q1+
110 voice,——] ~ ,ᴧ Q1+
113 Zones,] ~ ᴧ Q1+

113 him,——]~ ,ᴧ Q1+
116–117 of friendship] Q2;
  offriendship Q1
116–117 friend-|ship] friendship
  Q1+
125 Foote,] ~ ᴧ Q1+
126 us?——] ~ ,ᴧ Q1+
129 owne;——] ~ ;ᴧ Q1+
132 him:] ~ , Q1+
134 Exeunt] Exit Q1+
135–136 with?...darke,] Q2; ~ ,
  ...~; Q1
143–144 Devitry,——] ~ ,ᴧ Q1+
147 Foote,] F2; ~ ᴧ Q1–2
149 mee?] ~ , Q1+
152 for't;] ~ , Q1+
154 Sir;] ~ , Q1+

161 learning:] ~ , Q1+
161 bootes;] ~ , Q1+
166 you;] ~ , Q1+
171 live;] Q2; ~ , Q1
176 Foote,] ~ ᴧ Q1+
180 lost.——] ~ ,ᴧ Q1+
181 men——] ~ . Q1+
183 you;] ~ , Q1+
184 Foote,] ~ ᴧ Q1+
185 epistles;] ~ , Q1+
192 betraide;] ~ , Q1+
205 Foote,] ~ ᴧ Q1+
211 viper;——] ~ ;ᴧ Q1–2, F2±
212 Martell,——] ~ ,ᴧ Q1+
216 torture,——] ~ ,ᴧ Q1+
217.1 Exeunt] Exit Q1+

V.ii

In this scene prefixes for the Courtiers *are simple numerals in* Q1+

0.1 three] F2; 3 Q1–2
1 meanes?] ~ . Q1+
1 artᴧ] Q2; ~ , Q1
1 it?] ~ . Q1+
3 hawke;] ~ , Q1+
5 know:] ~ ᴧ Q1; ~ , Q2, F2
7–10 Armies...him] Q1+ *line*
  Armies...glisters, | Some...
  pills, | Twenty...drench, | As
  ...him (F2 *om*. As...him)

F2 *omission begins after* drench,
  line 10

19 out,] ~ ᴧ Q1–2
23–24 But...faile] Q1–2 *line* But
  ...honor | Has...faile
24 faile?] ~ . Q1–2
25 memory——] ~ . Q1–2
27 pension——] ~ . Q1–2
36–37 (and...truth;)] ᴧ ~ ...
  ~ ;ᴧ Q1–2
38 sleepe?] ~ , Q1–2
41 ever:] ~ , Q1–2

43 another?] ~ , Q1–2
50 ye:] ~ , Q1–2
53 ignorance?] ~ , Q1–2
60 slumber;] ~ , Q1–2
62 never;] ~ , Q1–2
67 set,——] ~ ,ᴧ Q1–2
67 No,] ~ ᴧ Q1–2
72 him,] ~ ᴧ Q1–2
75 wrongs,] ~ ᴧ Q1–2
80 baneᴧ] Q2; ~ , Q1
83 be:] ~ , Q1–2
91 now;——] ~ ;ᴧ Q1–2
95–96 (For...so;)] ᴧ~...~ ;ᴧ
  Q1–2
101 will——] ~ . Q1+
103 tendernes,] ~ ᴧ Q1–2
117 blasted;] ~ , Q1–2
120 scatter'd:] ~ , Q1–2
125 apparent:] ~ , Q1–2
125 taken,] ~ ᴧ Q1–2

F2 *omission ends after line* 127

134 miseries?] ~ , Q1+

135 horrors?] ~ , Q1+
137 poppy,——] ~ , ∧ Q1+
138 embraces ∧...quiet;] ~ ;...
　　~ ∧ Q1–2; ~ ;...~ , F2
141 sleepe?] F2; ~ . Q1–2
149 face——] ~ . Q1+
150 face——] ~ . Q1+
152 (I...perfectly)] ∧ ~ ...~ ∧
　　Q1+
153 there:] ~ , Q1+
154 comes!...substance!] ~ ,...
　　~ , Q1+
155 one,——] ~ , ∧ Q1+
156 comest——] ~ , Q1+
157 her,] ~ ∧ Q1+
158 againe,——] ~ , ∧ Q1+
159 ready,——] ~ , ∧ Q1+
163 honors——] ~ . Q1+
164 friend;] ~ , Q1+
167 her;——] ~ ; ∧ Q1–2, F2±

169 lips——] ~ ∧ Q1+
169 me,] ~ ∧ Q1+
169 brightnesse,] Q2; ~ ; Q1
173 Martell;——] ~ ; ∧ Q1+
173 sweete.] F2; ~ , Q1–2
175 me;] ~ , Q1+
178–179 No...her.] *one line in* Q1+
178 *Protaldye*] Q2; *Protaldie* Q1
179–180 Love...glasses] *one line in*
　　Q1+
181–182 My...too] Q1+ *line* My
　　...now | Close...too
182 woman,——] ~ , ∧ Q1–2, F2±
184 alive;——...Lady,——] ~ ; ∧
　　...~ , ∧ Q1+
189 loves,...lasteth;] ~ ;...~ ,
　　Q1–2; ~ ;...~ ∧ F2
191 us:] ~ , Q1+
196 on. They] ~ , they Q1+

HISTORICAL COLLATION

[This collation includes substantive and semi-substantive differences from the present text appearing in the two Quartos, the Folio of 1679, six later editions, and three commentaries. Sigla are as follows:

C   *The Dramatick Works*, ed. George Colman the Elder. London, 1778.
     Vol. 10.
D   *Works*, ed. Alexander Dyce. London, 1843. Vol. 1.
Dei K. Deighton, *The Old Dramatists: Conjectural Readings*. West-
     minster, 1896. Pp. 31–3.
F2   *Fifty Comedies and Tragedies*. London, 1679.
L   *Works*, ed. Gerard Langbaine the Younger. London, 1711. Vol. 7.
M   *Beaumont and Fletcher*, ed. J. St Loe Strachey (The Mermaid Edi-
     tion). London, 1887. Vol. 1.
Ma   J. Monck Mason, *Comments on the Plays of Beaumont and Fletcher*.
     London, 1798. Pp. 360–8.
Mi   John Mitford, *Cursory Notes on Various Passages in the Text of
     Beaumont and Fletcher*. London, 1856. P. 9.
Q1–2 The quartos of 1621 and 1648–9.
S   *Works*, ed. Theobald, Seward, and Sympson. London, 1750. Vol. 10
     (ed. Seward).
W   *Works*, ed. Henry Weber. Edinburgh, 1812. Vol. 12.]

Dramatis Personæ] *entirely omitted* Q1, Q2 (*first issue*), F2

I.i

0.1 *Bawdber*] *Bawdher* F2, L, S
1 tainters] tainturs Q1(c); tain-
    turs C+; taints Theobald (*qy
    in* S)
6 (And...Actions) followes] ∧
    And...Actions ∧ followes Q1–
    2, F2, L; ∧And...Actions ∧
    follow S, C; (And...actions
    follow,) W, D, M; (And...
    actions fellows) Dei
9 Opening...nothing] To noth-
    ing opening in the end S (*qy*)
13 yee] you C+
20 promises] promisse Q2, F2, L
22 take] rake Q1(u)

24 shewes] shew C+
24, 25 um] them Q2+
25 multiplyes] multiply C+
39 Suspitions] Suspitious Q1–2, F2
48 a] 'o F2+
52 dayes warmth] day's sudden
    warmth Dei (*qy*)
55–56 (And...it)] ∧ ~ ...~ ∧ Q2,
    F2, L, C
55 you, that] you so, that S
56, 81, 95, 109, 115 yee] you C+
59 Turning] Tucking S, C; girning
    Dei (*qy*)
64 place, almost ∧ in] ~ ∧ ~ ∧ of
    S; ~ ∧ ~ , ~ C

474

65 Are] And W
72 Lyes] Lie S+
98 payd] pray'd S
98 watchd] watch Q1–2
101 am I] I am F2, L
106 weepers‸] weeper, Q1+
110 suffers] succours S (qy fosters)
112 they] they'd Ma
114 Bawdber] Bawdher L, S
114 would] will S
118 servants] turned over in Q2 as though a part of line 120
121 Letchers, Leaches] Leachers, Letches Q1(u)–2, F2, L; Leachers, Leeches S, M

127 were,] ~ . Q2, F2, L
127, 161, 177 I am] I'm F2, L
136 women] woman F2
137 Bawdber] Bawdher F2, L, S
143 yee] you W
151 unlickt] unlikt F2, L, S
151 win] ginn S (qy); wean C (qy)
160 there] these L+ (−D, M)
160 Protaldye.] Bawd. Q1+(−D)
171 dosse] Dross S, C, W; Dolt S (qy)
171 you] ye C, W, M
171 glister] clisters C; glisters W
172 on] of C, W
174 are] om. Q1–2, F2, L

I.ii

1 Though] Thought Q1
2 no end] no other end W
3 I am] I'm F2
5 your] you Q1–2, F2, L
5 your...by] you...that S (qy)
7 weakenesses] weakness F2
14 her] the S
24 or] to F2, L
28 lost] loose S
35 reasons] reason F2, L, S
40 loose] lose F2
54 your] you Q1

54 grace done] Grace but done S
61 an enimy] an nimy Q1(u)
84 such] them Q2, F2, L, S
86 their foreheads] their high foreheads M
102 mothes] mothers Q1–2, F2, L
105 and...traine] and vertuous traine Q1(c)–2; and vertuous traine traine Q1(u)
106 worthy] worth S
111 its] ti's F2; it's L
124 powers] Power L, S

II.i

5 razed] raized Q2, F2
8 so neere a] a neere Q1–2, F2; a nearer L+
12 griefe‸] ~ , L, S
18 if or] or if F2, L; not if S
26 prizelesse] priceless D, M
28 owner] doner Q1–2; donor F2, L
34 may] must W
35 jealious] jelous F2+
41 them] 'em F2+
58 shall] should Q2+

61 Cator] Caterer S, C, W
65 a one] an one F2, L, S, C
69 em] them Q2+
70 em] them Q2, F2
91 em] him Q1–2, C, W
92 souldiers] soldier C, W
92 see me] seeme Q1–2, F2, L
96 rare...arts] care...acts Q1–2, F2, L; care... arts C, W
111 Austrachia] Astrucia L, S
113 With all] Withall Q2, F2
129 you,] your ‸ Q1–2, F2, L

144 art] are Q1–2
164 but] altho' Ma
189 affect] effect Q2, F2
201 texte] texde Q1–2, F2; tax L, S
223 scarabes] Scrabs L, S
228 trustde] trust Q2, F2, L
241 pleasde] plea'd Q2
242 blessings] blessing Q1
253 meant] meane Q1–2, F2

257 you mothes] you mothers Q1–2,
F2; your Mothers L; your
Mouths S, C, W
259 you] yon Q2
264 sonnes] Son F2
289 a] om. Q2, F2, L, S
303 what] om. F2
318 I am] I'm F2, L
321 I] om. Q1–2, F2, L
324 yet appeare] yet you appear W

II.ii

2 her] his S, C, W
4 Weary] weary'd L, S
5 thought] though Q1
6 I have snigled] I'll snigle S; I've
singled S (qy), C

12 desire] Design S, C
32 lost] lose W, M
36 You'le hunt] You I'll hunt F2
39 troope] troops S

II.iii

9 ath] o'th' F2+
11 take it] take't Q2+ (−W, D,
M)
12 *Martell.*] om. Q1–2, F2
15 ye] you C+
22 met a] met with a Q2, F2, L, S
43 two, man] two‸ man Q1; two‸
men Q2, F2, L, S
45 um] them Q2+ (−D, M)
46 set] whet Q2+ (−C)
47 um] them Q2+

50 fourescore] four scores M
50 they are] they're F2, L, S, C
64 and] an F2
67 a] o' F2+
68 too] two Q1
72 And] an S+
72 bawd] bawb Q2, F2
72 beast, barking] A Beast, a barking S
74 your] you Q1
79 mushrump] mushrum F2+

II.iv

0.1 *Bawdber*] *Bawdher* F2, L, S
24 him‸ with,] him, which‸ Q1–
2, F2, L
29 thy] thine Q2+
44 boy] Body S
52 Villaine] Villany F2, L, S
53 *Protaldye.*] om. Q1–2, F2
56 you] yon Q1
60 forsweare] swear C
65 rare] care Q1 (u)

73 fall] falls Q1–2, F2
77 his] this W
93 shall] should F2, L, S
95 by] from L, S
97 here] hear F2, L
106 You are] You're F2, L
108 you] yon Q1–2, F2, L
123 good] god Q1–2, F2, L
124 Follow as] Follow me as S
129 pray you] pray F2+ (−C)

130 you] your F2, L
131 *Martell*] *Mart.* [as speech-
    prefix] Q2, F2, L
131.1 Bawdber] Bawdher L, S
136 fearefull] *om.* F2
141 one] on Q2

149 *Brunhalt.*] *Prot.* Q1+ (−S)
164 not] no W
169 worde] worke Q1–2, F2
171 *Protaldye,* then] *Protaldye,* thou
    then S, C
173.1 *Exeunt.*] *om.* Q1(u)–2, F2

III.i

2 mandrake] mandrakes S+
14 temperate] intemperate W (*qy*)
15 do you not] don't you S
17 my] thy Q1+
32 your] you Q1(u)
34 selfe's] selfe is Q2+
37 forgot] forget W
44 beates∧] ~ , F2
52 lesse∧] ~ , Q2, F2, L
70 Nere] We are Q1+ (−D, M);
    'Twere Ma
84 nay my selfe,] my selfe, nay
    Q1–2, F2, L
93 thought] though Q1
99 inhabited] uninhabited S, C
101 borrowde] borrowed Q2, F2,
    S, C, M
104 one] own L
110 travaile] travel F2, L
113 to] unto S, C, W
114 Brother] My Brother S, C
115 inlarge] in large Q2

116 joyes are unbounded] Joy's
    unbounded S
116 insteed of question] 'stead of
    questioning S
117 to] *om.* Q1–2, F2, L
121 stage] stange Q2, F2
121 eye] ye Q2, F2, L
139 hope] hope's S
141 From] As Ma, W
143 where] whereas S
150 The example] Th'example F2,
    L, S, C
153 What∧] ~ , F2
167 *Forte*] *Forts* Q1–2, F2, L;
    Leforte S+
168 learnde] learned F2, L, C, M
168 Astronomer, great] Astronomer,
    and great S; Astronomer, a
    great C, W
176 conveiance] conveniance Q2,
    F2, L, S
183 *Bawdber*] *Bawdher* L, S

III.ii

0.1 Bawdber] Bawdher L, S
2 *Servant.*] *Lecure.* Q1+(−D,
    M)
3 Wind] Pray wind S
3 love] have Q2, F2, L; will have
    S
5 businesses] business L, S
6 *Servant.*] *Lecure.* Q1+ (−D,
    M)

7.1 *Exit.*] *following line* 6 Q1+
    (−D, M)
9 All that's] All's that F2, L
10–11 will gladly] gladly will S
13 do] to Q1–2; too F2, L
14 howsoever] However S
17 borne] born F2, L
21 should] shall F2, L
23 marcht] matcht Q1–2, F2, L

477

23 fought] sought F2, L
25 away] a way Q1
26 nay if] Nay, and if S
27 the‸ fast] thee; fast Q2, F2, L;
om. the S
31 em] them Q2, F2, L, W
38 sum's] son's Q1–2, F2
38 you] ye W
38 every] each S
40–41 the kingdome] the whole
Kingdom S
42 bawdery] bawdry F2+
42.1 Enter...Lady] Enter Protaldy, a Lady, and Revellers
Q1+(−D, M)
43 be long] belong Q1–2
43 earning your] earning of your S
46 What opinion] What an Opinion
S
74 chops] chaps C+
77 Ha[four times]] Ha[five times]
S
80 fie] fie, fie S
90 ide] I do Q1–2, F2, L, C; I S
91.1 Enter Revellers.] at line 42.1
Q1+(−D, M)
93 I had thought] I thought S
93 my] om. W

101 Me] See Sympson (qy in S)
109.1 The] They F2+
127 has] hath Q2+
128 palace] place Q1+
137 Withdraw...lights.] Withdraw
——but for your Lights. S;
Withdraw! But, for your lights
——C, W
140 do] om. S, W
142 incitement, not] incitement, and
not S+
143 Whither] Whether Q2, F2
144 so unlike] So much unlike S
149 thy] my Q2, F2, L
157 jealious] jealous Q2+
164 unlucky] unhappy L, S
169 Bequeathd] Bequeathe Q1+
(−W, D, M)
170 Austracia] Astrucia L
179 suffer'd double] suffer'd | A
double S
179 travaile] travel F2, L
187 fate] face F2, L
187 sweare‸ fell...hand;] ~ , to
fall...~ , S; ~ . Fell...~ ? C
187 fell] Tell Q2, F2, L
190.1 Enter Martell.] following line
189 Q1+(−W, D, M)

III.iii

7 figure which] Figure then |
Which S
18 loanes] loans F2, L
25 this] his F2
28 named] nam'd F2+ (−W, M)
46 your] you Q2
51 a] her Ma

52 at...paine] 't least ease my
Paine S
55 eye] eyes W
57 Diana] Dian S
69 virtue living] living virtue D
69.1 Exit] Exeunt Q1–2, F2, L, S

IV.i

1 Thierry.] Mart. Q2
3 toward] towards F2, L, S
5 Outrunne] Outrunnes Q1–2,
F2

5 on] om. S
7 sees] see M
16 Gives] Give Q1–2, F2
17 pleasure the‸] the pleasure, S+

478

25 comfort] comforts S+
30 thee] the F2+
40 a way] away Q2, F2
61 haile] hale Q2
62 thy] the F2, L, S
64 She is] Sh'is F2+
72 thinke] thing F2
84 It] I L, S
86 yee] you C+
96 with all] withall Q1(u)
109 staies] stay S+
111 um] them Q2+
113 Here is] Here's F2, L
115 venter] venture F2+
127 thou'rt] they'r Q1–2, F2, L;
    they've S (qy), D, M; they've
    made thee the D (qy)
135 Tell] 'Till S, Ma, W, D, M
149 amongst] among M
151 won] woue Q1; wove Q2, F2,
    L, S
159 *Martell.] Deui.* Q1–2, F2

163 kingdome] Kingdom's S
165 a] an F2+
173 dying] thing Q2, F2, L, S
179 makes] make C+
179 proceede] procreant S, C (qy
    breed), W; proud Theobald (qy
    in S), D, M
182 to] too C, W, M; 'tis Heath (in
    D)
185 worthines] worthies Q1–2, F2,
    L; worth S, C; worths W, D, M
199 it] om. S
202 knowes...loves] know...love
    L+
206 olives beare] olive beare Q2;
    Olive-bear F2, L; Olive bears S
211 'tis] is't F2, it is S
212 above?] above us? C, W
213 whither] whether Q2, F2
213 venter] venture F2+
226 hells ‸...mother;] ~ ;...~ ‸
    Q1–2, F2; ~ ;...~ : L, S

IV.ii

1 I am] I'm F2, L
3 *Enter* Lecure.] *following* death,
    line 4 Q1+ (–D, M)
13 it on] upon S
38 safe] safely D (qy)
47 our] your Q1–2, F2, L
55 a] no Sympson (qy in S)
92 bankerout] bankrupt F2+
95 In] I F2
130 from] from from F2
174 upon] on S
176 pleasures] pleasure Q2, F2, S
185 *Ordella,] Ordella,* is S

186 monument worthy] Monument
    only worthy S
186 the] a W
199 praiers] praises Q2, F2, L
216 up] om. C, W
220 That] For Ma
240 that] om. Q2, F2, L, M
247 Reveng'd] Revenge Q1–2
250 ill] all F2, L, S
264 *Austrachia] Astrucia* L, S
267 to] unto S
268 thought] though Q2

V.i

5 tonges] tones Q1+
12 part] om. Q1(u)
28 of god] of good Q1–2; of a good
    F2, L; of a gode S

29 sicker wombe] siking Womb S;
    siking wemb C, W
31 a] of Q2+
32 countriman] countrymen W

35 on, pead] one, pead Q1 (|)
39 nor] and Q2, F2, L, S
40 too] two F2+ (−D)
44 sowe] some F2, L
44 the] and M
70 bricke-kills] Brick-kilns S+
70 and feare] and the fear S, C
72 preferre it] preserve you from it
   S, C; prevent it Ma, W, D, M;
   defer it S (qy); prefer to it
   (omitting too't line 71) Mi
92 Come...a] Come, there are a
   Q1+ (−D, M)
92 em] them Q2
92.1 Souldiers] Soldier F2
95 am I] I am F2, L, S
96 adventures] adventure Q2
103 letters] letter Q1+ (−D, M)

106 love safety] love your safety
    Q2+
128 we] she Q1
129–130 owne;...heare,] ~ !...
    ~ ? C+
130 bind mee] bind me, bind me F2,
    L, S
132 lading] ladine Q2
148, 157, 160, 171 em] them Q2+
149 where, where] where [thre
    times] F2, L, S
155 wherefore] therefore Q2, F2,
    L, S
165 unbind] unbidd Q2
171 top] topt Q2+
180 I am] I'm F2, L, S, C
205 piecemeale] piece-meals F2, L,
    S, C

V.ii

3 hawke] Hawks F2, L
6 cures] cure F2+(−D, M)
8 glisters] clisters C, W, M

F2 omission begins after drench, line
   10

16 bloud] blond Q2
23 prayer] prayers Q1
29 now...selfe] feele your selfe
   now Q2, L, S
50 proclame] maintain Dei (qy)
51 above] from W
54 recalm'd] reclam'd Q1; reclaim'd
   Q2+, Ma; becalm'd S (qy)
62 never I, never;] never, never I!
   C, W
77 not feele] nor feel S
83 ye...ye] you...you C+
87 misery ∧...see,] ~ ∧...~ ∧
   Q2, L, S; ~ ,...~ ∧ C+
106 have] are Q1

106, 148 um] them Q2+
117 pleasure] pleasures Q2, L, S

   F2 omission ends after line 127

130 to, that] ~ ∧ ~ Q1+(−W, D,
    M)
133 then] thine Q1
138 give] gives Q2, F2, L
138.1 Enter Ordella.] following line
    136 Q1+(−W, D, M)
146 No,] Nor ∧ Q1+ (−W, D, M)
149 sweetely there?] sweetely?
    there's Q1+
161 sirs] Sir Q2, F2, L, S
162 soule: away,] ~ ∧ ~ , Q2, F2
167 She is] Shee's Q2, F2, L
169 me] om. Q1 (u)
170 Ordella.] Mart. Q1+(−D)
176.1 Enter...Memberge.] following
    line 175 Q1+(−D, M)
177 her] om. S

480

185 *Dies*] *Die* F2, L, S, C

187–188 um...um] them...them
 Q2+

188 unto] to Q2, F2, L, S

191 service] services C+

192 mad] bad D (*qy*)

195 tonge] tomb Theobald and
 Sympson (*qy in* S)

THE FAITHFUL SHEPHERDESS

edited by

CYRUS HOY

TEXTUAL INTRODUCTION

The Faithful Shepherdess (Greg, 287) was not entered in the Stationers' Register and its first quarto edition is undated. Limits for its date of publication are suggested by the relatively brief partnership of its publishers, Richard Bonian and Henry Walley, which is traceable from December 1608 to January 1610. The Q1 text was certainly in print by 3 May 1610 when Sir William Scipwith, to whom Fletcher had addressed an Ode among the quarto's prefatory verses, died. Later in the year the play is mentioned by John Davies of Hereford in Epigram 206 of his *Scourge of Folly* (entered in the Stationers' Register on 8 October 1610). Greg, on the evidence of the device which appears on the Q1 title-page (McKerrow, 284), suggests the printer 'to have been Edward Allde'.

Under the date of 8 December 1628 the Stationers' Register records the transfer of rights to the play from Walley to R. Meighen, and in the following year a second quarto, printed from Q1, appeared. A third edition, printed from Q2, was published in 1634, prompted presumably by the recent revival of the play at Court and at the Blackfriars; it is provided with verses by Shakerly Marmion to the actor Joseph Taylor, who had supervised the Court production, and with the new Prologue which William Davenant had written for the occasion. A fourth quarto edition, printed from Q3, appeared in 1656, and a fifth, printed from Q4, in 1665. The text of the play which appears in the folio of 1679 was printed from Q4.

The undated first quarto is, then, the only substantive text of the play and is the basis of the present edition. Despite the absence of a licensing entry in the Stationers' Register, the publication of Q1 clearly had the blessing of the dramatist. The play is set before the reading public with a bevy of prefatory verses wherein Fletcher is consoled by his fellow dramatists (Beaumont, Jonson, Chapman, Field) or consoles himself for the failure of the play on the stage; the prefatory material is climaxed with the famous epistle 'To the

485

Reader', signed by Fletcher, with its much-quoted definition of tragicomedy. Copy for Q1 must have been, if not the author's own manuscript, then a carefully prepared transcript of this.

The care that went into the preparation of printer's copy was matched by the care expended on it by Compositor *A* who began the job of setting it in type; using a single skeleton-forme, he set the whole of sheets B, C, D and E. It is tempting to over-praise the quality of Compositor *A*'s work because what follows, when his stint is finished, is so bad. Nonetheless, it is fair to say that the printing of sheets B through E is no worse, and on the whole rather better, than that of the average Elizabethan play quarto. A drastic change occurs with the beginning of sheet F. Two new skeleton-formes are added, and a second compositor (*B*) takes over. The quality of his work may be suggested by some of the running-titles he set for the skeleton-forme in which the inner formes of sheets G and H were printed: 'Sepheardesse' (G2), 'SheaPheardesse' (G3ᵛ, H4), 'ShePheardesse' (G4, H1ᵛ). Compositor *B*'s work is extremely careless, marked at virtually every line by one or more instances of foul case or wrong fount or turned letters, and characterized throughout by a quite indiscriminate use of periods, commas and colons. Fletcher's dramatic system of pointing is preserved with considerable fidelity by Compositor *A*, but is reduced to near chaos by Compositor *B*. His work extends through both the outer and the inner formes of sheets F, G and H. With sheet I, two new compositors appear, and with them two new skeleton-formes. Compositor *C* set sigs I1 through I2ᵛ, I4, K1–K1ᵛ, K4ᵛ–L1ᵛ. Compositor *D* set sigs I3–I3ᵛ, I4ᵛ, and K2–K4. Their treatment of Fletcher's punctuation is not markedly better than that accorded it by Compositor *B*.

The four compositors who set Q1 exhibit habits of spelling and abbreviation which make it possible to identify their shares with some precision. At the centre of the evidence is the work of Compositor *B*, conspicuous alike for its execrable quality and for certain spelling peculiarities that cause the section of Q1 set by him to stand out from all the others. Chief among these is Compositor *B*'s spelling of the word 'shepherd'. He spells this frequently recurring word in a variety of ways, but always with an *ea* in its first as well as in its second syllable, e.g., 'sheapeard', 'sheapheard', 'sheappeard'. Compositors *A* and *C* always spell the word 'shepheard'. On the other hand, Compositor *D*'s spelling ('sheepheard') is distinctly his own.

Compositor *B*'s spelling 'theise' is unique in Q 1; all three of the other compositors spell 'these'. So, too, with Compositor *B*'s spelling 'woeman' (or 'woemen'), spelled 'woman' (or 'women') by all the others. Other spellings characteristic of Compositor *B* are 'ther' (or 'ther's'), 'wher', 'ould', 'tould', 'thincke', 'banckes', 'darcknes', 'drincke', 'trewe', 'hygh', 'hydd', 'thyne', 'hayle', 'wayting', 'bytt', 'gydes', 'paynes', 'smyle', 'tyme', 'doeble', 'fier', 'freind'. The abbreviated speech prefix *Per.* (for *Perigot*) serves to differentiate Compositor *B* from Compositor *A* (who sets *Peri.*) if not from Compositors *C* and *D* (both of whom also set *Per.*). Compositor *A* sets the speech prefix *Clor.* Compositor *B*, while sometimes setting *Clor.*, more often sets the character's name in full, *Clorin*, as do Compositors *C* and *D*. Compositor *A* sets *Sul.*, while Compositors *B*, *C*, and *D* set the full word *Sullen* by way of designating the speech prefixes of the Sullen Shepherd. But the feature which most effectively distinguishes Compositor *B*'s setting of speech prefixes from the work of his fellow compositors is his use of a colon (instead of the usual period) following a speech prefix, a practice shared by none of the others.

A difference in spelling and a difference in method of setting prefixes taken together serve to differentiate Compositors *C* and *D* one from another. As has already been noted, Compositor *C*'s spelling *shepheard* contrasts with Compositor *D*'s *sheepheard*. In setting speech prefixes, Compositor *C* does what is normally done: indents the prefix some two or three spaces from the left-hand margin. Compositor *D* does not thus indent, but sets the prefix flush with the left-hand margin. Compositor *C* generally (but not invariably) sets the speech prefix *Satyre*; Compositor *D* generally (but not invariably) sets *Satire*. By way of designating speech prefixes for the Old Shepherd, Compositor *C* sets *Old*, Compositor *D* sets *Olde*.

The most formidable problem which Q 1 poses for the editor of *The Faithful Shepherdess* is the punctuation. The extent of the deterioration in the quarto's pointing after Compositor A's stint is ended will be clear from the fact that, while it has seemed necessary to emend the Q1 punctuation 64 times in Compositor A's share (sigs. B1 through E4^v, or from I.i.1 through III.i.197), some 536 emendations of the quarto pointing have been deemed necessary in the remainder of the play (sigs. F1 through L1^v) set by Compositors B, C, and D.

The present edition is based on a collation of the seven extant copies of Q1 preserved in the following collections: British Museum (wanting leaf [A4]), Bodleian Library (wanting leaves ¶1 and ¶2), the Dyce Collection in the Victoria and Albert Museum, Harvard University Library, the Henry E. Huntington Library (wanting leaf G3, which has been supplied from a copy of Q2), the Carl Pforzheimer Library, and an hitherto unrecorded copy in the possession of Mr Robert S. Pirie, Boston, Mass. Leaves ¶1 and ¶2 are missing from the Pirie copy. While the sheets of Q1 were going through the press a number of corrections were made, the substantive changes made in the inner and outer formes of sheet D, and the inner forme of sheet I being of particular importance.

THE FAITHFUL SHEPHERDESS

To my lov'd friend M. John Fletcher,
on his Pastorall

Can my approovement (Sir) be worth your thankes?
Whose unknowne name and muse (in swathing clowtes)
Is not yet growne to strength, among these rankes
To have a roome and beare off the sharpe flowtes
Of this our pregnant age, that does despise
All innocent verse, that lets alone her vice.

But I must justifie what privately,
I censur'd to you: my ambition is
(Even by my hopes and love to Poesie)
To live to perfect such a worke, as this,   10
Clad in such elegant proprietie
Of words, including a morallitie

So sweete and profitable, though each man that heares,
(And learning has enough to clap and hisse)
Arives not too't, so misty it appeares;
And to their filmed reasons, so amisse:
But let Art looke in truth, she like a mirror,
Reflects her comfort, ignorances terror

Sits in her owne brow, being made afraid,
Of her unnaturall complexion,   20
As ougly women (when they are araid
By glasses) loath their true reflection;
Then how can such opinions injure thee,
That tremble, at their owne deformitie?

12 morallitie] Q3; mortallitie Q1-2

Opinion, that great foole, makes fooles of all,
And (once) I feard her till I met a minde
Whose grave instructions philosophicall,
Toss'd it like dust upon a March strong winde:
He shall for ever my example be,
And his embraced doctrine grow in me.   30

His soule (and such commend this) that commaund
Such art, it should me better satisfie,
Then if the monster clapt his thousand hands,
And drownd the sceane with his confused cry;
And if doubts rise, loe their owne names to cleare 'em
Whilst I am happy but to stand so neere 'em.

                                                    N.F.

To my friend Maister *John Fletcher* upon his
Faithfull Shepheardesse

I know too well that no more then the man
That travels through the burning desarts, can
When he is beaten with the raging sunne,
Halfe smotherd with the dust, have power to runne
From a coole river, which himselfe doth finde,
Ere he be slak'd: no more can he whose minde
Joies in the muses, hold from that delight,
When nature, and his full thoughts bid him write,
Yet wish I those whome I for friends have knowne,
To sing their thoughts to no eares but their owne: 10
Why should the man, whose wit nere had a staine,
Upon the publike stage present his vaine,
And make a thousand men in judgement sit,
To call in question his undoubted wit,
Scarce two of which can understand the lawes
Which they should judge by, nor the parties cause,
Among the rout there is not one that hath
In his owne censure an explicite faith.

One company knowing they judgement lacke,
Ground their beliefe on the next man in blacke: 20
Others, on him that makes signes, and is mute,
Some like as he does in the fairest sute,
He as his mistres doth, and she by chance,
Nor wants there those, who as the boy doth dance
Betweene the actes, will censure the whole play:
Some like if the wax lights be new that day:
But multitudes there are whose judgements goes
Headlong according to the actors clothes.
For this, these publicke things and I, agree
So ill, that but to do aright to thee,   30
I had not bene perswaded to have hurld
These few, ill spoken lines, into the world,
Both to be read, and censurd of, by those,
Whose very reading makes verse senceles prose,
Such as must spend above an houre, to spell
A challenge on a post, to know it well:
But since it was thy happe to throw away,
Much wit, for which the people did not pay,
Because they saw it not, I not dislike
This second publication, which may strike   40
Their consciences, to see the thing they scornd,
To be with so much wit and art adornd.
Besides one vantage more in this I see,
Your censurers must have the quallitie
Of reading, which I am affraid is more
Then halfe your shreudest judges had before.

Fr. Beaumont.

42 wit] Q2; will Q1

To the worthy Author *M.*
John Fletcher.

The wise, and many-headed *Bench*, that sits
    Upon the Life, and Death of *Playes*, and *Wits*,
(Compos'd of *Gamester*, *Captaine*, *Knight*, *Knight's man*,
    Lady, or *Pusil*, that weares maske, or fan,
Velvet, or *Taffata* cap, rank'd in the darke
    With the shops *Foreman*, or some such *brave sparke*,
That may judge for his *six-pence*) had, before
    They saw it halfe, damd thy whole play, and more,
Their motives were, since it had not to do
    With vices, which they look'd for, and came to.   10
I, that am glad, thy Innocence was thy Guilt,
    And wish that all the *Muses* blood were spilt,
In such a *Martirdome*; To vexe their eyes,
    Do crowne thy murdred *Poëme*: which shall rise
A glorified worke to Time, when Fire,
    Or moathes shall eate, what all these Fooles admire.
                           Ben: Jonson.

To his loving friend M. *Jo. Fletcher*
concerning his Pastorall, being
both a Poeme and a play:

There are no suerties (good friend) Will be taken
For workes that vulgar-good-name hath forsaken:
A Poeme and a play too! why tis like
A scholler that's a Poet: their names strike
Their pestilence inward, when they take the aire;
And kill out right: one cannot both fates beare.
But, as a Poet thats no scholler, makes
Vulgarity his whiffler, and so takes
Passage with ease, and state through both sides prease
Of Pageant seers: or as schollers please   10
That are no Poets; more then Poets learnd;

Since their art solely, is by soules discernd;
The others fals within the common sence
And sheds (like common light) her influence:
So, were your play no Poeme, but a thing
That every Cobler to his patch might sing:
A rout of nifles (like the multitude)
With no one limme of any art indude:
Like would to like, and praise you: but because,
Your poeme onely hath by us applause,   20
Renews the golden world; and holds through all
The holy lawes of homely pastorall;
Where flowers, and founts, and Nimphs, and semi-Gods,
And all the Graces finde their old abods:
Where forrests flourish but in endlesse verse;
And meddowes, nothing fit for purchasers:
This Iron age that eates it selfe, will never
Bite at your golden world; that others, ever
Lov'd as it selfe: then like your Booke do you
Live in ould peace: and that for praise allow.   30

G. Chapman.

To that noble and true lover of learning,
Sir Walter Aston knight
of the Bath.

Sir I must aske your patience, and be trew.
This play was never liked, unlesse by few
That brought their judgements with um, for of late
First the infection, then the common prate
Of common people, have such customes got
Either to silence plaies, or like them not.
Under the last of which this interlude,
Had falne for ever prest downe by the rude
That like a torrent which the moist south feedes,

Drowne's both before him the ripe corne and weedes: 10
Had not the saving sence of better men
Redeem'd it from corruption: (deere Sir then)
Among the better soules, be you the best
In whome, as in a Center I take rest,
And propper being: from whose equall eye
And judgement, nothing growes but puritie:
(Nor do I flatter) for by all those dead,
Great in the muses, by *Apolloes* head,
He that ads any thing to you; tis done
Like his that lights a candle to the sunne: 20
Then be as you were ever, your selfe still
Moved by your judgement, not by love, or will,
And when I sing againe as who can tell
My next devotion to that holy well,
Your goodnesse to the muses shall be all,
Able to make a worke Heroyicall.

Given to your service
John Fletcher.

To the inheritour of all worthines,
Sir William Scipwith.
Ode.

If from servile hope or love,
                    I may prove
But so happy to be thought for
Such a one whose greatest ease
                    Is to please
(Worthy sir) I have all I sought for,

For no ich of greater name,
                    which some clame
By their verses do I show it

494

To the world; nor to protest   10
             Tis the best;
These are leane faults in a poet:

Nor to make it serve to feed
             at my neede,
Nor to gaine acquaintance by it,
Nor to ravish kinde Atturnies,
             in their journies,
Nor to read it after diet.

Farre from me are all these Ames,
             Fittest frames   20
To build weakenesse on and pitty.
Onely to your selfe, and such
             whose true touch
Makes all good, let me seeme witty.

             The Admirer of your vertues,
             John Fletcher.

To the perfect gentleman
Sir Robert Townesend.

If the greatest faults may crave
   Pardon where contrition is
(Noble Sir) I needes must have
A long one, for a long amisse.
If you aske me (how is this)
   Upon my faith Ile tell you frankely,
   You love above my meanes to thanke yee.
Yet according to my Talent,
As sowre fortune loves to use me,
A poore Shepheard I have sent,   10
In home-spun gray for to excuse me.

And may all my hopes refuse me:
   But when better comes ashore,
   You shall have better, newer, more.
Til when, like our desperate debters,
Or our three pild sweete protesters,
I must please you in bare letters,
And so pay my debts, like jesters;
Yet I oft have seene good feasters,
   Onely for to please the pallet,   20
   Leave great meat and chuse a sallet.

All yours
John Fletcher.

To the Reader.

If you be not reasonably assurde of your knowledge in this kinde of Poeme, lay downe the booke or read this, which I would wish had bene the prologue. It is a pastorall Tragie-comedie, which the people seeing when it was plaid, having ever had a singuler guift in defining, concluded to be a play of country hired Shepheards, in gray cloakes, with curtaild dogs in strings, sometimes laughing together, and sometimes killing one another: And missing whitsun ales, creame, wassel and morris-dances, began to be angry. In their error I would not have you fall, least you incurre their censure. Understand therefore a pastorall to be a representation of shep- 10 heards and shephearddesses, with their actions and passions, which must be such as may agree with their natures, at least not exceeding former fictions, and vulgar traditions: they are not to be adorn'd with any art, but such improper ones as nature is said to bestow, as singing and Poetry, or such as experience may teach them, as the vertues of hearbs, and fountaines: the ordinary course of the Sun, moone, and starres, and such like. But you are ever to remember Shepherds to be such, as all the ancient Poets and moderne of understanding have receaved them: that is, the owners of flockes and not hyerlings. A tragie-comedie is not so called in respect of 20 mirth and killing, but in respect it wants deaths, which is inough to make it no tragedie, yet brings some neere it, which is inough to make it no comedie: which must be a representation of familiar people, with such kinde of trouble as no life be questiond, so that a God is as lawfull in this as in a tragedie, and meane people as in a comedie. Thus much I hope will serve to justifie my Poeme, and make you understand it, to teach you more for nothing, I do not know that I am in conscience bound.

John Fletcher.

[From Q3

Unto his worthy friend M^r. *Joseph Taylor*
upon his presentment of the *Faithfull Shepherdesse*
before the King and Queene, at White-hall, on
Twelfth night last. 1633.

When this smooth Pastorall was first brought forth,
The Age twas borne in, did not know it's worth.
Since by thy cost, and industry reviv'd,
It hath a new fame, and new birth atchiv'd.
Happy in that shee found in her distresse,
A friend, as faithfull, as her Shepherdesse.
For having cur'd her from her courser rents,
And deckt her new with fresh habiliments,
Thou brought'st her to the Court, and made her be
A fitting spectacle for Majestie.   10
So have I seene a clowded beauty drest
In a rich vesture, shine above the rest.
Yet did it not receive more honour from
The glorious pompe, then thine owne action.
Expect no satisfaction for the same,
Poets can render no reward but Fame.
Yet this Ile prophesie, when thou shalt come
Into the confines of *Elysium*
Amidst the Quire of Muses, and the lists
Of famous Actors, and quicke Dramatists,   20
So much admir'd for gesture, and for wit,
That there on Seats of living Marble sit,
The blessed Consort of that numerous Traine,
Shall rise with an applause to entertaine
Thy happy welcome, causing thee sit downe,
And with a Lawrell-wreath thy temples crowne.
And meane time, while this Poeme shall be read,
Taylor, thy name shall be eternized:
For it is just, that thou, who first did'st give
Unto this booke a life, by it shouldst live.   30

Shack. Marmyon.

[From Q3

This Dialogue newly added, was spoken by way of Prologue
to both their Majesties at the first acting of
this Pastorall at *Somerset-house* on
Twelfe-night 1633.

Priest.

A Broyling Lambe on *Pans* chiefe Altar lies,
My Wreath, my Censor, Virge, and Incense by:
But I delay'd the pretious Sacrifice,
To shew thee here, a gentler Deity.

Nymph.

Nor was I to thy sacred Summons slow,
Hither I came as swift as th'Eagles wing,
Or threatning shaft from vext *Dianaes* bow,
To see this Islands God; the worlds best King.

Priest.

Blesse then that Queene, that doth his eyes envite
And eares, t'obey her Scepter, halfe this night.   10

Nymph.

Let's sing such welcomes, as shall make Her sway
Seeme easie to Him, though it last till day.

Welcome as Peace t'unwalled Citties, when
Famine and Sword leave them more graves then men.
As Spring to Birds, or Noone-dayes Sun to th'old
Poore mountayne Muscovite congeald with cold,
As Shore to'th Pilote in a safe knowne Coast
When's Carde is broken and his Rudder lost.

This Dialogue] Written by Sir William Davenant, and reprinted among the
'Poems on Several Occasions never before Printed' in the 1673 edition of his *Works*
(p. 305). For variants between this later version of the Dialogue and the Q3 text, see
the Historical Collation.

[Dramatis Personae

Perigot
Thenot
Daphnis
Alexis
Sullen Shepherd
Old Shepherd
Priest of Pan
God of the River
Satyr
Clorin
Amoret
Amarillis
Cloe
Shepherds, Shepherdesses]

THE FAITHFULL SHEPHEARDESSE

Enter Clorin *a Shepheardesse having buried her love in an Arbour.* **I. i**

Clorin. Haile holy earth, whose colde armes do embrace
The truest man that ever fed his flockes:
By the fat plaines of fruitfull Thessaly,
Thus I salute thy grave, thus do I pay
My early vowes and tribute of mine eies,
To thy still loved ashes: thus I free
My selfe from all ensuing heates and fires
Of love, all sports, delights and games,
That Shepheards hold full deare: thus put I off.
Now no more shall these smooth browes be girt,　　　　10
With youthfull coronals, and lead the dance,
No more the company of fresh faire Maids
And wanton shepheards be to me delightfull,
Nor the shrill pleasing sound of merry pipes,
Under some shady dell, when the coole winde
Plaies on the leaves: all be farre away,
Since thou art farre away, by whose deare side,
How often have I sat crownd with fresh flowers
For Summers queene, whilst every Shepheards boy,
Puts on his lusty greene with gaudy hooke,　　　　20
And hanging scrippe of finest cordevan:
But thou art gone, and these are gone with thee,
And all are dead but thy deare memorie:
That shall outlive thee, and shall ever spring,
Whilst there are pipes, or Jolly shepheards sing.
And heere will I, in honor of thy love,
Dwell by thy grave, forgetting all those joyes,
That former times made precious to mine eies:
Onely remembring what my youth did gaine,
In the darke hidden vertuous use of hearbs:　　　　30
That will I practise, and as freely give

All my endeavours, as I gaind them free.
Of all greene wounds I know the remedies,
In men or cattell, be they stung with snakes,
Or charmd with powerfull words of wicked art,
Or be they love-sicke, or through too much heat
Growne wilde or lunaticke, their eies or eares
Thickned with misty filme of dulling rume,
These I can cure, such secret vertue lies
In hearbs applyed by a virgins hand: 40
My meat shall be what these wilde woods affoord,
Berries, and Chesnuts, Plantains, on whose cheeks
The Sun sits smiling, and the lofty fruit
Puld from the faire head of the straite grown pine:
On these Ile feede with free content and rest,
When night shal blinde the world, by thy side blest.

Enter a Satyre.

Satyre.   Through yon same bending plaine,
That flings his armes downe to the maine,
And through these thicke woods have I runne,
Whose bottome never kist the Sunne   50
Since the lusty spring began,
All to please my Master *Pan*,
Have I trotted without rest
To get him fruit, for at a feast,
He entertaines this comming night,
His Paramoure, the *Syrinx* bright:
But behold a fairer sight,   *He stands amazed.*
By that heavenly forme of thine,
Brightest faire thou art devine:
Sprong from great immortall race   60
Of the Gods: for in thy face,
Shines more awfull majesty,
Then dull weake mortalitie
Dare with misty eies behould
And live, therefore on this mould,
Lowly do I bend my knee,

In worship of thy dietie,
Deigne it Goddesse from my hand,
To receive what ere this land,
From her firtile wombe doth send   70
Of her choise fruites: and but lend,
Beliefe to that the *Satyre* tels,
Fairer by the famous wells,
To this present day nere grewe,
Never better nor more true.
Heere be grapes whose lusty blood,
Is the learned Poets good,
Sweeter yet did never crowne,
The head of *Bacchus*, nuts more browne
Then the squirrels teeth that cracke them,   80
Deigne ô fairest faire to take them,
For these black ey'd *Driope*,
Hath often times commaunded me,
With my clasped knee to clime,
See how well the lusty time,
Hath deckt their rising cheekes in red,
Such as on your lips is spred,
Heere be berries for a Queene,
Some be red, some be greene:
These are of that lussious meat,   90
The great God *Pan*, himselfe doth eate:
All these, and what the woods can yeeld,
The hanging mountaine or the field,
I freely offer, and ere long,
Will bring you more, more sweet and strong.
Till when humbly leave I take,
Least the great *Pan* do awake,
That sleeping lies in a deepe glade,
Under a broad beeches shade:
I must goe, I must runne,   100
Swifter then the fiery Sunne.   *Exit.*
Clorin.   And all my feares goe with thee.
What greatnesse or what private hidden power,

Is there in me to draw submission,
From this rude man, and beast? sure I am mortall,
The daughter of a Shepheard, he was mortall:
And she that bore me mortall: pricke my hand
And it will bleed: a feaver shakes me,
And the selfsame winde that makes the young lambs shrinke,
Makes me a cold, my feare saies I am mortall: 110
Yet I have heard (my mother told it me)
And now I doe believe it, if I keepe
My virgin flower uncropt, pure, chaste, and faire,
No Goblin, wood-god, Faiery, Elfe, or Fiend,
Satyr or other power that haunts these groaves,
Shall hurt my body, or by vaine illusion,
Draw me to wander after idle fiers,
Or voices calling me in dead of night,
To make me followe, and so tole me on,
Through mires and standing pooles: 120
Else why should this rough thing, who never knew
Manners, nor smooth humanitie, whose heates
Are rougher then himselfe, and more mishapen,
Thus mildely kneele to me? sure there is a power
In that great name of virgin, that bindes fast
All rude uncivill bloods, all appetites
That breake their confines: then strong chastity,
Be thou my strongest guarde, for heere Il'e dwell
In opposition against Fate and Hell.

                                                    [*Exit.*]

        Enter an Olde Shepheard, *with foure couple of Shepheards*   [I. ii
            and Shepheardesses [*including* Perigot *and* Amoret].

Old Shepheard.   Now we have done this holy festivall,
In honor of our great God, and his rights
Perform'd, prepare your selves for chast
And uncorrupted fires: that as the priest,
With powerful hand shall sprinkle on your browes
His pure and holy water, ye may be

From all hot flames of lust, and loose thoughts free.
Kneele shepheards kneele, heere comes the Priest of *Pan*.

Enter Priest.

Priest.   Shepheards thus I purge away,
Whatsoever this great day,   10
Or the past houres gave not good,
To corrupt your maiden blood:
From the high rebellious heat,
Of the grapes and strength of meat,
From the wanton quicke desires,
They do kindle by their fires,
I do wash you with this water,
Be you pure and faire heereafter.
From your livers and your vaines,
Thus I take away the staines.   20
All your thoughts be smooth and faire,
Be ye fresh and free as ayre.
Never more let lustfull heat,
Through your purged conduits beate,
Or a plighted troth be broken,
Or a wanton verse be spoken
In a Shepheardesses eare:
Go your waies y'are all cleare.

                     They rise and sing in praise of Pan.

                     The Song.

        Sing his praises that doth keepe,
             Our Flockes from harme,
        Pan the Father of our sheepe,   30
             And arme in arme
        Tread we softly in a round,
        Whilst the hollow neighbouring ground,
        Fills the musicke with her sound,

             *29–42 Sing his praises . . . unyoke.

33   505   B D W

> Pan, *o great God,* Pan *to thee*
> *Thus do we sing:*
> *Thou that keepest us chaste and free,*
> *As the young spring,*
> *Ever be thy honor spoke,*   40
> *From that place the morne is broke,*
> *To that place Day doth unyoke.*
>
> *Exeunt omnes but* Perigot *and* Amoret.

Perigot.   Stay gentle *Amoret* thou faire browd maide,
Thy Shepheard praies thee stay, that holds thee deere,
Equall with his soules good.
Amoret.   Speake, I give
Thee freedome Shepheard, and thy tongue be still
The same it ever was: as free from ill
As he whose conversation never knew
The court or cittie: be thou ever true.
Perigot.   When I fall off from my affection,   50
Or mingle my cleane thoughts with foule desires,
First let our great God cease to keepe my flockes,
That being left alone without a guard,
The woolfe, or winters rage, sommers great heat,
And want of water, rots: or what to us
Of ill is yet unknowne, fall speedily,
And in their generall ruine let me goe.
Amoret.   I pray thee gentle Shepheard wish not soe,
I do believe thee: tis as hard for me
To thinke thee false, and harder then for thee   60
To holde me foule.
Perigot.   O you are fairer farre,
Then the chaste blushing morne, or that faire starre,
That guides the wandring seaman through the deepe:
Straighter then the straightest pine upon the steepe
Head of an aged mountaine, and more white,
Then the new milke we strip before day light
From the full fraighted bags of our faire flockes:

Your haire more beautious then those hanging lockes
Of young *Apollo*.
Amoret.   Shepheard be not lost,
Ye are saild too farre alreadie from the coast   70
Of our discourse.
Perigot.   Did you not tell me once
I should not love alone, I should not loose
Those many passions, vowes, and holy oathes,
I have sent to heaven: did you not give your hand,
Even that faire hand in hostage? do not then
Give backe againe those sweetes to other men,
You your selfe vowd were mine.
Amoret.   Shepheard so farre as maidens modesty
May give assurance, I am once more thine,
Once more I give my hand, be ever free   80
From that great foe to faith, foule jealosie.
Perigot.   I take it as my best good, and desire
For stronger confirmation of our love,
To meete this happy night in that faire grove,
Where all true shepheards have rewarded bene
For their long service: say sweet shall it hould?
Amoret.   Deere friend you must not blame me if I make
A doubt of what the silent night may doe,
Coupled with this dayes heat to moove your blood:
Maids must be fearefull, sure you have not bene   90
Washd white enough, for yet I see a staine
Sticke in your liver, goe and purge againe.
Perigot.   O do not wrong my honest simple truth,
My selfe and my affections are as pure,
As those chaste flames that burne before the shrine,
Of the great *Dian*: onely my intent
To draw you thither, was to plight our trothes,
With interchange of mutuall chaste imbraces,
And ceremonious tying of our soules:
For to that holy wood is consecrate,   100
A vertuous Well, about whose flowery bancks,
The nimble footed Faieries daunce their rounds,

By the pale mooneshine, dipping often times
Their stolen children, so to make them free
From dying flesh, and dull mortalitie:
By this faire Fount hath many a Shepheard sworne,
And given away his freedome, many a troth
Beene plight, which neither envy nor ould time
Could ever breake, with many a chaste kisse given,
In hope of comming happinesse: by this   110
Fresh Fountaine many a blushing maide
Hath crownd the head of her long loved shepheard,
With gaudy flowers, whilst he happy sung,
Laies of his love and deare captivitie:
There growes all hearbs fit to coole looser flames,
Our sensuall parts provoke chiding our bloodes,
And quenching by their power those hidden sparks,
That else would breake out, and provoke our sence,
To open fires, so vertuous is that place:
Then gentle Shepheardesse believe and grant,   120
In troth it fits not with that face to scant
Your faithfull Shepheard of those chaste desires,
He ever aimd at, and——
Amoret. Thou hast prevaild, farwell, this comming night,
Shal crowne thy chaste hopes with long wishd delight.
Perigot. Our great God *Pan* reward thee for that good
Thou hast given thy poore shepheard, fairest bud
Of maiden vertues: when I leave to be
The true admirer of thy chastitie,
Let me deserve the hot polluted name,   130
Of a wilde woodman, or affect some dame
Whose often prostitution hath begot,
More foule diseases, then ever yet the hot
Sun bred through his burnings, whilst the dog
Pursues the raging Lyon, throwing fog
And deadly vapor from his angry breath,
Filling the lower world with plague and death.

Exit Amoret.

Enter another Shepheardesse [Amarillis] *that is in love with Perigot.*

Amarillis.   Shepheard may I desire to be believed,
What I shall blushing tell?
Perigot.   Faire maide you may.
Amarillis.   Then softly thus, I love thee *Perigot,*   140
And would be gladder to be lov'd againe,
Then the colde earth is in his frozen armes
To clip the wanton spring: nay do not start,
Nor wonder that I woe thee! thou that art
The prime of our young groomes, even the top
Of all our lusty Shepheards: what dull eie
That never was acquainted with desire,
Hath seene thee wrastle, run, or cast the stone,
With nimble strength and faire delivery,
And hath not sparckled fire, and speedily   150
Sent secret heat to all the neighbouring vaines?
Who ever heard thee sing, that brought againe,
That freedome backe was lent unto thy voice?
Then do not blame me (shepheard) if I be
One to be numbred in this company,
Since none that ever saw thee yet, were free.
Perigot.   Faire Shepheardesse much pittie I can lend,
To your complaints: but sure I shal not love:
All that is mine, my selfe and my best hopes,
Are given already: do not love him then   160
That cannot love againe: on other men
Bestowe those heates more free, that may returne
You fire for fire, and in one flame equall burne.
Amarillis.   Shall I rewarded be so slenderly
For my affection, most unkinde of men?
If I were old, or had agreed with Art,
To give another nature to my cheekes,
Or were I common mistris to the love
Of every swaine, or could I with such ease
Call backe my love, as many a wanton doth,   170
Thou mightst refuse me Shepheard, but to thee

509

I am onely fixt and set, let it not be
A sport, thou gentle Shepheard, to abuse
The love of silly maide.
   Perigot.   Faire soule, ye use
These words to little end: for knowe, I may
Better call backe, that time was yesterday,
Or stay the comming night, then bring my love
Home to my selfe againe, or recreant prove.
I will no longer hold you with delaies,
This present night I have appointed bene,   180
To meet that chaste faire (that enjoyes my soule)
In yonder grove, there to make up our loves.
Be not deceav'd no longer, choose againe,
These neighbouring plaines have many a comely swaine,
Fresher and freer farre then I ere was,
Bestowe that love on them and let me passe,
Farwell, be happy in a better choise.   *Exit.*
  Amarillis.   Cruell, thou hast strucke me deader with thy voice
Then if the angry heavens with their quicke flames,
Had shot me through: I must not leave to love,   190
I cannot, no I must enjoy thee boy,
Though the great dangers twixt my hopes and that
Be infinite: there is a Shepheard dwels
Downe by the More, whose life hath ever showne
More sullen discontent then *Saturnes* browe,
When he sits frowning on the birthes of men:
One that doth weare himselfe away in lonenesse,
And never joyes unlesse it be in breaking
The holy plighted troths of mutuall soules:
One that lusts after every severall beauty,   200
But never yet was knowne to love or like,
Were the face fairer or more full of truth,
Then *Phœbe* in her fulnesse, or the youth
Of smooth *Lyeus*: whose nye starved flockes
Are alwaies scabby, and infect all sheepe
They feede withall, whose lambes are ever last,
And dye before their weaning, and whose dog,

Lookes like his Maister, leane, and full of scurffe,
Not caring for the pipe or whistle: this man may
(If he be wel wrought) do a deede of wonder, 210
Forcing me passage to my long desires:
And heere he comes, as fitly to my purpose
As my quicke thoughts could wish for.

Enter Sullen [Shepherd].

Sullen Shepherd.   Fresh beautie, let me not be thought uncivill,
Thus to be partner of your lonenesse: t'was
My love (that ever working passion) drew
Me to this place to seeke some remedie
For my sicke soule: be not unkinde and faire,
For such, the mightie *Cupid* in his dombe
Hath sworne to be aveng'd on, then give roome 220
To my consuming fires, that so I may
Injoy my long desires, and so allay
Those flames, that else would burne my life away.
Amarillis.   Shepheard, were I but sure thy heart were sound
As thy words seeme to be, meanes might be found
To cure thee of thy long paines: for to me
That heavy youth consuming miserie,
The love sicke soule endures, never was pleasing:
I could be well content with the quicke easing
Of thee and thy hot fires, might it procure 230
Thy faith, and farther service to be sure.
Sullen Shepherd.   Name but that great worke, danger, or what can
Be compast by the wit or art of man,
And if I faile in my performance, may
I never more kneele to the rysing day.
Amarillis.   Then thus I try thee shepheard, this same night,
That now comes stealing on, a gentle paire
Have promis'd equall love, and do appoint
To make yon wood the place, where hands and hearts
Are to be tied for ever: breake their meeting 240
And their strong faith, and I am ever thine.

232 *Sullen Shepherd.*] Q2; *om.* Q1

Sullen Shepherd.   Tell me their names, and if I doe not move
(By my great power) the center of their love
From his fixt being, let me never more,
Warme me, by those faire eies I thus adore.
Amarillis.   Come, as we goe Ile tell thee what they are,
And give thee fit directions for thy worke.

Exeunt.

Enter Cloe.   [I. iii]

Cloe.   How have I wrongd the times, or men, that thus,
After this holy feast I passe unknowne,
And unsaluted? t'was not wont to be
Thus frozen with the younger company
Of jolly shepheards: t'was not then held good,
For lusty groomes to mixe their quicker blood
With that dull humor: most unfit to be
The friend of man, cold and dull chastitie:
Sure I am held not faire, or am too ould,
Or else not free enough, or from my fould   10
Drive not a flocke sufficient great, to gaine
The greedy eies of wealth alluring swaine.
Yet if I may believe what others say,
My face has foile enough, nor can they lay
Justly too strict a coynesse to my charge.
My flockes are many, and the downes as large
They feed uppon: then let it ever be
Their coldnesse, not my virgin modesty
Makes me complaine.

Enter Thenot.

Thenot.   Was ever man but I,
Thus truely taken with uncertaintie?   20
Where shall that man be found that loves a minde
Made up in constancy, and dares not finde
His love rewarded? heere, let all men knowe,
A wretch that lives to love his mistres so.

512

Cloe.   Shepheard I pray thee stay, where hast thou bene,
Or whether goest thou? heere be woods as greene
As any, ayre as fresh and sweet,
As where smooth *Zephirus* plaies on the fleet
Face of the curled streames: with flowers as many
As the young spring gives, and as choise as any: 30
Heere be all new delights, coole streames and wels,
Arbors oregrowne with wood bines, Caves, and dels,
Chuse where thou wilt, whilst I sit by and sing,
Or gather rushes, to make many a ring
For thy long fingers, tell thee tales of love,
How the pale *Phœbe* hunting in a grove,
First saw the boy *Endimion*, from whose eyes,
She tooke eternall fire, that never dies,
How she convaid him softly in a sleepe,
His temples bound with poppy to the steep   40
Head of old *Latmus*, where she stoopes each night,
Gilding the mountaine with her brothers light
To kisse her sweetest.
Thenot.   Farre from me are these
Hot flashes bred from wanton heat and ease,
I have forgot what love and loving meant,
Rimes, Songs, and merry rounds, that oft are sent
To the soft eare of Maid, are strange to me:
Onely I live t'admire a chastity,
That neither pleasing age, smooth tongue, or gold,
Could ever breake upon, so sure the molde   50
Is, that her minde was cast in: tis to her
I onely am reserved, she is my forme, I stirre
By, breath, and moove: tis she and only she
Can make me happy or give misery.
Cloe.   Good Shepheard, may a stranger crave to know,
To whome this deare observance you do owe?
Thenot.   Ye may, and by her vertue learne to square
And levell out your life: for to be faire
And nothing vertuous, only fits the eye

25 hast] Q2; haste Q1   32 oregrowne] Q3; are growne Q1-2

Of gaudy youth, and swelling vanitie.   60
Then knowe, shee's cald the virgin of the grove,
She that hath long since buried her chaste love,
And now lives by his grave, for whose deare soule
She hath vowd her selfe into the holy role
Of strickt virginitie, tis her I so admire,
Not any looser blood or new desire.   [*Exit.*]
Cloe.   Farewell poore swaine, thou art not for my bend,
I must have quicker soules, whose words may tend,
To some free action: give me him dare love
At first encounter, and as soone dare proove.   70

The Song.

Come Shepheards come,
Come away without delay,
Whilste the gentle time doth stay,
Greene woods are dumme,
And will never tell to any,
Those deere kisses, and those many
Sweete imbraces that are given,
Dainty pleasures that would even
Raise in coldest age a fire,
And give virgin blood desire.   80
  Then if ever,
  Now or never,
  Come and have it,
  Thinke not I,
  Dare deny,
  If you crave it.

Enter Daphnis.

Heere comes another: better be my speede,
Thou God of blood, but certaine if I reade
Not false, this is that modest shepheard, he
That onely dare salute, but nere could be   90
Brought to kisse any, holde discourse, or sing,

514

Whisper, or boldly aske that wished thing
We all are borne for: one that makes loving faces,
And could be well content to covet graces,
Were they not got by boldnesse: in this thing
My hopes are frozen, and but fate doth bring
Him heather, I would sooner choose
A man made out of snowe, and freer use
An Eunenke to my endes: but since hee is heere,
Thus I attempt him:——Thou of men most deare,   100
Welcome to her, that onely for thy sake,
Hath bene content to live: here boldly take
My hand in pledge, this hand, that never yet
Was given away to any: and but sit
Downe on this rushy bancke, whilst I go pull
Fresh blossomes from the bowes, or quickly cull
The choisest delicates from yonder meade,
To make thee chaines or chaplets, or to spreade
Under our fainting bodies, when delight
Shall locke up all our sences! how the sight   110
Of those smooth rising cheekes renue the story
Of young Adonis, when in pride and glory
He lay infolded twixt the beating armes
Of willing Venus: me thinkes stronger charmes,
Dwell in those speaking eyes: and on that brow
More sweetnesse then the painters can allow,
To their best peeces: not *Narcissus* he:
That wept himselfe away in memorie
Of his owne beautie, nor *Silvanus* boy,
Nor the twice ravisht maide, for whome old *Troy*,   120
Fell by the hand of *Pirrhus*, may to thee,
Be otherwise compared then some dead tree
To a young fruitfull Olive.
Daphnis.   I can love,
But I am loth to say so, least I prove
Too soone unhappy.
Cloe.   Happy thou wouldst say,
My dearest *Daphnis*, blush not if the day

515

To thee and thy soft heates be enemie,
Then take the comming night, faire youth tis free
To all the world, shepheard Ile meet thee then
When darkenes hath shut up the eies of men,   130
In yonder grove: speake shall our meeting hold?
Indeed ye are too bashful, be more bold,
And tell me I.
Daphnis.   I am content to say so,
And would be glad to meet, might I but pray so
Much from your fairenes, that you would be true.
Cloe.   Shepheard thou hast thy wishe.
Daphnis.   Fresh maide aduie,
Yet one word more, since you have drawne me on
To come this night, feare not to meete alone,
That man that will not offer to be ill,
Though your bright selfe would aske it, for his fill   140
Of this worlds goodnesse: do not feare him then,
But keepe your pointed time, let other men
Set up their bloods to saile, mine shall be ever,
Faire as the soule it carries, and unchast never.   *Exit.*
Cloe.   Yet am I poorer then I was before.
Is it not strange, among so many a score
Of lusty bloods, I should picke out these thinges
Whose vaines like a dull river farre from springs,
Is still the same, slowe, heavy, and unfit
For streame or motion, though the strong windes hit   150
With their continuall power upon his sides?
O happy be your names that have bene brides:
And tasted those rare sweetes, for which I pine,
And farre more heavy be thy griefe and tine,
Thou lazy swaine that maist relieve my needes,
Then his uppon whose liver alwaies feedes
A hungry vulture.
                    Enter Alexis.

Alexis.   Can such beautie be
Safe in his owne guard, and not draw the eye

Of him that passeth on to greedy gaze,
Or covetous desire, whilst in a maze　　　　　　　160
The better part contemplates, giving raine
And wished freedome to the labouring vaine?
Fairest and whitest, may I crave to knowe,
The cause of your retirement, why ye goe
Thus all alone? me thinkes the downes are sweeter
And the young company of swaines more meeter,
Then these forsaken and untroden places.
Give not your selfe to lonenesse, and those graces
Hide from the eies of men, that were intended
To live amongst us swaines.
Cloe.　　　　　　　　　Thou art befriended——　　170
Shepheard in all my life, I have not seene,
A man in whome greater contents hath beene,
Then thou thy selfe art: I could tell thee more,
Were there but any hope left to restore
My freedome lost: ô lend me all thy red,
Thou shamefast morning, when from *Tithons* bed
Thou risest ever maiden.
Alexis.　　　　　　　　If for me,
Thou sweetest of all sweets, these flashes be,
Speake and be satisfied, ô guide her tongue,
My better angell, force my name among　　　　　180
Hir modest thoughts, that the first word may be——
Cloe.　*Alexis* when the sunne shall kisse the sea,
Taking his rest by the white *Thetis* side,
Meet in the holy wood, where Ile abide
Thy comming Shepheard.
Alexis.　　　　　　　　If I stay behinde,
An everlasting dulnesse and the winde,
That as he passeth by shuts up the streame,
Of *Reine* or *Volga* whilst the sunnes hot beame,
Beats backe againe, ceaze me, and let me turne
To coldenesse more then yce: oh how I burne　　190
And rise in youth and fier! I dare not stay.
Cloe.　My name shall be your word.

Alexis.   Fly fly thou day.   *Exit.*
Cloe. My griefe is great if both these boyes should faile,
He that will use all windes must shift his saile.

                                                      Exit.

Enter an olde shepheard with a bell ringing, and the   II. i
                Priest of Pan *following.*

Priest.   Shepheards all, and maidens faire,
    Fold your flockes up, for the Aire
    Ginns to thicken, and the Sunne
    Already his great course hath runne.
    See the dew drops how they kisse
    Every little flower that is,
    Hanging on their velvet heads,
    Like a rope of christal beades.
    See the heavy cloudes low falling
    And bright *Hesperus* downe calling,   10
    The dead night from under ground,
    At whose rysing mistes unsound,
    Damps, and vapours fly apace,
    Hovering ore the wanton face,
    Of these pastures, where they come,
    Striking dead both budd and bloome,
    Therefore from such danger locke
    Every one his loved flocke,
    And let your dogs lye loose without,
    Least the Woolfe come as a scout   20
    From the mountaine, and ere day
    Beare a Lambe or Kid away:
    Or the crafty theevish Foxe,
    Breake upon your simple flockes,
    To secure your selves from these,
    Be not too secure in ease,
    Let one eie his watches keepe,

9 low] Q4; lowde Q1–3   16 budd] Q1(c); bloud Q1(u)
27 watches] Q1 (c); walkes Q1 (u)

Whilst the tother eie doth sleepe.
So you shall good Shepheards prove,
And for ever hold the love   30
Of our great God: sweetest slumbers
And soft silence fall in numbers
On your eye-lids: so farewell,
Thus I end my evenings knell.

Exeunt.

Enter Clorin *the Shepheardesse sorting of hearbs, and telling the* [II. ii]
natures of them.

Clorin. Now let me know what my best Art hath done,
  Helpt by the great power of the vertuous moone,
  In her full light: ô you sonnes of earth,
  You onely brood, unto whose happy birth
  Virtue was given, holding more of nature
  Then man her first borne and most perfect creature.
  Let me adore you, you that onely can,
  Helpe or kill nature, drawing out that span
  Of life and breath, even to the end of time,
  You that these hands did crop, long before prime   10
  Of day, give me your names, and next your hidden power.
  This is the *Clote* bearing a yellowe flowre:
  And this blacke Horehound, both are very good,
  For sheepe or shepheard, bitten by a wood
  Dogs venomd tooth, these Ramnus branches are,
  Which stucke in entries, or about the barre
  That holds the dore fast, kill all inchantments, charmes,
  Were they *Medeas* verses that do harmes
  To men or cattel: these for frenzy be
  A speedy and a soveraigne remedie,   20
  The bitter Wormewood, Sage, and Marigold,

4 happy] Q1(c); high Q1(u)   6 and] Q1(c); a Q1(u)
10 crop] Q1(c); lop Q1(u)   11 give] Q1(c); told Q1(u)
15 tooth] Q1(c); teeth Q1(u)
15 Ramnus] Ramuns Q1(c); Ramuus Q1(u)
17 fast] Q1(c); *om.* Q1(u)

Such simpathy with mans good they do hold:
This Tormentil whose vertue is to part
All deadly killing poison from the heart,
And heere *Narcissus* roote, for swellings best:
Yellow *Lecimacus*, to give sweete rest
To the faint Shepheard, killing where it comes,
All busie gnats, and every fly that hummes,
For leprosie, Darnell, and Sellondine,
With Calamint, whose vertues do refine   30
The blood of Man, making it free and faire,
As the first houre it breath'd, or the best aire.
Heere other to, but your rebellious use,
Is not for me, whose goodnes is abuse,
Therefore foule Standergrasse, from me and mine
I banish thee, with lustfull Turpentine,
You that intice the vaines, and stirre the heat
To civill muteny, scaling the seate
Our reason moves in, and deluding it
With dreames and wanton fancies, till the fit   40
Of burning lust be quencht by appetite,
Robbing the soule of blessednes and light:
And thou light *Varvin* to, thou must goe after
Provoking easie soules to mirth and laughter,
No more shall I dip thee in water now,
And sprinckle every post, and every bow
With thy well pleasing juice, to make the gromes,
Swell with high mirth as with joy all the romes.

Enter Thenot.

Thenot.   This is the Cabin where the best of all
Her sex, that ever breathd, or ever shall   50

22 Such] Q 1 (c); Which Q 1 (u)
23 Tormentil] Q 1 (c); Formentill Q 1 (u)
35 Standergrasse] Q 1 (c); Sandergrasse Q 1 (u)
36 with] Q 1 (c); and Q 1 (u)   40 fancies] Q 1 (c); forces Q 1 (u)
48 as] Q 1 (c); and Q 1 (u)
48.1 Thenot] Q 1 (c); *Shepheard* Q 1 (u)
49 *Thenot*] Q 1 (c) (*The.*); *Shep.* Q 1 (u)

Give heat or happinesse to the Shepheards side,
Doth onely to her worthy selfe abide.
Thou blessed starre, I thank thee for thy light,
Thou by whose power the darkenesse of sad night
Is banisht from the earth, in whose dull place
Thy chaster beames play on the heavy face
Of all the world: making the blew sea smile,
To see how cunningly thou dost beguile
Thy brother of his brightnesse, giving day
Againe from *Chaos*, whiter then that way   60
That leades to *Joves* hye Court, and chaster farre
Then chastity it selfe: yon blessed starre
That nightly shines, thou all the constancy
That in all women was, or ere shal be:
From whose faire eye-balles flies that holy fire,
That poets stile the mother of desire,
Infusing into every gentle breast,
A soule of greater price, and farre more blest
Then that quicke power which gives a difference
Twixt man and creatures of a lower sence.   70
Clorin.   Shepheard how camst thou hether to this place?
No way is troden, all the verdent grasse
The spring shot up stands yet unbrused heere
Of any foote, onely the dappld deere
Farre from the feared sound of crooked horne
Dwels in this fastnesse.
Thenot.   Chaster then the morne,
I have not wandred, or by strong illusion
Into this vertuous place have made intrusion,
But hether am I come (believe me faire)
To seeke you out, of whose great good the Aire   80
Is full, and strongly labors, whilst the sound,
Breakes against heaven, and drives into a stound

57 making] Q1(c); make Q1(u)   62 yon] Q1(c); you Q1(u)
63 nightly] Q1(c); brightly Q1(u)   66 poets stile] Q1(c); stiled is Q1(u)
74 dappld] Q1(c); dapple Q1(u)   82 Breakes] Q1(c); Beates Q1(u)
82 stound] Q3; stround Q1–2

The amazed Shepheard, that such vertue can
Be resident in lesser then a man.
Clorin.   If any art I have, or hidden skill,
May cure thee of disease or festred ill,
Whose griefe or greenenesse to anothers eie,
May seeme unpossible of remedie,
I dare yet undertake it.
Thenot.   Tis no paine
I suffer through disease, no beating vaine   90
Convaies infection dangerous to the heart,
No part impostumde to be curde by Art,
This bodie holdes: and yet a feller griefe
Then ever skilfull hand did give reliefe
Dwels on my soule, and may be heald by you,
Faire beauteous virgin.
Clorin.   Then shepheard let me sue
To knowe thy griefe: that man yet never knew
The way to health, that durst not shew his sore.
Thenot.   Then fairest know I love you.
Clorin.   Swaine no more.
Thou hast abus'd the strictnes of this place,   100
And offred Sacriligeous foule disgrace
To the sweet rest of these interred bones,
For feare of whose ascending fly at once,
Thou and thy idle passions, that the sight
Of death and speedy vengeance may not fright
Thy very soule with horror.
Thenot.   Let me not
Thou all perfection merrit such a blot,
For my true zealous faith.
Clorin.   Darest thou abide
To see this holy earth at once devide
And give her bodie up, for sure it will,   110
If thou pursuest with wanton flames to fill
This hallowed place: therefore repent and goe,

89 *Thenot*] Q2; *Shep.* Q1   99 *Thenot*] Q2; *Shep.* Q1
106 *Thenot*] *Shep.* Q1(c); *om.* Q1(u)   111 flames] Q1(c); flame Q1(u)

Whilst I with praiers appease his Ghost belowe,
That else would tell thee what it were to be,
A rivall in that vertuous love, that he
Imbraces yet.
Thenot.   Tis not the white or red
Inhabits in your cheeke, that thus can wed
My minde to adoration: nor your eye,
Though it be full and faire, your forehead hye,
And smooth as *Pelops* shoulder: not the smile   120
Lies watching in those dimples, to beguile
The easie soule, your hands and fingers long,
With vaines inameld richly, nor your tongue,
Though it spoke sweeter then *Arions* Harpe,
Your haire woven into many a curious warpe,
Able in endles errour to infould
The wandring soule, not the true perfect mould,
Of all your bodie, which as pure doth showe,
In Maiden whitenes as the Alpsien snowe.
All these, were but your constancy away,   130
Would please me lesse then a blacke stormy day
The wretched Seaman toyling through the deepe.
But whilst this honourd strictnes you dare keepe,
Though all the plagues that ere begotten were,
In the great wombe of aire were setled here
In opposition, I would like the tree,
Shake off those drops of weakenes, and be free
Even in the arme of danger.
Clorin.   Wouldst thou have
Me raise againe fond man, from silent grave,
Those sparckes that long agoe were buried here,   140
With my dead friends cold ashes?
Thenot.   Deerest deare,
I dare not aske it, nor you must not graunt,

113 praiers] Seward; praies Q1; praise Q2–5, F, L
116 *Thenot*] Q2; *Shep.* Q1   124 *Arions*] Q1(c); *Orions* Q1(u)
126 infould] Q3; vnfould Q1–2   127 wandring] Q1(c); errant Q1(u)
129 Alpsien] Q1(c); Alpen Q1(u)   133 dare] Q1(c); do Q1(u)
141 *Thenot*] Q2; *Shep.* Q1

Stand strongly to your vow, and do not faint:
Remember how he lov'd ye, and be still,
The same opinion speakes ye, let not will,
And that great god of women, Appetite,
Set up your blood againe, do not invite
Desire, and fancy from their long exile,
To seat them once more in a pleasing smile:
Be like a Rocke made firmely up gainst all   150
The power of angry heaven, or the strong fall
Of *Neptunes* battery, if ye yeild I die
To all affection: tis that loialtie
Ye tie unto this grave I so admire,
And yet theres something else I would desire,
If you would heare me, but withall deny,
O *Pan*, what an uncertaine desteny
Hanges over all my hopes! I will retire,
For if I longer stay, this double fier,
Will licke my life up.

Clorin.   Do, and let time weare out,   160
What Art and Nature cannot bring about.

Thenot.   Farewell thou soule of virtue, and be blest
For ever, whilst I wretched rest
Thus to my selfe, yet graunt me leave to dwell
In kenning of this Arbor: yon same dell
Ore topt with mourning Cipresse and sad Ewe,
Shall be my Cabin, where I'le earely rew,
Before the Sunne hath kist this dewe away,
The hard uncertaine chance which Fate doth lay
Upon this head.

Clorin.   The Gods give quicke release   170
And happy cure unto thy hard disease.

                                             Exeunt.

143 strongly] Q1 (c); strong Q1 (u)   148 from] Q3; for Q1–2
162 *Thenot*] Q2; *Shep.* Q1

524

Enter Sullen Shepheard.

Sullen Shepherd.   I do not love this wench that I should meet,
For never did my unconstant eie yet greet
That beautie, were it sweeter or more faire,
Then the new blossomes, when the morning aire
Blowes gently on them, or the breaking light,
When many maiden blushes to our sight
Shootes from his early face: were all these set
In some neat forme before me, twould not get
The least love from me: some desire it might,
Or present burning: all to me in sight   10
Are equall, be they faire, or blacke, or browne,
Virgin, or carelesse wanton, I can crowne
My appetite with any: sweare as oft,
And weepe as any, melt my words as soft
Into a maidens eares, and tell how long
My heart has bene her servant, and how strong
My passions are: call her unkinde and cruell,
Offer her all I have to gaine the jewell
Maidens so highly praise: then loath and fly,
This do I hold a blessed destenie.   20

Enter Amarillis.

Amarillis.   Haile Shepheard, *Pan* blesse both thy flocke and thee,
For being mindefull of thy word to me.
Sullen Shepherd.   Welcome faire Shepheardesse, thy loving swaine
Gives thee the selfe same wishes backe againe:
Who till this present houre nere knew that eie,
Could make me crosse mine armes or daily dye
With fresh consumings: boldly tel me then,
How shall we part their faithfull loves, and when?
Shall I bely him to her, shall I sweare
His faith is false, and he loves every where?   30
Ile say he mockt her the other day to you,
Which will by your confirming shew as true,

10 Or] Q 1 (c); And Q 1 (u)

525

For she is of so pure an honesty,
To thinke (because she will not) none will lye.
Or else to him Ile slaunder *Amoret*,
And say, she but seemes chaste, Ile sweare she met
Me mongst the shadie sycamoures last night,
And loosely offerd up her flame and spright,
Into my bosome: made a wanton bed
Of leaves and many flowers, where she spred   40
Her willing bodie to be prest by me,
There have I carv'd her name on many a tree,
Together with mine owne, to make this show
More full of seeming: *Hobinal* you know,
Sonne to the aged Shepheard of the Glen
Him I have sorted out of many men,
To say he found us at our private sport,
And rouz'd us fore our time by his resort:
This to confirme, I have promis'd to the boy
Many a pretty knack, and many a toy,   50
As grinnes to catch him birds with: bowe, and bolt,
To shoote at nimble squirrels in the holt:
A paire of painted buskins and a lambe,
Soft as his owne lockes, or the downe of Swan.
This I have done to winne ye, which doth give
Me double pleasure, discord makes me live.
Amarillis. Loved swaine I thanke ye, these trickes might prevaile
With other rusticke shepheards, but will faile
Even once to stirre, much more to overthrow,
His fixed love from judgement, who doth know,   60
Your nature, my end, and his chosens merrit,
Therefore some stronger way must force his spirit
Which I have found: give second, and my love
Is everlasting thine.
Sullen Shepherd.   Try me and prove.
Amarillis. These happy paire of lovers meet straight way,
Soone as they fould their flockes up with the day
In the thicke grove bordering upon yon hill,

33, 34 she] Seward; he Q1–5, F, L   52 nimble] Q1(c); Conies, Q1(u)

In whose hard side Nature hath carv'd a well:
And but that matchlesse spring which Poets know,
Was nere the like to this: by it doth growe   70
About the sides, all hearbs which witches use,
All simples good for medicine or abuse,
All sweetes that crowne the happy nuptiall day,
With all their colours: there the month of May
Is ever dwelling, all is young and greene,
There's not a grasse on which was ever seene,
The falling *Autume* or cold winters hand,
So full of heate and virtue is the land
About this fountaine, which doth slowly breake
Below yon Mountanes foote, into a creeke   80
That waters all the valley, giving fish
Of many sorts, to fill the shepheards dish.
This holy well, my Grandame that is dead,
Right wise in charmes, hath often to me sed,
Hath power to change the forme of any creature,
Being thrice dipt over the head, into what feature,
Or shape t'would please the letter downe to crave,
Who must pronounce this charme to, which she gave
Me on her death bed, told me what and how
I should apply unto the patients brow,   90
That would be chang'd, casting them thrice a sleepe
Before I trusted them into this deepe.
All this she shew'd me, and did charge me prove,
This secret of her Art, if crost in love:
I'le this attempt, now Shepheard I have here
All her prescriptions, and I will not feare
To be my selfe dipt: come, my temples binde
With these sad hearbs, and when I sleepe you finde
As you do speake your charme, thrice downe me let,
And bid the water raise me *Amoret*,   100
Which being done, leave me to my affaire,
And ere the day shall quite it selfe out weare,
I will returne unto my Shepheards arme,
Dip me againe, and then repeat this charme,

And plucke me up my selfe, whome freely take,
And the hotst fire of thine affection slake.
Sullen Shepherd. And if I fit thee not, then fit not me,
I long the truth of this wels power to see.

Exeunt.

Enter Daphnis.   II. iv

Daphnis.   Heere will I stay, for this the covert is
Where I appointed *Cloe*: do not misse,
Thou bright ey'd virgin, come, ô come my faire,
Be not abus'd with feare, nor let cold care
Of honor stay thee from thy Shepheards arme,
Who would as hard be wonne to offer harme
To thy chaste thoughts, as whitenesse from the day,
Or yon great round to move another way.
My language shall be honest, full of truth,
My flame as smooth and spotlesse as my youth: 10
I will not entertaine that wandring thought,
Whose easie currant may at length be brought
To a loose vastenes.
Alexis (within).   *Cloe!*
Daphnis.   Tis her voice
And I must answere, *Cloe!* ô the choise
Of deare imbraces, chaste and holy straines
Our hands shall give! I charge you all my vaines
Through which the blood and spirit take their way,
Locke up your disobedient heats, and stay
Those mutinous desires, that else would growe
To strong rebellion: do not wilder showe   20
Then blushing modestie may entertaine.
Alexis (within). *Cloe!*
Daphnis.   There sounds that blessed name againe,
And I will meete it: let me not mistake,

Enter Alexis.

This is some Shepheard, sure I am awake,

What may this riddle meane? I will retire,
To give my selfe more knowledge.
Alexis.　　　　　　　　　　　　Oh my fier,
How thou consum'st me? *Cloe* answere me,
Alexis, strong *Alexis*, high, and free,
Cals upon *Cloe*: see mine armes are full
Of intertainement, ready for to pull　　　　　　　30
That golden fruit which too too long hath hung,
Tempting the greedy eye: thou stayest too long,
I am impatient of these mad delaies,
I must not leave unsought those many waies
That lead into this center, till I finde
Quench for my burning lust, I come unkinde.　　　*Exit* Alexis.
Daphnis.　　Can my imagination worke me so much ill,
That I may credit this for truth, and still
Believe mine eies, or shall I firmely hold
Her yet untainted, and these sights but bold　　　　40
Illusion? sure such fancies oft have bene
Sent to abuse true love, and yet are seene,
Daring to blinde the vertuous thought with error,
But be they farre from me with their fond terror:
I am resolvd my *Cloe* yet is true.
Cloe (within).　*Cloe!*
Daphnis.　　　　　　Harke *Cloe* sure this voice is new,
Whose shrilnes like the sounding of a bell,
Tels me it is a woman: *Cloe*, tell
Thy blessed name againe.
Cloe (within).　　　　　　Heere.
Daphnis.　Oh what a greefe is this to be so neere　　　50
And not incounter?

　　　　　　　　　　　　Enter Cloe.

Cloe.　　　　　　Shepheard we are met,
Draw close into the covert, least the wet
Which falles like lazy mistes uppon the ground,
Soake through your startups.

43 thought] Q3; though Q1-2　　　　*46 *Cloe (within). Cloe!*] Seward

529

Daphnis.   Fairest, are you found?
How have we wandred that the better part
Of this good night is perisht? oh my heart!
How have I longd to meet ye? how to kisse
Those lilly hands? how to receive the blisse
That charming tongue gives to the happy eare
Of him that drinkes your language? but I feare   60
I am too much unmannerd, farre to rude,
And almost growne lascivous to intrude
These hot behaviours, where regard of fame,
Honor, and modesty, a vertuous name,
And such discourse, as one faire sister may
Without offence unto the brother say,
Should rather have bene tenderd: but believe
Heere dwels a better temper, do not grieve
Then, ever kindest, that my first salute,
Seasons so much of fancy, I am mute   70
Henceforth to all discourses, but shall be
Suting to your sweet thoughts and modestie:
Indeede I will not aske a kisse of you,
No not to wring your fingers, nor to sue
To those blest paire of fixed starres for smiles:
All a young lovers cunning, all his wiles,
And pretty wanton dyings shall to me
Be strangers, onely to your *Chastity*
I am devoted ever.

Cloe.   Honest swaine,
First let me thanke you, then returne againe   80
As much of my love: [*aside*] no thou art too cold
Unhappy boy, not temperd to my mold,
Thy blood fals heavy downeward, tis not feare
To offend in boldnesse wins, they never weare
Deserved favours that deny to take
When they are offred freely: do I wake
To see a man of his youth, yeares and feature,
And such a one as we call goodly creature,
Thus backeward? what a world of precious Art,

Were meerely lost, to make him do his part?   90
But I will shake him off, that dares not hold,
Let men that hope to be belovd be bold——
Daphnis I do desire since we are met
So happily, our lives and fortunes set,
Uppon one stake to give assurance now,
By interchange of hands and holy vow,
Never to breake againe: walke you that way,
Whilst I in zealous meditation stray
A little this way: when wee both have ended
These rights and dueties by the woods befriended,   100
And secresie of night, retire and finde
An aged oake whose hollownes may binde
Us both within his bodie, thither goe:
It stands within yon bottome.
Daphnis.   Be it so.   *Exit* Daphnis.
Cloe.   And I will meete there never more with thee,
Thou idle shamefastnesse.
Alexis (*within*).   *Cloe!*
Cloe.   Tis hee
That dare I hope be bolder.
Alexis [*within*].   *Cloe.*
Cloe.   Now
Great *Pan* for *Sirinx* sake bid speed our plow.

                                        Exit Cloe.

         Enter the Sullen Shepheard *with* Amarillis *in a sleepe.*   III. i

Sullen Shepherd.   From thy forehead thus I take
These hearbs, and charge thee not awake,
Till in yonder holy well,
Thrice with powerfull magicke spell,
Fild with many a balefull word,
Thou hast bene dipt, thus with my cord
Of blasted hempe, by moone-light twinde,
I do thy sleepy body binde,
I turne thy head into the East,

                        531

And thy feete into the West, 10
Thy left arme to the South put forth,
And thy right unto the North:
I take thy body from the ground,
In this deepe and deadly sound:
And into this holy spring,
I let thee slide downe by my string:
Take this maide thou holy pit
To thy bottom, neerer yet,
In thy water pure and sweete,
By thy leave I dip her feete: 20
Thus I let her lower yet,
That her anckles may be wet:
Yet downe lower, let her knee
In thy waters washed bee,
There stop: Fly away
Every thing that loves the day,
Truth that hath but one face,
Thus I charme thee from this place.
Snakes that cast your coates for new,
Camelions, that alter hue, 30
Hares that yearely sexes change,
Proteus altring oft and strange,
Hæcatæ with shapes three,
Let this maiden changed be,
With this holy water wet,
To the shape of *Amoret*:
Cinthia worke thou with my charme,
Thus I draw thee free from harme,
Up out of this blessed lake,
Rise both like her and awake. *She awakeh.* 40

Amarillis. Speake shepheard, am I *Amoret* to sight?
Or hast thou mist in any magicke right?
For want of which any defect in me,
May make our practises discovered be?
Sullen Shepherd. By yonder moone, but that I heere do stand,

41 *Amarillis*] Q2; *Amo.* Q1

532

Whose breath hath thus reformd thee, and whose hand,
Let thee downe dry, and pluckt thee up thus wet,
I should my selfe take thee for *Amoret,*
Thou art in clothes, in feature, voice and hew
So like, that sence can not distinguish you.   50
Amarillis.   Then this deceit which cannot crossed be,
At once shall loose her him, and gaine thee me.
Hether she needes must come, by promise made,
And sure his nature never was so bad,
To bid a virgin meete him in the wood,
When night and feare are up, but understood,
T'was his part to come first: being come, Ile say
My constant love made me come first and stay,
Then will I leade him further to the grove,
But stay you here, and if his owne true love   60
Shall seeke him heere, set her in some wrong path,
Which say her lover lately troden hath:
Ile not be farre from hence, if neede there bee
Heere is another charme, whose power will free
The dazeled sence: read by the moone beames cleare,
And in my owne true shape make me appeare.

Enter Perigot.

Sullen Shepherd.   Stand close, heere's *Perigot,* whose constant
     heart,
Longs to behold her, in whose shape thou art.
Perigot.   This is the place (faire *Amoret*) the houre
Is yet scarce come, heere every silvane power   70
Delights to be, about yon sacred well,
Which they have blest with many a powerfull spell,
For never travailer in dead of night,
Nor straied beasts have falne in, but when sight
Hath faild them, then their right way they have found,
By helpe of them, so holy is the ground:
But I will farther seeke, least *Amoret*

51 *Amarillis*] Q2; *Amore.* Q1   66 owne] Q2; one Q1

Should be first come and so stray long unmet.
My *Amoret, Amoret!*   *Exit.*
Amarillis.   *Perigot!*
Perigot [*within*].   My love!
Amarillis.   I come my love.   *Exit.*
Sullen Shepherd.   Now she hath got   80
Her owne desires, and I shall gainer be
Of my long lookt for hopes aswel as she:
How bright the moone shines heere, as if she strove
To show her glory in this little grove

Enter Amoret.

To some new loved Shepheard: yonder is
Another *Amoret*: where differs this
From that, but that she *Perigot* hath met,
I should have tane this for the counterfeit:
Hearbs, woods, and springs, the power that in you lies,
If mortall men could know your properties.   90
Amoret.   Me thinkes it is not night, I have no feare,
Walking this wood, of Lyon, or of Beare,
Whose names at other times, have made me quake,
When any shepheardesse in her tale spake,
Of some of them, that underneath a wood
Have torne true lovers that together stood.
Me thinkes there are no goblins, and mens talke,
That in these woods the nimble Faieries walke,
Are fables, such a strong hart I have got,
Because I come to meete with *Perigot*,   100
My *Perigot*, whose that my *Perigot*?
Sullen Shepherd.   Faire Maid.
Amoret.   Ay me thou art not *Perigot.*
Sullen Shepherd.   But I can tell ye newes of *Perigot:*
An houre together under yonder tree,
He sat with wreathed armes and cald on thee,
And said, why *Amoret* staiest thou so long:
Then starting up downe yonder path he flung,
Least thou hadst mist thy way: were it day light

534

He could not yet have borne him out of sight.
Amoret.   Thankes gentle Shepheard and beshrew my stay,   110
That made me fearefull I had lost my way:
As fast as my weake legs, (that cannot be
Weary with seeking him) will carry me,
Ile followe, and for this thy care of me,
Pray *Pan* thy love may ever follow thee.   *Exit.*
Sullen Shepherd.   How bright she was? how lovely did she show?
Was it not pittie to deceive her so?
She pluckt her garments up and tript away,
And with a virgin innocence did pray
For me, that perjurd her: whilst she was heere,   120
Me thought the beames of light that did appeare,
Were shot from her: me thought the moone gave none,
But what it had from her: she was alone
With me, if then her presence did so move,
Why did not I assay to win her love?
She would not sure have yeilded unto me,
Woemen love onely oportunitie
And not the man, or if she had denied
Alone, I might have forcd her to have tried
Who had bene stronger: ô vaine foole, to let   130
Such blest occasion passe, Ile follow yet,
My blood is up, I cannot now forbeare.

Enter Alexis *and* Cloe.

I come sweete *Amoret*, soft who is heere?
A paire of lovers, he shall yeild her me,
Now lust is up, alike all women be.
Alexis.   Where shall we rest, but for the love of me,
Cloe I know ere this would weary be.
Cloe.   *Alexis* let us rest heere, if the place
Be private, and out of the common trace
Of every shepheard: for I understood,   140
This night a number are about the wood,
Then let us choose some place where out of sight,
We freely may injoy our stolne delight.

535

Alexis. Then boldly heere, where we shall nere be found,
No shepheards way lies heere, tis hallowed ground,
No maide seekes heere her straied Cow, or Sheepe,
Faieries and Fawnes, and Satires do it keepe,
Then carelessely rest heere, and clip and kisse,
And let no feare make us our pleasures misse.

Cloe. Then lye by me, the sooner we begin,   150
The longer ere day descry our sin.

Sullen Shepherd. Forbeare to touch my love, or by yon flame
The greatest power that Shepheards dare to name,
Heere where thou sitst under this holy tree,
Her to dishoner thou shalt buried be.

Alexis. If *Pan* himselfe should come out of the lawnes,
With al his troopes of Satyres and of Faunes,
And bid me leave I sweare by her two eies,
A greater oath then thine, I would not rise.

Sullen Shepherd. Then from the cold earth never thou shalt move, 160
But loose at one stroke both thy life and love.

                        [Knocks Alexis *down and injures him.]*

Cloe. Hold gentle Shepheard.

Sullen Shepherd.   Fairest Shepheardesse,
Come you with me, I do not love ye lesse
Then that fond man that would have kept you there
From me of more desert.

Alexis.   O yet forbeare
To take her from me, give me leave to die
By her.

The Satyre *enters*, he [*the* Sullen Shepherd] *runs one way and she*
[Cloe] *another*.

Satyre. Now whilst the moone doth rule the sky,
And the starres, whose feeble light
Give a pale shadow to the night,
Are up, great *Pan* commaunded me   170
To walke this grove about, whilst he
In a corner of the wood,
Where never mortall foote hath stood,

536

Keepes dancing, musicke and a feast,
To intertaine a lovely guest:
Where he gives her many a rose
Sweeter then the breath that blowes
The leaves: grapes, beries of the best,
I never saw so great a feast.
But to my charge: heere must I stay,   180
To see what mortalls loose their way,
And by a false fire seeming bright,
Traine them in and leave them right:
Then must I watch if any be
Forcing of a chastity,
If I finde it, then in haste,
Give my wreathed horne a blast,
And the faieries all will run,
Wildely dauncing by the moone,
And will pinch him to the bone,   190
Till his lustfull thoughts be gone.
Alexis.   O death!
Satyre.   Backe againe about this ground
Sure I heare a mortall sound:
I binde thee by this powerfull spell,
By the waters of this well:
By the glimmering moone beames bright,
Speake againe thou mortall wight.
Alexis.   Oh!
Satyre.   Heere the foolish mortall lies,
Sleeping on the ground, arise,   200
The poore wight is almost dead,
On the Ground his woundes have bled,
And his Clothes fould with his bloud:
To my Goddesse in the wood,
Will I lead him, whose hands pure,
Will helpe this mortall wight to cure.

[*Exeunt* Satyre *and* Alexis.]

197 Speake...wight.] *Repeated before line* 199, *at the beginning of the Satyre's*
following speech, in Q1; *corrected in* Q2.

Enter Cloe *againe.*

Cloe. Since I beheld yon shaggy Man, my brest
Doth pant, each bush me thinks should hide a Beast,
Yet my desire, keepes still above my feare,
I would faine meete some Sheapheard knew I where,   210
For from one cause of feare, I am most free,
It is Impossible to Ravish mee,
I am soe willing: here upon this ground,
I left my love all Bloody with his wound,
Yet till that fearefull shape made me be gone,
Though he were hurt, I furnisht was of one,
But now both lost: *Alexis* speake or move,
If thou hast any life thou art yet my love,
Hee's dead, or else is with his little might,
Crept from the Bancke for feare of that ill spright,   220
Then where art thou that struck'st my love, ô stay,
Bring mee thy selfe in Change, and then Ile say,
Thou hast some Justice, I will make thee trim,
With Flowers, and Garlands, that were ment for him,
Ile Clip thee round, with both mine armes as fast,
As I did meane, he should have bin imbraced.
But thou art fled, what hope is left for mee?
Ile run to *Daphnis* in the hollow tree,
Who I did meane to mocke: though hope be small,
To make him bolde, rather then none at all,   230
Ile try him, his heart, and my behaviour to
Perhapes may teach him, what he ought to doe.   *Exit.*

Enter the Sullen Sheappeard.

Sullen Shepherd. This was the place, twas but my feeble sight,
Mixt with the horror of my deed, and night,
That shapt theise feares, and made me run away,
And loose my Beautious hardly gotten Pray.
Speake Gentle Sheappardess I am alone,

207 yon] Q4; you Q1-3   221 stay] Q2; stray Q1
234 and] Q2; an Q1

And tender love, for love, but shee is gone
From me, that having struke her lover dead,
For silly feare left her a lone and fled: 240
And see the wounded Body is Removed
By her of whome it was so well beloved.

Enter Perigot *and* Amarillis *in the shape of Amoret.*

But all theise fancies must be quite forgott:
I must lye close, heere comes younge *Perigott*,
With subtill *Amarillis* in the shape
Of *Amoret*, pray love hee may not scape.   [*Retires.*]
Amarillis.   Beloved *Perigot*, show mee some place,
Where I may rest my Limbes, weake with the Chace
Of thee, an hower before thou cam'st at least.
Perigot.   Beshrewe my Tardy stepps, here shalt thou rest   250
Uppon this holy bancke: no deadly snake,
Uppon this Turffe her selfe in foulds doth make,
Here is no poyson, for the Toade to feed.
Here boldly spread thy handes, no venomd weed,
Dares blister them. No slymy snaile dare creepe,
Over thy face when thou art fast a sleepe,
Here never durst the bablinge Cuckoe spitt.
No slough of falling Starr did ever hitt
Uppon this Bancke. Let this thy Cabin bee,
This other set with violets for mee.   260
Amarillis.   Thou dost not love mee *Perigot?*
Perigot.   Faire mayde
You onely love to heare it often sayd;
You do not doubt.
Amarillis.   Beleeve mee, but I doe.
Perigot.   What shall wee now begin againe to woe,
Tis the best way to make your lover last,
To play with him, when you have caught him fast.

242.1 *of Amoret*] Q2; *of a Amore* Q1
247] *Here and to her exit at line* 318 (*excepting line* 285), *speech prefixes for* Amarillis
are printed as Amo. *in* Q1–2; *printed as* Amar./Ama. *in* Q3.

Amarillis.   By *Pan* I sweare, Beloved *Perigot*,
And by yon Moone, I thincke thou lovest me not.
Perigot.   By *Pan* I sweare and if I falcely sweare,
Let him not guard my flockes, let Foxes teare   270
My Earelyest lambes, and wolves whilst I doe sleepe
Fall on the rest, a Rott amonge my sheepe,
I love thee better, then the carefull Ewe,
The new yeand lambe that is of her owne hew:
I dote uppon thee, more then that young lambe
Doth on the Bagg, that feedes him from his dam.
Were there a sort of wolves gott in my fould,
And one Rann after thee, both young and ould
Should be devour'd, and it should bee my strife,
To save thee, whom I love above my life.   280
Amarillis.   Howe should I trust thee when I see thee chuse
Another bedd, and dost my side refuse?
Perigot.   Twas only that the chast thoughts might bee showen,
Twixt thee and mee, although we were alone.
Amarillis.   Come, *Perigot* will show his power that hee
Can make his *Amoret*, though she weary bee,
Rise nimbly from her Couch, and come to his.
Here take thy *Amoret*, imbrace and Kisse.
Perigot.   What meanes my love?
Amarillis.   To do as lovers shud,
That are to bee injoyed not to bee woed.   290
Ther's nere a Sheapardesse in all the playne,
Can kisse thee with more Art, ther's none can faine
More wanton trickes.
Perigot.   Forbeare deare soule to trye,
Whether my hart be pure: Ile rather dye,
Then nourish one thought to dishonor thee.
Amarillis.   Still thinkst thou such a thinge as Chastitie,
Is amongst woemen? *Perigot* thers none,
That with her love is in a wood alone,
And wood come home a Mayde: be not abusd,
With thy fond first beleife, let time be usd: 300
Why dost thou rise?

Perigot.   My true heart thou hast slaine.
Amarillis.   Fayth *Perigot*, Ile plucke thee downe againe.
Perigot.   Let goe thou Serpent, that into my brest,
  Hast with thy Cunning div'd, art not in jest?
Amarillis.   Sweete love lye downe.
Perigot.   Since this I live to see,
  Some bitter North wind blast my flocks and mee.
Amarillis.   You swore you lov'd yet will not doe my will.
Perigot.   O be as thou wert, once, Ile love thee still.
Amarillis.   I am, as still I was and all my kind,
  Though other showes wee have poore men to blynd.   310
Perigot.   Then here I end all love, and lest my vaine
  Beleeife should ever draw me in againe,
  Before thy face that hast my youth mislead,
  I end my life, my blood be on thy head.
Amarillis.   O hold thy hands thy *Amoret* doth cry.
Perigot.   Thou counsayl'st well, first *Amoret* shall dye,
  That is the cause of my Eternall smart.
Amarillis.   O hold.
Perigot.   This steele shall peirse thy lustfull hart.

                                        He runs after her.

    The Sullen Sheapheard *stepes out and uncharmes her.*

Sullen Shepherd.   Up and downe every where,
  I strewe the hearbs to purge the Ayer,   320
  Let your Odor drive hence,
  All mistes that dazell sence,
  Herbes and springs whose hydden might
  Alters shapes, and mocks the sight.
  Thus I charge ye to undo
  All before I brought yee to:
  Let her flye, let her scape,
  Give againe her owne shape.   [*Retires.*]

    Enter Amarillis *in her owne shape* [*followed by* Perigot].

Amarillis.   For beare thou gentle swayne thou dost mistake;

        328.1 *in her owne shape*] Q2; *om.* Q1

541

Shee whom thou followedst fled into the brake,   330
And as I crost thy way I mett thy wrath;
The only feare of which neere slayne me hath.
Perigot.   Pardon fayre Sheapardesse, my rage and night
Were both uppon me and beguild my sight;
But farr be it from mee to spill the blood
Of harmelesse maydes that wander in the wood.

                                        Exit [Amarillis].

                    Enter Amoret.

Amoret.   Many a weary stepp in yonder path
Poore hoplesse *Amoret* twice troden hath,
To seeke her *Perigot*, yet cannot heare
His voyce: my *Perigot*, shee loves thee deare   340
That calles.
Perigot.   See yonder where shee is, how faire
Shee showes, and yet her breath infects the Ayer.
Amoret.   My *Perigot*.
Perigot.   Here.
Amoret.   Happye.
Perigot.   Haplesse first:
It lights on thee, the next blowe is the worst.   [*Wounds her.*]
Amoret.   Stay *Perigot*, my love, thou art unjust.
Perigot.   Death is the best reward thats due to lust.

                                        Exit Perigot.

Sullen Shepherd [*aside*].   Now shall their love be crost; for being
    strucke,
Ile throwe her in the Fount least being tooke
By some Night Travayler, whose honest care,
May help to cure her.——Sheapardesse prepare   350
Your selfe to dye.
Amoret.   No mercy I doe crave,
Thou canst not give a worsse blowe then I have,
Tell him that gave mee this, who lov'd him to,
He strucke my soule and not my bodye through:

337 *Amoret*] *Printed to the right of line 337 in* Q1

Tell him when I am dead my soule shall bee
At peace if hee but thincke hee injurd mee.

He flinges her into the well.

Sullen Shepherd.   In this Fount bee thy Grave, thou wert not ment,
Sure for a woman, thou art so Innocent.
Shee cannot scape for underneath the ground,
In a longe hollowe the cleere spring is bound,   360
Till on yon syde where the Morns sunn doth looke,
The strugling water breakes out in a brooke.   *Exit.*

The God of the River *Riseth with* Amoret, *in his armes.*

God of the River.   What powerfull Charmes my streames doe
        bring
Backe againe unto their spring?
With such force that I their god,
Three times stricking with my rod,
Could not keepe them in their Rancks.
My fishes shute into the bankes.
Ther's not one, that stayes and feeds,
All have hidd them in the weedes.   370
Heres a Mortall almost dead,
Falne into my River head,
Hallowed so with many a spell,
That till now none ever fell.
Tis a Feamale young and cleare,
Cast in by some Ravisher,
See uppon her brest a wound,
On which there is no playster bound,
Yet shee's warme, her pulses beat,
Tis a signe of life and heate.   380
If thou bee'st a virgin pure,
I can give a present cure,
Take a drope into thy wound
From my watry locke more round
Then Orient Pearle, and farr more pure,
Then unchast flesh may endure.

373 Hallowed] Q3; Hollowed Q1–2   383 drope] Q2 (drop); droope Q1

See shee pants and from her flesh,
The warme blood gusheth out a fresh,
She is an unpoluted mayde:
I must have this bleeding stayde. 390
From my banckes, I plucke this flower,
With holy hand whose vertuous power,
Is at once to heale and draw.
The blood Returnes. I never saw
A fayrer Mortall. Now doth breake
Her deadly slumber: virgin, speake.
Amoret.   Who hath restor'd my sence, given mee new breath,
And brought mee backe out of the Armes of death?
God of the River.   I have heald thy wounds.
Amoret.   Aye mee.
God of the River.   Feare not him that succord thee: 400
I am this Fountaynes God, belowe,
My waters to a River growe,
And twixt two banckes with Osiers sett,
That only prosper in the wet,
Through the Meddowes do they glide,
Wheeling still on every syde,
Sometimes winding round about,
To find the Evenest channell out.
And if thou wilt go with mee,
Leaving Mortall company, 410
In the Coole streames shall thou lye,
Free from harme as well as I:
I will give thee for thy food,
No fish that useth in the mudd,
But Trout and Pike that love to swim,
Where the Gravell from the brim,
Through the pure streames may be seene:
Orient Pearle fit for a Queene,
Will I give thy love to winn,
And a shell to keepe them in: 420
Not a fish in all my brooke,

417 Through] Q2; Though Q1

That shall disobeye thy looke,
But when thou wilt come slyding bye,
And from thy white hand take a flye:
And to make thee understand,
How I can my waves commaund,
They shall Bubble whilst I sing,
Sweeter then the silver string.

The Song.

Doe not feare to put thy feete,
Naked in the River sweete,   430
Thinke not leach, or Neute, or Toad,
Will byte thy foote, when thou hast trod,
Nor let the water rising hye,
As thou wadest in make thee cry
And sobb, but ever live with mee,
And not a wave shall trouble thee.

Amoret.   Immortall power, that rul'st this holy flud,
I know my selfe unworthy to be woed,
By thee a God, for ere this, but for thee
I should have showne my weake Mortallitie: 440
Besides by holy Oath betwixt us twaine,
I am bethrothd unto a Sheaphard Swaine,
Whose comely face, I know the Gods above
May make mee leave to see, but not to love.
God of the River.   Maye hee prove to thee as trewe:
Fayrest virgin now adue,
I must make my waters flye,
Least they leave ther Channells dry,
And beasts, that come unto the spring
Misse ther mornings watringe,   450
Which I would not, for of late
All the Neighbour people sate
On my banckes and from the fold,

429–436 Doe not feare...trouble thee.   437 that] Q2; ther Q1

Two white Lambs of three weekes Old,
Offered to my *Dietie*,
For which this yeare they shall bee free
From raging floods that as they passe,
Leave their gravell in the grasse,
Nor shall their Meades be over flowne,
When their grasse is newly moane.   460

Amoret. For thy kindnesse to me showne,
Never from thy bancks be blowne,
Any Tree, with windy force,
Crosse thy streames to stopp thy Course:
May no Beast that comes to drincke
With his Hornes cast downe thy brincke:
May none that for thy fishe doe looke,
Cutt thy banckes to damme thy Brooke:
Bare-foote may no Neighbour wade
In thy coole streames, wife nor mayde,   470
When the spawnes on stones do lye,
To wash ther Hempe and spoyle the frye.

God of the River. Thankes Virgin, I must downe againe.
Thy wound will put thee to noe paine.
Wonder not, so soone tis gone;
A holy hand was layd uppon.   *Exit.*

Amoret. And I unhappye borne to bee,
Must follow him, that flyes from mee.

          [*Exit.*]

          Enter Perigot.   **IV. i**

Perigot. Shee is untrue, unconstant, and unkinde,
Shee's gone, shee's gone, blow hygh thou North west winde,
And rayse the Sea to Mountaynes: let the Trees,
That dare oppose thy Raging fury leese
Their firme foundation; Creepe into the earth,
And shake the world as at the monstrus birth,
Of some new Prodegey, whilst I constant stand,

Holdinge this trusty Bore-Speare in my hand,
And falling thus uppon it——

Enter to Perigot, Amarillis *running*.

Amarillis.   Stay thy dead doing hand, thou art to hott   10
Against thy selfe, believe me comely Swaine,
If that thou dyest, not all the showers of Rayne
The heavy Clowdes send downe can wash away
That foule unmanly guilt, the world will lay
Uppon thee. Yet thy love untainted stands:
Believe mee shee is constant, not the sands
Can bee so hardly numbred as shee wunn:
I do not triffle, Sheapard, by the Moone,
And all those lesser lights our eyes doe vewe,
All that I tould thee *Perigot* is true: 20
Then bee a free man, put away dispayre,
And will to dye, smooth gently up that fayre,
Dejected forehead: be as when those eyes,
Tooke the first heat.

Perigot.   Allas hee doeble dyes,
That would beleive, but cannot: tis not well,
Ye keepe mee thus from dying here to dwell,
With many worse companions: but oh death,
I am not yet inamourd of this breath,
So much, but I dare leave it: tis not payne,
In forcing of a wound: nor after gayne,   30
Of many dayes, can hold mee from my will,
Tis not my selfe, but *Amoret*, byds kille.

Amarillis.   Stay, but a little, little but one hower,
And if I do not showe thee through the power
Of hearbes and words I have, as darke as Night,
My selfe, turn'd to thy *Amoret*, in sight,
Her very figure, and the Robe shee weares;
With tawny Buskins, and the hooke she beares
Of thyne owne Carving, where your names are set,
Wrought underneath with many a Curious frett;   40

9.1 *Enter to Perigot*] *Perigot to Enter* Q 1   28 this] Q 3; his Q 1–2

The *prim-Rose* Chaplet, taudry-lace and Ring,
Thou gavest her for her singing, with each thing
Else that shee weares about her, lett mee feele
The first fell stroke of that Revenging steele!
Perigot.   I am contented if ther bee a hope,
To give it Entertaynement for the scope
Of one poore hower; goe you shall find me next
Under yon shady Beech, even thus perplext,
And thus beleeving.
Amarillis.   Bynde before I goe,
Thy soule by *Pan* unto mee, not to doe   50
Harme or outragious wrong uppon thy life,
Till my Returne.
Perigot.   By *Pan*, and by the strife,
Hee had with *Phoebus* for the Masterye,
When Goulden *Mydas* judg'd their *Minstralcye*;
I will not.

                              Exeunt [*severally*].

                    Enter Satyre *with* Alexis *hurt.*   [IV. ii

Satyre.   Softly glyding as I goe,
With this Burden full of woe,
Through still silence of the night,
Guided by the glooe-wormes light,
Hether am I come at last;
Many a Thicket have I past;
Not a twigg that durst deny mee;
Nor a bush that durst descry mee,
To the little Bird that sleepes
On the tender spray; nor creeps   10
That hardy worme with poynted Tayle,
But if I bee under sayle,
Flying faster then the wind,
Leavinge all the Clowdes behind,
But doth hide her tender head,
In some hollow Tree or bedd

Of seeded Nettells: not a Hare
Can be started from his fare
By my footing, nor a wish
Is more sudden, nor a fish   20
Can bee found, with greater ease,
Cut the vast unbounded seaes,
Leaving neither print nor sound,
Then I when nimbly on the ground,
I measure many a leage an howre;
But behold the happy bower,
That must ease me of my charge,
And by holy hand enlardge,
The soule of this sadd man that yet,
Lyes fast bound in deadly fitt,   30
Heaven and great *Pan* sucker it.
Hayle thou beauty of the Bower,
Whiter then the Paramore
Of my Maister; let me crave,
Thy virteous helpe to keepe from Grave,
This poore Mortall that here lyes,
Wayting when the destinyes
Will undo his thread of life;
Veiwe the wound by cruell knife,
Trencht into him.   40
                    [*Enter* Clorin.]

Clorin.   What art thou, call'st mee from my holy Rightes
And with the feared name of death afrightes
My tender Eares? Speake me thy name and will.
Satyre.   I am the *Satyre* that did fill,
Your lapp with early fruite and will,
When I happ to gather more,
Bring yee better, and more store:
Yet I come not empty now,
See a blossome from the bowe,
But beshrewe his hart that pulld it,   50

33 Whiter] Q3; Whither Q1-2

549

And his perfect Sight that Culld it,
From the other springinge bloomes,
For a sweeter youth the Groomes
Cannot show mee, nor the downes:
Nor the many neighbouring Townes:
Low in yonder glade I found him,
Softly in mine Armes I bound him,
Hether have I brought him sleeping,
In a Trance, his wounds fresh weepinge,
In remembrance such youth may   60
Spring and perish in a Day.
Clorin.   *Satyre*: they wrong thee, that doe tearme thee rude:
Though thou beest outward rough and tawny hued,
Thy manners are as gentle and as fayre,
As his who bragges himselfe, borne only heyre,
To all Humanity: let mee see thie wound:
This Hearb will stay the Currant being bound,
Fast to the Orephyse, and this restrayne
Ulcers, and Swellinges, and such inward payne,
As the cold Ayre hath forc'd into the sore,   70
This to drawe out such Putrifiing gore,
As inward falls.
Satyre.   Heaven grant it may doe good.
Clorin.   Fayrely wipe away the blood,
Hold him gently till I fling,
Water of a vertuous spring
On his Temples: turne him twice
To the Moone beames, pinch him thrice:
That the labouring soule may drawe,
From his great ecclipse.
Satyre.   I sawe   80
His Eye-lids mooving.
Clorin.   Give him breath,
All the danger of cold death
Now is vanisht: with this playster,
And this unction doe I maister
All the festred ill that maye

Give him greife another day.
Satyre.   See hee gathers up his spright
And begins to hunt for light,
Now a gapes and breathes agayne:
How the bloud runns to the vayne,   90
That earst was empty.
Alexis.   Oh my hart,
My dearest, dearest *Cloe* O the smart,
Runnes through my side: I feele some poynted thing,
Passe through my Bowels, sharper then the stinge
Of *Scorpion.*
            Pan preserve mee, what are you?
            Doe not hurt mee, I am true,
            To my *Cloe* though shee fly
            And leave mee to this Destiny.
            There shee stands, and will not lend,
            Her smooth white hand to helpe her freind.   100
But I am much mistaken, for that face,
Beares more Austeritye and modest grace,
            More reproving and more awe,
            Then theise Eyes yet ever sawe,
            In my *Cloe*, oh my payne:
            Eagerly Renewes againe:
Give mee your helpe for his sake you love best.
Clorin.   Sheapheard thou canst not possibly take rest,
Till thou hast layed a syde all heates, desiers,
Provoking thoughts, that stirr upp lusty fiers,   110
Commerse with wanton Eyes: strong bloud, and will
To execute, theise must bee purg'd untill
The vayne growe Whiter: then Repent and pray
Great *Pan*, to keepe you from the like decaye,
And I shall undertake your cure with ease,
Till when this verteous Playster will displease
Your tender sides. Give mee your hand and rise.

91 earst] Q2; east Q1
108 possibly] Q4; possible Q1–3
116 Playster] Q2; Playsters Q1

Helpe him a little *Satyre*, for his Thyghes
Yet are feeble.
Alexis.   Sure I have lost much blood.   120
Satyre.   Tis no matter, twas not good.
  Mortall you must leave your woing,
  Though ther be a Joye in doing,
  Yet it brings much griefe, behynd it,
  They best feele it, that doe find it.
Clorin.   Come bringe him in, I will attend his sore,
  When you are well, take heed you lust no more.
Satyre.   Sheapeard see what comes of kissinge,
  By my head twere better missing.
  Bryghtest if ther bee ramayning,   130
  Any service, without fayninge,
  I will do it, were I sett,
  To catch the nimble wind or gett,
  Shaddowes glydinge on the greene,
  Or to steale from the great Queene
  Of Fayryes, all her Beautye,
  I would do it, so much dutye
  Doe I owe those pretious Eyes.
Clorin.   I thancke thee honest Satyre, if the Cryes,
  Of any other that be hurt, or ill,   140
  Draw thee unto them, prithee do thy will,
  To bring them hether.
Satyre.   I will and when the weather
  Serves to Angle in the brooke,
  I will bring a silver hooke,
  With a lyne of finest silke,
  And a rodd, as white as milke,
  To deceive the little fishe:
  Soe I take my leave and wish,
  On this bowre may ever dwell,   150
  Springe, and sommer.
Clorin.   Friend farewell.
          Exit [Satyre *one way*, Clorin *with* Alexis *another*].

148 deceive] Q2; deserue Q1

552

Enter Amoret, *seeking her love.*

Amoret.   This place is Ominous for here I lost
My love and almost life, and since have crost
All theise woodes over, never a Nooke or dell,
Where any little Byrd, or beast doth dwell,
But I have sought it, never a bending browe,
Of any hill or Glade, the wind sings through,
Nor a greene bancke or shade where Sheapeards use
To sit and Riddle, sweetely pipe or chuse
Their valentynes, but I have mist to find
My love in. *Perigot*, Oh to unkind,   10
Why hast thou fled mee? Whether art thou gone,
Howe have I wrong'd thee? Was my love alone,
To thee, worthy this scorned Recompence? Tis well,
I am content to feele it; but I tell
Thee Sheapeard: and theise lusty woods shall heare,
Forsaken *Amoret* is yet as cleare,
Of any stranger fier, as Heaven is
From foule Corruption, or the deepe Abisse,
From light, and happynesse; and thou mayst knowe,
All this for truth and how that fatall blowe,   20
Thou gavest mee, never from desert of myne,
Fell on my life, but from suspect of thyne,
Or fury more then Madnes: therefore, here,
Since I have lost my life, my love, my deare,
Upon this cursed place, and on this greene,
That first devorced us, shortly shall bee seene,
A sight of so great pitty that each eye,
Shall dayly spend his spring in memorye
Of my untymely fall.
                    Enter Amarillis.

Amarillis.   I am not blynd,
Nor is it through the working of my Mynd,   30
That this showes *Amoret*: for sake me all,
That dwell uppon the soule, but what men call

36   553   B D W

Wonder, or more then wonder Miracle,
For sure so strange as this the Oracle,
Never gave answere of. It passeth dreames,
Or maddmens fancye, when the many streames,
Of newe Imagination rise and fall:
Tis but an howre since theise Eares heard her call,
For pitty to young *Perigot*; whilst hee,
Directed by his fury Bloodelye,   40
Lanch't upp her brest, which bloudlesse fell and cold,
And if beleife may Credit what was told,
After all this the Mellancholly Swayne,
Tooke her into his Armes being almost slayne,
And to the bottom of the holy well,
Flung her for ever with the waves to dwell.
Tis shee, the very same, tis *Amoret*,
And living yet, the great powers will not let
Their verteous love be Crost. Mayde wipe away
Those heavy dropps of sorrow, and allay   50
The storme that yet goes high, which not deprest,
Breakes hart, and life, and all before it rest:
Thy *Perigot*——
Amoret.   Where: which is *Perigot?*
Amarillis.   Sits there below lamenting much God wott,
Thee, and thy fortune: goe and comfort him,
And thou shalt finde him underneath a brim
Of sayling Pynes that edge yon Mountaine in.
Amoret.   I goe, I run, Heaven graunt mee I maye winn
His soule agayne.   [*Exit.*]
                    Enter Sullen [Shepherd].

Sullen Shepherd.   Stay *Amarillis*, stay,
Ye are to fleete, tis two howers yet to day;   60
I have perform'd my promise, lett us sitt
And warme our bloodes together till the fitt
Come lively on us.
Amarillis.   Freind you are to keene;

The Morning Riseth, and wee shall be seene,
For beare a little.
Sullen Shepherd.   I can staye no longer.
Amarillis.   Hold Sheapeard hold, learne not to bee a wronger
Of your word, was not your promise layed,
To break their loves first?
Sullen Shepherd.   I have done it Mayd!
Amarillis.   No they are yet unbroken, met againe,
And are as hard to part yet as the stayne   70
Is from the finest lawne.
Sullen Shepherd.   I say they are
Now at this present parted, and so farr,
That they shall never meete.
Amarillis.   Swayne tis not so,
For do but to yon hanging Mountayne goe,
And ther beleive your eyes.
Sullen Shepherd.   You doe but hold
Of with delayes and trifles, fare wel cold
And frozen bashfullnes, unfit for men,
Thus I sallute thee virgin.
Amarillis.   And thus then,
I bid you followe. Catch mee if ye can.   *Exit.*
Sullen Shepherd.   And if I stay behind I am no Man.   80
                                Exit running after her.

Enter Perigot.   [IV. iv]

Perigot.   Night do not steale away: I woe thee yet
To hold a hard hand ore the Rusty bytt,
That Gydes thy Lazy teame: goe backe againe,
Bootes thou that driv'st thy frozen wane,
Round as a Ringe and bring a second Night,
To hyde my sorowes from the comming light:
Let not the Eyes of men, stare on my face,
And read my falling, give mee some blacke place,
Where never sunn beame, shot his wholsome light,
That I may sitt, and powre out my sadd spright,   10

555   36-2

Like running water never to be knowne,
After the forced fall and sound is gone.

Enter Amoret *looking of Perigot.*

Amoret. This is the bottome: speake if thou be here,
My *Perigot*, thy *Amoret*, thy deare,
Calles on thy loved Name.
Perigot.   What art thou dare
Tread theise forbydden pathes, where death and care,
Dwell on the face of darcknes?
Amoret.   Tis thy friend,
Thy *Amoret* come hether to give end,
To theise consuminges: looke upp gentle Boye,
I have forgot those paynes, and deare annoy,   20
I sufferd for thy sake, and am content,
To bee thy love againe. Why hast thou rent,
Those curled lockes, wher I have often hunge,
Ribandes and damaske Roses, and have flunge,
Waters distilld to make thee fresh and gaye,
Sweeter then Nose-gayes on a Bridall daye?
Why dost thou crosse thyne Armes, and hang thy face,
Downe to thy Boosome, letting fall apace,
From those too little Heavens uppon the ground,
Showres of more price, more Orient, and more round   30
Then those that hange uppon the moones pale browe?
Cease theise complainings Sheapheard, I am nowe
The same, I ever was, as kinde and free,
And can forgive before you aske of mee,
Indeed I can, and will.
Perigot.   Soe spoke my fayre.
O you great working powers of Earth, and Ayre,
Water, and forming fier, why have you lent
Your hydden vertues of so ill intent?
Even such a face, so fayre so bright of hewe,
Had *Amoret*, such words soe smooth and newe,   40
Came flowing from her tongue, such was her eye,

15 art] Q2; *om.* Q1

556

And such the poynted sparckle that did flye,
Forth like a bleeding shaft, all is the same,
The Robe, and Buskins, painted hooke, and frame,
Of all her Body, O mee *Amoret*.

Amoret.   Sheapeard what meanes this Riddle, who hath sett,
So strange a difference, twixt my selfe and mee,
That I am growne annother? Looke and see,
The Ring thou gavest mee, and about my wrest,
That Curious Braeslet, thou thy selfe didst twist,   50
From those fayre Tresses: knowest thou *Amoret*?
Hath not some newer love forced thee forget,
Thy Auncient fayth?

Perigot.   Still nearer to my love;
Theise be the very words shee oft did prove,
Uppon my temper; so shee still wod take
Wonder into her face, and silent make
Signes with her head and hand as who wod saye,
Sheapeard remember this annother daye.

Amoret.   Am I not *Amoret*; where was I lost?
Can there be Heaven, and time, and men, and most   60
Of theise unconstant? Fayth where art thou fled?
Are all the vowes and protestations dead:
The hands held upp? the wishes and the hart?
Is ther not one remayninge, not a part
Of all theise to bee found? Why then I see:
Men never knewe that vertue constancye.

Perigot.   Men ever were most blessed, till Crosse fate,
Brought love, and woemen forth unfortunate,
To all that ever tasted of their smiles,
Whose Actions are all double, full of wiles,   70
Like to the subtill Hare, that fore the Houndes,
Makes many turnings, leapes and many roundes,
This waye and that waye, to deceave the sent,
Of her pursuers.

Amoret.   Tis but to prevent,
Ther speedy comminge on that seeke her fall,

60 men, and most] Q2; men, most Q1

557

The hands of Cruell men, more Bestiall,
And of a nature more refusing good,
Then beastes themselves, or fishes of the flood.

Perigot.   Thou art all theise, and more then nature ment,
When shee created all, frownes, joyes, content: 80
Extreame fier for an hower, and presentlye:
Colder then sleepy poyson: or the sea,
Uppon whose face sitts a continuall frost:
Your Actions ever driven to the most,
Then downe agayne as lowe, that none can find,
The rise or falling of a woemans minde.

Amoret.   Can ther bee any Age, or dayes, or time,
Or tongues of Men, guilty so great a crime
As wronging simple Mayde? O *Perigot*:
Thou that wast yesterday without a blott,   90
Thou that wast every good, and every thinge,
That men call blessed: thou that wast the spring,
From whence our looser groomes drew all their best:
Thou that wast alwaies Just, and alwaies blest,
In fayth and promise, thou that hadst the name,
Of vertuous given thee, and made good the same,
Even from thy Cradle: thou that wast that all,
That men delighted in, Oh what a fall,
Is this to have bene soe, and now to bee,
The onlye best in wrong, and infamye,   100
And I to live to know this, and by mee,
That lov'd thee dearer then myne Eyes or that,
Which wee esteeme our honour virgin state,
Dearer then swallowes love the early morne,
Or doggs of Chace the sound of merry Horne,
Dearer then thou canst love thy newe love, if thou hast
Another, and farr dearer then the last,
Dearer then thou can'st love thy selfe, though all
The selfe love were within thee, that did fall
With that coye swayne that now is made a flower,   110
For whose deare sake, Eccho weepes many a showre:

79 *Perigot.*] Q2; *om.* Q1

558

And am I thus rewarded for my flame,
Lov'd worthely to gett a wantons name?
Come thou forsaken willowe winde my head,
And noyse it to the world, my love is dead:
I am forsaken I am Cast awaye,
And left for every lazy Grome to saye,
I was unconstant light, and sooner lost,
Then the quicke Clowds wee see or the Chill frost,
When the hott sun beates on it. Tell mee yet,   120
Canst thou not love againe thy *Amorett?*
Perigot.   Thou art not worthy of that blessed name,
I must not knowe thee, flynge thy wanton flame,
Uppon some lighter blood: that may be hott,
With words and fayned passions, *Perigot,*
Was ever yet unstaynd, and shall not nowe,
Stoope to the meltings of a borrowed browe.
Amoret.   Then heare mee heaven, to whome I call for right,
And you fayre twinckling starres, that crowne the night,
And heare mee woods, and silence of this place,   130
And ye sad howers, that moove a sullen pace,
Heare mee ye shadowes, that delight to dwell,
In horred darknesse, and ye powers of Hell,
Whilst I breath out my last, I am that mayde,
That yet untaynted *Amoret* that played
The carelesse Prodigall, and gave awaye
My soule to this younge man that now dares saye:
I am a stranger, not the same, more wild,
And thus with much beleife, I was beguild.
I am that Mayde, that have delayd, denyed,   140
And almost scornd the loves of all that tryde
To win me but this swayne, and yet confesse,
I have bene woed by many with no lesse
Soule of affection and have often had
Ringes, Bellts and Cracknels sent me from the lad
That feeds his flockes downe westward, Lambes and Doves
By young *Alexis, Daphnis* sent me gloves,

140 denyed] Q2; denye Q1

559

All which I gave to thee: nor theise, nor they
That sent them, did I smyle on, or ere lay
Upp to my after memorye. But why   150
Do I resolve to grieve and not to dye?
Happy had bene the stroake thou gavest if home,
By this tyme had I found a quiet roome
Where every slave is free, and every brest,
That living bread new care, now lyes at rest,
And thether will poore *Amoret*.

Perigot.   Thou must.
Was ever any man soe loath to trust
His Eyes as I, or was ther ever yet,
Any so like, as this to *Amoret*,
For whose deare sake, I promise if ther bee   160
A living soule within thee, thus to free
Thy Body from it.   *He hurts her agayne.*

Amoret.   So this worke hath end.
Farewell and live, be constant to thy friend,
That loves thee next.

Enter Satyre: Perigot *runns off.*

Satyre.   See the day begins to breake,
And the light shutts like a streake
Of subtill fier, the wind blowes cold,
Whilst the morning doth unfold.
Nowe the Byrds begin to rouse,
And the Squyrrill from the boughes,   170
Leaps to gett him Nutts and fruite,
The early Larke that earst was mute,
Carrolls to the Risinge daye,
Many a Note, and manye a laye:
Therfore here I end my watch,
Least the wandering Swayne should catch
Harme or loose himselfe.

Amoret.   Ah mee.
Satyre.   Speake agayne what ere thou bee,

171 Leaps] Q3; Leps Q1–2   174 manye a laye] Q2; manye laye Q1

I am ready, speake I say,
By the dawning of the day,   180
By the power of Night and *Pan*;
I inforce thee speake againe.
Amoret.   O I am most unhappie.
Satyre.   Yet more blood,
Sure these wanton Swaynes are wood.
Can there be a hand, or hart,
Dare commit so vild a part,
As this Murder? By the Moone,
That hydd her selfe when this was done,
Never was a sweeter face.   190
I will beare her to the place,
Where my Goddess keepes, and crave
Her to give her life, or grave.

                                   Exeunt.

Enter Clorin.   [IV. v]

Clorin.   Here whilst one patient takes his rest secure
I steale a broad to doe annother Cure.
Pardon thou buryed body of my love,
That from thy side I dare so soone remoove,
I will not prove unconstant, nor will leave
Thee for an hower alone. When I deceave
My first made vowe, the wildest of the wood
Teare me, and ore thy Grave lett out my blood.
I goe by witt to Cure a lovers payne,
Which no hearb can, being done, Ile come againe.   *Exit.* 10

Enter Thenot.

Thenot.   Poore Sheapeard in this shade for ever lye,
And seeing thy fayre *Clorins* Cabin dye.
O happlesse love which being answered ends,
And as a little Infant cryes and bendes
His tender Browes, when rowling of his eye,
He hath espyed something that glisters nye,

Which he would have, yet give it him, away
He throwes it straight, and cryes a fresh to playe
With something else: such my affection sett,
On that which I should loath if I could geett.   20

Enter Clorin.

Clorin [*aside*].   See where hee lies; did ever man but hee,
Love any woeman for her Constancy,
To her dead lover, which she needs must end,
Before she can alowe him, for her freind,
And he himselfe, must needes the cause destroye,
For which he loves, before he can injoye.
Poore Sheapeard, Heaven grant I at once may free
Thee from thy payne, and keepe my loyalty:——
Sheapheard looke upp.
Thenot.   Thy brightnesse doth amaze,
Soe *Phoebus* may at Noone byd mortalls gaze.   30
Thy glorious constancy appeares so bright,
I dare not meete the Beames with my weake sight.
Clorin.   Why dost thou pyne away thy selfe for mee?
Thenot.   Why dost thou keepe such spottlesse constancy?
Clorin.   Thou holy Sheapheard see what for thy sake,
Clorin, thy *Clorin*, now dare undertake.   *He starts up.*
Thenot.   Stay ther, thou constant *Clorin* if ther bee,
Yet any part of woeman left in thee,
To make thee light: thincke yet before thou speake.
Clorin.   See what a holy vowe, for thee I breake,   40
I that already have my fame farr spread,
For beeing constant to my lover dead.
Thenot.   Thincke yet deare *Clorin* of your love, how trewe,
If you had dyed, he would have bene to you.
Clorin.   Yet all Ile loose for thee——
Thenot.   Thincke but how blest,
A constant woeman is above the rest.
Clorin.   And offer upp my selfe, here on this ground,
To be disposd by thee.
Thenot.   Why dost thou wound

His hart with Mallice, against woemen more,
That hated all the Sex but thee before?   50
How much more pleasant had it bene to mee,
To dye then to behold this change in thee!
Yet, yet, returne: let not the woeman swaye.
Clorin.   Insult not on her now, nor use delaye,
Who for thy sake hath venturd all her fame.
Thenot.   Thou hast not venturd but bought Certaine shame,
Your Sexes Curse, foule falshood, must and shall,
I see once in your lives light on you all:
I hate thee now: yet turne.
Clorin.   Be just to mee:
Shall I at once, loose both my fame and thee?   60
Thenot.   Thou hadst no fame, that which thou didst like good
Was but thy Appetite, that swayed thy bloud,
For that time to the best; for as a blast,
That through a house comes, usually doth cast
Things out of order: yet by chaunce may come,
And blowe some one thinge to his proper rome,
Soe did thy Appetite, and not thy zeale,
Swaye thee by chaunce to do some one thing well.
Yet turne.
Clorin.   Thou dost but trye me if I would
Forsake thy deere imbraces for my ould   70
Loves though he were alive, but doe not feare.
Thenot.   I doe contemne thee nowe, and dare come neare,
And gayse uppon thee, for me thinkes that grace,
Austeritye, which satt uppon that face,
Is gone, and thou like others. False mayde see,
This is the gaine of foule Inconstancy.   *Exit.*
Clorin.   Tis done: great *Pan*, I give thee thankes for it,
What Art could not have heald, is curd by witt.

52 then to behold] Q3; then behold Q1–2
76 Inconstancy] Q2; Inconstance Q1

Enter Thenot *agayne.*

Thenot.   Will yee be constant yet, will ye remoove,
  Into the Cabin to your buryed love?   80
Clorin.   Noe lett me dye, but by thy side remayne.
Thenot.   Ther's none shall knowe that thou didst ever stayne
  Thy worthy stricknes, but shalt honnerd bee,
  And I will lye againe under this tree,
  And pine and dye for thee with more delight,
  Then I have sorrow now to know thee light.
Clorin.   Let mee have thee, and Ile be where thou wilt.
Thenot.   Thou art of womens race and full of guilt.
  Farewell all hope of that sex, whilst I thought,
  There was one good, I feared to find one nought: 90
  But since there minds I all alike espie,
  Hencefoorth Ile chuse as others, by mine eye.   [*Exit.*]
Clorin.   Blest be yee powers that gave such quicke redresse,
  And for my labours sent so good successe.
  I rather chuse though I a woman bee,
  He should speake ill of all, then dye for me.

                                                        [*Exit.*]

Enter Priest, *and* old Shepheard.   V. i

Priest.   Shepheards, rise and shake of sleepe.
  See the blushing Morne doth peepe,
  Through the windowes, whilst the Sune
  To the Mountayne topps is runne,
  Gilding all the vales below,
  With his rising flames which grow,
  Greater by his climing still.
  Up yee lazy groomes and fill,
  Bagg and Bottle for the fielde,
  Claspe your cloakes fast lest they yeeld,   10
  To the bitter Northeast wind,
  Call the Maydens up and find,

              92 others] Q2; thers Q1

                         564

Who laye longest, that she may,
Go without a friend all daye.
Then reward your dogs and praye,
Pan to keepe you from decay,
So unfold, and then away.
What not a Shepheard stirring? Sure the groomes,
Have found their beds to easie, or the Roomes,
Fillde with such new delight, and heat that they,   20
Have both forgot their hungry sheepe, and day:
Knock that they may remember what a shame,
Sloath and neglect, layes on a Shepheards name.

Old Shepherd.   It is to little purpose, not a swayne,
This night hath knowne his lodging, heere; or layne,
Within these cotes: the woods or some neere towne,
That is a neighbour to the bordering downe,
Hath drawne them thether, bout some lusty sport,
Or spiced wassal Boule, to which resort,
All the young men and maydes of many a coate,   30
Whilst the Trim Minstrell strikes his merry note.

Priest.   God pardon sinne, showe me the way that leades,
To any of their haunts.

Old Shepherd.   This to the Meades,
And that downe to the woods.

Priest.   Then this for me,
Come Shepheard let me crave your company.

Exeunt.

Enter Clorin *in her Cabin*, Allexis *with her.*   [V. ii]

Clorin.   Now your thoughts are almost pure,
And your wound beginns to cure.
Strive to bannish all thats vaine,
Lest it should breake out againe.

16 decay] Q1(c); delay Q1(u)
18 Sure] Q1(c); saue Q1(u)   19 or] Q1(c); for Q1(u)
25 lodging, heere] Q1(c); longing, heard Q1(u)
31 note] Q1(c); notes Q1(u)   33 their] Q1(c); the Q1(u)
*0.1 *Enter* Clorin...Allexis *with her.*   1 thoughts] Q1(c); thought Q1(u)

Alexis.   Eternall thanks to thee, thou holy mayde:
I find my former wandring thoughts, well stayd,
Through thy wise precepts, and my outward payne,
By thy choyce hearbs is almost gone againe.
Thy sexes vice and vertue are reveald,
At once, for what one hurt another heald.   10
Clorin.   May thy griefe more apease,
Relapses, are the worst disease:
Take heede how you in thought offend,
So mind and body both will mend.

Enter Satyre *with* Amoret.

Amoret.   Beest thou the wildest creature of the Wood,
That bearst me thus a way drownd in my blood,
And dying, know I cannot injurd be:
I am a mayde, let that name fight for me.
Satyre.   Fayrest Virgine do not feare,
Me that doth thy body beare,   20
Not to hurt, but heald to be,
Men are ruder farre then we.
See fayre Goddesse in the wood,
They have let out yet more blood:
Some savadge man hath strucke her brest
So soft and white, that no wild beast,
Durst a toucht asleepe or wake,
So sweete that Adder, Neut, or Snake,
Would have layne from arme to arme,
On her Bossome to be warme,   30
All a night and being hot,
Gone away and stung her not.
Quickly clap hearbs to her brest,
A man sure is a kind of Beast.
Clorin.   With spottlesse hand, on spotlesse Brest,
I put these hearbs to give thee rest.
Which till it heale thee there wil bide
If both be pure, if not off slide.

21 heald] Q2; held Q1

566

See it falls off from the wound,
Shepheardesse thou art not sound,   40
Full of lust.
Satyre.   Who would have thought it,
So fayre a face.
Clorin.   Why that hath brought it.
Amoret. For ought I know or thinke, these words my last:
Yet *Pan*, so helpe me as my thoughts are chast.
Clorin. And so may *Pan* blesse this my cure,
As all my thoughts are just and pure,
Some uncleanesse nye doth lurke,
That will not let my medcines worke.
Satyre search if thou canst find it.
Satyre. Here away me thinks I wind it.   50
Stronger yet, Oh here they be,
Heere heere in a hollow tree,
Two fond mortalls have I found.
Clorin. Bring them out, they are unsound.

Enter Cloe, *and* Daphinis.

Satyre. By the fingers thus I wring yee,
To my Goddesse thus I bring yee.
Strife is vayne, come gently in,
I sented them, they are full of sinne.
Clorin. Hold *Satyre*, take this Glasse,
Sprinkle over all the place,   60
Purge the Ayre from lustfull breath,
To save this Shepheardesse from death.
And stand you still, whilst I do dresse
Her wound for feare the payne increase.
Satyre. From this glasse I throw a dropp,
Of Christall water on the topp,
Of every grasse, on flowers a payre:
Send a fume and keepe the Ayre,
Pure and wholesome, sweete and blest,
Till this virgins wound be drest.   70
Clorin. *Satyre* help to bring her in.

Satyre.   By *Pan*, I thinke shee hath no sinne,
                    [*Carries* Amoret *into the bower.*]
   She is so light: lye on these leaves,
   Sleepe that mortall sence deceaves,
   Crowne thine eyes, and ease thy paine,
   Mayst thou sone be well againe.
Clorin.   *Satyre* bring the Shepheard nere,
   Trye him if his mind be cleere.
Satyre.   Shepheard come.
Daphnis.   My thoughts are pure.
Satyre.   The better tryall to endure.   80
Clorin.   In this flame his finger thrust,
   Which will burne him if he lust.
   But if not away will turne,
   As loath unspotted flesh to burne:
   See it gives backe, let him go.
Satyre.   Farewell Mortall keepe thee so.   [*Exit* Daphnis.]
   Staye fayre Nymph, flye not so fast,
   Wee must trye if you be chaste:
   Heres a hand that quaks for feare,
   Sure she will not prove so cleare.   90
Clorin.   Hold her finger to the flame:
   That will yeeld her praise or shame.
Satyre.   To her doome shee dares not stand,
   But pluckes away her tender hand:
   And the Taper darting sends,
   His hot beames at her fingers ends.
   O thou art foule within, and hast
   A mind if nothing else unchast.
Alexis.   Is not that *Cloe?* tis my love; tis shee:
   Cloe, faire *Cloe*.
Cloe.   My *Alexis*.
Alexis.   He.   100
Cloe.   Let me imbrace thee.
Clorin.   Take her hence,
   Least her sight disturbe his sence.

86 Farewell...so.] Dyce; *printed as part of Clorin's preceding speech in* Q1–5, F

568

Alexis.   Take not her: take my life first.
Clorin.   See his wound againe is burst:
  Keepe her neere heere in the wood,
  Til I have stopt these streames of bloud.

[Exeunt Satyre with Cloe.]

  Soone againe he ease shall find,
  If I can but still his minde:
  This curtaine thus I do display,
  To keepe the pierceing Ayre away.   110

[Draws the curtain across the bower.]

Enter old Sheepheard, and Priest. [V. iii]

Priest.   Sure they are lost for ever, tis in vaine,
  To finde them out, with trouble and much paine,
  That have a Ripe desire, and forward will,
  To flye the company of all, but ill.
  What shall be counsaild? Now shall we retire?
  Or constant follow still, that first desire,
  We had to finde them?
Old Shepherd.   Stay a little while:
  For if the mornings mist do not beguile,
  My sight with shaddowes, sure I see a swaine,
  One of this jolly troopes come backe againe.   10

Enter Thenot.

Priest.   Doest thou not blush young sheepheard to be knowne,
  Thus without care, leaving thy flocks alone,
  And followinge what desire and present bloud,
  Shapes out before thy burning sence, for good,
  Havinge forgot what tongue hereafter may
  Tell to the world thy faleing off, and say
  Thou art regardlesse both of good and shame,
  Spurning at vertue, and a verteous name:
  And like a glorious desperat man, that buies,
  A poison of much price, by which he dyes,   20

<hr>

18 and a verteous name] Q 1 (c); and verteous names Q 1 (u)

Doest thou lay out for lust, whose only gaine,
Is foule disease, with present age and paine:
And then a Grave: these be the frutes that growe,
In such hot vaines that only beat to know,
Where they may take most ease and growe ambitious,
Through their owne wanton fire, and pride delitious.
Thenot.   Right holy Sir I have not knowen this night,
What the smooth face of Mirth was: or the sight,
Of any loosenesse: musicke, joy and ease,
Have bene to me, as bitter drugges to please   30
A Stomake lost with weakenesse, not a game
That I am skild at throughly: nor a dame,
Went her tongue smoother then the feete of Time,
Her beauty ever living like the Rime,
Our blessed *Tyterus* did singe of yore,
No, were shee more entising then the store
Of fruitfull Summer, when the loaden tree,
Bids the faint Traveller be bolde and free,
Twere but to me like Thunder gainst the bay,
Whose lightning may inclose, but never stay   40
Upon his charmed branches, such am I,
Against the catching flames of womans eye.
Priest.   Then wherefore hast thou wandred?
Thenot.   Twas a vowe,
That drew me out last night, which I have nowe,
Strictly perform'd, and homewards go to give
Fresh pasture to my sheepe, that they may live.
Priest.   Tis good to heare ye Sheepheard if the heart,
In this well sounding Musick beare his part.
Where have you left the rest?
Thenot.   I have not seene,
Since yesternight, we met upon this greene,   50
To fould our flocks up, any of that trayne:

23 growe] Q1(c); growes Q1(u)
37 Summer] Q1(c) (*Summr*); *Homer* Q1(u)
39 bay] Q1(c); raine Q1(u)   42 flames] Q1(c); flamer Q1(u)
51 flocks up, any] Q1(c); flocks, any Q1(u)

Yet have I walkt these woods round and have laine
All this long night under an aged tree:
Yet neyther wandring Shepheard did I see,
Or Shepheardesse, or drew into myne eare,
The sound of living thing unlesse it were,
The Nightingale, among the thicke leaved spring
That sits alone, in sorrow and doth sing,
Whole nights away in mourning, or the Owle,
Or our great Enemye that still doth howle   60
Against the Moones cold beames.

Priest.   Go and beware,
Of after falling.

Thenot.   Father tis my care.   *Exit* Thenot.

Enter Daphnis.

Old Shepherd.   Here comes another straggler, sure I see,
A shame in this young Shepheard.——*Daphnis*!

Daphnis.   Hee.

Priest.   Where hast thou left the rest, that should have bene
Long before this, grazing upon the greene
Their yet imprisond flocks?

Daphnis.   Thou holy man,
Give me a litle breathing till I can,
Be able to unfold what I have seene,
Such horror that the like hath never bene,   70
Knowne to the eare of Shepheard: oh my heart,
Labours a double motion to impart,
So heavy tydings! You all know the Bower,
Where the chast *Clorin* lives, by whose great power,
Sicke men and cattell have bene often cur'd,
There lovely *Amoret*, that was assur'd,
To lusty *Perrigot*, bleedes out her life,
Forced by some iron hand and fatall knife,
And by her young *Allexis.*

65 thou] Q3; *om.* Q1–2
73 So] Q1 (c); Of so Q1 (u)

Enter Amarillis *running from her* Sullen Sheepeheard.

Amarillis.   If there be
    Ever a Neighbour-brooke or hollow tree,   80
    Receive my body, close me up from lust,
    That follows at my heeles, be ever just,
    Thou God of sheepheards: *Pan* for her deare sake,
    That loves the Rivers brinks, and still doeth shake,
    In colde remembrance of thy quick pursute:
    Let me be made a reede, and ever mute,
    Nod to the waters fall, whilest every blast,
    Singes through my slender leaves that I was chaste.
Priest.   This is a night of wonder, *Amarill*,
    Be Comforted, the holy gods are still   90
    Revengers of these wrongs.
Amarillis.   Thou blessed man,
    Honourd upon these plaines and lov'd of *Pan*:
    Heare me, and save from endles infamy,
    My yet unblasted flower Virginitie:
    By all the Garlands that have croun'd that head,
    By thy chast office, and the mariage bed,
    That still is blest by thee: by all the rights
    Due to our God: and by those virgin lights,
    That burne before his Altar: let me not,
    Fall from my former state to gaine the blot   100
    That never shall be purged. I am not now,
    That wanton *Amarillis*: heere I vowe,
    To Heaven, and thee grave father, if I may,
    Scape this unhappy Night, to knowe the day,
    A virgin, never after to endure
    The tongues, or company of men unpure.
    I heare him, come, save me.
Priest.   Retire a while,
    Behinde this bush, till wee have knowen that vile
    Abuser of young maydens.   [*They retire.*]

79 *running*...Sheepeheard] Q 1 (c); *om.* Q 1 (u)

572

Enter Sullen [Shepherd].

Sullen Shepherd.   Stay thy pace,
Most loved *Amarillis*: let the chase,   110
Growe calme and milder, flye me not so fast,
I feare the pointed Brambles have unlac't
Thy golden Buskins: turne againe and see,
Thy Shepheard follow, that is strong and free,
Able to give thee all content and ease,
I am not bashfull virgin, I can please:
At first encounter hugg thee in mine arme,
And give thee many kisses, soft and warme,
As those the Sunne prints on the smiling cheeke,
Of Plummes or mellow peaches: I am sleeke,   120
And smooth as *Neptune* when stearne *Eolus*,
Locks up his surley winds and nimbly thus,
Can shew my Active youth: why doost thou flye?
Remember *Amarillis* it was I,
That kild *Alexis* for thy sake, and set,
An everlasting hate twixt *Amoret*,
And her beloved *Perigot*; twas I,
That drownd her in the well, where she must lye,
Till time shall leave to be: then turne againe,
Turne with thy open armes and clipp the swayne   130
That hath performd all this, turne turne I say:
I must not be deluded.
Priest [coming forward].   Monster stay,
Thou that art like a canker to the state,
Thou livest and brethest in, eating with debate,
Through every honest bosome, forcing still,
The vaynes of any men, may serve thy will,
Thou that hast offered with a sinfull hand,
To seaze upon this virgin that doth stand,
Yet trembling here.
Sullen Shepherd.   Good holynesse declare,
What had the danger bene if being bare,   140

119 the smiling] Q3; thy ~ Q1-2

I had imbracd her, tell me by your Art:
What comming wonders wood that sight impart?
Priest.   Lust, and branded soule.
Sullen Shepherd.   Yet tell me more,
  Hath not our Mother *Nature* for her store,
  And great increase, sayd it is good and just,
  And willd that every living creature must,
  Beget his like?
Priest.   Yee are better read then I,
  I must confesse in Blood and Letchery:
  Now to the Bowre and bring this beast along,
  Where he may suffer Pennance for his wrong.   150

[*Exeunt.*]

Enter Perigot *with his hand bloody.*   [V. iv

Perigot.   Here will I wash it in the mornings dewe,
  Which she on every litle grasse doth strewe,
  In silver dropps against the Sunnes appeare:
  Tis holy water and will make me cleere.
  My hand will not be cleansed, my wronged love,
  If thy chast spirit in the Ayre yet move,
  Looke mildly downe on him that yet doth stand,
  All full of guilt thy blood upon his hand,
  And though I strucke thee undeservedly,
  Let my revenge on her that Injurd thee,   10
  Make lesse a fault which I intended not,
  And let these dew dropps wash away my spot.
  It will not cleanse, O to what sacred flood,
  Shall I resort to wash away this blood:
  Amidst these Trees the holy *Clorin* dwells,
  In a low Cabin, of cut boughs, and heales
  All wounds: to her I will my selfe adresse,
  And my rash faultes repentantly confesse:
  Perhaps sheele find a meanes by Arte or prayer,
  To make my hand with chast blood stayned, fayre: 20
  That done not farre hence underneath some tree,

Ile have a little Cabin built since shee,
Whom I adorde is dead, there will I give,
My selfe to stricknesse and like *Clorin* live.

Exit.

The Curtayne is drawne, Clorin *appeares sitting in the Cabin,* Amoret [V. v]
sitting on the one side of her, Allexis *and* Cloe *on the other, the* Satyre
standing by.

Clorin.   Shepheard once more your blood is stayed,
Take example by this mayd,
Who is healde ere you be pure,
So hard it is lewd lust to cure,
Take heede then how you turne your eye,
On these other lustfully:
And sheepheardesse take heed least you,
Move his willing eye thereto,
Let no wring, nor pinch, nor smile
Of yours, his weaker sence beguyle.   10
Is your love yet true and chast,
And for ever so to last?
Alexis.   I have forgot all vaine desires,
All looser thoughts, ill tempred fires,
True love I find a pleasant fume,
Whose moderat heat can nere consume.
Cloe.   And I a newe fire feele in mee,
Whose base end is not quencht to be.
Clorin.   Joyne your hands with modest touch,
And for ever keepe you such.   20

Enter Perigot.

Perigot.   Yon is her cabin, thus far off ile stand,
And call her foorth, for my unhallowed hand,
I dare not bring so neere yon sacred place.
Clorin come foorth and do a timely grace,
To a poore swaine.
Clorin.   What art thou that doest call?

575

Clorin is ready to do good to all.
Come neere.
Perigot.   I dare not.
Clorin.   *Satyre*, see
Who it is that calls on mee.
Satyre.   Thers a hand some swaine doth stand,
Stretching out a bloudy hand.   30
Perigot.   Come *Clorin* bring thy holy waters clear,
To wash my hand.
Clorin.   What wonders have beene here
Tonight! Stretch foorth thy hand young swaine,
Wash and rubbe it whylst I raine
Holy water.
Perigot.   Still you power,
But my hand will never scoure.
Clorin.   *Satire*, bring him to the bowre,
Wee will try the soveragne power
Of other waters.
Satyre.   Mortall sure,
Tis the bloud of mayden pure   40
That staines thee soe.

The Satire *leadeth him to the Bower, where he spieth* Amoret *and*
kneeleth downe: shee knoweth him.

Perigot.   What e're thou be,
Beest thou her spright, or some divinitie,
That in her shape thinks good to walke this grove,
Pardon poore *Perigot*.
Amoret.   I am thy love,
Thy *Amoret*, for evermore thy love:
Strike once more on my naked brest, Ile proove
As constant still. O canst thou love me yet,
How soone could I my former griefes forget.
Perigot.   So over great with joy, that you live nowe   50
I am, that no desire of knowing how
Doeth seaze me; hast thou still power to forgive?

26 good] Q1(c); stood Q1(u)   47 Strike] Q3; Sticke Q1-2

Amoret.   Whil'st thou hast power to love, or I to live:
More welcome now then hadst thou never gone
Astray from me.
Perigot.   And when thou lov'st alone
And not I, death or some lingring paine
That's worse, light on me.
Clorin.   Now your staine
Perhaps will cleanse thee once againe:
See the bloud that erst did stay,
With the water drops away: 60
All the powers againe are pleas'd,
And with this newe knot are appeasd:
Joyne your hands, and rise together,
Pan be blest that brought you hether.

Enter Priest *and* olde Sheepheard.

Goe backe againe what ere thou art: unlesse
Smooth maiden thoughts possesse thee, doe not presse
This hallowed ground. Goe *Satire* take his hand,
And give him present triall.
Satyre.   Mortall stand,
Till by fire, I have made knowne
Whether thou be such a one,   70
That mayst freely tread this place,
Holde thy hand up: never was,
More untainted flesh then this.
Fairest he is full of blisse.
Clorin.   Then boldely speake why doest thou seeke this place.
Priest.   First honourd virgin to behold thy face,
Where all good dwells, that is: next for to try
The trueth of late report, was given to mee:
Those sheepheards that have met with foule mischance,
Through much neglect, and more ill governance,
Whether the wounds they have may yet endure   80
The open ayre, or stay a longer cure:
And lastly what the doome may be, shall light

74 full] Q2; fall Q1

577

Upon those guilty wretches, through whose spight
All this confusion fell. For to this place,
Thou holy mayden have I brought the race,
Of these offenders, who have freely tolde,
Both why, and by what meanes, they gave this bold
Attempt upon their lives.

Clorin.   Fume all the ground,
And sprinckle holy water, for unsound   90
And foule Infection ginnes to fill the Ayre:
It gathers yet more strongly, take a paire
Of Censors fild with Franckensence and Mirr,
Together with cold Camphire, quickly stirr
Thee gentle *Satire*, for the place beginns
To sweat and labour, with the abhorred sinnes
Of those offendors: let them not come nye,
For full of itching flame and leprosie,
Their very soules are, that the ground goes backe,
And shrinks to feele the sullen waight of black   100
And so unheard of vennome: hye thee fast,
Thou holy man, and bannish from the chast,
These manlike monsters, let them never more
Be knowen upon thes dounes, but longe before,
The next sunnes rising, put them from the sight,
And memory of every honest wight.
Be quicke in expedition, lest the sores
Of these weake patients, breake into newe gores.

                                        Exit Priest.

Perigot.   My deare deare *Amoret*, how happy are
Those blessed paires, in whom a little jarr   110
Hath bred an everlasting love, to strong
For time or steele, or envy to do wrong!
How do you feele your hurts? alasse poore heart
How much I was abusd, give me the smart
For it is justly mine.

Amoret.   I doe beleeve.

85 fell] Q2; full Q1   89 lives] Q2; live Q1
92 take a paire] Q2; *om.* Q1

578

It is enough deare friend, leave off to grieve,
And let us once more in despight of ill,
Give hands, and hearts againe.

Perigot.   With better will,
Then ere I went to finde, in hottest day
Coole Christall of the fountaine, to allay   120
My eager thirst: may this band never breake,
Heare us ô heaven.

Amoret.   Be constant.

Perigot.   Else *Pan* wreake
With double vengeance, my disloyalty.
Let me not dare to knowe the company
Of men, or any more behold those eyes.

Amoret.   Thus sheepheard with a kisse all envy dies.

Enter Priest.

Priest.   Bright Maid, I have perform'd your will, the swaine
In whom such heate, and blacke rebellions raigne
Hath undergone your sentence:
Only the maide I have reserv'd, whose face   130
Shewes much amendment, many a teare doth fall
In sorrow of her fault: great faire recall
Your heavie doome, in hope of better dayes
Which I dare promise: once again, upraise
Her heavy Spirit, that neere drowned lies
In selfe consuming care that never dies.

Clorin.   I am content to pardon: call her in,
The ayre growes coole againe, and doth beginn
To purge it selfe, how bright the day doth showe
After this stormy cloud! Goe *Satire* goe,   140
And with this taper boldly try her hand.
If she be pure and good, and firmely stand
To be so still: we have perfoormd a woorke
Worthy the gods them-selves.   Satire *brings* Amarillis *in.*

Satyre.   Come forward Maiden, do not lurke
Nor hide your face with griefe and shame,

144 Amarillis] Q1 (c); *Amoret* Q1 (u)

579

Now or never get a name,
That may raise thee, and recure,
All thy life that was impure:
Holde your hand unto the flame,   150
If thou beest a perfect dame,
Or hast truely vowd to mend,
This pale fire will be thy friend.
See the Taper hurts her not,
Goe thy waies, let never spot,
Hencefoorth ceaze upon thy bloode.
Thanke the Gods and still be good.

Clorin.   Yonge sheepheardesse now, ye are brought againe
To virgin state, be so, and so remaine
To thy last day, unlesse the faithfull love   160
Of some good sheepeheard force thee to remove,
Then labour to be true to him, and live
As such a one, that ever strives to give
A blessed memory to after Time:
Be famous for your good, not for your crime.
Now holy man, I offer up againe
These patients full of health, and free from paine:
Keepe them from after ills, be ever neere
Unto their actions: teach them how to cleare
The tedeous way they passe through, from suspect: 170
Keepe them from wrong in others, or neglect
Of duety in them selves, correct the bloud,
With thrifty bitts and laboure: let the flood,
Or the next neighbouring spring give remedy
To greedy thirst, and travaile, not the tree
That hanges with wanton clusters: let not wine,
Unlesse in sacrifice or rights devine,
Be ever knowen of shepheards: have a care,
Thou man of holy life, now do not spare
Their faults through much remissnes, nor forget   180
To cherish him, whose many paynes and sweat,
Hath given increase, and added to the downes.

170 through] Q2; though Q1   180 nor] Q2; not Q1

Sort all your Shepheards from the lazie clownes,
That feede their heafers in the budded Broomes,
Teach the young maydens stricknes that the grooms
May ever feare to tempt their blowing youth,
Banish all complement but single truth,
From every tongue, and every Shepheards heart,
Let them use perswading, but no Art:
Thus holy Priest, I wish to thee and these,   190
All the best goods and comforts that may please.
All.   And all those blessings Heaven did ever give,
Wee praye upon this Bower may ever live.
Priest.   Kneele every Shepheard, whilst with powerful hand,
I blesse your after labours, and the Land,
You feede your flocks upon. Great *Pan* defend you
From misfortune and amend you,
Keepe you from those dangers still,
That are followed by your will:
Give yee meanes to know at length,   200
All your Ritches: all your strength,
Cannot keepe your foot from falling,
To lewd lust, that still is calling,
At your cottage, till his power,
Bring againe that golden howre,
Of peace and rest, to every soule.
May his care of you controle,
All diseases, sores or payne,
That in after time may raigne,
Eyther in your flocks or you,   210
Give yee all affections new,
New desires and tempers new,
That yee may be ever true.
Now rise and go, and as ye passe away,
Sing to the God of sheepe, that happy laye,
That honest *Dorus* taught yee, *Dorus* hee,
That was the soule and God of melody.

195 your] Q2; you Q1

Song.   *They all sing.*

All yee Woodes, and Trees, and Bowers,
All ye vertues, and yee powers,
That inhabit in the lakes,   220
In the pleasant springs or brakes:
   Move your feete,
   To our sound,
   Whilst wee greete,
   All this ground,
With his honour and his name,
That defendes our flockes from blame.

Hee is great, and he is just,
Hee is ever good and must,
Thus be honnerd: Daffadillyes,   230
Roses, Pinckes, and loved Lillyes,
   Let us fling,
   Whilst wee sing,
   Ever holy,
   Ever holy,
Ever honerd, ever young,
Thus great Pan *is ever sung.*

      Exeunt [*all but* Clorin *and the* Satyre].

Satyre. Thou devinest, fayrest, brightest,
Thou most powerfull mayd, and whitest,
Thou most vertuous, and most blessed,   240
Eyes of Starrs and Golden Tressed,
Like *Apollo*, tell me sweetest,
What new service now is meetest,
For the *Satyre*? Shall I stray,
In the middle Ayre and staye,
The Sayling Racke or nimbly take,
Hold by the Moone, and gently make
Suite to the pale Queene of the night,
For a Beame to give thee light?

    217.1 *They*] Q2; *the* Q1

Shall I dive into the Sea,   250
And bring thee corrall, making way
Through the rising waves that fall,
In snowy fleeces? deerest shall
I catch thee wanton fawnes, or flyes,
Whose woven wings the Summer dyes,
For many coulours? get thee fruit,
Or steale from Heaven old *Orpheus* Lute?
All these I venter for and more,
To do her service, all these Woods adore.
Clorin.   No other Service *Satyre* but thy watch,   260
About these Thicks least harmlesse people catch,
Mischiefe or sad mischance.
Satyre.   Holy virgin, I will daunce,
Round about these woods as quick,
As the breaking light, and pricke,
Downe the lawnes, and downe the vales,
Faster then the Windmill sayles.
So I take my leave and praye,
All the comforts of the day:
Such as *Phœbus* heate doth send,   270
On the Earth may still befriend,
Thee and this Arbor.
Clorin.   And to thee,
All thy masters love be free.

                                        Exeunt.

          FINIS   *The Pastorall of the*
                          faithfull Shepheardesse.

          254 thee] Dyce; the Q 1-5, F

583

TEXTUAL NOTES

I.ii

29–42 *Sing his praises... unyoke.*]   Music by William Lawes for the song is
preserved in two places in Music MS. Dc. 1. 69 (nos. 15 and 126) in the
Edinburgh University Library. See John P. Cutts, 'Seventeenth-Century
Songs and Lyrics in Edinburgh University Library Music MS. Dc. 1. 69',
Musica Disciplina, 13 (1959), 181. Cutts suggests that Lawes' setting was
prepared for the 1634 revival of the play. He notes the following variants
between the text as given in the manuscript and that of Q1:

34 neighbouring] murmuringe
35 her] the

The last three lines, Cutts reports, 'are scored for a Chorus of Treble and
Bass'.

II.iv

46 *Cloe (within). Cloe!*]   Q1–5, F print the first two words in the margin to
the right of line 45, and the third at the beginning of line 46, thereby including it in Daphnis' speech which thus is not interrupted. But it is clear
from lines 48–9 that Cloe has just called out her own name.

III.i

429–436 *Doe not feare... trouble thee.*]   Music for the song is printed in John
Wilson's *Select Ayres and Dialogues* (1659), p. 98, and his *Cheerful Ayres*
(1660), pp. 24–5. At line 431, for Q1's 'leach, or Neute, or Toad', Wilson's
texts read 'Neute, nor Leech, nor Toade'. A manuscript version of the
setting is preserved in Edinburgh University Library Music MS. Dc. 1. 69
(no. 96); see Cutts, 'Seventeenth-Century Songs', p. 189.

V.ii

0.1 *Enter Clorin... Allexis with her.*]   To this stage direction, corrected
copies of Q1 add, erroneously, the words '*and Amorillis*'.

PRESS-VARIANTS

[Copies collated: BM (British Museum), Bodl (Bodleian Library), Dyce (Victoria and Albert Museum), CSmH (Henry E. Huntington Library), MH (Harvard University Library), Pforz (Carl Pforzheimer Library), Pirie (Robert S. Pirie, Boston, Mass.).

SHEET [A] (*outer forme*)

Corrected: BM (wants leaf [A4]), Bodl, Dyce, MH, Pforz, Pirie
Uncorrected: CSmH

Sig. [A3] (Field's verses)
line 2 vnknwne] nvknowne
line 2 mnfe] mufe
line 8 ambition] ambicio
line 9 loue to] louono
line 10 worke, as] work t as
line 18 comfort,] ~ :

Sig. [A4ᵛ] (Chapman's verses)
line 23 femi-Gods] femy-Gods

SHEET [A] (*inner forme*)

Corrected: Dyce, CSmH, Pforz
Uncorrected: BM, Bodl, MH, Pirie

Sig. [A3ᵛ] (Heading to Beaumont's verses)
lines 0.1–2 *Fletcher* ◠ vpon his | faithfull Shepheardeffe] *Fletceher,* | *vpon his faithfull Shepheardeffe*

HALF-SHEET (*inner forme*)

Corrected: Dyce, Pforz
Uncorrected: BM, CSmH, MH
(Both leaves of the half-sheet are
missing from Bodl and Pirie copies)

Sig. ¶ 1ᵛ (verses to Scipwith)
line 19 Farre] Fare

SHEET D (*outer forme*)

Corrected: BM, CSmH, Pirie
Uncorrected: Bodl, Dyce, MH, Pforz

Sig. D1
  II.i.16 budd] bloud
      27 watches] walkes
  II.ii.4 happy] high
      6 &] a
     10 crop] lop
     11 giue] told
     15 tooth...Ramuns] teeth...Ramuus
     17 dore fast,] dore,

Sig. D2ᵛ
  II.ii.106 *Shep.] omitted*
     111 flames] flame
     124 *Arions] Orions*
     127 wandring] errant
     129 Alpsien] Alpen

Sig. D3
  II.ii.132 toyling...deep] toylng...deepe
     133 dare] do
     143 strongly] strong

Sig. D4ᵛ
  II.iii.88 charmeto,] charme, to ∧

SHEET D (*inner forme*)

1st stage corrected: CSmH
Uncorrected: Bodl, Dyce, MH, Pforz

Sig. D2
  II.ii.70 fence.] ~ ∧
      72 graſſe∧] ~ .

2nd stage corrected: BM, Pirie

Sig. D1ᵛ
  II.ii.21 Sage,] ~ ∧
      22 Such] Which
      23 Tormentil] Formentill
      35 standergraſſe] Sandergraſſe
      36 with] and
      40 fancies] forces

586

48 as] and
48.1 *Thenot*] *Shepheard*
49 *The.*] *Shep.*

Sig. D2

II.ii.57 making] make
60 *Chaos.*] ~ ∧
62 yon] you
63 nightly] brightly
66 poets ſtile] ſtiled is
74 dappld] dapple
82 Breakes] Beates

Sig. D3ᵛ

II.iii.10 Or] And
28 when?] ~ ∧

Sig. D4

II.iii.37 ſycamoures] ſicamoures
52 nimble] Conies,

SHEET F (*outer forme*)

Corrected: BM, Bodl, Dyce, CSmH, Pforz, Pirie
Uncorrected: MH

Sig. F3

III.i.360 bound] bonud

SHEET H (*inner forme*)

1st stage corrected: Bodl, MH
Uncorrected: Dyce, Pforz

Sig. H1ᵛ

IV.iv.44 painted,] ~ ∧
47 difference,] ~ ∧

Sig. H2

IV.iv.71 Hare,] ~ ∧
74 preuent,] ~ .
79 theiſe,] ~ ∧
94. Iuſt,] ~ ∧

Sig. H4

IV.v.18 straight,] ~ ∧

2nd stage corrected: BM, CSmH, Pirie

Sig. H1ᵛ
  IV.iv.41 tongue,] ~ ∧,
      46 Riddle,] ~ ∧

SHEET I (*inner forme*)

1st stage corrected: Bodl
Uncorrected: CSmH, MH

Sig. I1ᵛ
  V.i.16 decay] delay
     18 fure] faue
     19 or] for
     20 Fillde] Filde
     24 not] uot
     25 lodging, heere] longing, heard
     29 Boule] Bowle
     31 note] notes
     33 their] the
  V.ii.0.1 *Clorin*] *Clorni*
     0.1 *with her. | and Amorillis*] *with her.*
     1 thoughts] thought
     2 cure] cnre
     8 hearbs] herbs
     11 *Clorin*] *Clorni*

Sig. I2
  V.ii.35 *Clorin*] *Clorni*
     42 *Clorin*] *Clormi*

Sig. I3ᵛ
  V.iii.18 and a verteous name] and verteous names
     23 growe] growes
     27 Sir] S.
     31 Stomake] Stomouke
     37 *Summr*] *Homer*
     39 bay] raine
     42 flames] flamer
     45 perform'd] perfoom'd
     45 homewards] homewords

Sig. I4
  V.iii.51 flocks vp, any] flocks, any
     62.1 *Daphnis*] *Daphinis*
     64.S.P. *Daphnis*] *Dalphinis*

65. *Preost*] *Priest*
68 breathing] brething
73 So] Of so
74 *Clorin*] *Cloeni*
77 *Perrigot*] *Perrogots*
78 iron] Iron
79 running from her fullen fheepeheard.] *omitted*

2nd stage corrected: Dyce, Pforz, Pirie

Sig. I1ᵛ
V.ii.1 *Clorin*] *Clorni*

Sig. I2
V.ii.45 *Glorin*] *Glormi*

3rd stage corrected: BM

Sig. I4
V.iii.69 to] ro

SHEET K (*inner forme*)

Corrected: BM, Dyce, Pforz, Pirie
Uncorrected: Bodl, CSmH, MH

Sig. K1ᵛ
V.iv.22 built] builts
V.v.O.2 *Allexis*] *Allepis*

Sig. K2
V.v.10 his] his his
26 good] stood

Sig. K3ᵛ
V.v.110 blessed] b.effed
113 your] yovr
134 promife:] ~ ₄
135 drowned] drouned

Sig. K4
V.v.144 *Amarillis*] *Amoret*
175 trauaile, not₄] ~ ₄ ~ ,

EMENDATIONS OF ACCIDENTALS

To my lov'd friend

2 unknowne] Q2; vnknwne Q1
2 muse] Q2; mnse Q1
12 morallitie‸] mortallitie. Q1–2; morallitie. Q3–5

22 reflection;] Q3; ~ , Q1–2
28 March] Q3; march Q1–2
28 winde:] Q4; ~ , Q1–3

To my friend Maister *John Fletcher*

0.2 Faithfull] Q5; faithfull Q1–4
19 knowing] Q2; kowing Q1

36 well:] Q3; ~ , Q1–2

To that noble and true lover of learning

22 will,] ~ ‸ Q1

To the inheritour of all worthines

11 best;] ~ ‸ Q1
12 poet:] ~ ‸ Q1
14 neede,] ~ ‸ Q1
15 it,] ~ ‸ Q1
17 journies,] ~ . Q1

18 diet.] ~ ‸ Q1
19 Ames,] ~ ‸ Q1
21 pitty.] ~ ‸ Q1
24 good,] ~ ; Q1

To the perfect gentleman

4 one,] ~ ; Q1
4 amisse.] ~ ‸ Q1
8 Talent,] ~ ‸ Q1
9 me,] ~ ‸ Q1

16 protesters,] ~ ‸ Q1
17 letters,] ~ ‸ Q1
18 debts,] ~ ; Q1
18 jesters;] ~ , Q1

To the Reader

20 hyerlings.] ~ ‸ Q1

I.i

I.i] Actus primi, Scena prima. Q1
5 eies,] Q2; ~ : Q1
13 delightfull,] Q3; ~ . Q1–2

16 leaves:] Q4; ~ , Q1–2; ~ ; Q3
16 away,] Q3; ~ : Q1–2
17 away,] Q2; ~ : Q1

31 will I] Q2; I will I Q1
52 *Pan*] Q3; Pan Q1–2
56 *Syrinx*] Q3; Syrinx Q1–2
72 *Satyre*] Satyre Q1–5, F
75 true.] Q4; ~ , Q1–3
79 *Bacchus*] Q3; Bacchus Q1–2

91 *Pan*] Q3; Pan Q1–2
97 awake,] Q3; ~ : Q1–2
99 Under] Q2; Vnde Q1
117 fiers,] Q3; ~ . Q1–2
125 virgin,] Q3; ~ ; Q1–2

I.ii

7 free.] Q3; ~ , Q1–2
14 meat,] Q3; ~ . Q1–2
16 fires,] Q3; ~ . Q1–2
26 spoken‿] Q3; ~ : Q1–2
27 eare:] ~ , Q1–2; ~ ; Q3–5, F
44 thee stay] Q3; theee ~ Q1; the ~ Q2
44 deere,] Q2; ~ . Q1
76 men,] Q2; ~ . Q1
96 *Dian*] Q3; Dian Q1–2

114 captivitie:] ~ , Q1–2; ~ ; Q3–5, F
121 scant‿] Q3; ~ . Q1–2
126 good‿] Q3; ~ , Q1–2
127 shepheard,] Q2; ~ ‿ Q1
185 freer] Q2; freeer Q1
195 *Saturnes*] Q3; Saturnes Q1–2
204 *Lyeus*:] ~ , Q1–3; ~ ; Q4–5, F
228 pleasing:] ~ , Q1; ~ ; Q2–4, F; ~ . Q5

I.iii

98 freer] Q3; freeer Q1–2
99 Eunenke] Euuenke Q1–2; Eunuch Q3–5, F
100 him:——] ~ : ‿ Q1–2; ~ . ‿ Q3–5, F
120 *Troy*] Q5; Troy Q1–4
123–124 I...prove] Q2; *one line in* Q1

154 tine,] Q2 (time); ~ . Q1
170 befriended——] ~ , Q1–2, 4–5, F; ~ ‿ Q3
181 be——] Q4; ~ , Q1–3
188 *Reine*] Q3 (*Rhine*); Reine Q1–2
192 *Exit*] Q3; *at the end of line* 191 *in* Q1–2

II.i

II.i] Actus secundus Scena prima. Q1
4 runne.] Q2; ~ , Q1

6 is,] ~ : Q1–5, F
31 sweetest] Q2; sweeeest Q1

II.ii

3 light:] ~ , Q1; ~ ; Q2–4, F; ~ . Q5
15 Ramnus] Ramuus Q1 (u); Ramuns Q1 (c), Q2–5, F
20 remedie,] Q3; ~ . Q1–2

60 *Chaos*,] Q2; ~ . Q1 (c); ~ ‿ Q1 (u)
74 deere‿] Q3; ~ : Q1–2
92 Art,] Q2; ~ : Q1
93 holdes:] ~ , Q1; ~ ; Q2–5, F

97 griefe:] ~ ⋏ Q1–2; ~ ; Q3–5, F
105 fright⋏] Q3; ~ . Q1; ~ , Q2

146 women,] Q3; wowen⋏ Q1; women ⋏ Q2
165 Arbor:] ~ , Q1–2; ~ ; Q3–5, F

II.iii

21 Shepheard,] Q2; ~ ⋏ Q1
34 not)] Q2; ~ ⋏ Q1
51 with:] ~ ⋏ Q1–5, F
54 Swan.] ~ , Q1; ~ ; Q2–5, F
73 day,] Q3; ~ . Q1–2
74 colours:] ~ , Q1–4, F; ~ ; Q5

77 hand,] Q3; ~ ⋏ Q1–2
78 land⋏] Q2; ~ : Q1
79 fountaine,] Q3; ~ : Q1–2
94 love:] Q5; ~ , Q1; ~ ; Q2; ~ . Q3–4

II.iv

II.iv] Actus secundus Scena quarta. Q1
 2 *Cloe*:] ~ , Q1–2; ~ ; Q3–5, F
 2 misse,] Q3; ~ : Q1; ~ ⋏ Q2
13 *Cloe*] Q5; Cloe Q1–4, F
14 *Cloe*] Q2; Cloe Q1
22 *Cloe*] Cloe Q1–5, F
27 *Cloe*] Q2; Cloe Q1
39–40 hold | Her] Q2; hold her | Her Q1
46 *Cloe*!] ~ ⋏ Q1–5, F
54 your] Q2; yous Q1
54 found?] Q2; ~ ⋏ Q1

57 kisse⋏] Q2; ~ : Q1
67 tenderd:] Q3; ~ , Q1; ~ ; Q2
68–69 grieve⋏ | Then, ever kindest,] Q3; ~ , | ~ ⋏ ~ ~ ⋏ Q1–2
75 smiles:] ~ , Q1–5, F
76 wiles,] Q3; ~ : Q1–2
92 bold——] ~ , Q1, 4; ~ . Q2–3, 5, F
99 way:] Q2; way ⋏ Q1
106, 107 *Cloe*] Q4; Cloe Q1–3
106 hee⋏] Q3; ~ . Q1–2
108 *Pan*] Q3; Pan Q1–2
108 *Sirinx*] Q3; Sirinx Q1–2

III.i

III.i] Actus tertius Scena prima. Q1
25–26] Q2; *one line in* Q1
35–36] Q2; *one line in* Q1
65 sence:] ~ ⋏ Q1–2; ~ , Q3–5, F
67 heere's] Q2 (here's); heeee's Q1
74 sight⋏] Q2; ~ , Q1
76 ground:] Q3; ~ , Q1; ~ ; Q2
79 *Amoret, Amoret*] Q3; Amoret, Amoret Q1–2
79 *Perigot*] Q3; Perigot Q1–2
103 *Perigot*:] Q3; ~ , Q1–2
115, 156 *Pan*] Q3; Pan Q1–2

193 sound:] ~ , Q1; ~ ; Q2–5, F
198 Oh!] Q2; ~ ⋏ Q1
203 bloud:] Q4; ~ , Q1; ~ ; Q2–3
207 beheld ⋏ yon] Q4; ~ , you Q1–2; ~ ⋏ you Q3
207 brest⋏] Q3; ~ , Q1–2
210 Sheapheard] Q3; *Sheapheard* Q1–2
213 willing:] ~ , Q1; ~ ; Q2; ~ . Q3–5, F
217 lost:] Q3; ~ , Q1–2

221 ô] Q2; o Q1

227 fled,] ~ ˄ Q1–2; ~ . Q3–5, F

228 tree,] Q3; ~ . Q1; ~ : Q2

229 mocke:] ~ , Q1–5, F

236 Pray.] Q2; ~ , Q1

238 gone˄] Q3; ~ , Q1–2

239 dead,] Q3; ~ : Q1–2

241 Removed˄] Q3; ~ . Q1–2

242.1 Amarillis˄] Q2; ~ . Q1

243 fancies˄] Q2; ~ , Q1

243 forgott:] ~ , Q1–5, F

244 close,] Q3; ~ ˄ Q1–2

245 *Amarillis*] Q3; Amarillis Q1–2

245 shape˄] Q3; ~ , Q1–2

246 *Amoret,*] Q2; ~ ˄ Q1

247 *Perigot*] Q3; Perigot Q1–2

248 Chace˄] Q2; ~ . Q1

251 bancke:] ~ ˄ Q1–2; ~ , Q3–5, F

255 them.] ~ , Q1–5, F

258 hitt˄] Q3; ~ . Q1–2

259 bee,] Q3; ~ . Q1–2

261 love] Q2; lone Q1

268 yon] Q2; you Q1

269 sweare,] Q3; ~ : Q1–2

270 teare˄] Q3; ~ , Q1–2

272 on] Q2; one Q1

272 rest,] Q2; ~ ˄ Q1

273 thee] Q2; the Q1

274 hew:] ~ , Q1–2; ~ ; Q3–5, F

275 lambe˄] Q3; ~ . Q1; ~ , Q2

278 thee,] Q2; ~ ˄ Q1

278 ould˄] Q3; ~ , Q1–2

280 above˄] Q3; ~ , Q1–2

282 refuse?] Q3; ~ , Q1–2

283 thoughts˄] Q3; ~ , Q1–2

285 Come, *Perigot*˄] Q3; ~ ˄ ~ , Q1–2

286 *Amoret*] Q3; Amoret Q1–2

288 *Amoret,* imbrace˄] Q3; Amoret˄ ~ , Q1; Amoret ˄ ~ ˄ Q2

289 love?] Q3; ~ ; Q1–2

289 shud,] Q3; ~ . Q1–2

292 faine˄] Q3; ~ . Q1–2

294 pure:] Q5; ~ , Q1–2; ~ ; Q3–4

297 woemen?] Q3; ~ , Q1–2

297 *Perigot*] Q3; Perigot Q1–2

299 Mayde:] ~ ˄ Q1; ~ , Q2; ~ ; Q3–5, F

300 usd:] Q3; ~ , Q1–2

301 rise?] Q3; ~ , Q1–2

301 heart˄] Q3; ~ , Q1–2

301 thou hast] Q2; thon ~ Q1

302 *Perigot*] Q2; Perigot Q1

304 div'd,] ~ ˄ Q1–2; ~ ; Q3–5, F

304 art] Q2; art, art Q1

304 jest?] Q2; ~ ; Q1

311 vaine˄] Q3; ~ , Q1–2

323 might˄] Q3; ~ : Q1–2

325 undo˄] Q3; ~ ; Q1–2

326 to:] Q4; ~ , Q1–2; ~ ; Q3

327 flye,] Q2; ~ ˄ Q1

328 shape.] Q2; ~ ? Q1

333 Sheapardesse, my rage and night˄] Q3; ~ ˄ ~ ~ ~ ~ , Q1–2

335 blood˄] Q3; ~ . Q1; ~ , Q2

338 hath,] Q2; ~ . Q1

339 heare˄] Q3; ~ , Q1–2

340 voyce:] ~ , Q1; ~ ; Q2–5, F

340 deare˄] Q2; ~ : Q1

341 is, how faire˄] Q2; ~ ˄ ~ ~ . Q1

344 lights˄] Q2; ~ , Q1

345 thou] Q2; thon Q1

346 reward˄] Q2; ~ . Q1

347 crost;] Q5; ~ , Q1–4

347 strucke,] Q3; ~ ; Q1–2

348 tooke˄] Q3; ~ : Q1–2

350 her.——] ~ , ˄ Q1–2; ~ . ˄ Q3–5, F

350 Sheapardesse] Q3; *Sherpardesse* Q1; *Shepheardesse* Q2

350 prepare˄] Q3; ~ , Q1–2

355 bee˄] Q2; ~ . Q1

361 yon] Q2; you Q1

367 Rancks.] Q2; ~ ˄ Q1

593

370 weedes.] Q3; ~ ‸ Q1; ~ , Q2
374 fell.] Q3; ~ , Q1; ~ ; Q2
380 heate.] Q3; ~ , Q1; ~ ; Q2
384 round‸] Q3; ~ , Q1–2
386 endure.] Q3; ~ , Q1; ~ : Q2
390 stayde.] Q3; ~ , Q1; ~ : Q2
391 flower,] Q2; ~ . Q1
393 draw.] Q3; ~ , Q1–2
394 saw‸] Q3; ~ , Q1–2
395 Mortall.] Q3; ~ , Q1–2
395 breake‸] Q3; ~ , Q1–2
396 slumber:] Q3; ~ , Q1–2
398 death?] Q3; ~ , Q1–2
407 about,] Q2; ~ . Q1
408 out.] Q3; ~ , Q1–2
410 company,] Q3; ~ . Q1; ~ :
    Q2
411 lye,] Q2; ~ : Q1
412 I:] Q2; ~ , Q1
417 seene:] Q2; ~ , Q1
420 in:] Q3; ~ , Q1; ~ ; Q2
424 flye:] ~ , Q1–2; ~ . Q3–5, F
425 understand,] Q3; ~ : Q1–2
432 *thou*] Q 2; thon Q1
434 *cry*‸] Q2; ~ : Q1
438 selfe‸] Q3; ~ , Q1–2

439 By thee] Q2; ~ the Q1
439 for thee‸] Q2; ~ ~ : Q1
440 Mortallitie:] Q3; ~ , Q1–2
442 bethrothd] Q2; be throthd Q1
442 Sheaphard] Q3; *Sheaphard* Q1–
    2
443 face,] Q3; ~ ; Q1–2
443 above‸] Q3; ~ : Q1–2
444 see,] Q3; ~ : Q1; ~ ; Q2
448 dry,] Q3; ~ . Q1; ~ ; Q2
450 watringe,] Q2; ~ . Q1
451 late‸] Q3; ~ . Q1; ~ , Q2
452 sate‸] Q3; ~ . Q1; ~ , Q2
453 On] Q2; One Q1
454 Two] Q2; Tow Q1
463 Tree,] Q3; ~ ; Q1–2
463 force,] Q2; ~ . Q1
464 Course:] Q2; ~ , Q1
466 brincke:] Q2; ~ ‸ Q1
467 none] Q2; non Q1
469 wade‸] Q3; ~ : Q1–2
470 streames,] Q5; ~ ? Q1; ~ ‸
    Q2–4
471 on] Q2; one Q1
477 bee,] Q2; ~ . Q1

IV.i

1 untrue,] Q3; ~ ‸ Q1–2
9 it——] ~ . Q1–5, F
10 hand,] Q2; ~ ‸ Q1
10 hott‸] Q3; ~ , Q1–2
11 selfe,] Q2; ~ ‸ Q1
12 Rayne‸] Q4; ~ . Q1–2; ~ ,
    Q3
13 away‸] Q3; ~ : Q1; ~ , Q2
14 lay‸] Q2; ~ , Q1
15 thee.] Q3; ~ , Q1; ~ ; Q2
15 Yet] Q3; yet Q1–2
16 sands‸] Q3; ~ , Q1–2
18 Sheapard] *Sheapard* Q1–5, F
18 the] Q2; thee Q1
20 true:] Q2; ~ , Q1

25 cannot:] ~ , Q1–2; ~ ; Q3–5,
    F
29 it:] ~ , Q1–4, F; ~ ; Q5
32 *Amoret*,] Q2; ~ . Q1
33 one] Q2; on Q1
34 power‸] Q3; ~ ? Q1; ~ , Q2
35 Night,] Q3; ~ ? Q1; ~ : Q2
36 sight,] Q3; ~ ? Q1; ~ ; Q2
38 the] Q2; thee Q1
40 frett;] ~ ‸ Q1–2; ~ , Q3–5, F
41 Chaplet,] Q2; ~ ? Q1
42 singing,] Q3; ~ ‸ Q1; ~ ; Q2
42 thing‸] Q3; ~ , Q1–2
43 her,] Q2; ~ ‸ Q1
43 feele‸] Q3; ~ ; Q1; ~ , Q2

44 steele !] ~ ? Q1
45 hope,] Q3; ~ ; Q1–2
46 scope∧] Q2; ~ ; Q1
47 next∧] Q3; ~ ? Q1; ~ , Q2
48 Beech,] Q2; ~ ? Q1

48 perplext,] Q3; ~ ; Q1–2
49 goe,] Q3; ~ ; Q1–2
50 doe∧] Q4; ~ , Q1–3
52 strife,] Q3; ~ ; Q1–2
54 *Mydas*∧] Q3; ~ , Q1–2

IV.ii

0.1 Alexis] Q3; *Alezis* Q1–2
1 goe,] Q3; ~ ; Q1–2
2 woe,] Q3; ~ ; Q1–2
3 night,] Q2; ~ ? Q1
4 light,] Q2; ~ . Q1
6 have] Q2; hane Q1
8 mee,] Q3; ~ . Q1–2
9 sleepes∧] Q3; ~ : Q1–2
10 spray;] Q2; ~ ∧ Q1
10 creeps∧] Q3; ~ , Q1–2
11 Tayle,] Q3; ~ ; Q1; ~ : Q2
12 sayle,] Q3; ~ ; Q1–2
13 wind,] Q3; ~ ; Q1–2
16 bedd∧] Q2; ~ ; Q1
17 Nettells:] Q3; ~ ∧ Q1; ~ ; Q2
18 fare∧] ~ ; Q1; ~ , Q2–5, F
19 footing,] Q2; ~ ∧ Q1
19 wish∧] Q3; ~ ; Q1; ~ , Q2
20 fish∧] Q2; ~ ? Q1
21 found,] Q2; ~ ; Q1
22 seaes,] Q2; ~ ; Q1
23 sound,] Q3; ~ . Q1; ~ : Q2
28 enlardge,] Q2; ~ ; Q1
31 it.] ~ , Q1; ~ : Q2; ~ ! Q3–5,
   F
33 Paramore∧] Q2; ~ : Q1
37 the] Q2; thee Q1
37 destinyes∧] Q3; ~ . Q1; ~ ,
   Q2
38 life;] Q2; ~ , Q1
41 thou,] ~ ? Q1; ~ ; Q2; ~ ∧
   Q3–5, F
43 Eares ?] Q3; ~ , Q1–2
43 Speake] speake Q1–5, F
44 *Satyre*] Q3; Statyre Q1; Satyre
   Q2

52 bloomes,] Q2; ~ ∧ Q1
53 Groomes] Q2; Gwomes Q1
55 Townes:] ~ , Q1; ~ ; Q2–4,
   F; ~ . Q5
62 *Satyre*] Q3; Satyre Q1–2
62 rude:] ~ , Q1–4, F;
   ~ ; Q5
63 hued,] Q5; ~ : Q1–4
68 restrayne∧] Q3; ~ , Q1–2
71 to∧] Q2; ~ , Q1
76 spring∧] Q2; ~ : Q1
77 Temples:] ~ ∧ Q1; ~ ; Q2–5,
   F
77 twice∧] Q2; ~ : Q1
79 drawe,] Q2; ~ . Q1
80 sawe∧] Q3; ~ . Q1; ~ , Q2
82 death∧] Q2; ~ : Q1
83 vanisht:] ~ , Q1–3; ~ ; Q4–5,
   F
83 playster,] Q2; ~ : Q1
84 maister∧] Q3; ~ : Q1; ~ , Q2
85 maye∧] Q3; ~ : Q1; ~ , Q2
90 vayne,] Q3; ~ : Q1–2
91 empty] Q3; emply Q1; emty
   Q2
93 Runnes∧] Q2; ~ , Q1
94 stinge∧] Q3; ~ , Q1–2
95 you ?] Q3; ~ , Q1–2
98 Destiny.] Q3; ~ , Q1–2
100 freind.] ~ , Q1; ~ : Q2–5, F
103 awe,] Q2; ~ . Q1
108 Sheapheard] Q3; *Sheapheard*
   Q1–2
110 fiers,] Q2; ~ . Q1
111 bloud, and will∧] Q3; ~ ∧ ~
   ~ , Q1–2

112 untill₄] Q2; ~ , Q1
113 Whiter:] ~ ₄ Q1; ~ ; Q2–5, F
113 pray₄] Q2; ~ : Q1
115 ease,] Q2; ~ . Q1
116 displease₄] Q3; ~ , Q1–2
117 Give] give Q1–5, F
118 Thyghes₄] Q3; ~ . Q1; ~ Q2
121 good.] Q3; ~ , Q1–2
128 Sheapeard] Q3; Sheapeard Q1–2

128 kissinge,] Q4; ~ ₄ Q1–3
129 missing.] Q3; ~ , Q1–2
130 ther₄] Q2; ~ , Q1
135 Queene₄] Q4; ~ , Q1–3
136 Fayryes] Fayryes Q1–5, F
137 it, so much dutye₄] Q3; ~ ₄ ~ ~ ~ , Q1; ~ , ~ ~ ~ , Q2
139 thee] Q2; the Q1
141 will,] Q2; ~ ? Q1
143 weather₄] Q2; ~ : Q1
148 fishe:] Q2; ~ , Q1

IV.iii

1 lost₄] Q2; ~ , Q1
2 crost₄] Q3; ~ , Q1–2
7 use₄] Q3; ~ , Q1–2
8 Riddle, sweetely] Q2; ~ ₄ s,weetely Q1
8 chuse₄] Q3; ~ , Q1–2
9 valentynes,] Q3; ~ : Q1–2
9 find₄] Q3; ~ . Q1; ~ , Q2
10 in.] Q3; ~ , Q1–2
10 unkind,] Q3; ~ . Q1; ~ : Q2
11 Whether] whether Q1–5, F
12 Was] was Q1–5, F
13 Tis] tis Q1–5, F
15 heare,] Q2; ~ . Q1
16 Amoret₄] Q3; ~ , Q1–2
17 is₄] Q3; ~ . Q1; ~ , Q2
18 deepe₄] Q2; ~ : Q1
19 happynesse;] Q2; ~ , Q1
23 Madnes:] ~ ₄ Q1; ~ ; Q2–5, F
28 memorye₄] Q3; ~ . Q1; ~ , Q2
29 Enter Amarillis] Q2; Enter Amarillsi Q1 (after line 28)
30 Mynd,] Q2; ~ . Q1
31 Amoret] Q3; Amoret Q1–2
31 Amoret:] ~ , Q1; ~ ; Q2–5, F
35 of.] ~ , Q1–5, F
38 howre₄] Q2; ~ , Q1
39 Perigot;] Q2; ~ ? Q1
44 slayne,] Q3; ~ . Q1; ~ : Q2
46 dwell.] Q3; ~ , Q1; ~ : Q2

47 Amoret,] Q3; ~ . Q1–2
48 let₄] Q3; ~ , Q1–2
49 Crost.] Q3; ~ , Q1; ~ ; Q2
49 Mayde] Q3; mayde Q1–2
49 away₄] Q3; ~ , Q1–2
50 allay₄] Q3; ~ , Q1–2
52 Breakes₄] Q3; ~ , Q1–2
53 Perigot——] Q4; ~ : Q1; ~ . Q2–3
53 Perigot?] Q3; ~ . Q1–2
54 wott,] Q2; ~ : Q1
55 fortune:] ~ , Q1–4, F; ~ ; Q5
56 brim₄] Q3; ~ , Q1–2
58 run,] Q3; ~ ₄ Q1–2
58 mee₄] Q3; ~ . Q1; ~ , Q2
58 winn₄] Q2; ~ : Q1
61 promise,] Q3; ~ ₄ Q1–2
61 sitt₄] Q3; ~ ; Q1–2
62 fitt₄] Q2; ~ ; Q1
64 Morning₄] Q2; ~ , Q1
66 Sheapeard] Sheapeard Q1–5, F
66 wronger₄] Q2; ~ ; Q1
68 first?] Q3; ~ : Q1; ~ . Q2
68 Mayd!] ~ ? Q1
70 stayne₄] Q2; ~ ? Q1
71 are₄] Q3; ~ . Q1–2
75 hold₄] Q3; ~ : Q1; ~ , Q2
76 delayes₄] Q2; ~ : Q1
76 cold₄] Q3; ~ , Q1–2
79 followe.] ~ , Q1–4, F; ~ ; Q5

IV.iv

1 yet‸] Q2; ~ ? Q1
3 teame:] Q3; ~ , Q1–2
4 *Bootes*] Q3; Bootes Q1–2
6 light:] Q5; ~ , Q1–2; ~ ; Q3–4
11 knowne,] Q2; ~ : Q1
14 *Perigot*] Q3; Perigot Q1–2
14 *Amoret*] Q3; Amoret Q1–2
15 dare‸] Q3; ~ , Q1–2
17 darcknes?] Q3; ~ , Q1–2
18 *Amoret*] Q3; Amoret Q1–2
19 consuminges:] ~ ‸ Q1; ~ ; Q2–5, F
22 againe.] ~ ‸ Q1; ~ ; Q2–4, F; ~ : Q5
22 Why] Q5; why Q1–4
26 daye?] Q2; ~ , Q1
29 ground,] ~ . Q1; ~ ‸ Q2–5, F
31 browe?] Q2; ~ ‸ Q1
32 Sheapheard,] Q2; ~ ‸ Q1
32 nowe‸] Q3; ~ , Q1–2
35 fayre.] Q4; ~ , Q1–3
37 lent‸] Q3; ~ , Q1–2
38 intent?] Q2; ~ , Q1
40 such‸] Q2; ~ , Q1
45 Body,] Q2; ~ ‸ Q1
48 annother?] Q3; ~ , Q1–2
48 Looke] looke Q1–5, F
48 see,] Q2; ~ . Q1
51 Tresses:] Q3; ~ , Q1–2
51 *Amoret*?] Q3; ~ . Q1; ~ , Q2
53 fayth?] Q3; ~ , Q1–2
55 temper;] Q5; ~ , Q1–4
55 take‸] Q3; ~ , Q1–2,
56 make‸] Q3; ~ , Q1–2
57 Signes] Q2; Singes Q1
57 with] Q2; whith Q1
57 saye,] Q3; ~ ‸ Q1–2
59 *Amoret*;] Q2; ~ . Q1
59 lost?] Q2; ~ , Q1
ɔFayth] F; faith Q1–5

64 a part‸] Q3; apart. Q1; apart, Q2
65 found?] Q3; ~ ‸ Q1; ~ , Q2
65 Why] why Q1–5, F
72 turnings,] Q3; ~ ‸ Q1–2
75 comminge‸] Q2; ~ , Q1
83 frost:] Q2; ~ ‸ Q1
85 lowe,] Q2; ~ ‸ Q1
88 tongues‸] Q2; ~ : Q1
88 crime‸] Q3; ~ : Q1–2
89 Mayde?] Q2; ~ , Q1
90 Thou] Q2; Thon Q1
91 good,] Q3; ~ : Q1–2
96 same,] Q2; ~ : Q1
101 mee,] Q2; ~ . Q1
102 then‸] Q3; ~ , Q1–2
105 sound] Q2; souud Q1
108 all‸] Q3; ~ , Q1–2
109 fall‸] Q3; ~ . Q1; ~ , Q2
110 swayne‸] Q3; ~ : Q1; ~ , Q2
110 flower,] Q2; ~ ‸ Q1
111 showre:] Q2; ~ ‸ Q1
113 name?] Q3; ~ , Q1; ~ ; Q2
120 it.] Q3; ~ , Q1–2
120 Tell] Q3; tell Q1–2
121 love] Q2; lone Q1
121 *Amorett*] Q3; Amorett Q1–2
122 Thou] Q2; Thon Q1
125 *Perigot*] Q3; Perigot Q1–2
126 nowe,] Q2; ~ . Q1
128 heaven,] Q3; ~ : Q1; ~ ‸ Q2
128 right,] Q2; ~ . Q1
130 woods,] Q2; ~ ‸ Q1
130 and] Q2; and and Q1
135 *Amoret*] Q3; Amoret Q1–2
135 played‸] Q3; ~ : Q1; ~ , Q2
136 Prodigall,] Q3; ~ : Q1–2
136 awaye‸] Q3; ~ : Q1; ~ , Q2
139 beguild.] Q3; ~ , Q1; ~ ; Q2
140 delayd,] Q3; ~ ‸ Q1–2

141 tryde‸] Q3; tryded, Q1; tryde, Q2
143 lesse‸] Q3; ~ . Q1; ~ , Q2
144 had‸] Q3; ~ : Q1; ~ , Q2
145 Ringes,] Q3; ~ ‸ Q1–2
145 Cracknels‸] Q3; ~ . Q1; ~ , Q2
145 lad‸] Q3; ~ . Q1; ~ , Q2
148 thee:] Q3; ~ ‸ Q1; ~ , Q2
148 theise,] Q2; ~ . Q1
149 on] Q2; one Q1
149 lay‸] Q2; ~ . Q1
150 after] Q2; af er Q1
150 memorye.] Q3; ~ ‸ Q1; ~ , Q2
150 But] Q3; but Q1–2
150 why‸] Q3; ~ , Q1–2
151 dye?] Q2; ~ ‸ Q1
153 roome‸] Q3; ~ . Q1; ~ , Q2
155 bread‸] Q3; ~ , Q1–2
156 *Amoret*] Q3; Amoret Q1–2
156 must.] Q3; ~ , Q1; ~ ; Q2

157 man‸] Q3; ~ , Q1–2
157 trust‸] Q3; ~ , Q1–2
159 *Amoret*] Q3; Amoret Q1–2
161 thee,] Q2; ~ ‸ Q1
161 free‸] Q2; ~ , Q1
163 live,] Q2; ~ ‸ Q1
164.1 *runns off*] Q3; *runus of* Q1; *runes off* Q2
166 streake‸] Q3; ~ , Q1–2
167 fier,] Q2; ~ ‸ Q1
168 unfold.] ~ , Q1; ~ ; Q2–5, F
174 laye:] Q3; ~ , Q1–2
176 catch‸] Q2; ~ , Q1
179 ready,] Q3; ~ ‸ Q1–2
185 wood.] Q3; ~ , Q1; ~ : Q2
188 Murder?] Q3; ~ , Q1–2
188 By] Q4; by Q1–3
190 face.] ~ , Q1; ~ ; Q2; ~ : Q3–5, F
192 keepes,] Q2; ~ ‸ Q1
192 crave‸] Q3; ~ , Q1–2

IV.v

2 Cure.] Q3; ~ , Q1–2
5 unconstant,] Q2; ~ ‸ Q1
5 leave‸] Q3; ~ , Q1–2
6 alone.] Q3; ~ , Q1–2
6 When] Q3; when Q1–2
6 deceave‸] Q3; ~ , Q1–2
7 wood‸] Q3; ~ , Q1–2
8 blood.] ~ , Q1; ~ ; Q2–4, F; ~ ? Q5
11 Sheapeard] Q4; *Sheapeard* Q1–3
12 *Clorins*‸] Q2; ~ , Q1
12 dye.] ~ , Q1; ~ ; Q2; ~ : Q3–5, F
14 bendes‸] Q3; ~ , Q1–2
16 nye,] Q2; ~ . Q1
17 away‸] Q3; ~ , Q1–2
19 else:] Q2; ~ ‸ Q1
21 lies;] Q2; ~ ‸ Q1
23 lover,] Q2; ~ ‸ Q1

26 injoye.] ~ , Q1; ~ ; Q2; ~ ? Q3–5, F
27 Sheapeard] *Sheapeard* Q1–5, F
27 free‸] Q2; ~ , Q1
28 loyalty:——] ~ , ‸ Q1; ~ : ‸ Q2–5, F
29 Sheapheard] *Sheapheard* Q1–5, F
30 gaze.] ~ , Q1–2, 4, F; ~ ; Q3, 5
31 bright,] Q2; ~ . Q1
33 mee?] Q2; ~ ‸ Q1
35 Sheapheard] *Sheapheard* Q1–5, F
36 *Clorin*...*Clorin*] Q3; Clorin... Clorin Q1–2
37, 43 *Clorin*] Q3; Clorin Q1–2
45 thee——] ~ . Q1–5, F
48 wound‸] Q3; ~ , Q1–2
49 more,] Q2; ~ . Q1
50 Sex‸] Q5; ~ , Q1–4

50 before?] Q3; ~ , Q1–2
52 thee!] ~ , Q1–2; ~ : Q3; ~ ?
   Q4–5, F
53 yet, returne] Q2; ~ . ~ Q1
54 delaye,] Q3; ~ ₐ Q1–2
60 thee?] Q3; ~ , Q1; ~ . Q2
61 Thou] Q2; Thon Q1
63 best;] Q2; ~ , Q1
64 castₐ] Q3; ~ , Q1–2
67 zeale,] Q2; ~ . Q1
68 thee] Q2; the Q1
69 wouldₐ] Q3; ~ . Q1; ~ , Q2
72 nowe,] Q3; ~ : Q1–2
72 neare,] Q2; ~ . Q1
73 grace,] Q2; ~ : Q1
75 False] false Q1–5, F

77 done: greatₐ] ~ ₐ ~ : Q1;
   ~ ₐ ~ ₐ Q2; ~ , ~ ₐ Q3–4,
   F; ~ ; ~ ₐ Q5
78.1 Enterₐ] Q2; ~ : Q1
79 constantₐ] Q3; ~ , Q1–2
80 love?] Q3; ~ , Q1; ~ . Q2
82 stayneₐ] Q3; ~ , Q1–2
83 bee,] Q2; ~ ₐ Q1
88 guilt.] Q3; ~ , Q1; ~ ; Q2
90 nought:] Q3; ~ ₐ Q1; ~ , Q2
91 espie,] Q3; ~ ₐ Q1–2
92 others] Q2; thers Q1
94 successe.] Q3; ~ , Q1–2
96 He...me] Q2; Q1 lines: He
   ...all, | then...me.
96.1 Finis Actus quartus Q1

V.i

V.i.] Actus Quintus. | Scena I. Q1
12 find,] Q2; ~ . Q1
15 your] Q2; yonr Q1
17 away.] Q2; ~ ₐ Q1
18 stirring?] Q3; ~ ₐ Q1; ~ , Q2
18 Sure] sure Q1–5, F
19 Roomes,] Q2; ~ . Q1

21 day:] ~ , Q1; ~ ; Q2–5, F
23 neglect] Q2; neclect Q1
27 downe,] Q3; ~ : Q1–2
28 sport,] Q2; ~ ; Q1
29 resort,] Q2; ~ . Q1
31 Trimₐ] Q2; ~ , Q1
33 Meades,] Q2; ~ . Q1

V.ii

1 pure,] Q3; ~ : Q1–2
16 blood,] Q2; ~ . Q1
17 be:] ~ ₐ Q1–2; ~ , Q3–4, F;
   ~ ; Q5
23 Goddesse] Goddesse Q1–5, F
28 Adder, Neut,...Snake] Adder,
   Neut,...Snake Q1–5, F
28 Snake,] Q2; ~ . Q1
37 thee] Q2; the Q1
38, 39 off] Q3; of Q1–2
40 Shepheardesse] Q3; Sepheardesse Q1; Shepheardesse Q2
52 tree,] Q2; ~ . Q1
54 out,] Q3; ~ ₐ Q1–2
57 vayne,] Q3; ~ ₐ Q1–2

66 topp,] ~ . Q1; ~ ₐ Q2–5, F
67 grasse,] Q2; ~ ₐ Q1
72 sinne,] Q2; ~ . Q1
73 light:] Q3; ~ , Q1; ~ ; Q2
74 deceaves,] Q2; ~ . Q1
81 finger] Q2; figer Q1
85 backe,] Q3; ~ ₐ Q1–2
87 Nymph] Q3; Nymph Q1–2
88 you] Q2; yon Q1
97 hastₐ] Q3; ~ ; Q1–2
101–102 Take...sence.] Q3; one
   line in Q1–2
104 burst:] Q3; ~ , Q1–2
105 wood,] Q2; ~ . Q1

V.iii

2 paine,] Q2; ~ : Q1
4 ill.] Q3; ~ : Q1-2
5 counsaild?] ~ : Q1; ~ ‸ Q2-5, F
9 shaddowes,] Q3; ~ : Q1-2
9 swaine,] Q2; ~ ‸ Q1
12 alone,] Q3; ~ : Q1-2
20 dyes,] Q3; ~ ‸ Q1-2
25 ambitious] Q2; ambtious Q1
29 loosenesse:] ~ , Q1-2; ~ ; Q3-5, F
32 throughly:] Q4; ~ , Q1-3 (throghly Q1-2)
34 beauty] Q2; beauy Q1
37 Summer] Q3; *Summr* Q1(c); *Summer* Q2
38 free,] Q2; ~ ‸ Q1
42 catching] Q2; catchiug Q1
43 wandred?] Q3; ~ . Q1-2
48 part.] Q3; ~ ; Q1-2
49 rest?] Q3; ~ , Q1; ~ . Q2
51 trayne:] Q2; ~ ‸ Q1
58 sing,] Q2; ~ : Q1
60 howle‸] Q3; ~ . Q1; ~ , Q2
64 Shepheard.——] ~ ‸‸ Q1; ~ :‸ Q2; ~ . ‸ Q3-5, F
64 *Daphnis*!] Q4; ~ , Q1 (*Daphinis*); ~ . Q2-3
66 greene‸] Q3; ~ : Q1; ~ , Q2
67 flocks?] Q3; ~ , Q1; ~ . Q2

73 tydings!] Q3; ~ ‸ Q1; ~ , Q2
73 You] Q4; you Q1-3
74 *Clorin* ‸ lives,] Q2; ~ , ~ ‸ Q1
74 power,] Q2; ~ . Q1
75 have] Q2; hane Q1
77 *Perrigot*,] Q2; ~ : Q1
77 life,] Q3; ~ : Q1-2
85 remembrance] Q3; remembrance Q1-2
90 still‸] Q3; ~ , Q1-2
92 and] Q2; aud Q1
94 Virginitie:] Q2; ~ ‸ Q1
94 Virginitie] *Virginitie* Q1-5, F
101] Q2; Q1 *lines*: That...purged. | I...now,
108 bush] Q2; bushk Q1
109 Abuser] Q2; Aboser Q1
113 Buskins:] ~ , Q1; ~ ; Q2-5, F
113 see,] Q2; ~ : Q1
120 peaches:] Q2; ~ ‸ Q1
123 youth:] ~ ‸ Q1; ~ ; Q2-5, F
123 flye?] Q3; ~ , Q1-2
124 Remember] Q2; Remmber Q1
127 *Perigot*;] Q3; ~ ‸ Q1; ~ : Q2
129 be:] ~ , Q1; ~ ; Q2-5, F
129 againe,] Q3; ~ : Q1-2
136 will,] Q3; ~ . Q1-2
142 impart?] Q2; ~ . Q1
147 like?] Q3; ~ . Q1-2

V.iv

10 thee,] Q2; ~ . Q1
12 spot.] Q3; ~ , Q1-2
15 *Clorin*‸] Q3; ~ . Q1; ~ , Q2
16 Cabin] Q3; *Cabin* Q1-2

16 boughs,...heales‸] Q2; ~ ‸ ...~ , Q1
17 wounds:] ~ , Q1; ~ ; Q2-5, F
20 fayre:] Q3; ~ ‸ Q1; ~ , Q2

V.v

0.2 *one side*] Q2; *on side* Q1
1 blood] Q2; bloold Q1
6 lustfully:] Q3; ~ , Q1; ~ ; Q2
10 beguyle.] Q3; ~ , Q1–2
12 last?] Q2; ~ . Q1
23 sacred] Q2; sacerd Q1
23 place.] Q2; ~ , Q1
33 Tonight!] Q3; ~ , Q1–2
33 Stretch] stretch Q1–5, F
37 *Satire*,] Q2; ~ . Q1
37 bowre,] Q3; ~ ₐ Q1–2
41 thee] Q2; hee Q1
42 be,] Q3; ~ . Q1–2
45 love,] Q3; ~ . Q1–2
46 *Amoret*,] Q3; ~ . Q1; ~ : Q2
48 still.] Q3; ~ , Q1–2
52 forgive?] Q2; ~ , Q1
53 live:] ~ , Q1; ~ ; Q2–5, F
58 cleanse ₐ...againe:] Q2; ~ ,
    ...~ ₐ Q1
67 ground.] Q3; ~ , Q1–2
67 Goe] Q3; goe Q1–2
68 stand,] Q3; ~ . Q1–2
72 up:] ~ , Q1; ~ ; Q2–5, F
73 this.] Q3; ~ , Q1–2
77 is:] Q4; ~ , Q1; ~ ; Q2–3
82 cure:] ~ , Q1; ~ ; Q2; ~ .
    Q3–5, F
91 Ayre:] Q3; ~ ₐ Q1; ~ , Q2
93 Mirr,] Q3; ~ : Q1–2
94 stirr ₐ] Q2; ~ . Q1
95 Thee] Q2; The Q1
97 offendors:] ~ , Q1–2; ~ ; Q3,
    5, F
101 vennome:] Q5; ~ , Q1; ~ ;
    Q2–4
107 expedition] Q3; expediton Q1–
    2
109 are ₐ] Q3; ~ , Q1–2
112 wrong!] ~ , Q1–2; ~ ? Q3–5,
    F
113 hurts?] Q3; ~ , Q1–2

121 thirst:] Q3; ~ , Q1–2
122 ô] Q2; o Q1
126 sheepheard] shheepheare Q1
132 fault:] ~ , Q1–4, F; ~ ; Q5
136 consuming] Q2; consnming Q1
140 cloud!] ~ , Q1–2; ~ ? Q3–5,
    F
140 Goe] goe Q1–5, F
149 impure:] Q3; ~ , Q1; ~ ; Q2
151 dame,] Q3; ~ : Q1–2
155 waies,] Q3; ~ ₐ Q1–2
167 paine:] Q2; ~ ₐ Q1
168 them ₐ] Q3; ~ , Q1–2
169 cleare ₐ] Q3; ~ , Q1–2
170 suspect:] ~ ₐ Q1; ~ , Q2–4,
    F; ~ ; Q5
173 laboure:] ~ , Q1–4, F; ~ ; Q5
174 neighbouring] Q3; neghbour-
    ing Q1–2
176 clusters:] ~ , Q1–4, F; ~ ; Q5
176 wine,] Q4; ~ ₐ Q1–3
178 shepheards:] ~ , Q1–4, F; ~ ;
    Q5
179 now] Now Q1–5, F
179 spare ₐ] Q3; ~ , Q1–2
180 forget ₐ] Q3; ~ , Q1–2
183 clownes,] Q2; ~ : Q1
187 truth,] Q2; ~ . Q1
188 tongue] Q2; tougue Q1
190 Priest] *Priest* Q1–5, F
195 Land,] Q2; ~ . Q1
196 upon.] Q2; ~ ₐ Q1
196 you ₐ] Q3; ~ . Q1; ~ , Q2
200 length] Q2; lenght Q1
201 Ritches:] ~ ₐ Q1; ~ , Q2–5, F
201 strength,] Q2; ~ . Q1 (strenght)
202 Cannot] Q2; Caunot Q1
205 howre,] ~ : Q1–2; ~ ₐ Q3–5, F
211 new,] Q3; ~ . Q1–2
215 laye,] Q3; ~ : Q1–2
219 *powers*,] ~ : Q1–2; ~ ₐ Q3–5,
    F

221 *brakes*:] ~ . Q1; ~ , Q3–5, F;
      bancks. Q2
223 *sound*,] Q3; ~ : Q1; ~ ; Q2
225 *ground*,] Q3; ~ . Q1–2
226 *name*,] ~ . Q1; ~ ᴧ Q2–5, F
229 *must*,] ~ : Q1; ~ ᴧ Q2–5, F
230 *honnerd*:] Q2; ~ , Q1
231 *Lillyes*,] Q3; ~ . Q1–2
235 *holy*,] Q3; ~ . Q1–2
239 whitest,] Q3; ~ . Q1; ~ : Q2
243 meetest,] Q2; ~ . Q1
244 the] Q; thee Q1
244 *Satyre* ?] Q3; ~ ᴧ Q1; ~ ; Q2
244 Shall] shall Q1–5, F

247 make ᴧ] Q2; ~ . Q1
249 light ?] Q2; ~ , Q1
251 thee] Q2; the Q1
251 corrall,] Q2; ~ ᴧ Q1
251 way ᴧ] Q3; ~ , Q1–2
253 fleeces ?] Q2; ~ , Q1
253 shall ᴧ] Q3; ~ , Q1–2
256 coulours ?] Q2; ~ ᴧ Q1
257 Lute ?] Q2; ~ ᴧ Q1
263 Holy virgin] Q2; *Holy virgin*
      Q1
271 befriend] Q3; be friend Q1–2
272 Arbor] Q2; *Arbor* Q1

HISTORICAL COLLATION

To construct the Historical Collation the Q1 copy-text has been collated against Q2 of 1629 in the Folger Shakespeare Library, Q3 of 1634 (Folger copy), Q4 of 1656 in the Huntington Library, Q5 of 1665 (Huntington copy), and a copy of the 1679 Folio in the possession of the editor. Later editions collated are the *Works*, 1711, edited by Langbaine (L); 1750, edited by Theobald, Seward, and Sympson (S); 1778, edited by George Colman the younger (C); 1812, edited by Henry Weber (W); 1843–6, edited by Alexander Dyce (D); the edition prepared by W. W. Greg for Vol. III of the Variorum Edition, 1908 (V); the edition of W. A. Neilson in *Chief Elizabethan Dramatists*, 1911 (N); the edition of C. R. Baskervill in *Elizabethan and Stuart Plays*, 1934 (B).

To my lov'd friend] *om.* F, L, S, C, N, B
  12 morallitie] mortallitie Q1–2, W
  18 Reflects] Reflect Q2–3
  18 comfort] confort Q2; consort Q3–5

22 true reflection] truer-flection Q2
28 it] is Q5
31 commaund] commands Q3–5, W, D, V
36.1 N. F.] *Nath. Field* Q2–5, W, D, V

To my friend] *om.* L, S, C, N, B
  4 with] in Q4–5, F
  6 slak'd] slack'd Q3–5, F
  24 wants] want F, W, D
  26 like] *om.* Q3–5, F
  26 be new] be not new Q4–5 F

27 judgements] judgement Q4–5, F, W, D, V
30 to thee] for thee Q4–5, F
42 wit] will Q1
44 must] now must Q3–5, F

To the worthy] *om.* L, S, C, N, B

To his loving] *om.* F, L, S, C, N, B
  0.2–3 concerning...a play] *om.* Q3–5

13 fals] fall Q3–5
30 for] far Q5

To that noble] *om.* Q2–5, F, L, S, C, N, B

3 um] em W, D, V

To the inheritour] *om.* Q2–5, F, L, S, C, N, B

6 I have] I've W, D, V
19 Farre] Fare Q1 (u)

To the perfect] *om.* Q2–5, F, L, S, C, N, B

To the Reader] *om.* Q2–5, F, L, S, C

9 least] lest W+

Unto his worthy friend] *om.* Q1–2, F, L–W, N, B

0.4 *last.* 1633.] *om.* Q5
24 to] and Q4–5

This Dialogue] *om.* Q1–2, L, S, C, N, B
4 gentler] gentle Q4–5, F
5 was I...thy] I was...the W
6 as swift] swift Davenant
6 th'Eagles] the Eagles Davenant
8 To see...King.] *Pan* sends his offering to this Islands King. Davenant, W
9–10 that doth his eyes...halfe this night.] whose Eies have brought that light | Which hither led and stays him here; | He now doth shine within her Sphear, | And must obey her Scepter half this night. Davenant, W

11 Let's sing] Sing we Davenant, W
12.1] Davenant, W *add*: Chorus of *both.*
13 t'unwalled] to wealthy Davenant, W
14 leave them] have left Davenant, W
15 Noone-dayes Sun to th'old] *Phebus* to the old Davenant, W
17 to'th Pilote] to Pilots Davenant, W
18 When's Carde is] Their Cards being Davenant, W
18 his Rudder] their Rudders Davenant, W

I.i

8 and games] and merry games Q2 (BM copy), V; and jolly games Q3–5, F, L, S, C, W, D, N
10 be girt] be begirt Q4–5, F, L, S, D, N
25 Whilst] While L, S, C
44 head] heap Q5
80 squirrels teeth that cracke] Squirril whose Teeth crack S, C

80, 81 them] 'em L–C
89 some] and some S
97 Least] Lest Q3+
115 these] the Q2–5, F, L–D
120 mires] mire Q2–5, F, L–V
120 pooles:] pooles, to find my ruine: Q2–5, F, L–N
124 there is] there's L–W

I.ii

0.1 *with foure*] *with him four* F

1 done] gone Q2–3

19 livers] liver Q4–5, F, L

28 y'are] ye are Q4–5, F, L–B

34 *Whilst*] While L–W

56 fall] full Q2–5, F, L

57 goe] feel Q4–5, F, L

63 seaman] Sea men F, L

64 then the] then Q2; than Q3–5, F, L–D

70 Ye are] Y'are Q4–5, F, N, B; You're L, S, C; You are W, D

72 loose] lose Q4+

74 I have] I've Q4–5, F, L, S, C, N, B

99 soules] selves Q2–5, F, L

115 growes] grow L–D

127 Thou hast] Thou'st S, C

131 a] the Q2–5, F, L–W

133 ever] e'er S–D

134 through] thorough S, W, D, N

134 whilst] while L–W

137.2 *Enter another...Perigot.*] *Enter Amarillis.* Q2–5, F

148 thee] the Q2

152 thee] the Q2

163 equall] *om.* S

174 ye] you C–V, B

184 These] The L, S

188 thou hast] thou'st L–C

200 every] ever F

207 weaning] waining Q2–4, F, L

232 *Sullen Shepherd*] *om.* Q1; *Sull.* Q2–5; *Shep.* F

I.iii

12 eies] eye Q5

14 foile] soile Q2–5, F, L

22 dares] dare F

25 hast] haste Q1

27 as fresh] is fresh Q2; likewise as fresh Q4–5, F, L–D, N

32 oregrowne] are growne Q1–2

32 wood bines] wood bins Q2–3; woodbinds Q4–5, F, L, S

47 eare] Ears F

47 Maid] Mayds Q4–5, F, L, S

48 live] love Q2–3

48 t'admire] to admire W, D

50 sure the] pure a F; sure a V, N, B

53 breath] breathe C–B

57 Ye] You Q2+

68 words] works F

99 hee is] he's Q3+

124 least] lest Q3+

132 ye] you F, C–D, N

133 I am] I'm Q3–4, F, L

154 tine] time Q2–5, F, L

164 ye] you C, W, D, N

166 more] far Q4–5, F, L–C

167 these] those Q2–5, F, L

169 Hide] hid Q4–5, F, L

172 hath] have Q4–5, F, L–V

176 shamefast] shamefac'd L–D

176 *Tithons*] *Titans* Q5

180 my] may Q2

184 Meet in] Meet me in V, N, B

188 whilst] while L–W

II.i

9 low] lowde Q1–3; down N
10 downe] loud N
16 budd] bloud Q1(u)
20 Least] Lest Q3+

27 watches] walkes Q1(u)
28 Whilst] While L–W
28 the tother] the other C, W
32 And…in] In…and S

II.ii

1 *Clorin*] *om.* Q1–5
2 great] *om.* Q5
3 you sonnes] you best sons S
4 happy] high Q1(u)
6 and] a Q1(u)
10 crop] lop Q1(u)
11 Of day] *om.* S
11 give] told Q1(u)
15 tooth] teeth Q1(u), N
15 Ramnus] Ramuus Q1(u);
    Ramuns Q1(c), Q2–5, F, L;
    Ramson's S, C, W; rhamnus'
    D, V, N, B
17 fast] *om.* Q1(u), W, N
22 Such] Which Q1(u)
23 Tormentil] Formentill Q1(u)
25 roote] roots F
25 best] be Q4, F
33 to] two Q3+
35 Standergrasse] Sandergrasse
    Q1(u)
36 with] and Q1(u)
40 fancies] forces Q1(u)
48 as] and Q1(u), W
48.1 Thenot] *Shepheard* Q1(u)
49 *Thenot*] *Shep* Q1(u)
57 making] make Q1(u), N
62 yon] you Q1(u), Q2, D, N;
    Thou S–W
63 nightly] brightly Q1(u), N
63 shines] shin'st S, C
66 poets stile] stiled is Q1(u), N
74 dappld] dapple Q1(u)
79 am I] I am Q2

81 whilst] while L–W
82 Breakes] Beates Q1(u)
82 stound] stround Q1–2
83 The amazed] Th' amazed L–D,
    N
87 eie] eies Q2
88 unpossible] impossible Q5
89 *Thenot*] *Shep.* Q1
98 The] Thy Q2
99 *Thenot*] *Shep.* Q1
106 *Thenot*] *Shep.* Q1(c); *om.* Q1(u)
111 flames] flame Q1(u)
113 praiers] praies Q1; praise Q2–5,
    F, L
116 *Thenot*] *Shep.* Q1
124 *Arions*] Orions Q1(u)
125 woven] wove Q4–5, F, L, S
126 infould] unfould Q1–2
127 wandring] errant Q1(u), W
127 not] nor Q4–5, F, L, S
129 Alpsien] Alpen Q1(u), D;
    Alpine W, N
133 whilst] while L, S, C
133 dare] do Q1(u), W, D, N
134 ere] are Q2, Q4, L
141 *Thenot*] *Shep.* Q1
143 strongly] strong Q1(u)
144 ye] you C–D, N
145 ye] you C–D, N
148 from] for Q1–2
149 seat] set Q3–5, F, L
150 gainst] against Q2
152 ye] you C–D, N

154 Ye] You C–D, N
160 and] *om.* Q4–5, F, L, S
162 *Thenot*] *Shep.* Q1

163 whilst I] whilst here I Q3, C;
whilst that here I Q4–5, F, W,
D, N; while that here I L, S

II.iii

2 never] ne'r Q4+
5 them] then F
7 Shootes] Shoot Q4+
7 his] its S–W
10 Or] And Q1(u), V–B
15 maidens] maiden Q3–4, F
19 praise] prise Q4+ (–V, B)
25 knew] knit Q2
31 the other] th'other Q3+(–V)
33, 34 she] he Q1–5, F, L

38 flame] shame Q2
49 I have] I've L, S–B
51 grinnes] gins F, L–N; gren B
52 nimble] Conies Q1(u), N
55 I have] have I W
55 ye] you C–D, N
57 ye] you C–D
62 stronger] stranger F
86 over] o're Q3+(–V, B)

II.iv

4 nor] or V, B
5 thy] the Q4–5, F, L
10 flame] flames Q2–5, F–D
22 blessed] blesseds F
34 those] these Q4–5, F, L, S
43 thought] though Q1–2
46 *Cloe (within). Cloe !*] *Cloe within.
| Cloe* ∧ Q1–5, F, L, N (*where the
second* Cloe *is printed as part of
Daphnis' preceding speech*)

49 Heere] Cloe! here S–D
52 least] lest Q3+
57 ye] you C–D, N
66 brother] tother V
84 To offend] T'offend Q5, S, C
97 you] thou L, S
106 shamefastnesse] Shamefac'dness
L–D

III.i

0.1 the] *om.* Q3–5, F
9, 10 into] unto D, N
10 thy] the Q2
25 There...away] There I stop.
Now fly away S, C; There I
stop.—Fly away W
27 hath] beareth S
40 *awakeh*] *awakes* Q3–5, F
41 *Amarillis*] *Amo.* Q1
46 reformd] transformed Q2+
(–V, B)
50 that] *om.* Q2–3

51 *Amarillis*] *Amore* Q1
52 loose] lose Q4+
59 will I] I will Q5
65 moone] Moones Q3–5, F, L–C
66 owne] one Q1
66 shape make] mape shake Q4;
map make F
71 yon] your Q2
77 least] lest Q3+
80 hath] has F
92 of Beare] the ~ Q2–5, F, L
103 ye] you C–D, N

607

108 Least] Lest Q3+
111 me] him V
114 Ile followe,...of me] *om.* Q2;
Ile seeke him out, and for thy
curtesie Q3–5, F, L, S, C; I'll
follow him; and for this thy
care of me W
119 a] her F
126 She would not] Would she not
N
145 hallowed] hollowed Q2
151 ere day] ere the day Q2+
160 thou shalt] shalt thou Q5, F
161 loose] lose Q3+
163 ye] you F, C–D, N
164 fond] found Q2
169 Give] Gives D, N, B
181 loose] lose Q3+
184 Then] Them Q2
207 yon] you Q1–3
215 till] still S
221 stay] stray Q1
229 Who] Whom F, D, N
231 him] *om.* C
232.1 *the*] *om.* Q3–5, F
234 and] an Q1
236 loose] lose Q3+
243 all] *om.* Q3–5, F, L
252 Turffe] trufe Q4
257 spitt] sit C
267 Beloved] I loved Q2–5, F, L–C
268 yon] you Q1

272 on] one Q1
273 thee] the Q1
275 that] the Q4–5, F, L–W
281 should] shall Q2–5, F, L–C
288 thy] my Q2
302 thee] the Q2
309 as still] still as Q5
310 other] others Q2
320 the hearbs] these ∼ S–W
321 hence] from hence S
325 ye] you F
327 flye, let] flye, and let S
328 owne] former S
331 thy way] the ∼ Q5
348 least] lest Q3+
356.1 *He*] *om.* Q4–5, F
358 woman] women Q4
361 yon] you Q1
373 Hallowed] Hollowed Q1–2
383 drope] droope Q1
384 locke] lockes Q2+
406 on] one Q4
411 shall] shalt Q2+
417 Through] Though Q1
428 string] spring Q3–5, F, L
437 that] ther Q1
438 be] by Q2
439 By thee] ∼ the Q1
449 Least] Lest Q3+
453 On] One Q1
471 on] one Q1

IV.i

9.1 *to Perigot*] *om.* Q2–5, F
18 the] thee Q1
24 dyes] dye Q4
26 Ye] You C–D, N

28 this] his Q1–2
33 one] on Q1
38 the] thee Q1
39 where] were Q2

608

IV.ii

26 bower] power Q4+(−V, B)
33 Whiter] Whither Q1–2
37 the] thee Q1
39 undo] cut off F
42 the] thy Q4–5, F, L
47 yee] you C–D, N
66 thie] the Q3+(−N, B)
73 doe] be L–W
89 a] he Q4–5, F, L–D
91 earst] east Q1

98 this] thy F
108 possibly] possible Q1, B
109 heates] hearts Q2–5, F, L
110 thoughts] thought F
110 lusty] lustful S
113 vayne] veins S–W
116 Playster] Playsters Q1
136 Of Fayryes] Of the fairies S–W
139 thee] the Q1
148 deceive] deserve Q1

IV.iii

3 never] ne'er S–D, N
5 it] him Q3–5, F, L–C
5 never] ne'er S–D, N
7 or] nor Q3–5, F, L–C, N
9 but] that Q3+(−V, B)
13 worthy] worth S–W
32 men] man Q4

34 as] is Q2
37 Imagination] Imaginations Q2+(−V)
39 whilst] while L–W
55 and thy] thy and F
60 Ye] You C–B
79 ye] you Q3+ (−V)

IV.iv

3 thy] the Q4–5, F
15 What art thou dare] What thou Q1; What art thou darest Q4–5, F, L; What art? Who dare S
24 Ribandes] Riband F
26 then Nose-gayes] then the Nose-gays Q3–5, F
38 of] to S–W
39 face] fact Q2
41 flowing] flying Q2–5, F, L–W
47 strange] stronge Q2+
60 men, and most] men, most Q1
62 the] thy Q5
64 not one] no one W
67 Crosse] crass F
72 Makes] Mares L
79 *Perigot.*] om. Q1
84 ever driven to] over driven for S
97 thy] the Q5

103 esteeme] esteemd Q2+(−D, V, B)
106 canst love] om. S, C
126 not] nor Q5
138 wild] vild D, N
140 denyed] denye Q1
147 me] my Q2
148 gave] give Q4–5
149 on] one Q1
155 bread] breds Q2; breeds Q3–5, F, L–W
168 Whilst] While L–W
171 Leaps] Leps Q1–2
174 manye a laye] manye laye Q1
176 Least] Lest Q3+
177 loose] lose Q3+
177 Ah] Ay Q5
187 vild] vile L–W

IV.v

5 unconstant] inconstant C, W
5 nor will leave] I will leave S
13 being] beings F
45 loose] lose Q3+
48 be] by Q2
49 woemen] woman Q4-5, F, L, S
52 then to behold] then behold Q1-2
60 loose both] both lose Q3-5, F-C, W; lose both D-B

68 by] be F
76 Inconstancy] Inconstance Q1
79 yee...ye] you...you C-D
83 shalt] shall Q4-5, F, N
86 thee] the Q4-5, F
88 womens] woman's W, V
92 others] thers Q1
93 gave] give Q4-5, F, L, S
95 a] om. Q5

V.i

1 of] off Q3+
3 windowes] windowe Q4-5, F, L, S
3 whilst] while L-W
16 decay] delay Q1(u)
18 Sure] save Q1(u)
19 or] for Q1(u)

25 lodging, heere] longing, heard Q1(u)
28 them] then Q2
28 bout] but Q2
31 note] notes Q1(u)
33 their] the Q1(u)

V.ii

0.1 her.] ~ . and Amorillis Q1(c), Q2-3
1 thoughts] thought Q1(u)
9 vice] voice Q2
20 doth] do F
21 heald] held Q1
27 a] ha' F, C, V, N; have W, D
37 it] I N

37 thee there wil bide] thee, will abide Q3-5, F, L, S, N
38, 39 off] of Q1-2
58 they are] they're Q3+
86 Farewell...so.] printed as part of Clorin's preceding speech Q1+ (−D, V, B)
102 Least] lest Q3+
106 I have] I ha' F, N; I've C

V.iii

2 them] 'em F
8 mornings] Morning F
18 and a verteous name] and verteous names Q1(u)
22 age] ache C
23 growe] growes Q1(u)

37 Summer] Homer Q1(u)
37 loaden] laden Q5
39 bay] raine Q1(u)
42 flames] flamer Q1(u)
47 ye] you C, W, D, N
51 flocks up, any] flocks, any Q1(u)

52 these] those Q2+(−F, V)
53 long] *om.* Q2; same Q3–5, F,
 L–W
55 eare] eares Q2
61 and] *om.* Q5
65 hast thou left] hast left Q1–2, B
73 So] Of so Q1 (u)
77 *Perrigot*] *Perrogots* Q1 (u)
79 *running...Sheepeheard*] *om.*
 Q1 (u)
88 was] am Q5
96 thy] the F

105 A virgin, never after to] A
 virgin, never to Q3; to live a
 virgin, never to Q4–5, F, L, S
106 unpure] impure Q4–5, F, L, S,
 W
119 the smiling] thy ∼ Q1–2
136 men] that Q2+(−B)
143 and branded] and a branded
 Q3+(−B)
146 willd] will Q2; wills Q3–5, F,
 L–W
147 Yee are] You're C–D, N
150.1 *Exeunt*] *om.* Q1–2

V.iv

0.1 *hand*] hands F
1 the] this Q2–5, F, L–C

5 hand] hands F

V.v

6 these] each Q4–5, F, L, S; this
 D, V, N
7 least] lest Q3+
18 base end] chast flame Q4+
26 good] stood Q1 (u)
29 Thers a hand some] Thers at
 hand some Q2; There at hand
 some Q3+
35 power] powre Q3–4; pour
 Q5+
41 thee] hee Q1
41.2 *kneeleth*] *kneeling* Q2–5, F
47 Strike] Sticke Q1–2
48 canst] couldst Q3+
48 love] leave Q2
49 could] should Q3–5, F, L, S, V
56 I, death] I thee, Death S–D, N
58 Perhaps...againe] this perhaps
 will cleanse again Q4–5, F, L,
 S; Perhaps will cleans'd be;
 once again. N
62 are] *om.* F
74 full] fall Q1

85 fell] full Q1
86 the race] a brace S, C
89 lives] live Q1
92 take a paire] *om.* Q1
96 the abhorred] th' abhorred L–D,
 N
129 sentence:] ∼ , and disgrace
 Q2+
136 consuming] confusing L
144 *Amarillis*] *Amoret* Q1 (u)
158 ye] you C–D
170 through] though Q1
171 wrong in] wronging Q3+
 (−V)
178 shepheards] Shepherd F
180 nor] not Q1
187 complement] complements Q3–
 5, F, L–C
189 them use] them still use Q3+
 (−V, B)
192 *All*] *Alex.* Q3–5, F
194 whilst] while L–W
195 your] you Q1

219 *ye vertues*] *you* ~ F
221 *brakes*] *bancks* Q2
229 *ever*] *even* Q2
248 of the night] of night Q2+
249 thee] me Q2

254 thee] the Q1–5, F, L, S
256 For] Of Q2+
258 I] Ile Q2+
261 Thicks] thickets Q3–5, F, L–C
261 least] lest Q3+